L&NWR LOCOMOTIVE NAMES

L&NWR LOCOMOTIVE NAMES

THE NAMED LOCOMOTIVES OF THE LONDON & NORTH WESTERN RAILWAY AND ITS AMALGAMATED COMPANIES

JOHN GOODMAN

THE RAILWAY CORRESPONDENCE AND TRAVEL SOCIETY

2002

ISBN 0901115908

www.rcts.org.uk

Published by the Railway Correspondence
and Travel Society
7 Cherryfields, Peterborough,
England, PE2 5XD

Cover Photo: Webb Precursor 2147 *Champion*
L&NWR Society photograph collection No.B16

Printed by Ebenezer Baylis & Son Ltd, Worcester

Alfred the Great class 1979 *Nelson* at No. 2 arrival platform, Euston.

(Allan Sommerfield Collection)

CONTENTS

PREFACE

There never has been a collection of locomotive names anything like those that appeared on the locomotives of the London & North Western Railway. Whosoever travelled by L&NWR and took an interest in "their engine" must have wondered at the extraordinary variety of the names they noticed. Even now many people find the selection of North Western names uplifting in their variety and purpose.

I remember to this day a week I spent at Colwyn Bay during the Easter school holidays of 1934, where I had gone with my mother to recuperate after a bout of influenza. It was supposed the sea air would do me good. That may have been so, but it was the trains passing by that did me the most good. The great moment of the day was the passing of the Up and the Down Irish Mails; To quote one day, 6163 *Civil Service Rifleman* sped through on the Down, and moments later 6162, then unnamed, on the Up. But it was the L&NWR names that fascinated. The first to go by was *Swiftsure*, then *Lord Byron, George Macpherson, Ptarmigan. Malta, C.J.Bowen Cooke, Wolfhound, Otterhound, Fame, Hotspur, Moor Hen, Staghound, Marmion* and *Boarhound*. Not bad for one day, and Friday the thirteenth of April at that! I deduced that there must have been a pack of hounds, and I supposed more than two birds. I knew that Lord Byron was the poet, but who were the other two men? What is more I found that not all the Claughtons were named, for 5972 and 5990 had none, nor had several Prince of Wales class. Was there some reason for that?

It once appeared in print quite correctly that the L&NWR locomotives were blessed with an amazing variety of names, but then immediately and in the same sentence and entirely incorrectly, it was asserted that they had been distributed at random. Nothing could be farther from the truth. For every L&NWR name, as always in the sphere of nomenclature, the choice was made after careful thought and deliberation. There are all manner of underlying reasons for their selection.

It is a fascinating exercise to study this great family of names one by one and attempt to work out the reasoning that must have lain behind the choice of each name.

The source of some are self-evident, others less so. The years roll by, and so it is probable that the sources of some of the very earliest names may never now be known. That in itself is good, for it causes the student to keep on searching, until a possible, or a probable, even maybe a certain solution comes to light. Anyone who has endeavoured to have seen a complete class of locomotive knows how keenly he looks at every one of the type until the moment of joy and triumph when he sees the final one, but he also knows that from then on he will never be able to look at that class in quite the same way. Until perchance one of them is renamed, and then, wonderful! He's off again in the hunt! So with the name-source project. It is good that there should always be some that we might have only partially solved, or are mistaken about, and a few others which we may never solve. For then the search goes on.

With L&NWR names going right back into the times of King William IV it would be a triumph indeed to have narrowed the elusive ones down to a mere handful.

J.G.

1

ABBREVIATIONS

B&L	Bolton & Leigh Railway
BL&CJR	Birkenhead, Lancashire & Cheshire Junction Railway
BS	Brockley Lane Sidings
C&B	Chester & Birkenhead Railway
C&W	Cockermouth & Workington Railway
FR	Furness Railway
GJR	Grand Junction Railway
GWR	Great Western Railway
H&M	Huddersfield & Manchester Railway
K&W	Kendal & Windermere Railway
L&B	London & Birmingham Railway
L&C	Lancaster & Carlisle Railway
L&CH	Ludlow & Clee Hill Railway
L&M	Liverpool & Manchester Railway
L&NWR	London & North Western Railway
L&PJR	Lancaster & Preston Junction Railway
L&Y	Lancashire & Yorkshire Railway
LMS	London Midland & Scottish Railway
M&B	Manchester & Birmingham Railway
MR	Midland Railway
NLR	North London Railway
NU	Northern Union
P&L	Preston & Longridge Railway
P&WHDR	Preston & Wyre Harbour Dock & Railway
S&D	Stockton & Darlington Railway
S&P	Sandy & Potton Railway
SS	South Staffordshire Railway
St.H	St.Helens Canal & Railway
V of C	Vale of Clwyd Railway
W&FJ	Whitehaven & Furness Junction Railway
WJ	Whitehaven Junction Railway
CD	Carriage Department
NG	Narrow Gauge
PW	Permanent Way Department
N Div	Northern Division
NE Div	North Eastern Division
S Div	Southern Division
CF	Crooked (or Curved) Frames
cyl	cylinder
DA	Direct Action (Rocking shaft eliminated)
DW	Driving wheel
LFB	Long (or Large) firebox type locomotives
Pass	Passenger engine
SF	Straight Frames
SFB	Short (or Small) firebox type locomotives

Chapter 1
INTRODUCTION

1. THE GENERAL PRINCIPLES OF NUMBERING AND NAMING

The London & North Western Railway was formed on 16th July 1846 by the amalgamation of the Manchester & Birmingham Railway, the Grand Junction Railway (which had absorbed the Liverpool & Manchester Railway and the Bolton & Leigh Railway in 1845) and the London & Birmingham Railway.

The L&M's first locomotive was their No 1 *Rocket*, built in 1829; the Grand Junction's was their No 1 *Saracen*, of 1837. Both of these companies gave numbers and names to their locomotives, whereas the M&B and L&B provided numbers only and the B&L names only.

Until July 1846 these Companies had control over their separate stocks.

The L&M and the GJ kept to its own distinct system of numbering and naming. In the case of the L&M when a locomotive had run its course, as happened in the case of eleven of them, the name was re-used on its successor, but a new higher serial number was given to it. Thus for example, their No 4 *Dart* was replaced in December 1836 by a No 48 *Dart*. With the GJ, on the other hand, when a locomotive was replaced, it was by another one bearing the same name and number as its predecessor, so their 2-2-2 No 1 *Saracen* was replaced in 1841 by an 0-4-2 No 1 *Saracen* built by John Melling, thus making it essential for the historian to indicate clearly which locomotive he was referring to, the first or the second.

The L&NWR adopted the GJ practice, and so came about the tradition which associated a number with a name. To give an example, the number 7 and the name *Scorpion* appeared together on the GJ 2-2-2 of 1837, on its replacement in 1842, on the LFB Goods DA of 1852, and finally on the Problem class locomotive of 1861 which was not withdrawn until 1904.

In course of time numbers and names went their separate ways, thus to take the case of *Saracen* instanced above, the third and fourth engines bearing this name also were No 1, but the fifth, of the Experiment class built in February 1909, was No 2624, No 1 no longer being available by virtue of having been used in June 1907 for the Precursor class named *Clive*.

In the case of the L&B the policy was to give numbers only for their locomotives. There was one exception. The company's ballast engines, used for permanent way maintenance were all named and one of these, *Harvey Combe* was included temporarily in the L&NWR stock list, but without a number.

The B&L's stock were named, and the four which come to the L&NWR brought their names with them, and were numbered in four gaps (Nos 123, 124, 125 and 127) existing in the L&NWR list; similarly the four coming named from the North Union in 1847 were numbered in the next available Nos 177-180.

This established another principle, that whenever a Company was absorbed into the L&NWR its stock was given either a number which had become available by the withdrawal of a locomotive which had borne that number, or if that number had an associated name, it was given that name as well, or if no number was available, then the next number above the highest in the L&NWR books at the time. Thus in 1859, when the Lancaster & Carlisle stock was added to that of the L&NWR, their No 1 *Rickerby* took the Number 377, following the sequence of the "Old Crewe Types" No 376 *Proserpine*.

Fig. 1 The fourth No.1 *Saracen*. Problem class built in November 1861.

(L&NWR Society Photograph Collection)

3

The L&C engines were already named, resulting in some clearly undesirable duplication with existing L&NWR names. This led to the renaming of several of the L&C engines. There are instances of two locomotives with the same name running simultaneously, but they are extremely rare.

When locomotives were built by Contractors, and not at Crewe, as in the case of the Sharp, Stewart 0-6-0s in 1857, they were given available running numbers and the associated names.

Throughout L&NWR days the engine with the highest running number gave the clue to the total number in Capital Stock. For example the Company's Capital Stock prior to the addition of that of the L&C had been 376; and. to instance another example many years later, when the Experiment class 2646 *Boniface* was completed in July 1909, the Capital Locomotive Stock (including unnamed locomotives of course) was 2646.

The policy of every locomotive having a name could not last, and early in John Ramsbottom's time in October 1858 universal naming began to come to an end, when the fourth DX Goods to be built (Crewe No 402) emerged unnamed, despite the fact that there were old names available for re-use. This was the first indication of a change in policy, one which was no doubt caused by the sheer number of engines that the rapidly expanding Company was proposing to build. To start with there was some hesitation, for the next eight (Crewe Nos 403-410) came out between then and the following June and were given names, five old, and three, *Trevithick*, *Roberts* and *Whitworth* new, maybe just through a whim by Ramsbottom. From then on until May 1862 numbers and names were provided only when they became available because of the withdrawal of their previous owners: there was a single exception in August 1861 when No 568 was given the name *Stewart*, after it had been removed from Lancaster & Carlisle's 2-2-2 No 398.

The last Goods engine to receive a name was No 532 *Grasmere* in May 1862, and their names were removed by Ramsbottom from 1863 onwards, resulting in many old names becoming available for re-use at an earlier date than anticipated.

Very few Southern Division engines were named, but Webb decided in 1872 that four classes of express engines, the Bury, Curtis & Kennedy 2-2-2s known as the "Low-domed Singles", "Small Bloomers", "Large Bloomers" and "Extra Large Bloomers" should be given some of the names which he had available from withdrawn Northern Division stock.

In the days of the independent Southern Division, before the amalgamation of the locomotive departments in 1862, the only engines in stock with names were the Cramptons *Liverpool* and *London*, and two which had been transferred from the Huddersfield & Manchester, *Saddleworth* and *Standedge*.

The Southern Division took over the 29 engines of the South Staffordshire Railway in 1858, all of which bore names at the time. It seems likely that they all lost their names in 1862, if not before.

2. 'CREWE' OR 'MOTION' NUMBERS

Until April 1851, the engine name was stamped on the various parts of the motion so that they might be reunited on the same engine after repair. It must be borne in mind that as yet standardisation was in its infancy, and one engine's motion parts did not necessarily fit those of another. This was a strong reason for the names that were chosen having as few letters as practicable.

From then on, progressive numbers were stamped on the motion. One result of this was that it became possible to keep count of the number of engines built at Crewe. The numbering began with the number 183 appearing on the motion of the engine with Running Number 267, named *Glyn*. 183 was no arbitrary choice, but was to establish that 182 engines had by then been built at Crewe, an essential part of the Company's evidence, to counter the pending claim by one John Gray for infringement of his link-motion patent. Precisely which these 182 were remains a matter for conjecture, and those listed in Table 2 are one possibility. An alternative explanation certainly exists.

Gray lost his case in December 1851, but the system of assigning motion numbers once started continued to be used. They were consecutive and never repeated, and continued not only to the end of the L&NWR in December 1922, but long into LMS days.

There was in fact a single break in this consecutive line, which occurred in 1897 when Crewe Numbers 3784 and 3785, which had been set aside for the renewal of two Precedents, were not used.

To illustrate the establishment of a locomotive's identity, consider, for instance, Engine No.150 *Linnet*. There have been at one time or another three with this number and name. The first was the Liverpool & Manchester 2-2-2 of February 1845 which had its name stamped on its Motion; the second and the third were in fact identical LFB Passenger locomotives of the Prince Ernest class, but one of them had Motion Number 257 (of August 1853) and the other Motion Number 379 (of April 1857), the former having gone to the Lancaster & Carlisle Railway in 1857 to become their No 29 *Linnet*. There exist lists of members of the Prince Ernest class which do not include Motion Numbers, and so appear at first sight to print by mistake a No 150 *Linnet* twice. But it is not an error, for there were indeed two of them, but not at the same time. No two engines having the same Running Number were ever in L&NWR stock at the same time.

Engines not built at Crewe, such as those built at Wolverton, did not have Motion numbers. neither did those supplied by outside contractors, as for example those of the Lancaster & Carlisle Railway built by Rothwell and by Fairbairn which came into L&NWR stock in 1859, or the 0-6-0s built by Sharp, Roberts & Co. in the very early days of John Ramsbottom's time at Crewe.

But there were exceptions: the twenty Prince of Wales class built by the North British Locomotive Company in 1915 and 1916 were provided with Crewe Motion numbers (5257-5276): and not only that, their nameplates clearly stated "CREWE WORKS". It seems that the powers-that-be at Crewe much preferred to build their own locomotives and to make one believe they had when they had not! Similarly when the Beardmore & Co.'s *Prince of Wales* was built in March 1924 it received a Crewe Motion Number 5752, but in this instance the nameplate stated the correct builder's name.

The highest Motion number on a *named* L&NWR engine was 5565 on the Claughton *Sir Charles Cust*.

It is fascinating to see how unerringly these earliest names laid the foundation for L&NWR names for years to come. As the tables demonstrate, there was a *Talisman* to be seen from 1838 on the L&M until 22nd May 1937 when the Claughton was withdrawn; and its younger sister *Thalaba* too from 1838 until 22nd September 1934. The B&L Railway provided a *Marquis Douro* from 1838, and the name was still used until September 1928 when the Waterloo class engine was withdrawn, a *Friar* from the NU probably built in late 1839 or 1840 until 13th September 1933, a *Stentor* from the sixth engine built for the GJR in 1837 until January 1936, and their *Sirocco* also from 1837 until, believe it or not, in British Railway times, **11th June 1949**.

3. THE QUEST FOR ACCURACY

Charles Williams in his preface to the 1922 Edition of "A Register of the Locomotives of the London & North-Western Railway" wrote "The very best endeavours have been made, involving many hours of careful checking, to ensure absolute accuracy, without which such a publication as this loses much, if not all, of its value, but in dealing with such an enormous mass of figures as is contained in these pages, it is perhaps too much to hope that there shall be no slips." As it turned out greatly to his credit, there were only twenty-one, mostly typographical errors which he listed in his Supplement published in 1924.

It was a great achievement, and he could not possibly have expressed my own feelings more clearly, as I prepare this work for publication.

Typographical, and straightforward mistakes inevitably occur in compiling lists of such length and complexity as these.

This work is an attempt to place in one volume the details of all the named locomotives of the L&NWR and its associated companies, and has involved a study of all the many details, lists and tables that have been compiled and published over the past century or more. During the course of my research I have found that many if not all of these, official publications included, have contained some errors and misprints, some obvious, but others less so.

In addition to that I have found quite a fair degree of divergence between virtually every list and every other one, causing me to compare one with another, and decide which one to enter in this volume. The differences appeared for very good reasons.

In the May 1936 Railway Observer, E.E.Robinson, Jnr., commenting on a series of articles by Mr W.L.Harris, writes:- "I gather that Mr.Harris's figures are from the Crewe Books, and thus are practically the same as my own records. In many cases there are alternative entries in the Works Books that make matters very confusing. and the only procedure one can take is to accept the entry that seems most likely to be correct in the light of subsequent happenings." The terminology he used was "Crewe Books" and "Works Books", which is itself misleading, for both must have been books compiled at Crewe. In fact there are known to be two lists, one compiled by the Works, and the other by the Running Department which for many locomotives records a later building date.

In addition to those two lists, a third was compiled by observers noting the dates that appeared on the nameplates, or "Plate Dates" and this produced still more differences. The nameplate would have been prepared in anticipation of a locomotive's month of completion, and a delay, for example, sometimes occured over the end of one month and the start of the next.

Naturally too, there are differences as between withdrawal dates and scrap or cut-up dates. Crewe did not live in an Alice's Wonderland in which the command for execution was carried out on the spot! A study of the withdrawal and scrap dates of the Webb Precursors, for example, shows that the average time-lag between the two was about eleven weeks, a calculation which excludes the ten members of the class withdrawn in September and October 1891 and not scrapped until December the following year.

All these differences of dating are perfectly understandable, so all that one can be certain of is that such and such an engine was built and went into service 'very close indeed to' such and such a date, and came to the end of its working life 'near to' another.

None of the lists that have ever been published, not excepting those in the tables in this volume, can be described as being correct or otherwise.

There is one field worth mentioning in which there is an extremely high degree of concurrence. It is that of Crewe Numbers (Motion Numbers) by which every individual locomotive can be identified; and during the course of my researches, I have found only three small areas of divergence. (See Appendix 8)

Other differences, alas, are known to have a more sinister cause, when enthusiasm overrides the quest for historical accuracy. There have also been instances of 'historians' inventing information which they could not find, and presenting them as facts. A quotation by William Lees in the Journal of the Stephenson Locomotive Society of October 1956 is pertinent here:- "John Evelyn unburdened himself of a great truth when in 1682 he remarked 'It is not imaginable to such as have not tried, what labour a historian (that would be exact) is condemned to; He must read all, good and bad, and remove a world of rubbish before he can lay the foundation.' His words echo a peculiar truth when applied to a study of the 'London and North Western' engine stock of what might be termed the 'Carboniferous age'."

We are all involved in this 'Quest for Accuracy', researchers, authors, editors, proof-readers and last but by no means least yourselves the readers.

If I have invented anything, I didn't mean to!

4. THE ILLUSTRATIONS

Great care has been taken to ensure that the illustrations are related to the text and are of a high standard, and I am indebted to Rodney Lissenden for his guidance over this.

Some however are reproductions of very early photographs and it is inevitable that they are less than good, but they have been included for their historical interest and because they relate closely to the text. This applies particularly to Figures 12, 13, 17, 20, 22, 39, 40, 65, 67, 68 and 71, many of which are of locomotives absorbed by the L&NWR and sold or scrapped soon afterwards.

Fig. 2   Precursor class 5297 *Sirocco* which survived to become the last former L&NWR named locomotive in service. It was allocated British Railways No.58010, but withdrawn without carrying it on 11th June 1949.

(Allan Sommerfield Collection)

Chapter 2
NAMING – A CHRONOLOGICAL APPROACH

1 THE EARLY YEARS 1829-1848

England was comparatively peaceful in the years following the Napoleonic Wars. The early days of the Industrial Revolution abounded in skilled craftsmen and mechanics, available to the Railway Company Directors and locomotive builders and to their Locomotive Superintendents. One such was George Stephenson of Wylam, who taught himself to read at the age of seventeen, and became a renowned skilled engineer and mechanic.

It was in the first instance it was the Directors who selected the names for their engines, and if we are to understand and appreciate the underlying reasons for the names they chose we must endeavour to enter into their minds, their ways of life, and know something about the times in which they lived, and their environment.

The country by that time had been divided by the industrial revolution into two distinct parts: there was the old rural life, and in pockets within it a number of 'manufacturing towns', especially in the North and in the West Midlands. A glance of Cheffin's Map of the London and Birmingham Railway of 1839 shows the whole of Coventry of a size able to fit neatly into the acreage of Althorpe (now Althorp) Park. The Borough of Birmingham was only slightly larger.

In general the railway company Directors were leaders in the industrial revolution. They were able men of business, and in the case of those who hailed from the Liverpool area often held directorships in the shipping world too. They lived in country houses with grounds and libraries in proportion to their size. Birds in plenty on the estate, and private libraries filled with leather-bound volumes of the classics, and the works of the great English writers and poets.

When and where were the names chosen? Some no doubt during the course of a Directors' Meeting, others maybe after dinner at a Director's country residence after the ladies had withdrawn. (Was this, I wonder, the underlying reason for engines being named after Directors' Residences?) They were often men of learning and well-read; the library was at hand, and on the shelves were copies of the ancient classics which must have been a facet of the popular reading of the time.

The giants of mythology, the strongest of men and beasts, the ear-splitting, the fierce and the fiery were obvious choices for these entirely new machines of awesome strength and fire.

It was not just the L&M and GJR that bore such names as these; it was nation-wide. In those early days the length and breadth of the country the infant railway system abounded in Atlases and Vulcans, Samsons and Goliaths.

Around these name-selectors lay the countryside, bringing bird life to the forefront of their minds. Country roads wound they way between town and village, the railway with cutting and embankment and bridges over rivers went from place to place more or less as the crow flies. and their flight was swifter than the horse. What better than a series of bird names? There were plenty from which to choose.

Smoke maybe rose and hung over the manufacturing towns, but an after-dinner stroll into the grounds in the country opened up the vista of the planets, stars, some passing comet, an eclipse or even the occasional thunderbolt. Rural man is ever conscious of the night sky, just as we were during the second world war blackout when we looked up to assess whether an air raid on Coventry was less or more likely.

All of this is purely surmise and relates to the early days of engine naming. As is usually the case, the early informal ways tend to become formalised, and in reply to a correspondent's general inquiry in 1922 the editor of the Railway Magazine replied:

"The policy (of naming locomotives) to be adopted is generally decided by the directors; the actual names to be used is a matter of arrangement, being usually in the hands of the locomotive department, though probably the directors and the general manager will indicate their desires in any particular connection." Not an imaginative reply, but likely to be well informed.

The Liverpool & Manchester Railway Locomotive Numbers and Names

It soon becomes evident that their very earliest names were chosen for the speed, the fire and vapour trail they emitted, the explosive sound of the exhaust and their very strength which caught the imagination. Stephenson's *Rocket* went off like the military weapon of that name, these new machines flew like the *Meteor* and the *Comet*, of which many had at that time been seen. They belched sparks, smoke and ash like *Hecla*. They roared like the *Lion*, equalled the speed of the *Leopard*, and the trains they hauled reached their destinations like the *Dart* to its board, the *Arrow* to its target.

The strength of this new method of propulsion brought to mind such characters as *Samson* and *Goliath*, and their power was that of many horses, and so naturally at the very outset we find such names as *Elephant*, *Mastodon*, *Buffalo* and *Rhinoceros*. To a large extent the names chose themselves, and we are left with a delightful series of them.

In actual fact, when it arrived on the line on 18th January 1830, Robert Stephenson's engine bore the name *Wildfire* which he himself had chosen for it. By the time the next engine arrived on 1st February, the Board had decided to choose their own names for their locomotives, and named it *Comet*, and *Wildfire* was renamed *Meteor*. Then followed *Arrow* and *Dart*. They were not numbered until June, somewhat curiously not in the order in which they had arrived, starting with No 1 *Rocket*, followed by Nos 2-8, *Arrow, Meteor, Dart, Comet, Phoenix, Northumbrian* and *North Star*. From then on all new arrivals received their numbers in strict sequence.

The Planets - Astronomy

The batch of engines that began to appear at the close of 1830 were given the names of the Planets, so providing us with the first 'class' name 'The Planet' class. The series began in September 1830 with *Planet*, followed in 1831 by *Mercury, Mars, Jupiter, Saturn, Sun*, and *Venus*; in the same vein, but not of the same class, we find *Orion*, and still looking heavenwards, *Meteor, Comet, Shooting Star*, and *Eclipse*. *Neptune* was not discovered until 1846 and had to wait until 1903, when the last of the Alfred the Great class was named after the warship of that time. One may wonder why there was never an L&M engine named 'Uranus', for it had been discovered in 1781 by Herschel, who first gave it the name Georgiani Sidus after King George III. In this country it was popularly known as Herschel, but by the 1830s it was almost universally known as Uranus. It is worth noting that the GWR "Firefly" class engines included a series in 1841 of these six L&M planets, and they also omitted Uranus. Maybe it was little known at this period.

Birds

The first of the series began in September 1841 with their 69 *Swallow*, and continued until July 1846. Most of these names were repeated time and time again as the years went by, a batch of four more being added in May 1854, and a further eight on members of the George the Fifth class in the autumn of 1911.

In 1851 one of the SFB Goods DA appeared with a new bird name, *Swift*. This was some five years after the earlier series had ended, leading one to look for a possible alternative source. It may have been a descriptive name, after the pattern of the old L&M pair *Rapid* and *Speedwell*, but it is more likely to have had connections with John Swift, the solicitor who had acted for the Company in the matter of

Fig. 3   Stephenson's *Rocket*. Built in 1829. L&NWR postcard set 10 "Famous Locomotives" No.1.

(Fred Gray Collection)

the purchase of the land upon which Crewe Works came to be built.

The *Nightingale* of 1855 must surely have been named in honour of Florence Nightingale whose nursing work in the Crimea would have been in the public mind at the time. As we have seen, the use of the surname only was a well established practice.

All in all the L&M provided an inspiring collection of names.

The Grand Junction Railway Engine Names and Numbers

These date from 1837, and differ from those of the L&M. In a word, they were fiercer! It would seem that someone on the GJ had a fire and brimstone fixation. It is interesting to note that they did not duplicate names given to the adjoining L&M, a fact which eliminated any possible confusion that might have occured on the several miles of the L&M line over which their engines ran, and obviated the need for renaming when the two Companies amalgamated and became the L&NWR.

Characters of Mythology

The Grand Junction men with real imagination provided within its first 25 engines eight names from mythology, and in doing so gave the impression that they associated them with emanations of evil; there was *Hecate* who presided over witchcraft, *Alecto* the goddess of curses on evil-doers, *Centaur* the beast which was half horse and half man, *Cerberus* the three-headed watch dog, *Harpy* the minister of divine vengeance, and *Zamiel* a demon forest-huntsman.

Other early names

Not only that, their fish was the voracious *Shark*, their birds, *Falcon* and *Eagle* of 1837, *Hawk* and *Vulture* of 1838 were birds of prey, and on the ground for good measure was that highly unpleasant tyrant *Phalaris* who heated his prisoners in a bronze bull, and a *Scorpion* for any who might have escaped his clutches. It is true that the name selection mellowed, but not until June 1845 when *Phlegethon*, the river of fire in Hades, was followed by the *Prince*. It reminds one of living happily ever after a somewhat grisly nightmare.

The L&M selection had been so much gentler, with the exception of *Samson* and *Goliath* so named because of their physical strength. Altogether they provided a noble collection of names, almost all of which happily came down through the years and well into the 20th Century.

Volcanoes

Hecla in Iceland, *Etna* In Sicily and *Vesuvius* in Italy were obviously suitable names for locomotives, which belched fire, and smoke and ash.

Shakespearean Characters

A possible group but one which must be regarded as doubtful because the characters are such minor ones. They were *Caliban* and *Prospero* of 1837. Maybe they are both in tune with other Grand Junction names of ill repute, for one was a deformed slave, and the other condemned to live in a cell.

Much later, in L&NWR days there were four more *Ariel* in 1848, *Hotspur* in 1851, *Falstaff* in 1855 and *Puck* in 1866.

The C&B *Touchstone* of 1840 and the W&FJ *Titania* are clearly not members of any L&NWR set.

The Works of Sir Walter Scott

Whereas there may be some doubt about a series of Shakespeare's characters there is none about Scott's works There are two sets, the first of which appears in the L&M list in 1838 with *Rokeby, Roderick* (The Vision of Don Roderick) and *Talisman*.

The second, numbering five in all, appeared on members of the Problem class of January and February 1863, *Lord of the Isles, Marmion, Ivanhoe, Red Gauntlet* and *Waverley*.

Another name associated with Scott is *Jeanie Deans* but this, as mentioned elsewhere, was the result of a visit Mr.Webb made to Edinburgh.

Directors' Residences

The idea of naming engines after the homes of those closely involved in the railway scene came in March 1846, with *Lonsdale* (possibly), *Dalemain* and *Greystoke*; followed by *Ingestre, Sandon, Lowther, Knowsley* and *Trentham* provided later that year by the newly formed L&NWR.

Not until February 1852 do we find the next, with *Allerton* and *Sefton*, and last but not least in 1870 comes *Bevere* in Worcestershire, the home of Richard Moon.

London & North Western Railway Names and Numbers

Titles

We come now to a curious group of names, provided in 1847 and 1848.

The Victorian age, we may suppose, was one in which persons in authority were respected, whether of high rank in the navy or the army, of high birth, or in the judiciary. The idea of naming engines with titles or rank might not have occurred to us, but it did to them, and unquestionaly these powerful machines commanded considerable respect, and like their namesakes were not to be trifled with. The first four were *Duke, Earl, Baronet* and *Marquis*, and it is conceivable that the titles were suggested by personalities. If *Senator* was one of this set of names, one wonders what prompted the choice. We then move to include civic authority with *Mayor* and *Councillor*, the armed forces with *Admiral* and *General* (they appropriately put the Senior Service first), and the Diplomatic Corps with *Envoy* and *Ambassador*, and yet higher to include *Emperor* and *Monarch*. There was a late addition with *Viceroy* in 1853.

The Twins

Names derived from mythology continue to be used. One pair of these are worth a mention. *Castor* and *Pollux* were the twin sons of Jupiter and Leda, and the locomotives which bore their names were inseparable in service and in due course nine years later passed their names and numbers to the last two members of the "Isis" class. They were however parted three years later when *Castor* was transferred to the Southern Division and lost his name at the time, leaving his brother in the North. The elder brother's name survived until April 1936 living to the hoary old age of eighty-eight, while that of his junior had lasted only until May 1887, passing away anonymously in his late thirties.

Prime Ministers

The first to be named after a Prime Minister was the B&L *Peel*, and the first two of L&NWR times were *Canning* and *Russell* in June 1847. Many of the engines were named when those concerned were in Office.

The probability is that the Duke of *Wellington* was named primarily for his pre-eminence as a soldier.

Several other Prime Ministers were honoured later on, as detailed in the next chapter.

In Memoriam (i)

The first which comes into this group was *Huskisson* through the naming came seventeen years after his tragic death at the opening of the L&M. For subsequent such names see below.

Precious Stones

1848 provides several examples of minor series, starting with a cluster of precious stones in February *Diamond, Ruby, Pearl* and *Emerald*.

Patron Saints

The patron saints of England, Wales and Ireland appeared in quick succession in April and May 1848.

Flowers

In September 1848 came a tiny bouquet consisting of a *Lily*, a *Rose* and a *Violet*.

2. THE REIGN OF FRANCIS TREVITHICK: GJR 1841-1846, L&NWR N DIV 1846-1857

Trevithick's time was notable for the country's wealth, progress and enlightenment, when the nation's sea power was unchallenged, and when the nation was justly proud of its superiority in technology; the Great Exhibition to be held in 1851 in Hyde Park was being planned, which the whole world was to visit and marvel at British work and workmanship. The names of this period reflect the nation's well-being.

Ocean-going Liners (i)

The Port of Liverpool was the place where the L&NWR and the Shipping lines of Victorian days met and exchanged their passengers. There was the most efficient cooperation between them regarding the times of Boat Trains, and of the arrival and departure of the Liners. and there is no doubt that the L&NWR was interested in capturing as much of the mail as possible.

It is not surprising therefore that many express locomotives received the names of liners.

Which was the first? Very possibly, but it is impossible to be certain, *Unicorn*, in 1849, for this was the name of the Royal Mail Steam Packet which had made the first mail run to the United States in 1840.

(If not *Unicorn*, then *Britannia* of 1869 might qualify, for she had been the first Cunard liner, also coincidentally dating from 1840, but the fact that the name *Britannia* was followed immediately by an *Hibernia* and a *Scotia* strongly suggests its name source was national and did not refer to any ship.)

Postmasters General

Before the railway age long distance mail had been conveyed by stage-coach. The very considerable increase in mail following the advent of Rowland Hill's Penny Post in May 1840 coincided with the expansion of the rail network, and it was obviously advantageous for the Post Office and the Railway authorities to work in harmony to their mutual advantage. Thus several Postmasters General enjoyed the privilege of having an engine named after them, the first taking place in 1849.

Date	Postmaster General
1849	*Clanricarde*
1852	*Hardwicke*
1857 (L&C)	*Lowther* }
	Lonsdale }
1857	*St.Germans*
1857	*Canning* (George)
(see note concerning Prime Ministers)	
1863	*Elgin*

Apart from Elgin named in 1863, they all belonged to Trevithick's time. (see also Indian Mutiny)

Although neither was a PMG, *Rowland Hill* and *Maberley*, both were closely associated with the efficiency (or otherwise) of the Royal Mail, and received their names in February 1854 on successive engines. It was generally known that there was fierce antipathy between the two men, so here we find the L&NWR behaving in a completely neutral manner by giving them equal honour, side by side. But they did place *Rowland Hill* first, and his name long outlived that of *Maberley*.

In passing it should be noted that *Rowland Hill* was a very early example of the use of Christian and Surname. Just *Hill* would have been all too brief, and have meant nothing to the travelling public.

In Memoriam (ii)

The tragic and accidental death of the Earl of Powis in January 1848 was the second engine to be remembered in this way when the name *Powis* appeared on an SFB Pass SF built at Edge Hill in April 1849; The engine so named was held in store for a while, and only briefly emerged into the light of day when sent to work on the S Div in the summer of 1849 as part of the north versus south locomotive exchange, eventually emerging in early 1850 renumbered and named *Soho*. The name *Powis* was used again in July 1850 on an SFB Goods SF built at Crewe.

It was some while, not until 1873 in fact, that more engines named in memoriam appeared, and details of these will be found in the following chapter.

The Crimean, or Russian War

The War had a great influence over the choice of names throughout 1854.

On 5th July 1853 the Russians invaded the Danubian Principalities, and Sir Charles *Napier* recommended that the Home Fleet be brought to a state of discipline and completeness. In February 1854 a fleet hastily assembled from ships at Lisbon sailed for the Baltic on 11th March 1854. On the 29th war was declared against Russia, Vice-Admiral Sir Charles *Napier* was sent to the Baltic Sea, and at the same time a British Fleet and a Military Force embarked for the Black Sea and The Crimea.

Why the name *Czar* came out that March it is hard to understand: on the other hand the troopship *Simoom* was on active service and was an obvious choice. *Aberdeen*, also in March, was Prime Minister. By July HMS *Miranda's* and HMS *Amphion's* great exploits must have been in the public eye. The Turks were our allies, hence the name *Turk*; *Varna* was Marshal *St.Arnaud's* headquarters, and *Alma* the river and place of a notable battle; Field Marshal *Raglan* commanded the British forces, and HMS *Euxine* was another troopship. There are two contenders for the origin of *Baltic*: if one of the seas of the Crimean War received a name, why not the other? On the other hand, the trans-Atlantic liner *Baltic* held the Blue Riband in 1854.

Arab and *Cossack* undoubtedly have wartime associations, but both names prove difficult as regards their origins. *Arab* may simply refer to the breed of horse, or to those who rode them; in support of this the GWR had given one of their engines this name in 1853. Alternatively it could relate to a small fortification known as "the Arab fortress", upon whose successful defence against the Russian forces it is no exaggeration to say that for months the war depended upon it, and we read that "all Europe held its breath until the British army arrived to relieve it". *Cossack*, which we find paired in the name order with *Arab*, might also have referred to famous horsemen, but we cannot overlook that the Russian ship being built at Northfleet and intended to be named "Witjas", was seized on the outbreak of war, completed, and "renamed" HMS *Cossack*. Perhaps we are mistaken if we suppose that locomotive names always had an exclusive source; just occasionally it might have been otherwise.

What becomes clear during this period is the striking similarity between the naming of the ships of the Royal Navy and of L&NWR locomotives. It is a fact that of the British Fleet in the Black Sea in October 1854, six of the eleven Ships of the Line, and 21 of the 40 Frigates, and that almost one third of the Baltic Fleet of 45 vessels had names in common with L&NWR engines of the time. Many of these names had been chosen quite independently, but those mentioned above were beyond doubt given to commemorate outstanding ships and their achievements.

There does not appear to have been a warship named *Warrior*, and all one can say is that the name had a wartime flavour to it.

Florence *Nightingale's* immense contribution to the nursing profession was not immediately recognised, for her name does not appear until June 1855, the same month as an old L&M name was revived and a new name appeared in *Majestic* and *Banshee*, both of which were Frigates that had engaged in battle in the Black Sea. As for *Bellerophon*, it is difficult to be sure whether it was decided to introduce one more mythological being into the name list, or to honour a ship in the news at the time.

The GWR "Caliph" class had a *Neptune* in March 1854, *Cyprus* in April, *Janus* in May, *Sphinx* and *Banshee* in September, and *Amphion* in April 1856, all of which were names of vessels serving in the Fleets either in the Baltic or the Black Sea in 1854. But the L&NWR list of names covering that war is far and away the most comprehensive.

There were of course an assortment of other names interspersed among those with wartime assocations, including two great engineers *Fairbairn* and *Nasmyth* and another five birds.

3. THE REIGN OF JOHN RAMSBOTTOM 1857-1871

One of Ramsbottom's early decisions late in 1858 was to end the naming of goods engines, with the result that many of the "Old Crewe Types" lost their names, some when they were rebuilt as tank engines, some when the were placed on the Duplicate List, and many not until 1872 and 1873 as recorded in the late D.H.Stuart's copy of a list he discovered at Crewe. Another result was that most of the DX Goods were never named, and before long many of those which had been named passed them in 1863 and 1864 to members of the Samson and other classes then being built.

The Indian Mutiny

Just as the Crimean War had provided a set of names, so did the Mutiny of 1857, as found in the Problems four years later in February 1863, with that distinguished and gallant company of *Havelock*, *Outram*, *Clive* and *Clyde*. *Elgin*, whose name appears next in the list was only indirectly involved in overcoming the mutiny, by transferring troop reinforcements from Hong Kong to Calcutta. The reason for choosing his name was that he was by 1863 Viceroy of India.

This is one more instance of a grouping of names identifying exactly after whom the engines were named. For this *Clyde* was not named after the river but after Lord Clyde, and *Outram* not after the pioneer rail engineer but General Sir James Outram.

The final batch of Problems

Some two and a half years later in July 1865 ten more Problems were built as additions to capital stock, all of which received new names. The first two were relatives of Richard Moon: *Edith* was his daughter, and *Eleanor* the name both of his wife and of their daughter who had died in 1859.

Edith was withdrawn in January 1907, and *Eleanor* the following July, in which month both names were given to Whale's Precursors. The family bond was strong, for once again the two locomotives had successive Motion Numbers. The third in the batch was named *Alfred Paget*, possibly because in his role as clerk-marshal to the Queen he worked closely with the Company in matter relating to the Queen's travels. (A predecessor of *Sir Charles Cust*). To complete the batch came a delightful set of seven women of mythology.

The Newtons of 1866-1869

It was in 1866, with the advent of the Newtons and at a time when old names were in short supply that a splendid batch of new names began to appear.

It seems to have been an age when the mid-Victorians had time to look back and consider our history. The Directors must have debated long and hard to decide as to who and what should be listed among the most outstanding people and events of the world's past and present; certainly they came out with a noble series.

In the case of the people they selected, only the surname was used: nameplates were to be short in length, as had been general.

Sir Isaac *Newton* heads the list, and his intended successor was the American Benjamin *Franklin*. But just then *The Duke of Edinburgh* visited Crewe Works, and his name on a plate appeared in place of Franklin's. There followed the versatile *Herschel*, by then an elderly man in his mid-seventies, and after him more names to conjure with, the great men of science and engineering *Newcomen, Telford, Smeaton, Dalton* and *Faraday*.

But what about *Franklin* and the nameplates that had been made? He came into his own six months later and the plate date was altered from MAY 1866 to NOVR 1866. He was still in good company, amidst four men of literary fame, two more 'titles', two prime ministers, some generals, admirals and explorers, and two parliamentarians.

Fifteen months after that the third batch were built, and the list of names chosen contains many that were highly topical, providing a good insight into what the country was concerned with in the summer of 1868 and the latter end of 1869: several battle honours, more great names, and near the end of the batch come *Baying, Tennyson,* the trio *Britannia, Hibernia* and *Scotia, Dunrobin* and *Goldsmith*.

Of these seven, only *Britannia* and *Hibernia* survived throughout their engine's life. *Tennyson* was renamed *John Mayall* in 1885; In January 1870 *Baying* was renamed *Bevere*, and at some unknown date that year (Samuel Scott's manuscript does not give a month.) *Scotia, Dunrobin* and *Goldsmith* were renamed *Sedgwick, Quernmore* and *Patterdale* respectively. The reason for the renaming of the last three lies in the fact that three former Lancaster & Carlisle goods engines nos 379, 380 and 381 had been withdrawn by or during December 1868 and their numbers were taken by these newly built Newtons; their associated names swiftly followed. But why *Baying* became *Bevere* so swiftly remains unknown; maybe there was a compelling reason for Richard Moon's residence to be displayed.

By the time of the final two batches there were plenty of old names available, and only three were given new ones.

4.THE LONG REIGN OF FRANCIS WEBB 1871-1903

The naming of the Southern Division Engines

It is evident that Webb was interested in names for his engines. Goods engines continued to lose the names, and theirs and many others were available for re-use. He decided they should go to express engines on the Southern Division. Thus in Spring 1872 McConnell's Low-domed Singles and the Bloomers (small, large and extra large) received names.

Three of these names were new. *Caithness* was given to one of the extra large Bloomers to honour a recently appointed Director, and two large Bloomer names were new, *Japan* and *Burmah*. for by 1872 trade was expanding with the countries of the Far East, and Japanese and Burmese delegations had arrived in Britain. The choice of these names was no doubt to encourage good diplomatic and business relationships, and no doubt to impress our visitors. It would not be surprising if we were to find that they were used on trains taking them to see British Industry at work.

The first Newton built during his time was, of course, named after his predecessor in office, *John Ramsbottom*. After which for the greater part, old names were re-used, the exceptions mostly being topical. But what was it that caused the name *Marquis* to be changed to *Isabella* in 1873?

A Trio of Virtues

Pluck, Patience and *Perseverance* were early members of the Precedent class built in March 1875, and all three went together to Edge Hill. It is hard to conceive a more imaginative trio of names for express engines. One may wonder if their names reflected Webb's feeling as he worked to produce the class, also how long they remained together.

The United States Presidents

During the spring of 1881 a party of L&NWR Directors including the Duke of Sutherland and organised largely on the initiative of Mr.Henry Crosfield paid a visit to the United States of America and met officials of the Pennsylvania Railroad, the Chicago & North Western, the Baltimore & Ohio and many other railroad Companies, learned a great deal about railway practice in the New World and established many good relationships. They paid a visit to the White House, and were most courteously received by *President Garfield*, This took place shortly before his assassination. The naming of three Precedents in January 1882, No 253 after him as a memorial, and Nos 254 and 256 after *President Lincoln* and *President Washington* were a fitting tribute to the newly forged links between British and American railways and railroads. All three were for many years shedded at Edge Hill, enabling visitors from the New World to have a good chance of seeing them and noting their names.

In their journey the Directors travelled widely and among other things, marvelled at the grandeur of the Niagara Falls. The naming in 1885 of *Niagara* does not appear to be associated with any ship, but the Falls, once seen, remain in the memory and so possibly we have a connection here with this tour. There is a full account of this journey in G.P.Neele's "Railway Reminiscences". He was one of the party.

New names come flooding in from 1882 onwards until 1890, not unsurprisingly those of many liners. By this time a third of the world's sea-going ships were on the British register, and the Port of Liverpool was exporting more British goods, not least Lancashire's cotton, than any other in the land. Passengers to and from the New World were multiplying. The Blue Riband was repeatedly being broken, and its holders were much in the news. What better than to name the Euston to Liverpool locomotives after the great ships that plied between Liverpool and New York.

So we have:-

Ocean-going Liners (ii)

In the first section under this heading the possibility was considered of *Unicorn* being the first ocean going liner to receive a name. By February 1884 we are on sure ground, when Webb brought out his Experiment Compound class and gave its second batch in February and March 1884 the names of nine liners, of which five had at one time or another won the Blue Riband. They came from no less than six different shipping companies, and all were sailing from Liverpool. One suspects there might have been ten ships' names chosen, but the sudden death of Richard Roberts caused the first of the batch to bear his name instead.

Webb's Dreadnoughts were built two years later and from March 1886 onwards came a series of Cities, nine of which were named after liners plying from Liverpool. Strangely no liner bore the name *City of Liverpool*, so this one was named after the City at the time of an Exhibition there in 1886; neither was there a liner of the name *City of Lichfield*.

Thirdly came the Teutonics in March 1889, nine of which received the names of White Star liners. It is reasonable to conject that a series of ten names had first been proposed, leading one to wonder which name had been chosen and then displaced by *Jeanie Deans*. Could it have been *Belgic*, which was substituted for *Germanic* in 1914? It would be good to think so.

In March 1893 the Inman and International Line transferred to the American Line and thereafter sailed from Southampton, thus bringing to a close the link between ship's and L&NWR locomotive's names.

An unusual development was the introduction of

Two-word Names

The winter of 1891 presented the Company with an entirely new problem. A new and larger class of Webb's Compounds was emerging, with separate splashers over the driving wheels. They were known as the Greater Britain class, after the prototype and were ten in number. They were followed in 1894 and 1898 by another ten of similar splasher design known as the John Hick class. Very possibly the question arose as to which splasher should have the nameplate (as was the case years later on the LMS with their Jubilees) and the L&NWR opted for two-word names, with one word on each splasher. All twenty were double-named. The days of the short single name on the 2-2-2s were long past.

Apart from *Henry Cort* and *John Rennie*, all the names chosen were new, and this, of course, is how *Bessemer* was reunited with his Christian name!

Queen Victoria's Diamond Jubilee and Ships of the Royal Navy

And so we approach the end both of the reign of Queen Victoria, and of that of Francis Webb. The Queen had been on the throne for an astonishing 60 years. The word Jubilee was on people's lips as Millennium has recently been on ours. The British were conscious of and proud of the Empire, and of the Navy and its men of war which ruled the waves. So we find the *Iron Duke* of June 1897 renamed in the December *Jubilee* and being provided with a unique nameplate engraved with a red diamond at each end of the lettering. That was followed by a most comprehensive roll call of the ships of the Royal Navy in the Jubilee and Alfred the Great classes, led by *Black Prince* in June 1897 and culminating in *Neptune*, in the month of Francis Webb's retirement, August 1903.

Reality and Legend

Not all the Jubilee class were named after warships of the day. *Black Diamond* might have had a loose assocation with the red diamonds on Jubilee's nameplate, and Black Watch was known to be Queen Victoria's favourite regiment. We seem to have some lateral thinking here.

The names *King Edward VII* and *Queen Alexandra* were an obvious choice, and the reasoning behind *T.H.Ismay*, *La France*, *Francis Stevenson* and *Charles H.Mason* is evident and dealt with elsewhere. What lay behind the choice of *Crusader* and *Cavalier* is obscure: they do not seem to have been warships.

But what about the five remaining seemingly assorted new names?

Rob Roy	of 3.99
Robin Hood	of 4.99
Alfred the Great	of 5.01
King Arthur	of 6.01
Lady Godiva	of 8.03

Have these names anything in common? The only possible, indeed, highly probable answer lies in the fact that all five are real people to whom popular legendary tales have accumulated over the years. No longer, therefore, do we need to search for some connection between the L&NWR and Coventry. Legends abound around Rob Roy and Robin Hood; Alfred the Great burnt some cakes, and there are the

Arthurian legends (vide *Merrie Carlisle*); Lady Godiva's exploits in Coventry have been embellished in the course of time. I am particularly grateful to Clive Holden for spotting this series of names.

5. THE SHORT REIGN OF GEORGE WHALE 1903-1908

We now have reached Edwardian times.

Maybe George Whale had locomotive matters of a more serious nature than the naming of his engines. Many of the difficulties he was faced with were those he inherited from his predecessor, causing him to break with tradition by not naming his first new engine after him.

As a result of the swift withdrawal of Webb's Compounds, their names were queueing up to be re-used, so at no time did he have to set his mind on deciding upon any new names. If there were topical events, there was no room to include them, a fact which, as far as past Director's names were concerned, was swiftly put right in Bowen Cooke's time.

Only the final members of his Experiment class which went to traffic in 1909 after his retirement received new names, and it is unlikely that he took any part in their choice. They were the batches built in 1909 with names starting with "B" and the Counties, and thus strictly speaking they belong to:-

6. THE REIGN OF C.J.BOWEN COOKE 1909-1920
The Names beginning with "B"

An over-spill from Whale's days, and what a fascinating miscellany consisting of names guaranteed to excite the traveller's curiosity, and not even appearing in alphabetical order.

The Experiment class Counties

From November 1909 until January 1910 a very neat series appeared which began with a series of seventeen English Counties in alphabetical order situated northwards and westwards from Euston, and ended with the three Welsh Counties served by the Company.

So we come to Bowen Cooke's own selection of names.

The George the Fifth and Queen Mary classes Royalty, Directors, Chief Mechanical Engineers

He had not long been in charge of locomotive building at Crewe when on May 6th 1910, King Edward VII died, and King George V ascended to the throne, leading to his first choice of names, *George the Fifth* and *Queen Mary*. They had only been on the throne for two months.

His next move was to honour his predecessor-but-one, *F.W.Webb* and in so doing made good Whale's omission, and immediately after that he honoured his immediate predecessor *George Whale*. That was in the October, which happened to be the month in which George Whale died, and so that name may thus be regarded also as being In Memoriam.

After which came the names of fourteen past Directors, a most fitting tribute to those great men who had ensured the success of the Company so faithfully before his time as CME.

In 1912 came the death of *Lord Stalbridge*, and the engine which had been ordered as *Caliban* was in May 1913 named after him. He had been a most highly respected Chairman. The inclusion of *S.R.Graves* the previous March was of course just an instance of the re-use of a former director's name.

The Hounds

A series of ten "hounds" came out in April and May 1911. The first of these, somewhat curiously, was only the non-English *Dachshund*, and the name lasted only until December 1915, when the letters were defaced by a red line scored through them and another plate worded *Bull Dog* placed above. There could be no doubt which was to be master over the other.

Vessels of Discovery

After the 1911 series with *Coronation* and nine patriotic names which are dealt with in the next chapter, came a series of ten names which at first sight do not appear to cohere. But the several series of names which preceded them, as well as the birds which immediately followed, and the resorts (built in 1915) served by the Company on the last members of the class, were obvious groups of ten. It is logical to surmise that there ought to be a common bond. It is worth while to list them here:-

Beagle	*Perseus*	*Traveller*
Challenger	*Nubian*	*Vanguard*
Fire Queen	*Racehorse*	
Harrier	*Roebuck*	

Only *Roebuck* was a name that had been used before, on a "Columbine" class of November 1847 withdrawn in 1879, and there is no reason to suppose it had referred to anything other than the small swiftly running deer.

What, if any, could be the connection between these names? The answer begins to emerge when one remembers that *Beagle* was the name of the ship in which Darwin made his great voyage of exploration, and that *Challenger* was the name of the Royal Naval vessel used in the late 1870s for experiments in deep sea soundings. Might the others be vessels used in exploration and discovery?

Racehorse and *Roebuck* neatly fit into this category, the former used in Arctic exploation, and the latter in exploration of Australia. Of the other six of the set, the best that can be said is that *Harrier, Traveller* and *Vanguard* are the right sort of names. Research up to the present has failed to find anything more.

The Resorts

The final batch of ten George the Fifth class which came out in the summer of 1915 were given the names of popular resorts served by the Company. One of them, *Dovedale* had been ordered as *Ashbourne*, and, presumably because of local protests about accuracy *Leamington* swiftly was altered to *Leamington Spa*.

To sum up, the naming of the George the Fifth class was most orderly. There were ten Directors, ten hounds, ten associated with the Coronation and the year 1911, ten birds (five new and five old), what would have been twenty traditional names, had it not been for the inclusion of *Loyalty* and *Lord Stalbridge* in place of the names *Plynlimmon* and *Caliban* that had been ordered for them; and finally the ten resorts.

The Prince of Wales

In October 1911 the prototype of a new class of 4-6-0 express engines was completed, and it was decided that it should be named after the Prince of Wales.

So the nameplates from Experiment class No 1676 were removed, and the building date on it altered from NOVR 1906 to OCTR 1911. The change is quite evident because the brass mix then used differed slightly from the original one.

The new name for the No 1676 was *Shakespeare*.

The Prince of Wales's Warships

If, as we have seen, names were often chosen in batches of ten, it is arguable that the nine names which followed the 1911 *Prince of Wales* might have had some connection with him, and it has been suggested that they were the names of the warships or shore establishments on or at which the Prince had served during his naval training.

Eight of these names fit the bill. *Andromeda* was a Training Ship, *Bonaventure* and *Hermione* were Cruisers, *Coquette* and *Wolverine* were Destroyers, *Enchantress* was the Admiralty Yacht, *Pathfinder* a Scout Cruiser, and *Defiance* was the Torpedo Training School at Devonport. Only *Conqueror*, a Battleship built in 1911 does not. Whatever be the truth of this theory anyone who had served in the other eight would have been thoroughly trained.

This is certainly an explanation that is, to say the least, intriguing, and indeed may be regarded as quite plausible.

The Claughton class Directors

Then very early in 1913 came the Claughton class, and with them an almost complete change of policy, for apart from *Ralph Brocklebank* who died in 1895, all the Directors were, as far as can be ascertained, very much alive.

Men and Women of Literature

Later in October 1913 more Prince of Wales class came out, bearing a fine series of new names, arguably the best ever devised, commemorating famous poets, authors, historians and playwrights. All included either a christian name, or the initials by which the person had popularly been known; this was a great improvement on the use of the surname only, as had been the case with *Milton* and *Goldsmith* when previously commemorated.

There were to have been thirty in all, but it was decided in March 1914 to honour the veteran Mr.Neele, their famous Superintendent of the Line who was by then approaching his nineties, and so *Francis Bacon* whose name had been chosen to end the series, graciously stepped down and gave place to *G.P.Neele*.

The Great War 1914-1918

War was declared on the 4th of August 1914 and two months later the nameplate *Germanic* was scored out and another plate worded *Belgic* placed above it. The second batch of Claughtons was under construction just then, and *Lord Kitchener's* name appears in the middle of the series of names of Directors of the Company. It was an obvious choice, for no one was more vividly in the public eye than he. In November 1914 *Teutonic* was renamed *The Tsar* and in December 1915 *Dachshund* received the same treatment as *Germanic* had received, with the name *Bull Dog* superimposed. Understandably anything with a German flavour was to be expunged.

The War affected every aspect of life, and locomotive building was severely curtailed. No more Prince of Wales class were built until locomotive shortage made it imperative to have more, so another twenty were constructed by the North British Locomotive Company between October 1915 and January 1916, all of which were given old names, but of course with new straight plates to suit the long splashers on this class.

At the same time, but extending to April 1916 thirty more of the class came out from Crewe, ten with old names and the other twenty with clear wartime associations. The first ten comprised the names of outstanding men and women, including the nursing heroine *Edith Cavell,* whose execution by the Germans had caused such a shock to the public: and the second group of ten included three which commemorated the Dardanelles campaign, and seven of ships lost by enemy action, two of which, *Anglia* and *Tara* had historical connections with the Company. The name *Arethusa* presents a difficulty of identity, in that her loss was a comparatively minor instance of the many terrible naval losses suffered during the war, in that she had gone down almost by accident with little loss of life. It has not proved possible to find what if any connection there may have been between her and her crew and the L&NWR.

By mid-March 1916 brass was in short supply, the country was passing through a time of severe austerity and the policy of naming express engines came to a halt. The subsequent batches of the Princes were never named.

In the Claughton class *Captain Fryatt*'s name appears. That was in March 1917 a few months after his gallantry and execution.

Almost the conclusion of these wartime names was the honouring of three L&NWR Employees who had won the Victoria Cross, once more on Claughtons.

After the War

In January 1920 the name *Patriot, In Memory of the Fallen L&NWR Employees 1914 - 1919* was given; it was a splendid War Memorial, which appeared first briefly on a Claughton, but was soon transferred to another member of the same class. It was for many years used for the observance of the two minutes' silence at Rugby Shed on Remembrance Day, wreathed in poppies.

This was a start, albeit a brief one, to providing once again names for the Company's express engines.

According to the published lists, five months later the name *C.J.Bowen Cooke* appeared on engine 2059 in honour of their highly esteemed Chief Mechanical Engineer, and the nameplates were dated MAY 1920. It was a great shock when he died in office on the 18th of October. The old plates were scrappped and in his memory new ones were substituted, bearing the date OCTR 1920.

In the tables that follow the date of building of 2059 is given as May 1920, and appears in its proper sequence as *5530* in the Crewe or Motion numbers; but it has been established that the previous owner of 2059, a 1400 class "Bill Bailey" 4-6-0 Compound with Crewe No.*4439*, was not withdrawn until September 1920, from Monument Lane shed. Crewe Works was under severe strain during 1920 owing to the transition from wartime work to locomotive and general railway requirements, and it is possible with the 1920 Claughtons there was some variation between plate dates and dates of building, and that *C.J.Bowen Cooke* did not emerge until the September.

A year later in December 1921, Claughton 207 received the name *Sir Charles Cust.* This was done to promote a better relationship between the Company and the Royal Household in planning and executing royal journeys, and possibly also to maintain the subsidiary policy of always providing a named engine for a royal journey, one which had been under strain because of the plethora of new and unnamed Claughtons. It is said that Sir Charles first saw his name when 'inspecting' the engines the Company had provided for one of the journeys mentioned above! The nameplate itself was not new, for it had been used temporarily on the occasion of a Royal Train working on 8th October 1921.

Four more wartime commemorations followed, three bearing the rank and names of L&NWR employees who had won the Victoria Cross during the war, the fourth that of the Cruiser *Vindictive,* well known for her self-sacrifice at Zeebrugge on St.George's Day 1918, named at about the time she was being raised to the surface.

Finally the age old policy of re-using names of yore was resumed at an unhurried pace well into 1923 and for a couple of months after the Minute 53 of the LMS Rolling Stock Committee dated 31st May 1923 was promulgated. This Minute stipulated "new engines" (were) "not to be named but those with names will continue to do so." The nameplates of the Claughtons until the end of January 1923 had the inscription "L & N W R Co.", and those after then had "L M S".

How fortunate that that old and very long standing pair of names *Talisman* and *Thalaba* should reappear in the nick of time; and when *Patience* was reborn, surely *Pluck* and *Perseverance* could not have been far behind. As will be seen below Pluck missed by a hair's breadth, while *Perseverance* failed to make it under Minute 1714 of the LMS

Board in 1927 because of some Royal Scot name-juggling, and as it transpired had to wait patiently until its revival in October 1936 on an LMS Jubilee. It got there in the end, a splendid witness to its own name!

So by July 1923 many old names had reappeared, twelve on Princes and twenty on Claughtons, but there were to be no more. The last two were *Bevere* and *Baltic,* Some more names had been chosen but, alas, it was too late. According to C.Williams's Register they would have been:-

The Prince of Wales class

Richard Francis Roberts	Cook
Shah of Persia	City of New York
St.Patrick	Euxine
The Duke of Edinburgh	Florence
William Baker	Isabella
Belted Will	Liver

The Claughton class

Duke of Albany	Magdala
Eden	Marchioness of Stafford
Firefly	Outram
Hardman	Pluck
Joshua Radcliffe	Quernmore

A Postscript

The Beardmore LMS No 5845 Prince of Wales

Strictly speaking this is not a L&NWR locomotive, except in design, and it never received an L&NWR Number. It was exhibited at the British Empire Exhibition in 1924, and was named only for its duration. The nameplate was of a different design from the one that first appeared on the Experiment 1676 in November 1906, and which had been adapted to appear on the prototype Prince of Wales Class locomotive 819 in October 1911. This latter pair of plates were removed from 819 when it arrived in October 1924 at Derby for repair, but returned sometime after January 1925 to what was by then LMS No 5600.

Chapter 3
NAMING – A THEMATIC APPROACH

Fig. 4   Group of L.N.W. Officers 1879. L&NWR Official Photograph. Some of the men whose names appeared on the Company's engines.
"Mr.F.W.Webb Loco Dept" Left hand end with arms resting on the stone.
"George Findlay Genl.Manager" Standing above Mr.Webb's cuffs, wearing hat.
"Mr.G.P.Neele Supt.of Line" Fifth from left in top row, with dark moustache and beard.
"Mr.Whale Loco Dept" With sideburns, standing behind and to the right of Mr.Neele.
"Mr.F.Harrison Assist Supt of Line" Right hand end of front row, with watch chain.
Also in the photograph is "Adimiral Dent Marine Dept", whose two sons, Sir Francis' and Charles' names appeared in 1916. His head appears immediately to the right of Mr.Webb's hands.

Company Directors

The first Director's name, *Sutherland*, appeared in February 1851 and undoubtedly related to the 2nd Duke who had been a Director of the Liverpool & Manchester Railway. This was followed two months later by *Glyn* and *Allerton* in 1852, and *Anson* in 1853, the honour being bestowed on the last of these after he had resigned from the office of Chairman in 1853 on being appointed Commander in Chief, India. Next came *Chandos* a highly influential man not only in his directorship of the Company but in many other respects too.

No more are found until 1873, when the sudden death of Samuel Graves was remembered by 'Improved Precedent' No 1141 *S.R.Graves,* and the year after 'Precedent' No 2176 *Robert Benson,* that old veteran who had served on the Board since 1844 until his death in the autumn of 1874, and No 2177 *Edward Tootal*, having served since 1851. They were the two grand old men of the Board, and in this way their CME expressed appreciation. The same happened again in 1877 after the

death of *Sir Hardman Earle.* The next came in 1894 when Sir Richard Moon who had been Chairman of the Board from 1861 until 1891, and knighted in 1887, was given the name, simply *Richard Moon.* Maybe that was his wish. At the same time *William Cawkwell* the Board's Deputy Chairman received a name.

The name *T.H.Ismay* comes next in February 1900, on Jubilee No 1921, most probably because of his renown as a founder of the White Star line as well as L&NWR Director, and in memory of his recent death.

More Director's names appeared in 1910 and 1911 on early members of the George the Fifth and Queen Mary classes, followed in 1913 by the name *S.R.Graves* once again, and as the result of his recent death *Lord Stalbridge.*

Also in 1913 came the Claughton class, and with them another long series, including *Ralph Brocklebank* who had died in 1895. In the case of the *Duke of Sutherland* it is difficult to know whether he knew about the choice of name before he died. The locomotive chosen was the first of three of the class to carry the date June 1913 and so might therefore have emerged from Crewe early that month, and the Duke himself died on the 26th.

The Company's Officers

From first to last it was the splendid custom to reward Company officers either during their lifetime, or as often was the case, as a fitting memorial to their outstanding and long service. As will be seen from the table below Joseph *Locke* was the first to receive the honour, with Captain Mark *Huish* following a couple of years later. James Edward *McConnell* whose face was set so sternly against the naming of engines had his name on a South Staffordshire engine, but sometime after its arrival on the Southern Division and had come into his charge, its name was removed, never to appear again.

There were many, and this table provides an excellent summary of many of the prominent and faithful servants of the Company.

		Date of name	Duration of office
Chief Mechanical Engineer, (or equivalent title).			
James Edward *McConnell*	Locomotive Supt.	1858(SS)	1847-1862
Francis *Trevithick*	ditto	1859	1843-1857
John Ramsbottom	ditto	1872	1857-1871
F.W.Webb		1910	1871-1903
George Whale		1910	1903-1909
C.J.Bowen Cooke		1920	1909-1920
Superintendent of the Line			
G.P. Neele		1914	1862-1895
Sir Robert Turnbull		1913	1895-1914
Chief Engineer			
Joseph *Locke*	Engineer in Chief GJ	1851	1835-1837
	Engineer in Chief L&C		1841-1846
Robert *Stephenson*	Engineer L&M	1851	1827-1833
	Engineer L&B		1833-1838
William Baker		1879	1859-1878
Francis Stevenson		1902	1879-1902
E.C.Trench		1916	1909-1922
General Manager			
Captain Mark *Huish*		1853	1846-1858
George Findlay		1894	1880-1893
I.T.Williams		1917	1917-1919 (Acting)
Sir Thomas Williams		1919	1919-1920
Sir Robert Turnbull		1913	1914
Guy Calthrop		1916	1914
Sir Guy Calthrop		1919	-1919
Sir Frank Ree		1913	1909-1914
Solicitor			
John *Swift*		1851	Early days-1861
James *Blenkinsop*		1873	1861-1872
Richd Francis Roberts		1884	1874-1883
Charles H.Mason		1903	1883-1903
Company Secretary			
Henry *Booth*		1853	
Manager of L&M, Secretary of GJR, Joint Secretary (Northern)			1846-1859
Charles Edward *Stewart*		1861	1859-1866
Thomas Houghton		1910	1890-1902
James Bishop		1916	1904-1921
Auditor			
Henry Crosfield		1871}	1864-1882
The Auditor		1878]	

The Ladies

Beyond question the Ladies' names present the greatest difficulty when it comes to discovering who they actually were. It is all too easy to state that Eleanor was the wife of King Henry II. Indeed she was, but that is highly unlikely to be the source of the name.

It is extremely probable that the ladies in question have some close connection with the influential gentlemen of the Company.

There is little doubt who *Madge* (April 1871) was, and the identity of *Mabel* (October 1880) after some confusion as to her precise relationship with George Stephenson, has been resolved. She was his mother, and Robert's grandmother, but precisely why she was chosen for the honour is unresolved. There seems to be no doubt however that *Florence* (April 1872) was the eldest daughter of the Duke of Sutherland.

Neither is there any problem concerning *Edith, Eleanor* or *Isabella.* As will be seen in the Glossary, all three were close relations of Sir Richard Moon.

Ida (May 1853) is most unlikely to relate to a living relative of a Company Director or high officer, for it appeared twelve years before any other such names, and the identity of *Adelaide* (January 1866) remains unsolved, but with a Crewe Number only two figures distant from *Henrietta* and *Constance* (both also January 1866) she must surely fit into the L&NWR family somewhere.

In Memoriam (iii)

As mentioned in the previous chapter *Huskisson* and *Powis* were names resulting from a death. From Webb's day onwards more engines were named after men who had had long and close association of one kind or another with the Company and had passed on. The shock of *S.R.Graves'* sudden death in January 1873 was most heavy, causing his name to appear on the first of Webb's "Improved" Precedents in the August; The name *Blenkinsop,* who died shortly after Graves, was given to the next one of this batch.

The roll of honour is:-

Aug 1873	*S.R.Graves*	Jan 1884	*Richd Francis Roberts*
Aug 1873	*Blenkinsop*	April 1894	*George Findlay*
Feb 1875	*Robert Benson*	Feb 1900	*T.H.Ismay*
March 1875	*Edward Tootal*	March 1902	*Francis Stevenson*
April 1877	*Sir Hardman Earle*	Feb 1903	*Charles H.Mason*
Feb 1879	*William Baker*	Oct 1910	*George Whale*
Nov 1880	*Lawrence*	May 1913	*Lord Stalbridge*
Feb 1882	*Henry Pease*	June 1913	*Duke of Sutherland*
	and, last but not least,	Oct 1920	*C.J.Bowen Cooke*

The last two are worth special attention.

Duke of Sutherland must be considered a border-line case, for the locomotive was the first of three Claughtons to carry the date June 1913 and might therefore have emerged from Crewe early that month. The Duke died on the 26th. It would be good to think that he knew about the proposed naming before he died, but, of course if that were the case, the name was not given in his memory.

C.J.Bowen Cooke The locomotive's official building date is given as May 1920, but it was not completed until the October, and was possibly still in the Paint Shop when Bowen Cooke died, unexpectedly, on 18th October.

Locomotive Engineers

It is hardly surprising that we find few locomotive builders in the list of names, because after the establishment of the Company's Works at Crewe, there was little need for outside builders, and in the case of the Southern Division who bought the majority of their locomotives from such firms until Wolverton Works went into production. Wolverton-built locomotives were unnamed.

Bury of Edward Bury & Co. was a name which appeared very early on on a B&L locomotive, in 1832 in fact, but was promptly renamed *Bee*. (Did he prefer to hide behind his Initial, one may wonder, or did the engine buzz as kettles sometimes do?) Another possibility is the name *Stephenson,* Robert, of R.Stephenson & Co. whose firm's output was prolific.

We are on sure ground with *Fairbairn* and *Nasmyth* which appeared in May 1854. Had these two names not appeared together there might have been a problem in identifying the latter, for there was more than one Nasmyth in the public domain at that time, but only one possible Fairbairn. The Nasmyth to be eliminated was the South India Company's Lieutenant whose name must have appeared frequently in The Times because of his outstanding leadership at the Arab fortress in the Crimea. The position of a name in relation to those around it not infrequently gives a sure clue to the name's source, and here we have a good example.

Famous Engineers, Inventors and Scientists

It is only to be expected that such folk as these found their names on steam locomotives, for they were true partners with the Railways in the Industrial Revolution . *James Watt,* a very early name first introduced in 1848, and *Richard Trevithick* were pioneers in the use of steam power. *Wheatstone* whose electric telegraph helped significantly in rail safety had intimate connections with the L&NWR, as also did *Henry Bessemer,* one of whose steel plants was installed at Crewe and *William Siemens* who had one of his furnaces there. *Whitworth,* whose development of standardisation had such an impact of mechanical engineering, also had close personal connections with Crewe. Great civil engineers, such as Thomas *Telford* and *John Rennie* were included as was *Richard Arkwright,* whose contribution to the Lancashire cotton industry brought so much business to the L&NWR together with *Murdock,* pioneer in the gas industry, and underpinning them all that most brilliant of mathematicians, Isaac *Newton* himself.

There are many more numbered among the great, who will I trust forgive me for having recorded their names only in the Glossary and the Tables.

Locomotive Developments, Precedents, etc.

In the English language the word "precedent" has many synonyms. Through the L&NWR years we find the names *Precedent, Premier. Precursor, Pioneer* and *Forerunner,* all genuine successors of the *Novelty* of yore. Another delightful pair are *Problem* and *Theorem,* reflecting the draughtsmen and engineers wrestling with new designs and developments; *Experiment, Compound* and *Triplex* are all in the same vein. These delightful groups of names are typical of the fertile imagination in the minds of the Chief Mechanical Engineers of the day, who were unceasingly experimenting. Both the *Experiment* of Sharp, Roberts & Co. for the Liverpool & Manchester Railway built in February 1833, and Francis Webb's of the same name (the first of the divided drive compounds) completed in January 1882, were, to say the least, true experiments in locomotive design and were aptly named; on the other hand many might contend that there was very little experimentation about Whale's No 66 of April 1905. Certainly O.S,Nock was correct in describing Whale's 513 *Precursor* as the "Precursor of an entirely new era at Crewe".

In passing it is worth noting that the Company was not alone in providing such names. The first locomotive delivered to the GWR from Mather, Dixon was a *Premier,* as well as the first locomotive to be built at Swindon Works some while later.

Miniatures

The Narrow-Gauge locomotives, seven in all, built for the Crewe Works were diminutive compared with their standard gauge sisters amidst whom they ran and which towered over them. The first was aptly named *Tiny;* then came *Pet* and *Nipper,* and so on. The last two were named *Billy* and *Dickie* and were the shortest possible form of denoting Mr.William Rylance, the foreman at Crewe whom Webb used for special projects, and his son Richard. For all we know these names were those by which the two men were popularly known.

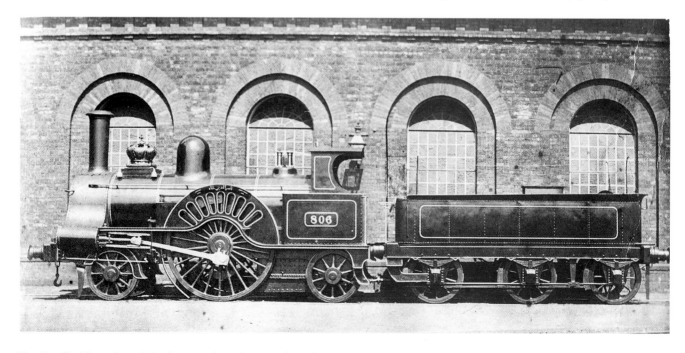

Fig. 5   Problem class 806, decorated on the occasion of the visit of the Shah of Persia to Crewe works on 27th June 1873, and temporarily bearing the name *Nasr Ed Din* in Persian script.

(Norman Lee Collection)

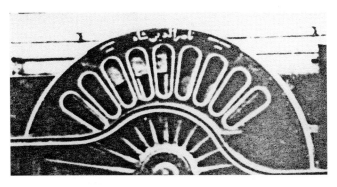

Fig. 6   The nameplate *Nasr Ed Din*. The plate is black with white lettering, and contains the usual building details and the date Feb 1863.

(Allan Sommerfield Collection)

Visits to Crewe Works by Important Personages

From time to time Royalty and other important people were invited to Crewe to be shown round the Works, and if they were of sufficient stature the occasion was marked with a named engine.

One of the first was the visit of *Prince Oscar* of Sweden in May 1862.

Another early example was the visit by H.R.H. *The Duke of Edinburgh* in June 1866, when the Newton Class engine 1481, which was intended to be Franklin received his name. However the name *Franklin* appeared that November on one of the second batch of Newtons, 1520.

Another was occasioned by the memorable visit of the Shah of Persia on 27th June 1873 when Problem 806 Waverley was temporarily given nameplates *Nasr Ed Din* inscribed in Persian script, this being the name of the Shah of Persia who was visiting the country, and Crewe Works, at the time. These plates were dated June 1873. In addition Improved Precedent 942 was provided with nameplates *Shah of Persia* worded in the standard L&NWR lettering style.

Three years later Precedent class 858 received the name *Sir Salar Jung*, after the Oriental Potentate who came as the guest of the Duke of Sutherland during a visit he was making to the country which caused great public interest. He did in fact visit Crewe twice, coming again in July 1878.

The last instance was the name given to George the Fifth class 1680 *Loyalty.* chosen to mark the visit by His Majesty King George V and Her Majesty Queen Mary on 21st April 1913.

Royalty

Throughout the whole life of the L&NWR, members of the British Royal Family were honoured with a name, as were a few members of foreign royalty. It is known that the B&L had a *Victoria* in 1837, and possible, but not certain, that the L&M had a *Victoria* in 1839. The Grand Junction had a *Prince* and a *Princess* in June and July 1845, and renamed the former *Prince Albert* sometime in 1847. The GJR and the L&M were not alone, for the Chester & Birkenhead Railway had a *Victoria* and an *Albert* in November 1845, but neither came into L&NWR stock.

It has been asserted that the nameplates of *Prince Albert* were removed from the engine after his death and later restored, but this is not borne out by Crewe records and must be discounted.

As the years went by many of the children and grandchildren of the Queen and Prince Consort are to be found in the list of names, the *Prince of Wales* and *Princess Royal* by their titles, and the others by name. They were not named in order of age, and so for example we find *Prince Arthur's* name preceding that of his brother, who was ten years older. Understandably *Princess May* becomes *Queen Mary*, and the *Prince of Wales* relates in turn to three successive Heirs to the Throne. Others remembered by their titles are *The Queen, Queen Empress, The Duke of Edinburgh, Duke of Albany, Duke of Connaught* and *The Earl of Chester.*

The Royal Family travelled frequently by rail, including among their number that wholly imaginary title the *Duchess of Lancaster* for an exceedingly important person.

Worth a mention is the strange turn of events in 1853, when *Prince Arthur, Prince Ernest* and *Prince Eugene* form a sequence in the 'Prince Ernest' class names. The first of them was the third son of the Queen, a boy of three; the second in all probability was his eight year old uncle, the Prince Consort's elder brother who was visiting London that year; but the third cames from the past and does not seem to be any other person than Prince Eugene, Duke of Savoy, who fought in battle beside Marlborough. The only explanation that comes to mind is that one 'Prince' name led to another.

Dagmar was another name connected with royalty.

As we have seen *Prince Oscar* of Sweden was named at the time he visited Crewe Works; and that many years later, in 1915, four members of foreign royal families were honoured because they represented our allies in The Great War, namely the King and Queen of the Belgians, and the Kings of Italy and Serbia.

Other manifestations of loyalty to the Royal Family occurred from time to time.

It is said that in 1862 when Problem class 291 *Prince of Wales* was built it was provided with solid splashers with the Prince's feather's painted on them. A retired LNWR Painter told Mr.C.Williams that the painting was done by a clever artist among the workmen, who had a large screen erected round him in order that his work might be uninterrupted. He added that the decoration lasted for a few years only, and Ramsbottom then reverted to the earlier practice of perforated splashers. Unfortunately no photographic evidence has come to light to support this story, and a photograph of the engine 'as built' shows perforated splashers.

Then, in 1888, came the Race to Edinburgh in competition with the East Coast route. One of the Tucks L&NWR series of postcards (Set 10 "Famous Locomotives") of 1904 is of Problem class 134 *Princess Royal,* for which an official photograph was taken at some time after its rebuilding in April 1896. The wording on the card reads "During the race to Edinburgh in 1888 this engine took the 10 a.m. from Euston to Crewe at an average speed of 57.1 miles per hour" The booked time was 52 3/4 mph. I know of no records of when this renaming took place, or for how long. *Owl* was the name with which No 134 both began and ended its life, and *Princess Royal's* number similarly was 610. Might it have been that a royal name was deemed to be a better one to commemorate this very fast run?

Thirdly in 1897 to mark Queen Victoria's Diamond Jubilee, both 2053 *Greater Britain* and 2054 *Queen Empress* had the Royal Coat of Arms painted in the rear splashers instead of the Company's one, this at the time when 2053 was painted in Post Office red with yellow and black lining, and the smokebox, chimney and wheels in royal blue, and when 2054 appeared in creamy-white with brass bands around the boiler, and a lavender smokebox. For good measure the tender of *Queen Empress* was decorated with a brass plaque.

Patriotism

L&NWR engine names consistently reflected the spirit of the nation.

Apart from the *Wellington* and the *Victory* of the B&L, this spirit of patriotism is not so very evident at the very start of engine naming. It is nowhere to be found in the Liverpool & Manchester's or the Grand Junction's names lists.

Later Victorians were undoubtedly patriotic and for very good reasons, and so were the Edwardians and Georgians. Thus we find running thought L&NWR lists many names of Admirals and Generals, victories in battle, warships that had achieved fame, and so forth.

One of the most patriotic names is that of *Greater Britain* of October 1891, a two word name cleverly devised to suit the pair of splashers of this prototype locomotive. It is not difficult to envisage the Directors or their naming committee debating how best to adorn this larger-than-ever Compound locomotive of which they were so proud.

Patriotism was fervent at the time the ten George the Fifth class engines appeared in June and July 1911, and the series of ten names began with *Coronation,* whose nameplate included the words *5000th Engine built at the Locomotive Works Crewe June 1911* and was surmounted by a crown. It is arguably one of the finest nameplates ever made, and the locomotive was beautifully complemented by much more ornate red lining than the normal L&NWR Pattern. Then came *British Empire* and the names of the Empire of *India,* the Commonwealth of *Australia,* the Dominions of *Canada, New Zealand* and *South Africa,* the Crown Possession *Gibraltar,* and the two Crown Colonies of *Malta* and *Cyprus.*

Proud folk travelled behind locomotives bearing proud names.

Incidentally the inclusion of *Australia* provides us with an instance of a change in the name's origin; Alfred the Great 1947 *Australia* had been named after the warship of the time, but when it was transferred to the George the Fifth class 1218 it was related of course directly to the Commonwealth.

Warships

What was the first engine to be named after a Royal Naval vessel? At a guess it may have been the Bolton & Leigh *Victory* on the grounds that they also possessed a *Nelson.* That said, it is exceedingly difficult to be certain which names were derived from which warship, and more than that, whether the names had been chosen independently by the L&NWR and the Admiralty, both of whom had a penchant for the names of mythology and astronomy. What is more there was a strong link between The Company and the Admiralty, as instanced by the fact that the Earl of Hardwicke and the Marquis of Chandos were members of a Royal Commission set up in 1858 to report on recruitment to the Navy.

Some of these names were undoubtedly identifiable as having warships as their source, particularly those the 1854 series during the Crimean War.

The Jubilee series make warship origins crystal clear, but even so the matter is not altogether straightforward because in certain cases there was no warship in service, or even on the stocks when a name was chosen. Some must be just traditional warship names. A study of *Dreadnought* illustrates the point.

In the glossary an attempt has been made to differentiate between certainly, probability and possibility in this hazardous exercise. The danger of hitting a mine is only too real!

Finally, another mention should appear here of the possibility of the nine members of the Prince of Wales class being either warships or naval establishments.

Prime Ministers and Politicians

Ten Prime Ministers find themselves in the name list, the first four early on. Two years before he became Prime Minister, Lord *Stanley* was granted a name in 1850 for his excellence as a politician; in 1852 he inherited the title Lord *Derby.* and thus achieved the distinction of having two engines named after him.

Pitt was included in 1866 in the Problem list of the distinguished and the great.

The ten were:-

Name	Date of naming	Years of Office
Peel	1840(B&L) 1850	1834-5/41-6
Canning	1847	1827
Russell	1847	1846-52/65-6
Wellington	1848	1828-30
Stanley	1850	1852/8-9/66-8
Derby	1852	ditto
Aberdeen	1854	1852-5
Pitt	1866	1783-1801/4-6
Palmerston	1863	1855-8/9-65
Disraeli	1877	1868/74-80
Gladstone	1868	1868-74/80-5/6/92-4

Several more Members of the Cabinet and Parliament were included, the first being *Clarendon* in 1851; others included *Harrowby,* and *Brougham* in the 1850s, and later on *John Bright* and *Richard Cobden.* Many of the Company Directors were also Members of Parliament, but this was not necessarily the main reason for the choice of their names.

Famous Persons

The list is nigh endless. Included in the roll call of the famous are to be found Admirals, Field Marshals, Generals, men and women of the past and who were contemporary; figures, some well known to us, others who do not come to our minds quite so readily after the passing of a century and more. There are great statesmen, explorers, adventurers, warriors, foreign dignitaries, and so on. The Directors' and CMEs' wide sense not only of British and World history is truly remarkable, as a study of the Glossary will show.

Racehorses

It seems strange in the light of the practice of other railway companies and in view of the similarity between the racehorse and the express engine, that the L&NWR had but a single racehorse name. They had acquired two from the Birkenhead, Cheshire & Lancashire Junction Railway, *Volante* and *Voltigeur,* and it is true that *Cossack* had won the Derby in 1847, but we may safely discount that as the name's source, as also in the case of *Eclipse* where the association with the rcaehorse must be reckoned a remote possibilty.

But when the Company Director, the Duke of Westminster's horse in 1899 won the Derby, the 2000 Guineas and the St.Leger, it was felt there was no option. Jubilee 1920 had to be named *Flying Fox.*

It should be noted that the George the Fifth 1631 *Racehorse* was named after the Ship of Discovery, and not a racehorse.

Chapter 4

THE NAMES CONTRIBUTED BY THE AMALGAMATED COMPANIES OF THE L&NWR

The Warrington & Newton Railway

The Company was incorporated in 1831 and absorbed into the Grand Junction in 1834 but its locomotives, all of which were built by Robert Stephenson & Co. in 1831, were not taken into GJ stock. They were named *Warrington, Newton, Achilles* and *Shrigley*. The first three appeared later on in the L&NWR names list in their own right, but, as a matter of general interest, the last of them was named after a racehorse.

The London & Birmingham Railway

It was the policy of this railway not to name its engines. The Contractors building the line named theirs, and one of them, *Harvey Combe* started as a traffic engine, being used mostly on passenger trains, in December 1840 and continuing thus until September 1841. It was briefly included in their passenger stock list in 1840/1.

The Bolton & Leigh Railway

Absorbed together with the Liverpool & Manchester Railway by the Grand Junction Railway in 1845.

Records show that their locomotives received a variety of names, the earliest in 1829 being the aptly named *Sans Pareil*, for the world truly had never seen its like before. *Lancashire Witch* perfectly reflected the folk-lore of the town and County Palatine of Lancaster, *Twin Sisters* delightfully epitomised the two boilers of the locomotive that bore the name. Another was named *Victoria* at the time of the young Queen's Accession to the Throne; *Nelson, Wellington, Marquis Douro* and *Victory* commemorated the naval and military heros whose victories were still uppermost in the nation's consciousness, and *Victory* must surely have been named after Admiral Nelson's flagship. The name *Castle* deserves a mention: The crest of the old Bolton coat-of-arms was an elephant with a castle on its back (as by a pure coincidence is that of Coventry), and the B&L had two carriages named *Elephant* and *Castle*, and the adjoining L&M had an engine named *Elephant*, which probably ran on the B&L at times,

Only *Victory,* together with *Marquis Douro, Peel* the Prime Minister, and *Soho,* the name of Benjamin Hick & Son's Works, became part of the L&NWR stock.

The Manchester & Birmingham Railway

Amalgamated with London & Birmingham and Grand Junction on 16th July 1846 to become the Manchester & Birmingham Division of the L&NWR and in 1849 the North Eastern Division, which became part of the L&NWR (Northern Division) in 1857.

Although there were no named locomotives, one of them received a name after it had been sold. This was No 23, an 0-4-2 built in 1842 by Sharp Roberts & Co., which became N.Div 423, and was sold in April 1860 to the St.Helens Railway, to be their No 2 *Trent* being named after the river. When St.Helens Railway was absorbed it was allocated L&NWR 1368.

The Huddersfield & Manchester Railway & Canal Company

This was a small Company whose line passed through the Pennine range, which was absorbed into the Northern Division in August 1847. There were five named locomotives. As might be expected all were of a local flavour. *Aldam* was the Company Chairman and *Brook* his deputy, and *Huddersfield* was an obvious choice. These three went to the Northern Eastern Division. The rail and canal tunnels under *Saddleworth* Moor at *Standedge* were great engineering feats, and the engines with this names were transferred early on to the Southern Division, where they kept their names at least until 1849.

The North Union Railway

In 1847 their nineteen locomotives were divided between the L&Y and the L&NWR. Information is scarce, but it is believed the L&NWR took possession in 1847 of thirteen of them. In June 1838 the NU Board had decided to have numbers only on their engines and the only names mentioned in their records are *Ranger, Liver* and *St.George.* Only four of the thirteen came into L&NWR stock, and were named *Chimera, Friar, Nun* and *Monk.* A more unlikely quartet would be hard to imagine, except by putting a cat amongst pigeons. Be that as it may, the L&NWR succeeded in introducing another vicious monster to join the GJ company of horrors.

According to S.S.Scott other named engines of the NU were, *Ace of Spades, Tayleur, Stephenson* and *Novelty*; and, according to Thomas S.Steel (SLS Journal 1954 p.208) *General, Commodore, Courier* and possibly *Ambassador.* In the light of the NU Board's decision in 1838, these may have been names carried only in the early years of the Company.

The Preston & Wyre Railway, Harbour & Dock Company

Only two of their locomotive stock came to the L&NWR in April 1850, named after a river and a lake, *Ribble* and *Windermere.*

The Lancaster & Carlisle Railway

Twenty goods and five passenger engines were built for them during 1857, and a further ten passenger and two goods in 1859, all of which were named, and came into L&NWR stock in 1859, together with four that they had themselves received earlier from the Kendal & Windermere Railway.

There was a distinctly Lake District flavour about these 41 engines.

It is impossible to be certain about the reasons lying behind some of the names, but there appear to be ten or maybe eleven director's residences, five rivers, five mountains, three lakes and several towns, villages and places of interest. And there are some real gems, names to cause travellers to return home to their books to read again about their local history, folklore and poetry, such as *Belted Will, John O'Gaunt, Lady of the Lake, Luck of Edenhall, Merrie Carlisle* and, most intriguing of all, *Duchess of Lancaster.*

Their arrival into L&NWR stock caused some duplication of names, which is hardly surprising because of the L&NWR's close association with the L&C for many years previously. So in December 1859 twelve lost their names, and two were renamed, namely *Lowther* which became *Ulleswater*, and *Dalemain* which took on an entirely new L&NWR name *Stewart*.

The Chester & Birkenhead Railway

The Company had ten named engines in all. The first six built in 1840 and 1841 had a curious assortment of names. *Wirral* was geographical, but *Lupus*, unless you lived in Cheshire was obscure. 'Lupus' is Latin for 'Wolf', and was the nickname of Hugh, who became in the 1070s the 1st Earl of Chester and who died in 1101; It is of L&NWR interest, for it was the middle (and a family) name of the first Duke of Westminster, elevated from a Marquisate in 1874, Hugh Lupus Grosvenor, for many years a Director until just before the end of the 19th century. The others were *Zillah, Touchstone, Commodore* and *Hirondelle*. In fact none of these six came to the L&NWR, but *Zillah* re-appeared on a BL&CJR engine in June 1857 and so finds a niche among L&NWR names. There had already been a *Commodore* of the L&NWR since 1847. The other four names date from 1845, and were *Victoria, Albert, Druid* and *Monk*, and all four survived to the time when the Company was amalgamated on 22nd July 1857 with the

The Birkenhead, Lancashire & Cheshire Junction Railway

Victoria and *Albert* eventually went to the GWR and so pass beyond the bounds of this work; whereas the other two *Druid* and *Monk* came into L&NWR ownership.

As regards engine names the amalgamation brought problems. Both Companies had a *Birkenhead*, causing the C&B one to be renamed *Monk*; and when the line was leased on 1st January 1860 jointly by the GWR and the L&NWR, and the latter had had a *Druid* since 1851 they renamed it *Glendower* in November 1860. Similarly since they also had already acquired their own *Monk* from the North Union, the BC&LJ's one took the name *Violet*. As it turned out these last two names only lasted for three months, passing on to DX Goods engines in February 1861.

Following the amalgamation of these two Companies, their stock consisted of 33 engines, twelve of which went to the GWR and 21 to the L&NWR of which eleven were named.

Of these it is worth noting that BL&CJR No 13 had been renamed from *Mersey* to *Forerunner* and that it became L&NWR 442; and that *Hawkstone*, the name of an estate not far distant in Shropshire. was preferred to *Gheber*.

The L&NWR named the unnamed ten in November 1860 (and gave them their associated numbers) which had become available through withdrawal. BL&CJR 34, 35 and 36 fitted neatly into both the numbers and names of the recently withdrawn *Phœbus, Talisman* and *Thalaba*.

Since the twelve which eventually went to the GWR had been jointly owned with the L&NWR, their names qualify to be listed in this volume. They form a strangely assorted bunch:- *Touchstone,*

Blazer, Gnome, Weaver, Volante and *Voltigeur, Thunderer, Dreadnought, Cricket* and *Grasshopper*. Of these only *Thunderer* and *Dreadnought* find their way back into the name lists, appearing by coincidence together once again in 1884.

Volante and *Voltigeur* were racehorses, and the 'Vol' at the beginning seems to have been the only connection between them, for they had won their races and achieved fame fifty eight years apart while the other pair *Cricket* and *Grasshopper* might have been so named because of the appearance of their moving parts, in the same vein as "Tishies" was the nickname of the Prince of Wales class engines that had been rebuilt with Beames derived valve gear.

Finally mention should be made of the four "Z"s *Zeno, Zopyrus, Zygia* and *Zillah* built in 1857 by Robert Stephenson & Co. What an extraordinarily popular name *Zillah* was in those early days.

The South Staffordshire Railway

Their locomotives were built by a wide assortment of firms. The majority of their names were of towns on the line. But there were exceptions, for example *McConnell* of 1858, so named "presumably by an appreciative management", as O.S.Nock expressed it, despite his well known aversion to naming. He soon got his way however, because the name was smartly removed when the locomotive went with all the others into his charge in the Southern Division. Probably *Tipton*, the last of the six built by W.Fairbairn & Sons holds the record for the shortest time a name lasted.

It would seem that there was a link between the manufacturer and the name, For the locomotives were ordered and delivered in pairs, and although it is not immediately apparent, the names are similarly paired.

Belvidere and *Angerstein* were built in or about 1850 by Garforth & Co. and at the time of writing the link seems to lie in Kent.

Viper and *Stag* were 2-4-0s which came from E.B.Wilson & Co, in late 1852 and early 1853. and the common factor is that both are of wildlife. They were followed by 0-6-0s *Esk* and *Justin* in May 1853, and there is some evidence that the source of this strange pair of names might be found, surprisingly, in Scotland.

Priam and *Ajax* from Vulcan Foundry in 1855, originally intended for the Shrewsbury and Hereford Railway, are names from mythology.

The Sandy & Potton Railway

The line was leased to the L&NWR in 1864. One was named *Shannon*, which had become L&NWR Duplicate list 1104 in March 1862. The other was *Little England* so named because it was a small engine built by George England & Co. and which had gone to the L&NWR in 1863 as a Departmental locomotive.

The Knighton Railway

The L&NWR worked the line from 1863, and it was absorbed in 1868. There was one engine, which carried the name *Knighton*.

The Ludlow & Clee Hill Railway

The line was finally absorbed by the L&NWR in 1892, and its sole engine was named *Sir Charles* after the Chairman of its Trustees.

Fig. 7   St.Helens Canal & Railway Company No.22 *Shannon.* One of their many engines named after rivers.

(John Ward Collection)

The St.Helens Canal & Railway Company

Their engine names clearly indicate a predominance of rivers, fifteen in all; four birds, *Swan, Lapwing* and *Swallow* (coming from the L&NWR series) and a fourth of their own, *Raven* which has very strong associations with the locality, with the name of the Inn and the Road adjacent to St.Helens Station.

Of the other names, two, *Saracen* and *Scorpion* came unchanged when purchased from the L&NWR, and a similar engine whose L&NWR name is uncertain was named *Alma* after the river and battle of Crimean War fame; *Star* and *Britain* were new names given to two more engines purchased from Crewe and *John Smith* was one of their Company Directors. And there was a *Hero* and a *Goliath.*

The Whitehaven & Furness Junction Railway

Ten of their locomotives entered the L&NWR Stock list in 1866, with an assortment of names. Five might be described as 'usual' that is to say that had appeared over time in many a locomotive name list; Their *Tubal Cain* reminds us who the L&NWR *Tubal* was, while *Queen Mab* and *Kelpie* take us into the mysterious, and who or what was *Big Ben* the year before the bell was cast? It is a bewildering assortment of quite delightful names. It must have been adventurous to travel on the line, in and out of fairyland. And who would have guessed that both *Cedric* and *Gurth* spring together from the mind of Sir Walter Scott?

The Cockermouth & Workington Railway The

Company confined their names to Rivers, five in all.

The Vale of Clwyd Railway and The Carnarvonshire Railway

The small Welsh and Welsh border lines provided local and Welsh names, and one has to be careful to get the spelling right.

GREENBANK SIDINGS, PRESTON

One locomotive was named *Greenbank*, the other *Tomlinson*, after the owner of the sidings.

.. ..

The following railways absorbed into the L&NWR at one time or another or jointly taken over, had no named engines in the L&M, GJR or L&NWR lists:-

The Anglesey Central Railway
The Aylesbury Railway
The Chester & Holyhead Railway
The Cromford & High Peak Railway
The Denbigh, Ruthin & Corwen Railway
The Manchester & Birmingham Railway
The North & South Western Junction Railway
The North London Railway
The Shrewsbury & Hereford Railway
The Sirhowy Railway
The Warrington & Newton Railway
The Whitehaven Cleator & Egremont Railway

Chapter 5
INTRODUCTION TO THE TABLES

The tables list all the name-bearing locomotives of the Companies which came together to form the L&NWR, of the L&NWR itself and of all those Companies which were at one time or another absorbed into it.

They summarise their names, their "Crewe" (or "Motion") numbers, their Running numbers, types, builders, dates of building, and where applicable rebuilding, and the dates of their disposal, sale, replacement, withdrawal or scrapping.

To distinguish Crewe Numbers from Running Numbers, the former are always printed in italics.

Where the name appears in bold type it is an indication that this is the first time it appeared on a locomotive. Subsequent uses of the name are in ordinary type.

Tables 3 to 12 provide in addition the details of locomotives which subsequently carried the same name, enabling the reader to follow the line of succession of the names carried on L&NWR locomotives from the earliest days until the withdrawal of the last of them in the days of British Railways on 11th June 1949. Subsequent name-holders are listed against each name together with the date when it was so named. An asterisk before an entry indicates a re-use of a name, but with a change in engine number.

For the most part dates are recorded in months and years (e.g. 2.42). Where only the year is recorded the year is entered in full (e.g.1841).

Numbers appearing in brackets are Duplicate Numbers, followed by the date of renumbering. For the most part these are not listed after the engine has lost its name.

Table 1 lists the locomotive of the Contributory Companies prior to the formation of the L&NWR.

Table 2 lists those known as the "Old Crewe Types" built at Crewe and Edge Hill from October 1843 until May 1858.

Table 3 lists in numerical order locomotives numbers 1 to 376, built from the earliest days until January 1856, giving the name associated with each number, and is designed to illustrate the L&NWR custom of handing on the name from one locomotive to another.

Table 4 concerns the years 1857 to 1859, and the locomotives which went to and returned from the L&NWR to the Lancaster & Carlisle Railway.

Table 5 The locomotives which went to the North London Railway and back.

Table 6 gives the details resulting from the transfer of locomotives from the Northern to the Southern Division in 1860.

Table 7 lists those built during the time of John Ramsbottom from 1857 to 1871,

Table 8 those from the Southern Division, and those named by Francis Webb,

Table 9 those built by Francis Webb between 1871 and 1903,

Table 10 those built by George Whale from 1903 until his retirement in 1908,

Table 11 those built by C.J.Bowen Cooke.

Table 12 gives details of the locomotives of the Engineering Department, Carriage and Wagon Department, Narrow Gauge, etc.

Table 13 concerns the named locomotives of all the Companies absorbed by the L&NWR from 1847 through to 1906.

In Tables 4 to 10, where a name appears for the first time, details of the subsequent holders of that name are provided in the same manner as in Table 3.

Details concerning the early years of locomotive building and nomenclature are sometimes obscure, but fortunately years of observation and a great amount of research have taken place concerning L&NWR engines, and within that, their names. In the case of some of the absorbed companies evidence is incomplete.

It is a sobering thought that very little if anything in these tables is the result of any original research on my own part, for what appears in them is a collation of the work of many enthusiasts and expert historians, past and present, and tribute is especially due to

M.C.V.Allchin	W.L.Harris	Samuel S.Scott
Bertram Baxter	S.H.P.Higgins	Donald H.Stuart
W.Beckerlegge	Harry Jack	Edward Talbot
Roger Bell	H.F.F.Livesey	Dudley Whitworth
Alan G.Dunbar	F.Mike Page	Charles Williams
F.E.A.Eades	E.E.Robinson, Jnr.	Willie Yeadon
F.C.Hambleton	J.W.P.Rowledge	

TABLE 1
THE CONTRIBUTING COMPANIES

(1) GRAND JUNCTION RAILWAY

The numbers and names given to Grand Junction Railway locomotives purchased from outside firms from the opening of the line on 4th July 1837 until February 1842 were:-

1 *Saracen*	19 *Doctor Dalton*	37 *Hawk*	55 *Lucifer*
2 *Hecla*	20 *Eagle*	38 *Camilla*	56 *Phantom*
3 *Shark*	21 *Wizard*	39 *Tartarus*	57 *Sultan*
4 *Hecate*	22 *Basilisk*	40 *Jason*	58 *Syren*
5 *Falcon*	23 *Vizier*	41 *Gorgon*	59 *Vandal*
6 *Stentor*	24 *Sirocco*	42 *Sunbeam*	60 *Tantalus*
7 *Scorpion*	25 *Harpy*	43 *Vampire*	61 *Phosphorus*
8 *Wildfire*	26 *Aeolus*	44 *Harlequin*	62 *Hyperion*
9 *Alecto*	27 *Merlin*	45 *Sybil*	63 *Herod*
10 *Dragon*	28 *Prometheus*	46 *Medea*	64 *Odin*
11 *Zamiel*	29 *Alaric*	47 *Vulture*	65 *Charon*
12 *Centaur*	30 *Sirius*	48 *Oberon*	66 *Colossus*
13 *Prospero*	31 *Pegasus*	49 *Columbine*	67 *Briareus*
14 *Witch*	32 *Tamerlane*	50 *Hornet*	68 *Antæus*
15 *Phalaris*	33 *Erebus*	51 *Torch*	69 *Python*
16 *Lynx*	34 *Phœbus*	52 *Diomed*	70 *Sphinx*
17 *Caliban*	35 *Talisman*	53 *Clio*	71 *Typhon*
18 *Cerberus*	36 *Thalaba*	54 *Medusa*	72 *Phlegethon*

During this period two engines, No 1 *Saracen* and No 7 *Scorpion* were replaced by two bearing the same numbers and names, and No 19 *Doctor Dalton* was sold.

Nos 28, 34, 35 and 36 had been overhauled by Jones, Turner and Evans and No 26 rebuilt with outside cylinders at Edge Hill by August 1841.

A new No 42 and No 39 were built at the Grand Junction Edge Hill Works in June 1842, and Jones & Potts, as the firm had become known, completed Nos 23, 24, 31 and 12. All these new engines were provided with outside cylinders and bore the former names related to their numbers.

From then until April 1846 nineteen new engines were built at Crewe, of which five were replacements.

The following were built:-

73	*Prince*	6.45	78	*Lonsdale*	2.46	83	*Windermere*	4.46
74	*Deva*	10.45	79	*Belted Will*	2.46	84	*Saddleback*	4.46
75	*Apollo*	9.45	80	*Dalemain*	3.46	85	*Ingestre*	5.46
76	*Albion*	9.45	81	*Greystoke*	3.46	86	*Sandon*	6.46
77	*Mersey*	11.45	82	*Wordsworth*	4.46			

The following were built as replacements:-

19	**Princess**	7.45	(for 19 *Doctor Dalton* Sold 1839)
4	*Hecate*	1.46	
25	*Harpy*	2.46	
14	*Witch*	6.46	
16	*Lynx*	7.46	

The GJ stock in April 1846 was 83 locomotives. Their numbers are deduced as being:-
1 - 32/4 - 43/5 - 53/5 - 86
excluding:-

54	*Medusa*	Sold 4.46 and not replaced until	1.6.46
44	*Harlequin*	Sold 4.46	9.46
33	*Erebus*	Scrapped 4.46	10.46

The Grand Junction numbers (1-83) and names were retained on the Northern Division of the L&NWR after 16th July 1846.

79 *Belted Will* did not enter traffic until July 1846, but was included in the last official Grand Junction list issued in April 1846.
73 *Prince* was renamed **Prince Albert** in 1847.
83 *Windermere* was renamed **Skiddaw** in May 1850

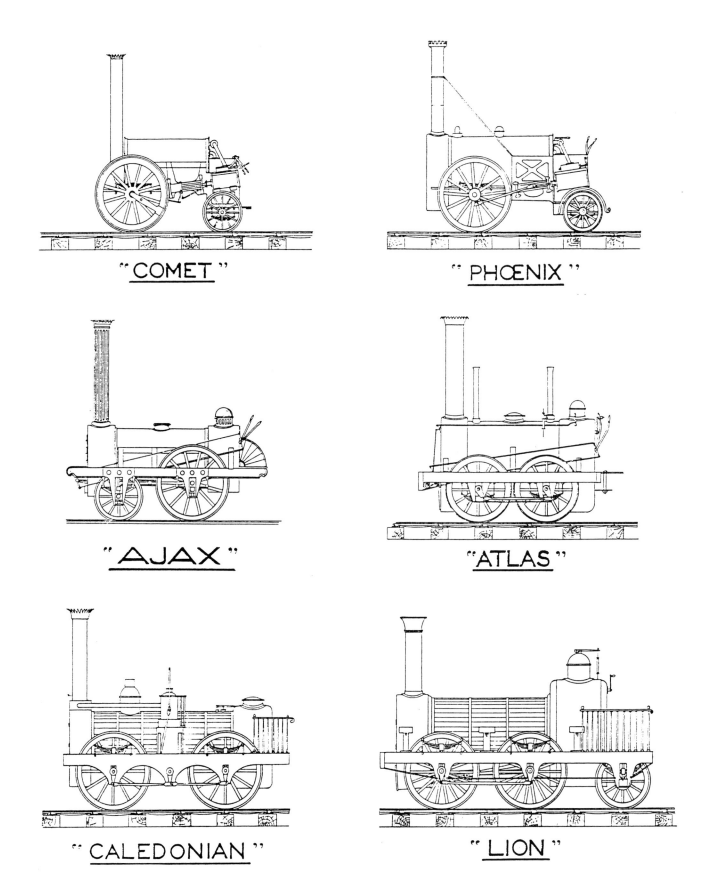

"COMET"

"PHŒNIX"

"AJAX"

"ATLAS"

"CALEDONIAN"

"LION"

Fig. 8 From line drawings prepared at Crewe in 1928 for the plaques for locomotives of the Royal Scot class

Built in 1835 for the Liverpool and Manchester Railway.
The first engine with inside cylinders.

Fig. 9   Old Passenger Locomotive Driving wheel 5ft diam. Built in 1835 for the Liverpool & Manchester Railway.
L&NWR Postcard Set 2 No.1.

(Fred Gray Collection)

(2) THE LIVERPOOL & MANCHESTER RAILWAY

The numbers and names of their locomotives in the chronological order in which they started to work on the line were:-

Number	First Name	Building date	Type (L&M)	Disposal
1	*Rocket*	1829	0-2-2	Sold 1836
				To Patent Office Museum 1862
				Now in Science Museum, South Kensington.
3	*Meteor**	18.1.30	0-2-2	Hired to B&L 8.31 Withdrawn by 1836 Sold 3.37
5	*Comet**	1.2.30	0-2-2	Sold 1832
2	*Arrow**	2.30	0-2-2	Hired to B&L 8.31 Withdrawn 1837 Sold 1840
4	*Dart**	2.30	0-2-2	Scrapped by 4.33
6	*Phœnix**	6.30	0-2-2	Scrapped by 4.33
7	*Northumbrian**	7.30	0-2-2	'Done with' 1836 Broken up
8	*North Star*	8.30	0-2-2	Sold 12.33
9	*Planet*	4.10.30	2-2-0	Hired to B&L 1831 or early 1832 Withdrawn 1840-1
10	*Majestic*	11.30	0-2-2	Withdrawn by 4.33
11	*Mercury*	1.31	2-2-0	Rebuilt 2-2-2 12.33 Withdrawn 1840-1
12	*Mars*	1.31	2-2-0	Sold 9.39
13	*Samson*	1.31	0-4-0	Withdrawn by 1836
14	*Jupiter*	2.31	2-2-0	Withdrawn c 1840
15	*Goliah*	3.31	0-4-0	Sold 9.35
16	*Saturn**	4.31	2-2-0	'Done with' 4.33 Broken up 1834
17	*Sun**	4.31	2-2-0	Sold 9.35
18	*Venus**	4.31	2-2-0	'Done with' 4.33 Withdrawn by 1836
19	*Vulcan*	5.31	2-2-0	Sold 3.41
20	*Etna*	6.31	2-2-0	Broken up c 1841
21	*Fury*	8.31	2-2-0	Withdrawn 1840 Broken up c.1842
22	*Victory*	9.31	2-2-0	Withdrawn 1840-1 Broken up c.1842, or sold to B&L as 2-2-2 in 1842

No.	Name	Date	Type	Notes	Second L&M No.	L&NWR No.	Disposal
23	*Atlas*	10.31	0-4-0	Hired to B&L 1831 or early 1932 Rebuilt 0-4-2 by 8.34 Renewed as No 81 11.42 (See also Note 1)			
24	*Vesta*	11.31	2-2-0	'On sale' 11.36			
25	*Milo**	2.32	0-4-0	Withdrawn 10.34			
26	*Liver**	4.33	2-2-0	Sold 10.37			
27	*Pluto*	8.32	2-2-0	Rebuilt 1842 (3.6.42)	9	(127)	Withdrawn 1847
28	*Caledonian**	8.32	0-4-0	Sold to L&B 5.37			
29	*Ajax*	11.32	2-2-0	Withdrawn 1840-1			
30	*Leeds**	1.33	2-2-0	Sold to C&B 9.40			
31	*Firefly*	4.33	2-2-0	Withdrawn 1840-1			
32	*Experiment*	2.34	2-2-0	Sold to GJR 12.36			
33	*Patentee**	9.34	2-2-2	Blew up 11.38			
34	*Titan*	9.34	0-4-0	Ballast engine 1842 Broken up c.1844			
35	*Orion*	10.34	0-4-0	Withdrawn c.1840			
36	*Swiftsure*	10.34	2-2-0	Withdrawn c.1843			
37	*Rapid**	5.35	2-2-2	Withdrawn c.1843			
38	*Speedwell**	6.35	2-2-2	Withdrawn c.1843			
39	*Hercules*	12.35	0-4-0	Withdrawn c.1842			
40	*Eclipse*	28.12.35	0-4-0	Withdrawn c.1842			
41	*Star*	2.36	2-2-2	Ballast engine 1842	53	(124)	Withdrawn 1848
42	*York**	2.36	0-4-2	Withdrawn ?1843-4			
43	*Vesuvius*	2.36	2-2-2		54	(125)	Withdrawn 1848
44	*Thunderer*	2.36	0-4-2	Withdrawn c.1842			
45	*Lightning*	6.36	2-2-2		21	114	Scrapped 11.49
46	*Cyclops*	6.36	2-2-2	Withdrawn 1842-3 Broken up ?1843			
47	*Milo**	21.11.36	2-2-2	Broken up 1841			
48	*Dart**	12.36	2-2-2	Broken up c.1843			
49	*Phoenix***	12.36	2-2-2	Broken up c.1842			
50	*Majestic*	12.36	2-2-2	Broken up c.1841			
51	*Etna*	1.37	2-2-2	Broken up c.1841			
52	*Arrow**	2.37	2-2-2	Withdrawn 1845			
53	*Sun**	3.37	2-2-2	Broken up 1842			
54	*Meteor*	3.37	2-2-2		n/k	115	Scrapped 5.49
55	*Comet**	3.37	2-2-2	Withdrawn 1845			
56	*Vesta*	3.37	2-2-2	Broken up c.1841			
57	*Lion*	7.38	0-4-2	Withdrawn 1857	36	116	Preserved
58	*Tiger*	7.38	0-4-2		37	(117)	To L&NWR 7.47 Withdrawn 1850
59	*Rokeby**	10.38	2-2-2		52	(123)	To L&NWR 7.47 Withdrawn 1848
60	*Roderic*	10.38	2-2-2		20	118	Scrapped 9.47

Listed by Scott both as *Roderic*, and as *Roderick* in "The List of Locomotives up to 1840 inclusive".   Sold to Mr.Morris 1.48

No.	Name	Date	Type	Notes	Second L&M No.	L&NWR No.	Disposal
61	*Mammoth*	12.38	0-4-2	Broken up 1843	30		
62	*Leopard**	12.38	2-2-2	Broken up 1845	3		
63	*Mastodon*	12.38	0-4-2		56	119	Scrapped 3.49
64	*Panther**	12.38	2-2-2	Withdrawn c.1844			
65	*Elephant*	3.39	0-4-2		34	113	Withdrawn 6.47 For sale 1.48
66	*Samson*	3.39	0-4-2		35	120	Withdrawn 11.47 For sale 1.48
67	*Buffalo*	3.39	0-4-2		50	121	?Sold 5.67
68	*Goliah*	3.39	0-4-2		51	122	Scrapped 9.47
69	*Victoria*	1839	0-4-2?	(See Note 3 below)	1		

'Bird' class 2-2-2 and 2-4-0, built by L&M at Edge Hill

No.	Name	Date	Type	Notes	Second L&M No.	L&NWR No.	Disposal
69	*Swallow*	8.9.41	2-2-2		128	Sold St.Helens 3.50	

No.	Name	Date	Wheels	Note	No.	Disposal
70	*Martin*	1.42	2-2-2	(Note 2)	129	Rebuilt 5.49
71	*Heron*	11.41	2-2-2		130	Scrapped 5.52
72	*Kingfisher*	9.41	2-2-2		131	Scrapped 5.51
73	*Pelican*	12.41	2-2-2		132	Scrapped 5.52
74	*Ostrich*	2.42	2-2-2	(Note 4)	133	On sale 5.54
75	*Owl*	3.42	2-4-0		134	Replaced 11.53
76	*Bat*	6.42	2-4-0		135	Sold 9.52
77	*Stork*	5.42	2-2-2		136	Scrapped 5.52
78	*Crane*	10.42	2-2-2		137	Sold 3.54
79	*Swan*	9.42	2-2-2		138	Sold St.Helens 5.55
80	*Cygnet*	12.42	2-2-2		139	Scrapped 9.52
81	*Atlas*	1.11.42	2-2-2	(Renewal of 23)	140	Sold St.Helens 2.52
82	*Pheasant*	11.42	2-2-2		141	Scrapped 5.51
83	*Partridge*	6.43	2-2-2	(Note 4)	126	'On sale' 5.54
84	*Bittern*	4.43	2-4-0		142	Sold St.Helens 12.52
85	*Lapwing*	10.43	2-4-0		143	Sold 9.53
86	*Raven*	12.43	2-4-0		144	Replaced 11.53
87	*Crow*	1.44	2-4-0		145	Replaced 10.53
88	*Redwing*	4.44	2-2-2	(Note 4)	146	Scrapped 5.54?
89	*Woodlark*	1.45	2-2-2		147	Sold 2.52
90	*Penguin*	10.44	2-4-0		148	Replaced 11.53
91	*Petrel*	7.44	2-4-0		149	Sold 4.56
92	*Linnet*	2.45	2-2-2		150	Sold 9.53
93	*Goldfinch*	2.45	2-2-2		151	Scrapped 10.53
94	*Bullfinch*	5.45	2-2-2		152	Replaced 1855
95	*Chaffinch*	5.45	2-2-2		153	Sold 3.54
96	*Starling*	7.45	2-4-0		154	Replaced 11.54
97	*Owzell*	11.45	2-4-0		155	Replaced 11.54
98	*Redstart*	12.45	2-4-0		156	Replaced 3.56
99	*Redbreast*	9.45	2-4-0		157	Scrapped 5.51
100	*Condor*	3.46	2-2-2		158	Scrapped 3.53
101	*Adjutant*	3.46	2-4-0		159	Replaced 1.57
102	*Flamingo*	3.46	2-4-0		160	Replaced 5.53
103	*Cuckoo*	3.46	2-4-0		161	Replaced 3.56
104	*Albatross*	6.46	2-4-0		162	Replaced 6.56
106	*Osprey*	7.46	2-4-0		163	Replaced 6.56

Fig. 10 "Old Crewe Passenger Engine Driving wheel 6ft. of 1846".
L&NWR Postcard Set 2 No.1.

(Fred Gray Collection)

* Names marked with an asterisk do not appear in L&NWR locomotive stock lists.

** The name *Phoenix* came into the L&NWR Stock List in 1866: Whitehaven and Furness Joint Stock No 6, a 2-4-0 built 9.47 by R.& W.Hawthorn and rebuilt as a 2-2-2T. L&NWR No (1559) 1586 in 1866 (1265 6.67) Scrapped 6.68

Notes:-

1)   Scott writes ""No 140 ATLAS was apparently rebuilt in 1842, and had the L. & M. number altered from 23 to 55 when rebuilt; the name proves that it was not a new engine: no classical names were given to new engines."

2)   129 *Martin* was rebuilt in 5.49, as 242 *Giraffe*, then held in store until 11.50, to emerge as SFB Pass SF 'Onyx' class 129 *Martin*.

3)   (69 *Victoria*   1839   2-2-2 or 0-4-2   Renumbered 1 in 1841)
     This locomotive's existence is doubtful. True that it is included in Whishaw's list, but is not mentioned in L&M records, nor in Woods' Complete List of Locomotives as at 16th December 1842. It is nevertheless included in Scott's list, as having been built in 1839 by Mather, Dixon (Works No 53, Driving Wheel diameter 4ft 6in, cylinders 12 1/2 x 18, renumbered No 1 ?0-4-2). The compilation and content of Mather, Dixon's list might not be authentic.

4)   One of these three engines was sold to the St.Helens Railway but it is not possible to identify which.

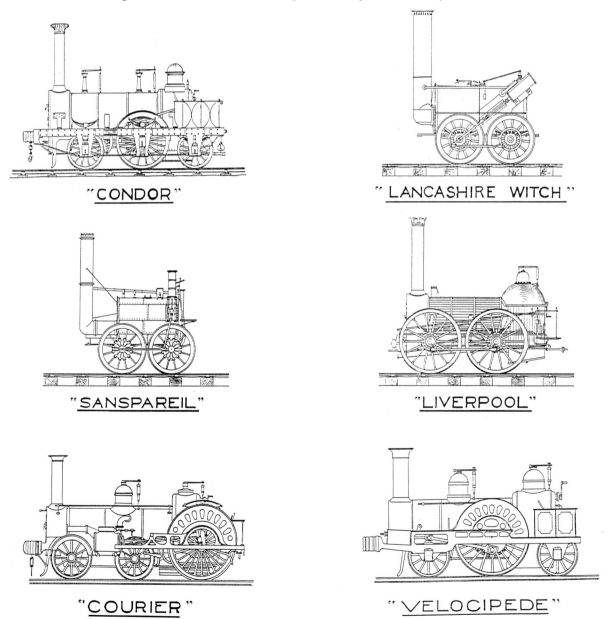

Fig. 11   From line drawings prepared at Crewe in 1928 for the plaques for locomotives of the Royal Scot class

Robert Stephenson & Co.	1-18/20/2-5/7/9/31/3
Fenton, Murray & Co.	19/21/30
Edward Bury & Co.	26
Galloway, Bowman & Glasgow	28
Sharp, Roberts & Co.	32
Tayleur & Co.	34-5/7-8/40-2/7/9-51
George Forrester & Co.	36
Mather, Dixon & Co.	39/44/8/52/4-5
Haigh Foundry	43/5-6
R. & W. Hawthorn & Co.	53/6
Todd, Kitson & Laird	57-8/62/4-5/7
Rothwell, Hick & Rothwell	59-60
T.Banks & Co.	61/3
B.Hick & Son	66/8

L&M Locomotives thereafter were built at Edge Hill, the first being No 69 *Swallow*

(3) BOLTON & LEIGH RAILWAY

The Bolton & Leigh Railway was initially worked under contract by John Hargreaves, Junior. It was amalgamated with the Grand Junction Railway in 1845.

The Company' policy was to provide names only for their engines. There is one however listed as "No 1", and by a stretch of imagination this might be regarded as a name, of the group "Pioneer", or "Precursor". It seems illogical to exclude this engine from the B&L Stock Lists below, and following Shill's Table, I have taken the liberty of printing "No 1" in italics.

Research into the B&L Locomotive List has continued unabated from Whishaw's time in 1840 right through to the present day, producing any number of deductions, corrections and additions, so that it is impossible to claim that this list (or any other) is definitive or final. This is just a collection of some of the facts and suggestions which seem most likely to come reasonably close to what took place some one hundred and seventy years or so ago. It is to be hoped that further research may take place in the years to come.

In approximate chronological order of building, we have:-

DATE	NAME	TYPE	BUILDER	DISPOSAL
7.28	*Lancashire Witch* (Named 1.8.28) On hire from L&M when new.	0-4-0	Robert Stephenson & Co.	Scrapped by 1840 Returned to L&M c11.29
8.28	*Twin Sisters* On hire from L&M.	0-6-0 (Makers drawing) 0-4-0 (Shill)	Robert Stephenson.& Co.	Returned to L&M
1829	*Sans Pareil* 0-4-0, rebuilt 2-2-0 Timothy Hackworth Preserved On hire from L&M, then purchased by Hargreaves at end of its loan to the S&D; Preserved first in Patents Office Museum London, later in Science Museum.			
1829	*Dreadnought*	Six-wheeled ?0-4-2 (Ahrons)	Edward Bury & Co. (Clarence Foundry)	Sold or scrapped before 1840
22.7.30	*Liverpool*	0-4-0	Edward Bury & Co.	Scrapped before 1840
	See the Ackermann 'long print' of November 1831			
1830	*Union*	2-2-0 Vertical boiler	Rothwell Hick & Rothwell (Union Foundry)	Sold or scrapped before 1841
5.31	*Phoenix*	0-4-0	Crook & Dean for William Hulton	
7.31	*Nelson*	2-2-0	Robert Stephenson & Co.	
4.32	Rebuilt	2-2-2	"New" to Hargreaves	Scrapped c1842
4.32	*Bury* renamed *Bee*	0-4-0	Edward Bury & Co. (No.4) purchased by Hargreaves	Sold to Hulton Collieries

4.32	*Clarence*	0-4-0	Edward Bury & Co. (No.5) (Clarence Foundry, Liverpool) On hire from L&M , then purchased by Hargreaves Rebuilt 0-4-2 before 1840 Scrapped by 1845
5.32	*Bolton*	0-4-0	Crook & Dean, of Bolton possibly renamed *Veteran* by 1838 (Whishaw 0-4-0/Baxter 0-6-0) Rebuilt 0-4-2 1838 William Dean Sold or scrapped 12.45
1832	*Salamander*	0-4-0	Crook & Dean Sold or scrapped after 1840
1834	*Soho*	0-4-2	Benjamin Hick & Son Sold to GJR 1.46, later to become L&NWR 125
1836	*Utilis*	0-4-2	For Hargreaves Rebuilt 2-4-2 1837 ?Sold to Lancaster & Preston Junction Railway 27.7.46
1836	*Wellington*	0-4-2	Tayleur & Co. Sold 12.45 to Birmingham & Gloucester/Bristol & Gloucester Joint Board No 39 and name *Wellington* retained 2.47 MR 295
1837	*Victoria*	0-4-2	For Hargreaves Retained to work Coppull Colliery traffic. Scrapped c.1864
1838	*Pandora*	0-4-2	Tayleur & Co. Sold 12.45 to Birmingham & Gloucester/Bristol & Gloucester Joint Board No 60 and name *Pandora* retained. 2.47 MR 297
1838	*Castle*	0-4-2	Benjamin Hick & Son for Hargreaves ?Sold to Lancaster & Preston Junction Railway 27.7.46
1838	*Marquis Douro* or *Marquis of Douro*	0-4-2	Tayleur & Co. Sold to GJR 1.46 and used on NU, later to become L&NWR 124
1838	*Vixen*	2-2-0	Acquired second hand after 1841 Sold or scrapped 12.45
1839	*St.David*	2-2-2	Bourne & Bartley, or Summers Grove & Day, Southampton, and purchased at auction by Hargreaves Sold or scrapped before 1845
1839	*Prince*	2-2-2	Sold or scrapped 12.45

Note. Ted Craven was confident that *St.David* was the later *Prince*

1840 (1844 - LNWR Archives)	*Peel*	2-2-2 (Baxter 0-4-2)	Edward Bury & Co Sold to GJR 1.46, later to become L&NWR 127
c1840	*Liverpool*	0-4-0	William Dean Sold or scrapped before 1845 Possibly a "replacement" for the earlier *Liverpool*
1840 (1839 - LNWR Archives)	*No 1*	2-2-2	Nasmyth, Gaskell & Co.(Works No 9) Sold 12.45 to Birmingham & Gloucester/Bristol & Gloucester Joint Board No 5 and named (or renamed) *Camilla* 2.47 MR 104
1842	*Victory*	2-2-2	"New" to Hargreaves "in 1842 apart from a few plates in the Boiler" Sold to GJR 1.46 to become L&NWR 123

This engine might possibly be the engine built by Robert Stephenson & Co.
in September 1831 for the L&M, their No 22, subsequently acquired in 1842 by the B&L.

Five L&M engines were hired by the B&L during 1831 and 1832: These were:-

L&M No 2 *Arrow*
3 *Meteor*
9 *Planet*
22 *Victory*
23 *Atlas*

Thus it will be seen that only four Bolton & Leigh engines came into L&NWR Stock in 1847:-

No 123 *Victory*
No 124 *Marquis Douro*
No 125 *Soho*
No 127 *Peel*

The origin of some of these names is clear:-

Bolton was built in Bolton at the Phoenix Foundry of John Crook and William Dean, *Bury* and *Clarence* at Bury's Clarence Foundry, *Phoenix* at the Phoenix Foundry, Little Bolton, Lancashire, *Soho* at the Soho Foundry of Benjamin Hick & Co. and *Union* at the Union Foundry of Rothwell Hick and Rothwell.

(4) NORTH UNION RAILWAY

The Company was leased jointly by the Manchester and Leeds and the Grand Junction on 1st January 1846.

Their nineteen locomotives were divided on 31st December 1846, Nos 5/6/9/12/7/8 going to the L&Y and the remainder to the L&NWR. Their condition was described as being "very defective from the start", and only four are definitely known to have been taken into L&NWR Stock around the end of September 1847, as Nos 177-180 and being named at the time.

These were:-

L&NWR Number	Name	Type	NU Number	Builder	Date
177	*Chimera*	2-2-0	Not known	Not known	
178	*Friar*	2-2-0	Not known	Not known	
179	*Nun*	2-2-0	One of NU 14	Edward Bury & Co	1841
			or NU 15	Tayleur & Co	1841
			or NU 16	Tayleur & Co	1841
180	*Monk*	0-4-2	NU 19	Bury, Curtis & Kennedy	1846

Others which came to the L&NWR may have included:-

NU 1 Formerly *Ranger*	2-2-0			Haigh Foundry	1841
NU 13 Formerly *St.George*	2-2-2			Bourne & Bartley	
				(or Haigh Foundry) Purchased	5.39

The B&L 0-4-2 *Marquis Douro* (or *Marquis of Douro*) was used on the NU between the time it had been sold to the GJR in January 1846 and the time it became L&NWR No 124 in 1847.

(5) LONDON & BIRMINGHAM RAILWAY

Harvey Combe A 2-2-2 built in 1835 by Robert Stephenson & Co. not numbered in L&B stock, but listed in passenger stock between December 1840 and September 1841.

TABLE 2
THE "OLD CREWE TYPES"

The number in brackets indicate the order in which it is considered possible that the first one hundred and eighty two of these engines may have been built at Crewe. I am greatly indebted to the late Mr.W.L.Harris for his article in Premier News in 1988 "The First 182 Engines Built at Crewe" for the details which follow.

An asterisk denotes an engine sold in January 1857 to the Lancaster & Carlisle Railway.

The engine name always appears in italics, and in bold type when the name first appeared on a L&NWR engine.

"Old Crewe" Types built at Crewe October 1843 - March 1845
2-2-2 5ft 6in Passenger engines

(1)	32	*Tamerlane*	(6)	20	*Eagle*	(12)	17	*Caliban*
(2)	27	*Merlin*	(7)	5	*Falcon*	(13)	3	*Shark*
(3)	13	*Prospero*	(8)	15	*Phalaris*	(14)	10	*Dragon*
(4)	6	*Stentor*	(9)	30	*Sirius*	(15)	21	*Wizard*
(5)	8	*Cerberus*	(11)	8	*Wildfire*	(16)	11	*Zamiel*

2-4-0 5ft Goods engine

(10) 2 *Hecla*

"Columbine" or "Old Crewe Passenger" class 2-2-2 6ft Passenger, curved frames, small (3ft 7 1/2in) firebox, Indirect Action Motion
April 1845 - February 1848   61 engines

(17)	22	*Basilisk*	(38)	16	*Lynx*	(63)	104	**Phaeton**
(18)	73	**Prince #**	(43)	44	*Harlequin*	(64)	40	*Jason**
(19)	19	**Princess**	(44)	38	*Camilla*	(70)	109	**The Queen**
(20)	49	*Columbine*	(45)	33	*Erebus*	(71)	110	**Canning**
(21)	75	**Apollo**	(46)	91	**Knowsley**	(72)	111	**Russell**
(22)	76	**Albion**	(47)	92	**Trentham**	(73)	37	*Hawk*
(23)	74	**Deva**	(48)	93	**Premier**	(87)	26	*Aeolus*
(24)	77	**Mersey**	(49)	94	**Helvellyn**	(88)	188	**Colonel**
(25)	4	*Hecate*	(50)	29	*Alaric*	(89)	189	**Elector**
(26)	25	*Harpy*	(51)	95	**Hydra**	(90)	190	*Peerless*
(28)	79	**Belted Will**	(52)	96	**Polyphemus**	(91)	191	**Diamond**
(29)	80	**Dalemain**	(53)	97	**Atalanta**	(92)	192	**Hero**
(33)	84	**Saddleback**	(54)	9	*Alecto*	(93)	193	**Pearl ***
(34)	85	**Ingestre**	(55)	98	**Dædalus**	(94)	194	**Ruby**
(35)	54	*Medusa*	(56)	99	**Duke**	(95)	195	**Emerald ***
(36)	86	**Sandon**	(61)	47	*Vulture*	(96)	196	*Leander*
(37)	14	*Witch*	(62)	103	**Archimedes**			

The following eleven were built at Edge Hill

164	*Sun*	168	**Dromedary**	183	**Theorem**
165	*Star*	169	**Huskisson ***	184	**Problem**
166	*Comet*	118	*Roderic*	185	**Alderman**
167	**Rhinoceros**	182	**Roebuck**		

\# 73 *Prince* was renamed *Prince Albert* in 1847.

"Lonsdale" class 2-4-0 5ft Goods, curved frames, small firebox
February 1846 - June 1848   38 engines

(27)	78	*Lonsdale*	(66)	106	*Senator*	(83)	186	*Narcissus*
(30)	81	*Greystoke*	(67)	107	*Magistrate*	(97)	197	*Fame*
(31)	82	*Wordsworth*	(68)	113	*Elephant*	(98)	198	*Avon*
(32)	83	*Windermere*	(69)	108	*Mayor*	(99)	199	*Castor**
(39)	87	*Eden*	(74)	112	*Councillor*	(100)	200	*Pollux**
(40)	88	*Lune*	(75)	170	*Candidate*	(101)	201	*Ariel*
(41)	89	*Bela*	(76)	171	*North Western*	(102)	202	*Eclipse*
(42)	90	*Lowther*	(77)	122	*Goliath*	(103)	203	*St. George*
(57)	100	*Earl*	(78)	172	*Admiral*	(104)	204	*Thunderbolt*
(58)	101	*Baronet*	(79)	174	*General*	(105)	46	*Medea*
(59)	41	*Gorgon*	(80)	120	*Samson*	(106)	55	*Lucifer*
(60)	102	*Marquis*	(81)	175	*Commodore*	(107)	57	*Sultan*
(65)	105	*Viscount*	(82)	181	*Pilot*			

"Cornwall" 8ft 6in Passenger Built as 2-2-2 October 1847 1 engine

(84) 173 *Cornwall*

"Courier" 4-2-0 7ft Passenger (T.R.Crampton) Built November 1847 1 engine

(85) 176 *Courier*

"Velocipede" 2-2-2 7ft Passenger   Built November 1847 1 engine

(86) 187 *Velocipede*

"Onyx" class 2-2-2 6ft Passenger, straight frames, small firebox
May 1848 - November 1850   42 engines

(116)	216	*Ambassador*	(125)	224	*Violet*	(144)	28	*Prometheus*
(117)	217	*Emperor**	(136)	51	*Torch*	(145)	178	*Friar**
(118)	218	*Wellington*	(137)	233	*Unicorn*	(146)	52	*Diomed*
(119)	219	*Nelson*	(138)	234	*Mazeppa*	(147)	11	*Lightning*
(120)	177	*Chimera*	(139)	45	*Sybil*	(148)	35	*Talisman*
(121)	220	*Waterloo*	(140)	235	*Clanricarde*	(156)	179	*Nun **
(122)	221	*Trafalgar*	(141)	236	*Hawkstone*	(157)	128	*Swallow*
(123)	222	*Lily*	(142)	237	*Blenheim*	(176)	36	*Thalaba*
(124)	223	*Rose**	(143)	115	*Meteor*	(177)	61	*Phosphorus*

A further fifteen were built at Edge Hill:-

211	*Onyx*	230	*Monarch*	124	*Marquis Douro*
212	*Megatherion*	231	*Firefly*	129	*Martin*
213	*Talbot*	34	*Phœbus*	117	*Tiger*
59	*Vandal*	125	*Soho*	60	*Tantalus*
229	*Watt*	127	*Peel*	141	*Pheasant*

"Vampire" class 2-4-0 5ft Goods, straight frames, small firebox
May 1848 - May 1851   48 engines

(108)	50	*Hornet*	(134)	232	*Ixion*	(165)	240	*Bee*
(109	205	*St.David*	(135)	119	*Mastodon*	(166)	241	*Wasp*
(110)	58	*Siren #*	(149)	244	*Leviathan*	(167)	257	*Stanley*
(111)	206	*Menai*	(150)	245	*Ellesmere*	(168)	260	*Anglesea*
(112)	207	*Conway*	(151)	246	*Caradoc*	(169)	238	*President*
(113)	208	*St.Patrick*	(152)	247	*Mammoth* (Tank)	(170)	239	*Powis*
(114	209	*Envoy **	(153)	248	*Salopian*	(171)	261	*Hercules*
(115)	210	*Alchymist **	(154)	249	*Cambrian*	(172)	262	*Liver*

(126)	225	*Llewellyn*		(155)	250	*John o'Gaunt*		(173)	253	*Bucephalus*
(127)	53	*Clio*		(158)	251	*Vernon*		(174)	242	*Giraffe*
(128)	43	*Vampire*		(159)	252	*John o'Groat*		(175)	62	*Hyperion*
(129)	48	*Oberon*		(160)	254	*Theseus*		(178)	263	*Herald*
(130)	226	*Champion*		(161)	102	*Marquis*		(179)	264	*Clarendon*
(131)	227	*Snowdon*		(162)	255	*Precursor*		(180)	265	*Napier*
(132)	228	*Delamere*		(163)	256	*Cadmus*		(181)	266	*Sutherland*
(133)	56	*Phantom*		(164)	243	*Chillington*		(182)	70	*Sphinx*

Baxter and Nock record the change of spelling from the Grand Junction 58 Siren to the L&NWR 58 Siren above.

247 Mammoth was the first Tank engine to be built at Crewe, in October 1849.

"Glyn" class 2-4-0 5ft Goods, small firebox, direct action
April 1851 - April 1853 47 engines

As stated in Chapter 1, engines from now on had their motion stamped not with its name, but with a number.

Crewe Motion numbers, printed in italics, begin at Number *183*.

183	267	**Glyn**		*195*	275	**Vulcan** *		*216*	287	**Eglinton**		*233*	301	**Giant**
184	268	**Cyclops**		*196*	277	**Hotspur**		*217*	288	**Loadstone**		*234*	302	**Fly**
185	269	**Wyre**		*197*	276	**Pluto** *		*218*	289	**Director**		*235*	303	**Achilles**
186	270	**Dee**		*203*	281	**Allerton**		*224*	292	**Hardwicke**		*236*	305	**Peacock**
187	157	*Redbreast*		*204*	282	**Irwell**		*225*	293	**Quicksilver**		*237*	304	**Hector** *
188	67	*Briareus*		*205*	140	*Atlas*		*226*	294	**Magnet**		*238*	306	**Bulldog**
189	131	*Kingfisher*		*206*	283	**Croxteth**		*227*	295	**Penmaenmawr** *		*239*	142	*Bittern*
190	271	**Minotaur** *		*207*	284	**Harbinger**		*228*	296	**Bellerophon**		*240*	307	*Fury*
191	272	**Druid**		*212*	68	*Antæus*		*229*	297	**Una**		*241*	308	**Booth** *
192	273	**Hope**		*213*	286	**Derby**		*230*	298	**Don**		*242*	158	*Condor*
193	66	*Colossus*		*214*	132	*Pelican*		*231*	299	**Elk**		*243*	309	**Huish** *
194	274	**Swift**		*215*	136	*Stork*		*232*	300	**Ant**				

Many of the "Crewe Goods" with the small firebox were rebuilt as named side tanks from 1856 onwards, and until 1869 the curved nameplates were removed from the splashers and fitted to the tanks. Some, but not all of those converted after 1868 lost their names in the process.

Fig. 12   3097 2-4-0T Ex Glyn class 5ft Goods SFB DA 295 *Penmaemawr*
Photographed after November 1887

(John Ward Collection)

Fig. 13   Isis class 5ft LFB Goods DA 159 *Adjutant*

(Allan Sommerfield Collection)

Fig. 14   946 Ex Isis class 215 *Spitfire* after rebuilding as 2-4-0ST in lined livery. Believed to be a photograph taken at Monument Lane during the time it was station shunter at New Street Birmingham.

(John Ward Collection)

"Odin" class 2-2-2 6ft Passenger, small firebox, direct action
November 1851 - November 1852   13 engines

198	64	Odin	202	280	**Glendower**	211	130	Heron	222 291 ***Prince of***
199	147	Woodlark	208	1	Saracen	219	139	Cygnet	***Wales***
200	278	**Locke**	209	7	Scorpion	220	135	Bat	
201	279	**Stephenson**	210	285	**Sefton** *	221	65	Charon	

"Rocket" 2-2-2 7ft Passenger, small firebox, direct action
August 1852   1 engine

223 290 Rocket

"Isis" class 2-4-0 5ft Goods, large (4ft 5in) firebox, direct action
May 1853 - November 1857   106 engines

244	310	**Isis**	295	336	**Woodcock**	329	361	**Umpire**
245	72	Phlegethon	296	337	**Snipe**	330	362	**Cato**
246	71	Typhon	297	338	**Fairbairn**	341	152	Bullfinch *
247	311	**Ida** *	298	339	**Nasmyth**	342	373	**Snake** *
248	312	**Tubal**	299	23	Vizier	343	372	**Centipede**
249	69	Python	300	126	Partridge	344	374	**Serpent**
250	160	Flamingo	301	345	**Turk**	346	375	**Virago**
251	138	Swan	302	347	**Cossack** #	348	63	Herod
252	314	**Crewe**	303	346	**Arab** #	349	5	Falcon
253	137	Crane	304	348	**Varna**	350	10	Dragon
258	319	**Anson**	305	349	**Warrior**	354	21	Wizard
259	317	**Antelope**	306	352	**Raglan**	356	376	**Proserpine**
260	318	**Reynard**	307	350	**Baltic**	357	156	**Redstart** *
261	320	**Viceroy**	308	351	**Alma**	358	149	Petrel
262	321	**Autocrat** *	309	27	Merlin	359	11	Zamiel
263	322	**Harrowby**	310	18	Cerberus later 17 Caliban	360	161	Cuckoo
264	143	Lapwing	311	13	Prospero	361	180	Monk
265	151	Goldfinch *	312	20	Eagle *	362	163	Osprey
266	145	Crow	313	176	Courier	363	258	Ribble
267	153	Chaffinch	314	6	Stentor	364	162	Albatross
271	326	**Rowland Hill**	315	154	Starling *	365	18	Cerberus *
272	327	**Maberley**	316	155	**Ousel**	366	215	Spitfire
273	328	**Czar**	317	15	Phalaris	369	159	Adjutant
274	329	**Simoon**	318	353	**St.Arnaud** *	370	116	Lion
275	330	**Hurricane**	319	3	Shark	371	152	Bullfinch
276	331	**St.Germans**	320	354	**Euxine**	372	154	Starling
277	332	**Aberdeen**	321	30	Sirius	373	156	Redstart (Tank)
278	333	**Hardinge** *	322	8	Wildfire	374	209	Envoy (Tank)
279	24	Sirocco	323	355	**Hardman** *	375	199	Castor
280	133	Ostrich	324	356	**Memnon**	376	200	Pollux
291	146	Redwing	325	357	**Terrier** *			
292	32	Tamerlane	326	358	**Falstaff** *			Motion Numbers
293	334	**Ptarmigan**	327	359	**Glowworm** *			*345/7/51-3/5/67/8*
294	335	**Quail**	328	360	**Theodore**			went to the N.E.Div.
								and were unnamed

373 156 Redstart and *374 209 Envoy* were built 2-4-0Ts for the Bolton Branch.
  Many of the class were rebuilt, and some converted to Tank engines, and after 1858 most lost their names when this took place.
  # Another version is that *302 347* was *Arab*, and *303 346 Cossack*.
  * Sold to Lancaster & Carlisle Railway in January 1857.

"Prince Ernest" class 2-2-2 6ft Passenger, large firebox, direct action
June 1853 - May 1858   34 engines

254	313	**Prince Ernest** *	336	367	**Nightingale**	389	217	Emperor
255	315	**Prince Arthur**	337	368	Majestic	390	223	Rose

256	316	*Prince Eugene*	338	369	**Banshee** *	391	285	*Sefton*
257	150	*Linnet* *	339	371	**Mercury**	392	313	*Prince Ernest*
268	148	*Penguin*	340	370	**Gazelle**	393	259	*Windermere*
269	323	**Greyhound**	377	42	*Sunbeam*	394	311	*Ida*
270	324	**Messenger**	378	110	*Canning*	395	321	*Autocrat*
331	363	**Empress**	379	150	*Linnet*	396	333	*Hardinge*
332	364	**Latona**	380	169	*Huskisson*	397	353	*St.Arnaud*
333	259	*Windermere* *	381	178	*Friar*	398	373	*Snake*
334	365	**Vesta**	382	193	*Pearl*			
335	366	**Nestor**	383	179	*Nun*			

* Sold to Lancaster & Carlisle Railway in January 1857.

Fig. 15   Raven class 1840 *Pegasus*, which had been L&NWR No 31 until May 1876.

(Allan Sommerfield Collection)

"Raven" class 2-2-2 7ft Passenger, large firebox, direct action
November 1853 - September 1857   15 engines

281	144	*Raven*	286	340	**Euston**	384	18	*Cerberus*
282	134	*Owl*	287	341	**Miranda**	385	20	*Eagle*
283	12	*Centaur*	288	342	**Amphion**	386	40	*Jason*
284	325	**Chandos**	289	343	*Etna*	387	151	*Goldfinch*
285	31	*Pegasus*	290	344	**Kestrel**	388	195	*Emerald*

In addition, 187 *Velocipede* and 223 290 *Rocket* were assimilated to this class, after being rebuilt with 4ft 5in fireboxes.
All this class retained their names even in the Duplicate List.

TABLE 3
THE EARLY YEARS

CREWE MOTION AND ENGINE RUNNING NUMBERS, AND NAMES
and
SUBSEQUENT ENGINES BEARING THE SAME NAME
Subsequent name bearers are listed in the entries offset to the right, and the asterisk denotes a change in their running number

1 *Saracen*
      Grand Junction 2-2-2 (R.Stephenson & Co.) 1837 Replaced 1841
      GJ 0-4-2 (John Melling) 2.42 (May have been intended to have the name *Prince*) Sold to St.Helens
      Railway 2.52, No 12 *Saracen*
208   SFB Pass DA 4.52 Replaced 1861
          Problem 11.61
          *Experiment No 2624 2.09

2 *Hecla*
      GJ 2-2-2 (Haigh Foundry) 1837 Replaced 10.44
      GJ 2-4-0 Completed Crewe 10.44 (No 2A 1860) Replaced 2.60 Sold 11.61
          DX 9.60
          *Samson No 732 7.64
          *Whitehaven & Furness Junction 0-4-2 No 2 1866
          *Waterloo No 732 1.95

3 *Shark*
      GJ 2-2-2 (R.Stephenson & Co.) 1837 Replaced 1.45
      GJ 2-2-2 Completed Crewe 1.45 Replaced 12.54
319   LFB Goods DA 30.11.54 2-4-0ST 11.73 and name removed. Withdrawn 2.87
          *Samson No 2159 11.74
          *Waterloo No 2159 5.94
          *Prince of Wales No 1084 1.16

4 *Hecate*
      GJ 2-2-2 (Haigh Foundry) 1837 Replaced 1846
      SFB Pass CF 1.46 (1823 1.71 and 1895 12.71) Presumably unnamed by 4.72 Withdrawn 5.73
          *Large Bloomer No 848 4.72
          *Experiment Compound No 1113 6.84
          *Precursor No 688 7.05

5 *Falcon*
      GJ 2-2-2 (Haigh Foundry) 1837 Replaced 4.44
      GJ 2-2-2 Completed Crewe 4.44 Replaced 9.55
349   LFB Goods DA 9.55 Name removed 21.6.72. Withdrawn 7.84 (Ordered as 378 *Palmerston*)

6 *Stentor*
      GJ 2-2-2 (Rothwell, Hick) 1837 Replaced 1844
      GJ 2-2-2 Completed Crewe 1.44 Replaced 11.54
314   LFB Goods DA 27.11.54 2-4-0ST 11.73 and name removed. Withdrawn 4.87
          *Prince of Wales No 522 7.22

7 *Scorpion*
      GJ 2-2-2 (R.Stephenson & Co) 1837 Replaced 1841
      GJ 0-4-2 (John Melling) 2.42 (May have been intended to have the name *Princess* in 1847)
      Sold to St.Helens Railway 2.52 No 15 *Scorpion*
209   SFB Pass DA 4.52 (No 7A 11.61) Scrapped 9.76
          Problem 11.61
          *Precursor No 1723 8.0

8 *Wildfire*
      L&M No 2 0-2-2 1.30 (Robert Stephenson & Co) Renamed *Meteor*
      GJ 2-2-2 (R.Stephenson & Co) 1837 Completely renewed 10.44
      GJ 2-2-2 Completed Crewe 10.44 Replaced 1.54 Sold 9.2.55
322   LFB Goods DA 2.2.55 2-4-0ST 2.73 and name removed. Withdrawn 5.87
          *Samson No 468 10.74
          *Waterloo No 468 11.90

9 *Alecto*	GJ 2-2-2 (Rothwell, Hick) 1837 Sold 12.46
	SFB Pass CF 1.47 (1824 1.71 and 1900 12.71) Withdrawn 12.72
	*Newton No 2003 4.71
	*Renewed Precedent No 2003 6.91
	*Precursor No 1516 8.07

10 *Dragon*	GJ 2-2-2 (Rothwell, Hick) 1837 Replaced 2.45
	GJ 2-2-2 Completed Crewe 2.45 Replaced 9.55
350	LFB Goods DA 9.55 Rebuilt 10.69 Name removed 15.10.72 Withdrawn 10.86. (Ordered as 377 *Diana*)
	*Webb Precursor No 1155 9.74
	*Precursor No 60 10.04

11 *Zamiel*	GJ 2-2-2 (Rothwell, Hick) 1837 Replaced 3.45
	GJ 2-2-2 Completed Crewe 3.45 Replaced 3.56
359	LFB Goods DA 3.56 Rebuilt 12.68 Name removed by 1873 Withdrawn 2.84
	*Samson No 635 9.73
	*Waterloo No 635 1.90
	*Prince of Wales No 401 12.15

12 *Centaur*	GJ 2-2-2 (Sharp, Roberts & Co.) 1837 Replaced 1842
	GJ 2-2-2 Outside cylinders (Jones, Turner & Evans) 11.42 On sale 1853
283	LFB Pass (Raven class) 2.54 Rebuilt 1.63 and 1871 (1806 11.76) and name retained Withdrawn 3.79
	*Samson No 773 5.79 (3200 11.94)
	*Waterloo No 773 7.95

13 *Prospero*	GJ 2-2-2 (R.Stephenson & Co.) 1837 Replaced 12.43
	GJ 2-2-2 Completed Crewe 12.43 Replaced 11.54
311	LFB Goods DA 17.11.54 Rebuilt 5.70 Name removed 3.7.72 or 26.8.72 Withdrawn 11.86
	*Samson No 414 9.73 (3271 8.95)
	*Waterloo No 414 1.96
	*Experiment No 1361 10.07

14 *Witch*	GJ 2-2-2 (R.Stephenson & Co.) 1837 Scrapped by 6.46
	SFB Pass CF 6.46 (1825 1.71 and 1906 12.71) Withdrawn 1.73
	*Newton No 2004 4.71
	*Renewed Precedent No 2004 5.91
	*Prince of Wales No 1379 1.16

15 *Phalaris*	GJ 2-2-2 (Rothwell, Hick) 1837 Replaced 4.44
	GJ 2-2-2 Completed Crewe 4.44 On sale 11.54
317	LFB Goods DA 30.11.54 Name removed 9.6.73 Withdrawn 8.80
	*Samson No 285 9.73
	*Waterloo No 285 3.93
	*Precursor No 1297 8.07

16 *Lynx*	GJ 2-2-2 (Rothwell, Hick) 1837 Scrapped by 7.46
	SFB Pass CF 7.46 (1826 1.71 and 1877 1.72) Withdrawn 1.78
	*Newton No.2005 4.71
	*Renewed Precedent No 2005 1.94

17 *Caliban*	GJ 2-2-2 (Sharp, Roberts & Co.) 1837 Replaced 10.44
	GJ 2-2-2 Completed Crewe 10.44 Sold 10.59
310	LFB Goods DA 17.1.57 Ex No 18 *Cerberus* Rebuilt 2.72 Name removed 12.2.72 Withdrawn 6.97
	*Small Bloomer No 602 4.72
	*Samson No 805 -.84
	*Waterloo No 805 4.93
	*Prince of Wales No 2392 12.15

18 *Cerberus*	GJ 2-2-2 (Sharp, Roberts & Co.) 1837 Replaced 2.44
	GJ 2-2-2 Completed Crewe 2.44 Withdrawn 1854
310	LFB Goods DA 28.10.54 - 17.1.57 when renumbered 17 and renamed *Caliban*
365	LFB Goods DA 1.57 L&C No 49 1.57 LNWR No 512 and name removed 12.59 Scrapped 1.83
384	LFB Pass (Raven class) 7.57 Rebuilt 6.69 (No 1829 11.76) and name retained Withdrawn 6.77

*Webb Precursor No 1174 10.78
*Precursor No 1111 3.05

19 **Doctor Dalton**   GJ 2-2-2 (Sharp, Roberts & Co.) 1837 Sold 1839

19 **Princess**   GJ 2-2-2 (Crewe) 7.45 (1827 1.71 and 1873 1.72) Withdrawn 7.79
This engine was a replacement for 2-2-2 GJ No 19
*Newton No 2006 4.71
*Renewed Precedent No 2006 11.90

20 **Eagle**   GJ 2-2-2 (Sharp, Roberts & Co.) 1837 Replaced 3.44
GJ 2-2-2 Completed Crewe 3.44 Replaced 11.54
312   LFB Goods DA 20.11.54 L&C No 44 1.57 LNWR No 507 and name removed 12.59 Scrapped 5.86
385   LFB Pass (Raven class) 7.57 Rebuilt 4.69 Withdrawn 4.76

21 **Wizard**   GJ 2-2-2 (Sharp, Roberts & Co.) 1837 Replaced 2.45
GJ 2-2-2 Completed Crewe 2.45 Replaced 1.56
354   LFB Goods DA 2.56 Rebuilt 11.68 and name removed Scrapped 3.80 (Ordered as 381 *Sardinian*)
*Precedent No 872 6.77
*Renewed Precedent No 872 8.95

22 **Basilisk**   GJ 2-2-2 (Sharp, Roberts & Co.) 1837 Replaced 4.45
GJ 2-2-2 Completed Crewe 4.45 Renewed 1.57 as 6ft single SFB Pass CF (1828 1.71 and 1878 1.72)
Scrapped 12.76
*Large Bloomer No 852 4.72

23 **Vizier**   GJ 2-2-2 (Sharp, Roberts & Co.) 1837 Replaced 1842
GJ 2-2-2 Outside cylinders (Jones, Turner & Evans) 11.42 On sale 5.54
299   LFB Goods DA 5.54 Name removed 4.11.72 Scrapped 2.86
*Webb Precursor No 2148 8.74
*Precursor No 2202 10.05

24 **Sirocco**   GJ 2-2-2 (Sharp, Roberts & Co.) 1837 Replaced 1842
GJ 2-2-2 Outside cylinders (Jones, Turner & Evans) 11.42 On sale 5.54
279   LFB Goods DA 5.54 Rebuilt 11.68 Name removed 25.10.72 Scrapped 9.86
*Webb Precursor No 1153 9.74
*Precursor No 643 11.04

25 **Harpy**   GJ 2-2-2 (Sharp, Roberts & Co.) 1837 Replaced 1846
SFB Pass CF 2.46 (1129 2.71 and 1870 12.71) Withdrawn 11.75
*Large Bloomer No 893 4.72
*Dreadnought No 2061 12.85
*Precursor No 1396 11.05

26 **Aeolus**   GJ 2-2-2 (Tayleur & Co.) 1838 Rebuilt at Edge Hill with outside cylinders 8.41 Sold 9.47
SFB Pass CF 11.47 (1200 2.71 and 1898 1.72)
*Large Bloomer No 849 3.72

27 **Merlin**   GJ 2-2-2 (Tayleur & Co.) 1838 Replaced 10.43
GJ 2-2-2 Completed Crewe 10.43 On sale 10.54
309   LFB Goods DA 22.10.54 Rebuilt 4.71 (1889 1.80) Withdrawn 5.85
*Alfred the Great No 1978 8.03

28 **Prometheus**   GJ 2-2-2 (Tayleur & Co.) 1838 Repaired (Jones, Turner & Evans) 1840-1, and returned to stock 8.41 Scrapped 11.49
SFB Pass SF 11.49 (28A 11.61) Scrapped 12.78
Problem 11.61
*Experiment No 1304 11.06

29 **Alaric**   GJ 2-2-2 (Sharp, Roberts & Co.) 1838 Sold 11.46
SFB Pass CF 11.46 (1221 2.71 and 1899 1.72) Withdrawn 7.74
*Large Bloomer No 990 4.72
*Precursor No 282 4.06

30 *Sirius*	GJ 0-4-2 (Jones, Turner & Evans) 1838 Renewed at Crewe 9.44	
321	GJ 2-2-2 Completed Crewe 9.44 Replaced 1.55 Sold 9.2.55	
	LFB Goods DA 28.1.55 Name removed 30.7.72 Scrapped 6.87	

30 *Sirius*
321

GJ 0-4-2 (Jones, Turner & Evans) 1838 Renewed at Crewe 9.44
GJ 2-2-2 Completed Crewe 9.44 Replaced 1.55 Sold 9.2.55
LFB Goods DA 28.1.55 Name removed 30.7.72 Scrapped 6.87
      *Whitehaven & Furness 0-4-2 No 13 *Sirius* 1866
      *Samson No 424 9.73 (3206 1.95)
      *Waterloo No 424 7.95

31 *Pegasus*
285

GJ 2-2-2 (Tayleur & Co.) 1838 Replaced 1842
GJ 2-2-2 Outside cylinders (Jones, Turner & Evans) 11.42 On sale 11.53
LFB Pass (Raven class) 12.53 (Scott 2.54) Rebuilt 8.65 (1840 5.76) and name retained Withdrawn 1.80
      *Precedent No 482 11.80
      *Renewed Precedent No 482 1.94
      *Prince of Wales No 446 11.15

32 *Tamerlane*
292

GJ 2-2-2 (Tayleur & Co.) 1838 Replaced 10.43
GJ 2-2-2 Completed Crewe 20.10.1843 On sale 5.54
LFB Goods DA 5.54 Name removed 19.2.72 Scrapped 7.88
      *Large Bloomer No 1003 4.72
      *Dreadnought No 545 7.86
      *Precursor No 1419 3.04

33 *Erebus*

GJ 2-2-2 (Sharp, Roberts & Co.) 1838 Scrapped 4.46
SFB Pass CF 10.46 Southern Division No 339 1.60 and name removed Scrapped 8.73
      Problem 2.60
      *Precursor No 564 6.07

34 *Phoebus*

GJ 2-2-2 (Tayleur & Co.) 1838 Repaired (Jones, Turner & Evans) 1840-1 and returned to stock 8.41 Scrapped 5.50
SFB Pass SF Built Edge Hill 5.49, as 238 *President*, renumbered and renamed 34 *Phoebus* 1/2 year 5.50
  Replaced 11.60
      BL&CJ 2-4-0T No 34 L&NWR No 34 *Phoebus* 11.60
      DX 5.62

35 *Talisman*

GJ 2-2-2 (Tayleur & Co.) 1838 Repaired (Jones, Turner & Evans) 1840-1 and returned to stock 8.41 Scrapped 9.49
SFB Pass SF 9.49 Replaced 11.60
      BL&CJ 0-4-2 No 35 L&NWR No 35 *Talisman* 11.60
      Samson 2.65
      Waterloo 10.90
      *Claughton No 12 1.23

36 *Thalaba*

GJ 2-2-2 (Tayleur & Co.) 1838 Repaired (Jones, Turner & Evans) 1840-1 and returned to stock 8.41 Replaced 11.50
Sold 4.51 to St.Helens Railway No 16 *Mersey* Sold 7.57
SFB Pass SF 12.50 (36A 11.60 and 1103 5.62) and rebuilt 5.64 (1884 1.72) Scrapped 9.76
      BL&CJ 0-4-2 No 36 L&NWR No 36 *Thalaba* 11.60
      Samson 2.65
      Waterloo 10.90
      *Claughton No 30 4.23

37 *Hawk*

GJ 2-2-2 (Mather, Dixon & Co.) 1838 Sold 8.47
SFB Pass CF 7.47 (37A 12.60?) Replaced 9.61
SFB Goods SF No 240 *Bee*, Rebuilt 2-4-0T 10.59 North London Railway No 31 On return 11 or 12.60 it became
  No 37 *Hawk* (1968 6.75) Scrapped 5.80

38 *Camilla*

GJ 2-2-2 (Sharp, Roberts & Co.) 1838 Sold 7.46
SFB Pass CF 9.46 (1106 6.71 and 1897 1.72) Withdrawn 1.76
      *Large Bloomer No 889 4.72

39 *Tartarus*

GJ 2-2-2 (Tayleur & Co.) 1838 Renewed 6.42
GJ 2-2-2 Outside cylinders Edge Hill 7.42 (39A 1859 and 1104 4.62) Withdrawn by 10.62
      DX 5.59
      *Samson No 628 2.64
      *Waterloo No 628 4.93

40 *Jason*	GJ 2-2-2 (Sharp, Roberts & Co.) 1838 Sold 4.47
	SFB Pass CF 5.47 L&C No 38 1.57 L&NWR No.501 and name removed 12.59 Renamed *Bellerophon* 1864 Withdrawn 10.78
386	LFB Pass (Raven class) 8.57 Rebuilt 3.70 (1852 11.76 and name *Jason* retained) Withdrawn 10.78
	*Webb Precursor No 718 2.79
	*Precursor No 2064 3.05

| 41 *Gorgon* | GJ 0-4-2 (Jones, Turner & Evans) 1838 Sold 2.47 |
| | SFB Goods CF 3.47 Name removed 1864 2-4-0T 7.66 Sold 12.81 |

42 *Sunbeam*	GJ 2-2-2 (Tayleur & Co.) 1838 Renewed 6.42
	GJ 2-2-2 Outside cylinders Edge Hill 7.42 Lasted until 1857
377	LFB Pass (Prince Ernest class) No 40 1.57 (Plate date 12.56) No 42 8.57 Rebuilt 3.67 (1860 7.83 and 3077 5.87)
	Engineer's Department (Spare engine) 2.93 *Engineer Northampton* 4.95 until scrapped 11.01
	*Experiment Compound No 1104 6.84
	*Precursor No 2062 8.05

43 *Vampire*	GJ 2-2-2 (R.& W.Hawthorn & Co.) 1838 Scrapped 10.48
	SFB Goods SF 10.48 2-4-0T 1.70 and name removed Scrapped 1.88
	*Samson No 885 10.74 (3269 5.95)
	*Waterloo No 885 1.96

44 *Harlequin*	GJ 2-2-2 (Rothwell, Hick) 1838 Sold 4.46
	SFB Pass CF 9.46 Southern Division No 342 1.60 and name removed Scrapped 8.73
	Problem 3.60
	*Experiment No 496 9.07

45 *Sybil*	GJ 2-2-2 (R.& W.Hawthorn & Co.) 1838 Scrapped 4.49
	SFB Pass SF 4.49 (Possibly 45A 12.60) Replaced 9.61
	SFB Goods SF No 206 *Menai*, Rebuilt 2-4-0T 2.60 North London Railway No 36 On return 11 or 12.60 it becam No 45 *Sybil* Presumably unnamed by 11.74 (1840 1.81) Scrapped 5.86
	*Samson No 2152 11.74
	*Waterloo No 2152 6.94

46 *Medea*	GJ 2-2-2 (Sharp, Roberts & Co.) 1838 Scrapped 4.48
	SFB Goods CF 4.48 2-4-0T 1870 and name removed Withdrawn 6.88
	*Small Bloomer No 623 4.72
	*Samson No 995 5.79
	*Waterloo No 995 2.95

47 *Vulture*	GJ 2-2-2 (Mather, Dixon & Co.) 1838 Sold 4.47
	SFB Pass CF 5.47 (1184 6.71 and 1871 1.72) Withdrawn 10.77
	*Large Bloomer No 853 4.72
	*Webb Precursor No 1165 11.78
	*Precursor No 2257 8.05

48 *Oberon*	GJ 2-2-2 (R.& W.Hawthorn & Co.) 1838 Replaced 10.48 Sold 11.49
	SFB Goods SF 10.48 Name retained when converted to Tank engine in 1868 but presumably unnamed by 10.74 Scrapped 10.81
	*Webb Precursor No 425 10.74
	*Precursor No 2164 4.04

49 *Columbine*	GJ 2-2-2 (Rothwell, Hick) 1838 Replaced 1845
	GJ 2-2-2 (Crewe) 20.7.45 (1198 6.71 and 1868 12.71)
	Engineer. Bangor 11.77 - 1.02 Withdrawn and preserved as 49 *Columbine*
	*Large Bloomer No 850 4.72

| 50 *Hornet* | GJ 2-2-2 (Mather, Dixon & Co.) 1838 Scrapped 5.48 |
| | SFB Goods CF 5.48 Name removed 22.10.74 Withdrawn 3.81 |

51 *Torch*	GJ 2-2-2 (R.& W.Hawthorn & Co.) 1838 Scrapped 2.49
	SFB Pass SF 2.49 (1829 7.71 and 1901 1.72) *Engineer Stafford* 9.73 until withdrawal 3.91
	*Large Bloomer No 895 4.72

52 **Diomed** GJ 2-2-2 (Walker & Co.) 1838-9 Replaced 11.49
SFB Pass SF 7.49 Replaced 8.60
          DX 9.60
          *Samson No 821 5.63
          *Waterloo No 821 1.92

53 **Clio** GJ 2-2-2 (R.& W.Hawthorn & Co.) 1838 Scrapped 10.48
SFB Goods SF 10.48 Name retained when converted to Tank engine 4.60 (1940 3.81) Sold 10.81
          *Claughton No 2230 7.22

54 **Medusa** GJ 2-2-2 (Walker & Co.) 1838-9 Sold 4.46
SFB Pass CF 1.6.46 Rebuilt 1856 (1830 6.71, 1874 1.72 and 3088 7.87) Rebuilt 2 cylinder compound 1878 Rebuilt
    Triple Compound and renamed *Triplex* 8.95 Scrapped 10.03
          *Large Bloomer No 999 4.72
          *Dreadnought No 2058 12.85
          *Precursor No 366 5.05

55 **Lucifer** GJ 2-2-2 (Sharp, Roberts & Co.) 1839 Scrapped 5.48
SFB Goods CF 5.48 2-4-0T 1860 Presumably unnamed by 3.72 Withdrawn 10.78
          *Large Bloomer No 1004 4.72

56 **Phantom** GJ 2-2-2 (Sharp, Roberts & Co.) 1839 Sold 11.48
SFB Goods SF 11.48 2-4-0T 1871 and name removed Scrapped 4.83
          *Precedent No 883 5.77
          *Renewed Precedent No 883 11.94

57 **Sultan** GJ 2-2-2 (Sharp, Roberts & Co.) 1839 Scrapped 5.48
SFB Goods SF 6.48 2-4-0T 1865 (1935 7.81) Scrapped 8.89
          *Small Bloomer No 977 4.72
          *Jubilee No 1938 10.00

58 **Syren** GJ 2-2-2 (Sharp, Roberts & Co.) 1839 Scrapped 6.48
   Siren SFB Goods CF 6.48 2-4-0T 1862 (1965 6.75) Withdrawn 12.76
          *Samson No 446 9.73
          *Waterloo No 446 4.93

59 **Vandal** GJ 2-2-2 (Sharp, Roberts & Co.) 1839 Sold by 7.48
SFB Pass SF Edge Hill 7.48 (1831 6.71 and 1896 1.72) Withdrawn 2.77
          *Small Bloomer No 980 4.72
          *Dreadnought No 2060 12.85
          *Precursor No 1117 11.04

60 **Tantalus** GJ 2-2-2 (Haigh Foundry) 2.40 Scrapped 11.50
SFB Pass SF Edge Hill 11.49 as 253 *Bucephalus*, renumbered and renamed 60 *Tantalus* 1/2 year 11.50
   Southern Division No 337 1.60 and name removed Scrapped 20.1.73
          Problem 3.60
          *Precursor No 1469 3.05

61 **Phosphorus** GJ 2-2-2 (Mather, Dixon & Co.) 6.40 Scrapped 11.50
SFB Pass SF 11.50 Southern Division No 331 1.60 and name removed Scrapped 4.9.78
          Problem 3.60
          *Experiment No 830 9.07

62 **Hyperion** GJ 2-2-2 (Mather, Dixon & Co.) 7.40 Scrapped 11.50
SFB Goods SF 11.50 2-4-0T 4.58 (1804 3.76) Scrapped 3.78
          *Precursor No 1787 5.06

63 **Herod** GJ 2-2-2 (Geo.Forrester & Co.) 6.40 Replaced 1855
348 LFB Goods DA 9.55 Name removed 15.10.72 Withdrawn 8.87

64 **Odin** GJ 2-2-2 (Geo.Forrester & Co.) 7.40 On sale 11.51
198 SFB Pass DA 11.51 (1875 7.71) *Engineer Northampton* c.1879 until withdrawal 1.91
          *Large Bloomer No 847 4.72
          *Samson No 1164 5.79
          *Waterloo No 1164 2.95
          *Prince of Wales No 2442 2.16

	65 *Charon*	GJ 2-2-2 (R.Stephenson & Co.) 7.40 Scrapped 10.52
221		SFB Pass DA 10.52 (Possibly 65A 10.61) Scrapped 6.75
		DX 10.61
		*Samson No 735 5.63
		*Waterloo No 735 1.92

	66 *Colossus*	GJ 0-4-2 (Tayleur & Co.) 1.41 Converted to static works engine 10.51
193		SFB Goods DA 10.51 2-4-0T 5.69 Presumably unnamed by 8.74 Withdrawn 7.83
		*Webb Precursor No 1154 9.74
		*Jubilee No 1912 6.99

	67 *Briareus*	GJ 0-4-2 (Tayleur & Co.) 1.41 Scrapped 5.51
188		SFB Goods DA 5.51 2-4-0T 7.62 Presumably unnamed by 3.72 Withdrawn 6.94
		*Large Bloomer No 995 4.72

	68 *Antaeus*	GJ 0-4-2 (Tayleur & Co.) 3.41 Scrapped 5.52
212		SFB Goods DA 5.52 2-4-0T 4.65 Withdrawn 11.81
		*Precursor No 561 4.06

	69 *Python*	GJ 2-2-2 (R.Stephenson & Co.) 4.41 On sale 5.53
249		LFB Goods DA 5.53 Rebuilt 11.58 Name removed 10.9.73 Scrapped 12.79
		*Webb Precursor No 413 10.74
		*Precursor No 1784 10.05

	70 *Sphinx*	GJ 0-4-2 (John Melling) 1.41 Sold to St.Helens Railway 4.51, who retained the name
		SFB Goods SF 3.51 2-4-0T 10.68 Presumably unnamed by 11.74 Carriage Department Wolverton No 2
		12.77 until withdrawal 2.95
		*Samson No 2156 11.74
		*Waterloo No 2156 2.95 (3488 6.14)
		*Prince of Wales No 1466 1.16

	71 *Typhon*	GJ 2-2-2 (R.Stephenson & Co.) 5.41 On sale 5.53
246		LFB Goods DA 5.53 Rebuilt 12.63 Name removed 15.10.72 Scrapped 12.78
		*Samson No 444 9.73
		*Waterloo No 444 10.90
		*George the Fifth No 1481 4.13

	72 *Phlegethon*	GJ 2-2-2 (R.Stephenson & Co.) 7.41 Scrapped 4.53
245		LFB Goods DA 4.53 2-4-0T 2.60 Name removed 25.11.72 Scrapped 5.87

	73 *Prince*	GJ 2-2-2 (Crewe) 6.45
	Prince Albert	Renamed *Prince Albert* 1847 Rebuilt 4.57 and name removed 1861 Withdrawn 3.78
		*Newton No 1214 4.72
		*Renewed Precedent No 1214 11.90
		*Prince of Wales No 1178 2.22

	74 *Deva*	GJ 2-2-2 (Crewe) 10.45 Rebuilt 10.56 Scrapped 6.69

	75 *Apollo*	GJ 2-2-2 (Crewe) 9.45 Rebuilt 2.59 (1833 7.71 and 1869 1.72) Sold 5.72
		*Large Bloomer No 851 4.72
		*Experiment Compound No 1120 6.84
		*Precursor No 1115 4.05

	76 *Albion*	GJ 2-2-2 (Crewe) 9.45 Rebuilt 2.58 (1834 7.71 and 1902 1.72) Withdrawn 8.76
		*Newton No 1215 4.72
		*Renewed Precedent No 1215 8.93
		*Prince of Wales No 610 12.15

	77 *Mersey*	GJ 2-2-2 (Crewe) 11.45 Southern Division No 343 1.60 and name removed Scrapped 22.6.72
		*St.Helens 0-6-0 No 16 *Mersey*
		Problem 5.60
		*Precursor No 665 6.07

	78 *Lonsdale*	GJ 2-4-0 (Crewe) 2.46 Rebuilt 9.57 Rebuilt 2-4-0T 9.69 Presumably unnamed by 4.72 (1967 6.75)
		Withdrawn 11.84

*L&C No 11 1857
*Small Bloomer No 840 4.72

79 **Belted Will**	SFB Pass CF 2.46 (1835 7.71 and 1903 1.72) This locomotive did not enter traffic until July 1846, but was included in the last official list of the GJR issued in April 1846. Withdrawn 8.77	

        *L&C No 24 1857
        *Newton No 1220 4.72
        *Renewed Precedent No 1220 6.87

80 **Dalemain** GJ 2-2-2 (Crewe) 3.46 Rebuilt 10.57 (1836 7.71 and 1904 1.72) Withdrawn 9.74
        *L&C No 22 1857
        *Large Bloomer No 854 4.72

81 **Greystoke** GJ 2-4-0 (Crewe) 2.46 Sold 11.64
        *L&C No 23 1857
        Waterloo 1.92
        *Experiment No 2116 1.09

Greystock Samson 1.65 - Renamed *Greystoke* 4.12.91

82 **Wordsworth** GJ 2-4-0 (Crewe) 4.46 2-4-0T 2.59 Presumably unnamed by 8.73 (1969 6.75) Withdrawn 8.80
        *Newton No 1020 8.73
        *Renewed Precedent No 1020 5.91
        *Experiment No 1661 5.09

83 **Windermere** GJ 2-4-0 (Crewe) 4.46 Renamed *Skiddaw* 4.50
        (*For continuation of the name* Windermere, *see* No 259)

Skiddaw Named *Windermere* until 4.50 2-4-0T 9.71 and name removed (1978 6.75) Withdrawn 11.86
        *L&C No 9 1857
        *Samson No 486 10.74
        *Waterloo No 486 6.93

84 **Saddleback** SFB Pass CF 4.46 (1837 7.71 and 1905 1.72) Withdrawn 1.74
        *L&C No 10 1857
        *Samson No 1162 5.79
        *Waterloo No 1162 6.93
        *George the Fifth No 845 3.13

85 **Ingestre** SFB Pass CF 5.46 (1839 1.72) Withdrawn 6.72
        *Large Bloomer No 856 4.72
        *Claughton No 2420 1.23

86 **Sandon** SFB Pass CF 6.46 (1907 1.72) Withdrawn 7.75
        *Large Bloomer No 855 4.72

87 **Eden** SFB Goods CF 15.7.46 Rebuilt Tank 6.58 Wagon Department 5.59 and renamed *Earlestown* Withdrawn 1.81
        *L&C No 7 1857
        DX 5.59
        *Samson No 724 2.64
        *St.Helens No 7
        *Waterloo No 724 3.93

88 **Lune** SFB Goods CF 8.46 Presumably unnamed by 4.72 2-4-0T 1873 (1861 12.75) Sold 11.81
        *L&C No 6 1857
        *St.Helens No 28
        *Small Bloomer No 615 4.72

89 **Bela** SFB Goods CF 8.46 2-4-0T 1869 Presumably unnamed by 4.72 Withdrawn 11.86
        *Small Bloomer No 621 4.72

90 **Lowther** SFB Goods CF 9.46 2-4-0T 3.59 Withdrawn 11.74
        *L&C No 21 1857
        *Precedent No 2186 4.75
        *Renewed Precedent No 2186 2.96

91 **Knowsley** SFB Pass CF 10.46 (1908 1.72) Withdrawn 7.78
        *Large Bloomer No 887 4.72
        *Experiment Compound No 306 7.83
        *Precursor No 1114 9.05

92 *Trentham*	SFB Pass CF 10.46 (1909 1.72) *Engineer Swansea* 10.80 Withdrawn 7.89
	*Large Bloomer No 894 4.72
	*Experiment Compound No 305 7.83
	*Precursor No 2120 5.05

93 *Premier*	SFB Pass CF 10.46 (1911 1.72) *Engineer Swansea* 10.80 Withdrawn 6.78
	*Newton No 1216 4.72
	*Renewed Precedent No 1216 11.88
	*Prince of Wales No 1694 4.23

94 *Helvellyn*	SFB Pass CF 11.46 (1912 1.72) Withdrawn 6.78
	*Large Bloomer No 890 4.72
	*Webb Precursor No 1149 9.78
	*Precursor No 2023 4.04

95 *Hydra*	SFB Pass CF 12.46 (1913 1.72) Withdrawn 10.74
	*Large Bloomer No 888 4.72
	*Experiment Compound No 303 4.83
	*Precursor No 1617 8.05

96 *Polyphemus*	SFB Pass CF 12.46 (1914 1.72) Withdrawn 7.78
	*Large Bloomer No 892 4.72
	*Jubilee No 1929 4.00

97 *Atalanta*	SFB Pass CF 12.46 Southern Division No 344 1.60 and name removed Scrapped 17.10.72
	Problem 5.60
	*Experiment No 61 11.06

| 98 *Dædalus* | SFB Pass CF 1.47 (1915 1.72) Withdrawn 2.80 |
| | *Large Bloomer No 896 4.72 |

In S.Scott's Duplicate List under the heading "DAEDALUS (or DÆDALUS)" he has a footnote:-
"Note No.1915 (old 98). I remember this engine still carried the nameplate 'Daedalus' for some time after the Bloomer 896 had been given the same name in 1872 & 1873. S.Scott"

| 99 *Duke* | SFB Pass CF 2.47 (1916 1.72) Withdrawn 3.73 |
| | *Large Bloomer No 891 4.72 |

| 100 *Earl* | SFB Goods CF 2.47 2-4-0T 3.59 Presumably unnamed by 4.72 Withdrawn 7.81 |
| | *Small Bloomer No 626 4.72 |

| 101 *Baronet* | SFB Goods CF 2.47 2-4-0T 4.61 Presumably unnamed by 3.72 Withdrawn 3.79 |
| | *Large Bloomer No 997 4.72 |

| 102 *Marquis* | SFB Goods CF 12.3.47 To NE Division No 31 3.47 Renumbered and renamed 261 *Hercules* in 1863 (1911 3.79) Sold 5.81 |

102 *Marquis*	SFB Goods SF 2.50 This was a replacement for the above engine, and charged to the Capital Account because it had not been paid for. Rebuilt 2-4-0T 6.61 and not known if the name was retained. Name removed by 8.73. Scrapped 12.83
	*Newton No 403 8.73
	*Webb Precursor No 1143 8.74
	*Precursor No 412 11.04

103 *Archimedes*	SFB Pass CF 5.47 (1917 2.72) Withdrawn 1.76
	*Large Bloomer No 989 4.72
	*Dreadnought No 1395 6.86
	*Precursor No 648 10.04

104 *Phaeton*	SFB Pass CF 5.47 (1918 2.72) Withdrawn 12.75
	*Newton No 1218 4.72
	*Renewed Precedent No 1218 11.90
	*George the Fifth No 2086 4.13

105 *Viscount*		SFB Goods CF 5.47 2-4-0T 3.57 Name removed 2.1.73 Withdrawn 7.85
		*Webb Precursor No 402 9.74
		*Precursor No 1737 3.05
106 *Senator*		SFB Goods CF 5.47 2-4-0T 6.61 Presumably unnamed by 9.74 Withdrawn 5.79
		*Webb Precursor No 406 9.74
		*Precursor No 305 11.04
107 *Magistrate*		SFB Goods CF 6.47 Name removed 10.12.73 Withdrawn 12.73
108 *Mayor*		SFB Goods CF 6.47 2-4-0T 1869 Name removed, date unknown Withdrawn 8.81
109 *The Queen*		SFB Pass CF 6.47 (1827 8.72) Withdrawn 10.72
		*Newton No 1213 4.72
		*Renewed Precedent No 1213 4.92

378 110 *Canning* SFB Pass CF 30.6.47 L&C No 39 1.57 L&NWR No 502 and name removed 12.59 Withdrawn 8.73
LFB Pass (Prince Ernest class) 28.1.57 (1883 8.83 and 3027 3.88) *Engineer Watford* 12.91 *Engineer Lancaster* 4.94
until withdrawal 4.03
*Prince of Wales No 504 8.22

111 *Russell* SFB Pass CF 7.47 Southern Division 1.60 No 340 and name removed Scrapped 10.74
Problem 5.60

112 *Councillor* SFB Goods CF 9.47 2-4-0T 1860 Presumably unnamed by 4.72 (1845 7.75) Withdrawn 9.82
*Small Bloomer No 981 4.72

113 *Elephant* L&M No 65 0-4-2 3.39 (Todd, Kitson & Laird) Renumbered 34 L&NWR No 113 1847 Scrapped 6.47
SFB Goods CF 6.47 Name removed 27.11.73 Withdrawn 11.73

114 *Lightning* L&M No 45 2-2-2 6.36 (Haigh Foundry) Renumbered 21 L&NWR No 114 1847 Scrapped 11.49
SFB Pass SF 8.49 (1829 8.72) Withdrawn 7.74
*Newton No 1219 4.72
*Renewed Precedent No 1219 1.88
*Experiment No 1781 5.09

Meteor L&M No 2 0-2-2 1.30 (Robert Stephenson & Co) Sold 3.37
Meteor L&M No 54 2-2-2 3.37 (Mather, Dixon & Co) Allotted L&NWR No 115 Scrapped 5.49

115 *Meteor* SFB Pass SF 5.49 (1839 8.72) Scrapped 1.79
*Precedent No 863 5.77
*George the Fifth No 2242 5.13

116 *Lion* L&M No 57 0-4-2 7.38 (Todd, Kitson & Laird) Renumbered 36 L&NWR No 116 1847 Sold 5.59,
370 but subsequently preserved
LFB Goods DA Built 1.57 (Stored as No 20) 8.57 Rebuilt 11.66 (1883 1.80) Scrapped 3.82

117 *Tiger* L&M No 58 0-4-2 3.38 (Todd, Kitson & Laird) renumbered 37 L&NWR No 117 1847
Probably replaced or rebuilt as SFB Pass SF 5.49 Edge Hill, as 243 *Chillington*,
renumbered and renamed 117 *Tiger* half year to 11.49 Replaced 11.60
Problem 11.60
*Precursor No 1439 11.05

118 *Roderic* L&M No 60 2-2-2 3.38 (Rothwell, Hick & Rothwell) renumbered 20 L&NWR No 118 1847 Scrapped 9.47
SFB Pass CF Edge Hill 9.47 (1842 8.72) Withdrawn 7.74

119 *Mastodon* L&M No 63 0-4-2 3.39 (T.Banks & Co.) renumbered 56 L&NWR No 119 1847 Scrapped 3.49
SFB Goods SF 3.49 2-4-0T 5.70 and name removed Scrapped 3.94
*Small Bloomer No 625 4.72
*Samson No 479 5.79
*Waterloo No 479 3.92

120 *Samson* L&M No 13 0-4-0 (Robert Stephenson & Co.) 1.31 Rebuilt 1834 Withdrawn by 1839
L&M 0-4-2 No 66 3.39 (B.Hick & Son) Renumbered 35 L&NWR No 120 1847 Scrapped 11.47

SFB Goods SF 11.47 2-4-0T 10.59 North London Railway No 32 11.59 Returned to L&NWR 11 or 12.60 to become No 364 *Buffalo* Replaced 2.82 Scrapped 7.83

     DX 11.59
     *Samson No 633 5.63
     *Waterloo No 633 1.92
     *Prince of Wales No 2339 1.16

121 *Buffalo*

L&M No 67 0-4-2 3.39 (Todd, Kitson & Laird) Renumbered 50 L&NWR No 121 1847 (121A 1860 and 1106 4.62) Sold 5.67

     DX 9.60

*SFB Goods SF No 120 *Samson*, Rebuilt 2-4-0T 10.59 North London Railway No 32 22.11.59 On return 11 or 12.60 it became No 364 *Buffalo* Presumably unnamed by 3.75 (1865 2.82) Scrapped 7.83

     *Precedent No 2181 3.75
     *Experiment No 2630 3.09

122 *Goliah*

L&M No 15 0-4-0 3.31 (Robert Stephenson & Co.) Sold 9.35
L&M No 68 0-4-2 3.39 (B.Hick & Son) Renumbered 51 L&NWR No 122 1847 Scrapped 9.47
SFB Goods CF 10.47 Name *Goliah* removed 9.8.75 Withdrawn 4.79

Goliath

     *St.Helens No 25 *Goliath*
     *Jubilee No 1927 3.00

—- *Victory*

L&M No 22 2-2-0 9.31 (Robert Stephenson & Co.) Withdrawn 1840-1
Bolton & Leigh 0-6-0 (John Hargreaves) 1832. Rebuilt 0-4-2 L&NWR 123 1847 (123A 1860 and 1107 1862). Some sources give the name as having been *Victoria*, but the fact that the DX which inherited the name was *Victory* supports the view that the latter name is correct. Sold 1862

123 *Victory*

     DX 9.60

124 *Marquis Douro*

Bolton & Leigh 0-4-2 (Tayleur & Co.) 1838 L&NWR No 124 Sold 3.50
  The name is sometimes given as *Marquis of Douro*
SFB Pass SF Edge Hill Built 5.49 as No 241 *Wasp*, renumbered and renamed 124 *Marquis Douro* during the half year ending 5.50 Replaced 11.60

     Birkenhead, Lancashire & Cheshire Junction 0-4-2 (Sharp, Stewart & Co.) Built 8.58 No 41 (unnamed) L&NWR No 124 and named 11.60
     Samson 2.65
     Waterloo 3.93

125 *Soho*

Bolton & Leigh 0-4-2 (Benjamin Hick & Son) 1838 L&NWR No 125 1847 Sold 3.50, and subsequently to Robert Daglish 1852, who may possibly have rebuilt it and sold it to St.Helens Railway to become their *Garston*
SFB Pass SF Built Edge Hill 4.49 as 239 *Powis*, renumbered and renamed 125 *Soho* during the half year ending 5.50 (125A 11.61, 1108 5.62 and 1885 12.71) Scrapped 10.78

     DX 11.61

126 *Partridge*

L&M No 83 2-2-2 6.43 L&NWR No 126 1847 and either scrapped or sold to St.Helens No 24 *Alma* 5.54
  (See No 133 *Ostrich* and No 146 *Redwing*)

300

LFB Goods DA 5.54 To traffic 1.7.54 Name removed 19.2.72 Scrapped 4.90

     *Small Bloomer No 617 4.72
     *George the Fifth No 1713 9.11

127 *Peel*

Bolton & Leigh 0-4-2 1840 (Edward Bury & Co.) L&NWR No 127 1847 Sold 3.50
SFB Pass SF Built Edge Hill 5.49 as 240 *Bee*, renumbered and renamed 127 *Peel* during the half year ending 5.50 (127A 3.62, 1109 5.62 and 1886 12.71) Scrapped 1.78

     Problem 3.62
     *Precursor No 2581 12.05

128 *Swallow*

L&M No 69 2-2-2 9.41 L&NWR No 128 1847
  Sold to St.Helens Railway 3.50 (having been rebuilt before purchase as a 2-4-0, or subsequently by them by 1855), to become their No 9 *Swallow* L&NWR No 1375 7.64 (1200 10.11.66) Sold 8.2.71
SFB Pass SF 11.49 (1843 8.72) Scrapped 12.76

	129 *Martin*	L&M No 70 2-2-2 1.42 L&NWR No 129 1847 Rebuilt as 242 Giraffe in 5.49 and held in store until 11.50, when it entered traffic with its former number and name

129 *Martin*

L&M No 70 2-2-2 1.42 L&NWR No 129 1847 Rebuilt as 242 Giraffe in 5.49 and held in store until 11.50, when it entered traffic with its former number and name
    Replaced 9.61
        DX 9.61
          *Samson No 793 2.64
          *Waterloo No 793 5.94

211   130 *Heron*

L&M No 72 2-2-2 11.41 L&NWR No 130 1847 Scrapped 5.52
SFB Pass DA 5.52 (130A 11.61)
    DX 11.61

189   131 *Kingfisher*

L&M No 71 2-2-2 9.41 L&NWR No 131 1847 Scrapped 5.51
SFB Goods DA 28.7.51 Name removed 4.9.72 Rebuilt Crane Tank 9.73 Scrapped 11.92

214   132 *Pelican*

L&M No 73 2-2-2 12.41 L&NWR No 132 1847 Withdrawn 5.52
SFB Goods DA 5.52 2-4-0T 12.61 (1939 5.82) Scrapped 6.88

280   133 *Ostrich*

L&M No 74 2-2-2 2.42 L&NWR No 133 1847 On sale 5.54 and possibly sold to St.Helens Railway
    (See 126 *Partridge* and 146 *Redwing*)
LFB Goods DA 5.54 Southern Division 1.60 No 349 and name removed Scrapped 7.91
      Beyer, Peacock 0-6-0 Early 1860 Name removed 12.65
        *Samson No 632 12.65
        *Waterloo No 632 6.90
        *Waterloo No 739 13.8.13

282   134 *Owl*

L&M No 75 2-4-0 3.42 L&NWR No 134 1847 Replaced 11.53 On sale 3.55
LFB Pass (Raven Class) 11.53 Southern Division No 324 1.60 and name removed Renumbered 924 4.62 and
    renamed *Marathon* 9.64 (See under)
      Problem 5.60

924 *Marathon*

Formerly No.134 *Owl*, renamed *Marathon* after return from Southern Division 9.64 Rebuilt 7.68
    (1880 11.76) *282* and name *Marathon* retained Scrapped 20.8.77
      *Precedent No 517 9.78
      *Renewed Precedent No 517 3.96
      *Prince of Wales No 1542 1.23

220   135 *Bat*

L&M No 76 2-4-0 6.42 L&NWR No 135 1847 Sold 9.52
SFB Pass DA 9.52 (1138 5.62) Rebuilt 1870 (1867 12.71 and 3082 2.87) and renamed *Locomotion* for use with
    the Engineer's Saloon Reboilered 2.06 Out of Stock 5.11 *Engineer South Wales* 7.11 Scrapped 12.20
      DX 5.62

215   136 *Stork*

L&M No 77 2-2-2 5.42 L&NWR No 136 1847 Scrapped 5.52
SFB Goods DA 5.52 2-4-0T 9.67 Withdrawn 4.84
      *Large Bloomer No 992 4.72
      *Dreadnought No 1379 6.86
      *Precursor No 229 11.05

253   137 *Crane*

L&M No 78 2-2-2 10.42 L&NWR No 137 1847 Sold 3.54
LFB Goods DA 5.53 Rebuilt 2.63 (1962 1.80) Scrapped 2.83

138 *Swan*

L&M No 79 2-2-2 9.42 L&NWR No 138 1847 Crewe 1855 list gives 'cut up' 5.55, but it could have been
    sold to St.Helens Railway to be their first No 5, then sold on to the Balaklava Railway 8.55. St.Helens
    Railway appears to have replaced it with a second No 5 *Swan*, which became L&NWR No 1371 7.64 Sold
    to Isaac Watt Boulton 11.64

251   LFB Goods DA 5.53 Rebuilt 2.68 Name removed 12.2.72 Scrapped 1.84
      *Small Bloomer No 629 4.72

219   139 *Cygnet*

L&M No 80 2-2-2 12.42 L&NWR No 139 1847 Scrapped 9.52
SFB Pass DA 9.52 Replaced 11.61
    Problem 11.61

140 **Atlas**   L&M No 23 0-4-0 10.31 Rebuilt 0-4-2 by 8.34 Renewed as 2-2-2 No 81 11.42 L&NWR No 140 1847
Sold to St.Helens 2.52, who may have renamed it *Sutton*, but this is not confirmed.

205   SFB Goods DA 3.52 2-4-0T 1867 Name presumed removed by 11.74 Withdrawn 5.83
   *Samson No 2150 11.74
   *Waterloo No 2150 6.93
   *Prince of Wales No 2417 2.16

141 **Pheasant**   L&M No 82 2-2-2 11.42 L&NWR No 141 1847 Scrapped 5.51
SFB Pass SF Built Edge Hill 11.49 as 264 *Clarendon*, renumbered and renamed 141 *Pheasant* during the half
year ending 5.51 Possibly (141A), and out of service 11.60 Replaced 9.61
SFB Goods SF No 245 *Ellesmere*, Rebuilt 2-4-0T 11.59 North London Railway No 35 Returned 11 or
12.60 to become No 141 *Pheasant* Hired to Contractor 9.62 Presumably unnamed by 4.72
   *Small Bloomer No 666 4.72
   *Samson No 263 5.79
   *Waterloo No 263 1.95
   *Experiment No 2076 1.09

142 **Bittern**   L&M No 84 2-4-0 4.43 L&NWR No 142 1847 Replaced 7.52 Sold 12.52 to St.Helens Railway as a
2-4-0 and very likely was their No 17 renamed *Britain*, but this is not confirmed. Allotted L&NWR
No 1383 7.64 Scrapped 9.64

239   SFB Goods DA 3.53 2-4-0T 9.66 Withdrawn 11.81

143 **Lapwing**   L&M No 85 2-4-0 10.43 L&NWR No 143 1847 Sold 9.53 to St.Helens Railway as a 2-4-0 to become their No 18
Lapwing L&NWR No 1384 7.64 Sold 15.2.65

264   LFB Goods DA 10.53 2-4-0T 5.70 Name removed 9.6.73 Scrapped 3.83
   *Webb Precursor No 1151 10.78
   *Precursor No 1642 3.06

144 **Raven**   L&M No 86 2-4-0 12.43 L&NWR No 144 1847 Replaced 11.53 'On sale' 2.55

281   LFB Pass (Raven class) 2.54 Rebuilt 2.63 and 1872 (1899 2.77) and name retained Withdrawn 12.80
   *St.Helens No 21
   *Dreadnought No 643 5.88

145 **Crow**   L&M No 87 2-4-0 1.44 L&NWR No 145 1847 Replaced 10.53 Sold 4.54

266   LFB Goods DA 10.53 Rebuilt 4.64 and 2-4-0ST 9.76 (1815 9.84 and 3037 11.86) Scrapped 9.90

146 **Redwing**   L&M No 88 2-2-2 4.44 L&NWR No 146 1847 Scrapped 5.54 or sold to St.Helens Railway
(See 126 *Partridge* and 133 *Ostrich*)

291   LFB Goods DA 5.54 Rebuilt 9.71 and name removed Scrapped 2.84

147 **Woodlark**   L&M No 89 2-2-2 1.45 L&NWR No 147 1847 Sold 2.52 to St.Helens Railway 2.52 No 14 *Star*

199   SFB Pass DA 11.51 (1137 5.62) Scrapped 12.78
  DX 5.62
   *Samson No 794 3.64
   *Waterloo No 794 1.95

148 **Penguin**   L&M No 90 2-4-0 10.44 (or 1.45) L&NWR No 148 1847 Replaced 11.53 'On sale' 3.55

268   LFB Pass (Prince Ernest class) 12.53 Reb.7.68 (1934 8.83) Withdrawn 3.85
   *Experiment Compound No 1117 7.84
   *Precursor No 2012 11.05

149 **Petrel**   L&M No 91 2-4-0 7.44 L&NWR No 149 1847 Sold 4.56

358   LFB Goods DA 2.56 2-4-0T 2.57 Presumably unnamed by 4.72 Scrapped 1.84 (Ordered as 379
Combermere)
   *Small Bloomer No 838 4.72
   *Samson No 209 5.79 (3198 11.94)
   *Waterloo No 209 8.95 (3496 7.14)
   *Prince of Wales No 1744 1.16

150 **Linnet**   L&M No 92 2-2-2 2.45 L&NWR No 150 1847 Sold 9.53

257   LFB Pass (Prince Ernest class) 8.53 L&C No 29 1.57 L&NWR No 492 Name *Linnet* removed 12.59 Renamed
Trevithick 1864 Rebuilt 7.62 (1829 1.84) Withdrawn 3.86

379   LFB Pass (Prince Ernest class) 4.57 Rebuilt 10.70 (1951 8.83) Withdrawn 12.84

	151 *Goldfinch*	L&M No 93 2-2-2 2.45 L&NWR No 151 1847 Scrapped 10.53
265		LFB Goods DA 10.53 L&C No 51 1.57 L&NWR No 514 and name removed 12.59 Withdrawn 4.82
387		LFB Pass (Raven class) 8.57 Rebuilt 4.69 and name retained (1918 2.77) Withdrawn 7.82
	152 *Bullfinch*	L&M No 94 2-2-2 5.45 L&NWR No 152 1847 Replaced 1855
341		LFB Goods DA 7.55 L&C No 47 1.57 L&NWR No 510 and name removed 12.59 Scrapped 1.88
371		LFB Goods DA 14.2.57 Name removed 31.10.72 Scrapped 7.84
	153 *Chaffinch*	L&M No 95 2-2-2 5.45 L&NWR No 153 1847 Sold 3.54
267		LFB Goods DA 11.53 Rebuilt 10.69 and name removed Withdrawn 6.86
	154 *Starling*	L&M No 96 2-4-0 7.45 L&NWR No 154 1847 Replaced 11.54
315		LFB Goods DA 17.11.54 L&C No 50 1.57 L&NWR No 513 and name removed 12.59 Scrapped 7.91
372		LFB Goods DA 2.57 Rebuilt 12.66 Name removed 10.9.73
	155 *Owzell*	L&M No 97 2-4-0 11.45 L&NWR No 155 1847 Replaced 11.54 'On sale' 3.55
316	155 *Ousel*	LFB Goods DA 30.11.54 Rebuilt 11.67 Name removed 14.7.74 Withdrawn 8.80
	156 *Redstart*	L&M No 98 2-4-0 12.45 L&NWR No 156 1847 Replaced 3.56
357		LFB Goods DA 3.56 L&C No 48 1.57 L&NWR No 511 and name removed 12.59 Scrapped 7.91
		(Ordered as 380 *Napoleon*)
373		'Isis' class 2-4-0T 2.57 (1830 9.84 and 3052 11.86) Scrapped 11.86
	157 *Redbreast*	L&M No 99 2-4-0 9.45 L&NWR No 157 1847 Scrapped 5.51
187		SFB Goods DA 5.51 2-4-0T 8.69 and name removed Withdrawn 3.83
	158 *Condor*	L&M No 100 2-2-2 3.46 L&NWR No 158 1847 Scrapped 3.53
242		SFB Goods DA 3.53 2-4-0T 3.65 Presumably unnamed by 6.77 Sold 8.83
		*Precedent No 868 6.77
		*Renewed Precedent No 868 11.96
		*Prince of Wales No 867 1.16
	159 *Adjutant*	L&M No 101 2-4-0 3.46 L&NWR No 159 1847 Replaced 1.57
369		LFB Goods DA Built 1.57 (Stored) 8.57 Rebuilt 5.71 and name removed Scrapped 5.87
		*Precursor No 675 4.06
	160 *Flamingo*	L&M No 102 2-4-0 3.46 L&NWR No 160 1847 Replaced 5.53 'On sale' 3.55
250		LFB Goods DA 5.53 2-4-0T 11.60, or 11.69 and name removed Scrapped 3.80
	161 *Cuckoo*	L&M No 103 2-4-0 3.46 L&NWR No 161 1847 Replaced 3.56
360		LFB Goods DA 3.56 Name removed 16.5.72 Scrapped 7.86
		*Bury "Low-domed Single" No 1185 1872
		*Samson No 1168 7.79
		*Waterloo No 1168 6.94
	162 *Albatross*	L&M No 104 2-4-0 6.46 L&NWR No 162 1847 Replaced 6.56
364		LFB Goods DA 6.56 Rebuilt 9.71 and name removed Scrapped 11.82
		*Webb Precursor No 1169 10.78
		*Precursor No 510 6.04
	163 *Osprey*	L&M No 106 2-4-0 7.46 L&NWR No 163 1847 Replaced 6.56
362		LFB Goods DA 6.56 Name removed 19.2.72 Rebuilt 3.72 Scrapped 4.84
		*Small Bloomer No 703 4.72
	—- *Sun*	L&M 2-2-0 (Robert Stephenson & Co.) No 17 4.31 Sold 9.35
		L&M 2-2-2 (R.& W.Hawthorn & Co) No 53 3.37 Broken up 1842
	164 *Sun*	SFB Pass CF Edge Hill 7.47 (No 1859 8.72) Withdrawn 3.76
		*St.Helens No 20
	—- *Star*	L&M 2-2-2 (Tayleur & Co.) No 41 2.36 Renumbered 53 To L&NWR 7.47 and scrapped

Fig. 16   3020 *Cornwall* Running with Ramsbottom chimney c.1886.

Locomotive & General 15106. (Allan Sommerfield Collection)

Fig. 17   *Maintenance* Formerly Prince Ernest class 178 *Friar.*

(L&NWR Society Photograph Collection No 00042)

165 *Star*	SFB Pass CF Edge Hill 5.47 Sold 10.60
	*St.Helens No 14, purchased 2.52 from L&NWR, ex No 147 *Woodlark*
	Problem 11.60

—- **Comet** L&M 0-2-2 (Robert Stephenson & Co.) No 5 1.30 Sold 1832
L&M 2-2-2 (Mather, Dixon & Co.) No 55 3.37 Withdrawn 1845

166 *Comet* SFB Pass CF Edge Hill 5.47 (1869 8.72) Withdrawn 4.75

167 **Rhinoceros** SFB Pass CF Edge Hill 8.47 (1910 8.72) Withdrawn 1.73

168 **Dromedary** SFB Pass CF Edge Hill 8.47 (1947 8.72) Withdrawn 4.75

169 **Huskisson** SFB Pass CF Edge Hill 9.47 L&C No 37 1.57 L&NWR No 500 and name *Huskisson* removed 12.59
Renamed *Menai* 1864 Name removed 30.12.72 Withdrawn 11.75

380 LFB Pass (Prince Ernest Class) 4.57 Rebuilt 6.72 (1817 8.83) Withdrawn 8.84
*Dreadnought No 2063 12.85
*Precursor No 638 12.04

170 **Candidate** SFB Goods CF 9.47 Name removed 6.11.72 Withdrawn 1.76
*Webb Precursor No 2149 8.74
*Precursor No 1301 10.05

171 **North Western** SFB Goods CF 9.47 2-4-0T 1858 Presumably unnamed by 8.73 Withdrawn 11.86
*Newton No 1132 8.73
*Renewed Precedent No 1132 6.87
*Experiment No 1990 10.06

172 **Admiral** SFB Goods CF 10.47 Name removed 8.10.73 (1848 5.75) Withdrawn 6.82
*Precursor No 772 4.06

173 **Cornwall** Trevithick design 2-2-2 11.47; Altered to (2+2)-2-2 after
9.48, and exhibited thus at the Great Exhibition of 1851, held in London 1st May to 15th October where
it was awarded a medal; Rebuilt as 2-2-2 Raven class 11.58. Rebuilt/reboilered twice between 1871 and 1887
(3020 3.86) Out of traffic 1904 and name presumably removed by 10.05
Withdrawn to store for preservation 12.07 Reinstated 5.11 Withdrawn again 3.13 Preserved 1933
*Precursor No 1363 10.05 - 5.11 when renamed *Brindley* and name *Cornwall* restored to the 2-2-2
above

174 **General** SFB Goods CF 10.47 2-4-0T 1862 Presumably unnamed by 1872 (1926 7.75) Withdrawn 8.84
*Bury "Low-domed Single" No 1184 1872
*Precedent No 1170 9.78

175 **Commodore** SFB Goods CF 11.47 (1947 5.75) Withdrawn 7.78
Scott gives the name *Commodore* to 529, originally 261 *Hercules* and then North London Railway No 33,
on its return 9.61. See Table 5.
*Precedent No 478 11.80
*Renewed Precedent No 478 12.96

176 **Courier** 4-2-0 Crampton 11.47 Withdrawn 11.54
313 LFB Goods DA 24.11.54 Rebuilt 2.70 and name removed Withdrawn 7.82
*Precedent No 866 5.77
*Renewed Precedent No 866 2.96

177 **Chimera** North Union Railway 2-2-0 Building date, builder and number unknown L&NWR No 177 1847
Replaced 8.48, and sold 11.48
SFB Pass SF 8.48 Withdrawn 9.60
DX 9.60
*Samson No 733 5.63
*Waterloo No 733 1.90

178 **Friar** North Union Railway 2-2-0 Built 1838, builder and number unknown L&NWR No 178 1847
SFB Pass SF 6.49 L&C No 32 1.57 L&NWR 495 and name *Friar* removed 9.59 Renamed *Trafalgar* 1864
Scrapped 10.80

381 LFB Pass (Prince Ernest class) 5.57 Rebuilt 6.69 and 12.79 (1970 8.83) Transferred to Mr.Footner, Chief

Permanent Way Engineer 8.90 and became *Maintenance*, and *Engineer South Wales* 5.97 Withdrawn 7.11
*Experiment Compound No 1116 7.84
*Precursor No 837 2.06

179 *Nun*   North Union Railway 2-2-0 (One of Nos 14-17, built either by E.Bury & Co or Tayleur & Co.) 1841
L&NWR No 179 1847 Disposal not recorded
SFB Pass SF 11.49 L&C No 31 1.57 L&NWR No 494 and name removed 12.59 Probably sold by 4.62

383   LFB Pass (Prince Ernest class) 5.57 Rebuilt 3.74 (1945 5.83) Withdrawn 11.86

180 *Monk*   North Union Railway 0-4-2 No 19 (Bury, Curtis and Kennedy) 3.46 L&NWR No 180 1847 Disposal not
recorded

361   LFB Goods DA 5.56 Rebuilt 4.69 (1948 4.80) Scrapped 5.85

181 *Pilot*   SFB Goods CF 11.47 Name removed 9.6.73 (1976 4.75) Withdrawn 2.83
*Precedent No 864 5.77
*Renewed Precedent No 864 6.96

182 *Roebuck*   SFB Pass CF Edge Hill 11.47 (1948 9.72) Withdrawn 2.79
*George the Fifth No 1644 8.11

183 *Theorem*   SFB Pass CF Edge Hill 11.47 Replaced 9.60
DX 9.60
*Samson No 792 2.64
*Waterloo No 792 6.93

184 *Problem*   SFB Pass CF Edge Hill 2.48 Replaced 11.59
Problem 11.59
*Precursor No 2580 12.05

185 *Alderman*   SFB Pass CF Edge Hill 2.48 Withdrawn 12.71

186 *Narcissus*   SFB Goods CF 11.47 2-4-0T 1860 Presumably unnamed by 9.73 Withdrawn 7.78
*Samson No 604 9.73
*Waterloo No 604 11.90

Fig. 18   1932 *Velocipede* L&NWR Postcard Nov 1904 Revised Series.

(Allan Sommerfield Collection)

187 *Velocipede*		SFB Pass Enlarged 11.47 Rebuilt Raven class 11.69 (1932 2.77) and name retained. (Scott gives 10.47 building date) Withdrawn 11.81

187 *Velocipede* SFB Pass Enlarged 11.47 Rebuilt Raven class 11.69 (1932 2.77) and name retained. (Scott gives 10.47 building date) Withdrawn 11.81
  *Experiment Compound No 302 4.83
  *Precursor No 2584 1.06

188 *Colonel* SFB Pass CF 12.47 Name removed 31.12.72 Withdrawn 12.75

189 *Elector* SFB Pass CF 1.48 (1953 9.72) Withdrawn 12.79

190 *Peerless* SFB Pass CF 1.48 (1951 9.72) Withdrawn 10.77

191 *Diamond* SFB Pass CF 1.48 (1952 9.72) Withdrawn 7.78

192 *Hero* SFB Pass CF 1.48 Southern Division No 335 1.60 and name removed Scrapped 14.8.78
  DX 8.60
  *Samson No 901 1.64
  *St.Helens No 23
  *Waterloo No 901 10.90

382
193 *Pearl* SFB Pass CF 2.48 L&C No 35 1.57 L&NWR No 498 and name removed 12.59 Sold 10.61
  LFB Pass (Prince Ernest class) 5.57 Rebuilt 7.69 Withdrawn 11.78
  *Webb Precursor No 1180 2.79
  *Precursor No 234 3.06

194 *Ruby* SFB Pass CF 2.48 (1950 9.72) Withdrawn 7.78

388
195 *Emerald* SFB Pass CF 2.48 L&C No 36 1.57 L&NWR No 499 and name removed 12.59 Scrapped 12.71
  LFB Pass (Raven class) 9.57 Rebuilt 5.70 (1928 2.77) and name retained Withdrawn 9.7
  *Webb Precursor No 626 1.79
  *Precursor No 300 7.05

196 *Leander* SFB Pass CF 2.48 Sold 11.60
  Problem 11.60
  *Experiment No 291 11.06

197 *Fame* SFB Goods CF 3.48 2-4-0T 1859 Presumably unnamed by 10.74 Sold 11.82
  *Webb Precursor No 427 10.74
  *Precursor No 2578 12.05

198 *Avon* SFB Goods CF 3.48 2-4-0T 1867 Presumably unnamed by 4.75 Withdrawn 1.85
  *Precedent No 2189 4.75
  *Renewed Precedent No 2189 8.97

375
199 *Castor* SFB Goods CF 3.48 L&C No 62 1.57 L&NWR No 525 and name removed 12.59 Scrapped 1.78
  LFB Goods DA 3.57 Southern Division 1.60 No 345 and name removed Scrapped 7.87
  *Beyer, Peacock 0-6-0 No 199 Early 1860
  *Samson No 746 1.66
  *Waterloo No 746 6.94
  *Prince of Wales No 606 1.16

200 *Pollux* SFB Goods CF 3.48 L&C No 63 1.57 Rebuilt CF to SF DA, L&NWR No 526 and name removed 12.59 Scrapped 9.76
376 LFB Goods DA 11.57 Name removed 22.6.74 Scrapped 5.87

201 *Ariel* SFB Goods CF 4.48 2-4-0T 1870 and name removed Withdrawn 4.85
  *Large Bloomer No 994 4.72

—- *Eclipse* L&M 0-4-0 (Mather, Dixon & Co.) No 40 12.35 Withdrawn 1840-1

202 *Eclipse* SFB Goods CF 4.48 2-4-0T 1870 and name removed Withdrawn 8.85
  *Samson No 636 9.73
  *Waterloo No 636 4.93
  *George the Fifth No 404 4.13

203 *St. George*	SFB Goods CF 4.48 Name removed 4.11.72 Withdrawn 2.85
	*Samson No 469 10.74
	*Waterloo No 469 6.93
	*George the Fifth No 681 3.13

203 *St. George*   SFB Goods CF 4.48 Name removed 4.11.72 Withdrawn 2.85
     *Samson No 469 10.74
     *Waterloo No 469 6.93
     *George the Fifth No 681 3.13

204 *Thunderbolt*   SFB Goods CF 4.48 2-4-0T 1871 and name removed Withdrawn 10.82
     *Webb Precursor No 409 10.74
     *Precursor No 1102 11.04

205 *St. David*   SFB Goods SF 5.48 Name retained when converted to Tank engine 9.63 Presumably unnamed by 4.72
     *Small Bloomer No 740 4.72

206 *Menai*   SFB Goods SF 6.48 Rebuilt 2-4-0T 2.60 North London No 36 2.60 Returned to L&NWR 11 or 12.60 to become No 45 *Sybil* (1840 1.81) Scrapped 5.86
     DX 4.60
     *SFB pass CF No 500 (ex 169 *Huskisson*) 1864 Name removed 30.12.72

207 *Conway*   SFB Goods SF 5.48 Name retained when converted to Tank engine 7.63 Presumably unnamed by 4.72 Scrapped 9.85
     *Bury "Low-domed Single" No 1183 1872
     *George the Fifth No 1086 6.15

208 *St. Patrick*   SFB Goods SF 5.48 Name retained when converted to Tank engine 1867 Presumably unnamed by 10.74 Scrapped 11.83
     *Samson No 434 10.74
     *Waterloo No 434 4.93

209 *Envoy*   SFB Goods SF 7.48 Rebuilt 2-4-0T L&C No 64 1.57 Rebuilt 2-4-0 1858 L&NWR No 527 and name removed 12.59 Scrapped 6.84
374   'Isis' class 2-4-0T 2.57 Scrapped 1.79
     *Precedent No 865 5.77
     *Renewed Precedent No 865 9.94

210 *Alchymist*   SFB Goods SF 7.48 Rebuilt 2-4-0T L&C No 65 1.57 Rebuilt 2-4-0 1858 L&NWR No 528 and name removed 12.59 Scrapped 4.77
     DX 6.59
     *Prince Ernest class No 489 1864 (formerly No 369 *Banshee*) (1823 1.84 and 3045 11.86) Scrapped 12.87
     *Dreadnought No 645 6.88
     *Precursor No 365 4.05

211 *Onyx*   SFB Pass SF Edge Hill 5.48 Southern Division 1.60 No 334 and name removed Scrapped 20.2.79
     DX 8.60
     *Samson No 902 2.64
     *Waterloo No 902 4.93
     *Prince of Wales No 810 1.16

212 *Megatherion*   SFB Pass SF Edge Hill 5.48 (1954 9.72) Scrapped 8.77

213 *Talbot*   SFB Pass SF Edge Hill 5.48 (1955 9.72) Scrapped 9.79

214 *Shap*   L&C 0-6-0 No 1 (Unnamed) Date of building by Jones & Potts, or receipt 9.46 Driving Wheels 5ft 0in Purchased by L&NW 11.47, and numbered and named 214 *Shap* 214A 11.57, and replaced. Sold 20.12.60 to Richard Evans & Co.
     *L&C No 20 1857
     Class D 0-6-0 3.59
     *Samson No 764 2.64
     *Waterloo No 764 3.93

215 *Spitfire*   L&C 0-6-0 No 2 (Unnamed) Date of building by Jones & Potts, or receipt 9.46 Driving Wheels 5ft 0in Purchased by L&NWR 11.47, and numbered and named 215 *Spitfire* Sold 11.56 to John Taylor & Co. of Liverpool
366   LFB Goods DA 8.56 Southern Division No 346 1.60 and name removed 946 4.62 Reb 2-4-0ST 5.74 Scrapped 4.84
     DX 4.60
     *Samson No 742 7.64
     *Waterloo No 742 3.93

216 *Ambassador*		SFB Pass SF 7.48 Replaced 1860
		DX 10.60
		*LFB Pass (Prince Ernest class) No 490 1864 (ex *Windermere*) (No 1828 1.84) Scrapped 8.84
		*Dreadnought No 647 6.88
		*Precursor No 333 12.04
217 *Emperor*		SFB Pass SF 7.48 L&C No 33 1.57 L&NWR No 496 12.59 and name removed Renamed *Quicksilver* 1864
389		Name removed 30.12.72 Scrapped 12.78
		LFB Pass (Prince Ernest class) 10.57 Withdrawn 5.82
		*Experiment Compound No 374 7.84
		*Precursor No 311 9.05
218 *Wellington*		SFB Pass SF 8.48 (218A 2.62 and 1111 9.62)
		Problem 2.62
		*Experiment No 1490 1.09
219 *Nelson*		SFB Pass SF 8.48 (1956 9.72) Scrapped 9.78
		*Alfred the Great No 1979 8.03
220 *Waterloo*		SFB Pass SF 8.48 Southern Division No 338 1.60 and name removed Scrapped 15.12.77
		DX 8.60
		*Samson No 748 2.64
		*Waterloo No 748 11.89
221 *Trafalgar*		SFB Pass SF 9.48 Southern Division No 341 1.60 and name removed Scrapped 18.4.78
		DX 8.60
		*SFB Pass SF No 495 (Formerly No 178 *Friar*) 12.59 Named *Trafalgar* 1864 (1862 2.73) Scrapped
		10.80
		*Jubilee No 1940 10.00
222 *Lily*		SFB Pass SF 9.48 (222A 11.60) Scrapped 5.76
		Problem 11.60
223 *Rose*		SFB Pass SF 9.48 L&C No 34 1.57 L&NWR No 497 and name removed 12.59 Scrapped 8.78
390		LFB Pass (Prince Ernest class) 11.57 (1927 7.83) Withdrawn 10.88
224 *Violet*		SFB Pass SF 9.48 Southern Division No 333 1.60 and name removed Scrapped 4.10.78
		C&B 2-2-2 No 8 *Birkenhead*, renamed *Monk* by the BL&CJ c.7.47 L&NWR No 224 and renamed
		Violet 11.60
		DX 2.61
		*Samson No 763 5.63
		*Waterloo No 763 3.93
225 *Llewellyn*		SFB Goods SF 10.48 Name removed 22.10.73 Scrapped 1.76
		*Precedent No 869 6.77
		*Renewed Precedent No 869 1.97
		*Claughton No 180 4.23
226 *Champion*		SFB Goods SF 11.48 2-4-0T 6.60 Presumably unnamed by 8.74 Replaced 11.80
		*Webb Precursor No 2147 8.74
		*Precursor No 515 12.04
227 *Snowdon*		SFB Goods SF 11.48 Name probably retained when converted to Tank engine 1865 and if so, presumably
		unnamed by 4.75 Scrapped 4.87
		*Precedent No 2191 4.75
228 *Delamere*		SFB Goods SF 11.48 2-4-0T 5.59 Presumably unnamed by 4.72 Scrapped 1.80
		*Extra Large Bloomer No 1198 4.72
		*Precursor No 2051 8.07
229 *Watt*		SFB Pass SF Edge Hill 11.48 (229A 11.59?) Replaced 11.59
		Problem 11.59
		*Precursor No 2585 1.06
230 *Monarch*		SFB Pass SF Edge Hill 12.48 (230A 11.60) Replaced 11.60
		Problem 11.60
		*Precursor No 419 6.07

—- *Firefly*	L&M No 31 2-2-0 (Robert Stephenson & Co.) 3.33 Withdrawn 1840-1

231 *Firefly*

SFB Pass SF Edge Hill 12.48 Southern Division No 336 1.60 and name removed Scrapped 1.74
  BL&CJ 0-4-2 No 42 L&NWR No 231 and named *Firefly* 11.60
  Samson 2.65
  Waterloo 6.90

232 **Ixion**

SFB Goods SF 11.48 Name retained when converted to Tank engine 2.62 (1876 11.81) Scrapped 2.87
  *Samson No 445 9.73
  *Waterloo No 445 4.93

233 **Unicorn**

SFB Pass SF 3.49 (Possibly 233A 9.61, 1113 5.62 and 1881 1.72) Scrapped 12.77
SFB Goods SF No 266 *Sutherland*, Rebuilt 2-4-0T 11.59 North London Railway No 34 On return 11 or
  12.60 it became No 233 *Unicorn*
    *Samson No 2157 11.74
    *Waterloo No 2157 1.96

234 **Mazeppa**

SFB Pass SF 3.49 (Possibly 234A 11.61, 1114 4.62) Scrapped 1.78
  Problem 11.61
  *Experiment No 667 11.06

235 **Clanricarde**

SFB Pass SF 4.49 Name possibly removed when converted to Tank engine 1870 (1957 9.72) Scrapped 12.77
  *Experiment No 1986 9.06

236 **Hawkstone**

SFB Pass SF 4.49 Southern Division No 332 1.60 and name removed Scrapped 1.78
  BL&CJ 0-6-0 No 14 *Gheber*, formerly *Dee*, L&NWR No 236 and named *Hawkstone* 11.60
  DX 4.61

237 **Blenheim**

SFB Pass SF 5.49 (Possibly 237A 9.60) Replaced 9.60
  DX 9.60
LFB Pass No 491 12.59 1864 (Formerly No 313 *Prince Ernest* Motion No 254) Named *Blenheim* 1864
  Scrapped 1.84
    *Jubilee No 1934 9.00

238 **President**

SFB Pass SF Edge Hill 5.49, in store, and entered stock renumbered and renamed 34 *Phoebus* during the
  half year ending 5.50
SFB Goods SF 7.50 2-4-0T and name removed 3.71 Sold 5.81
  *Large Bloomer No 1007 4.72
  *Experiment No 1992 10.06

239 **Powis**

SFB Pass SF Edge Hill 4.49, in store, and entered stock renumbered and renamed 125 *Soho* during the half
  year ending 5.50
SFB Goods SF 7.50 Name retained when converted to Tank engine 5.65 (1930 11.81) Scrapped 3.83

240 **Bee**

SFB Pass SF Edge Hill 5.49. in store, and entered stock renumbered and renamed 127 *Peel* during the half
  year ending 5.50
SFB Goods SF 4.50 Rebuilt 2-4-0T 10.59 North London No 31 11.59 Returned to L&NWR 11 or 12.60
  to become No 37 *Hawk* Withdrawn 5.80
    DX 10.59
    *Samson No 642 7.64
    *Waterloo No 642 8.90

241 **Wasp**

SFB Pass SF Edge Hill 5.49, in store, and entered stock renumbered and renamed 124 *Marquis Douro* during
  the half year ending 5.50
SFB Goods SF 4.50 Name retained when converted to Tank engine 12.58 but presumably removed by 4.72
  Scrapped 7.86
    *Small Bloomer No 979 4.72

242 **Giraffe**

A rebuild of 129 *Martin* to SFB Pass SF Edge Hill 5.49, in store until 11.50, when it entered traffic renumbered
  and renamed 129 *Martin*
SFB Goods SF 11.50 Name removed when converted to Tank engine 8.69 Withdrawn 9.85
  *Precedent No 2182 3.75
  *Renewed Precedent No 2182 5.95

243 *Chillington* SFB Pass SF Edge Hill 5.49. in store, renumbered and renamed 117 *Tiger* during the half year ending 11.49
SFB Goods SF 3.50 Name retained when converted to Tank engine 11.61 but presumably unnamed by 4.75 Sold 12.86
  *Precedent No 2188 4.75
  *Renewed Precedent No 2188 2.95
  *Experiment No 2626 2.09

244 *Leviathan* SFB Goods SF 9.49 2-4-0T 3.59 Presumably unnamed by 3.72 Scrapped 10.86
  *Large Bloomer No 1001 4.72
  *Dreadnought No 510 4.85
  *Precursor No 301 11.04

245 *Ellesmere* SFB Goods SF 8.49 Rebuilt 2-4-0T 11.59 North London No 35 2.60 Returned to L&NWR 11 or 12.60
  to become No 141 *Pheasant* Sold 3.82
  DX 11.59
  *Samson No 634 5.63
  *Waterloo No 634 3.93

246 *Caradoc* SFB Goods SF 10.49 Name retained when converted to Tank engine 7.62 (Baxter 7.63) but presumably
  unnamed by 4.75 Scrapped 7.82
  *Precedent No 2192 4.75
  *Renewed Precedent No 2192 5.94

247 *Mammoth* L&M 0-4-2 (T.Banks & Co.) No 61 3.39 Renumbered 30 L&NWR 7.47 and scrapped
SFB Goods SF 2-4-0T 10.49 (1901 11.81) Scrapped 5.86
  *Small Bloomer No 978 4.72
  *Dreadnought No 513 5.85
  *Precursor No 645 1.05

248 *Salopian* SFB Goods SF 10.49 Name removed when converted to Tank engine 1871 Scrapped 9.87
  *Precedent No 2193 5.75
  *Renewed Precedent No 2193 2.96

249 *Cambrian* SFB Goods SF 10.49 Name retained when converted to Tank engine 11.58 but presumably unnamed by 5.75
  Scrapped 3.86
  *Precedent No 2194 5.75
  *Renewed Precedent No 2194 10.96

250 *John O'Gaunt* SFB Goods SF 11.49 Name removed when converted to Tank engine 1869 (Scott 1869 Baxter 12.60) Sold 5.81
  *L&C No 74 1859
  *Samson No 1163 10.74
  *Waterloo No 1163 2.95

John OGaunt *Jubilee No 1921 2.13

251 *Vernon* SFB Goods SF 12.49 Name retained when converted to Tank engine 1864 (Baxter 4.60) (1952 12.81)
  Scrapped 1.84

252 *John O'Groat* SFB Goods SF 11.49 Name retained when converted to Tank engine 10.64 but presumably unnamed by 10.74
  Scrapped 3.85
  *Samson No 487 10.74
  *Waterloo No 487 8.95
  *Claughton No 1599 8.22

253 *Bucephalus* SFB Pass SF Edge Hill 11.49, in store, renumbered and renamed 60 *Tantalus* during the half year ending 11.50
SFB Goods SF 11.50 Name retained when converted to Tank engine 3.63 but presumably unnamed by 4.72
  Scrapped 6.90
  *Small Bloomer No 780 4.72
  *Precursor No 990 4.06

254 *Theseus* SFB Goods SF 12.49 Name retained when converted to Tank engine 8.59 but presumably unnamed by 4.72
  Scrapped 5.86
  *Large Bloomer No 1002 4.72

255 *Precursor* SFB Goods SF 3.50 2-4-0T 3.63 Presumably unnamed by 4.74 Replaced 5.79
  *Webb Precursor No 2145 4.74
  *Precursor No 513 3.04

| | 256 *Cadmus* | SFB Goods SF 3.50 Name retained when converted to Tank engine 8.62 but presumably unnamed by 4.72 Sold 11.83 |
| | | *Small Bloomer No 789 4.72 |

| | 257 *Stanley* | SFB Goods SF 5.50 2-4-0T 5.60 (1981 1.82) Scrapped 1.86 |

	258 *Ribble*	Preston & Wyre Railway, Harbour, & Dock 0-4-0 L&NWR No 258 4.50 Replaced 5.56
363		LFB Goods DA 5.56 Name removed 12.2.72 Scrapped 6.88
		*L&C No 19 1857
		*Small Bloomer No 630 4.72

	259 *Windermere*	(*Continuation of the name Windermere from* No 83)
		Preston & Wyre Railway, Harbour & Dock, L&NWR No 259 4.50 Replaced 1855
333		LFB Pass (Prince Ernest class) 18.4.55 L&C No 27 1.57 L&NWR No 490 and name *Windermere* removed 12.59 Renamed *Ambassador* 1864 Rebuilt 1.72 and 7.80 (1828 1.84) Scrapped 8.84
		*Kendal & Windermere Railway L&C No 67 5.57
393		LFB Pass 11.57 (Prince Ernest class) (Allotted No 214 but not carried) Rebuilt 10.73 (1911 8.83) Withdrawn 7.88
		*George the Fifth No 789 5.15
		(There appears to be duplication of the name *Windermere*, on L&C Nos 27 and 67 between 8.57 and 12.59.

| | 260 *Anglesea* | SFB Goods SF 5.50 Name retained when converted to Tank engine 3.62 (1907 1.82) Scrapped 10.83 |

| | —- *Hercules* | L&M No 39 0-4-0 (Mather, Dixon & Co.) 12.35 Withdrawn 1840-1 |

	261 *Hercules*	SFB Goods SF 10.50 Rebuilt Tank 10.59 North London No 33 1.60 Returned to L&NWR No 529 11 or 12.60 and renamed *Langdale* (1827 5.83) Scrapped 6.86 (Harris does not give the name *Langdale*) Scott: *Commodore*
		DX 11.59
		*SFB Goods CF No 431 (Formerly No 102 *Marquis*) 1863 (1911 3.79) Presumably unnamed by 5.77 Sold 5.81
		*St.Helens 0-4-2T No 4
		*Precedent No 1105 5.77
		*Renewed Precedent No 1105 12.97

	262 *Liver*	L&M No 26 4.33 Sold 10.37
		SFB Goods SF 10.50 Name retained when converted to Tank engine 8.60 but presumably removed by 11.74 Scrapped 5.86
		*Samson No 2155 11.74
		*Waterloo No 2155 1.95

	263 *Herald*	SFB Goods SF 1.51 2-4-0T 11.60 Presumably unnamed by 4.72 Scrapped 1.79
		*Small Bloomer No 765 4.72
		*Dreadnought No 2062 12.85
		*Precursor No 911 9.05

	264 *Clarendon*	SFB Pass SF Edge Hill 11.49, in store, renumbered and renamed 141 *Pheasant* during the half year ending 5.51
		SFB Goods SF 1.51 Name removed when converted to Tank engine 3.69 Scrapped 12.85
		*Newton No 787 8.73
		*Renewed Precedent No 787 8.93

| | 265 *Napier* | SFB Goods SF 2.51 Name retained when converted to Tank engine 6.64 but presumably unnamed by 4.72 Scrapped 7.82 |
| | | *Small Bloomer No 917 4.72 |

	266 *Sutherland*	SFB Goods SF 2.51 Rebuilt 2-4-0T 11.59 North London No 34 11.59 Returned to L&NWR 11 or 12.60 to become No 233 *Unicorn* Replaced 2.81
		DX 11.59
		*Samson No 739 7.64
		*Waterloo No 739 4.93

From this date, Motions were no longer stamped with the name of the engine, but with numbers, known as Crewe Works or Motion Numbers,

| 183 | 267 *Glyn* | SFB Goods DA 4.51 2-4-0T 2.70 and name removed Sold 10.89 |
| | | *Small Bloomer No 768 4.72 |

—- *Cyclops*	L&M 2-2-2 (Haigh Foundry) No 46 8.36 Withdrawn 1842-4	

184 268 *Cyclops*   SFB Goods DA 5.51 2-4-0T 4.64 (1861 9.82) Withdrawn 7.83
        *Samson No 805 9.73
        *Experiment Compound No 1102 5.84
        *Precursor No 1545 4.05

185 269 *Wyre*   SFB Goods DA 6.51 2-4-0T 7.68 Presumably unnamed by 4.72 Withdrawn 6.85
        *Small Bloomer No 614 4.72
        *Samson No 1166 6.79
        *Waterloo No 1166 1.96

186 270 *Dee*   SFB Goods DA 6.51 2-4-0T 7.64 (1974 9.82) To Carriage Department, Crewe No 4 5.86 (Scott 3.86)
  Withdrawn 8.95
        *St.Helens 0-6-0 No 27

190 271 *Minotaur*   SFB Goods DA 8.51 L&C No 61 1.57 L&NWR No 524 and name removed Withdrawn 6.82
        Sharp, Stewart & Co. 0-6-0 8.57
        Newton 9.70
        Renewed Precedent 6.87

191 272 *Druid*   SFB Goods DA 8.51 2-4-0T 5.62 Presumably unnamed by 8.74 Withdrawn 4.83
        *Webb Precursor No 1144 8.74
        *Precursor No 106 10.04

192 273 *Hope*   SFB Goods DA 10.9.51 Crane Tank 1.66 Name removed 1873-5 Scrapped 11.92

194 274 *Swift*   SFB Goods DA 11.51 2-4-0T 2.63 Presumably unnamed by 4.72 Withdrawn 1.86
        *Small Bloomer No 717 4.72

—- *Vulcan*   L&M 2-2-0 (Fenton, Murray & Jackson) No 19 5.31 Sold 3.41
195 275 *Vulcan*   SFB Goods DA 11.51 L&C No 60 1.57 L&NWR No 523 and name removed 12.59 Withdrawn 9.85
        Sharp, Stewart & Co. 0-6-0 8.57
        *Whitehaven Junction No 14
        Newton 9.70
        Renewed Precedent 1.88
        *Prince of Wales No 525 12.15

276 *Pluto*   L&M 2-2-0 (Robert Stephenson & Co.) No 27 8.32 Renumbered 9 c1841 Allotted L&NWR No 127 but
  withdrawn 1847
197   SFB Goods DA 11.51 L&C No 59 1.57 L&NWR No 522 and name removed 12.59 Withdrawn 7.84
        Sharp, Stewart & Co. 0-6-0 8.57
        Newton 9.70
        Renewed Precedent 11.88
        *Prince of Wales No 745 1.16

196 277 *Hotspur*   SFB Goods DA 10.51 2-4-0T 3.65 Presumably unnamed by 10.74 Withdrawn 6.85
        *Samson No 631 10.74
        *Waterloo No 631 1.96
        *Prince of Wales No 2300 12.15

200 278 *Locke*   SFB Pass DA 4.52 Southern Division No 330 1.60 and name removed Scrapped 14.8.78
        BL&CJ 2-2-2 No 20 L&NWR No 278 *Locke* 11.60
        DX 2.61
        *Problem No 762 11.62
        *Precursor No 1011 7.07

201 279 *Stephenson*   SFB Pass DA 12.51 (279A 2.62)
        Problem 2.62
        *Experiment No 2052 12.06

202 280 *Glendower*   SFB Pass DA 4.52 Southern Division 1.60 No 329 and name removed Name not restored on return from
  Southern Division. 929 4.62 Rebuilt 11.63 and name restored 1873 (1831 3.73) Scrapped 10.12.78
        C&B 2-2-2 No 7 *Druid* L&NWR No 280 and renamed *Glendower* 11.60
        DX 2.61

203 281 **Allerton**	*Experiment No 1987 9.06	
	SFB Goods DA 2.52 2-4-0T 8.66 Presumably unnamed by 4.72 Withdrawn 11.90	
	*Bury "Low-domed Single" No 1186 1872	

204 282 **Irwell**
SFB Goods DA 3.52 2-4-0T 8.67 Name presumably removed after 1871 (1859 5.83 and 3076 5.87)
To Carriage Department, Wolverton No 3 3.90 Withdrawn 2.97
St.Helens No 3

206 283 **Croxteth**
SFB Goods DA 4.52 Southern Division No 353 1.60 and name removed Sold 6.92
DX 4.60
*Samson No 731 7.64
*Waterloo No 731 11.89
*Claughton No 2511 6.23

207 284 **Harbinger**
SFB Goods DA 4.52 2-4-0T 10.67 Presumably unnamed by 8.74 Withdrawn 4.86
*Webb Precursor No 2146 8.74
*Precursor No 1395 3.04

210 285 **Sefton**
SFB Pass DA 5.52 L&C No 30 1.57 L&NWR No 493 and name removed 12.59 Withdrawn 1864
BL&CJ 2-2-2 No 22 L&NWR No 285 *Sefton* 11.60 Name removed 1862

391
LFB Pass (Prince Ernest class) 11.57 Southern Division No 325 1.60 and name removed Name restored to
No 925 1873 Rebuilt 3.75 (1848 1.84 and 3068 2.87) Withdrawn 11.88

213 286 **Derby**
SFB Goods DA 6.52 2-4-0T 12.68 Presumably unnamed by 1872 Withdrawn 6.85
*South Staffs No 23
*Bury "Low-domed Single" No 1187 1872
*Precedent No 506 11.80

216 287 **Eglinton**
SFB Goods DA 7.52 2-4-0T 12.66 Presumably unnamed by 1872 Withdrawn 8.94
*Bury "Low-domed Single" No 1182 1872
*Webb Precursor No 255 1.79
*Precursor No 2061 4.05

217 288 **Loadstone**
SFB Goods DA 8.52 2-4-0T 9.64 Presumably unnamed by 11.74 (1866 5.83) To Carriage Department
Wolverton No 5 9.85 until withdrawal 2.95
*Samson No 2154 11.74
*Waterloo No 2154 3.94
*Prince of Wales No 2175 11.15

218 289 **Director**
SFB Goods DA 8.52 2-4-0T 9.64 Presumably unnamed by 8.73 Withdrawn 1.81
*Newton No 696 8.73
*Renewed Precedent No 696 11.88

—- **Rocket**
Liverpool & Manchester 0-2-2 (Robert Stephenson & Co.) No 1 1829
Laid up c.1840 Sold in 1862 to Patent Office Museum. Now in Science Museum.

223 290 *Rocket*
Prototype SFB 7ft 2-2-2 cyl 15 x 20 8.52 Rebuilt LFB cyl 15 1/4 x 20 9.64 (1810 5.76) and name retained
Withdrawn 9.78 and scrapped 12.78
*Precedent No 193 9.78
*Renewed Precedent No 193 5.97

222 291 **Prince of Wales**
SFB Pass DA 11.52 (291A 2.62; 1117 4.62; 1876 12.71) *Engineer-Crewe* 1879 - 9.99 Scrapped 13.10.99
Problem 2.62
*Experiment No 1676 11.06
*Prince of Wales No 819 10.11

224 292 **Hardwicke**
SFB Goods DA 11.52 2-4-0T 1.64 Withdrawn 1.82 Scrapped 9.82
*Newton No 790 8.73
*Renewed Precedent No 790 4.92

225 293 **Quicksilver**
SFB Goods DA 11.52 Southern Division No 352 1.60 and name removed Sold 4.92
DX 5.60
*SFB pass No 496 (ex 217 *Emperor*) 1864 Name removed 30.12.72

226 294 **Magnet**
SFB Goods DA 11.52 2-4-0T 9.64 (1836 6.83 and 3059 2.87) Sold 7.92

227 295 **Penmaenmawr**
SFB Goods DA 11.52 L&C No 58 1.57 L&NWR No 521 and name removed 12.59 Reb 2-4-0T 1870

(1875 4.83, 3097 11.87) Sold 1.03
    Sharp, Stewart & Co. 0-6-0 9.57
    Newton 9.70
    Renewed Precedent 6.93
    *George the Fifth No 1188 4.13

228 296 **Bellerophon**   SFB Goods DA 20.11.52 Southern Division No 351 1.60 and name removed Renumbered 951 4.62 Rebuilt Crane Tank 8.68 To Carriage Department, Wolverton No 1 7.77 (or 1.77) Withdrawn 6.96
Or CD4 Crewe 8.77; CD 2 Wolverton 3.86 Scrapped 3.95 (Williams, Harris, Craven).
    DX 5.60
    *SFB Pass CF No 501 (ex No 40 *Jason*) 1864 (1846 3.73) Withdrawn 10.78
    *Precursor No 988 4.06

229 297 **Una**   SFB Goods DA 11.52 2-4-0T 11.65 Presumably unnamed by 3.72 Withdrawn 8.83
    *Large Bloomer No 998 4.72

230 298 **Don**   SFB Goods DA 11.52 2-4-0T 10.70 and name removed Withdrawn 11.03

231 299 **Elk**   SFB Goods DA 11.52 2-4-0T 11.64 (1855 6.83) Withdrawn 11.83

232 300 **Ant**   SFB Goods DA 1.53 Rebuilt 2-4-0T 7.61, rebuilt again 1873 Withdrawn 11.87
337   *LFB Pass (Prince Ernest class) No 926 (ex No 368 *Majestic*) Renamed *Ant* in 1873 (1858 1.84)
    and 3075 5.87 Scrapped 11.89

233 301 **Giant**   SFB Goods DA 2.53 2-4-0T 3.68 (1864 3.83 and 3079 2.87) Sold 4.90

234 302 **Fly**   SFB Goods DA 2.53 2-4-0T 7.65 (1811 4.83 and 3033 11.86) Withdrawn 5.90

—- **Achilles**   Warrington & Newton 2-2-0 12.31 Absorbed by Grand Junction in 1834
235 303 *Achilles*   SFB Goods DA 2.53 2-4-0T 8.70 and name removed Withdrawn 11.03
    *Large Bloomer No 1005 4.72
    *Dreadnought No 511 5.85
    *Precursor No 310 12.04

237 304 **Hector**   SFB Goods DA 2.53 L&C No 55 1.57 L&NWR No 518 and name removed 12.59 Withdrawn 7.83
    Sharp, Stewart & Co. 0-6-0 9.57
    Newton 9.70
    Renewed Precedent 6.92

236 305 **Peacock**   SFB Goods DA 2.53 2-4-0T 7.65 (1804 7.83 and 3026 11.86) Withdrawn 8.88

238 306 **Bulldog**   SFB Goods DA 2.53 2-4-0T 5.62 Presumably unnamed by 4.72 Sold 9.92
    *Small Bloomer No 627 4.72
    Bull Dog   *George the Fifth No 956 12.15
    Bulldog   *George the Fifth No 956 Late 1921

—- *Fury*   L&M 2-2-0 (Fenton, Murray & Jackson) No 21 8.31 Withdrawn 1840

240 307 *Fury*   SFB Goods DA 3.53 2-4-0T 1.67 (1879 7.83 and 3022 4.87) Withdrawn 6.04

241 308 **Booth**   SFB Goods DA 14.3.53 L&C No 56 1.57 L&NWR No 519 and name removed 12.59 Rebuilt Crane Tank 8.73
Scrapped 1.93
    Sharp, Stewart & Co. 0-6-0 9.57
    Newton 9.70
    Renewed Precedent 6.90

243 309 **Huish**   SFB Goods DA 4.53 L&C No 57 1.57 L&NWR No 520 and name removed 12.59 Withdrawn 9.84
    Sharp, Stewart & Co. 0-6-0 9.57

244 310 **Isis**   LFB Goods DA 5.53 Rebuilt 3.64 (or 1859) Also 2-4-0ST 4.74 and name removed Scrapped 9.91
    *Samson No 2153 11.74
    *Waterloo No 2153 6.93

247 311 **Ida**   LFB Goods DA 5.53 L&C No 53 1.57 L&NWR No 516 12.59 and name removed Scrapped 12.77
394   LFB Pass (Prince Ernest class) 2.58 Rebuilt 6.75 (1871 2.84 and 3085 2.87) Withdrawn 3.90

248 312 **Tubal**	LFB Goods DA 31.5.53 Southern Division No 350 1.60 and name removed Scrapped 4.85	

248 312 **Tubal** LFB Goods DA 31.5.53 Southern Division No 350 1.60 and name removed Scrapped 4.85
 DX 5.60
 *Samson No 828 8.64
 *Waterloo No 828 7.90
 *Precursor No 2017 3.06

254 313 **Prince Ernest** LFB Pass (Prince Ernest class) 6.53 L&C No 28 1.57 L&NWRNo.491 and name *Prince Ernest* removed
 12.59 Renamed *Blenheim* 1864 Withdrawn 1.84

392 LFB Pass (Prince Ernest Class) No 39, later No 313 11.57 Withdrawn 10.81

252 314 **Crewe** LFB Goods DA 7.53 Rebuilt 22.1.69. If rebuilt in 1.69 the name was then removed Scrapped 12.94

255 315 **Prince Arthur** LFB Pass (Prince Ernest class) 7.53 Rebuilt 1.68 and 8.78 (1872 2.84 and 3086 6.87) *Engineer South Wales*
 7.89 and *Engineer Stafford* 5.97 until withdrawn 4.01

256 316 **Prince Eugene** LFB Pass (Prince Ernest class) 8.53 Southern Division No 328 1.60 and name removed Renumbered 928 4.62 Name
 restored 1872 (1870 1.84) Scrapped 7.86
 BL&CJ 2-2-2 No 21 L&NWR No 316 named *Prince Eugene* 11.60 Name removed 1862

259 317 **Antelope** LFB Goods DA 9.53 Rebuilt 5.70 and name removed
 *Precedent No 2183 3.75
 *Renewed Precedent No 2183 6.95

260 318 **Reynard** LFB Goods DA 9.53 Rebuilt 9.71 and name removed Scrapped 7.88
 *Precedent No 2184 3.75
 *Renewed Precedent No 2184 5.97

258 319 **Anson** LFB Goods DA Built 11.53 (Stored) 5.54 Rebuilt 10.68 Name removed 26.2.73 Scrapped 1.84
 *Jubilee No 1932 9.00

261 320 **Viceroy** LFB Goods DA Built 11.53 (Stored) 5.54 Rebuilt 1.68 Name removed 10.9.73 Scrapped 5.86

262 321 **Autocrat** LFB Goods DA Built 11.53 (Stored) 5.54 L&C No 54 1.57 L&NWR No 517 12.59 and name removed
 Scrapped 9.78

395 LFB Pass (Prince Ernest class) 3.58 Rebuilt 6.72 (1881 2.84) Withdrawn 11.84
 *Dreadnought No 2064 12.85
 *Experiment No 306 6.05

263 322 **Harrowby** LFB Goods DA Built 11.53 (Store) 5.54 Rebuilt 1.66 Name removed 9.6.73 Scrapped 2.83
 *Webb Precursor No 697 10.78
 *Precursor No 315 7.05

269 323 **Greyhound** LFB Pass (Prince Ernest class) 11.53; To Traffic 12.53 (1884 2.84 and 3028 5.88) *Engineer Manchester* 10.88
 Withdrawn 9.01
 *Dreadnought No 2059 12.85
 *Precursor No 302 7.05

270 324 **Messenger** LFB Pass (Prince Ernest class) 11.53; To Traffic 14.12.53 Withdrawn 10.83
 *Experiment Compound No 1111 6.84
 *Precursor No 519 5.05

284 325 **Chandos** LFB Pass (Raven class) 1.54 Southern Division No 323 1.60 and name removed 923 4.62
 Rebuilt and name restored 1864 (1835 5.76) Scrapped 31.4.77
 BL&CJ 2-4-0 No 38 *Dee* L&NWR No 325 11.60 and renamed *Chandos*
 DX 5.62
 *Precedent No 1187 9.78
 *Renewed Precedent No 1187 6.96

271 326 **Rowland Hill** LFB Goods DA 2.54 Rebuilt 2.72 Name removed 19.2.72 Scrapped 12.86
 *Large Bloomer No 1008 4.72
 *Dreadnought No 659 7.86
 *Precursor No 2582 12.05

272 327 **Maberley** LFB Goods DA 2.54 2-4-0T 12.67 Presumably unnamed by 1872 Scrapped 1.84

		*'Extra Large' Bloomer No 1200 1872
273	328 *Czar*	LFB Goods DA 3.54 Rebuilt 10.71 Name removed 18.9.73 Scrapped 1.83
274	329 *Simoom*	LFB Goods DA 3.54 Rebuilt 7.69 Name *Simoom* removed 13.12.72 Scrapped 2.83
	Simoon	*Webb Precursor No 408 9.74
	Simoom	*Precursor No 2 6.04
275	330 *Hurricane*	LFB Goods DA 3.54 Rebuilt 9.67 Name removed 10.9.73 Scrapped 3.85
		*Experiment No 1988 9.06
276	331 *St.Germans*	LFB Goods DA 3.54 Rebuilt 7.68 Scrapped 10.79
277	332 *Aberdeen*	LFB Goods DA 3.54 Rebuilt 9.71 and name removed Scrapped 9.96
278	333 *Hardinge*	LFB Goods DA 4.54 L&C No 52 1.57 L&NWR No 515 and name removed 12.59 Scrapped 3.85
396		LFB Pass (Prince Ernest class) 3.58 Rebuilt 4.72 (1885 2.84 and 3029 5.88) Withdrawn 11.89
293	334 *Ptarmigan*	LFB Goods DA 5.54 Rebuilt 2.70 and name removed Scrapped 6.87
		*George the Fifth No 1681 9.11
294	335 *Quail*	LFB Goods DA 5.54 Rebuilt 12.68 Scrapped 7.85
		*George the Fifth No 1371 9.11
295	336 *Woodcock*	LFB Goods DA 5.54 Rebuilt 3.70 Name removed 9.6.73 Scrapped 4.87
		*George the Fifth No 1799 10.11
296	337 *Snipe*	LFB Goods DA 5.54 Rebuilt 10.71 and name removed Scrapped 6.92
		*George the Fifth No 1730 10.11
297	338 *Fairbairn*	LFB Goods DA 5.54 Rebuilt 4.69 Presumably unnamed by 6.77 Scrapped 1.79
		*Precedent No 870 6.77
		*Renewed Precedent No 870 5.98
298	339 *Nasmyth*	LFB Goods DA 5.54 Rebuilt 3.67 Name removed 15.3.73 Scrapped 12.80
		*Precedent No 919 9.78
		*Renewed Precedent No 919 12.93
286	340 *Euston*	LFB Pass (Raven class) 22.7.54 Rebuilt 12.66 (1941 2.77) and name retained Withdrawn 1.78
		*Special Tank (No 3186) 6.95
287	341 *Miranda*	LFB Pass (Raven class) 29.7.54 Rebuilt 11.67 (1897 3.77) and name retained Withdrawn 5.78
		*Precedent No 1194 9.78
		*Renewed Precedent No 1194 2.97
288	342 *Amphion*	LFB Pass (Raven class) 8.8.54 Scrapped 5.76
		*Precursor No 804 4.06
	—- *Etna*	L&M 2-2-0 (Robert Stephenson & Co.) No 20 6.31 Sold 9.35
		L&M 2-2-2 (Tayleur & Co.) No 51 1.37 Broken up c1841
289	343 *Etna*	LFB Pass (Raven class) 27.8.54 Southern Division No 320 1.60 and name removed 920 4.62 Name restored 1864
		Rebuilt 8.67 (1853 11.76) Scrapped 5.1.78
		BL&CJ 2-4-0 No 23 *Mersey* L&NWR No 343 and renamed *Etna* 11.60
		DX 5.62
		*Webb Precursor No 481 1.79
		*Precursor No 2287 12.05, No 2577 1.06
290	344 *Kestrel*	LFB Pass (Raven class) 20.8.54 Rebuilt 9.68 (1917 3.77) and name retained Withdrawn 9.77
		*Samson No 852 5.79
		*Waterloo No 852 2.95
		*Prince of Wales No 90 12.15
301	345 *Turk*	LFB Goods DA 29.9.54 Southern Division No 348 1.60 and name removed Scrapped 7.84
		DX 4.60
		*Samson No 829 8.64

*Waterloo No 829 1.92

303 346 **Arab** — LFB Goods DA 12.9.54 Rebuilt 12.71 and name removed Scrapped 8.91
*Webb Precursor No 1152 9.74
*Precursor No 1307 12.05 and No 2576 1.06

302 347 **Cossack** — LFB Goods DA 12.9.54 Rebuilt 11.69 and name removed Scrapped 7.87
*Webb Precursor No 1145 9.74
*Precursor No 685 10.04

304 348 **Varna** — LFB Goods DA 16.9.54 Rebuilt 12.71 Name removed 10.9.73 Scrapped 2.87

305 349 **Warrior** — LFB Goods DA 23.9.54 Rebuilt 7.68 Name removed 6.12.72 Scrapped 8.83
*Webb Precursor No 426 10.74
*Jubilee No 1925 3.00

307 350 **Baltic** — LFB Goods DA 30.9.54 Rebuilt 5.70 and name removed Scrapped 11.84
*Samson No 2151 11.74
*Waterloo No 2151 12.95
*Claughton No 2445 7.23

308 351 **Alma** — LFB Goods DA 8.10.54 Rebuilt 10.67 Presumably unnamed by 4.75 Scrapped 1.79
*St.Helens No 24
*Precedent No 2185 4.75
*Renewed Precedent No 2185 3.96

306 352 **Raglan** — LFB Goods DA 13.10.54 Rebuilt 11.63 Name removed 19.2.72 Scrapped 12.82
*Large Bloomer No 996 4.72

318 353 **St.Arnaud** — LFB Goods DA 30.11.54 L&C No 46 1.57 L&NWR No 509 and name removed 1859 Scrapped 4.86
397 — LFB Pass (Prince Ernest class) 4.58 Rebuilt 8.69 and 8.80 (1910 2.84 and 3089 3.89) *Engineer Stafford* 4.91
Withdrawn 6.97

320 354 **Euxine** — LFB Goods DA 30.11.54 2-4-0T 4.70 Name removed 12.12.72 Scrapped 6.92
*Samson No 485 10.74
*Waterloo No 485 3.93

323 355 **Hardman** — LFB Goods DA 6.2.55 L&C No 40 1.57 L&NWR No 503 and name removed 12.59 Scrapped 6.91
DX 3.9.58
*Samson No.758 5.63
*Waterloo No 758 1.90

324 356 **Memnon** — LFB Goods DA 16.2.55 Southern Division No 347 1.60 and name removed Scrapped 8.85
BL&CJ 0-4-0T No 27 L&NWR No 356 *Memnon* 11.60
DX 4.61
*Samson No 736 7.64
*Waterloo No 736 1.92

325 357 **Terrier** — LFB Goods DA 24.2.55 L&C No 41 1.57 L&NWR No 504 and name removed 12.59 Scrapped 4.87
DX 14.9.58
*Samson No 738 5.63
*Waterloo No 738 1.90
*Experiment No 2629 3.09

326 358 **Falstaff** — LFB Goods DA 1.3.55 L&C No 43 1.57 L&NWR No 506 and name removed 12.59 Scrapped 6.86
DX 11.58
*Samson No 795 3.64
*Waterloo No 795 6.93
*Prince of Wales No 2203 11.15

327 359 **Glowworm** — LFB Goods DA 20.3.55 L&C No 42 1.57 L&NWR No 505 and name removed 12.59 Scrapped 10.78
(Scott has *Glow-worm*)
DX 11.58
*Samson No 752 5.63
*Waterloo No 752 3.92
*Renewed Precedent No 1745 7.14

328	360	**Theodore**	LFB Goods DA 20.3.55 Rebuilt 2.72 and name removed Scrapped 10.90
329	361	**Umpire**	LFB Goods DA 20.3.55 Name removed 12.2.72 Scrapped 6.80 *Large Bloomer No 1000 4.72
330	362	**Cato**	LFB Goods DA 18.4.55 Rebuilt 7.70 and name removed Scrapped 4.81
331	363	**Empress**	LFB Pass (Prince Ernest class) 18.4.55 (1918 2.84) Withdrawn 12.84 *Experiment Compound No 372 7.84 *Precursor No 374 9.05
332	364	**Latona**	LFB Pass (Prince Ernest class) 18.4.55 Southern Division No 327 1.60 and name removed 927 4.62 Name restored 1864 Rebuilt 8.70 (1863 1.84) Scrapped 8.85 BL&CJ 2-2-2 No 15 L&NWR No 364 named *Latona* 11.60
——		**Vesta**	L&M 2-2-0 (Robert Stephenson & Co.) No 24 11.31 'On Sale' 11.36 L&M 2-2-2 (R.& W.Hawthorn & Co.) No 56 3.37 To L&NWR 7.47 and scrapped
334	365	*Vesta*	LFB Pass (Prince Ernest class) 5.55 Rebuilt 7.70 (1919 2.84) Withdrawn 8.84
335	366	**Nestor**	LFB Pass (Prince Ernest class) 5.55 Rebuilt 2.66 and 4.76 (1920 3.84 and 3045 6.89) *Engineer Northampton* 2.91 Scrapped 4.95
336	367	**Nightingale**	LFB Pass (Prince Ernest class) 5.55 Rebuilt 3.66 and 6.76 (1819 1.84 and 3041 11.86) *Engineer Lancaster* 11.91 *Engineer Watford* 1894 Withdrawn 5.95
—-		**Majestic**	L&M 2-2-0 (Robert Stephenson & Co.) No 10 11.30 Withdrawn by 4.33 L&M 2-2-2 (Tayleur & Co.) No 50 12.36 To L&NWR 7.47 and scrapped
337	368	*Majestic*	LFB Pass (Prince Ernest class) 9.6.55 Southern Division No 326 1.60 and name removed; as No 926 renamed *Ant* 1873 (1858 1.84 and 3075 5.87) Withdrawn 11.89 BL&CJ 2-4-0 (Robert Stephenson & Co.) No 24 L&NWR No 368 and named *Majestic* 11.60 DX 5.62 *Problem No 564 1863 *Experiment No 1020 1.09
338	369	**Banshee**	LFB Pass (Prince Ernest class) 12.6.55 L&C No 26 1.57 L&NWR No 489 and name *Banshee* removed 12.59 Renamed *Alchymist* 1864 Rebuilt 9.74 (1823 1.84 and 3045 11.86) Withdrawn 12.87 DX 6.59 *Samson No 757 5.63 *Waterloo No 757 1.92 *Experiment No 2628 3.09
340	370	**Gazelle**	LFB Pass (Prince Ernest class) 14.6.55 Withdrawn 8.76
—-		**Mercury**	L.M 2-2-0 No 11 1.1831 Robert Stephenson & Co. Withdrawn 1840-1
339	371	*Mercury*	LFB Pass (Prince Ernest class) 16.6.55 Withdrawn 12.77 *Precedent No 749 9.78 *Renewed Precedent No 749 6.95
343	372	**Centipede**	LFB Goods DA 9.55 2-4-0ST 3.73 Name removed 6.73 Scrapped 10.88
342 *398*	373	**Snake**	LFB Goods DA 8.55 L&C No 45 1.57 L&NWR No 508 Name removed 1859 Scrapped 12.83 LFB Pass (Prince Ernest class) 5.58 Scrapped 12.83 *Experiment Compound No 1115 7.84 *Precursor No 127 11.05
344	374	**Serpent**	LFB Goods DA 8.55 Name removed 9.6.73 Scrapped 9.84 *Samson No 2158 11.74
346	375	**Virago**	LFB Goods DA 10.55 Rebuilt 8.67 Scrapped 11.86
356	376	**Proserpine**	LFB Goods DA 11.55 Name removed 19.2.72 Scrapped 6.82 *Large Bloomer No 1006 4.72 *Precedent No 871 6.77 *Renewed Precedent No 871 8.94

LFB Goods DA

Number and name ordered:-			Changed to:-		
349	378	*Palmerston*	5	*Falcon*	9.55
350	377	*Diana*	10	*Dragon*	9.55
354	381	*Sardinian*	21	*Wizard*	2.56
357	380	*Napoleon*	156	*Redstart*	3.56
358	379	*Combermere*	149	*Petrel*	2.56

The numbers 377-381 were given to L&C 1-5, and the names *Diana* and *Sardinian* were not subsequently used.

TABLE 4
LANCASTER & CARLISLE RAILWAY

The L&C contracted with the L&NWR for the provision of locomotives for five years from its opening in 1846 and then for a further period until in 1857 forty locomotives were purchased from the L&NWR (N Div). The Company was leased by the L&NWR on 10th September 1859 (effective from 1st August 1859) and the L&NWR took possession of eighty-three locomotives. These eighty-three comprised thirty-nine built in 1857-9 (Numbers 1-25 and 70-83), four from K&W (Numbers 66-9) and the forty (Numbers 26-65) purchased from the L&NWR in 1857.

This entailed a certain number of duplicate names, and caused some to be renamed and others to have them removed.

1) L&C Numbers 1 and 2

Locomotives bought to supplement the L&NWR ones working the line under contract.

Date of building by Jones & Potts, or receipt 9.46
1 (Unnamed) 0-6-0 Sold to L&NWR 11.47 to become 214 *Shap*
2 (Unnamed) 0-6-0 Sold to L&NWR 11.47 to become 215 *Spitfire*

No 1 has in some records been associated with the name *Vizier*. In an account of an accident on 11th October 1847 at Milnthorpe, an engine of the name *Vizier* was in head-on collision with an Up cattle train hauled by the L&C's "No 1" engine. It would be too much of a coincidence for two Viziers to meet thus. More than likely the northbound one was the ex GJ No 23 working on the L&C under the L&NWR Contract in operation at that time.

2) L&C Numbers 1 - 25
5ft 0in 2-4-0 Goods Built in 1857 by Rothwell & Co.

L&C Number Name	L&NWR Number	12.59 Name	(until date)	Subsequent name-holders	
1 **Rickerby**	377	*Rickerby*	9.69		
2 **Newby**	378	*Newby*	9.69		
3 **Sedgwick**	379	*Sedgwick*	7.69	Newton	-.70
				Renewed Precedent	10.88
4 **Quernmore**	380	*Quernmore*	12.69	Newton	-.70
				Renewed Precedent	6.91
5 **Patterdale**	381	*Patterdale*	12.69	Newton	-.70
				Renewed Precedent	7.93
6 *Lune*	382	Name removed	12.59	*Small Bloomer No 615	4.72
to avoid duplication with SFB Goods CF No 88					
				*DX No 87	5.59
				*Samson No 724	2.64
				*Waterloo No 724	3.93
7 *Eden*	383	Name removed	12.59		
to avoid duplication with SFB Goods CF No 87					

8 **Luck of Edenhall**	384	*Luck of Edenhall*	(1112 12.71)	*Samson No 90	10.74
				*Waterloo No 90	6.94
		Name removed	26.2.73		
9 *Skiddaw*	385	Name removed	12.59	*Samson No 486	10.74
to avoid duplication with GJ 2-4-0 No 83				*Waterloo No 486	6.93
10 *Saddleback*	386	Name removed	12.59		
to avoid duplication with SFB Pass CF No 84				*Samson No 1162	5.79
				*Waterloo No 1162	6.93
				*George the Fifth No 845	3.13
11 *Lonsdale*	387	Name removed	12.59	*Small Bloomer No 840	4.72
to avoid duplication with GJ 2-4-0 No 78					
12 **Petteril**	388	Name removed	12.59		
13 **Inglewood**	389	*Inglewood*	(1807 2.70)	*Small Bloomer No 607	4.72
			1117 12.71		
14 **Ingleboro**	390	*Ingleboro*			

Name removed shortly after to avoid duplication with L&C No 24, L&NWR No 400 See below

15 **Levens**	391	*Levens*	(1809 3.70)	*Webb Precursor No 338	2.79
		1119 12.71 Name removed 9.6.73		*Precursor No 2513	3.06
16 **Fylde**	392	*Fylde*	(1810 3.70)		
		1120 12.71 Scrapped 2.84			
17 **Brougham**	393	*Brougham*	(1119 8.70)	Newton	8.70
				Renewed Precedent	4.93
				*Precursor No 2011	8.07
18 **Eamont**	394	*Eamont*	(1121 9.70)	Newton	8.70
		1104 12.71 Name removed 19.4.75		Renewed Precedent	4.93

(There was an overlap of names between building and naming of Newton 394 in 8.70 and removal of name from 1104 on 19.4.75)

19 *Ribble*	395	Name removed	12.59	St.Helens 0-4-0 No 10,	
to avoid duplication with LFB Goods DA No 258				L&NWR No 1376 8.64 Scrapped 9.64	
				*Small Bloomer No 630	4.72
20 *Shap*	396	Name removed	12.59	*Samson No 764	2.64
to avoid duplication with Class D 0-6-0 No 214 named 3.59				*Waterloo No 764	3.93

6ft 0in 2-2-2 Built in 1857 by Rothwell & Co.

L&C Number Name	L&NWR Number	12.59 Name	(until date)	Subsequent name-holders	
21 *Lowther* #	397	**Ulleswater**			

The name *Ulleswater* was removed by 1872

The name *Lowther* was removed 12.59 to avoid duplication with SFB Goods CF (2-4-0T) No 90, and the engine renamed *Ulleswater* see No L&C No 81, L&NWR No 544 below

| 22 *Dalemain* # | 398 | **Stewart** | | | |

The name *Dalemain* was removed 12.59 to avoid duplication with GJ 2-2-2 No 80 and the engine renamed *Stewart*

The name *Stewart* was removed by 1861

				*DX No 568	8.61
				*Precedent No 1189	5.77
				*Renewed Precedent No 1189	8.97
23 *Greystoke*	399	Name removed	12.59		
to avoid duplication with GJ 2-4-0 No 81				Waterloo	1.92
				*Experiment No 2116	1.09

24 *Belted Will*   400   *Ingleboro*

   The name *Belted Will* was removed to avoid duplication with SFB Pass CF No 79, and renamed *Ingleboro* c.12.59

   The name *Ingleboro* was removed by 1872

25 *Lazonby*   488   **Lazonby**   (1285 1.69)
                                             1192 12.71 (1949 1.79) Scrapped 4.80   *Precedent No 512   11.80

                      # Note made by Baxter: "Some records give renaming of No 21 as *Stewart*, and No 22 Name removed 1859"

3) L&C Numbers 26 - 65
Purchased from the L&NWR January 1857and taken back in 1859

The locomotives were taken back on 22nd December 1859, and were first shown in L&NWR Stock in January 1860, by which time not one of the original names was available, all having rapidly gone to newly built engines as indicated in columns 6 and 7 below. How swiftly the former names were removed is unclear, but it was probably done as quickly as possible to avoid duplications. Only eight passenger engines were given names on their return, and this not until 1863 or 1864.

The passenger engines 497, 499 and 502 which survived into the 1870s were not renamed.

L&C No	L&NWR	Number and name before sale		Type	Recipient of former name and date		L&NWR number 12.59	Name 1864
26	338	369	*Banshee*	LFB Pass DA	DX	6.59	489	*Alchymist*
27	333	259	*Windermere*	"	**Prince Ernest**	11.57	490	*Ambassador*
28	254	313	*Prince Ernest*	"	P.E.	11.57	491	*Blenheim*
29	257	150	*Linnet*	"	P.E.	4.57	492	*Trevithick*
30	210	285	*Sefton*	SFB Pass DA	P.E.	11.57	493	
31		179	*Nun*	SFB Pass SF	P.E.	5.57	494	
32		178	*Friar*	"	P.E.	5.57	495	*Trafalgar*
33		217	*Emperor*	"	P.E.	10.57	496	*Quicksilver*
34		223	*Rose*	"	P.E.	5.57	497	
35		193	*Pearl*	SFB Pass CF	P.E.	5.57	498	
36		195	*Emerald*	"	Raven	9.57	499	
37		169	*Huskisson*	"	P.E.	11.57	500	*Menai*
38		40	*Jason*	"	Raven	8.57	501	*Bellerophon*
39		110	*Canning*	"	P.E.	1.57	502	
40	323	355	*Hardman*	LFB Goods DA	DX	9.58	503	
41	325	357	*Terrier*	"	DX	9.58	504	
42	327	359	*Glowworm*	"	DX	10.58	505	
43	326	358	*Falstaff*	"	DX	10.58	506	
44	312	20	*Eagle*	"	Raven	7.57	507	
45	342	373	*Snake*	"	P.E.	5.58	508	
46	318	353	*St.Arnaud*	"	P.E.	11.58	509	
47	341	152	*Bullfinch*	"	Isis	2.57	510	
48	357	156	*Redstart*	"	Isis	2.57	511	
49	365	18	*Cerberus*	"	Raven	7.57	512	
50	315	154	*Starling*	"	Isis	2.57	513	
51	265	151	*Goldfinch*	"	Raven	8.57	514	
52	278	333	*Hardinge*	"	P.E.	3.58	515	
53	247	311	*Ida*	"	P.E.	2.58	516	
54	262	321	*Autocrat*	"	P.E.	3.58	517	
55	237	304	*Hector*	SFB Goods DA	SS 0-6-0	9.57	518	
56	241	308	*Booth*	"	SS 0-6-0	9.57	519	
57	243	309	*Huish*	"	SS 0-6-0	9.57	520	
58	227	295	*Penmaenmawr*	"	SS 0-6-0	9.57	521	
59	197	276	*Pluto*	"	SS 0-6-0	9.57	522	
60	195	275	*Vulcan*	"	SS 0-6-0	8.57	523	

61	*190*	271	*Minotaur*	"	SS 0-6-0	8.57	524
62		199	*Castor*	SFB Goods CF	BP 0-6-0	1859	525
63		200	*Pollux*	"	Isis	11.57	526
64		209	*Envoy*	SFB Goods SF	Isis	2.57	527
65		210	*Alchymist*	"	DX	6.59	
					and P.E.	9.59	528

4) L&C Numbers 66 - 69
Received from the Kendal & Windermere Railway via the L&C

L&C Number	L&NWR 12.59 Name	

66 *Langdale*   Kendal & Windermere 0-4-0T 5ft 6in (E.B.Wilson & Co.) 10.50

     529   **Langdale**   L&C No 66 5.57 L&NWR No 529 12.59 (529A 1861 and 1132 4.62) At Cromford & High Peak
31.1.65 - 24.4.65 Sold to the Mersey Docks & Harbour Board 8.65.

Subsequent name-holders: SFB Goods SF No 261 *Hercules* 10.50 Rebuilt Tank 12.59 North London Railway No 33 1.60 Returned to
L&NWR No 529 and according to some sources, named *Langdale* after 3.65 (1827 5.83) Scrapped   6.86

*Small Bloomer No 603 4.72

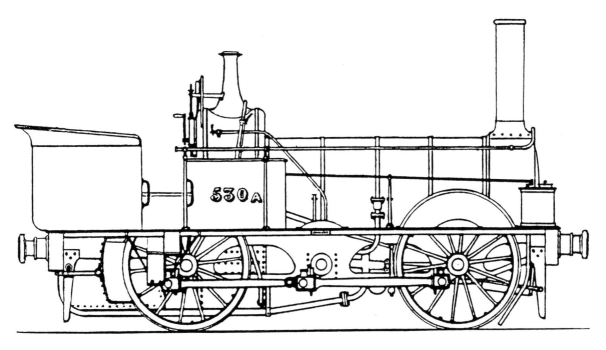

Ex-Kendal & Windermere Railway: E.B.Wilson dummy-
crank 0-4-0T: conjectural LNWR appearance, 1861-2.

Fig. 19   Ex K&W, and L&C 67 *Windermere*

(Author's Collection)

67 *Windermere*   Kendal & Windermere 0-4-0T 5ft (E.B.Wilson & Co.) 11.50

     530   (Unnamed)   L&C No 67 5.57 L&NWR No 530 12.59 and name removed, as recorded in the Crewe list of
L&C engines "in Stock Jany 1/60". The name removed to avoid duplication with L&NWR
333 259. (530A 2.61 and 1133 4.62). At Cromford & High Peak 14.12.64 - 11.4.65. Sold
11.5.65.

68 *Lady of the Lake*   Kendal & Windermere 0-4-2T 5ft (R.& W.Hawthorn) 1850
L&C No 68 5.57 L&NWR 12.59 Sold 8.3.60

531 *Lady of the Lake*
Subsequent name-holders: DX No 531 4.60 Renumbered 494 and name removed by 2.62
Problem 2.62
*Experiment No 1989 10.06

69 *Grasmere*   Kendal & Windermere 2-4-0T 5ft (Carrett Marshall & Co.) 8.56 L&C No 69 5.57 L&NWR
532 **Grasmere**   12.59 (1142 5.62) Sold 15.12.64
Subsequent name-holder: DX No 532 5.62

5) L&C Numbers 70 - 83
6ft 0in 2-2-2 Built in 1859 by William Fairbairn & Sons

L&C Number Name	L&NWR 12.59 Number Name		Subsequent name-holders
70 **Wennington**	533 *Wennington*	(1286 1.69) 1193 12.71 Scrapped 9.78	
71 **Duchess of Lancaster**	534 *Duchess of Lancaster* Name removed by 1872	(1287 1.69) 1194 12.71	*Precedent No 480 11.80 *Renewed Precedent No 480 4.97
72 **Merrie Carlisle**	535 *Merrie Carlisle*	(1288 1.69) 1195 12.71 Scrapped 4.76	*Precedent No 860 5.77 *Renewed Precedent No 860 3.95
73 **Lang Meg**	536 *Lang Meg*	(1289 2.69) 1196 12.71 Name removed by 1872	*Webb Precursor No 1150 10.78 *Precursor No 1387 3.06
74 **John OGaunt**	537 *John O'Gaunt*	(1290 2.69) 1197 12.71 Scrapped 9.75	

(Name removed 12.59 to avoid duplication with SFB Goods SF No 250)
SS: Sharp, Steward & Co. BP: Buyer, Peacock & Co.

5ft 0in 2-4-0 Built in 1859 by William Fairbairn & Sons

75 **Penrith Beacon**	538 *Penrith Beacon*	(1291 2.69) 1126 12.71 Name removed 9.6.73	*Precedent No 2187 4.75 *Renewed Precedent No 2187 2.97
76 **Preston**	539 *Preston*	(1115 12.69) 1121 12.71 (1958 1.75) Scrapped 9.87	
77 **Kendal**	540 *Kendal*	(1157 7.69) 1122 12.71 (1816 1.75) Scrapped 1.79	
78 **Sedbergh**	541 *Sedbergh*	(1160 8.69) 1123 12.71 (1961 1.75) Scrapped 2.79	
79 **Tebay**	542 *Tebay*	(1216 7.69) 1125 12.71 Name removed 31.12.72	
80 **Cross Fell**	543 *Cross Fell*	(1292 7.69) 1127 12.71 (1805 4.75) Scrapped 2.77	
81 *Ulleswater*	544 *Ulleswater*	Name later removed (1203 8.69) 1124 12.71 (1962 1.75) Scrapped 4.76	

(The name was removed c.12.59 to avoid duplication when L&NWR 397 was named *Ulleswater*)

5ft 0in 2-4-0 Goods Built in 1859 by Robert Stephenson & Co.

82 *Morecambe*	545 *Morecambe*	(1184 8.66)	Scrapped 1871
83 *Underley*	546 *Underley*	(1223 8.66 and 1866 12.71)	Scrapped 5.73

Note. There was duplication of the name *Windermere* between 8.57 and 12.59 on L&C Nos.27 and 67, and according to the Crewe list of L&C engines "in stock Jany 1/60" both No 490 (formerly L&C 27 and No 530 (formerly L&C 67) are given the name *Windermere*. It may be supposed that No 530 remained on the K&W and the duplication was overlooked, or regarded as unimportant.

TABLE 5
NORTH LONDON RAILWAY

In 1859 the NLR bought from the L&NWR (Northern Division) six named 2-4-0Ts, and numbered them 31 - 36.

It was not the practice of the North London Railway to provide their engines with names, and they did not, as has sometimes been supposed, name these six.

They were:-

L&NWR N Div Number and Name prior to the sale	Date to NLR	Subsequent Crewe Number and Name-holder and date	NLR Number	L&NWR N Div Number and Name at some date after return
240 *Bee*	11.59	DX *418* 10.59	31	37 *Hawk*
120 *Samson*	22.11.59	DX *419* 11.59	32	364 *Buffalo*
261 *Hercules*	1.60	DX *420* 11.59	33	529 See below
266 *Sutherland*	11.59	DX *422* 11.59	34	233 *Unicorn*
245 *Ellesmere*	2.60	DX *423* 11.59	35	141 *Pheasant*
206 *Menai*	2.60	DX *432* 4.60	36	45 *Sybil*

It is reasonable to assume that the choice of the six and their removal from the Capital Account list was made a month or more before they left Crewe to work on the NLR; their numbers and names were swiftly passed on to the DX locomotives being built just then.

As it turned out, their sojourn on the NLR was short lived. Following an accident on 16th May 1860, the Government Inspector recommended their withdrawal, and a Mr. Chubb of the NLR wanted the L&NWR to take them back. Ramsbottom reported on 12th July 1860 that they were in poor condition, thus after negotiation between the two Companies it was agreed that repairs should be carried out at Crewe, with an appropriate financial deduction. Four had been returned by 30th November and the other two in the December. Precisely which were the four and which the two is unknown.

Sometime later, presumably after the necessary repairs had been completed, five received new numbers and names, and the sixth a new number (529). There are three differing accounts about this. All agree on its number being 529; some say that it had no name, others record it as being named *Langdale*, the name carried by the previous No 529, and yet another has written in that it was named *Commodore*. (See Appendix 9)

It is not possible to determine precisely when these six numbers 37, 364, 529, 233, 141 and 45 became available for re-use, but it must have been sometime around September 1861. Number 364 had been available since sometime in September 1861 when its former owner, a Birkenhead, Lancashire & Cheshire Junction 2-2-2 was replaced. It is not known for certain if 37 became 37A in the Duplicate List in 12.60, but it was replaced in 9.61; 233 became 233A in 9.61; 141 had been withdrawn in 11.60, and 45 may have become 45A in 12.60 and was replaced in 9.61. A note found in an old Crewe foreman's ledger listing the six locomotives' numbers is headed "Tank Engines returned from North London Line Sept/61", does not necessarily mean that

Sept/61 was the date of their return, but was rather the date of their returning to the L&NWR stock list.

That number 364 received the name *Buffalo* had never been in doubt, but why it was not named *Latona* remains a mystery, since both number and name were available by virtue of its previous owner having gone to the Southern Division in 1.60. What is more DX *452* 121 had been given the name *Buffalo* as recently as 9.60, just two to three months before NLR No 32 came back home. It seems unlikely that the name was removed after just twelve months, so perchance the name did not go to the NLR returnee until the time between May 1863 and January 1865 when the bulk of the DXs lost their names. In this connection it is noted that the Crewe foreman's ledger mentioned above uses the expression "No & Name given them March/65".

Fig. 20 37 *Hawk*. Possibly the only photogragh of an SFB Goods with the original nameplates curved to fit the splasher placed on the side tanks after its conversion to 2-4-0T. Taken at the opening of the Kirkheaton Branch.

(Author's Collection)

TABLE 6
LOCOMOTIVE TRANSFERS FROM NORTHERN TO SOUTHERN DIVISION

The boundary between the Northern and Southern Divisions was moved northwards from Rugby to Stafford at the end of 1859, after which the Trent Valley Line was worked by S.Div engines.

Thirty two named Crewe-built engines, together with two unnamed Beyer, Peacock 0-6-0s which had been built in 1859 and intended for the Northern Division, were transferred to the Southern Division in January 1860. This move entailed the removal of their current numbers and names and they were renumbered in the Southern Division list, as shown below:

a) Northern Division engines transferred to Southern Division:-

Class	Motion Number (if any)	Engine Number	Name Removed	S.Division Number 1860	4.62
LFB Raven class 2-2-2	289	343	Etna	320	920
	284	325	Chandos	323	923
	282	134	Owl	324	924
LFB Prince Ernest class 2-2-2	391	285	Sefton	325	925
	337	368	Majestic	326	926
	332	364	Latona	327	927
	256	316	Prince Eugene	328	928
SFB Passenger DA 2-2-2	202	280	Glendower	329	929
	200	278	Locke	330	930
SFB Passenger 2-2-2 SF		61	Phosphorus	331	931
SF		236	Hawkstone	332	932
SF		224	Violet	333	933
SF		211	Onyx	334	934
CF		192	Hero	335	935
SF		231	Firefly	336	936
SF		60	Tantalus	337	937
SF		220	Waterloo	338	938
CF		33	Erebus	339	939
CF		111	Russell	340	940
SF		221	Trafalgar	341	941
CF		44	Harlequin	342	942
CF		77	Mersey	343	943
CF		97	Atalanta	344	944
LFB Goods DA 2-4-0	375	199	Castor	345	945
	366	215	Spitfire	346	946
	324	356	Memnon	347	947
	301	345	Turk	348	948
	280	133	Ostrich	349	949
	248	312	Tubal	350	950
SFB Goods DA 2-4-0	228	296	Bellerophon	351	951
	225	293	Quicksilver	352	952
	206	283	Croxteth	353	953

The two unnamed Beyer, Peacock 0-6-0s were numbered   321   921
(BP Works Nos 124/5. See Table 7)   and   322   922

...   .

This left in the N.Div. books thirty-two vacant numbers and their associated names. All were used again during 1860, first on the two Beyer Peacock 0-6-0s built in 1859 and taken into stock early in 1860, after that on the Problem Class and DXs being turned out at Crewe between February and August, and thirdly on twelve of the Birkenhead, Lancashire and Cheshire Junction Railway engines which came into L&NWR stock in the November.

Apart from the names and numbers which went to the Problem class engines under construction in the first half of 1860, these renamings and numbers did not last long. Goods engines ceased to carry names after about 1863-1864, and the BL&CJ engines had but a short life in NWR stock, and were placed on the Duplicate List, withdrawn, replaced or sold at the dates shown in the last column of the table below.

b) Names given to Northern Division engines after removal from those transferred to Southern Division

Class		Engine Number & Name		Naming date		
Beyer Peacock 0-6-0		133	*Ostrich*	Early in 1860		
		199	*Castor*	Early in 1860		
Problem Class 2-2-2		33	*Erebus*	2.60		
		44	*Harlequin*	3.60		
		60	*Tantalus*	3.60		
		61	*Phosphorus*	3.60		
		77	*Mersey*	5.60		
		97	*Atalanta*	5.60		
		111	*Russell*	5.60		
		134	*Owl*	5.60		
DX 0-6-0		345	*Turk*	4.60		
		215	*Spitfire*	4.60		
		283	*Croxteth*	4.60		
		296	*Bellerophon*	5.60		
		293	*Quicksilver*	5.60		
		312	*Tubal*	5.60		
		192	*Hero*	8.60		
		211	*Onyx*	8.60		
		220	*Waterloo*	8.60		
		221	*Trafalgar*	8.60		
Birkenhead,	No 7	280	*Glendower*	11.60	Name removed	2.61
Lancashire &	8	224	*Violet*	11.60	Name removed	2.61
Cheshire Junction	14	236	*Hawkstone*	11.60	Name removed	4.61
Railway	15	364	*Latona*	11.60	Replaced	9.61
	20	278	*Locke*	11.60	Replaced	2.61
	21	316	*Prince Eugene*	11.60	Name removed	1862
	22	285	*Sefton*	11.60	(1901 9.73)	and name removed
	23	343	*Etna*	11.60		and name removed
	24	368	*Majestic*	11.60	(1140 5.62)	and name removed
	27	356	*Memnon*	11.60	(356A 4.61)	and name removed.
	38	325	*Chandos*	11.60	(1136 5.62)	and name removed
	42	231	*Firefly*	11.60	(1178 2.65)	and name removed

Eight ex Northern Division engines which had lost their names upon transfer to the Southern Division later regained names, six receiving their former ones, and two being renamed:-

Class	S.Division Number & name		Name restored date	Renamed date
LFB Raven Class	920	*Etna*	1864	
	923	*Chandos*	9.64	
	924	**Marathon**		9.64
LFB Prince Ernest Class	925	*Sefton*	1873	
	926	*Ant*		1873
	927	*Latona*	1864	
	* 928	*Prince Eugene*	1872	
SFB Passenger DA 2-2-2	929	*Glendower*	1873	

The name *Owl* had gone immediately to Problem class engine *443* No 134, and thus was not available for restoration on No 924, and so probably in September 1864 a new name **Marathon** was provided.

The name *Majestic* went in November 1860 on to ex BL&CJ No 368, and when it became (1140) in the Duplicate List the name was given in May 1862 to DX 368. Sometime in 1863 it appeared again, this time on Problem Class *492* 564, and thus it was not available for restoration to Prince Ernest Class 926, which sometime in 1873 was eventually renamed *Ant*.

The name changes caused by these transfers were many. To cite one example, the name *Locke* appeared on four successive engines in less than three years, being removed from the SFB Pass 278 in January 1860, passed to the BL&CJR No 20 in the November, on to DX 278 three months later in February 1861, and because of the policy of removing names from Goods engines, thence to Problem class engine 762 in November 1862. It is interesting to note in passing that Problem 762 lasted until in February 1907, after which just five months or so later in the July the name went to Webb Precursor 1011. There certainly was a determined attempt to keep the great engineer's name alive and in the public eye.

Fig. 21   Prince Ernest class after restoration of the name *Sefton* in 1873, and bearing Duplicate No 1848 given in 1884.

F. Moore (Allan Sommerfield Collection)

TABLE 7
JOHN RAMSBOTTOM Appointed 1st August 1857 - Retired 1871

5ft 0in 0-6-0 Built by Sharp, Stewart & Co.

(Makers' nos. 1009-1015)
All received both old numbers and names

	Built	Duplicate Number		Disposal	Next Name-holder
271 *Minotaur.*	8.57	1811	9.70	Scrapped 5.78	Newton 9.70
275 *Vulcan.*	8.57	1812	"	Scrapped 3.78	Newton 9.70
276 *Pluto.*	8.57	1134	"	Scrapped 6.78	Newton 9.70
295 *Penmaenmawr.*	9.57	1813	"	Sold 1.80	Newton 9.70
304 *Hector.*	9.57	1814	"	Sold 4.75	Newton 9.70
308 *Booth.*	9.57	1815	"	Sold 7.74	Newton 9.70
309 *Huish.*	9.57	1816	10.70	Sold 5.75	-

Class D 5ft 0in 0-6-0 Built at Longsight in March 1859

214 *Shap.*   Rebuilt Saddle Tank 1863 Name removed 2.64 (1126 6.66)
Restored to Capital List 1139 12.71 Scrapped 7.78
Next name-holder   *Samson No 764 2.64

5ft 0in 0-6-0 Built by Beyer, Peacock & Co. in 1859

These were part of BP Order 362, placed by the Danube & Black Sea Railway for six locomotives, of which only two, Works Nos 120/1, went overseas. Nos 133 and 199, below, were Works Nos 122/3; and Nos 124/5 went to the Southern Division. See Table 6.

According to Beyer, Peacock records they were delivered in 1.1860, and each of them received an old number and name very early in 1860

133 *Ostrich.*		Presumably unnamed by 12.65 (1250 1.67) Restored to Capital List 1178 12.71 Scrapped 6.79	
		Next name-holder *Samson No 632 12.65	
199 *Castor.*		Presumably unnamed by 1.66 (1251 1.67) Restored to Capital List 1179 12.71 Scrapped 7.76	
		Next name-holder *Samson No 746 1.66	

DX 5ft 0in 0-6-0 Built at Crewe 942 engines

The first five of the class were built on DX account, which explains the origin of the term by which they were known.

By no means all received a name, but most of those which did received the old number as well. The names were removed from the DX Class by Mr. Ramsbottom in 1863 and 1864.

			Built	Next name-holder(s)	Date
399	355	*Hardman.*	3.9.58	*Samson No 758	5.63
400	357	*Terrier.*	14.9.58	*Samson No 738	5.63
401	358	*Falstaff.*	10.58	*Samson No 795	3.64
403	359	*Glowworm.*	11.58	*Samson No 752	5.63
404	87	*Eden.*	5.59	*Samson No 724	2.64
405	39	*Tartarus.*	5.59	*Samson No 628	2.64
406	428	**Trevithick.**	5.59	*Prince Ernest *257* No 150 *Linnet*	6.53
				Renumbered 492 8.53, and named *Trevithick*	1864
407	429	**Roberts.**	5.59	*Samson No 737	7.64
				*Waterloo No 737	5.94
408	447	**Whitworth.**	5.59	*Samson No 1045	1.65
				*Waterloo No 1045	9.89
409	210	*Alchymist.*	6.59	*Prince Ernest No 489	1864
410	369	*Banshee.*	6.59	*Samson No 757	5.63
418	240	*Bee.*	10.59	*Samson No 642	7.64
419	120	*Samson.*	11.59	*Samson No 633	5.63
420	261	*Hercules.*	11.59	St.Helens No 4	1860
422	266	*Sutherland.*	11.59	*Samson No 739	7.64
423	245	*Ellesmere.*	11.59	*Samson No 634	5.63
432	206	*Menai.*	4.60	*SFB Pass No 500	1864
433	531	*Lady of the Lake.*	4.60	*Renumbered 494 and name removed	2.62
434	345	*Turk.*	4.60	*Samson No 829	8.64
435	215	*Spitfire.*	4.60	*Samson No 742	7.64
436	283	*Croxteth.*	4.60	*Samson No 731	7.64
437	296	*Bellerophon.*	5.60	*SFB Pass No 501	1864
438	293	*Quicksilver.*	5.60	*SFB Pass No 496	1864
439	312	*Tubal.*	5.60	*Samson No 828	8.64
444	192	*Hero.*	8.60	*Samson No 901	1.64
445	211	*Onyx.*	8.60	*Samson No 902	2.64
446	220	*Waterloo.*	8.60	*Samson No 748	2.64
448	221	*Trafalgar.*	8.60	*SFB Pass No 495	1864
449	52	*Diomed.*	9.60	*Samson No 821	5.63
450	2	*Hecla.*	9.60	*Samson No 732	7.64
451	237	*Blenheim.*	9.60	*LFB Pass No 491	1864
452	121	*Buffalo.*	9.60	*SFB Goods SF (Tank) No 364 ex NLR By	3.65
453	123	*Victory.*	9.60	-	
454	183	*Theorem.*	9.60	*Samson No 792	2.64
455	177	*Chimera.*	9.60	*Samson No 733	5.63
456	216	*Ambassador.*	10.60	*Prince Ernest No 490	1864
469	224	*Violet.*	2.61	*Samson No 763	5.63
470	280	*Glendower.*	2.61	*Restored to SFB Pass 929	1873

471	278	*Locke.*	2.61	*Problem No 762	11.62
479	442	*Forerunner.* #	3.61	-	
483	236	*Hawkstone.*	4.61	-	
485	356	*Memnon.*	4.61	*Samson No 736	7.64
498	568	*Stewart.* ##	8.61	*Precedent No 1189	5.77
510	129	*Martin.*	9.61	*Samson No 793	2.64
513	65	*Charon.*	10.61	*Samson No 735	5.63
522	125	*Soho.*	11.61	-	
523	130	*Heron.*	11.61	-	
547	325	*Chandos.*	5.62	*Restored to Raven No 923	10.9.64
548	147	*Woodlark.*	5.62	*Samson No 794	3.64
549	135	*Bat.*	5.62	-	
550	343	*Etna.*	5.62	*Restored to Raven No 920	1864
551	368	*Majestic.*	5.62	*Problem No. 564 5.61, not named until	1863
552	34	*Phoebus.*	5.62	-	
553	532	*Grasmere.*	5.62	-	

442 **Forerunner** — Birkenhead, Lancashire & Cheshire Junction 0-6-0 (B.Hick & Co.) 3.49 No 13 *Mersey* L&NWR No 442 and renamed *Forerunner* 11.60 Sold 3.61 to Brassey & Co. (See Chapter 8)

Stewart This is the only DX name not to go more or less immediately to some other engine, making it a curious exception. Records differ concerning the name *Stewart* on L&NWR 398, formerly L&C No 22 *Dalemain.* This locomotive was withdrawn in April 1877. The fact that the name was used on Precedent 1189, built in May 1877 leads one to wonder if 398 carried the name to the end. This raises the possibilty that the name might have gone back from the DX and been restored to its former owner.

Two formerly named members of the class were still in service in 1923:-

401	358	*Falstaff*	LMS Number 8000	Withdrawn 11.28
404	87	*Eden*	(8001)	Withdrawn 6.25

Fig. 22   DX 568 *Stewart* Crewe As built. A rare photograph of a named DX Goods engine.

(Everard Beauchamp Collection)

PROBLEM CLASS 7ft 6in 2-2-2 60 engines

				Built	Withdrawn	Next Name-holder and date		
424	184	Problem.		11.59	- 5.05	*Precursor	No 2580	12.05
425	229	Watt.		11.59	-11.05	*Precursor	No 2585	1.06
426	33	Erebus.		2.60	- 9.06	*Precursor	No 564	6.07
427	44	Harlequin.		3.60	- 1.07	*Experiment	No 496	9.07
428	60	Tantalus.		3.60	-10.04	*Precursor	No 1469	3.05
429	61	Phosphorus.		3.60	- 9.06	*Experiment	No 830	9.07
440	77	Mersey.		5.60	- 1.07	*Precursor	No 665	6.07
441	97	Atalanta.		5.60	- 7.06	*Experiment	No 61	11.06
442	111	Russell.		5.60	- 7.06	-		
443	134	Owl.(x)		5.60	-10.03	-		
464	165	Star.		11.60	- 2.06			
465	117	Tiger		11.60	- 0.05	*Precursor	No 1439	11.05
466	222	Lily.		11.60	- 9.06	-		
467	196	Leander.		11.60	- 7.06	*Experiment	No 291	11.06
468	230	Monarch.		11.60	- 9.06	*Precursor	No 419	6.07
489	561	**Prince Oscar.**	(y)	5.61	- 4.06	-		
490	562	**Palmerston.**	(z)	5.61	- 7.06	*Experiment	No 1991	10.06
491	563	**Combermere.**	(z)	5.61	- 5.06	*Experiment	No 902	9.07
492	564	**Majestic.**	(z)	5.61	- 6.07	*Experiment	No 1020	1.09
493	565	**Napoleon.**	(z)	5.61	- 1.06	*Precursor	No 1311	3.06
524	234	Mazeppa.		11.61	- 3.06	*Experiment	No 667	11.06
525	28	Prometheus.		11.61	- 9.06	*Experiment	No 1304	11.06
526	1	Saracen.		11.61	- 6.07	*Experiment	No 2624	2.09
527	7	Scorpion.		11.61	- 5.04	*Precursor	No 1723	8.05
528	139	Cygnet.		11.61	- 8.06	-		
529	218	Wellington.		2.62	- 7.07	*Experiment	No 1490	1.09
530	279	Stephenson.		2.62	- 9.06	*Experiment	No 2052	12.06
531	531	Lady of the Lake.		2.62	- 6.06	*Experiment	No 1989	10.06

(Bronze Medallist 'for excellence of workmanship' at the 1862 International Exhibition in London. A replica of the medal was carried for many years on the cab sides.)

				Built	Withdrawn			
532	291	Prince of Wales.		2.62	- 9.06	*Experiment	No 1676	11.06
533	127	Peel.		3.62	- 11.5	*Precursor	No 2581	12.05

Note x An official photograph taken after rebuilding in 4.96 has the name *Princess Royal*
　　　 y Unnamed until May 1862
　　　 z Unnamed until 1863

Replacements for Southern Division Locomotives

			Built	Withdrawn	Next Name-holder and date		
584	762	Locke.	11.62	- 2.07	*Precursor	No 1011	7.07
585	803	**Tornado.**	11.62	- 7.06	*Experiment	No 1995	10.06
586	804	**Soult.**	11.62	- 4.98	-		
587	754	**Ethelred.**	11.62	- 7.07	*Experiment	No 2621	2.09
588	837	**Faerie Queene.**	11.62	- 2.06	*Precursor	No 1433	4.06
589	827	Victoria.	12.62	- 3.07	*Experiment	No 2112	9.07
590	610	**Princess Royal.**	12.62	- 2.05	-		
591	612	**Princess Alice.**	1.63	- 7.07	*Experiment	No 937	9.07
592	618	**Princess Alexandra.**	1.63	-11.07	*Experiment	No 1603	5.09
593	622	**Prince Alfred.**	1.63	-12.04	-		
594	665	**Lord of the Isles**	1.63	- 6.07	*Experiment	No 2623	2.09
595	667	**Marmion.**	1.63	- 9.06	*Precursor	No 469	6.07
596	675	**Ivanhoe.**	2.63	- 4.06	*Experiment	No 222	11.06
597	802	**Red Gauntlet.**	2.63	- 7.07	*Experiment	No 1483	1.09
598	806	**Waverley.**	2.63	- 1.05	*Precursor	No 2031	3.05
		Nasr Ed Din	June 1873, temporarily				
599	818	**Havelock.**	2.63	- 5.04	*Precursor	No 184	5.05
600	719	**Outram.**	2.63	-11.07	-		
601	723	**Clive.**	2.63	- 2.06	*Precursor	No 1	6.07
602	833	**Clyde.**	2.63	-12.06	*Precursor	No 1364	7.07
603	834	**Elgin.**	2.63	- 9.06			
830	1427	**Edith.**	7.65	- 1.07	*Precursor	No 2053	7.07
831	1428	**Eleanor.**	7.65	- 7.07	*Precursor	No 2181	7.07
832	1429	**Alfred Paget.**	7.65	-12.03	*Precursor	No 412	6.04

Fig. 23   Problem class 291 *Prince of Wales* in original condition. Note slotted splashers.

(L&NWR Society Photograph Collection No 1845)

Fig. 24   Problem class 291 *Prince of Wales* at Shrewsbury in final condition.

F. Moore's R.P (Everard Beauchamp Collection)

Fig. 25   Problem class 7ft 6in Passenger. 134 *Owl* of 1860.

(Allan Sommerfield Collection)

During the race to Edinburgh in 1888
this engine took the 10. am. train from Euston to Crewe
at an average speed of 57.1 miles per hour.

Fig. 26   Problem class 134 *Princess Royal*. The real name of No.134 is *Owl*. It would seem that the engine was named *Princess Royal* for a brief while after its exploits during the race to Edinburgh. The name was borrowed from No.610 for this official photograph.

L&NWR Postcard Set 10 "Famous Locomotives" No.3. (Fred Gray Collection).

833	1430	*Pandora.*	7.65 - 7.05	*Precursor	No 1116	9.05
834	1431	*Psyche.*	7.65 - 2.05	*Precursor	No 1510	9.05
835	1432	*Panopea.*	7.65 - 7.04	*Precursor	No 520	3.05
836	1433	*Daphne.*	7.65 - 5.06	*Precursor	No 218	6.07
837	1434	*Eunomia.*	7.65 -10.07	*Experiment	No 2622	2.09
838	1435	*Fortuna.*	7.65 -10.07	*Experiment	No 887	1.09
839	1436	*Egeria.*	7.65 - 8.04	*Precursor	No 1431	3.05

SAMSON CLASS 6ft 0in 2-4-0 50 engines
(1863-1866)

The number and name of every one of this batch of Samsons were passed to engines of the Waterloo Class on the dates shown.

			Built	Scrapped					Built	Scrapped
624	633	*Samson.*	5.63 -	1.92		736	828	*Tubal.*	8.64 -	7.90
625	634	*Ellesmere.*	5.63 -	12.92		737	829	*Turk.*	8.64 -	1.92
626	733	*Chimera.*	5.63 -	1.90		738	830	**Trent.**	8.64 -	1.90
627	735	*Charon.*	5.63 -	1.92		739	642	*Bee.*	7.64 -	8.90
628	738	*Terrier.*	5.63 -	1.90		780	81	*Greystock.*	1.65	-
629	52	*Glowworm.*	5.63 -	2.91				Some records have *Greystoke.*		
630	757	*Banshee.*	5.63 -	1.92				Renamed *Greystoke.* 4.12.91		
631	758	*Hardman.*	5.63 -	1.90		781	1045	*Whitworth.*	1.65 -	9.89
632	763	*Violet.*	5.63 -	3.93		782	401	*Zeno.*	1.65 -	3.94
633	821	*Diomed.*	5.63 -	1.92		783	404	*Zopyrus.*	1.65 -	3.94
680	901	*Hero.*	1.64 -	10.90		784	418	*Zygia*	1.65 -	12.92
681	902	*Onyx.*	2.64 -	3.93		785	419	*Zillah.*	2.65 -	1.90
682	628	*Tartarus.*	2.64 -	4.93		786	35	*Talisman.*	2.65 -	10.90
683	724	*Eden.*	2.64 -	12.92		787	36	*Thalaba.*	2.65 -	10.90
684	748	*Waterloo.*	2.64 -	11.89		788	124	*Marquis Douro.*	2.65 -	12.92
685	764	*Shap.*	2.64 -	12.92		789	231	*Firefly.*	2.65 -	6.90
686	792	*Theorem.*	2.64 -	6.93		880	609	**The Earl of Chester.**	1.66 -	4.93
687	793	*Martin.*	2.64 -	5.94		881	632	*Ostrich.*	12.65 -	6.90
688	794	*Woodlark.*	3.64 -	8.94		882	746	*Castor.*	1.66 -	4.94
689	795	*Falstaff.*	3.64 -	6.93		883	814	**Henrietta.**	1.66 -	1.90
730	731	*Croxteth.*	7.64 -	11.89		884	817	**Constance.**	1.66 -	4.93
731	732	*Hecla.*	7.64 -	8.94		885	819	**Puck.**	1.66 -	12.92
732	736	*Memnon.*	7.64 -	1.92		886	824	**Adelaide.**	1.66 -	4.93
733	737	*Roberts.*	7.64 -	5.94		887	832	**Sanspareil.**	1.66 -	4.93
734	739	*Sutherland.*	7.64 -	4.93		888	934	*North Star.*	1.66 -	3.92
735	742	*Spitfire.*	7.64 -	12.92		889	935	*Planet.*	1.66 -	4.93

Two members of the class were given a name which had come to the L&NWR via an Absorbed Company:-
  1392 *Clyde* *St.Helens 0-4-2 No 26 *Clyde* L&NWR No 1392 7.64 Sold 7.65
  1368 *Trent* *St.Helens No 2 *Trent* L&NWR 1368 7.64 Sold shortly afterwards.
Two Liverpool & Manchester Railway names were re-used:-
North Star 0-2-2 (Robert Stephenson & Co.) No 7 8.30 Sold 12.33
Planet 2-2-0 (Robert Stephenson & Co.) No 9 9.30 Withdrawn 1840-1841

Fig. 27   Close up of the nameplate *Violet* showing the re-brazing done to the year to change the '1' into a '3' when the plate was transferred from DX of February 1861 to Samson of May 1863.

(Roger Bell Collection).

Fig. 28   633 *Samson* as originally built. Note the ornamental rim around the chimney.

(Allan Sommerfield Collection).

NEWTON CLASS   6ft 6in   2-4-0

The number and name of all these Newtons were members of the Renewed Precedent class.

			Built Scrapped				Built Scrapped
920	1480	*Newton.*	4.66 - 11.88	1169	1675	*Vimiera.*	4.68 - 5.91
921	1481	*Franklin.*	5.66	1170	1676	*The Nile.*	4.68 - 5.91
		Name changed before entering service		1171	1677	*Badajos.*	4.68 - 1.90
		Plate date 6.66		1172	1678	*Airey.*	4.68 - 4.92
		The Duke of Edinburgh.	6.66 - 10.88	1173	1679	*Bunsen.*	4.68 - 1.88
922	1482	*Herschel*	5.66 - 1.90	1174	1680	*Livingstone.*	5.68 - 6.91
923	1483	*Newcomen.*	5.66 - 3.90	1175	1681	*Minerva.*	5.68 - 2.88
924	1484	*Telford.*	5.66 - 11.90	1176	1682	*Novelty.*	5.68 - 6.92
925	1485	*Smeaton.*	5.66 - 12.87	1177	1683	*Sisyphus.*	5.68 - 5.91
926	1486	*Dalton.*	5.66 - 3.90	1178	1684	*Speke.*	5.68 - 6.91
927	1487	*Faraday.*	5.66 - 6.87	1179	1685	*Gladiator.*	5.68 - 11.88
928	1488	*Murdock.*	5.66 - 11.88	1280	1744	*Magdala.*	10.69 - 3.92
929	1489	*Brindley.*	5.66 - 4.93	1281	1745	*John Bright.*	10.69 - 3.92
980	1513	*Shakespeare.*	10.66 - 2.90	1282	1746	*Baying.*	11.69 - 1.70
981	1514	*Scott.*	10.66 - 11.90		Renamed	*Bevere.*	1.70 - 1.90
982	1515	*Milton.*	10.66 - 5.90	1283	1747	*Tennyson.*	11.69
983	1516	*Byron.*	10.66 - 6.91		Renamed	*John Mayall.*	
984	1517	*Princess Helena*	11.66 - 11.88	1284	1748	*Britannia.*	11.69 - 6.89
985	1518	*Countess.*	11.66 - 5.91	1285	1749	*Hibernia.*	11.69 - 11.87
986	1519	*Duchess.*	11.66 - 6.91	1286	379	*Scotia.*	12.69 - -.70
987	1520	*Franklin.*	11.66 - 5.91		Renamed	*Sedgwick*	-.70 - 8.88
		(Date on nameplate altered from '5.66' to '11.66')		1287	380	*Dunrobin.*	12.69 - -.70

988	1521	*Gladstone.*	11.66 - 9.89	Renamed		*Quernmore.*	-.70 - 5.91
989	1522	*Pitt.*	11.66 - 1.88	1288	381	*Goldsmith.*	12.69 - -.70
990	1523	*Marlborough.*	11.66 - 4.93	Renamed		*Patterdale.*	-.70 - 6.93
991	1524	*Wolfe.*	11.66 - 3.90	1289	382	*Buckingham.*	1.70 - 5.90
992	1525	*Abercrombie.*	11.66 - 5.91	1300	393	*Brougham.*	8.70 - 5.93
993	1526	*Drake.*	11.66 - 1.90	1301	394	*Eamont.*	8.70 - 5.93
994	1527	*Raleigh.*	11.66 - 2.88	1302	395	*Scotia.*	9.70 - 5.92
995	1528	*Frobisher.*	11.66 - 2.88	1303	396	*Dunrobin.*	9.70
996	1529	*Cook.*	11.66 - 9.89	Renamed		*Tennyson.*	12.85 - 4.91
997	1530	*Columbus.*	11.66 - 11.88	1304	271	*Minotaur.*	9.70 - 5.87
998	1531	*Cromwell.*	11.66 - 11.90	1305	275	*Vulcan.*	9.70 - 11.87
999	1532	*Hampden.*	11.66 - 6.92	1306	276	*Pluto.*	9.70 - 10.88
1160	1666	*Ariadne.*	3.68 - 6.91	1307	295	*Penmaenmawr.*	9.70 - 6.93
1161	1667	*Corunna.*	3.68 - 6.93	1308	304	*Hector.*	9.70 - 5.92
1162	1668	*Dagmar.*	3.68 - 5.91	1309	308	*Booth.*	9.70 - 5.90
1163	1669	*Ilion.*	3.68 - 3.88	1380	2001	*Henry Crosfield.*	4.71 - 11.90
1164	1670	*Ganymede.*	3.68 - 7.87	1381	2002	*Madge.*	4.71 - 6.91
1165	1671	*Shamrock.*	3.68 - 6.91	1382	2003	*Alecto.*	4.71 - 6.91
1166	1672	*Talavera.*	3.68 - 2.90	1383	2004	*Witch.*	4.71 - 5.91
1167	1673	*Lucknow.*	4.68 - 5.91	1384	2005	*Lynx.*	4.71 - 1.94
1168	1674	*Delhi.*	4.68 - 11.90	1385	2006	*Princess.*	4.71 - 11.90

The number and name of all these Newtons were inherited by members of the Renewed Precedent class

TABLE 8
JAMES EDWARD McCONNELL Wolverton Appointed 15th February 1847
Resigned 20th February 1862

CRAMPTON 8ft 0in 4-2-0
Built by Tulk & Ley

200 **London.**   Built 17.6.47 L&NWR No 800 Rebuilt 0-4-2 Goods 5.55 (1201 9.63 and 1828 12.71) Scrapped 7.74
(S Div. No)   The name was not used again

CRAMPTON 8ft 0in 6-2-0
Built by Bury, Curtis & Kennedy

245 **Liverpool.** Built 6.48 Scrapped 9.58
(S Div. No)   Exhibited at the Great Exhibition at the Crystal Palace which took place between 1st May and 15th October 1851, and
            awarded a Council Medal for originality
         "Rebuilt" 4.59 McConnell Standard Goods 0-6-0
         5ft 6in   LNWR No 845 4.62 Scrapped 2.81
            The name was used again on Special Tank Duplicate Number (3021) 6.95

6ft. 0in. 2-2-2 "Low-domed" Singles
Built by Bury, Curtis & Kennedy and unnamed until sometime in 1872

Built	S Div Numbers	Duplicate Number	Capital list No	Name	Disposal	Subsequent name-holder and date
		4.62	1.63	12.71		
5.48	65	665	(1144)	1184	*General.*	Withdrawn 26.6.77	*Precedent No 1170 9.78
6.48	67	667	(1145)	1185	*Cuckoo.*	Withdrawn 26.6.77	*Samson No 1168 7.79
6.48	75	675	(1146)	1186	*Allerton.*	Withdrawn 8.5.78	-
8.48	12	612	(1128)	1182	*Eglinton.*	Withdrawn 5.12.77	*Webb Precursor No 255 1.79
8.48	18	618	(1139)	1183	*Conway.* (1810 9.78)	Scrapped 30.9.79	*George the Fifth No 1086 6.15
8.48	218	818	(1149)	1187	*Derby.* (1811 9.78)	Scrapped 14.5.80	*Precedent No 506 11.80

Fig. 29   Passenger Engine 1007 *President* Driving wheel 7ft. "Large Bloomer"

L&NWR Postcard Set 2 No.4. (Fred Gray Collection).

Fig. 30   The nameplate of "Large Bloomer" *Briareus.*

(Harry Jack Collection).

7ft 0in   2-2-2   "Large Bloomers"
Unnamed until March and April 1872

The numbers given in the first column are those of 1862, carried at the time the engines received names.

Batch i. Sharp Brothers between August 1851 and February 1853

			Date delivered	Scrapped		Subsequent name-holder			Date
847	Odin		30.8.51	- 12.78		Samson	No	1164	5.79
848	Hecate.		9.9.51	- 10.83		*Experiment Compound	No	1113	6.84
849	Aœlus.		18.9.51	- 12.79		-			
850	Columbine.		29.9.51	- 11.81		-			
851	Apollo.		6.10.51	- 3.81		*Experiment Compound	No	1120	6.84
852	Basilisk.		20.10.51	- 9.79		-			
853	Vulture.		8.11.51	- 1.77		*Webb Precursor	No	1165	11.78
854	Dalemain.		22.11.51	- 12.77		-			
855	Sandon.		16.12.51	- 12.77		-			
856	Ingestre.		31.12.51	- 6.76		*Claughton	No	2420	1.23
887	Knowsley.		13.10.52	- 5.82		*Experiment Compound	No	306	7.83
888	Hydra.		15.10.52	- 4.82		*Experiment Compound	No	303	4.83
889	Camilla.		2.11.52	- 2.84		-			
890	Helvellyn.		19.11.52	- 3.77		*Webb Precursor	No	1149	9.78
891	Duke.		26.11.52	- 4.83		-			
892	Polyphemus.		24.12.52	- 9.77		*Jubilee	No	1929	4.00
893	Harpy.	(x)	24.12.52	- 3.85	(1817 12.84)	*Dreadnought	No	2061	12.85
894	Trentham.		8.2.53	- 4.83		*Experiment Compound	No	305	7.83
895	Torch.	(x)	14.2.53	- 3.87	(1828 12.84 and 3050 11.86)	-			
896	Dædalus.		28.2.53	- 7.77		-			

Batch ii. Sharp, Stewart & Co in October and November 1861

999	Medusa.	(x)	21.10.61	- 9.87	(1898 11.84)	*Dreadnought	No	2058	12.85
1000	Umpire.	(x)	28.10.61	- 3.85	(1902 11.84)	-			
1001	Leviathan.		2.11.61	- 12.84		*Dreadnought	No	510	4.85
1002	Theseus.		7.11.61	- 6.82		-			
1003	Tamerlane.	(x)	13.11.61	- 5.86	(1905 11.84)	*Dreadnought	No	545	7.86

Batch iii. Kitson & Co in October 1861

			Date of works trial						
1004	Lucifer.		14.9.61	- 7.83		-			
1005	Achilles.		19.9.61	- 10.84		*Dreadnought	No	511	5.85
1006	Proserpine.		5.10.61	- 10.76		*Precedent	No	871	6.77
1007	President.		16.10.61	- 12.77		*Experiment	No	1992	10.06
1008	Rowland Hill.	(x)	25.10.61	- 2.85	(1907 11.84)	*Dreadnought	No	659	7.86

Batch iv. Wolverton Works between March and May 1862

989	Archimedes.	(x)	3.62	- 9.87	(1853 11.84 and 3071 11.86)	*Dreadnought	No	1395	6.86
990	Alaric.	(x)	3.62	- 6.86	(1881 11.84)	*Whale Precursor	No	282	4.06
991	**Japan.**		3.62	- 1.82		-			
992	Stork.	(x)	3.62	- 11.88	(1882 11.84 and 3023 5.87)	*Dreadnought	No	1379	6.86
993	**Burmah.**		4.62	- 2.81		-			
994	Ariel.		4.62	- 9.84		-			
995	Briareus.		4.62	- 9.79		-			
996	Raglan.		5.62	- 6.82		-			
997	Baronet.		4.62	- 1.82		-			
998	Una.	(x)	5.62	- 6.85	(1897 11.84)	-			

x These ten nameplates were removed in 1885

6ft 6in 2-2-2 "Small Bloomers"
Names allotted 18th April 1872

Batch i. Vulcan Foundry Co

		Built Scrapped		Subsequent name-holder and date			
614	*Wyre.*	6.54 - 2.79		*Samson	No	1166	6.79
615	*Lune.*	7.54 - 2.83		-			
617	*Partridge.*	7.54 - 6.83		-			

Batch ii. R & W Hawthorn & Co

623	*Medea.*	4.54 - 12.77		*Samson	No	995	5.79
625	*Mastodon.*	5.54 - 7.78		*Samson	No	479	5.79
626	*Earl.*	6.54 - 5.79		-			
627	*Bulldog.*	6.54 - 8.81		*George the Fifth	No	956 late 1921	
629	*Swan.*	6.54 - 1.83		-			
630	*Ribble.*	7.54 - 2.82		-			

Batch iii. Wolverton Works

703	*Osprey.*	5.57 - 9.81		-			
621	*Bela*	7.57 - 2.82		-			
607	*Inglewood.*	8.57 - 2.83		-			
740	*St.David.*	8.57 - 11.86 (1947 11.84)		-			
838	*Petrel.*	10.57 - 3.79		*Samson	No	209	5.79
840	*Lonsdale.*	1857 - 3.78		-			
768	*Glyn.*	2.58 - 3.84 (1963 3.84)		-			
602	*Caliban.*	7.58 - 8.81		*Samson	No	805	-.84
765	*Herald.*	10.58 - 3.85 (1952 11.84)					
				*Dreadnought	No	2062	12.85
780	*Bucephalus.*	12.58 - 8.83		*Whale Precursor	No	990	4.06
717	*Swift.*	5.59 - 9.82		-			
789	*Cadmus.*	7.59 - 12.80		-			
666	*Pheasant*	8.59 - 12.77		*Samson	No	263	5.79
603	*Langdale.*	10.59 - 12.84 (1941 11.84)-					
917	*Napier.*	1.60 - 6.80		-			
977	*Sultan.*	9.61 - 2.87 (1954 11.84)					
				*Jubilee	No	1938	10.00
978	*Mammoth.*	10.61 - 2.85 (1957 11.84)					
				*Dreadnought	No	513	5.85
979	*Wasp.*	10.61 - 6.80		-			
980	*Vandal.* (x)	11.61 - 3.87 (1816 12.84 and 3038 11.86)					
				*Dreadnought	No	2060	12.85
981	*Councillor.*	11.61 - 1.84 (1925 12.83)		-			

x   Nameplates were removed in 1885

Both Nos. 613 and 624 were withdrawn in 12.66 and were never named .

7ft 6in 2-2-2 "Extra Large Bloomers"
Built at Wolverton in 1861 and not named until 1872

1200	*Maberley.*	5.61 - Named 1872 (1871 10.79) Scrapped 3.82
		Name not used again
1198	*Delamere.*	8.61 - Named 1872 (1940 10.79) Scrapped 1.80
		*Whale Precursor No 2051 8.07
1199	**Caithness.**	11.61 - Named 5.72 (1885 10.79) Scrapped 3.82
		Name not used again

TABLE 9
FRANCIS WEBB   Appointed September 1871 - Retired May 1903

NEWTON CLASS 6ft 6in 2-4-0 20 engines

			Built	Scrapped				Built	Scrapped
1479	1211	**John Ramsbottom.**	3.72	11.88	1683	941	**Blenkinsop.**	8.73	10.88
1480	1212	**Pioneer.**	3.72	11.88	1684	942	**Shah of Persia.**	8.73	4.93
1481	1213	The Queen.	4.72	1.92	1685	974	**Richard Cobden.**	8.73	1.90
1482	1214	Prince Albert.	4.72	11.90	1686	696	Director.	8.73	11.88
1483	1215	Albion.	4.72	8.93	1687	787	Clarendon.	8.73	4.93
1484	1216	Premier.	4.72	11.88	1688	790	Hardwicke.	8.73	1.92
1485	1217	**Florence.**	4.72	4.91	1689	1132	North Western.	8.73	6.87
1486	1218	Phaeton.	4.72	11.90	1690	1141	**S.R.Graves.**	8.73	11.88
1487	1219	Lightning.	4.72	1.88	1691	403	Marquis	8.73	
1488	1220	Belted Will.	4.72	6.87			Name changed to **Isabella.**	-.73	1.92
1682	1020	Wordsworth.	8.73	5.91					

The number and name of all these were passed to members of the Renewed Precedent class.

Fig. 31   Samson class 90 *Luck of Edenhall.*

Real Photographs Co.Ltd.14145 (Allan Sommerfield Collection).

SAMSON CLASS 6ft 0in 2-4-0 40 engines

(1873-1874 and 1879)

			Built	Duplicate List number and date	Scrap date
1692	414	*Prospero.*	9.73	(3271 8.95)	
		Engineer Lancaster	4.03		2.24
1693	424	*Sirius.*	9.73	(3206 7.95)	
		Engineer-Crewe	9.99		7.14
1694	604	*Narcissus.*	9.73		11.90
1695	635	*Zamiel.*	9.73		1.90
1696	636	*Eclipse.*	9.73		4.93
1697	805	*Cyclops.*	9.7		
Renamed		*Caliban.* -.84			4.93
1698	444	*Typhon.*	9.73		11.90
1699	445	*Ixion.*	9.73		12.92
1700	446	*Siren.*	9.73		4.93
1701	285	*Phalaris.*	9.73		12.92
1842	434	*St.Patrick.*	10.74		4.93
1843	468	*Wildfire.*	10.74		11.90
1844	469	*St.George.*	10.74		6.93
1845	485	*Euxine.*	10.74		12.92
1846	486	*Skiddaw.*	10.74		6.93
1847	487	*John O'Groat.*	10.74	(3199 11.94)	
		'Spare Engine'	8.95		
		Engineer Liverpool	10.05		7.21
1848	631	*Hotspur.*	10.74	(3273 1.96)	
		Engineer Manchester	11.01		6.14
1849	1163	*John O'Gaunt.*	10.74		11.94
1850	90	*Luck of Edenhall.*	10.74		3.94
1851	885	*Vampire.*	10.74	(3269 5.95)	
		Engineer	5.97		
		'Spare Engine'	5.23		3.25
1852	2150	*Atlas.*	11.74		6.93
1853	2151	*Baltic.*	11.74	(3268 5.95)	
		Engineer Stafford	4.01		6.23
		later *Engineer Walsall*			
1854	2152	*Sybil.*	11.74		3.94
1855	2153	*Isis.*	11.74		4.93
1856	2154	*Loadstone.*	11.74		11.93
1857	2155	*Liver.*	11.74		8.94
1858	2156	*Sphinx.*	11.74		11.94
1859	2157	*Unicorn.*	11.74	(3272 11.95)	
		'Spare Engine'	11.05		5.23
1860	2158	*Serpent.*	11.74		8.94
1861	2159	*Shark.*	11.74		3.94
2279	773	*Centaur.*	5.79	(3200 11.94)	
		Engineer Watford	7.95		5.23
2280	1162	*Saddleback.*	5.79		4.93
2281	1164	*Odin.*	5.79		11.94
2282	1166	*Wyre.*	6.79	(3270 5.95)	
		Engineer.Bangor	1.02		12.25
2283	1168	*Cuckoo.*	7.79		3.94
2284	852	*Kestrel.*	5.79		11.94
2285	209	*Petrel.*	5.79	(3198 11.94)	
		Engineer Northampton	1.02		5.23
2286	995	*Medea.*	5.79		11.94
2287	479	*Mastodon.*	5.79		1.92
2288	263	*Pheasant.*	5.79		6.94

The ten which became Engineers, or 'Spare engine', lost their names at the time they were placed on the Duplicate List.

The final batch of ten were intended to carry numbers 2350 - 2359, but were numbered as above when put into traffic.

Apart from those which became 'Engineers', all the numbers and names of the class were inherited by Waterloo Class engines.

WEBB PRECURSOR CLASS 5ft 6in 2-4-0 40 engines

			Period of naming	Subsequent name-holder and date		
1802	2145	*Precursor.*	4.74 - 2.94	*Precursor	No 513	3.04
1803	2146	*Harbinger.*	8.74 - 3.93	*Precursor	No 1395	3.04
1804	2147	*Champion.*	8.74 - 3.95	*Precursor	No 515	12.04
1805	2148	*Vizier.*	8.74 - 3.93	*Precursor	No 2202	10.05
1806	2149	*Candidate.*	8.74 - 3.93	*Precursor	No 1301	10.05
1807	1143	*Marquis.*	8.74 - 2.94	*Precursor (formerly *Alfred Paget.*)	No 412	11.04
1808	1144	*Druid.*	8.74 - 10.91	*Precursor	No 106	10.04
1809	1145	*Cossack.*	9.74 - 2.94	*Precursor	No 685	10.04
1810	1152	*Arab.*	9.74 - 10.91	*Precursor	No 2576	12.05
1811	1153	*Sirocco.*	9.74 - 3.95	*Precursor	No 643	11.04
1812	1154	*Colossus.*	9.74 - 10.91	*Jubilee	No 1912	6.99
1813	1155	*Dragon.*	9.74 - 2.94	*Precursor	No 60	10.04
1814	402	*Viscount.*	9.74 - 3.93	*Precursor	No 1737	3.05
1815	406	*Senator.*	9.74 - 9.91	*Precursor	No 305	11.04
1816	408	*Simoon.*	9.74 - 3.94	*Precursor	No 2 (*Simoom*)	6.04
1817	409	*Thunderbolt.*	10.74 - 10.91	*Precursor	No 1102	11.04
1818	413	*Python.*	10.74 - 3.93	*Precursor	No 1784	10.05
1819	425	*Oberon.*	10.74 - 3.93	*Precursor	No 2164	4.04
1820	426	*Warrior.*	10.74 - 1.95	*Jubilee	No 1925	3.00
1821	427	*Fame.*	10.74 - 2.94	*Precursor	No 2578	12.05
2229	1147	**John Rennie.**	10.78 - 2.94	*John Hick	No 1549	3.98
2230	1148	**Boadicea.**	10.78 - 2.94	*Alfred the Great	No 1963	2.03
2231	1149	*Helvellyn.*	9.78 - 2.94	*Precursor	No 2023	4.04
2232	1150	*Lang Meg.*	10.78 - 3.93	*Precursor	No 1387	3.06
2233	1151	*Lapwing.*	10.78 - 3.95	*Precursor	No 1642	3.06
2234	1165	*Vulture.*	11.78 - 10.91	*Precursor	No 2257	8.05
2235	1169	*Albatross.*	10.78 - 10.91	*Precursor	No 510	6.04
2236	1174	*Cerberus.*	10.78 - 3.93	*Precursor	No 1111	3.05
2237	697	*Harrowby.*	10.78 - 2.94	*Precursor	No 315	7.05
2238	847	*Cedric.*	10.78 - 1.95	*Precursor	No 1104	2.05
2249	431	**Bessemer.**	1.79 - 10.91	-		
2250	838	**Henry Cort.**	1.79 - 3.95	*John Hick	No 1512	2.98
				*Experiment	No 1413	4.09
2251	779	**William Baker.**	3.79 - 2.93	-		
2252	680	**Giffard.**	3.79 - 1.95	-		
2253	255	*Eglinton.*	5.79 - 2.95	*Precursor	No 2061	4.05
2254	481	*Etna.*	5.79 - 10.91	*Precursor	No 2577	12.05
2255	626	*Emerald.*	5.79 - 2.95	*Precursor	No 300	7.05
2256	718	*Jason.*	5.79 - 3.93	*Precursor	No 2064	3.05
2257	338	*Levens.*	5.79 - 10.91	*Precursor	No 2513	3.06
2258	1180	*Pearl.*	5.79 - 2.95	*Precursor	No 234	3.06

Note: An alternative version, discarded by S.S.Scott, for Crewe numbers *2249-2258,* had the running number sequence <u>431</u>, <u>838</u>, 481, 626, <u>255</u>, 680, 338, <u>718</u>, 779 and <u>1180</u>. The numbers underlined indicate those where there was no change.

One member of the class was given a name which had come to the L&NWR via an Absorbed Company:-
1581 **Cedric** Whitehaven & Furness Joint Stock No 18 L&NWR No (1554)
1581 1866 (1263 6.67 and 1824 12.71) Scrapped 3.77

THE LMS RENUMBERING SCHEME

From this point to the end of this Table 9, and throughout Tables 10 and 11 two new columns appear, giving details of the LMS number, and the date of its application. A renumbering scheme was introduced soon after the grouping and, of named engines, the first to be done was L&NWR No 2511 *Croxteth* which then became LMS 5971 in July 1923, after which time the work went forward somewhat hesitantly. Because of industrial action in the Paint Shop at Crewe only three named engines were recorded as having been renumbered between June 1924 and February 1926, the three exceptions being L&NWR No 819 *Prince of Wales* which was painted and renumbered 5600 at Derby in October 1924, and L&NWR Nos 2222 *Sir Gilbert Claughton* and 1161 *Sir Robert Turnbull*, becoming LMS Nos 5900 and 5901 in June and December 1925 respectively. A report in the September 1925 issue of the Railway Magazine says "The paint shop at Crewe is now in full swing again; engines of all types (both passenger and goods) being in for painting and renumbering", in the light of which it seems strange that several months then elapsed before the next recorded renumbering. The task was completed in September 1928.

Note that where the LMS number appears in brackets, (e.g. (5004)) the number was allocated, but the engine was withdrawn before it had been applied.

Fig. 32   25001 *Snowdon* photographed between April and November 1934.

(L&NWR Society Photograph Collection No 9382).

PRECEDENT CLASS 6ft 6in 2-4-0

			Period of naming		Subsequent name-holder(s) and date		LMS Number	Date applied
			Built	Withdrawn				
1902	2175	*Precedent.*	12.74 -	11.94	Renewed Precedent *Prince of Wales	No 1749		11.15
1903	2176	*Robert Benson.*	2.75 -	4.96	Renewed Precedent			
1904	2177	*Edward Tootal.*	3.75 -	8.95	Renewed Precedent *George the Fifth	No 1193		3.13
1905	2178	*Pluck.*	3.75 -	1.94	Renewed Precedent			
1906	2179	*Patience.*	3.75 -	5.97	Renewed Precedent *Claughton	No 2499		8.22
1907	2180	*Perseverance.*	3.75 -	5.97	Renewed Precedent			
1908	2181	*Buffalo.*	3.75 -	7.07	*Experiment	No 2630		3.09
1909	2182	*Giraffe.*	3.75 -	5.95	Renewed Precedent			
1910	2183	*Antelope.*	3.75 -	6.95	"			
1911	2184	*Reynard.*	3.75 -	5.97	"			
1912	2185	*Alma.*	4.75 -	3.96	"			
1913	2186	*Lowther.*	4.75 -	2.96	"			
1914	2187	*Penrith Beacon.*	4.75 -	2.97	"			
1915	2188	*Chillington.*	4.75 -	2.95	"			
1916	2189	*Avon.*	4.75 -	8.97	"			
1917	2190	*Beatrice.*	4.75	briefly				
		Lady Beatrice.	1875 -	13.3.77				
		Princess Beatrice.	-	7.6.32	(Reb 11.95)		5000	7.28
1918	2191	*Snowdon.*	4.75 -	3.11.34	(Reb 11.92)		5001	3.28
							25001	24.4.34
1919	2192	*Caradoc.*	4.75 -	5.94	Renewed Precedent			
1920	2193	*Salopian.*	5.75 -	2.96	"			
1921	2194	*Cambrian.*	5.75 -	11.96	"			
2034	890	*Sir Hardman Earle.*	4.77 -	4.95	"			
2035	1177	*Princess Louise.*	4.77 -	3.96	Renewed Precedent *Claughton	No 42		2.22
2036	857	*Prince Leopold.*	4.77 -	9.97	Renewed Precedent			
2037	858	*Sir Salar Jung.*	5.77 -	5.97	"			
2038	860	*Merrie Carlisle.*	5.77 -	1.95	"			

2039	861	**Amazon.**	5.77 - 9.01	"			
2040	862	**Balmoral.**	5.77 - 7.97	Renewed Precedent			
2041	863	*Meteor.*	5.77 - 10.07	*George the Fifth No 2242	5.13		
2042	864	*Pilot.*	5.77 - 6.96	Renewed Precedent			
2043	865	*Envoy.*	5.77 - 9.94	"			
2044	866	*Courier.*	5.77 - 2.96	"			
2045	1189	*Stewart.*	5.77 - 8.97	"			
2046	883	*Phantom.*	5.77 - 11.94	"			
2047	1105	*Hercules.*	5.77 - 12.97	"			
2048	867	**Disraeli.**	6.77 - 7.94	Renewed Precedent *Prince of Wales No 1325	5.22		
2049	868	*Condor.*	6.77 - 11.96	Renewed Precedent			
2050	869	*Llewellyn.*	6.77 - 1.97	"			
2051	870	*Fairbairn.*	6.77 - 5.98	"			
2052	871	*Proserpine.*	6.77 - 8.94	"			
2053	872	*Wizard.*	6.77 - 8.95	"			
2219	1173	**The Auditor.**	8.78 - 1.94	"			
2220	1193	**Joshua Radcliffe.**	8.78 - 8.96	"			
2221	1194	*Miranda.*	9.78 - 2.97	"			
2222	749	**Mercury.**	9.78 - 6.95	"			
2223	517	*Marathon.*	9.78 - 1.96	Renewed Precedent *Prince of Wales No 1542	1.23		
2224	1170	*General.*	9.78 - 24.10.31			5002	3.26
2225	919	*Nasmyth.*	9.78 - 12.93	Renewed Precedent			
2226	193	*Rocket.*	9.78 - 3.97	"			
2227	1183	**Plynlimmon.**	9.78 - 8.96	Renewed Precedent *Prince of Wales No 257	11.15		
2228	1187	*Chandos.*	9.78 - 6.96	Renewed Precedent			
2400	619	**Mabel.**	10.80 - 3.96	"			
2401	789	**Breadalbane.**	10.80 - 7.94	Renewed Precedent *Claughton No 169	3.23		
2402	477	**Caractacus.**	10.80 - 3.96	Renewed Precedent			
2403	478	*Commodore.*	11.80 - 10.96	"			
2404	480	*Duchess of Lancaster.*	11.80 - 4.97	"			
2405	482	*Pegasus.*	11.80 - 1.94	Renewed Precedent *Prince of Wales No 446	11.15		
2406	506	*Derby.*	11.80 "for a short time only"				
		Sir Alexander Cockburn.	1880/1 - 6.96	Renewed Precedent			
2407	512	*Lazonby.*	11.80 - 11.8.29			5003	9.26
2408	514	**Lawrence.**	11.80 - 12.95	Renewed Precedent			
2409	945	*Humphrey Davy.*	11.80 - 6.95	"			
2501	253	**President Garfield.**	1.82 - 2.95	"			
2502	254	**President Lincoln.**	1.82 - 2.95	Renewed Precedent *Experiment No 2627	2.09		
2503	256	**President Washington.**	1.82 - 8.94	Renewed Precedent			
2504	257	**Duke of Albany.**	1.82 - 4.15				
2505	260	**Duke of Connaught.**	1.82 - 10.95	Renewed Precedent 2.96 *Claughton No 2427	1.22		
2506	262	**Wheatstone.**	1.82 - 4.97	Renewed Precedent			
2507	264	**Buckland.**	1.82 - 1.96	Renewed Precedent *Experiment No 2625	2.09		
2508	265	**Thomas Carlyle.**	1.82 - 8.94	Renewed Precedent			
2509	364	**Henry Pease.**	2.82 - 8.94	Renewed Precedent			
2510	955	**Charles Dickens.**	6.2.82 - 10.12	*George the Fifth No 82	1.13		

Eight "Precedents" were rebuilt and so did not become "Renewed Precedents"; nor did they receive new Crewe numbers.

They were:-

1908	2181	*Buffalo.*	Rebuilt 11.87, 11.93 and 1.02
1917	2190	*Princess Beatrice.*	Rebuilt 11.95
1918	2191	*Snowdon.*	Rebuilt 11.92
2041	863	*Meteor.*	Rebuilt sometime during the 1890s
2224	1170	*General.*	" " " " " " "
2407	512	*Lazonby.*	Rebuilt 12.99
2504	257	*Duke of Albany.*	Rebuilt 3.02
2510	955	*Charles Dickens.*	Rebuilt 5.02

See also the note at the foot of the "Renewed Precedent" table.

Fig. 33 Renewed Precedent class 2004 *Witch.*

F. Moore Railway Photographs (Allan Sommerfield Collection).

RENEWED PRECEDENT CLASS 6ft 6in 2-4-0 158 engines

			Date Renewed	Date Withdrawn	LMS Number	Date Applied
2996	271	*Minotaur.*	6.87 -	4.12.27	(5004)	
2997	1132	*North Western.*	6.87 -	5.06		
2998	1220	*Belted Will.*	6.87 -	3.21		
2999	1487	*Faraday.*	6.87 -	4.07		
3001	1670	*Ganymede.*	7.87 -	12.05		
3022	1485	*Smeaton.*	12.87 -	5.14		
3023	1749	*Hibernia.*	1.88 -	5.15		
3024	275	*Vulcan.*	1.88 -	12.09		
3025	1522	*Pitt.*	1.88 -	4.6.32	5005	6.27
3026	1679	*Bunsen.*	1.88 -	10.13		
3027	1219	*Lightning.*	1.88 -	2.09		
3028	1681	*Minerva.*	2.88 -	9.11		
3029	1528	*Frobisher.*	2.88 -	2.16		
3030	1527	*Raleigh.*	2.88 -	26.5.25	(5006)	
3031	1669	*Ilion.*	3.88 -	1.06		
3042	941	*Blenkinsop.*	10.88 -	4.25	(5008)	
3043	1481	*The Duke of Edinburgh.*	10.88 -	5.13		
3044	379	*Sedgwick.*	10.88 -	2.28	5007	3.27
3045	1517	*Princess Helena.*	11.88 -	11.28	5009	6.26
3046	1216	*Premier.*	11.88 -	3.21		
3047	1480	*Newton.*	11.88 -	22.3.28	(5010)	
3048	1685	*Gladiator.*	11.88 -	12.27	(5015)	
3049	1212	*Pioneer.*	11.88 -	1.28	5013	8.26
3050	1211	*John Ramsbottom.*	11.88 -	31.12.30	5012	12.23
3051	1141	*S.R.Graves.*	11.88 -	2.07		
3052	1488	*Murdock.*	11.88 -	6 4.32	5014	4.28
3053	276	*Pluto.*	11.88 -	7.07		
3054	696	*Director.*	11.88 -	24.12.32	5011	9.27

3055	1530	Columbus.	11.88 -	11.21		
3056	1748	Britannia.	7.89 -	6.28	5016	9.27
3060	1529	Cook.	9.89 -	12.12		
3061	1521	Gladstone.	9.89 -	3.3.26	(5017)	
3057	1482	Herschel.	1.90 -	7.08		
3058	1677	Badajos.	1.90 -	10.22		
3059	1526	Drake.	1.90 -	8.07		
3062	974	Richard Cobden.	1.90 -	3.19		
3063	1746	Bevere.	2.90 -	7.12		
3064	1513	Shakespeare.	2.90 -	4.11		
3065	1672	Talavera.	2.90 -	24.12.32	5018	3.28
3066	1486	Dalton.	3.90 -	4.14		
3067	1524	Wolfe.	3.90 -	7.08		
3068	1483	Newcomen.	3.90 -	1.09		
3069	1515	Milton.	5.90 -	11.14		
3070	382	Buckingham.	5.90 -	11.21		
3071	308	Booth.	6.90 -	10.22		
3142	2006	Princess.	11.90 -	31.3.32	5021	7.26
3143	1514	Scott.	11.90 -	12.14		
3144	1214	Prince Albert.	11.90 -	4.14		
3145	1218	Phaeton.	11.90 -	5.11		
3146	1674	Delhi.	11.90 -	31.11.30	5020	6.27
3147	2001	Henry Crosfield.	11.90 -	1.12		
3148	1531	Cromwell.	11.90 -	1.7.28	5019	10.27
3149	1484	Telford.	11.90 -	8.15		
3150	1683	Sisyphus.	5.91 -	1.08		
3151	396	Tennyson.	5.91 -	11.21		
3192	1675	Vimiera.	5.91 -	28.9.26	(5024)	
3193	1747	John Mayall.	5.91 -	12.05		
3194	1673	Lucknow.	5.91 -	2.19		
3195	1525	Abercrombie.	5.91 -	12.28	5022	1.27
3196	1668	Dagmar.	5.91 -	6.2.32	5023	4.27
3197	1676	The Nile.	5.91 -	9.06		
3198	2004	Witch.	5.91 -	8.12		
3199	1020	Wordsworth.	5.91 -	1.09		
3200	1518	Countess.	5.91 -	23.1.26	(5025)	
3201	1520	Franklin.	5.91 -	24.12.32	5027	1.27
3242	380	Quernmore.	6.91 -	10.22		
3243	1666	Ariadne.	6.91 -	17.9.25	(5028)	
3244	1680	Livingstone.	6.91 -	4.13		
3245	1217	Florence.	6.91 -	11.15		
3246	2003	Alecto.	6.91 -	1.07		
3247	2002	Madge.	6.91 -	31.12.28	5030	8.26
3248	1516	Byron.	6.91 -	7.07		
3249	1684	Speke.	6.91 -	15.8.31	5029	12.26
3250	1671	Shamrock.	6.91 -	8.06		
3251	1519	Duchess.	6.91 -	11.28	5026	6.26
3282	1744	Magdala.	4.92 -	8.15		
3283	1745	John Bright.	4.92			
Renamed		Glowworm 7.14	-	15.11.30	5034	2.28
3284	1532	Hampden.	6.92 -	4.11		
3285	304	Hector.	6.92 -	1.7.28	5035	7.28
3286	790	Hardwicke.	4.92 -	17.1.32	5031	5.28
3287	1213	The Queen.	4.92 -	20.2.32	5032	3.27
3288	403	Isabella.	4.92 -	9.22		
3289	1678	Airey.	4.92 -	11.2.27	(5033)	
3290	395	Scotia.	6.92 -	11.19		
3291	1682	Novelty.	6.92 -	1.7.28	5036	1.24
3343	1489	Brindley.	4.93 -	4.11		
3344	394	Eamont.	4.93 -	9.21		
3345	942	Shah of Persia.	4.93 -	1.16		
3346	393	Brougham.	4.93 -	3.07		
3347	1667	Corunna.	6.93 -	4.28	5039	3.24
3348	295	Penmaenmawr.	6.93 -	3.09		
3349	1523	Marlborough.	6.93 -	2.09		
3350	381	Patterdale.	7.93 -	11.12.27	(5037)	
3351	787	Clarendon.	8.93 -	7.27	(5038)	
3352	1215	Albion.	8.93 -	3.08		

3353	2005	*Lynx.*	1.94 - 18.12.30	5041	6.28
3490	919	*Nasmyth.*	12.93 - 8.28	5040	9.26
3491	2178	*Pluck.*	1.94 - 9.22		
3492	1173	*The Auditor.*	1.94 - 6.6.30	5042	5.26
3493	482	*Pegasus.*	1.94 - 10.14		
3494	2192	*Caradoc.*	5.94 - 7.27	(5043)	
3506	871	*Proserpine.*	8.94 - 28.8.25	(5044)	
3507	265	*Thomas Carlyle.*	8.94 - 30.4.30	5045	5.27
3508	789	*Breadalbane.*	7.94 - 12.14		
3509	865	*Envoy.*	9.94 - 11.28	5046	8.28
3510	867	*Disraeli.*	9.94 - 8.15		
3531	364	*Henry Pease.*	10.94 - 30.9.30	5048	4.28
3532	883	*Phantom.*	11.94 - 10.28	(5049)	
3533	256	*President Washington.*	10.94 - 2.23	(5047)	
3534	2175	*Precedent.*	11.94 - 4.15		
3535	860	*Merrie Carlisle.*	3.95 - 24.6.33	5050	10.23
3556	253	*President Garfield.*	2.95 - 8.21		
3557	2188	*Chillington.*	2.95 - 7.08		
3558	254	*President Lincoln.*	2.95 - 7.08		
3559	890	*Sir Hardman Earle.*	4.95 - 11.28	5051	11.26
3560	2182	*Giraffe.*	5.95 - 5.22		
3571	749	*Mercury.*	6.95 - 5.27	(5052)	
3572	2183	*Antelope.*	6.95 - 13.6.30	5054	1.27
3573	945	*Humphrey Davy.*	6.95 - 20.12.30	5053	4.28
3574	872	*Wizard.*	8.95 - 5.22		
3575	2177	*Edward Tootal.*	8.95 - 7.11		
3596	514	*Lawrence.*	12.95 -		
Renamed		*Puck* 6.13	- 12.8.26	(5055)	
3597	260	*Duke of Connaught.*	2.96 - 8.14		
3598	866	*Courier.*	2.96 - 12.28	5057	6.26
3599	2186	*Lowther.*	2.96 - 12.27	(5067)	
3600	2193	*Salopian.*	2.96 - 12.10.25	(5059)	
3611	517	*Marathon.*	3.96 - 4.21		
3612	2185	*Alma.*	3.96 - 12.28	5058	2.27
3613	477	*Caractacus.*	3.96 - 9.27	(5056)	
3614	619	*Mabel.*	3.96 - 19.5.26	(5060)	
3615	2176	*Robert Benson.*	4.96 - 6.27	(5061)	
3656	1177	*Princess Louise.*	3.96 - 2.20		
3657	264	*Buckland.*	4.96 - 4.07		
3658	864	*Pilot.*	6.96 - 7.27	(5063)	
3659	1187	*Chandos.*	6.96 - 30.10.30	5064	3.27
3660	506	*Sir Alexander Cockburn.*	6.96 - 3.2.32	5062	6.28
3681	1183	*Plynlimmon.*	8.96 - 1.11		
3682	1193	*Joshua Radcliffe.*	8.96 - 3.13		
3683	478	*Commodore.*	12.96 - 15.9.26	(5065)	
3684	2194	*Cambrian.*	11.96 - 26.5.25	(5066)	
3685	868	*Condor.*	11.96 - 5.11		
3726	869	*Llewellyn.*	1.97 - 1.22		
3727	2187	*Penrith Beacon.*	2.97 - 6.6.32	5069	2.24
3728	1194	*Miranda.*	2.97 - 24.5.30	5068	2.28
3729	262	*Wheatstone.*	4.97 - 6.6.32	5070	2.28
3730	480	*Duchess of Lancaster.*	4.97 - 9.27	(5071)	
3742	2180	*Perseverance.*	5.97 - 8.2.26	(5073)	
3743	193	*Rocket.*	5.97 - 28.1.26	(5072)	
3744	2184	*Reynard.*	5.97 - 2.19		
3745	858	*Sir Salar Jung.*	5.97 - 8.12		
3746	2179	*Patience.*	5.97 - 3.20		
3777	1189	*Stewart.*	8.97 - 12.22		
3778	2189	*Avon.*	8.97 - 12.8.27	(5076)	
3779	862	*Balmoral.*	9.97 - 1.8.31	5075	9.28
3780	857	*Prince Leopold.*	9.97 - 1.7.28	(5074)	
3781	1105	*Hercules.*	12.97 - 1.7.28	(5077)	
3782	870	*Fairbairn.*	5.98 - 27.12.28	5078	9.28
3783	861	*Amazon.*	9.01 - 25.8.25	(5079)	

In 1897 Crewe numbers *3777-3785* were reserved for intended rebuilds of "Precedents", but in the event only seven were used, and numbers *3784* and *3785* which had been allocated to 512 *Lazonby* and 863 *Meteor* were never used.

The name *John Bright* was removed from 1745 to avoid confusion with Claughton class 250 *J.A.Bright* built in August 1914.

The name *Lawrence* was removed from 514 to avoid confusion with Claughton class 2046 *Charles N.Lawrence* built in June 1913.

Note: In the 1935 Railway Magazine Volume 76 Mr.C.Williams writes that the earliest "Newton" class renewals were provided with new nameplates, until about 1890 after which the original nameplates were retained.

Fig. 34   Waterloo class 609 *The Earl of Chester* at Mancester (London Road).

(Allan Sommerfield Collection).

WATERLOO (or WHITWORTH) CLASS 6ft 0in 2-4-0 90 engines

			Date Renewed	Date Withdrawn	LMS No	Date applied	Subsequent Name-holder and date
3112	748	Waterloo	11.89 -	4.25	5080	3.24	
3113	1045	Whitworth.	9.89 -	9.2.26	(5081)		
3114	731	Croxteth.	11.89 -	1.23			*Claughton No 2511 6.23
3115	830	Trent.	1.90 -	9.07			*Prince of Wales No 1346 1.16
3116	733	Chimera.	1.90 -	29.9.26	(5082)		
3117	814	Henrietta.	1.90 -	24.6.28	5083	5.28	
3118	738	Terrier.	1.90 -	5.08			*Experiment No 2629 3.09
3119	419	Zillah.	1.90 -	6.07			*Alfred the Great No 1947 6.11
3120	635	Zamiel.	1.90 -	10.08			*Prince of Wales No 401 12.15
3121	758	Hardman.	1.90 -	8.22			
3122	632	Ostrich.	6.90 -	3.11			*Waterloo No 739 8.13
3123	231	Firefly.	6.90 -	8.22			
3124	828	Tubal.	7.90 -	2.06			*Precursor No 2017 3.06
3125	642	Bee.	8.90 -	16.1.32	5084	3.28	
3126	901	Hero.	10.90 -	31.12.28	5085	3.27	
3127	35	Talisman.	10.90 -	11.09			*Claughton No 12 1.23
3128	36	Thalaba.	10.90 -	7.22			*Claughton No 30 4.23
3129	444	Typhon.	10.90 -	3.09			
3130	468	Wildfire.	11.90 -				
Became		Engineer Northampton 5.23	-	12.27	(5086)		
3131	604	Narcissus.	11.90 -	1.10.30	5087	10.26	

3132	736	*Memnon.*	1.92 -	2.15			
3133	735	*Charon.*	1.92 -	31.12.28	5088	10.26	
3134	757	*Banshee.*	1.92 -	3.08			*Experiment No 2628 3.09
3135	633	*Samson.*	1.92 -	1.13			*Prince of Wales No 2339 1.16
3136	821	*Diomed.*	1.92 -	5.08			
3137	81	*Greystoke.*	1.92 -	5.08			*Experiment No 2116 1.09
3138	829	*Turk.*	1.92 -	8.09			
3139	934	*North Star.*	3.92 -	1.28	(5089)		
3140	752	*Glowworm.*	3.92 -	2.13			*Renewed Precedent No 1745 7.14
3141	479	*Mastodon.*	3.92 -	12.13			
3354	634	*Ellesmere.*	3.93 -	24.6.28	5091	5.28	
3355	485	*Euxine.*	3.93				
Became		*Engineer South Wales* 2.21 -		12.31			
3356	724	*Eden.*	3.93 -	9.08			
3357	763	*Violet.*	3.93 -	8.4.30	5092	8.27	
3358	764	*Shap.*	3.93 -	1.2.26	(5093)		
3359	819	*Puck.*	3.93 -	10.11			*Renewed Precedent No 514 6.13
3360	742	*Spitfire.*	3.93 -				
Became		*Engineer Liverpool* 7.21 -		3.10.32			
3361	285	*Phalaris.*	3.93 -	10.06			*Precursor No 1297 8.07
3362	418	*Zygia.*	3.93 -	5.08			
3363	124	*Marquis Douro.*	3.93 -	10.28	5090	5.28	
3365	628	*Tartarus.*	4.93 -	29.2.32	5095	4.26	
3366	445	*Ixion.*	4.93 -	1.11			
3367	817	*Constance.*	4.93 -	6.27	(5096)		
3368	609	*The Earl of Chester.*	4.93 -				
Became		*Engineer Walsall* 6.23 -		2.28	(5094)		
3369	739	*Sutherland.*	4.93 -				
Renamed		*Ostrich.* 13.8.13 -		1.23			
3370	636	*Eclipse.*	4.93 -	3.08			*George the Fifth No 404 4.13
3371	935	*Planet.*	4.93 -	2.09			*George the Fifth No 2197 4.13
3372	902	*Onyx.*	4.93 -	9.07			*Prince of Wales No 810 1.16
3373	832	*Sanspareil.*	4.93 -	1.07			*Experiment No 1526 10.07
3374	446	*Siren.*	4.93 -	8.15			
3375	434	*St.Patrick.*	4.93 -	8.21			
3376	805	*Caliban.*	4.93 -	3.09			*Prince of Wales No 2392 12.15
3377	824	*Adelaide.*	6.93 -	9.4.29	5097	7.28	
3378	1162	*Saddleback.*	6.93 -	5.12			*George the Fifth No 845 3.13
3379	2150	*Atlas.*	6.93 -	10.08			*Prince of Wales No 2417 2.16
3380	2153	*Isis.*	6.93 -	11.14			
3381	795	*Falstaff.*	6.93 -	3.14			*Prince of Wales No 2203 11.15
3382	469	*St.George.*	6.93 -	7.07			
3383	486	*Skiddaw.*	6.93 -	4.12.26	(5098)		
3384	792	*Theorem.*	6.93				
Became		*Engineer* 5.23 -		6.32	(5099)		
3441	737	*Roberts*	5.94 -				
Became		*Engineer Lancaster* 2.24 -		7.35	(5100)		
3442	404	*Zopyrus.*	3.94 -	4.13			
3443	2154	*Loadstone.*	3.94 -	3.13			*Prince of Wales No 2175 11.15
3444	2159	*Shark.*	5.94 -	1.08			*Prince of Wales No 1084 1.16
3445	793	*Martin.*	5.94 -		(5101)		
Became		*Engineer Watford* 5.23 -		4.36			
3446	2152	*Sybil.*	6.94 -	2.14			
3447	90	*Luck of Edenhall.*	6.94 -	9.15			
3448	401	*Zeno.*	6.94 -	6.15			
3449	1168	*Cuckoo.*	6.94 -	27.6.31	5102	2.26	
3450	746	*Castor.*	6.94 -	3.08			*Prince of Wales No 606 1.16
3451	263	*Pheasant.*	1.95 -	4.07			*Experiment No 2076 1.09
3452	794	*Woodlark.*	1.95 -	12.9.31	5104	3.27	
3453	2158	**Sister Dora.**	19.11.94 -	9.27	(5105)		
3454	732	*Hecla.*	1.95 -	9.27	(5103)		
3455	2155	*Liver.*	1.95 -	11.10			
3456	2156	*Sphinx.*	2.95 -				*Prince of Wales No 2175 11.15
Became		*Engineer Manchester* 6.14 -		9.27			
3457	852	*Kestrel.*	2.95 -	8.08			*Prince of Wales No 90 12.15
3458	1163	*John O'Gaunt.*	2.95 -	1.12			*Jubilee No 1921 2.13
3459	1164	*Odin.*	2.95 -	3.09			*Prince of Wales No 2442 2.16
3460	995	*Medea.*	2.95 -	4.08			

			Date Built	Date Withdrawn			Subsequent name-holder	
3461	209	*Petrel.*	8.95 -	9.14			*Prince of Wales No 1744	1.16
Became		*Engineer-Crewe*	7.14					
Became		*Engineer South Wales* 1.32	-	8.33				
3462	487	*John O'Groat.*	8.95 -	9.19			*Claughton No 1599	8.22
3463	773	*Centaur.*	7.95 -	12.24	(5106)			
3464	424	*Sirius.*	7.95 -	9.27	(5107)			
3465	2151	*Baltic.*	12.95 -	10.10			*Claughton No 2445	7.23
3466	885	*Vampire.*	1.96 -	3.16				
3467	1166	*Wyre.*	1.96 -	12.27	5108	3.24		
3468	414	*Prospero.*	1.96 -	10.06			*Experiment No 1361	10.07
3469	2157	*Unicorn.*	1.96 -	7.25	(5109)			
3470	631	*Hotspur.*	1.96 -	12.12			*Prince of Wales No 2300	12.15

The final batch of ten, Crewe Numbers *3461-70* received the numbers and names of members of the Samson class as they became available when placed on the Duplicate List prior to becoming "Engineers".

One of the first Compounds built for the L. & N. W. R.

Fig. 35   66 *Experiment* "One of the first Compounds built for the L&NWR".

L&NWR Postcard Set 2 No.6.   (Fred Gray Collection).

EXPERIMENT COMPOUND CLASS 6ft 6in 2-(2-2)-0 30 engines

			Date Built	Date Withdrawn	Subsequent name-holder		
2500	66	*Experiment.*	1.82 -	2.05			
		(Appeared in January 1882 as No 2500)			Experiment No	66	4.05
2625	300	**Compound.**	2.83 -	7.05			
2626	301	**Economist.**	3.83 -	10.04			
2627	302	*Velocipede.*	4.83 -	7.05	*Precursor No	2584	1.06
2628	303	*Hydra.*	4.83 -	1.05	*Precursor No	1617	8.05
2669	305	*Trentham.*	7.83 -	10.04	*Precursor No	2120	5.05

2670	306	*Knowsley.*	7.83 -	7.05
2671	307	**Victor.**	7.83 -	2.05
2672	520	**Express.**	7.83 -	2.05
2673	519	**Shooting Star.**	7.83 -	4.05
2734	311	**Richd Francis Roberts.**	1.84 -	7.05
2735	315	**Alaska.**	2.84 -	7.05
2736	321	**Servia.**	2.84 -	1.05
2737	323	**Britannic.**	2.84 -	3.05
2738	333	**Germanic.**	2.84 -	11.04
2739	353	**Oregon.**	2.84 -	7.05
2740	363	**Aurania.**	2.84 -	2.05
2741	365	**America.**	3.84 -	4.05
2742	366	**City of Chicago.**	3.84 -	5.05
2743	310	**Sarmatian.**	3.84 -	11.04
2744	1102	*Cyclops.*	5.84 -	10.04
2745	1120	*Apollo.*	6.84 -	12.04
2746	1104	*Sunbeam.*	6.84 -	1.05
2747	1113	*Hecate.*	6.84 -	8.04
2748	1111	*Messenger.*	6.84 -	2.05
2749	1115	*Snake.*	7.84 -	3.05
2750	1116	*Friar.*	7.84 -	8.05
2751	1117	*Penguin.*	7.84 -	10.04
2752	372	*Empress.*	7.84 -	6.05
2753	374	*Emperor.*	7.84 -	9.05

*Precursor	No	1114	9.05
*Precursor	No	1430	5.05
*Precursor	No	811	9.05
*Precursor	No	2166	10.05
*Precursor	No	117	10.05
*Precursor	No	2115	11.05
*Experiment	No	353	6.05
*Experiment	No	372	6.05
*Precursor	No	2007	11.05
*Precursor	No	113	7.05
*Precursor	No	1509	7.05
*Experiment	No	507	6.05
*Precursor	No	1545	4.05
*Precursor	No	1115	4.05
*Precursor	No	2062	8.05
*Precursor	No	688	7.05
*Precursor	No	519	5.05
*Precursor	No	127	11.05
*Precursor	No	837	2.06
*Precursor	No	2012	11.05
*Precursor	No	374	9.05
*Precursor	No	311	9.05

One Liverpool & Manchester Railway name was used again:-
Experiment 2-2-0 (Sharp, Roberts & Co.) No 32 2.33 Sold 12.36

Fig. 36   Experiment Compound 1104 *Sunbeam* at Manchester (London Road).

(Allan Sommerfield Collection).

Fig. 37 Dreadnought class 410 *City of Liverpool.*

F. Moore Railway Photographs (Allan Sommerfield Collection).

DREADNOUGHT CLASS 6ft 0in Compound 2-(2-2)-0 40 engines

			Date Built	Date Withdrawn	Subsequent name-holder			
2795	503	*Dreadnought.*	9.84 -	4.04	*Precursor	No	659	6.04
2796	508	*Titan.*	10.84 -	2.04	*Precursor	No	7	6.04
2797	504	*Thunderer.*	2.85 -	8.04	*Precursor	No	1120	1.05
2798	507	*Marchioness of Stafford.*	3.85 -	7.05				
		(Carried No 2798 for the 1885 Inventions Exhibition, South Kensington and awarded a Gold Medal)						
2799	509	*Ajax.*	2.85 -	4.04	*Precursor	No	639	10.04
2800	510	*Leviathan.*	4.85 -	5.04	*Precursor	No	301	11.04
2801	511	*Achilles.*	5.85 -	8.04	*Precursor	No	310	12.04
2802	513	*Mammoth.*	5.85 -	3.04	*Precursor	No	645	1.05
2803	515	*Niagara.*	5.85 -	11.04	*Precursor	No	40	3.05
2804	685	*Himalaya.*	5.85 -	10.04	*Precursor	No	303	1.05
2886	2055	*Dunrobin.*	12.85 -	1.05	*Precursor	No	1573	4.05
2887	2056	*Argus.*	12.85 -	4.04	*Precursor	No	323	2.05
2888	2057	*Euphrates.*	12.85 -	7.04	*Precursor	No	622	12.04
2889	2058	*Medusa.*	12.85 -	2.05	*Precursor	No	355	5.05
2890	2059	*Greyhound.*	12.85 -	2.05	*Precursor	No	302	7.05
2891	2060	*Vandal.*	12.85 -	7.04	*Precursor	No	1117	11.04
2892	2061	*Harpy.*	12.85 -	4.05	*Precursor	No	1396	11.05
2893	2062	*Herald.*	12.85 -	7.05	*Precursor	No	911	9.05
2894	2063	*Huskisson.*	12.85 -	9.04	*Precursor	No	638	12.04
2895	2064	*Autocrat.*	12.85 -	3.05	*Experiment	No	306	6.05
2896	173	*City of Manchester.*	3.86 -	8.04	*Experiment	No	1405	2.06
2897	2	*City of Carlisle.*	3.86 -	6.04	*Experiment	No	565	1.06
2898	1539	*City of Chester.*	6.86		renumbered 437			11.86
	437	*City of Chester.*	11.86 -	7.04	*Experiment	No	893	1.06
2899	410	*City of Liverpool.*	6.86 -	4.04	*Experiment	No	828	2.06
		(Exhibited at the Liverpool Exhibition in 1886)						
2900	1353	*City of Edinburgh.*	6.86 -	7.04	*Experiment	No	1357	1.06
2901	1370	*City of Glasgow.*	6.86 -	1.04	*Experiment	No	1669	1.06
2902	1395	*Archimedes.*	6.86 -	3.04	*Precursor	No	648	10.04
2903	1379	*Stork.*	6.86 -	2.05	*Precursor	No	229	11.05

2904	545	*Tamerlane.*	7.86 - 12.03			*Precursor	No	1419	3.04
2905	659	*Rowland Hill.*	7.86 - 5.04			*Precursor	No	2582	12.05
3012	637	**City of New York.**	3.88 - 8.04						
013	638	**City of Paris.**	4.88 - 11.04			*Experiment	No	1575	2.06
3014	639	**City of London.**	5.88 - 10.04			*Experiment	No	978	2.06
3015	640	**City of Dublin.**	5.88 - 1.04			*Experiment	No	1074	1.06
3016	641	**City of Lichfield.**	5.88 - 2.04			*Experiment	No	165	2.06
3017	643	*Raven.*	5.88 - 10.04						
3018	644	*Vesuvius.*	6.88 - 7.04			*Precursor	No	1137	2.05
3019	645	*Alchymist.*	6.88 - 1.05						
3020	647	*Ambassador.*	6.88 - 4.04						
3021	648	*Swiftsure.*	6.88 - 10.04			*Precursor	No	806	1.05

Five Liverpool & Manchester Railway names were re-used:-

Titan   0-4-0 (Tayleur & Co.) No 34 1834 Withdrawn 1840-1
Thunderer 0-4-2 (Mather, Dixon & Co.) No 44 2.36 Withdrawn 1842-4
Ajax   2-2-0 (Robert Stephenson & Co.) No 29 11.32 Withdrawn 1840-1
Vesuvius   2-2-2 (Haigh Foundry) No 43 2.36 Renumbered 54 To L&NWR 7.47 and scrapped
Swiftsure 2-2-0 (E.Forrester & Co.) No 36 10.34 Withdrawn 1842-4

Fig. 38   Teutonic class 1303 *Pacific.* (The one alleged to have been built experimentally as a triple compound engine, but not known to have been in service as such).

(John Ward Collection).

TEUTONIC CLASS 6ft 10in Compound 2-(2-2)-0 10 engines

			Date Built	Date Withdrawn		Subsequent name-holder			
3102	1301	**Teutonic.**	3.89 -	10.05		*Precursor	No	2583	1.06
3103	1302	**Oceanic.**	5.89 -	1.07		*Precursor	No	807	8.07
3104	1303	**Pacific.**	6.89 -	1.07		*Precursor	No	976	8.07
3105	1304	**Jeanie Deans.**	3.90 -	9.06		*Experiment	No	2161	10.07

(Exhibited carrying No 3105 at the Edinburgh "International Exposition of Electrical Engineering, General Invention and Industries" - opened 1.5.1890)

3106	1305	**Doric.**	5.90 -	6.06		*Precursor	No	276	7.07
3107	1306	**Ionic.**	6.90 -	12.05		*Precursor	No	1312	2.06
3108	1307	**Coptic.**	6.90 -	12.05		*Precursor	No	723	2.06
3109	1309	**Adriatic.**	6.90 -	7.07		*Experiment	No	322	12.08
3110	1311	**Celtic.**	6.90 -	3.06		*Precursor	No	754	7.07
3111	1312	**Gaelic.**	6.90 -	3.06		*Precursor	No	802	7.07

Fig. 39   Greater Britain class 2054 *Queen Empress*. Note also the engraved plate on the tender.

Fig. 40   Drawing of the engraved plate on the tender of 2054 *Queen Empress*.

GREATER BRITAIN CLASS 6ft 10in Compound 2-(2-2)-2 10 engines

			Date Built	Date Withdrawn		Subsequent Name-holder		
3292	2525	*Greater Britain.*	10.91	Renumbered		2053		15.12.91
		(Carried No 3292 for a short while after completion)						
	2053	*Greater Britain*	15.12.91 -	7.07		*Experiment	No 884	12.08
3435	2054	*Queen Empress.*	5.93 -	9.06		*Experiment	No 2027	11.06
		(Exhibited at The World's Fair in Chicago in 1893 carrying No 3435, and awarded a Gold Medal.)						
3472	2051	*George Findlay.*	4.94 -	7.07		*Experiment	No 1406	4.09
3473	2052	*Prince George.*	5.94 -	9.06		*Experiment	No 1135	9.07
3474	525	*Princess May.*	5.94 -	9.06		*Experiment	No 1709	11.06
3475	526	*Scottish Chief.*	5.94 -	3.06		*Experiment	No 1994	10.06
3476	527	*Henry Bessemer.*	5.94 -	1.07		*Experiment	No 1014	9.07
3477	528	*Richard Moon.*	5.94 -	3.06		*Experiment	No 1993	10.06
3478	767	*William Cawkwell.*	5.94 -	9.06		*Experiment	No 2269	12.06
3479	772	*Richard Trevithick.*	5.94 -	4.06		*Precursor	No 1650	5.06

JOHN HICK CLASS 6ft 0in Compound 2-(2-2)-2 10 engines

			Date Built	Date Withdrawn		Subsequent name-holder		
3505	20	*John Hick*	2.94 -	4.10		*George the Fifth	No 752	2.13
3858	1505	*Richard Arkwright.*	1.98 -	5.12		*George the Fifth	No 2282	2.13
3859	1512	*Henry Cort.*	2.98 -	10.07		*Experiment	No 1413	4.09
3860	1534	*William Froude.*	2.98 -	12.09		*George the Fifth	No 1138	2.13
3861	1535	*Henry Maudslay.*	2.98 -	8.10		*George the Fifth	No 2168	1.11
3862	1536	*Hugh Myddleton.*	3.98 -	2.09		*Experiment	No 1477	5.09
3863	1548	*John Penn.*	3.98 -	3.09		*Experiment	No 1566	5.09
3864	1549	*John Rennie.*	3.98 -	8.09		*George the Fifth	No 2124	2.13
3865	1557	*Thomas Savery.*	3.98 -	3.09		*Experiment	No 1498	5.09
3866	1559	*William Siemens.*	4.98 -	10.10		*George the Fifth	No 2154	2.13

Fig. 41   Special Tank 3186 *Euston.*

(Allan Sommerfield Collection).

SPECIAL TANK 4ft 3in 0-6-0T (Condensers and Square Tanks)

1960 528 *Euston*   Built 12.75 (No 3186 5.94) Named 6.95 (Allotted LMS No 7335) Scrapped 7.28

1961 50 *Liverpool* Built 1.76 (No 3021 5.93) Named 6.95 LMS No 7334 8.27, 27334 1938 Withdrawn 3.39

The term "Special Tank" was the official designation for the class, used by Ramsbottom in 1869 when he was reporting to the Locomotive Committee, the engines being specially designed for traffic in the Central Wales area, and the first batch being ordered as such.

TRIPLEX 6ft 0in Triple Compound 2-4-0

(3088) **Triplex.**   8.95 - 10.03 (Ex 54 *Medusa*)

JUBILEE CLASS 7ft 1in Compound 4-4-0 40 engines

Fig. 42 1501 *Jubilee* Photographed between December 1897 when it was renamed, and March 1899, when it was renumbered 1901.

Locomotive & General 2288 (Allan Sommerfield Collection).

			Built	Withdrawn	Dates Cut up	Converted to RENOWN	LMS Number	Date Applied
3856	1501	*Iron Duke.*	6.97 -					
		Renamed *Jubilee.*12.97						
		Renumbered 1901	3.99 -	12.31a	10.12.31	4.19	5156	3.28
3857	1502	*Black Prince.*	6.97 -					
		Renumbered 1902	3.99 -	21.6.30	22.8.30	8.19	5157	1.28
3928	1903	*Iron Duke.*	3.99 -	7.11.31	19.11.31	5.24	5110	6.26
3929	1904	*Rob Roy.*	3.99 -	5.23			(5111)	
3930	1905	*Black Diamond.*	3.99 -	20.11.30	27.11.30	8.14	5137	8.27
3931	1906	*Robin Hood.*	4.99 -	10.12.31	17.12.31	5.17	5149	2.27
3932	1907	*Black Watch.*	4.99 -	25.6.26	29.6.26	2.22	(5178)	
3933	1908	*Royal George.*	4.99 -	1.23				
3934	1909	*Crusader.*	4.99 -	4.28	?	11.19	(5159)	
3935	1910	*Cavalier.*	4.99 -	4.4.31		8.21	5172	10.26
3936	1911	*Centurion.*	6.99 -	5.12.31b	9.12.31	12.24	5112	2.28
3937	1912	*Colossus.*	6.99 -	22.11.29	19.12.29	5.24	5113	6.26
3938	1913	*Canopus.*	6.99 -	9.28	24.9.28	3.10	(5132)	
3939	1914	*Invincible.*	6.99	9.16				
		Renumbered 1257	4.20 -	27.10.31	5.1.32		5144	9.27
3940	1915	*Implacable.*	7.99 -	1.7.28	13.7.28	11.23	5114	7.26
3941	1916	*Irresistible.*	7.99 -	4.10.30	31.10.30	2.19	5155	1.28
3942	1917	*Inflexible.*	7.99 -	10.12.31	16.12.31	8.22	5184	7.27
3943	1918	*Renown.*	7.99 -	8.28	30.8.28	6.08	5131	4.26
3944	1919	*Resolution.*	8.99 -	21.12.28	21.12.28	11.19	5160	6.27
3945	1920	*Flying Fox.*	8.99 -	20.12.30	?	12.20	5166	8.28
3995	1921	*T.H.Ismay.*	2.00 -					
		Renamed *John o Gaunt* 2.13	-	23.7.26	23.7.26	4.13	(5134)	
3996	1922	*Intrepid.*	2.00 -	12.27	?	10.16	5146)	
3997	1923	*Agamemnon.*	3.00 -	14.3.25	14.3.25	-	(5115)	
3998	1924	*Powerful.*	3.00 -	8.12.31	18.12.31	6.22	5183	6.28
3999	1925	*Warrior.*	3.00 -	28.2.28	28.2.28	4.17	(5147)	
4000	1926	*La France.*	3.00 -	12.31c	8.12.31	3.22	5180	1.27
		(Exhibited carrying No 4000 at the Paris Universal Exposition, Parc de Vincennes, Summer 1900, and awarded a Gold Medal)						
4001	1927	*Goliath.*	3.00 -	10.12.31	23.12.31	1.24	5116	11.26
4002	1928	*Glatton.*	4.00 -	19.12.31	22.12.31	8.21	5173	7.27
4003	1929	*Polyphemus.*	4.00 -	5.12.30	5.12.30	2.24	5117	5.28
4004	1930	*Ramillies.*	4.00 -	20.11.30	25.11.30	4.16	5142	10.26
4045	1931	*Agincourt.*	9.00 -	13.6.30	24.7.30	12.21	5176	4.26
4046	1932	*Anson.*	9.00 -	4.25	4.25	6.20	(5162)	
4047	1933	*Barfleur.*	9.00 -	31.1.28	31.1.28	4.21	(5169)	
4048	1934	*Blenheim.*	9.00 -	19.12.31	23.12.31	9.20	5165	7.27
4049	1935	*Collingwood.*	10.00 -	28.11.29	5.12.29	3.10	5133	10.27
4050	1936	*Royal Sovereign.*	10.00 -	17.6.25	17.6.25	6.17	(5150)	
4051	1937	*Superb.*	10.00 -	10.28	15.11.28	1.19	5154	11.27
4052	1938	*Sultan.*	10.00 -	10.28	5.12.28	2.20	5161	11.27
4053	1939	*Temeraire.*	10.00 -	10.28	5.11.28	8.19	5158	8.27
4054	1940	*Trafalgar.*	10.00 -	23.11.29	19.12.29	4.21	5170	9.28

a. Out of Stock 12.20 - 11.31   b. Out of Stock 12.30 - 9.31   c. Out of Stock 12.30 - 12.31

Fig. 43   1901 *Jubilee.*

L&NWR Society Photograph Collection No B63.

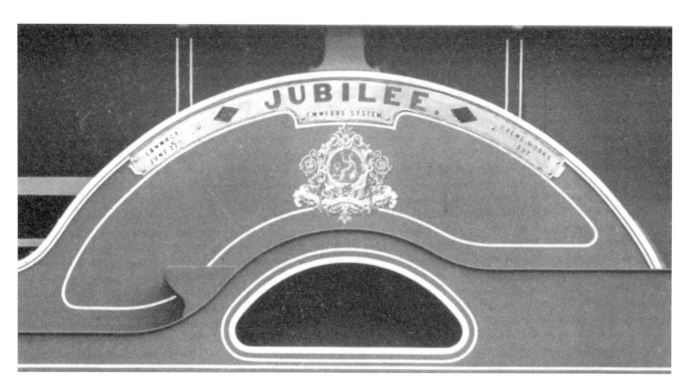

Fig. 44   The nameplate of *Jubilee.* Note the red diamonds, and the date June 22 1897. The normal practice was to place only the month contracted to three letters, and the year.

L&NWR Society Photograph Collection No. B63.

Fig. 45   Jubilee class 1914 *Invincible* on Scotch Express in Rugby Station. "The Royal Mail Route".

L&NWR Postcard Set 5 "Trains in Motion" No.5. (Fred Gray Collection).

Fig. 46   Reown class 1257 *Invincible* at Manchester London Road, near the turntable and under the water tower. Note the water gauge above the dome.

(Allan Sommerfield Collection).

Fig. 49   1941 *Alfred the Great,* described on the card as the Type of Engine used to convey Royalty.

L&NWR Postcard Set 8 "Modern Locomotives" No.4. (Fred Gray Collection).

ALFRED THE GREAT CLASS 7ft 1in 4-4-0 40 engines

Date			Built	Withdrawn	Cut up	BENBOW	RENOWN	Number	applied
			Dates			**Converted to**		**LMS**	
4125	1941	*Alfred the Great.*	5.01-	15.8.31	11.9.31	9.04	2.22	5179	9.27
4126	1942	*King Edward VII.*	5.01-	18.2.30	11.3.30	6.05	9.22	5185	9.26
4127	1943	*Queen Alexandra.*	6.01-	11.28	8.11.28	10.05	9.16	5145	11.26
4128	1944	*Victoria and Albert.*	6.01-	21.2.27	21.2.27	11.04		(5118)	
4129	1945	*Magnificent.*	6.01-	14.6.30	30.7.30	2.05	9.15	5139	5.27
4130	1946	*Diadem.*	6.01-	0.12.31	17.12.31	3.07	10.14	5138	9.28
4131	1947	*Australia.*	6.01-	6.11					
		Renamed *Zillah.* 6.11	-	7.10.25	7.10.25	1.05	9.21	(5174)	
4132	1948	*Camperdown.*	6.01-	13.8.30	29.8.30	7.05	10.15	5141	10.26

4133	1949	King Arthur.	6.01-	3.5.30	20.5.30	2.07	1.18	5152	1.28
4134	1950	Victorious.	6.01-	15.12.31	15.12.31	12.04	10.22	5186	10.27
4195	1951	Bacchante.	1.02-	4.25	4.25	3.04	10.13	(5136)	
4196	1952	Benbow.	1.02-	2.28	28.2.28	9.03	11.23	(5119)	
4197	1953	Formidable.	2.02-	11.28	27.11.28	11.07	12.23	5120	12.26
4198	1954	Galatea.	2.02-	27.6.30	12.8.30	4.04	10.24	5121	3.28
4199	1955	Hannibal.	2.02-	8.23		3.05		(5122)	
4200	1956	Illustrious.	2.02-	1.23		3.04			
4201	1957	Orion.	3.02-	1.28	3.2.28	6.04	4.17	5148	9.26
4202	1958	Royal Oak.	3.02-	10.28	30.10.28	11.05	4.22	5181	10.26
4203	1959	Revenge.	3.02-	25.1.30	22.2.30	8.04	4.16	5143	10.27
4204	1960	Francis Stevenson.	3.02-	11.28	12.12.28	4.04	2.18	5153	10.26
4285	1961	Albemarle.	2.03-	11.28	8.12.28	8.07	9.15	5140	11.27
4286	1962	Aurora.	2.03-	18.3.26	18.3.26	9.07	6.21	(5171)	
4287	1963	Boadicea.	2.03-	12.28	4.12.28	9.04	6.20	5163	11.26
4288	1964	Cæsar.	2.03-	3.11.29	12.12.29	12.04	9.24	5123	10.26
4289	1965	Charles H.Mason.	2.03-	17.6.25	17.6.25	6.04	8.17	(5151)	
4290	1966	Commonwealth.	2.03-	1.4.25	1.4.25	8.04		(5124)	
4291	1967	Cressy.	3.03-	2.28	18.2.28	4.04	12.23	(5125)	
4292	1968	Cumberland.	3.03-	10.28	28.9.28	10.04	6.20	5164	1.27
4293	1969	Dominion.	3.03-	9.4.30	15.4.30	10.04	4.24	5126	3.27
4294	1970	Good Hope.	3.03-	11.27	30.11.27	5.05	4.24	5127	4.26
4335	1971	Euryalus.	7.03-	8.11.30	3.12.30	9.05	4.13	5135	10.27
4336	1972	Hindostan.	7.03-	3.4.25	3.4.25	3.07	3.21	(5168)	
4337	1973	Hood.	7.03-	22.7.26	22.7.26	4.07	9.21	(5175)	
4338	1974	Howe.	7.03-	12.3.28		5.05		(5128)	
4339	1975	Jupiter.	8.03-	12.28	28.11.28	8.05	1.21	5167	11.27
4340	1976	Lady Godiva.	8.03-	12.22		9.06			
4341	1977	Mars.	8.03-	7.12.30	7.1.31	8.05	2.24	5129	6.27
4342	1978	Merlin.	8.03-	7.5.30	4.6.30	12.06	12.21	5177	8.27
4343	1979	Nelson.	8.03-	8.23		1.07		(5130)	
4344	1980	Neptune.	8.03-	8.12.31	18.12.31	11.05	5.22	5182	6.26

1961 was named *Albermarle* "for a few weeks when new".

Three Liverpool & Manchester Railway names were used again:-

Orion 0-4-0 (Tayleur & Co.) No 35 Built 1834 Withdrawn 1840-1

Jupiter 2-2-0 (R.Stephenson & Co.) No 14 2.Built 1831 'Done with' 4.1833

Mars 2-2-0 (R.Stephenson & Co.) No 12 Built 1.1831 Sold 9.1839

Two names were used again, almost immediately

   Illustrious   *Claughton No 150 5.23 - 2.33

   Lady Godiva   *Claughton No 110 5.23 - 12.32

L&NWR 1921 LMS (5134) was named *John O Gaunt*, and the nameplates did not include either the apostrophe or the full stop.

TABLE 10
GEORGE WHALE
Appointed May 1903 - Retired End of 1908

WHALE PRECURSOR CLASS 6ft 6in 4-4-0

Fig. 50   513 *Precursor*

L&NWR Postcard Set 8 "Modern Locomotives" No.4. (Fred Gray Collection).

Every locomotive in the class was in the first instance given an old name

			Period the name was applied		First LMS Number	Date	Second LMS Number	Date
			Built	Withdrawn				
4415	513	*Precursor.*	3.04 -	4.7.36	5278	5.27		
4416	1395	*Harbinger.*	3.04 -	26.6.37	5291	3.27	25291	11.36
4417	1419	*Tamerlane.*	3.04 -	14.3.36	5285	8.26		
4418	2023	*Helvellyn.*	4.04 -	28.3.36	5187	6.26	25187	11.34
4419	2164	*Oberon.*	4.04 -	17.8.46	5277	11.27	25277	8.36
4440	2	*Simoom.*	6.04 -	24.10.36	5308	10.27		
4441	7	*Titan.*	6.04 -	2.11.35	5276	4.28		

Fig. 51 Precursor class 412 *Alfred Paget,* photographed between June and November 1904, before being renamed *Marquis.*
A rare photograph, possibly a snapshot.

(Allan Sommerfield Collection).

4442	*412*	*Alfred Paget.*	6.04 -						
Renamed		*Marquis*	11.04 -	6.4.40	5188	4.26	25188	11.34	
4443	*510*	*Albatross.*	6.04 -	29.7.33	5189	7.28			
4444	*659*	*Dreadnought.*	6.04 -	9.5.36	5296	6.24			
4445	*639*	*Ajax.*	10.04 -	9.9.28	5190	11.26			
4446	*648*	*Archimedes.*	10.04 -	1.28	5191	2.27			
4447	*685*	*Cossack.*	10.04 -	18.4.32	5192	11.26			
4448	*60*	*Dragon.*	10.04 -	5.11.38	5298	4.27	25298	8.36	
4449	*106*	*Druid.*	10.04 -	1.5.37	5294	1.28	25294	12.36	
4450	*301*	*Leviathan.*	11.04 -	2.5.36	5289	9.27			
4451	*305*	*Senator.*	11.04 -	30.1.37	5307	4.28	25307	1.37	
445	*2643*	*Sirocco.*	11.04 -	11.6.49	5297	11.27	25297	12.36	
							(58010) B.R.		
4453	*1102*	*Thunderbolt.*	11.04 -	15.8.31	5193	11.26			
4454	*1117*	*Vandal.*	11.04 -	31.10.31	5194	2.26			
4455	*310*	*Achilles.*	12.04 -	10.10.36	5290	6.24			
445	*6333*	*Ambassador.*	12.04 -	22.8.36	5284	6.24	25284	8.36	
Renumbered 25284 11.8.36 at Rugby Works, shortly before withdrawal									
4457	*515*	*Champion.*	12.04 -	23.12.39	5282	11.27	25282	5.36	
4458	*622*	*Euphrates.*	12.04 -	12.27	(5195)				
4459	*638*	*Huskisson.*	12.04 -	15.4.33	5196	7.27			
4460	*303*	*Himalaya.*	1.05 -	1.2.36	5305	5.28			
4461	*645*	*Mammoth.*	1.05 -	8.11.30	5197	5.27			

4462	806	Swiftsure.	1.05 - 2.11.35	5318	5.26		

(Renumbered 5318 temporarily in March 1924)

4463	1120	Thunderer.	1.05 - 29.7.39	5310	6.26	25310	7.36

Name removed 9.36 to end duplication with LMS Jubilee 5703 named 6.5.36

4464	1137	Vesuvius.	2.05 - 29.8.36	5299	4.27	25299	4.36
4465	323	Argus.	2.05 - 24.10.36	5303	2.27		
4466	1104	Cedric.	2.05 - 12.33a	5199	8.28		
4467	1111	Cerberus.	3.05 - 6.10.34	5200	2.26		
4468	1431	Egeria.	3.05 - 18.11.30	5201	11.26		
4469	2064	Jason.	3.05 - 25.7.31	5273	6.24		
4470	40	Niagara.	3.05 - 15.11.30	5198	1.28		
4471	520	Panopea.	3.05 - 20.1.34	5202	8.27		
4472	1469	Tantalus.	3.05 - 20.3.37	5288	2.27	25288	11.36
4473	1737	Viscount.	3.05 - 1.8.36	5316	3.27		
4474	2031	Waverley.	3.05 - 21.11.31	5203	4.27		
4475	365	Alchymist.	4.05 - 5.6.37	5287	12.27	25287	4.36
4476	1115	Apollo.	4.05 - 2.28	5205	6.26		
4477	1545	Cyclops.	4.05 - 26.4.32	5206	10.27		
4478	1573	Dunrobin.	4.05 - 11.9.37	5286	4.26	25286	4.36
4479	2061	Eglinton.	4.05 - 8.8.36	5207	8.27	25207	11.34
4480	184	Havelock.	5.05 - 5.9.31	5204	6.27		
4481	366	Medusa.	5.05 - 14.4.45	5292	7.26	25292	12.36
4482	519	Messenger.	5.05 - 7.11.31	5208	10.27		
4483	2120	Trentham.	5.05 - 10.27	(5209)			
4484	1430	Victor.	5.05 - 26.9.31	5210	9.27		
4485	113	Aurania.	7.05 - 19.9.36	5211	11.27	25211	11.34
4486	300	Emerald.	7.05 - 2.11.35	5301	2.28		
4487	302	Greyhound.	7.05 - 25.1.47	5304	1.27	25304	8.36
4488	315	Harrowby.	7.05 - 31.12.36	5212	2.27	25212	11.34
4489	688	Hecate.	7.05 - 2.11.35	5274	6.27		
4490	1509	America.	7.05 - 1.3.28	5214	5.26		
4491	1617	Hydra.	8.05 - 13.7.40	5300	1.28	25300	12.36
4492	1723	Scorpion.	8.05 - 28.11.36	5295	5.27		
4493	2062	Sunbeam.	8.05 - 29.7.39	5279	10.27	25279	5.36
4494	2257	Vulture.	8.05 - 23.12.33	5215	2.27		
4495	311	Emperor.	9.05 - 29.4.33	5213	9.27		
4496	374	Empress.	9.05 - 6.6.36	5317	9.27		
4497	811	Express.	9.05 - 1.3.41	5311	11.27	25311	12.36

Name removed 9.36 to end duplication with LMS Jubilee 5706 named 26.5.36

4498	911	Herald.	9.05 - 8.2.36	5216	9.27	25216	11.34
4499	1114	Knowsley.	9.05 - 11.2.33	5217	11.26		
4500	1116	Pandora.	9.05 - 25.4.36	5218	2.26	25218	11.34
4501	1510	Psyche.	9.05 - 17.12.30	5219	10.27		
4502	1784	Python.	10.05 - 7.11.31	5220	10.27		
4503	2166	Shooting Star.	10.05 - 16.11.35	5280	5.27		
4504	2202	Vizier.	10.05 - 17.12.30	5221	6.27		
4510	117	Alaska.	10.05 - 2.9.33	5222	10.27		
4511	1301	Candidate.	10.05 - 7.11.36	5225	10.27	25225	5.36
4512	1363	Cornwall.	10.05 -				
Renamed		Brindley.	5.11 - 30.12.39	5272	8.27	25272	9.36
4513	1396	Harpy.	11.05 - 8.11.30	5226	12.27		
4514	2007	Oregon.	11.05 - 10.27	(5227)			
4515	2012	Penguin.	11.05 - 10.10.31	5228	5.28		
4516	2115	Servia.	11.05 - 16.4.32	5229	5.27		
4517	127	Snake.	11.05 - 28.11.36	5223	4.28	25223	11.34
4518	229	Stork.	11.05 - 11.27	(5224)			
4519	1439	Tiger.	11.05 - 14.1.33	5275	6.24		
4520	2576	Arab.	12.05 - 6.9.33	5230	10.26		

Numbered 1307 until 1.06

4521	2577	*Etna.*	12.05 -	8.2.36	5313	8.27		

Numbered 2287 until 1.06

4522	2578	*Fame.*	12.05 -	8.8.36	5309	6.24		
4523	2579	*Ganymede.*	12.05 -	8.2.36	5231	6.27		
4524	2580	*Problem.*	12.05 -	21.11.31	5232	5.28		
4525	2581	*Peel.*	12.05 -	21.7.34	5233	11.26		
4526	2582	*Rowland Hill.*	12.05 -	12.28	5234	12.26		
4527	2583	*Teutonic.*	1.06 -					
Renamed		**The Tsar.**	11.14 -					
Renamed		**Moonstone.**	12.15 -	13.4.35	5235	4.28		
4528	2584	*Velocipede.*	1.06 -	31.12.35	5312	5.27		

Name removed 7.33 to end duplication with Royal Scot 6148 named by 4.28

4529	2585	*Watt.*	1.06 -	30.12.33	5236	9.27		
4530	723	*Coptic.*	2.06 -	4.1.36	5239	1.28		
4531	837	*Friar.*	2.06 -	13.9.33	5240	12.27		
4532	1312	*Ionic.*	2.06 -	11.11.30	5242	3.27		
4533	1387	*Lang Meg.*	3.06 -	8.2.36	5306	4.28		
4534	1642	*Lapwing.*	3.06 -	9.11.35	5243	1.28		
4535	2513	*Levens*	3.06 -	3.6.39	5293	7.26	25293	
4536	234	*Pearl.*	3.06 -	20.2.32	5237	12.27		
4537	526	*Ilion.*	3.06 -	12.28	5238	12.26		
4538	1311	*Napoleon.*	3.06 -	1.2.36	5241	8.28		
4539	2017	*Tubal.*	3.06 -	9.11.35	5244	11.26		
4540	282	*Alaric.*	4.06 -	9.11.35	5314	2.28		
4541	561	*Antæus.*	4.06 -	22.3.41	5245	1.27	25245	5.36

Antaeus. The nameplate at first was spelt without a diphthong

4542	675	*Adjutant.*	4.06 -	8.2.36	5246	6.26		
4543	772	*Admiral.*	4.06 -	10.27	(5247)			
4544	804	*Amphion.*	4.06 -	2.11.35	5248	6.27		
4545	990	*Bucephalus.*	4.06 -	7.12.40	5319	7.27	25319	5.36
4546	988	*Bellerophon.*	4.06 -	3.6.33	5249	9.26		
4547	1433	*Faerie Queene.*	4.06 -	1.2.36	5250	6.27		
4548	1650	*Richard Trevithick.*	5.06 -	2.28	(5251)			
4549	1787	*Hyperion.*	5.06 -	18.12.30	5252	2.27		
4660	1	*Clive.*	6.07 -	8.11.30	5253	8.28		
4661	218	*Daphne.*	6.07 -	29.7.33	5254	11.26		
4662	419	*Monarch.*	6.07 -	20.12.30	5255	5.28		
4663	564	*Erebus.*	6.07 -	12.9.36	5281	9.27		
4664	665	*Mersey.*	6.07 -	10.27	(5256)			
4665	469	*Marmion.*	6.07 -	9.5.36	5270	8.26		

(Renumbered 25270 prematurely in 1934 for a short while until 21st April.)

4666	1011	*Locke.*	7.07 -	21.1.33	5257	11.27		
4667	1364	*Clyde.*	7.07 -	22.11.30	5258	10.26		
4668	2053	*Edith.*	7.07 -	10.3.34	5259	11.27		
4669	2181	*Eleanor.*	7.07 -	9.12.33	5260	1.28		
4670	276	*Doric.*	7.07 -	11.27	5261	12.26		
4671	754	*Celtic.*	7.07 -	23.12.30	5262	8.27		
4672	802	*Gaelic.*	7.07 -	14.11.33	5271	7.27		
4673	807	*Oceanic.*	8.07 -	2.12.32	5263	11.26		
4674	976	*Pacific.*	8.07 -	12.28	5264	11.26		
4675	1297	*Phalaris.*	8.07 -	24.10.31	5265	5.27		
4676	1309	*Shamrock.*	8.07 -	2.5.37	5302	4.28	25302	8.36
4677	1516	*Alecto.*	8.07 -	24.10.31	5266	5.28		
4678	2011	*Brougham.*	8.07 -	14.3.36	5283	8.27		
4679	2051	*Delamere.*	8.07 -	5.9.36	5315	4.26		

a 1104 *Cedric* Out of Stock   12.30 - 7.31

5278   *Precursor.* had the date of rebuilding (Feb 1913) stamped in its nameplates; as far as is known none of the others did.

5235   *Moonstone.* was the last of the original unaltered Precursors to be scrapped.

25188 emerged from Crewe Works in the autumn of 1937 bearing the name *Antæus.* the name which properly belonged to 25245. It is known that 25245 was in service nameless in November that year, and that the correct plates were restored by February 1938. It is uncertain if 25245 ever carried the name *Marquis.*

EXPERIMENT CLASS 6ft 0in 4-6-0

			Period the name was applied		First LMS Number	Date	Second LMS Number	Date
			Built	Withdrawn				
4505	66	Experiment	4.05 -	27.6.31	5450	6.26		
4506	306	Autocrat	6.05 -	13.12.30	5451	7.27		
4507	353	Britannic	6.05 -	20.12.30	5452	2.27		
4508	372	Germanic	6.05 -					
Renamed		*Belgic*	10.14 -	9.28	5453	11.26		
4509	507	Sarmatian	6.05 -	20.8.32	5454	6.26		
4550	565	City of Carlisle	1.06 -	6.25	(5455)			
4551	893	City of Chester	1.06 -	31.8.35	5456	2.28	25456	4.34
4552	1074	City of Dublin	1.06 -	29.9.34	5457	2.28	(25457)	
4553	1357	City of Edinburgh	1.06 -	9.12.33	5458	8.27		
4554	1669	City of Glasgow	1.06 -	20.12.30	5464	9.26		
4555	165	City of Lichfield	2.06 -	13.12.30	5459	6.26		
4556	828	City of Liverpool	2.06 -	27.10.34	5460	5.27	(25460)	
4557	978	City of London	2.06 -	12.5.34	5461	9.27	(25461)	
4558	1405	City of Manchester	2.06 -	10.11.34	5462	5.26	(25462)	
4559	1575	City of Paris	2.06 -	10.28	5463	7.27		
4620	1986	Clanricarde	9.06 -	10.25	(5465)			
4621	1987	Glendower	9.06 -	1.12.34	5466	6.26	(25466)	
4622	1988	Hurricane	9.06 -	9.28	5467	2.27		
4623	1989	Lady of the Lake	10.06 -	7.12.29	5468	4.27		

Name removed 12.28 to end duplication with Royal Scot No 6149 named by 4.28

			Period the name was applied		First LMS Number	Date	Second LMS Number	Date
4624	1990	North Western	10.06 -	19.3.32	5469	4.26		
4625	1991	Palmerston	10.06 -	2.28	5470	6.27		
4626	1992	President	10.06 -	30.12.33	5471	8.26		
4627	1993	Richard Moon	10.06 -	9.12.33	5472	12.26		
4628	1994	Scottish Chief	10.06 -	19.9.35 *	5473	4.26	25473	6.34
4629	1995	Tornado	10.06 -	28.9.25	(5481)			
4630	61	Atalanta	11.06 -	30.12.33	5474	11.27		
4631	222	Ivanhoe	11.06 -	22.6.35	5475	6.27	(25475)	
4632	291	Leander	11.06 -	22.8.31	5476	9.27		
4633	667	Mazeppa	11.06 -	30.12.33	5477	4.27		
4634	1304	Prometheus	11.06 -	16.5.31	5478	3.27		
4635	1676	Prince of Wales	11.06 -					
Renamed		Shakespeare	7.11 -	11.34 *	5479	9.27	(25479)	
4636	1709	Princess May	11.06 -	23.2.28	5480	4.27		
4637	2027	Queen Empress	11.06 -	10.10.31	5482	1.28		
4638	2052	Stephenson	12.06 -	18.12.30	5483	8.26		
4639	2269	William Cawkwell	12.06 -	25.7.31	5484	8.26		
4680	496	Harlequin	9.07 -	2.8.30	5485	11.26		
4681	830	Phosphorus	9.07 -	30.7.25	(5486)			
4682	902	Combermere	9.07 -	20.10.34	5487	2.27	(25487)	
4683	937	Princess Alice	9.07 -	24.3.34	5488	7.26	(25488)	
4684	2112	Victoria	9.07 -	20.12.30	5490	2.27		
4685	1014	Henry Bessemer	9.07 -	19.3.28	5489	10.26		
4686	1135	Prince George	9.07 -	9.6.34	5491	3.27	(25491)	
4687	1361	Prospero	10.07 -	9.6.33 *	5554	2.27		
4688	1526	Sanspareil	10.07 -	11.28	5492	11.26		
4689	2161	Jeanie Deans	10.07 -	8.25	(5493)			
4770	322	Adriatic	12.08 -	21.5.29	5494	6.27		
4771	884	Greater Britain	12.08 -	23.12.30	5495	1.28		
4772	887	Fortuna	1.09 -	19.3.32	5496	1.28		
4773	1020	Majestic	1.09 -	17.11.34	5497	9.27	(25497)	
4774	1483	Red Gauntlet	1.09 -	30.12.33	5498	6.27		
4775	1490	Wellington	1.09 -	30.12.33	5499	12.27		
4776	1553	Faraday	1.09 -	26.3.31	5500	6.27		
4777	1571	Herschel	1.09 -	23.1.29	5501	4.26		
4778	2076	Pheasant	1.09 -	27.10.34	5502	12.26	25502	5.34
4779	2116	Greystoke	1.09 -	31.7.25	(5503)			
4780	2621	Ethelred	2.09 -	10.11.34	5504	5.27	25504	5.34
4781	2622	Eunomia	2.09 -	4.28	5505	8.26		

4782	2623	*Lord of the Isles*	2.09 -	24.3.34	5506	10.26	(25506)	
4783	2624	*Saracen*	2.09 -	2.28	(5507)			
4784	2625	*Buckland*	2.09 -	7.9.35	5508	5.27	25508	4.34
4785	2626	*Chillington*	2.09 -	4.5.35	5509	2.27	25509	4.34
4786	2627	*President Lincoln*	3.09 -	17.5.28	5510	4.26		
4787	2628	*Banshee*	3.09 -	22.6.35	5511	8.27	25511	4.34
4788	2629	*Terrier*	3.09 -	2.28	5512	7.26		
4789	2630	*Buffalo*	3.09 -	19.3.32	5513	7.27		
4830	1406	*George Findlay*	4.09 -	17.8.35	5514	6.27	25514	4.34
4831	1413	*Henry Cort*	4.09 -	15.9.25	(5515)			
4832	1477	*Hugh Myddleton*	5.09 -	4.28	5516	7.26		
4833	1498	*Thomas Savery*	5.09 -	23.9.25	(5517)			
4834	1566	*John Penn*	5.09 -	30.12.33	5518	11.26		
4835	1603	*Princess Alexandra*	5.09 -	17.12.30	5519	3.27		
4836	1649	*Sisyphus*	5.09 -	20.8.32	5520	6.27		
4837	1661	*Wordsworth*	5.09 -	6.28	5521	12.26		
4838	1781	*Lightning*	5.09 -	2.5.30	5522	7.27		
4839	2022	*Marlborough*	5.09 -	14.4.34	5523	6.27	(25523)	
4840	2637	**Babylon**	6.09 -	3.1.32	5524	2.27		
4841	2638	**Byzantium**	6.09 -	16.6.34	5525	2.27	25525	5.34
4842	2639	**Bactria**	6.09 -	21.4.34	5526	6.27	(25526)	
4843	2640	**Belisarius**	6.09 -	9.25	(5527)			
4844	2641	**Bellona**	6.09 -	24.8.35	5528	1.28	25528	4.34
4845	2642	**Berenice**	6.09 -	30.12.33	5529	9.27		
4846	2643	**Bacchus**	6.09 -	10.27	(5530)			
4847	2644	**Berengaria**	6.09 -	28.7.34	5531	7.26	25531	6.34
4848	2645	**Britomart**	7.09 -	29.9.34	5532	6.27	25532	5.34
4849	2646	**Boniface**	7.09 -	9.9.28	5533	2.27		
4850	1412	**Bedfordshire**	11.09 -	16.1.32	5534	10.27		
4851	1418	**Cheshire**	11.09 -	19.12.31	5535	2.27		
4852	1420	**Derbyshire**	11.09 -	30.12.33	5536	6.27		
4853	1455	**Herefordshire**	11.09 -	9.12.33	5537	7.27		
4854	1611	**Hertfordshire**	11.09 -	23.9.25	(5538)			
4855	1616	**Lancashire**	11.09 -	24.3.34	5539	1.28	(25539)	
4856	1624	**Leicestershire**	11.09 -	30.12.33	5545	6.26		
4857	1652	**Middlesex**	11.09 -	30.12.33	5546	8.27		
4858	1689	**Monmouthshire**	12.09 -	19.3.32	5547	6.26		
4859	1703	**Northumberland**	12.09 -	10.3.34	5548	6.26	(25548)	
4860	71	**Oxfordshire**	12.09 -	4.28	5540	9.26		
4861	275	**Shropshire**	12.09 -	9.28	5541	10.26		
4862	677	**Staffordshire**	12.09 -	30.12.33	5542	8.27		
4863	1002	**Warwickshire**	12.09 -	20.12.30	5543	6.27		
4864	1534	**Westmorland**	12.09 -	18.9.25	(5544)			
4865	1471	**Worcestershire**	1.10 -	4.32	5549	7.27		
4866	1561	**Yorkshire**	1.10 -	9.28	5550	10.26		
4867	1618	**Carnarvonshire**	1.10 -	3.3.34	5551	12.27	(25551)	
4868	1621	**Denbighshire**	1.10 -	25.5.35	5552	7.27	25552	3.34
4869	1658	**Flintshire**	1.10 -	30.5.31	5553	4.27		

The replacement plate *Belgic* for L&NWR No.372 had stamped on it to the left of the name the inscription 'RE-NAMED SEPR 1914' in letters about 1/4 in high as used for the rebuilding dates on 'Jumbos'.

* 25473 *Scottish Chief* was the last of the class to be withdrawn, and according to C.Williams, the official withdrawal date was 14th September 1935, and the scrap date 19th September.

5479 *Shakespeare* (formerly *Prince of Wales*) which was withdrawn on 1st December 1934, was the last of the class to be scrapped, on 17th October 1935.

5554 *Prospero* was rebuilt in March 1915 as a four cylinder 4-6-0 with the Dendy Marshall valve-gear, withdrawn 3rd June 1933, and scrapped six days later.

TABLE 11

C.J.BOWEN COOKE   Appointed 1st March 1909 - Died 19th October 1920

GEORGE THE FIFTH CLASS 6ft 6in 4-4-0 80 engines
(Superheated)

			Period the name was applied		First LMS Number	Date	Second LMS Number	Date
			Built	Withdrawn				
4970	2663	*George the Fifth*	7.10 -	8.2.36	5320	3.27	(25320)	
4972	1294	*F.S.P.Wolferstan*	11.10 -	10.12.38	5322	11.27	25322	31.7.36
4973	1725	*John Bateson*	11.10 -	26.11.38	5324	3.28	25324	2.37
4974	2155	*W.C.Brocklehurst*	11.10 -	31.12.36	5326	6.27	25326	6.36
4975	1059	*Lord Loch*	11.10 -	7.2.48	5321	7.27	25321	1.37
4976	1583	*Henry Ward*	11.10 -	16.9.39	5323	3.27	25323	1.37
4977	2025	*Sir Thomas Brooke*	12.10 -	1.5.37	5325	12.27	25325	1.7.36
4978	228	*E.Nettlefold.*	1.11 -	12.9.36	5327	1.27	(25327)	
4979	445	*P.H.Chambres*	1.11 -	9.11.35	5328	11.27	(25328)	
4980	2168	*Henry Maudslay*	1.11 -	10.4.37	5339	12.27	25339	10.9.36
4990	956	*Dachshund*	4.11 -					
		Bull Dog 12.15						
		Bulldog late 1921			5340	12.27	(25340)	
4991	1489	*Wolfhound*	4.11 -	14.3.36	5341	7.27	(25341)	
4992	1504	*Boarhound*	4.11 -	9.11.35	5342	2.28	(25342)	
4993	1513	*Otterhound*	5.11 -	2.5.36	5343	4.26	(25343)	
4994	1532	*Bloodhound*	5.11 -	16.1.37	5344	5.27	(25344)	
4995	1628	*Foxhound*	5.11 -	19.12.36	5345	9.27	25345	10.6.36
4996	1662	*Deerhound*	5.11 -	29.2.36	5346	4.28	(25346)	
4997	1706	*Elkhound*	5.11 -	14.12.40	5347	3.27	25347	4.37
4998	1792	*Staghound*	5.11 -	20.6.36	5353	9.27	(25353)	
4999	2495	*Bassethound*	5.11 -	7.1.39	5357	2.27	25357	4.37
5000	1800	*Coronation*	6.11 -	22.6.40	5348	6.27	25348	16.8.36

Ran trials with the allotted No 1800, but was given No 5000 when put into regular service, until June 1927, when renumbered LMS 5348.
      5000   It was not broken up until April 1942

5001	502	*British Empire*	6.11 -	11.7.36	5349	12.26	(25349)	
5002	868	*India*	6.11 -	22.5.48	5350	7.27	25350	30.6.36

Name removed by 10.11.36 to end duplication with Jubilee No 5574 named 26.5.36

							(58011) B.R.	
5003	882	*Canada*	6.11 -	8.2.36	5351	5.28	(25351)	
5004	1218	*Australia*	6.11 -	9.11.35	5352	5.26	(25352)	
5005	2081	*New Zealand*	6.11 -	11.1.36	5354	12.26	(25354)	
5006	2212	*South Africa*	6.11 -	4.7.36	5355	9.27	(25355)	
5007	2291	*Gibraltar*	6.11 -	16.8.41	5356	11.27	25356	3.9.36

Name removed 9.36 to end duplication with Jubilee No 5608 named 13.3.36

5008	2177	*Malta*	7.11 -	21.11.36	5358	10.27	(25358)	

Name removed 9.36 to end duplication with Jubilee No 5616 named 6.8.36

5009	2498	*Cyprus*	7.11 -	5.12.36	5359	9.27	(25359)	

Name removed 9.36 to end duplication with Jubilee No 5605 named 28.7.36

5010	361	*Beagle*	7.11 -	25.9.37	5360	10.27	25360	4.37
5011	888	*Challenger*	7.11 -	9.11.35	5361	3.27	(25361)	
5012	1360	*Fire Queen*	7.11 -	18.3.39	5362	8.27	25362	4.37
5013	1394	*Harrier*	7.11 -	8.2.36	5363	9.27	(25363)	
5014	2494	*Perseus*	8.11 -	7.11.36	5368	9.27	(25368)	

(Renumbered 25368 prematurely in 1934 for a short while until 14th April)

5015	1623	*Nubian*	8.11 -	7.11.36	5364	10.27	(25364)	
5016	1631	*Racehorse*	8.11 -	17.4.37	5365	3.24	25365	3.7.36
5017	1644	*Roebuck*	8.11 -	14.11.36	5366	3.27	(25366)	
5018	2089	*Traveller*	8.11 -	12.12.36	5367	7.26	(25367)	
5019	2220	*Vanguard*	8.11 -	26.11.38	5374	6.27	25374	6.4.36
5020	1371	*Quail*	9.11 -	12.8.36	5369	6.27	25369	4.5.36
5021	1417	*Landrail*	9.11 -	5.12.36	5370	12.27	(25370)	

5022	1472	**Moor Hen**	9.11 -	4.10.39	5371	7.27	25371	6.8.36
5023	1595	**Wild Duck**	9.11 -	31.12.36	5372	9.27	25372	15.6.36
5024	1681	*Ptarmigan*	9.11 -	8.5.48	5373	5.26	25373	29.5.36
							(58012) B.R.	
5025	1713	*Partridge*	9.11 -	14.12.35	5375	11.27	(25375)	
5026	1730	*Snipe*	10.11 -	31.12.47	5376	7.27	25376	1.10.36
5027	1733	**Grouse**	10.11 -	24.7.37	5377	11.23	25377	8.36
5028	1777	**Widgeon**	10.11 -	26.6.37	5378	10.27	25378	11.8.36
5029	1799	*Woodcock*	10.11 -	22.8.36	5379	1.27	(25379)	
5118	82	*Charles Dickens*	1.13 -	6.2.37	5380	9.27	(25380)	
5119	752	*John Hick*	2.13 -	9.11.35	5381	12.27	(25381)	
5120	2124	*John Rennie*	2.13 -	3.7.37	5382	7.27	25382	9.9.36
5121	1138	*William Froude*	2.13 -	8.8.36	5385	7.27	(25385)	
5122	2154	*William Siemens*	2.13 -	6.2.37	5387	6.27	25387	24.6.36
5123	2282	*Richard Arkwright*	3.13 -	25.4.36	5388	9.27	(25388)	
5124	89	*John Mayall*	3.13 -	30.5.36	5383	11.27	(25383)	

(Renumbered 25383 prematurely in 1934 for a short while until April)

5125	132	*S.R.Graves*	3.13 -	29.2.36	5384	4.27	(25384)
5126	1193	*Edward Tootal*	3.13 -	1.2.36	5386	3.27	(25386)
5127	2279	*Henry Crosfield*	3.13 -	30.1.37	5395	6.27	(25395)

(Renumbered 25395 prematurely in 1934 for a short while until April)

5128	681	*St.George*	3.13 -	9.11.35	5390	4.26	(25390)
5129	845	*Saddleback*	3.13 -	29.2.36	5391	1.27	(25391)
5130	1188	*Penmaenmawr*	4.13 -	1.3.41	5392	2.28	25392	16.8.36
5131	1680	**Loyalty**	4.13 -	31.5.41	5393	2.24	25393	25.2.36
5132	2086	*Phaeton*	4.13 -	25.7.36	5394	2.24	(25394)
5133	404	*Eclipse*	4.13 -	10.7.37	5389	9.27	25389	27.4.36
5134	1481	*Typhon*	4.13 -	10.10.36	5396	6.28	(25396)
5135	2197	*Planet*	4.13 -	21.12.35	5397	3.28	(25397)

Name removed 7.33 to end duplication with Royal Scot 6131 named by 4.28

5136	2242	*Meteor*	5.13 -	17.10.36	5398	7.27	(25398)

Name removed 7.33 to end duplication with Royal Scot 6128 named by 4.28

5137	2428	**Lord Stalbridge**	5.13 -	4.7.36	5399	9.27	(25399)
5237	363	**Llandudno**	5.15 -	9.11.35	5400	8.27	
5238	789	*Windermere*	5.15 -	29.2.36	5401	6.27	
5239	984	**Carnarvon**	5.15 -	13.6.36	5402	2.27	

(Renumbered 25402 prematurely in 1934 for a short while until April)

5240	2153	**Llandrindod**	6.15 -	3.4.37	5406	6.26	
5241	2233	**Blackpool**	6.15 -	9.11.35	5407	12.27	
5242	104	**Leamington**	6.15 -				
Renamed		**Leamington Spa** 12.15	-	9.11.35	5403	2.24	
5243	226	**Colwyn Bay**	6.15 -	29.2.36	5404	10.23	
5244	1086	*Conway*	6.15 -	4.1.36	5405	2.28	
5245	2106	**Holyhead**	7.15 -	24.4.37	5408	9.27	
5246	2370	**Dovedale**	7.15 -	3.6.39	5409	9.26	25409	4.6.37

The nameplates of *Coronation* bore the words "*5000th engine built at the locomotive works Crewe June 1911*", but strictly speaking it was not in fact the 5,000th, but somewhere near it. Crewe numbers *3784* and *3785* were never used.

QUEEN MARY CLASS 6ft 6in 4-4-0 10 engines

(Non-superheated: Converted later to George the Fifth class)

			Period the name was applied		Conversion Date	First LMS Number	Date	Second LMS Number	Date
			Built	Withdrawn					
4971	2664	*Queen Mary*	7.10 -	21.3.36	6.13	5329	2.24	(25329)	
4981	238	*F.W.Webb*	10.10 -	14.3.36	9.14	5336	3.28	(25336)	
4982	896	*George Whale*	10.10 -	29.2.36	1.14	5332	11.26	(25332)	
4983	1195	*T.J.Hare*	10.10 -	11.7.36	9.14	5337	8.26	(25337)	
4984	1550	*Westminster*	10.10 -	12.9.36	9.13	5330	2.28	(25330)	
4985	1559	*Drake*	10.10 -	14.3.36	1.14	5333	1.27	(25333)	
4986	2151	*Newcomen*	10.10 -	27.11.37	4.14	5334	9.26	25334	2.37
4987	2271	*J.P.Bickersteth*	10.10 -	12.11.38	11.13	5331	7.27	25331	8.36
4988	2507	*Miles MacInnes.*	10.10 -	30.11.35	1.14	5335	12.27	(25335)	
4989	2512	*Thomas Houghton*	10.10 -	9.11.35	10.14	5338	9.27	(25338)	

PRINCE OF WALES CLASS 6ft 0in 4-6-0 245 engines

			Period the name was applied		First LMS Number	Date	Second LMS Number	Date
			Built	Withdrawn				
5030	819	*Prince of Wales* and 12.24	10.11 - 2.24	21.10.33	5600	10.24		
5031	1388	*Andromeda*	10.11 -	23.3.35	5601	2.27	25601	4.34
5032	1452	*Bonaventure*	11.11 -	26.6.37	5602	5.26	25602	5.34
5033	1454	*Coquette*	11.11 -	19.1.35	5603	5.27	25603	5.34
5034	1537	*Enchantress*	11.11 -	27.10.34	5604	11.26	25604	5.34
5035	1691	*Pathfinder*	11.11 -	10.11.34	5605	6.27	25605	5.34
5036	1704	*Conqueror*	11.11 -	25.9.33	5606	2.27		
5037	1721	*Defiance*	11.11 -	22.12.34	5607	4.26	25607	6.34
5038	2021	*Wolverine*	12.11 -	9.2.35	5608	4.26	25608	5.34
5039	2359	*Hermione*	12.11 -	14.10.33	5609	8.27		
5167	362	*Robert Southey*	10.13 -	9.10.33	5610	4.27		
5168	892	*Charles Wolfe*	10.13 -	25.5.35	5611	3.27	25611	7.34
5169	1081	*John Keats*	10.13 -	25.1.36	5612	2.26	25612	5.35
5170	1089	*Sydney Smith*	10.13 -	16.2.35	5613	11.26	25613	6.34
5171	1134	*Victor Hugo*	10.13 -	29.12.34	5614	6.26	25614	5.34
5172	2040	*Oliver Goldsmith*	11.13 -	9.3.35	5615	2.27	25615	5.34
5173	2075	*Robert Burns*	11.13 -	1.12.34	5616	2.27	25616	5.34
5174	2198	*John Ruskin*	11.13 -	14.3.36	5620	4.27	25620	5.34
5175	2205	*Thomas Moore*	11.13 -	1.9.34	5621	1.27	25621	5.34
5176	2213	*Charles Kingsley*	11.13 -	18.9.33	5622	4.27		
5177	321	*Henry W.Longfellow*	11.13 -	18.1.35	5617	3.27	25617	5.34
5178	479	*Thomas B.Macaulay*	11.13 -	23.2.35	5618	5.27	25618	6.34
5179	951	*Bulwer Lytton*	12.13 -	4.8.34	5619	5.27	25619	6.34
5180	1679	*Lord Byron*	12.13 -	18.5.35	5623	11.27	25623	5.34
5181	2249	*Thomas Campbell*	12.13 -	27.2.37	5624	3.27	25624	5.34
5182	2283	*Robert L.Stevenson*	12.13 -	12.12.36	5625	4.27	25625	5.34
5183	307	*R.B.Sheridan*	1.14 -	1.12.34	5628	6.26	25628	5.34
5184	637	*Thomas Gray*	1.14 -	15.12.34	5629	5.27	25629	4.34
5185	979	*W.M.Thackeray*	1.14 -	15.9.34	5630	4.26	25630	6.34
5186	1400	*Felicia Hemans*	1.14 -	6.6.36	5631	2.27	25631	6.34
5187	86	*Mark Twain*	1.14 -	30.5.36	5626	1.27	25626	5.34
5188	146	*Lewis Carroll*	1.14 -	25.7.36	5627	5.27	25627	6.34
5189	964	*Bret Harte*	2.14 -	5.9.33	5632	9.26		

Modified with Beames derived gear valve motion 3.23

5190	985	*Sir W.S.Gilbert*	2.14 -	7.9.35	5633	10.27	25633	6.34
5191	1321	*William Cowper*	2.14 -	29.9.34	5634	2.27	25634	5.34

5192	2152	*Charles Lamb*	2.14 -	17.3.34	5635	9.26	(25635)	
5193	2293	*Percy Bysshe Shelley*	2.14 -	26.1.35	5636	1.27	25636	5.34
5194	2377	*Edward Gibbon*	2.14 -	31.12.36	5637	3.27	25637	6.34
5195	2443	*Charles James Lever*	3.14 -	18.4.36	5638	4.26	25638	5.34
5196	2520	*G.P.Neele.*	3.14 -	7.10.33	5639	9.26		

Batch built by North British Locomotive Company. Works Numbers *21256-21275 5257-66* were built at Hyde Parks Works, and *5267-76* at Queens Parks Works. The stock dates were March 1916 for all except *5265-6* which were to stock in   April 1916.

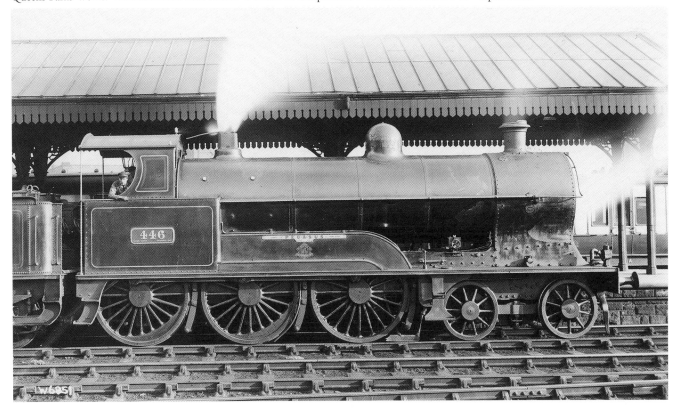

Fig. 52   Prince of Wales class 446 *Pegasus*. One of the batch built by the North British Locomotive Company at their Hyde Park Works. Note the contradiction. The name plate has "Built Crewe Works", whereas the round plate on the smokebox tells the truth!

Real Photographs Co.Ltd.   (Allan Sommerield Collection).

5257	136	*Minerva*	10.15 -	26.1.35	5663	6.27	25663	5.34
5258	173	*Livingstone*	10.15 -	2.2.35	5664	8.27	25664	6.34
5259	257	*Plynlimmon*	11.15 -	15.9.34	5666	5.26	(25666)	
5260	446	*Pegasus*	11.15 -	20.7.35	5668	1.24	25668	6.34
5261	1749	*Precedent*	11.15 -	26.1.35	5677	5.27	(25677)	
5262	2063	*Hibernia*	11.15 -	18.5.35	5679	6.27	25679	7.34
5263	2175	*Loadstone*	11.15 -	12.6.37	5680	5.27	25680	3.35
5264	2203	*Falstaff*	11.15 -	25.5.35	5681	3.24	25681	10.34
5265	2300	*Hotspur*	12.15 -	22.9.34	5687	3.27		
5266	2392	*Caliban*	12.15 -	12.9.36	5689	5.28	25689	8.34
5267	90	*Kestrel*	12.15 -	8.8.36	5660	10.26	25660	5.34
5268	401	*Zamiel*	12.15 -	10.11.34	5667	5.27	(25667)	
5269	525	*Vulcan*	12.15 -	17.4.37	5669	7.27	25669	6.34
5270	610	*Albion*	12.15 -	19.10.35	5670	4.27	25670	10.34
5271	867	*Condor*	1.16 -	5.12.36	5672	10.26	25672	3.4.34

Modified with Beames derived gear valve motion 6.23
Name removed 7.33 to end duplication with Royal Scot 6145 named 2.28

5272	1132	*Scott*	1.16 -	9.2.46	5674	4.26	25674	2.35
5273	1466	*Sphinx*	1.16 -	22.8.36	5675	7.26	25675	5.35
5274	1744	*Petrel*	1.16 -	20.4.35	5676	5.27	25676	8.34
5275	2055	*Milton*	1.16 -	30.3.35	5678	12.26	25678	5.34
5276	2339	*Samson*	1.16 -	13.4.35	5682	3.27	25682	6.34

Name removed 7.33 to end duplication with Royal Scot 6135 named by 4.28

Batch built at Crewe

			Plate Date	Stock Date					
5297	27	*General Joffre*	10.15	10.15 -	13.2.37	5640	2.27	25640	5.34
5298	88	*Czar of Russia*	10.15	10.15 -	12.9.36	5641	7.26	25641	5.34
5299	122	*King of the Belgians*	0.15	11.15 -	7.3.36	5642	3.27	25642	5.34
5300	160	*King of Serbia*	11.15	11.15 -	3.11.34	5643	11.26	25643	5.34
5301	185	*King of Italy*	11.15	11.15 -	7.3.36	5644	12.26	25644	5.34
5302	877	*Raymond Poincaré*	11.15	11.15 -	13.6.36	5645	8.26	25645	5.34
5303	1333	*Sir John French*	11.15	11.15 -	22.12.34	5646	10.26	25646	5.34
5304	2275	*Edith Cavell*	11.15	11.15 -	19.1.35	5647	2.27	25647	5.34
5305	2396	*Queen of the Belgians*	12.15	11.15 -	16.10.48	5648	5.27	25648	5.34
5306	2408	*Admiral Jellicoe*	12.15	11.15 -	7.10.33	5649	11.27		
5307	606	*Castor*	1.161	1.16 -	2.5.36	5650	3.24	25650	5.34
5308	745	*Pluto*	1.16	1.16 -	7.7.34	5651	5.26	25651	5.34
5309	1352	*The Nile*	1.16	1.16 -	5.10.35	5653	5.27	25653	5.34
5310	1379	*Witch*	1.16	1.16 -	9.3.35	5654	3.27	25654	6.34
5311	1484	*Smeaton*	1.16	1.16 -	8.12.34	5655	4.26	25655	5.34
5312	810	*Onyx*	1.16	1.16 -	11.9.33	5652	1.27		
5313	1084	*Shark*	1.16	2.16 -	3.9.38	5656	3.26	25656	4.34
5314	1346	*Trent*	1.16	2.16 -	11.4.36	5657	4.27	25657	4.34
5315	2417	*Atlas*	2.16	2.16 -	26.10.35	5658	1.27	25658	5.34

Name removed 7.33 to end duplication with Royal Scot 6134 3.28

5316	2442	*Odin*	2.16	2.16 -	23.3.35	5659	3.27	25659	4.34
5317	95	*Gallipoli*	3.16	3.16 -	9.2.35	5661	6.26	25661	4.34
5318	126	*Anzac*	3.16	3.16 -	22.8.36	5662	3.24	25662	8.34
5319	233	*Suvla Bay*	3.16	3.16 -	18.4.36	5665	5.27	25665	6.34
5320	849	*Arethusa*	3.16	3.16 -	31.12.36	5671	5.26	25671	5.34

Name removed 9.36 to end duplication with Jubilee 5696 named 2.4.36

5321	1100	*Lusitania*	3.16	3.16 -	29.1.49	5673	11.27	25673	8.34
5322	1324	*Falaba*	4.16	4.16 -	26.1.46	5683	5.27	25683	1.35
5323	2092	*Arabic*	4.16	4.16 -	4.4.36	5684	6.27	25684	4.35
5324	2276	*Persia*	4.16	4.16 -	8.8.36	5685	2.28	25685	5.34
5325	2295	*Anglia*	4.16	4.16 -	24.11.34	5686	11.23	(25686)	
5326	2340	*Tara*	4.16	4.16 -	9.9.33	5688	3.27		

Modified with Beames derived gear valve motion 4.24

			Plate Date	Stock Date	Period of naming				
5444	940	*Richard Cobden.*	1.19	2.19	6.22 - 18.7.36	5697	6.28	25697	4.34
5447	621	*Telford*	2.19	3.19	4.22 - 28.3.36	5700	5.27	25700	9.34
5451	1584	*Scotia*	3.19	3.19	5.22 - 3.10.36	5704	11.27	25704	9.34
5453	504	*Canning*	3.19	4.19	8.22 - 31.12.36	5706	1.27	25706	5.35
5454	974	*Hampden*	3.19	4.19	2.22 - 20.4.35	5707	9.27	25707	6.34
5470	522	*Stentor*	6.19	8.19	7.22 - 25.1.36	5723	4.27	25723	4.34
5475	1290	*Lucknow*	7.19	9.19	7.22 - 16.2.35	5729	2.24	25729	8.34
5483	1325	*Disraeli*	8.19	11.19	5.22 - 1.6.35	5736	3.27	25736	5.34
5489	1178	*Prince Albert*	9.19	12.19	2.22 - 22.9.34	5743	2.26	(25743)	
5497	1542	*Marathon*	11.19	3.20	8.22 - 28.3.36	5750	6.26	25750	10.34
5500	1694	*Premier*	11.19	4.20	4.23 - 22.2.36	5753	12.27	25753	5.34
5501	2516	*Dalton*		4.20	8.22 - 4.5.35	5754	1.28	25754	6.34

* 964 *Bret Harte* was specially named *Sir John French* for four days in January 1918

Renumbering into the 25xxx series took place between April 1934 and September 1935, the last to be dealt with being 25791 (unnamed) shortly before the 21st.

Fig. 53   Claughton class 1191 *Sir Frank Ree*

CLAUGHTON CLASS   6ft 6in   4-6-0   130 engines

			Built	Withdrawn	LMS Number	Date
5117	2222	Sir Gilbert Claughton	1.13 -	2.3.35	5900	6.25
5138	1161	Sir Robert Turnbull	5.13 -	5.33	5901	12.25
5139	1191	Sir Frank Ree	5.13 -	11.30	5902	12.26
5140	1319	Sir Frederick Harrison	5.13 -	7.1.33	5907	6.26
5141	1327	Alfred Fletcher	5.13 -	19.9.36	5908	8.26
5142	21	Duke of Sutherland	6.13 -	5.33	5903	4.27
5143	163	Holland Hibbert	6.13 -	8.12.34	5904	7.26
5144	650	Lord Rathmore	6.13 -	2.33	5905	5.27
5145	1159	Ralph Brocklebank	6.13 -	27.2.37	5906	2.26
5146	2046	Charles N.Lawrence	6.13 -	2.2.35	5909	3.27
5227	250	J.A.Bright	8.14 -	10.4.37	5910	4.27
5228	260	W.E.Dorrington	8.14 -	5.3.34	5911	5.26
5229	1131	Lord Faber	8.14 -	9.2.35	5912	2.26
5230	1429	Colonel Lockwood	9.14 -	8.8.34	5913	6.27
5231	2239	Frederick Baynes	9.14 -	23.3.35	5918	4.27
5232	209	J.Bruce Ismay	9.14 -	8.12.34	5914	12.26
5233	668	Rupert Guinness	9.14 -	24.11.34	5915	6.27
5234	856	E.Tootal Broadhurst	9.14 -	3.12.32	5916	6.27
5235	1567	Charles J.Cropper	10.14 -	22.9.34	5917	8.26
5236	2401	Lord Kitchener *	10.14 -	8.9.34	5919	4.27
5337	511	George Macpherson	7.16 -	6.4.35	5920	1.27
5338	695	Sir Arthur Lawley	7.16 -	1.12.34	5921	1.27
5339	968	Lord Kenyon	7.16 -	22.9.34	5922	12.26
5340	1093	Guy Calthrop	7.16 -			
Renamed		Sir Guy Calthrop	3.19	29.6.35	5923	3.28
5341	1345	James Bishop	8.16 -	29.9.34	5924	2.27
5342	2174	E.C.Trench	8.16 -	3.33	5925	2.27
5343	2204	Sir Herbert Walker	8.16 -			
Renamed		Sir Herbert Walker K.C.B.	4.17	14.1.33	5926	6.26
5344	2221	Sir Francis Dent	8.16 -	5.12.36	5927	6.26
5345	2338	Charles H.Dent	8.16 -	27.1.34	5928	9.26
5346	2395	J.A.F.Aspinall	9.16 -	2.3.35	5929	2.27

5367	37	*G.R.Jebb*	2.17 -		3.11.34		5930	3.27
5368	154	*Captain Fryatt*	3.17 -		12.5.34		5931	4.26
5369	155	*I.T.Williams*	3.17 -					
Renamed		*Sir Thomas Williams*	12.19 -		13.4.35		5932	2.27

			Plate Date	Stock Date	Period of naming			
5375	2097	*Patriot In Memory of the Fallen L & N W R Employees 1914-1919*	4.17	5.17	Briefly in 1.20		5938	1.27
5376	2230	*Clio*	5.17	5.17	7.22 -	1.6.35	5939	3.24
5377	1019	*Columbus*	5.17	6.17	2.22 -	22.9.34	5940	2.27
5380	2373	*Tennyson*	5.17	6.17	1.22 -	11.8.34	5943	7.26
5382	2420	*Ingestre*	6.17	7.17	1.23 -	14.4.34	5945	6.27
5383	2427	*Duke of Connaught.*	6.17	7.17	1.22 -	15.2.41	5946	5.27
5385	2445	*Baltic* #	7.17	8.17	7.23 -	3.4.37	5948	3.27
5390	986	*Buckingham.*	8.17	9.17	3.22 -	26.9.36	5953	2.27
5502	1914	*Patriot In Memory of the Fallen L & N W R Employees 1914-1919*	1.20	5.20	5.20 -	23.6.34	5964	6.26
5507	1177	*Bunsen.*	1.20	5.20	3.22 -	10.32	5966	2.26
5509	2499	*Patience*	2.20	6.20	8.22 -	3.12.35	5970	2.27
5510	2511	*Croxteth* #	2.20	6.20	6.23 -	11.30	5971	7.23
5511	1599	*John O'Groat*	2.20	6.20	8.22 -	26.1.35	5968	11.26
5513	1407	*L/Corpl J.A. Christie V.C.*	2.20	6.20	2.22 -	1.12.34	5967	2.27
5517	2035	*Private E.Sykes V.C.*	3.20	8.20	2.22 -	4.26	(5976	1.27)
5520	2268	*Frobisher*	3.20	8.20	8.22 -	14.4.34	5979	3.24
5521	12	*Talisman*	4.20	8.20	1.23 -	22.5.37	5975	1.27

(Renumbered 25975 briefly and prematurely during March and April 1934)

5530	1097	*Private W.Wood V.C.*	5.20	10.20	2.22 -	4.26	(5988	1.27)
5532	2059	*C.J.Bowen Cooke*	10.20	11.20	10.20 -	23.2.35	5991	7.28
5541	13	*Vindictive*	7.20	12.20	7.22 -	10.22		
	2430	*Vindictive* Renumbered			10.22 -	9.36	5999	3.27

Name removed 9.36 to avoid duplication with Jubilee Class 5725, built and   named 9.10.36.

| 5544 | 30 | *Thalaba* # | 8.20 | 2.21 | 4.23 - | 22.9.34 | 6002 | 3.27 |
| 5546 | 42 | *Princess Louise.* | 8.20 | 2.21 | 2.22 - | 7.35 | 6004 | 11.26 |

Name removed 7.35 to avoid duplication with Princess Royal Class 6204, built and named in 8.35.

5550	110	*Lady Godiva* #	9.20	3.21	5.23 -	3.12.32	6008	2.27
5553	150	*Illustrious* #	3.21	3.21	5.23 -	3.2.33	6011	1.27
5557	158	*Private E.Sykes V.C.*	4.21	4.21	4.26 -	3.33	6015	5.26
5559	169	*Breadalbane* #	4.21	5.21	3.23 -	26.10.40	6017	11.26
5560	179	*Private W.Wood V.C.*	4.21	5.21	4.26 -	6.2.33	6018	1.28
5561	180	*Llewellyn* #	4.21	5.21	4.23 -	15.12.34	6019	4.26
5563	192	*Bevere* #	5.21	5.21	7.23 -	24.2.34	6021	5.27
5565	207	*Sir Charles Cust*	5.21	5.21	12.21 -	26.7.41	6023	6.27
		See Appendix 6						

* 5236 2401 *Lord Kenyon* was renamed *Lord Kitchener* before going into service

These nameplates were lettered L M S

The nameplates *L/CORPL J.A.CHRISTIE V.C.* have in the abbreviated `Corporal` two dots under a raised smaller capital `L`

POST L&NWR ERA.

4-6-0 Built by Beardmore & Co. (Makers Number 304) 3.24, with Beames derived gear valve motion.

5752		*Prince of Wales*	5.24				5845	
		(Named for the British Empire Exhibition 6.24 - 1.25)					25845	1.35
		Withdrawn 15.11.47						

TABLE 12

THE ENGINEER'S AND CARRIAGE DEPARTMENT LOCOMOTIVES

A locomotive was set aside for the use of each of the District Engineers and provided with a nameplate, except where stated otherwise. The following is a list of the standard gauge engines, showing the names, the year from which it was so used and the former identity of each engine. A 'Spare Engine' was also kept available, but none received either a number or a name.

Fig. 54   The Permanent Way Department 2-2-2WT *Carlisle* built in 1856.

(Allan Sommerield Collection).

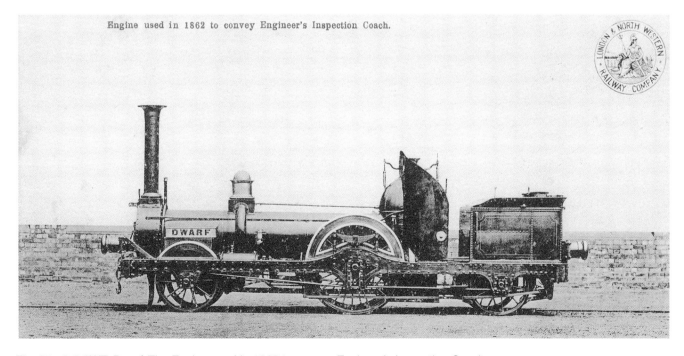

Fig. 55   2-2-2WT *Dwarf*. The Engine used in 1862 to convey Engineer's Inspection Coach.

L&NWR Postcard Set 2 No.3. (Fred Gray Collection).

Acton (Wolverton) 1869

This locomotive was an 0-4-0T built in 1850 by Sharp Bros. for a colliery near Mold purchased in March 1852 by the Chester & Holyhead Railway and named *Diamond*, then sold to the Birkenhead, Lancashire & Cheshire Junction Railway, so coming to the L&NWR in November 1860 to be their 356 *Memnon*. It went to the Duplicate List as 356A in April 1861 and 1118 in May 1862. John Ramsbottom reported in a Minute dated 23.9.1869 as follows "Wolverton Engine No 1118. This engine has been for a long time employed in shunting for the Carriage Dept and recommends that it be transferred to that Dept. Approved". It was then named *Acton*. On 10th March 1871 it was sold to the Shropshire Union Railways & Canal Co. to work the line to the Llwynenion brickworks which the S.U.C and the L&NWR had jointly converted from a tramroad. It was cut up at Crewe March 1883.

Carlisle (PW Dept) 1863

A George England 2-2-2WT built in 5.56 for the Manchester, Sheffield & Lincolnshire Railway as an inspection engine, with small saloon attached and at that time named *Watkin*. It was sold to the L&NWR Engineer's Department on 9th January 1863, renamed *Carlisle* (after the City) and used from then on by the Northern Division Engineer, at Manchester. Withdrawn 1888.

Dwarf (PW Dept) 1853

A George England 2-2-2WT , built in 1849 at Hatcham Iron Works, London, and delivered that September to the London and Blackwall Railway, who sold it back to the makers in August 1851. It was then sold to the Eastern Counties Railway, from whom the L&NWR purchased it in July 1853 for the use of Mr.H.Woodhouse the District Engineer in charge of all the lines south of Stafford, until 1873 when it was replaced by No 51 *Torch*. During this time although not named as such, it was in fact the original "Engineer Stafford". After overhaul it went to the P.W.Dept, Bangor until November 1877, when it was withdrawn, and brought to Crewe and, being considered worthy of preservation, was exhibited at the George Stephenson Centenary celebrations at Newcastle on 9th June 1881, but sadly and finally it was broken up at Crewe around 1888 after suffering fire damage in the tender shop. It was replaced at Bangor by *Columbine*.

Earlestown (Wagon Works)

SFB Goods CF Rebuilt 2-4-0T 6.58	87 *Eden*	
Renamed **Earlestown**		5.59 - 1.81
Special Tank *2308* 2359 *Earlestown*		3.81
Transferred to Wolverton CD No 8		1938

Note: The nameplates *Earlestown* are made of brass.

Fig. 56 *Engineer.Bangor* Formerly 49 *Columbine.* Note the full stop between *Engineer* and *Bangor.*

(Allan Sommerield Collection).

Fig. 57 *Engineer Liverpool* Formerly 742 *Spitfire*, with tender cab, and LMS crest on the splasher.

(Allan Sommerield Collection).

Fig. 58 *Engineer Manchester* Formerly LFB Passenger 3028 *Greyhound*.

(Allan Sommerield Collection).

Engineer	Samson	*1851*	(3269),	ex	885	*Vampire*	5.97 -	5.23
	Waterloo	*3384*	(3624),	ex	792	*Theorem*	5.23 -	6.32
Engineer.Bangor	Grand Junction		(1868),	ex	49	*Columbine*	11.77 -	1.02
	Samson	*2282*	(3270),	ex	1166	*Wyre*	1.02 -	14.12.25
Engineer Birmingham	* See note below beside *Engineer Wolverton*							
Engineer-Crewe	SFB Pass DA	*222*	(1876),	ex	291	*Prince of Wales*	1879 -	9.99
	Samson	*1693*	(3206),	ex	424	*Sirius*	9.99 -	7.14
	Waterloo	*3461*	(3496),	ex	209	*Petrel*	7.14 -	5.32
Engineer Lancaster	LFB Pass DA	*336*	(3041),	ex	367	*Nightingale*	11.91 -	1894
	LFB Pass DA	*378*		ex		*Engineer Watford*	4.94 -	4.03
	Samson	*1692*	(3271),	ex	414	*Prospero*	4.03 -	2.24
	Waterloo	*3441*	737			*Roberts*	2.24 -	7.35
Engineer Liverpool	Samson	*1847*		ex		'Spare Engine'	10.05 -	7.21
	Waterloo	*3360*	742			*Spitfire*	7.21 -	3.10.32
Engineer Manchester	LFB Pass DA	*269*	(3028),	ex	323	*Greyhound*	10.88 -	9.01
	Samson	*1848*	(3273),	ex	631	*Hotspur*	11.01 -	6.14
	Waterloo	*3456*	(3488),	ex	2156	*Sphinx*	6.14 -	9.27
Engineer Northampton	SFB Pass SF	*198*	(1875),	ex	64	*Odin*	c.1879 -	1.91
	LFB Pass DA	*335*	(3045),	ex	366	*Nestor*	2.91 -	4.95
	LFB Pass DA	*377*	(3077),	ex		'Spare Engine'	4.95 -	11.01
	Samson	*2285*	(3198),	ex	209	*Petrel*	1.02 -	5.23
	Waterloo	*3130*	468			*Wildfire*	5.23 -	12.27
Engineer South Wales	LFB Pass DA	*255*	(3086),	ex	315	*Prince Arthur*	7.89 -	5.97
	LFB Pass DA	*381*		ex		*Maintenance*	5.97 -	7.11
	SFB Pass DA	*220*	(3082),	ex	135	*Bat*		
			named			*Locomotion*	7.11 -	12.20
	Waterloo	*3355*	(3760),	ex	485	*Euxine*	2.21 -	12.31
	Waterloo	*3461*		ex		*Engineer-Crewe*	5.32 -	8.33

(Replaced by M.R. 155, later 20155 Withdrawn 28.10.1950)

Fig. 59   Samson class 'Spare Engine' Note the mark on the cab side where an ordinary ENGINEER plate appears to have been fixed. This means that the engine can only have been *1851* 885 *Vampire,* becoming first *Engineer,* and then ' Spare Engine' in May 1897.

(L&NWR Society Photograph Collection No. 1853).

Engineer Stafford	SFB Pass SF		(1901),	ex	51	*Torch* (1)	9.73 -	3.91
	LFB Pass DA	397	(3089),	ex	353	*St.Arnaud*	4.91 -	6.97
	LFB Pass DA	255		ex		*Engineer South Wales*	5.97 -	4.01
	Samson	1853	(3268),	ex	2151	*Baltic* (2)	4.01 -	c1904
Engineer Swansea	SFB Pass CF		(1909),	ex	92	*Trentham*	10.80 -	7.89
Engineer Walsall	Samson	1853	(3268),	ex	2151	*Baltic* (2)	c1904 -	6.23
	Waterloo	3368			609	*The Earl of Chester*	6.23 -	2.28
Engineer Watford	LFB Pass DA	378	(3027),	ex	110	*Canning*	12.91 -	4.94
	LFB Pass DA	336		ex		*Engineer Lancaster*	1894 -	5.95
	Samson	2279	(3200),	ex	773	*Centaur*	7.95 -	5.23
	Waterloo	3445			793	*Martin*	5.23 -	13.12.35

(Withdrawn from service as *Engineer Watford* and replaced by M.R.20008 on that date, but not withdrawn until P4.36)

Engineer Wolverton			* According to C.Williams, *Engineer Birmingham* and *Engineer Wolverton* are the two oldest but unfortunately they cannot now be identified. (SLS Journal 1951 page 178)					

'Engineer's Dept.Spare'	LFB Pass DA	377	(3077),	ex	42	*Sunbeam*	2.93 -	4.95
'Spare Engine'	Samson	1847	(3199),	ex	487	*John O'Groat*	8.95 -	10.05
	Samson	1859	(3272),	ex	2157	*Unicorn*	11.05 -	5.23
	Samson	1851		ex		*Engineer*	5.23 -	3.25

Notes:-

(1) Although used by the District Engineer at Stafford, it received the name *Engineer*.

(2) When the depot for the No 3 (Birmingham) District was transferred from Stafford to Walsall sometime around 1904, the plates *Engineer Stafford* were replaced by new ones *Engineer Walsall*.

Carriage Department (Wolverton)

No 1	SFB Goods DA	228(3)	951,	ex	296	*Bellerophon*	7.77 -	6.96
	Special Tank	2107	(3260)				6.96 -	20.2.37
No 2	SFB Goods SF	(4)	70			*Sphinx*	12.77 -	2.95
	0-4-2WT Crane	3437(5)	144				2.95 -	4.29
No 3	SFB Goods DA	204	(3076),	ex	282	*Irwell*	3.90 -	2.97
	Special Tank	2342	(1860)				2.97 -	8.59
No 5	SFB Goods DA	217	(1866),	ex	288	*Loadstone*	9.85 -	2.95
	0-4-2WT Crane	3438(5)	(3310)				2.98 -	5.29
No 6	Special Tank	1944	(3155)				5.01 -	5.59
No 7	Special Tank	2200	(3416)				12.11 -	11.59
No 8	Special Tank	2308				*Earlestown*	1938 -	11.57

Carriage Department (Crewe)

No 4	SFB Goods DA	186	(1974),	ex	270	*Dee*	5.86 -	8.95
	0-4-2WT Crane	3438(5)	195				8.95 -	2.96
	Special Tank	2154	(1842)				2.96 -	1931

Notes:-

(3) Harris gives "1-77" (Railway Observer 1935 page 232), and see Table 3

(4) 70 *Sphinx* was rebuilt 2-4-0T immediately prior to its transfer to the Carriage Department.

(5) *3437* 0-4-2T 4ft 0in Crane Shunter 144 Built 11.94; CD No 2 2.95 (3250 12.94, book entry only) Scrapped 15.4.1929
3438 0-4-2T 4ft 0in Crane Shunter 195 passed through a rapid succession of changes of identity. Built 11.94 ; (1808   8.95, book entry only); CD No 4 8.95; (1842 2.96); Renumbered (3310) 4.97 and CD No 5 2.98. Scrapped 10.5.1929.

THE PERMANENT WAY DEPARTMENT LOCOMOTIVES

Maintenance	LFB Pass DA	381	(1970),	ex	178	*Friar* 8.90 - 5.97

Danby Lodge

An 0-6-0ST built in March 1903 by Manning, Wardle No 1595 for John Scott (later Sir John) for the Grassholme Reservoir construction. It was bought in 1919 by the L&NWR from the Ministry of Munitions, Chilwell, and was used in widening the Standedge Tunnel, then in 1928-9 on work at Rolleston west curve, Notts. and in 1930-2 on widening at Mirfield, Yorks. It ended its days at Beeston in 1948. It had typical Manning, Wardle nameplates, cast, with raised lettering and fixed to the locomotive's saddle tanks. It was not included in the departmental stock, but was listed, together with other engines, (e.g. *Kitchener* and *Platelayer* of the P.W.Dept. and the narrow gauge Horwich works engines) under "Miscellaneous Vehicles".

NARROW-GAUGE LOCOMOTIVES

2ft 6in gauge

Name	Type	Built	
Jim Crow	0-4-2ST	3.1894	Hudswell, Clarke & Co. (340) A painted name.
Kitchener	0-4-0ST	3.1915	W.G.Bagnall & Co. (1999)
Platelayer	0-4-0ST	1893	W.G.Bagnall & Co. (1410 and delivered in November 1895 to Crewe with the name *Haulier*. Probably sold in 1941 to T.W.Ward Ltd., Templeborough. A photograph dated 27th March 1938 shows a nameplate riveted or bolted to the cabside.

Fig. 60   0-4-0ST Narrow gauge *Platelayer,* Permanent Way Department, Crewe

(John Ward Collection).

18in gauge in Crewe Works

Name	Type	Built	Withdrawn	
Tiny	0-4-0T	5.1862	25.3.1928	and cut up 2.5.1928
Pet	0-4-0T	6.1865	4.1929	Preserved
Nipper.	0-4-0T	1.1867	P10.1929	and not cut up until 12.2.1931
Topsy.	0-4-0T	1.1867	P10.1929	ditto
Midge	0-4-0T	11.1870	P10.1929	ditto
Billy.	0-4-0T	7.1875	P1.1931	Sold
Dickie	0-4-0T	5.1876	P10.1929	and not cut up until 12.2.1931

Except for *Dickie* for which there is photographic evidence, these building dates are taken from C.Williams' 1922 Register. Some of these differ from those in his 1912 Register, indicating that he had done some research between those years.

None were allotted Crewe (Motion) numbers.

In May 1888 *Billy.* was used on a mile long stretch beside the Middlewich branch of the Shropshire Union Canal near Worlston in an unsuccessful experiment to ascertain the viability of using steam engines to haul narrow boats.

Nipper, Topsy, Midge and *Dickie* A Minute dated 24.9.1929 authorises their withdrawal.

Billy was sold in January 1931 to J.Cashmore, Scrap Merchants, Great Bridge, near Dudley.

Fig. 61   Crewe works Narrow gauge *Nipper*.

(Norman Lee Collection).

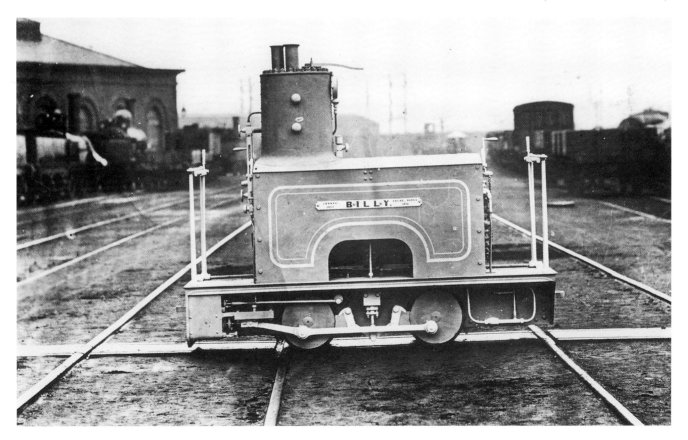

Fig. 62   Crewe works Narrow gauge *Billy*.

(Allan Sommerield Collection).

TABLE 13
ABSORBED RAILWAYS 1847 - 1906

THE PRESTON & WYRE RAILWAY, HARBOUR & DOCK COMPANY

The Preston & Wyre Railway, Harbour & Dock Co was leased to the Manchester & Leeds Railway in 1847, with the latter changing its name later that year to the Lancashire & Yorkshire Railway. On 28th July 1849 the Preston & Wyre lines were vested jointly in the LYR and LNWR and it remained a joint line until the LYR and LNWR amalgamated on 1 January 1922, just prior to the Grouping.

Only two of the Company's locomotives came to the L&NWR Northern Division:

Ribble 0-4-0 Built E.Bury & Co. and named 1847 L&NWR No 258 4.50
Replaced 5.56, probably to St.Helens Railway to become their No 10.

Windermere Wheel arrangement uncertain, built and named 1846-7
L&NWR No 259 4.50 Replaced 1855

THE HUDDERSFIELD & MANCHESTER RAILWAY & CANAL COMPANY

Absorbed by L&NWR into North Eastern Division on 9th July 1847.
The Huddersfield & Manchester Railway and the Leeds, Dewsbury & Manchester Railway were added to the former Manchester & Birmingham section to create an enlarged North-Eastern Division.

Fig. 63   2-2-2ST 446, which began life as Huddersfield & Manchester Railway 2-2-2 No.3 *Brook*. Built by Sharp Brothers & Co. in 1847. Photographed at Addison Road Station, Kensington c.1870 from Locomotive Magazine April 1901.

(Harry Jack Collection).

No. Name	Sharp Works Numbers	L&NWR 7.49	Numbers 8.57	Rebuilt 2-2-2ST		Disposal
		NE Div	N Div			
1 *Aldam*	415	44	444	1862		Scrapped 9.73
2 *Huddersfield*	417	45	445	1862	Reboilered 1870 (1939 9.73)	Scrapped 8.79
3 *Brook*	437	46	446	1862	Reboilered 1870 (1958 9.73)	Scrapped 6.74
		S Div (1850-2)				
Saddleworth	473	(52) Allotted	4	L&NWR 604 4.62 (1900 9.73)		Scrapped 8.75

5ft 0in 0-6-0 built in 1846 by R.& W.Hawthorn & Co.

Standedge		S Div (1850-1) 246		L&NWR 846 4.62 (1216 12.63)		Scrapped 3.69

Aldam and *Huddersfield* were ceremonially named on 2nd August 1847, and *Aldam* was used prior to withdrawal for shunting when the new offices at Crewe Works were built.

THE CHESTER & BIRKENHEAD RAILWAY

The Chester & Birkenhead Railway was opened on 22nd September 1840 and by the middle of 1841 owned six 2-2-2 locomotives.

No 1 *Wirral*   Tayleur & Co.   9.40 Converted to stationary engine 1854
No 2 *Zillah*   Mather, Dixon & Co. 9.40 Withdrawn 6.55
No 3 *Touchstone*   Mather, Dixon & Co. 9.40 Rebuilt 3.53 Jointly leased from 1.1.60 until 11.60, then to GWR No 114
No 4 *Commodore*   Tayleur & Co.   6.41 Withdrawn 6.55
No 5 *Hirondelle*   Tayleur & Co.   12.40 Withdrawn 6.55
No 6 *Lupus*   Tayleur & Co.   9.40 Withdrawn 6.55

By the end of 1845 the Stock had risen to ten, with the addition of

No 7 *Druid*   2-2-2 built 1843 by Jones & Potts, and delivered 12.44. Rebuilt 2-2-2T 1856. It went to L&NWR N Div as No 280 *Glendower* 11.60 Name removed 2.61

No 8 *Birkenhead*   A similar engine built 1843 by Jones & Potts and delivered 4.45, renamed *Monk*, rebuilt 2-2-2T and which became L&NWR No 224 *Violet* 11.60 Name removed 2.61

No 9 *Victoria*   2-2-2 built 1843 by Tayleur & Co.(219), purchased 11.45, rebuilt 3.58, jointly leased 1.1.60 - 11.60 then to GWR No 115

No 10 *Albert*   A similar build and history to No 9 above. Tayleur & Co.(220) GWR No 116 Rebuilt 1.57

It was amalgamated with the Birkenhead, Lancashire & Cheshire Junction on 22nd July 1847, when their five surviving locomotives Nos 3/7-10 were numbered in the Birkenhead, Lancashire & Cheshire Junction list.

THE BIRKENHEAD, LANCASHIRE & CHESHIRE JUNCTION RAILWAY
(Name changed to THE BIRKENHEAD RAILWAY 1st August 1859)

The Company was jointly leased by the GWR and the L&NWR by an Agreement dated 1st January 1860, which took effect on 20th November that year, and was vested jointly in the two companies by an Act of Parliament of 11th July 1861.
The locomotives were divided equally between these two companies, and not separately owned until 20th November 1860.

Not all the locomotives were named, some of those named went to the GWR, some to the L&NWR, and the unnamed ones were given names when they entered L&NWR ownership.

0-6-0 built by B.Hick & Co. and delivered 3.49

No 11 *Birkenhead* Renamed *Blazer* Jointly leased, then to GWR No 108
No 12 *Chester* Renamed *Gnome* Jointly leased, then to GWR No 109
No 13 *Mersey* Renamed *Forerunner* Jointly leased, then L&NWR No 442 Sold 3.61
No 14 *Dee* Renamed *Gheber* Jointly leased, then L&NWR No 236
   and renamed *Hawkstone* 11.60 (236A 4.61 and 1115 5.62) Sold 10.65
   The name *Hawkstone* went on to DX class 236 4.61

These four went to the Shrewsbury & Chester Railway in an exchange from 11.51 to 4.53 and were given new names on their return.

2-2-2 built by B.Hick & Co. 8.49 to 1850.

No 15 (unnamed) Purchased 3.51 L&NWR No 364 *Latona* 11.60 Replaced 9.61
     Name returned to Prince Ernest class No 927 1864

Nos 16-9 (unnamed) Jointly leased, then to GWR Nos 110-3
No 20 (unnamed) Purchased 9.51 L&NWR No 278 *Locke* 11.60 Replaced 2.61. Name went to DX class No 278 2.61

2-2-2 built by Sharp, Stewart & Co. (777/8)

No 21 (unnamed) Built 4.54 L&NWR No 316 *Prince Eugene* 11.60. Name removed 1862 Scrapped 9.77
     Name restored to Prince Ernest class No 928 1872

No 22 (unnamed) Built 4.54 L&NWR No 285 *Sefton* 11.60 name removed 1862. Scrapped 9.78 Name restored to Prince Ernest
     class No 925 1873

2-4-0 built by Robert Stephenson & Co. (820/1; 871/2)

No 23 *Mersey* Built 6.52 Delivered 8.52 L&NWR No 343 renamed *Etna* 11.60
     (1139 5.62) and name removed. Sold 12.62
     The name *Etna* went to DX No 343 5.62 and Raven class No 920 1864
No 24 (unnamed) Built 6.52 Delivered 8.52 L&NWR No 368 *Majestic* 11.60 (1140 5.62) and name removed Sold 11.71
     The name went to DX No 368 5.62 and Problem No 564 1863

No 25 *Birkenhead* Built 1.53 Jointly leased, then to GWR No 99

No 26 *Weaver* Built 1.53 Jointly leased, then to GWR No 100

0-4-0T built by Sharp Brothers (663) 12.50

No 27 (unnamed) Built for Mr.Edward Oakley for his colliery in Mold, purchased by the Chester & Holyhead Railway and named
     Diamond. Purchased 1.54 by the Birkenhead, Lancashire & Cheshire Junction Railway. L&NWR 356 *Memnon*
     11.60 (356A 4.61 and 1118 5.62) To Wolverton Works 1869 and there named *Acton* Sold to the Shropshire
     Union Railways and Canal 1871 Cut up at Crewe 3.83

0-4-2 built by Sharp, Stewart & Co. (783/4) 4.54 & 5.54

Nos 28-9 (unnamed) Jointly leased, then to GWR Nos 104/5

2-4-0 built by W.Fairbairn & Sons 1854 Delivered 1.55

Nos 30/1 (unnamed) Jointly leased, then to GWR Nos 106/7

2-4-0T built by Robert Stephenson & Co. (1049/50)

No 32 *Volante* Built 1.56 Jointly leased, then to GWR No 97
No 33 *Voltigeur* Built 2.56 Jointly leased, then to GWR No 98

2-4-0T built by W.Fairbairn & Sons 1855

No 34 (unnamed) Purchased 7.56 L&NWR No 34 *Phoebus* 11.60 (1141 5.62) Withdrawn 1864 and Sold 3.65
     The name went to No DX class No 34 5.62

0-4-2 built by Sharp, Stewart & Co. (953/4)

No 35 (unnamed)	Built 9.56 L&NWR No 35 *Talisman* 11.60 (1172 2.65 and 1836 12.71) Scrapped 8.82
	The name went to Samson class No 35 2.65
No 36 (unnamed)	Built 10.56 L&NWR No 36 *Thalaba* 11.60 (1164 2.65 and 1835 12.71) Scrapped 3.75
	The name went to Samson class No 36 2.65

0-6-0 built by Robert Stephenson & Co. (1055/60)

No 37 *Thunderer*	Built 8.56 Jointly leased, then to GWR No 101
No 40 *Dreadnought*	Built 9.56 Jointly leased, then to GWR No 102

2-4-0 ordered from Jones & Potts 4.55 by the Shrewsbury & Hereford Railway

No 38 Dee	Purchased 8.56 L&NWR No 325 renamed *Chandos* 11.60 (1136 5.62) Sold 12.65 to Denbigh, Ruthin & Corwen Railway, and when this company was taken over by the L&NWR in 1879 was allotted No 2349 (1860 4.79) Scrapped 8.79.
	The name *Chandos* went to DX No 325 5.62, and to Raven class No 923 9.64

0-4-0ST built by Sharp, Stewart & Co. (964 & 1026)

No 6* *Cricket*	Built 9.56 Jointly leased, then to GWR No 95
No 39* *Grasshopper*	Built 11.57 Jointly leased, then to GWR No 96

0-4-2 built by Sharp, Stewart & Co. (1071/2)

No 41 (unnamed)	Built 8.58 L&NWR No 124 *Marquis Douro* 11.60 (1176 2.65 and 1837 12.71) Rebuilt 0-6-0 1869 Sold 3.74 to Malines Terneuzen Railway No 9 and still at work in 1937
No 42 (unnamed)	Built 9.58 L&NWR No 231 *Firefly* 11.60 (1178 2.65 and 1838 12.71) Rebuilt 0-6-0 by 1865 Sold 3.74 to Malines Terneuzen Railway No 10 and still at work in 1937

2-4-0T built by Robert Stephenson & Co. (Nos 1081 and 1082)

No 1 *Zeno*	Built 2.57 L&NWR 401 11.60 (1142 1.65)
	Sold 8.65 to James Livesey, then to Central Uruguay Railway No 6 Scrapped 1895
	Samson No 401 1.65
	Waterloo No 401 3.94
No 2 **Zopyrus**	Built 2.57 L&NWR 404 11.60 (1129 1.65 and 1133 5.65)
	Sold 8.65 to James Livesey, then to Central Uruguay Railway No 7 Scrapped 1895
	Samson No 404 1.65
	Waterloo No 404 3.94

2-4-0 built by Robert Stephenson & Co. (Nos 1097 and 1098)

No 4 **Zygia**	Built 4.57 L&NWR 418 11.60 (1130 1.65 and 1813 12.71) Scrapped 12.78
	Samson No 418 1.65
	Waterloo No 418 3.93
No 5 **Zillah**	Built 6.57 L&NWR 419 11.60 (1174 1.65 and 1814 12.71) Scrapped 9.79
	Samson No 419 2.65
	Waterloo No 419 1.90
	Alfred the Great No 1947 6.11

* There is conflicting evidence surrounding these two. One was delivered in 1856, the other in 1857, and their names were *Cricket* and *Grasshopper*. But which was No 6 and which No 39 is uncertain. *Cricket* was the first to be delivered, in 1856, and *Grasshopper* the following year.

THE SOUTH STAFFORDSHIRE RAILWAY

From 5th July 1852 L&NWR (N Div) operated the line and maintained the locomotives, but these remained SS property.
The S Div took over the SSR working in April 1856; the SSR engines were transferred to the Southern Division but were not renumbered into the S Div list until (probably) July 1859.

It is most likely that they lost their names at that time. In April 1862 they were renumbered in the L&NWR series by the addition of 600.

Southern Division Number	South Staffordshire Number & Name		Building Date	D. W. Diam.	Type	Builder	Disposal	
7.59								
297	1	Dudley	2.49	5ft 9in	2-2-2	W.Fairbairn & Sons	Scrapped	3.81
298	2	Walsall	3.49	5ft 9in	2-2-2	"	Scrapped	4.78
299	3	Wednesbury	4.49	5ft 9in	2-2-2	"	Scrapped	8.81
300	4	Lichfield	5.49	5ft 9in	2-2-2	"	Scrapped	4.74
53	5	Burton	5.49	5ft 6in	2-2-2	Sharp Bros. & Co.	Scrapped	3.77
84	6	Stafford	5.49	5ft 6in	2-2-2	"	Scrapped	1.79
116	7	Bescot	6.49	5ft 6in	2-2-2	"	Scrapped	4.79
307	8	Birmingham	7.49	5ft 0in	0-6-0	W.Fairbairn & Sons	Scrapped	4.80
308	9	Wolverhampton	7.49	5ft 0in	0-6-0	"	Sold	8.75
(None)	10	Belvidere	1850	5ft 0in	0-4-2	W.J.& J.Garforth & Co. allotted)	Scrapped	1859
221	11	Angerstein	1850	5ft 0in	0-4-2	"	Scrapped	2.76
309	12	Pelsall	1.51	5ft 0in	0-6-0	R.Stephenson & Co.	Sold	3.74
310	13	Alrewas	1.51	5ft 0in	0-6-0	"	Sold	3.75
111	14	Sylph	7.51	5ft 0in	2-4-0 T	Sharp Bros. & Co.	Sold	8.73
112	15	Safety	7.51	5ft 0in	2-4-0 T	"	Sold	4.73
301	16	Viper	12.52	5ft 0in	0-6-0	E.B.Wilson & Co.	Scrapped	1.64
302	17	Stag	1.53	5ft 0in	0-6-0	"	Scrapped	1.74
160	18	Esk	5.53	6ft 0in*	2-4-0	"	Scrapped	4.76
181	19	Justin	5.53	6ft 0in*	2-4-0	"	Scrapped	10.74
305	20	Priam	4.55	5ft 0in	0-6-0	Vulcan Foundry	Withdrawn	1867
306	21	Ajax	4.55	5ft 0in	0-6-0	"	Sold	6.72
304	22	Bilston	7.56	5ft 0in	0-4-2	Beyer, Peacock & Co.	Scrapped	4.77
303	23	Derby	7.56	5ft 0in	0-4-2	"	Scrapped	7.77
311	(24)	Cannock	3.58	5ft 0in	0-6-0	W.Fairbairn & Sons	Scrapped	7.79
312	(25)	Bloxwich	3.58	5ft 0in	0-6-0	"	Scrapped	12.79
313	(26)	McConnell	4.58	5ft 0in	0-6-0	"	Scrapped	3.81
314	(27)	Vauxhall	5.58	5ft 0in	0-6-0	"	Scrapped	1.81
315	(28)	Aston	5.58	5ft 0in	0-6-0	"	Scrapped	10.78
316	(29)	Tipton	6.58	5ft 0in	0-6-0	"	Scrapped	8.78

* This is Clive Hardy's figure (E.B.Wilson & Co. Locomotive Works List); Baxter states "5ft 9in (not confirmed)" and E.E.Robinson Jnr. in the Railway Magazine for September 1935 has "6ft 6in".
According to H.F.F.Livesey and E.E.Robinson Jnr. Nos 24-29 had Southern Division numbers from the outset.

This line was taken over by the Bedford & Cambridge Railway on 7th July 1862, leased to the L&NWR on 23rd June 1864 and absorbed by them in 1870.

Shannon   0-4-0WT 3ft 0ins driving wheels Built 5.57 by George England & Co. To L&NWR 3.62 (1104 8.10.62 and 1863 12.71)
Sold to Wantage Tramway Company 5.78, to be their No 5.
Withdrawn and preserved in December 1945, and currently with the Great Western Society at Didcot.

Little England   2-2-2T Built 1848 by George England & Co. To L&NWR 1863 as Departmental Locomotive.

Fig. 64   0-4-0WT *Shannon* built in 1857 by George England & Co. L&NWR 1104. In steam aged 113 years at Didcot 2nd May 1970.

(John Goodman).

THE KNIGHTON RAILWAY COMPANY

The Company was incorporated in 1858, merged with the Central Wales Railway by an Act of 22nd June 1863. It had been worked by the L&NWR from 21st May 1863, and was absorbed by them in 1868.

1328 *Knighton*   0-4-2ST 4ft 0ins driving wheels Built by Beyer, Peacock 2.61 L&NWR 7.64 (1115 11.65)
Sold 5.69 to Messrs Partridge & Jones of Pontypool.

Fig. 65 0-4-2ST *Knighton* built by Beyer, Peacock in 1861, for the Knighton Railway Company.

(L&NWR Society Photograph Collection No. 9665).

THE LUDLOW & CLEE HILL RAILWAY

The line was authorised in 1861. Its owners made a Working Agreement with the GWR and the L&NWR jointly on 1st June 1867, and these two absorbed the line with effect from 1st January 1893, by an Act of 28th June 1892. It remained a joint line until 1948.

(1634) *Sir Charles*   0-6-0WT 3ft 10in driving wheels Built by Sharp, Stewart & Co. 11.63 (Works No.1477) L&NWR 7.64
(1189 12.67 and 1839 12.71)
Sold 7.72 to Bournes and Robinson, colliery proprietors, St.Helens. Later owned by Whitecross Co.Ltd.
at Sherdley Colliery, and by 1898 known to be at Glengarnock Steel Works.

Fig. 66 *Sir Charles* 0-6-0WT Ludlow & Clee Hill Railway. At Sherdley Colliery, Peasleycross on 1st February 1887 when owned by Whitecross Co. Ltd.

Copyright Wigan Heritage Service (J.A.Peden Collection).

Fig. 67 St.Helens Canal & Railway Company No. 4 *Hercules*.

Copright (St.Helens Local History and Archives Library).

THE ST.HELENS CANAL & RAILWAY COMPANY

The Warrington - Garston line was leased to the L&NWR with effect from 1st July 1860, and the whole line was absorbed by them on 29th July 1864.

L&NWR 1864 Number	Name	Type when built	Building Date / History	Disposal
1 1367	**Navvie** (or *Navvy*)	0-4-0?	1834 ?Bury Extensively reconstructed Sutton Works 1855-7	Sold 3.65
2 1368	**Trent**	0-4-2	1842 "Sharp, Stewart 0-4-2 from L&NWR" Rebuilt 1857 Purchased 4.60 Sold 9.64 to I.W.Boulton The identity of the Sharp Stewart (or Sharp, Roberts) 0-4-2 purchased from the L&NWR in April 1860 and which became No 2 *Trent* was originally M&B No 23, then L&NWR N.Div No 423	Sold 9.64
3 1369	*Irwell*	0-6-0	1856	Scrapped 9.64
4 1370	*Hercules*	0-4-2	1856 Sutton Works Rebuilt 0-4-2T by 7.64	Sold 1.65
5 1371	*Swan*	2-2-2	L&M No 79 9.42 L&NWR No 138, purchased from L&NWR 5.55 Crewe 1855 list gives "cut up 5.55", but it could have been sold to St.Helens Railway to be their first No 5, then sold on to the Balaklava Railway 8.55. St.Helens appear to have replaced it with a second ?2-2-2 No 5 *Swan*, L&NWR No 1371 7.64 A *Swan*, an 0-4-0 built 1838 by Jones Turner & Evans, appears on a St.Helens list in 1849, and again in January 1855, so strictly speaking the above two were the second and third engines of that name.	Sold 12.64

Fig. 68   St. Helens Canal & Railway Company No. 9 *Swallow*. Formerly L&M No. 69. of 1841.

6	1372	**John Smith**	0-4-0	Built 1830s or 40s by Bury. Purchased from Crewe. Extensively rebuilt 1855 at Sutton Works (1197 9.65)	Sold 12.71
7	1373	*Eden*	0-4-2	Built 1849 Sutton Works	Sold 1.65
8	(1374)	**Sankey**	2-2-0T?	Possibly built by Adams in 1865	Scrapped 4.64
9	1375	*Swallow*	2-2-2	L&M No 69 9.41 L&NWR No 128, purchased from L&NWR 3.50 Rebuilt 2-4-0 either before purchase, or by St.Helens by 1855 Rebuilt 1857 (1200 1.66)	Sold 2.71
10	1376	*Ribble*	0-4-0	Built E.Bury & Co. and named 1847 for the Preston & Wyre Railway, Harbour & Dock L&NWR No 258 4.50 Replaced 5.56 Sold to St.Helens Railway 4 or 5.56 No 10 *Ribble* L&NWR No 1376 7.64	Scrapped 9.64
11	1377	**Tyne**	0-6-0	Possibly built by E.Bury & Co.	Sold 9.65
12	1378	*Saracen*	0-4-2	Built J.Melling 2.42 for the Grand Junction Railway L&NWR No 1 *Saracen* 1847, purchased 2.52, to become No 12 Rebuilt 0-6-0 at some time L&NWR No 1378 7.64	Sold 5.65
13	1379	**Forth**	0-4-2	Built 1852 Daglish	Scrapped 1.65
14	(1380)	*Star*	2-2-2	1.45 Edge Hill L&M No 89 *Woodlark* L&NWR No 147 1847 Purchased 2.52 to become No 14 *Star* Rebuilt 0-4-2 at some time	Sold 11.64
15	1381	*Scorpion*	2-2-2	Built J.Melling 2.42 for the Grand Junction Railway L&NWR No 7 *Scorpion* 1847, purchased 2.52, to become No 15 Rebuilt 0-6-0 at some time, L&NWR No 1381 7.64	Sold to Bishops Castle Railway 6.65
16	1382	*Mersey*	0-6-0	(The second) No 16 *Mersey* might have been Bury, Curtis & Kennedy's 0-6-0, built 12.46 Southern Division No 168, and purchased 2.58, L&NWR No 1382 7.64 (1132 2.65) Reboilered Wolverton 9.64	Sold 4.1.70
				(The first St.Helens No 16 *Mersey* had been a 2-2-2 built by Tayleur & Co for the Grand Junction in 1838 L&NWR No 36 *Thalaba*, purchased in 4.51 It was replaced by another engine having the same number and name)	Sold 7.57
17	1383	**Britain**	2-4-0	L&M No 84 4.43 L&NWR No 142 *Bittern* 1847 Replaced 7.52 Purchased 12.52 to become St.Helens No 17 and renamed *Britain*, but this is not confirmed.	Scrapped 9.64
18	1384	*Lapwing*	2-2-2	L&M No 85 10.43 L&NWR No 143 *Lapwing* 1847 Purchased 9.53 as a 2-4-0 to become their No 18 *Lapwing* Rebuilt 0-6-0T 1857 L&NWR No 1384 7.64	Sold 2.65
19 (No 30 until late 1859)	1385	**Severn**	0-6-0	Built 4.59 Sharp, Stewart & Co (1129) (1210 12.67 and 1817 11.71)	Scrapped 1.83
20	(1386)	*Sun*	2-2-2?	Built c1859 Sharp, Stewart & Co.	Sold 9.64
21	1387	*Raven**	2-4-2T	Built 11.63 Sutton Works (1226 12.67, 1818 11.71 and 3040 11.86) Rebuilt 2-4-0 in the 1870s	Scrapped 7.88
22 (No 31 until late 1859)	1388	*Shannon*	0-6-0	Built 4.59 Sharp, Stewart & Co. (1130) (1267 12.67) Rebuilt 0-6-0T 1871 (1819 11.71)	Scrapped 3.80
23	1389	*Hero*	0-4-2	Built 1853 Sutton Works	Sold 2.65
24	1390	*Alma*	2-2-2	1842/4 Edge Hill 'Bird' class purchased 1854 Rebuilt 2-4-0 at some time (1125 1.66) Rebuilt 12.67 (1816 11.71)	Sold 1.74
25	1391	*Goliath*	0-4-2	Built 1854 Sutton Works	Scrapped 5.65

Fig. 69   St.Helens Canal & Railway Company No. 26. *Clyde.*

St.Helens Local History and Archives Library (Allan Sommerfield Collection).

26	1392	**_Clyde_**	0-4-2	Built 1850 Sutton Works	Sold 7.65
27	1393	_Dee_	0-4-2	Built 1860 Sutton Works	Sold 2.65
28	(1394)	_Lune_	0-4-0?	Possibly built by E.Bury	Scrapped Wolverton 12.64

* 21 _Raven_ was generally known as "White Raven" because at one time it was painted in white livery. It is given as "White Raven" in the Crewe workshop book entry listing engines taken over in August 1864.
GJ 0-4-2 No 70 _Sphinx_ built by J.Melling 1.41 was purchased 4.51, and the name retained. The number given to it is not known, and it appears to have gone by July 1864.

L&M 0-4-0 No 23 _Atlas_ 10.31 Rebuilt 0-4-2 by 8.34 Renewed as 2-2-2 No 81 11.42 L&NWR No 140 1847 Sold to St.Helens 2.52, who may have renamed it _Sutton_ (after the name of their Works), but this is not confirmed. It did not survive to return to L&NWR ownership.

The following were purchased from the L&NWR:-

Date	St.Helens No and Name		L&NWR No and Name	
4.51	16	_Mersey_	36	_Thalaba_
4.51	n/k	_Sphinx_	70	_Sphinx_
2.52	14	_Star_	147	_Woodlark_
2.52	12	_Saracen_	1	_Saracen_
2.52	15	_Scorpion_	7	_Scorpion_
12.52	17	_Britain_	142	_Bittern_ or 140 _Atlas_
9.53	18	_Lapwing_	143	_Lapwing_
4 or 5.56	10	_Ribble_	258	_Ribble_

Tolson writes "Probably a further 5 "Birds" purchased from L&NWR in 1854 and 1855" It is impossible to identify them precisely because of the time lag between withdrawal, a sale offer and eventual transaction, but the most likely candidates for St.Helens No 24 *Alma* are 126 *Partridge*, 133 *Ostrich* and 146 *Redwing*.

Postscript.

Early names were *King William IV, Queen Adelaide, Collier* (1832), *Star* (1833), *Greenall* (1833) (named after Peter Greenall, Chairman of the Directors in 1830), *Widnes* (1834), *Director* (1834), *Viaduct* (1834), *Sutton* and *Parr* (1838), *St.Helens* and *Runcorn* (1838-54), *Swan* (1849), *Eagle* (possibly purchased from L&NWR), *Blackbrook* (1849), *Garston, Queen* and *Resurgam* (1850). Apart from *Eagle*, none of these came from L&NWR stock.

Fig. 70   *Eller* Cockermouth & Workington Junction Railway. The name is just visible, painted on the boiler.

Hudswell Clarke Official Photograph   (Frank Jones Collection).

THE COCKERMOUTH & WORKINGTON RAILWAY

The Company was incorporated in 1845, and opened in 1847. It was absorbed by the L&NWR on 16th July 1866, and the five locomotives then in service went into L&NWR stock in December 1866.
These five were always referred to by their names only, and it is possible that they were never numbered.

C&WR (Number) and name	Number allotted 26.7.66	Renumbered Duplicate			Type	Built	Builder	Disposal
		1.4.67	6.67	12.71				
1 *Derwent*	(1548)	1575	1192		2-4-0T	1854	Neilson (75)	Scrapped 6.68
2 *Cocker*	(1550)	1577	1259	1821	0-4-2	1846-7	W.& A.Kitching.	Sold 3.74 to J.Firbank
3 *Marron*	(1549)	1576	1147	1822	0-4-2	1847	W.& A.Kitching	Sold as 0-4-2T 2.74 to W.Horsley
4 *Solway*	(1547)	1574	1183		0-4-0ST	1856	Neilson (324)	
	Rebuilt 0-4-2ST in late 1856, and according to Crewe records later rebuilt 2-4-0							Scrapped 6.68
5 *Eller*	(1546)	1573	1185	1823	0-6-0	8.62	Hudswell & Clarke	Scrapped 5.81

An earlier locomotive named *Derwent* built by Tulk & Ley (No 8) in 1846 had gone to the Whitehaven & Furness Junction Railway in 1853

THE WHITEHAVEN JUNCTION RAILWAY
and
THE WHITEHAVEN & FURNESS JUNCTION RAILWAY

The Whitehaven Junction Railway was opened for all traffic by 19th March 1847, and the Whitehaven & Furness Junction Railway was opened throughout on 1st November 1850.

During 1852 while each company remained independent of the other an arrangement was made for the joint use of all rolling stock but each retained ownership of its own stock. At the time the Whitehaven and Furness Junction Stock consisted of three locomotives and the Whitehaven Junction Stock of four, The former kept their old numbers 1-3, while the latter were increased by 3, (i.e. from 1-4, to 4-7).

The Whitehaven & Furness Junction Railway

		Built	Type	Builder	
1	*Lonsdale*	1847	2-4-0	R.Stephenson & Co.	(701 Baxter)
2	*Carlisle*	1847	2-4-0	R.Stephenson & Co.	(702 Baxter)
3	*Derwent*	10.46	0-4-2	Tulk & Ley (8)	

Purchased from the Cockermouth & Workington Railway in 1853

The Whitehaven Junction Railway

		Built	Type	Builder	
1	*Lowther*	8.46	0-4-2	Tulk & Ley (6)	To Joint Stock No 4
2	*Whitehaven*	8.46	0-4-2	Tulk & Ley (7)	To Joint Stock No 5
3	*Lonsdale*	7.47	2-4-0 #	Hawthorn (600)	To Joint Stock No 6 *Phœnix*
4	*Maryport*	7.47	2-4-0	Hawthorn (601)	To Joint Stock No 7 *Petrel*

Fig. 71 Whitehaven & Furness Junction Railway 2-2-2 No. 6 *Phœnix* at St.Bees. The nameplate with diphthong is on the boiler above the driving wheel.

F.Moore's Railway Photographs (Everard Beauchamp Collection).

The Joint Stock was numbered and named as under:-

1   *Lonsdale* Sold 1854 to become Stockton & Darlington No 78 *Lonsdale*
2   *Carlisle* Sold 1854 to become Stockton & Darlington No 79 *Carlisle*
3   *Derwent*   On sale 7.57 Scrapped 1859
4   *Lowther* (ex WJ No 1) Replaced 1856
5   *Whitehaven* (ex WJ No 2 Replaced 1856
6   *Phœnix* (ex WJ No 3 *Lonsdale*) Rebuilt 2-2-2# and 2-2-2T L&NWR
7   *Petrel* (ex WJ No 4 *Maryport*)   "   "   "   "   "   "   FR No 48

\# The driving wheel and the rear wheel of No 6 *Phoenix* were the same diameter, and this and probably No 7 *Petrel* also were easily convertible into a 2-2-2. In a Minute dated 18.11.1856 the Locomotive Superintendent was asked to submit an estimate for altering Nos 6 and 7 to tank engines. A Minute of 5.12.1856 noted that new tanks were required for Nos 6 and 7, followed by another a fortnight later which indicated that both engines required new boilers.

As the years went by each company added to its own stock, but the locomotive numbering remained common.

Owner			Purchased	Built	Type	Builder	Disposal
WJR	8	*Tubal Cain*	1854	3-4.47	0-6-0	Hawthorn (465)	L&NWR
WJR	9	*King Lear* *	1854	3-4.47	0-6-0	Hawthorn (466) (Scott)	L&NWR
							(Baxter FR No 43)
WJR	10	(unnamed)	1854	2.45	2-2-0	E.Bury & Co	Sold 11.60
WJR	11	*Kelpie*	1855	7.48	0-4-2	Tayleur & Co. (320)	L&NWR
WJR	12	*Big Ben*		8.55	0-6-0	Tulk & Ley (20)	L&NWR
WFJR	1	*Excelsior*		10.56	0-4-2	Hawthorn (975)	FR No 44
WFJR	2	*Hecla* *		11.56	0-4-2	Hawthorn (976) (Baxter)	L&NWR
							(Scott "LNWR to FR")
WFJR	3	*Mars*		7.57	2-4-0	Hawthorn (997	FR No 45
WJR	13	*Sirius*		7.57	0-4-2	Hawthorn (998)	L&NWR
WFJR	4	*Oberon*		1859	2-2-2WT	E.B.Wilson & Co.	FR No 46
WFJR	5	*Titania*		1859	2-2-2WT	E.B.Wilson & Co.	FR No 47
WJR	14	*Vulcan*		6.60	0-6-0	Hawthorn (1104)	L&NWR
WJR	10	*Queen Mab* **		11.60	2-2-2T	Hawthorn (1128)	L&NWR
WFJR	15	*Banshee* Ordered	10.62	4.63	0-4-0ST	Fletcher, Jennings & Co.(29)	FR No 49
WFJR	16	*Bob Ridley*	1862	1860	0-4-0ST	Neilson & Co.(571)	R No 50
WJR	17	*Gurth*		1863	0-6-0	R.Stephenson & Co. (1486)	L&NWR
WJR	18	*Cedric*		1864	0-6-0	Hawthorn (1245)	&NWR
WFJR	19	*Lonsdale*		1864	0-6-0	Hawthorn (1269)	FR No 42

* Scott records 2 *Hecla* as ("LNWR to FR"). It seems probable that Nos 8 *Tubal Cain* and 9 *King Lear* were purchased at the same time, and that both were owned by the WJR; and similarly that 1 *Excelsior* and 2 *Hecla* were delivered under the same Order from Hawthorn. In which case 8 and 9 would have gone to the LNWR, and 1 and 2 to the FR.

** There is some confusion about the wheel arrangement of *Queen Mab*. Scott gives 2-4-0; it is listed in his Sales List as sold in 6.74 as a 2-2-2 passenger engine. Beyond question it went to the Isle of Wight (Newport Junction), Railway as a 2-2-2T. It became their No 6 *Newport*, and was scrapped in 1895.

In 1866 the locomotives were shared between the L&NWR and the Furness Railway, the former receiving the Whitehaven Junction Stock, and the latter the Whitehaven & Furness Junction Stock.

Thus the following were numbered in the L&NWR Stock List:-

	Numbers			Duplicate Numbers		Disposal
Joint Stock	L&NWR 1866	Name		6.67	12.71	
6	(1559)	1586	*Phœnix*	1265		Scrapped 6.68
8	(1558)	1585	**Tubal Cain**	1196		Scrapped 6.68
9	(1551)	1578	*King Lear* *	1260		Scrapped 11.69
10	(1553)	1580	**Queen Mab**	1262	1825	Sold 6.74
11	(1560)	1587	**Kelpie**	1266		Scrapped 6.68

12	(1557)	1584 *Big Ben*	1127		Scrapped 7.68
13	(1556)	1583 *Sirius*	1106		Scrapped 7.70
14	(1555)	1582 *Vulcan*	1264		Scrapped 7.68
17	(1552)	1579 *Gurth*	1261	1820	Allotted No 3042, but scrapped 7.86
18	(1554)	1581 *Cedric*	1263	1824	Scrapped 3.77

* Scott writes "One engine, which became L.N.W. 1551, and 1578, and 1260 (7/67), built in 1857 by R.& W.Hawthorn, 6-wheels coupled, DW 4'9", cyls 15 x 24, is not positively identified in the L.N.W. records in the Works Office at Crewe; all the other engines are identified with their original names etc., but it would appear from the particulars given that it was the Whitehaven Junc.Ry. engine No. 9 "KING LEAR": though it is possible that it was originally No.4, or No.7, it was most probably No.9 as stated." Scott's Register Typescript Part 3, page 56. Note that in line 1 of this quotation, Scott has 1857 for the building date of this engine; it was actually built in 1847 as recorded above.

THE VALE OF CLWYD RAILWAY

The line was incorporated in 1856 and opened in 1858.
The working and management of the line by the L&NWR was made statutory by an Act of 25th July 1864, with full vesting and dissolution on 15th July 1867.

The locomotives were taken into L&NWR stock in April 1868.

Three 0-4-2ST engines, built by Sharp, Stewart & Co. built in 9.58 (1079), 10.58 (1080) and 8.59 (1136) respectively.

1   1686 *Clwyd*   (1183 6.68) 1164 11.71 (1866 5.79) Name removed 9.8.75 Scrapped 8.8.82

2   1687 *Elwy*   (1192 6.68) 1166 11.71 (1877 7.79) Possibly allotted No 3090 2.87 Scrapped 25.5.87

3   1688 *Galtfaenan*   (1204 6.68) 1168 11.71 (1853 7.79) Name removed 9.8.75 Scrapped 20.6.83

The name *Galtfaenan* has been spelt differently, as *Galtfarenan* in the ledger Donald Stuart discovered at Crewe (Appendix 2), and as *Galltfaenan* by Baxter, Goodall and by J.M.Dunn in the Railway Magazine of February 1957.

THE CARNARVONSHIRE RAILWAY

Absorbed by the L&NWR as the result of an Act of 4th July 1870. There were two locomotives, of which only one, a 2-4-0 built by Sharp, Stewart & Co. was named,

1790 *Glynllivon*   Built 1867 (1167 12.70 and 1861 12.71) Sold 11.72

GREENBANK SIDINGS, PRESTON

THE BROCKLEY LANE BRANCH
Acquired by the L&NWR on 1st November 1906

Two 0-4-0STs:-

2586 *Greenbank*   3ft.2in. Built by Andrew Barclay No.721 and delivered to the Brockley Lane Branch on 11th October 1894.
To Locomotive Tools Department 6.07, and sold soon afterwards.
At Skinningrove Iron Works (No.9) until scrapped in 1961

2587 *Tomlinson*   3ft.6in. Built by Barclays & Co., No.304 of February 1884.
To Locomotive Tools Department 6.07. Disposal unknown.

Note that over the years much contradictory evidence has been published regarding these two locomotives, but the above details are the most probable correct version. It is possible that neither carried the L&NWR numbers allocated.

Fig. 72 0-4-0ST *Greenbank* of Greenbank Sidings, formerly L&NWR 2586, at the Skinningrove Iron Co., Carlin How, Brotton, N.Yorks. The locomotive is parked at the quayside.

Copyright W.A.Brown, Beech Road, Chorlton, Manchester 21. (John Ward Collection).

THE SHROPSHIRE UNION RAILWAYS & CANAL COMPANY

Acton See Engineering Department Table 12.

THE FLEETWOOD, PRESTON & WEST RIDING JUNCTION RAILWAY COMPANY

OTHERWISE KNOWN AS THE PRESTON & LONGRIDGE RAILWAY

Purchased jointly with the L&Y on 17th June 1867, when the locomotive stock was taken over by the L&NWR.

Gardner   0-4-0ST Built by Beyer, Peacock & Co.(No 42) 12.56 DW 4ft.0in.
Addison   0-4-2 Built by Sharp, Stewart & Co. (No 1233) 12.60 DW 5ft.
          Both sold to Wigtownshire Railway 5.76.

Note. Due to instability, *Gardner* was converted to 0-4-2ST.

"Old Crewe Types":-

	Type	Wheel arrangement	Date introduced
"Columbine"	6ft Passenger, curved frames (SFB Pass CF)	2-2-2	7.45
"Lonsdale"	5ft Goods, curved frames (SFB Goods CF)	2-4-0	2.46
"Cornwall"	8ft 6in Passenger	4-2-2	8.47
"Velocipede"	7ft Passenger	2-2-2	11.47
"Courier"	7ft Passenger (Crampton)	4-2-0	11.47
"Onyx"	6ft Passenger, straight frames (SFB Pass SF)	2-2-2	5.48
"Vampire"	5ft Goods, straight frames (SFB Goods SF)	2-4-0	10.48

The remaining small firebox engines (which had direct action) were:-

	Type	Wheel arrangement	Date introduced
"Odin"	6ft Passenger	2-2-2	11.51
"Glyn"	5ft Goods	2-4-0	4.51
"Rocket"	7ft Passenger	2-2-2	8.52

From March 1853, all new engines were of the large firebox type:-

	Type	Wheel arrangement	Date introduced
"Isis"	5ft Goods	2-4-0	4.53
"Prince Ernest"	6ft Passenger	2-2-2	7.53
"Raven"	7ft Passenger	2-2-2	1.54

Later Classes:-

		Type	Wheel arrangement	Date introduced
"Low-Domed" Singles Nickname	(McConnell)	6ft 0in	2-2-2	5.48
"Large Bloomers" Nickname		7ft	2-2-2	8.51
"Small Bloomers" Nickname		6ft 6in	2-2-2	1854
"Extra Large Bloomers" Nickname		7ft 6in	2-2-2	5.61
"Problem" (or "Lady of the Lake")	(Ramsbottom)	7ft 6in	2-2-2	11.59
"Samson"		6ft	2-4-0	5.63
"Newton"		6ft 6in	2-4-0	4.66
"DX Goods"		5ft	0-6-0	9.58
"Precursor"	(Webb)	5ft 6in	2-4-0	4.74
"Precedent"		6ft 6in	2-4-0	12.74
"Renewed (or Improved) Precedent"		6ft 6in	2-4-0	6.87
"Waterloo" (or "Whitworth")		6ft	2-4-0	11.89
"Experiment"	(Webb)	6ft 6in	2-(2-2)-0	1.82
"Dreadnought"		6ft	2-(2-2)-0	9.84
"Teutonic"		6ft 10in	2-(2-2)-0	3.89
"Greater Britain"		6ft 10in	2-(2-2)-2	10.91
"John Hick"		6ft	2-(2-2)-2	2.94
"Jubilee"		7ft 1in	4-4-0	6.97
"Alfred the Great"		7ft 1in	4-4-0	5.01
"Precursor"	(Whale)	6ft 6in	4-4-0	3.04
"Experiment"	(Whale)	6ft	4-6-0	4.05
"George the Fifth"	(Bowen Cooke)	6ft 6in	4-4-0	7.10
"Queen Mary"		6ft 6in	4-4-0	7.10
"Prince of Wales"		6ft	4-6-0	10.11
"Claughton"		6ft 6in	4-6-0	1.13

Appendix 2

A Copy of two pages from a ledger discovered by the late Donald H.Stuart at Crewe in the 1960s.

Spelling - 'Galtfarenan' etc. as given

Name Plates Taken Off following Goods Engines at the dates
named below

Dates	Nos	Names	Dates	Nos	Names
Feby 12/72	138	Swan	Decr 31/72	188	Colonel
" "	361	Umpire	" "	1125	Tebay
" "	17	Caliban	July 30/72	30	Sirius
" "	258	Ribble	Aug 26/72	13	Prospero
Feby 19/72	326	Rowland Hill	Jany 2/73	105	Viscount
" "	126	Partridge	Feby 26/73	319	Anson
" "	352	Raglan	" "	1112	Luck of Edenhall
" "	163	Osprey	March 15/73	339	Nasmyth
" "	32	Tamerlane	June 9/73	1126	Penrith Beacon
" "	376	Proserpine	" "	1119	Levens
May 16/72	161	Cuckoo	" "	336	Woodcock
June 21/72	5	Falcon	" "	15	Phalaris
July 3/72	13	Prospero	" "	322	Harrowby
Sept 4	131	Kingfisher	" "	143	Lapwing
Octbr 15/72	10	Dragon	" "	374	Serpent
" "	63	Herod	" "	181	Pilot
" "	71	Typhon	Sept 10/73	69	Python
" 25 "	24	Sirocco	" "	154	Starling
" 31 "	152	Bullfinch	" "	320	Viceroy
Novr 4	203	St.George	" "	330	Hurricane
" "	23	Vizier	" "	348	Varna
" 6	170	Candidate	Sept 18/73	328	Czar
" 25	72	Phlegethon	Octbr 8/73	172	Admiral
Decr 6	349	Warrior	" 22/73	225	Llewellyn
" 12	354	Euxine	Novr 27/73	113	Elephant
" 13	329	Simoom	Decr 10/73	107	Magistrate
" 30	496	Quicksilver	June 22/74	200	Pollux
" "	500	Menai	July 14/74	155	Ousel

————————————(Second page)————————————

Dates	Nos	Names
Oct 22/74	50	Hornet
Apr 19/75	1104	Eamont
Aug 9/75	122	Goliah
" "	1168	Galtfarenan
" "	1164	Clwyd

(END)

Note that 13 *Prospero* is listed twice, on 3rd July and 26th August 1872 and that 30 *Sirius* and 13 *Prospero* (second mention) are not listed in chronological order.

496 *Quicksilver*, and 500 *Menai* were Passenger engines.

Fig. 73   Problem class 531 *Lady of the Lake.* Note replica of the bronze medal above the number plate.

(Allan Sommerfield Collection).

Fig. 74   Teutonic class 3105 *Jeanie Deans.* As numbered for the Edinburgh Exhibition in 1890.

L&NWR Postcard Set 10 "Famous Locomotives" No. 6.   (Fred Gray Collection).

Appendix 3
EXHIBITIONS

Several locomotives, each one the pride of the Line at the time, were exhibited. They were:-

173 *Cornwall.*

The Great Exhibition of 1851, held in London at the Crystal Palace 1st May to 15th October where it was awarded a medal. Preserved 1933.

245 *Liverpool.*

(S Div. No) The Crampton 6-2-0. The Great Exhibition of 1851. Awarded a Council Medal for originality.

531 *Lady of the Lake.*

The International Exhibition of 1862, in London. Bronze Medallist 'for excellence of workmanship'.
A replica of the medal was carried first on the footplate side-sheets, and when the cab was fitted, above the painted engine number, later numberplate.

373 Southern Division.

McConnell's H class, later named *Caithness.*
The International Exhibition of 1862.

507 *Marchioness of Stafford.*

Carried No 2798 for the 1885 Inventions Exhibition, South Kensington and was awarded a Gold Medal.

410 *City of Liverpool.*

The Liverpool Exhibition in 1886.

1304 *Jeanie Deans.*

Exhibited carrying No 3105 at the Edinburgh "International Exposition of Electrical Engineering, General Invention and Industries" - opened 1.5.1890.

2054 *Queen Empress.*

The World's Fair in Chicago in 1893 carrying No 3435, and awarded a Gold Medal.

1926 *La France.*

Exhibited carrying No 4000 at the Paris Universal Exposition, Parc de Vincennes, Summer 1900, and awarded a Gold Medal.

Sent to the Paris Exhibition in 1900 and gained the gold medal for excellence of workmanship.
Has run 224,872 miles to end of Dec., 1905.

FOUR CYLINDER COMPOUND ENGINE 'LA FRANCE'.
BUILT IN MARCH 1900.(L.& N.W. RAILWAY.)

Fig. 75   Jubilee class No 4000 *La France* Note the reproduction of the Gold Medal awarded at the Paris Exposition for excellence of workmanship in the place of the usual Company Coat of Arms.

L&NWR Postcard (Allan Sommerfield Collection).

Appendix 4
SURNAMES

There was no standard policy for the style of personal names. More often than not only the surname was used, but in other cases initials, or Christian or First names, Rank and Decoration, or Titles such as 'Lord' or 'Sir' were included in the nameplate. The following list may assist the reader to identify the people concerned.

SURNAME	LOCOMOTIVE NAME
Arkwright	*Richard Arkwright*
Aspinall	*J.A.F.Aspinall*
Baker	*William Baker*
Bateson	*John Bateson*
Baynes	*Frederick Baynes*
Benson	*Robert Benson*
Bickersteth	*J.P.Bickersteth*
Bishop	*James Bishop*
Bright	*J.A.Bright*
Bright	*John Bright*
Broadhurst	*E.Tootal Broadhurst*
Brocklebank	*Ralph Brocklebank*
Brocklehurst	*W.C.Brocklehurst*
Brooke	*Sir Thomas Brooke*
Calthrop	*Guy Calthrop*
	Sir Guy Calthrop
Cawkwell	*William Cawkwell*
Chambres	*P.H.Chambres*
Christie	*L/Corpl.J.A.Christie V.C.*
Claughton	*Sir Gilbert Claughton*
Cobden	*Richard Cobden*
Cockburn	*Sir Alexnder Cockburn*
Combe	*Harvey Combe*
Cooke	*C.J.Bowen Cooke*
Cort	*Henry Cort*
Cropper	*Charles J.Cropper*
Crosfield	*Henry Crosfield*
Cust	*Sir Charles Cust*
Davy	*Humphrey Davy*
Dent	*Charles H.Dent*
Dent	*Sir Francis Dent*
Dorrington	*W.E.Dorrington*
Earle	*Sir Hardman Earle*
Faber	*Lord Faber*
Findlay	*George Findlay*
Fletcher	*Alfred Fletcher*
French	*Sir John French*
Froude	*William Froude*
Graves	*S.R.Graves*
Guinness	*Rupert Guinness*
Harrison	*Sir Frederick Harrison*
Hibbert	*Holland Hibbert*
Hick	*John Hick*

Hill	*Rowland Hill*
Houghton	*Thomas Houghton*
Ismay	*J. Bruce Ismay*
Ismay	*T.H. Ismay*
Jebb	*G.R. Jebb*
Jung	*Sir Salar Jung*
Kenyon	*Lord Kenyon*
Lawley	*Sir Arthur Lawley*
Loch	*Lord Loch*
Lockwood	*Colonel Lockwood*
Lawrence	*Charles N. Lawrence*
MacInnes	*Miles MacInnes*
Macpherson	*George Macpherson*
Mason	*Charles H. Mason*
Maudslay	*Henry Maudslay*
Mayall	*John Mayall*
Moon	*Richard Moon*
Myddleton	*Hugh Myddleton*
Neele	*G.P. Neele*
Nettlefold	*E. Nettlefold*
Paget	*Alfred Paget*
Pease	*Henry Pease*
Penn	*John Penn*
Poincaré	*Raymond Poincaré*
Radcliffe	*Joshua Radcliffe*
Ramsbottom	*John Ramsbottom*
Rathmore	*Lord Rathmore*
Ree	*Sir Frank Ree*
Rennie	*John Rennie*
Roberts	*Richd Francis Roberts*
Rouse-Boughton	*Sir Charles*
Savery	*Thomas Savery*
Siemens	*William Siemens*
Smith	*John Smith*
Stalbridge	*Lord Stalbridge*
Stevenson	*Francis Stevenson*
Sykes	*Private E. Sykes V.C.*
Tootal	*Edward Tootal*
Trench	*E.C. Trench*
Trevithick	*Richard Trevithick*
Turnbull	*Sir Robert Turnbull*
Walker	*Sir Herbert Walker*
	Sir Herbert Walker K.C.B.
Ward	*Henry Ward*
Webb	*F.W. Webb*
Whale	*George Whale*
Williams	*I.T. Williams*
	Sir Thomas Williams
Wolferstan	*F.S.P. Wolferstan*
Wood	*Private W. Wood V.C.*

This appendix appears following a suggestion made by the late Professor Mike Page

Appendix 5
NAMES IN ALPHABETICAL ORDER

The first instance of this becomes apparent just before the turn of the century in the naming of the Jubilee and Alfred the Great classes. It starts with Jubilee Nos 1931-40, then with Alfred the Great Nos 1947-50, and 1951-9. After which to mark his death the name *Francis Stevenson* is inserted in alphabetical order, a happy event for the strictly alphabetically minded, for the ordered name of the warship *Repulse* would actually have spoilt the sequence - by a hair's breadth! Then followed a splendid run of twenty to end the Class. It is noteworthy that *Charles H.Mason* and *Lady Godiva* appear in strict alphabetical order amidst lines of warships.

In the case of the Whale Precursors the earliest members of the Class appear to have been named as their namesakes were withdrawn, but then, starting with 310 *Achilles* these were being withdrawn in such vast numbers that Whale held, as it were, a fistful of names, and so with the very occasional exception we find them in alphabetically arranged batches of ten. And what a good thing that proved to be, for by this means *Edith* and *Eleanor*, wife and daughter, continued to be inseparable.

We find the same at the outset with the Whale Experiments, when the Cities, formerly higgledy piggledy, found themselves splendidly tidied up. This was followed by the last and final block of ten ending with *William Cawkwell*, by which time old names were not coming in in such prolific quantities and there was a return to the ad hoc principle. It does however seem strange that the series of new names beginning with "B" did not emerge in alphabetic order, whereas the Counties which ended the class did, by completing the English ones before turning to the Welsh ones for the final three.

Appendix 6
SUBSTITUTIONS OF NAMES FOR ROYAL TRAIN WORKINGS

The Company and very likely members of the Royal Family were accustomed to their train being hauled on the main lines by one or more usually two of the latest and most reliable name-bearing locomotives. This was not so much a tradition as an inevitability because all passenger locomotives were named anyway.

But the Great War had its effects, and austerity meant that not only the 1917 batch of Claughtons were unnamed, but so were the batches of 1920 and 1921. Sooner or later it was bound to happen; a nameless Claughton as the best available candidate to be rostered for a Royal duty.

The solution was simple, to transfer to it temporarily the nameplates from some other member of the class.

Many such occasions may have taken place, some to be unnoticed, some to have been noticed but not recognised (for the observer had to know both a name and a number and recognise them as an abnormal pairing), some to be noted but never reported in the Railway press, and happily a few to be recorded. Records are scarce, and do not always tally.

When a Royal Train working was to take place, the King's Equerry would be consulted about the details of its working, was normally present on each occasion, and would take it upon himself to inspect the train and the locomotives for the journey. The Equerry at this time was a certain Sir Charles Cust who was said to be something of a martinet; there were times when the programme of the Royal Party and the requirements of railway operation were difficult to harmonise.

This led to Claughton 207 receiving his name *Sir Charles Cust*, which it was hoped he would accept as a compliment when he first set eyes on 'his' nameplate at Crewe as he carried out his duties. It is said that having no doubt approved of this, he went on forward to inspect the pilot engine to discover that it bore the name *Vindictive*. Was this a deliberate pairing of names? Who knows?

It is interesting to note that according to the table below that on 10th October 1922 207's rightful name was itself transferred temporarily to 1747, and that on the same day there was no name available for 2431 to borrow.

A study of the available evidence provides some examples and these are summarised as follows:-

No.	Named for the occasion	Number of rightful name owner	Train details
8th October 1921			
150	*Holland Hibbert*	163	UP from Scotland
161	*Ralph Brocklebank*	1159	UP from Scotland
205	*Charles N.Lawrence*	2046 (failed en route)	UP from Scotland
179	*J.A.F.Aspinall*	2395 (replacement for 205)	UP from Scotland
207	*Sir Charles Cust*	See below.	

<u>10th October 1921</u>

207	*Sir Charles Cust*	See below.

<u>8th August 1922</u>

2411	*Colonel Lockwood*	1429	DOWN Euston - Crewe
2431	*Charles N.Lawrence*	2046	DOWN Euston - Crewe
13	*Vindictive*	(correct number and name)	DOWN From Crewe
207	*Sir Charles Cust*	(correct name)	DOWN From Crewe

<u>?10th August 1922</u>

2411	*Colonel Lockwood*	1429	UP
207	*Sir Charles Cust*	(correct name)	UP

<u>8th October 1922</u>

1747	*Sir Charles Cust*	(then unnamed)	DOWN

<u>10th October 1922</u>

155	*Sir Thomas Williams*	(correct name)	UP Carlisle - Crewe
2431	nameless		UP Carlisle - Crewe
1747	*Sir Charles Cust*	(then unnamed)	UP Crewe - Euston
2046	*Charles N.Lawrence*	(correct name)	UP Crewe - Euston

<u>Date not stated</u>

2431	*Charles N.Lawrence*	2046

<u>1922 or 1923</u>

163	*Holland Hibbert*	(correct name)	DOWN Crewe - Manchester
2431	*Charles N.Lawrence* 2046, then in Works "		Crewe - Manchester

Photographs exist of 2431 still with the name *Charles N.Lawrence* taken on 8th and 19th August 1922.

The events surrounding the number 207 and the name *Sir Charles Cust* are somewhat complicated.

In The Railway Magazine 1921 Volume XLIX on page 424 the Editor in reply to a correspondent's query states "Name-plates of 1159 were transferred to 161 for the time being for the Royal train on October 8. At the same time three other unnamed engines of the same class were named for the occasion. 150 was *Holland Hibbert* ex 163; 179 was *J.A.F.Aspinall* ex 2395, and 205 was *Charles N.Lawrence* ex 2046. There was another engine named for the same purpose, viz., 207 *Sir Charles Cust*. The name was not a transfer from another locomotive."

This was followed in 1922 Volume L on page 218 in the section "What the railways are doing" by the statement "207, named *Sir Charles Cust* temporarily for the Royal Train working on October 8 last, and which has continued to run as such, has now been named permanently as above." Charles Williams was a regular contributor to the Magazine at that time.

Years later, in the Journal of the Stephenson Locomotive Society of October 1970 at a time when these Royal Train temporary renamings was the subject of some correspondence, a Mr.I.W.Perkins writes, on page 325 "Referring to the letter concerning the above in the September Journal, there are one or two errors which should be corrected. It was stated that 207 was allocated the name *Sir Charles Cust* and used for the Royal Train working on 8/10/1921. 207 was **not** used, or named and in fact neither was this engine used for the Royal Train of 10/10/1921. 1747 being the engine concerned, which had, for the occasion beem given the number **and** nameplates of 207 *Sir Charles Cust* (in **both** directions)".

The two accounts, one being contemporary and the other appearing almost fifty years after the event cannot be reconciled. Mr.Perkins' account must have been derived from an internal source, for no observer could perceive that the engine he saw carrying number plates 207 was in fact 1747, unless of course he had sight of its Crewe Number, which seems improbable.

Naming of new engines was strongly discouraged in May 1923, and the long established practice of naming express engines came to an end. Royal Trains were bound sooner or later to be hauled by un-named ones. There is a photograph in the January 1924 Railway Magazine of Claughtons Nos 32 (un-named) piloting 42 *Princess Louise* leaving Euston on the Royal Train destined for Ballater; The date was 16th August 1923, and on 26th March 1924 The Royal Train was observed being hauled by un-named Claughton 2450, leaving Euston from Platform 7.

Appendix 7
NAME CHANGES MADE AFTER ORDERING

Motion Number	Running Number	Name ordered	Name given	Date
921	1481	*Franklin*	*The Duke of Edinburgh*	6.66
3945	1920	*Rodney*	*Flying Fox*	8.99
4204	1960	*Repulse*	*Francis Stevenson*	3.02
5131	1680	*Plynlimmon*	*Loyalty*	4.13
5137	2428	*Caliban*	*Lord Stalbridge*	5.13
5138	1161	*Lord Stalbridge*	*Sir Robert Turnbull*	5.13
5139	1191	*Ralph Brocklebank*	*Sir Frank Ree*	5.13
5140	1319	*W.E.Dorrington*	*Sir Frederick Harrison*	6.13
5142	21	*A.H.Holland Hibbert*	*Duke of Sutherland*	6.13
5143	163	*J.Bruce Ismay*	*Holland Hibbert*	6.13
5144	650	*Charles N.Lawrence*	*Lord Rathmore*	6.13
5145	1159	*Colonel Lockwood*	*Ralph Brocklebank*	6.13
5146	2046	*Sir Frederick Harrison*	*Charles N.Lawrence*	6.13
5196	2520	*Francis Bacon*	*G.P.Neele*	3.14
5236	2401	*Lord Kenyon*	*Lord Kitchener*	10.14
5246	2370	*Ashbourne*	*Dovedale*	7.15
5382	2420	No name ordered	*Ingestre*	1.23
5509	2499	*Ingestre*	*Patience*	8.22
5516	1747	*Frobisher*	Unnamed	
5520	2268	*Patience*	*Frobisher*	8.22
5521	12	*Vindictive*	*Talisman*	1.23
5529	1096	*Talisman*	Unnamed	

There was always a reason for these changes.

The delay in the use of the name *Franklin* was caused by the visit to Crewe of the *Duke of Edinburgh* in the summer of 1866.

Thirty three years later, the outstanding prowess in 1899 of the Duke of Westminster's racehorse *Flying Fox* resulted in the removal of *Rodney* from the series of warships; and *Francis Stevenson*'s death on 1st February 1902 moved the Directors so deeply that they commemorated him the following month, instead of the name of another warship *Repulse*. Neither warship name was ever used.

It was the visit of the King and Queen to Crewe on 21st April 1913 which had the greatest impact on the names. The George the Fifth class locomotive for which the name *Plynlimmon* had been intended was in the erecting shop and just being finished on the day of the Royal visit, and was given instead the name *Loyalty*. That evening, at a banquet in Crewe Hall, the King gave knighthoods to Robert Turnbull and Frank Ree, and it was decided that the next two Claughtons 1191 and 1161, for whom the names *Ralph Brocklebank* and *Lord Stalbridge* had been selected should instead be named *Sir Robert Turnbull* and *Sir Frank Ree*. The displaced nameplates had already been made, and it was decided to use them, the former on a later member of the batch of Claughtons being built at the time. the latter on the George the Fifth class No 2428, for which the name *Caliban* had been chosen. No doubt the change in Mr.Holland Hibbert's name came about at his instigation.

The names *Plynlimmon* and *Caliban* were used on two of the Prince of Wales class locomotives, No 257 of November 1915, and No 2392 of December 1915.

The inclusion in the list of the name *Duke of Sutherland* took place at a time very close to his death, so close in fact that it is difficult to decide whether it came beforehand so that he should know of the honour, or as an immediate response to his passing.

The names *J.Bruce Ismay*, and *Colonel Lockwood*. were used on locomotives of the next batch in 1914.

The result of these changes was that the Plate Date on *Sir Frederick Harrison*, and *Ralph Brocklebank*, which went into Stock in June, was "May 1913."

In 1914 that most venerable servant of the Company, *G.P.Neele* was considered worthy to replace *Francis Bacon*; the engine originally bore the name *Francis Bacon*, but was renamed before leaving the works. And the extraordinarily great impact *Lord Kitchener* had on the public mind during the early months of the Great War, caused his name to displace that of *Lord Kenyon*. 2401 was renamed before going into service. So Lord Kenyon had to wait until July 1916 until his name appeared.

The change from *Ashbourne* to *Dovedale* is believed to arise from the fact that interesting though the town of *Ashbourne* is, it was really only the base from which people visited *Dovedale*.

Appendix 8
DISCREPANCIES BETWEEN CREWE NUMBERS LISTS

As stated in Chapter 1, only three instances of divergence between the published lists have been found. None of these has any connection with the list compiled in the running department, for these did not show the Crewe numbers.

L&NWR Crewe Numbers and Building Dates

Disparities in sources - A Comparison

		Samuel Scott's Manuscript		Baxter Vol 2B		Rowledge Locos Illust No 121		Hambleton SLS Jnl 7/1940	
NEWTON class Built in August 1873									
1020	*Wordsworth*		*1689*		*1689*		*1682*		
1132	*North Western*		*1690*		*1690*		*1689*		
1141	*S.R.Graves*		*1682*		*1682*		*1690*		
SAMSON class Built in September 1873									
805	*Caliban*		*1697*		*1701*		*1697*		
285	*Phalaris*		*1701*		*1697*		*1701*		
WEBB PRECURSOR class Built between January and May 1879									
779	*William Baker*	5/79	*2251*	2/79	*2257*	3/79	*2251*	3/79	*2251*
680	*Giffard*	1/79	*2252*	1/79	*2254*	3/79	*2252*	3/79	*2252*
255	*Eglinton*	1/79	*2253*	1/79	*2253*	5/79	*2253*	5/79	*2253*
481	*Etna*	1/79	*2254*	1/79	*2251*	5/79	*2254*	5/79	*2254*
626	*Emerald*	1/79	*2255*	1/79	*2252*	5/79	*2255*	5/79	*2255*
718	*Jason*	2/79	*2256*	2/79	*2256*	5/79	*2256*	5/79	*2256*
338	*Levens*	2/79	*2255*	2/79	*2255*	5/79	*2257*	5/79	*2257*
1180	*Pearl*	2/79	*2258*	2/79	*2258*	5/79	*2258*	5/79	*2258*

The Stephenson Locomotive Society Journal for July 1940 contains an article by Mr.F.C.Hambleton containing a list of the twenty engines of the class, at the start of which he wrote "I am much indebted to Mr.E.Eades for valuable assistance in compiling the table. The figures quoted are from the personal notes of the late S.S.Scott, copied from Crewe official records."

Despite what he writes, Hambleton didn't follow Scott's building dates.
In the lists set out in Table 9 in the case of the Newton class I have used Rowledge's Crewe numbers, in the Samson class Scott's and Rowledge's, and in that of the Webb Precursors those of Hambleton and Rowledge. In this last instance Scott has altered his entry for the Crewe number of 338 *Levens* from *2257* to *2255*.

Appendix 9
COMMODORE

The name *Commodore* has a history which, to say the least, is somewhat unusual.

It belonged in the first instance to the Chester & Birkenhead 2-2-2 built by Tayleur & Co. in June 1841, an engine which was withdrawn in June 1855 and thus never entered L&NWR Stock.

The name was also given to the SFB Goods 175 built in November 1847, which remained in service until July 1878. As a Goods engine it might have lost its name at any time after the early 1860s when John Ramsbottom decided that they should no longer be named, but I have no record of when, if it happened, this took place in the case of *Commodore*.

In the early 1920s Samuel Scott produced a Register entitled "The Locomotives of the London & North Western Railway." and in part 3, in his page on the North London Railway, he gives the details of the numbers and names of six 2-4-0Ts which went to that Company from the L&NWR and back. (See figures 184A and 184B)

One of the six was L&NWR 261 *Hercules*, which became N.L.R. No 33 and, contrary to Scott's entry did not have a name. On its return it received L&NWR 529. Some have listed it as then being named *Langdale*, which stems no doubt from the fact that the number 529 and the name *Langdale* had been linked previously on the former Kendal & Windermere 0-4-0T. It had been transferred to the Duplicate List as 529A in 1861.

Scott's manuscript shows 529 with a blank line in the names column. The typescript differs slightly, by entering in brackets the words "no name", on which is superimposed an ink double line, and to the right appears in bold handwritten capital letters *COMMODORE*.

(See figure....)

The questions immediately arise, by whom and on what authority was this entry made? After some research, the identity of the person who did this has been solved.

It proved impossible to find a solution by a study of the six letters *C.O.M.D.R.E*, and comparing them with the handwriting of those who were known to have had close association with Samuel Scott at the time he was producing his manuscript. But all was not lost. Here and there throughout the typescript are entries made in the same hand and ink, by someone who presumably was proof-reading. And a "2" on page 21, the date "1836" on page 25 and the phrase "7 + 26 in 1905" on page 65 give the clue. The handwritten numbers in a sample page of the works of Donald H.Stuart exactly and repeatedly match those in the typescript.

Where he hit on this name in this context we do not know, but the entry is very likely to be correct.

If he is right, then logically, SFB 175 must have lost its name at some time late in 1861.

A Crewe drawing dated 29.10.1861 of new 15 1/4in cylinders "for old goods engines of the class of *Commodore, Lonsdale* etc." has recently come to light which would indicate that they still carried their names at the time. The class name is unusual, in that *Commodore* was a member of the *Lonsdale* class, and incites one to speculate that it might have been in Crewe at the time. Might this have been when it passed on its name to 529?

Who can tell?

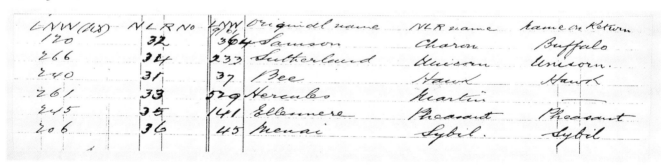

Fig. 76   The COMMODORE entry in Scott's Handwriting.

Orig.No.on L.N.W. N.Div.	Original name.	No. on N.L.R.	Name on N.L.R.	L.N.W.(N.Div.) No. and Name, on return (9/61).	
120	Samson	32	Charon	364	Buffalo
266	Sutherland	34	Unicorn	233	Unicorn
240	Bee	31	Hawk	37	Hawk
261	Hercules	33	Martin	529	(no name) COMMODORE
245	Ellesmere	35	Pheasant	141	Pheasant
206	Menai	36	Sybil	45	Sybil

Crewe Goods engines to N.L.R. 1859/1861.

Fig. 77   The COMMODORE entry in Scott's Typescript.
Scott's work is not without error. No names were carried while on the NLR, so how he gave 32 as *Charon* and 33 as *Martin* remains a mystery.

Appendix 10
THE L.&.N.W.R. WAR MEMORIAL LOCOMOTIVE
1914 *Patriot*

The asterisk on page 36 of "LMS Locomotive Names" which reads "* 2097, later 5938 carried the name *Patriot* for a short while until the plates were transferred to 1914" caused interest and produced some degree of research, particularly by the late Harold D.Bowtell. What was written is quite correct, but the phrase "for a short while" reminds one of the old conundrum "How long is a piece of string?"

What follows is a resume of a memorandum written by Mr.Bowtell in August 1994.

The Company decided early in 1920 that the first of the new batch of Claughtons under construction at the time should receive the name *Patriot*. It was to be Crewe number *5502*, and would be the prototype of a developed design, having a uniformly sloping grate, and Ross type safety valves. When completed it ran trials to assess the effect of the modifications, and because there were steaming problems, these trials took some while and Crewe numbers *5503-6* were the first to enter service. This was reflected at the time LMS numbers *5960-4* were applied to Crewe numbers *5503-6/2*. *Patriot* became No *5964*.

Precisely when the special name plates were made is not recorded, but had they been fixed on the engine during its trials there would surely have been photographs in the railway press.

In the ordinary course of events *5502* would have been given the number 69, from Coal Tank No 69 withdrawn in January 1920 but in the event it was handed down to *5503*, later *5960*, and the very appropriate number 1914 was decided upon. But it was not until April 1920 that Renown 1914 was renumbered 1257 and the chosen number became available.

No 1914 *Patriot* first entered service as such sometime in April or early May 1920.

So where does No 2097 fit in?

It was one of an earlier batch, Crewe number *5397* of 4.1917. It was shedded at Camden during April and May 1920, and was kept in immaculate condition, according to a paragraph in "Locomotive News" of 25th May 1920 which singled it out "for the unwonted splendour of its turnout". So far we are on sure ground.

In the same issue of "Locomotive News" under the heading "Shed changes" there appears "2097 *Patriot* (8)", 8 being the number of Rugby Shed, and there is no reason to doubt the truth of the entry. Harold Bowtell wrote that Rugby was unlikely to qualify for one of the limited number of Claughtons then in service, thus giving rise to speculation about why this transfer took place.

It cannot have remained long at Rugby, for this same issue reported that 2097 was no longer named *Patriot*, "although it was so named for a short while recently" and that since May 3rd it had shared with 1161 *Sir Robert Turnbull* the Scotch corridor express leaving Euston at 1.15 p.m.

The L&NWR War Memorial plaque was located on the inside back wall of Rugby steam shed, and always featured prominently in the Company's mind. As is well known the L&NWR and later the LMS traditionally made sure that an appropriate engine, the L&NWR *Patriot*, its successors LMS 5500 *Patriot*, and 6170 (later 46170) *British Legion* attended the Remembrance Day ceremony at Rugby shed.

It has not so far proved possible to determine the precise date on which this memorial was unveiled or dedicated, but supposing 1914 was for some reason not ready to attend a ceremony at Rugby, might not the splendid 2097 have played understudy?

If so, then "for a short while" might mean "just for the occasion", and maybe the piece of string was scarcely long enough in which to tie a knot!

Fig. 78   Claughton class 1914 *Patriot* in unlined black livery.

Photograph by H.Gordon Tidey
(Allan Sommerfield Collection).

Appendix 11
THE PRESERVATION OF NAMEPLATES

One of the more regrettable quirks of history is that apart from Cornwall, Hardwicke and Pet, no named L&NWR locomotives have survived. In the case of many of the other railway companies it is possible to take a preserved nameplate, and place it temporarily on a preserved locomotive of the same class. But when Sirocco was scrapped, the entire remaining L&NWR nameplates, as it were, became homeless, save for their honoured resting places in museums, or on some study wall, there to be polished and admired.

L&NWR nameplates and maybe a whistle or some such engine part are all that remain, often with the best photograph of the locomotive itself framed close by, and are greatly treasured and from time to time are displayed to the public or come up for sale at auction. One such plate (but alas not an L&NWR one) was placed at one time on the wall above the coat pegs in the hall of its owner opposite the staircase, and one day his small son brought in a school friend, took him half way up the stairs, and pointed to it and said in a tone of reverence and pride "This is the family treasure". He was right.

It has been suggested that a list of known nameplate survivors be included in this volume, and with full acknowledgement of the work of Roger Bell and Edward Talbot I append it, in order of age, and listing the Crewe numbers of the locomotives which carried them.

1847						
No 172 Cornwall.		2044 Courier.	3598	4459 Thunderbolt.		
		2046 Phantom.	3532	**1905**		
		2047 Hercules.	3781	4464 Vesuvius.		
1861		**1878**		4474 Waverley.		
469 Violet. 632	3357	2219 The Auditor.	3492	4476 Apollo.		
1864		2221 Miranda.	3738	4477 Cyclops.		
731 Hecla.	3454	2225 Nasmyth.	3490	4481 Medusa.		
739 Bee.	3125	**1879**		4487 Greyhound.		
1866		2282 Wyre.		4491 Hydra.		
928 Murdock.	3052	**1880**		4495 Emperor.		
986 Duchess.	3251	2404 Duchess of		4505 Experiment.		
1868		Lancaster.	3730	4514 Oregon.		
1161 Corunna.	3347	**1882**		4515 Penguin.		
1168 Delhi.	3146	2509 Henry Pease.		4519 Tiger.		
1176 Novelty.	3291	**1897**		4526 Rowland Hill.		
1179 Gladiator.	3048	3857 Black Prince		**1906**		
1869		**1899**		4529 Watt.		
1284 Britannia.	3056	3831 Robin Hood.		4548 Richard Trevithick.		
1870		3832 Black Watch.		4553 City of Edinburgh		
1308 Hector.	3285	3834 Crusader		4555 City of Lichfield		
1871		3843 Renown.		4556 City of Liverpool		
1384 Lynx.	3353	**1900**		4557 City of London		
1385 Princess.	3142	3999 Warrior.		4558 City of Manchester		
1872		4001 Goliath.		4559 City of Paris		
1481 The Queen.	3287	**1901**		4623 Lady of the Lake		
1873		4125 Alfred the Great.		4624 North Western		
1688 Hardwicke.	3286	4128 Victoria and Albert.		4630 Atalanta		
1694 Narcissus.	3131	**1902**		4632 Leander		
1874		**1903**		4635 Prince of Wales	5030
1846 Skiddaw.	3383	4202 Royal Oak.		4639 William Cawkwell		
1875		4203 Revenge.		**1907**		
1910 Antelope.	3572	4292 Cumberland.		4660 Clive		
1914 Penrith		4336 Hindostan.		4661 Daphne		
Beacon.	3727	4338 Howe.		4675 Phalaris		
1917 Princess		4340 Lady Godiva.		4676 Shamrock		
Beatrice.		4344 Neptune.		4686 Henry Bessemer		
1917 Snowdon.		**1904**		4687 Prospero		
1920 Salopian.	3600	4418 Helvellyn.		4688 Sanspareil		
1877		4419 Oberon.		**1909**		
2034 Sir Hardman		4440 Simoom.		4776 Faraday		
Earle.	3559	4445 Ajax.		4789 Buffalo		
2038 Marrie		4448 Dragon.		4838 Lightning		
Carlisle.	3525	4452 Sirocco.		4852 Derbyshire		

158

4857 Middlesex
4858 Monmouthshire
4860 Oxfordshire
4861 Shropshire
4862 Staffordshire
4863 Warwickshire

1910

4865 Worcestershire
4866 Yorkshire
4988 Miles MacInnes

1911

5000 Coronation
5009 Cyprus
5012 Fire Queen
5014 Pereus
5023 Wild Duck
5024 Ptarmigan
5026 Snipe
5032 Bonaventure

1913

5117 Sir Gilbert Claughton
5118 Charles Dickens
5129 Saddleback
5139 Sir Frank Ree
5140 Sir Frederick Harrison
5141 Alfred Fletcher
5142 Duke of Sutherland
5144 Lord Rathbone

5145 Ralph Brocklebank
5178 Thomas B.Macaulay
3595 Puck

1914

5193 Percy Bysshe Shelley
5196 G.P.Neele
5236 Lord Kitchener
3283 Glowworm

1915

5246 Dovedale
5267 Kestrel
4527 Moonstone
5304 Edith Cavell
5305 Queen of the Belgians

1916

5272 Scott
5321 Lusitania
5322 Falaba
5344 Sir Francis Dent

1919

5340 Sir Guy Calthrop

1920

5532 C.J.Bowen Cooke

1922

5390 Buckingham.
5517 Private E.Sykes V.C.
& 5557
5530 Private W.Wood V.C.
& 5560

1923

5380 Tennyson
5382 Ingestre
5385 Baltic
5497 Marathon
5521 Talisman
5550 Lady Godiva
5563 Bevere

1857

No 87 Earlestown   2308

1865

Pet

1867

Topsy

1895

Engineer Watford

1899

Engineer-Crewe

1903

Engineer Lancaster

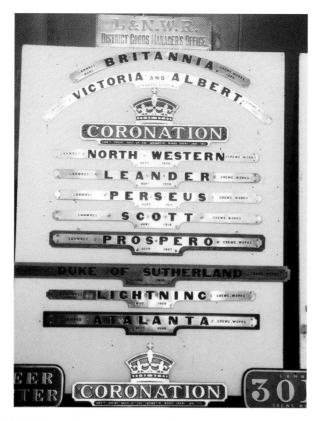

Fig. 79   L&NWR Nameplates on display at Crewe Works 16th August 1996

Copyright Hugh Ballantyne.

Fig. 80   L&NWR Nameplates on display at Crewe Works 16th August 1996

Copyright Hugh Ballantyne.

CHAPTER SEVEN
INTRODUCTION TO THE GLOSSARY

Almost a quarter of a century ago, the late Mr.A.G.Dunbar, who wrote articles in the Stephenson Locomotive Society Journals on the origins of some Scottish engines names, expressed the hope that some L.N.W.R. enthusiast might throw some light on some of the L.N.W.R. names, particularly what he called the "obscure" ones, but sadly this glossary has come too late to fulfil his hopes.

It is an alphabetical list of the names borne by the locomotives of the Liverpool and Manchester Railway, the Grand Junction, and the other companies which merged to form the London & North Western Railway, together with the names of those which from then on were built by or bought by them, and of those of the companies which they absorbed over the years.

The first column gives the name, the second gives the first and the subsequent dates on which that name was applied to a locomotive, and the third gives the details of the name's source.

Most of the sources are obviously correct, others less so, and a few are unclear or unknown. From the start of locomotive naming to the present day, billions of gallons of water have flowed out to sea from the Mersey past Liverpool, and from the Thames through London, so a very few sources may never be discovered.

Every attempt has been made in phrasing the sources to avoid being dogmatic.

Since the publication of the LMS Locomotive Names Book in 1994 in which the glossary included the names of those L&NWR engines which passed into LMS Stock, a considerable amount of new information has come in, a number of necessary corrections have been pointed out, and I have greatly appreciated all who have helped in this way to make the present Glossary more accurate.

Some of the entries are brief, while others go into greater detail. A few needed some form of amplification, and these appear in the chapter immediately following this one.

Once again I wish to record my sincere thanks to all who have helped me to compile this lengthy chapter.

THE GLOSSARY

Name	Dates of application	The source of the name
Abercrombie	1866 1891	1734-1801. General Sir Ralph died on HMS Foudroyant of wounds while commanding the British Army in the Egypt expedition of 1801.
Aberdeen	1854	1784-1860. George Hamilton Gordon, 4th Earl of Aberdeen was Foreign Secretary 1828-1830 and 1841-1846, Colonial Secretary 1834-1835, and Prime Minister of Great Britain and Ireland 1852-1855.
Achilles	W&N1831, 1853,1872,1885,1904	The hero of Homer's Iliad, whose weak point was his heel.
Acton	1869	Possibly named after John Acton (1834-1902), the historian who was created Baron Acton in 1869.
Addison	P&L1860	The Preston & Longridge Railway was formed by a committee which met in 1835 under the chairmanship of Thomas B.Addison.
Adelaide	1866 1893	This is one of three ladies' names first applied in January 1866. She is likely to be a relative of a Director or of some important person connected with the Company. There is just a possibility she was related to Constance, and maybe to Henrietta. (See *Constance*).
Adjutant	L&M1846 1857,1906	An Indian stork.
Admiral	1847,1906	The chief commander of a fleet of warships.
Admiral Jellicoe	1915,	1859-1935 The Right Honourable John Rushworth Jellicoe was promoted Admiral in 1914 and commanded the Grand Fleet 1914-1916.
Adriatic	1890 1908	The White Star liner of 1872-1898, named after the Adriatic Sea; Iron vessel of 3,850 gross tons. The White Star liner of 1907-1934; 24,550 gross tons.
Aeolus	GJ1838,1847,1872	The god of the winds in Greek mythology.

Agamemnon	*1900*	The Battleship of 1879-1903, named after the King of Mycenae who commanded the siege of Troy.
Agincourt	*1900*	The Iron ship of 10,600 tons built by Laird in 1861. She was renamed 'Agincourt' in 1866. She became a Harbour Service vessel in 1904, and a Coal Hulk 'C109' in 1908, was extraordinarily long lived, and not broken up until October 1960, aged 99. The ship was renamed to commemorate the English victory over the French at Agincourt on St.Crispin's Day 25th October 1415.
Airey	*1868,1892*	1803-1881. Richard, Baron Airey served with distinction in the Crimea, becoming a General in 1871.
Ajax	*L&M1832, SS1855,1886,1904*	The mythological King of Salamis and hero of the Trojan War, famous for his size, physical strength and beauty.
Alaric	*GJ1838. 1846,1872,1906*	Chief of the Visigoths, born c.AD376, sacked Rome in AD410 and died that same year.
Alaska	*1884* *1905*	The Guion liner of 1882-1894, named after the United States' territory at the north western tip of North America; a single screw 6,950 gross tons. Holder of the Blue Riband 1882-1884.
Albatross	*L&M1846, 1856,1878,1904*	A long-winged petrel; the largest of living sea fowl.
Albemarle	*1903*	The Battleship of 1901-1919, named after George Monck of 1608-1670, 1st Duke. He was a general whom Cromwell appointed Admiral and who played a leading part in three English naval victories in the first Dutch War. He also raised the Coldstream Guards.
Albermarle	*1903*	A name carried in error. New plates were made with correct spelling and were fixed shortly after the engine had entered service.
Albert	*L&PJ1840, C&B1845*	1819-1861. The Prince Consort was the younger son of Ernest I, Duke of Saxe-Coburg and Gotha, who married Queen Victoria 10th February 1840.
Albion	*GJ1845, 1872,1893* *1915*	The ancient and poetical name for Britain, derived from the Latin 'Albus' meaning 'White' referring to the White Cliffs of Dover. An alternative explanation is that Albion, a son of Neptune by Amphitrite, is said to have established the kingdom of Britain. The Battleship of 1901-1919.
Alchymist	*1848,1859, 1864,1888,1905*	The opera "The Alchymist" was composed in 1829-1830 by Louis Spohr. After Mendelssohn, Spohr was the most popular composer in England. He made visits to England in 1848 and 1853.
Aldam	*H&M1847*	1813-1890. William Aldam, junior, was Chairman of the Huddersfield & Manchester Railway & Canal Company and MP for Leeds.
Alderman	*1848*	One of a body of civic dignitaries.
Alecto	*GJ1837, 1847,1871,1891,1907*	'One who rests not'; One of the three Furies, having a head wreathed with snakes, and who breathed vengeance, war and pestilence. The goddess of curse on evil-doers.
Alfred Fletcher	*1913*	He was appointed a Director (Liverpool) of the L&NWR in 1875, and was Chairman of the newly formed "Passenger Traffic Committee" in 1891. He was also a Director of the Dundalk, Newry & Greenore Railway. He died aged 70 in 1919.
Alfred Paget	*1865* *1904*	1816-1888. General Lord Alfred Henry Paget, CB, MP., the fifth son of the 1st Marquis of Anglesey was chief equerry to Queen Victoria for most of the period 1846-1874, and clerk-marshal to the Queen 1846-1888, in which capacity he may have liaised with the Company over her travelling arrangements. He was included in a list of Directors in 1869. The name was carried in 1904 only between June, when the locomotive was built, and November, when it was renamed *Marquis*. The reason for the renaming is uncertain.
Alfred the Great	*1901*	He was born at Wantage in 849 and became King of Wessex 871-899,900 or 901, known as 'The Father of the British Navy', and who, so it is said, burnt some cakes whilst on the run from the Danes. One of the series of Jubilee class locomotives named after historical folk who have attracted legends to their name. (See also *King Arthur, Lady Godiva, Robin Hood* and *Rob Roy*)

Allerton	*1852* *1872*	Theodore Woolman Rathbone lived at Allerton Priory, Liverpool. He was a Director of no less than six railway Companies, the London & Birmingham, the Liverpool & Manchester, the Midland Counties, the London & North Western, the Lancaster & Carlisle Railways and the North Union. A busy man. Allerton Tower was the home of Sir Hardman Earle.
Alma *St.Helens 1854, 1875,1896*	*10.1854*	To commemorate the Battle of the Alma which took place by the River Alma (Crimea) on 20th September 1854.
Alrewas	*SS1851*	A village four miles north-east of Lichfield served by the South Staffordshire Railway.
Amazon	*1877,1901*	One of a race of female warriors, mentioned by the historian Herodotus. (Possibly legendary.)
Ambassador *1860,1864,1888,1894*	*1848*	The highest rank in the Diplomatic Service.
America	*1884* *1905*	The National liner of 1884-1887, named after the Continent; single screw 5,550 gross tons, holder of the Blue Riband for two months in 1884, and later sold to the Italian Navy.
Amphion	*1854* *1906*	The Wooden Steam Frigate of 1846-1864, named after the King of Thebes, the son of Zeus and Antiope, so musical that he could make stones dance, and which served in the Baltic 1854-5. On 17th May 1854, her captain and crew took possession of the town of Libau, and captured eight Russian merchant vessels, with no loss of life and without a shot being fired.
Andromeda	*1911*	The Cruiser of 1897-1913, when it became a Training Ship. The ship was named after the daughter of Cepheus and Cassiopeia, who, after death, was placed among the stars
Angerstein	*SS1850*	The most probable source is an industrialist Mr.John Angerstein who had a wharf on the Thames named after him, and must have been known to John Robinson McClean who probably ordered both this locomotive and its sister *Belvidere* for use on the South Staffordshire Railway. Alternatively, but less likely John Julius Angerstein, 1735-1823. A Russian born merchant, philanthropist whose art collection formed the nucleus of the National Gallery in 1824. (See *Belvidere*)

Fig. 81   The L&NWR Company's SS *Anglia.*

L&NWR Postcard Set 9 "Steamships" No. 3.   (Fred Gray Collection).

Anglesea	*1850*	The island off the north-western tip of North Wales was called 'Anglesea' at one time, and is spelt thus in the town in Victoria, Australia on the coast west of Geelong. It was in the spring of 1850 that the Britannia Tubular Bridge over the Menai Straits was opened; it is overlooked by the 1816 statue of the 1st Marquis of Anglesey, Field Marshal Henry William Paget (1768-1854), who lost a leg at Waterloo.
Anglia	*1916*	To commemorate the loss of the L&NWR vessel, the T.S.S. Anglia, of 1,862 gross tons, built in 1900, which became a hospital ship. The ship, incidentally, had the distinction of bringing His Majesty King George V home from France shortly before being mined in the English Channel on 17th November 1915 while bringing back wounded servicemen. 134 lives were lost.
Anson	*1853*	Major General the Hon.George Anson was born in 1797 the third son of Viscount Anson, and was MP for South Staffs in 1818. He was a Director of the London & Birmingham Railway, and thus one of the members of the Amalgamated L&NWR Board, becoming Chairman in 1852, and then Commander in Chief, India, the following year. He died of cholera at Karnal on 27th May 1857.
	1900	The Screw ship of 1883-1904, named after the Admiral of the Fleet (1697-1762).
Ant	*1852,1873*	A social hymenopterous insect, like the bee, regarded as busy and hard working.
Antæus	*GJ1841, 1852,1906*	The son of Earth and Sea; a Libyan giant and wrestler who was killed by Hercules.
Antelope	*1853, 1875,1895*	The hollow horned ruminant, akin to the deer.
Anzac	*1916*	Acronym for "The Australian and New Zealand Army Corps", which served with honour in Gallipoli from 25th April to 19th December 1915, with heavy loss of life.
Apollo	*GJ1845* *1872,1884,1905*	One of the great Olympian gods, son of Zeus, representing the life-giving and the destructive power of the sun. The god of music, poetry and healing.
Arab	*9.1854* *1874,1905*	Apart from the indigenous North African tribesmen several sources are possible:- 1. The name of an earthwork fortress which held out against the Russian Army during the Crimean War. 2. The breed of horse, famous because of the horsemanship of the Arabs in battle. 3. The name of a warship in service at the time. 4. A stagecoach name.
Arabic	*1916*	The White Star liner of 15,200 gross tons built in 1903. She was torpedoed by U-24 at close range off the Head of Kinsale on 19th August 1915. 44 lives were lost of whom several were United States citizens, a fact which caused public alarm. An apology was eventually made by the German Ambassador to the American Secretary of State, and diplomatic relations between the two countries was precariously maintained for another year. She was a sister ship to the 'Coptic'.
Archimedes	*1847* *1872,1886,1904*	The Greek philosopher, 287-211BC. The celebrated mathematician and engineer of antiquity.
Arethusa	*1916*	To commemorate the loss of the British Light Cruiser, built in 1913, which was officially the flagship of the 5th Light Cruiser Squadron and commanded by Cdre.R.Y.Tyrwhitt commanding the Harwich Force of light cruisers and destroyers during the first World War, and in this capacity she made a name for herself in the first half of the war. In February 1916 there were signs of great activity in the German High Seas Fleet and Cdre. Tyrwhitt was ordered to maintain a watch at the mouth of the Texel. Within a few days the German activity died away and on the 11th the light forces were returning to Harwich when the Arethusa ran upon a mine in the Sledwa Channel which had been regarded as clear. Despite heavy seas only ten men were lost. The cruiser was named after one of the Nereids who was changed into a fountain to help her escape the attentions of a river-god.
Argus	*1885,1905*	The nom de plume of Mr William H.Moss who wrote letters in "The Engineer" between September 1885 and January 1886 concerning the efficiency of Compound engines. This nom de plume was well chosen, for Argus was the hundred eyed monster employed by Hera (Juno) to watch Io of whom she was jealous, and the content of Moss's letters was distinctly bellicose.
Ariadne	*1868, 1891*	The daughter of Minos, King of Crete, who was abandoned by Theseus on the island of Naxos.
Ariel	*1848, 1872*	The name of a spirit of the air. The slave of Caliban, liberated by Prospero, in Shakespeare's "The Tempest".

Arrow	L&M1830/7	A straight, slender, pointed, barbed and flighted weapon, designed to be shot by a bow.
Aston	SS1858	The town in the West Midlands, now part of Birmingham, served by the South Staffordshire Railway.
Atalanta	1846 1860,1906	The daughter of Iasus, who in mythology was nursed in infancy by a she-bear, and who became a great huntress, famed for her fleetness of foot. An ideal name for an express passenger locomotive.
Atlas	L&M1832/42 1852,1874, 1893,1916	One of the Titans and brother of Prometheus, condemned to support the heavens with his head and hands. The title of Sharp, Roberts & Co's factory in Manchester.
Aurania	1884 1905	The Cunard liner of 1882, steel, single screw of 7,270 tons gross, built by J.& G.Thomson. She was a troopship to South Africa 1899-1902, and was sold in 1905. Aurania is the land of south-west Syria, and east of the River Jordan. The word literally means 'The hollow or cavernous land' from the Hebrew 'Hauran'. The kingdom of Basham, later the Roman province of Aurantis.
Aurora	1903	The Cruiser of 1887-1907, named after the mythological Roman goddess of the dawn, rising with rosy fingers.
Australia	1901 1911	The Armoured Cruiser of 1886-1905, in the year when the Commonwealth was established. The Commonwealth, and so named to celebrate the coronation year.
Autocrat	1853 1858,1885,1905	An absolute ruler; a description of the Tsars.
Avon	1848 1875,1897	The name is derived from the much earlier word 'afon' meaning 'river', therefore "River Avon" is a tautology. There are many "Avons". This is one of the earliest L&NWR 'river' names, and its identity is obscure. The Warwickshire Avon is the most likely one, for it is crossed by the London & Birmingham Railway viaduct at Brandon.
Babylon	1909	The ancient city of Mesopotamia; also a town in Egypt near Cairo, which was founded by immigrants from there.
Bacchante	1902	The Cruiser of 1901-1920, named after a priestess of Bacchus.
Bacchus	1909	The Roman god of wine.
Bactria	1909	The name of ancient Persia. The area north-west of Kabul in the north of modern Afghanistan.
Badajos	1868 1890	A fortress town on the Portugese-Spanish border stormed and captured on 6th/7th April 1812 during the Peninsular War.
Balmoral	1877 1897	The private Scottish residence of Queen Victoria and subsequent sovereigns. She laid the foundation stone on 19th September 1853.
Baltic	10.1854 1874 1895 1923	Royal Navy ships were in action in the Baltic Sea in 1854 and 1855 during the Crimean War. The New York and Liverpool United States Mail Steamship Line (commonly known as "the Collins Line") ship of 1851, which made the fastest crossing westbound that year. The name was reintroduced. The White Star liner of 1874. An inherited name. The White Star liner of 1874. By 1923 there was a White Star liner 1904-1933 of 23,900 gross tons, in service from Liverpool.
Banshee	1855 1859,W&FJ1863 1863,1892 1909	HMS Banshee was a paddle packet built at Rotherhithe in 1847, fitted with John Penn's improved oscillating engine. She was one of four naval Holyhead packets built that year, named Banshee, Caradoc, Llewellyn and St.Columba, representative, it would seem, of Ireland, England, Wales and Scotland. The locomotive was named after her in 1855 by virtue of her active service in the Black Sea 1854-1855. She was broken up in 1864. A Banshee was a female elf or fairy, the domestic spirit of Irish and Scots families, whose wail portends death. The Destroyer of 1894-1912.
Barfleur	1900	The Battleship of 1892-1910, named after the naval battle which lasted for six days off Cherbourg in May 1692 to prevent the sailing of French invasion troops.
Baronet	1847, 1872	An hereditary order of commoners, taking precedence next below a baron.
Basilisk	GJ1837 1845,1872	A fabulous monster with body and wings of a dragon, head and legs of a cockerel, whose breath or look was alleged by the ancients to be fatal.

Bassethound	*1911*	The short legged, or badger hound.

Bassethound   *1911*   The short legged, or badger hound.

Bat   *L&M1842*   *1852,1862*   A noctural mammal with a body like a mouse and with forelimbs modified to form wings. The L&M locomotive was somewhat misleadingly a member of the "Bird" class.

Baying   *1869*   A name carried for only about two months in 1869-1870.
The source has not been found.

Beagle   *1911*   One of the few locomotives named after vessels of exploration or discovery. The 'Beagle', built in 1820, was used as a 'Survey Ship' between 1825 and 1846, and took Charles Darwin to South America and Australasia in 1831. A small hound used to hunt hares by scent.

Beatrice   *1875*   1857-1944. She was the fifth daughter and youngest child of Queen Victoria, who married in 1885 Prince Henry of Battenburg. The fact that the locomotive was named *Beatrice* when new in April 1875 and renamed *Lady Beatrice* within months, strongly suggests that it honoured one and the same person. The same reasoning applies when it was renamed once again *Princess Beatrice* on the 13th March 1877.
If we take this view, it is strange that the title 'Princess' was not used from the start as in the case of the other daughters of Queen Victoria. (See *Lady Beatrice* and *Princess Beatrice*)

Bedfordshire   *1909*   An English County served by the Company.

Bee   *B&L1832*   *1849,1859,1864,1890*   A social insect, especially the honey bee, noted for being busy.

Bela   *1846,1872*   The river in Westmorland which flows about a dozen miles to the Kent estuary at Milnthorpe.

Belgic   *1914*   To honour our Belgian Allies. The name was placed above 'Germanic' (which had been defaced with a red line) soon after the outbreak of The Great War. It was an appropriate substitution, for there had been a White Star 'Belgic' of 4,200 gross tons from 1885-1898 whose name had not appeared among the 'Teutonics'.

Belisarius   *1909*   AD505-565. The greatest of the Roman Emperor Justinian's generals.

Bellerophon   *1852*   *1860,1864,1906*   The Greek hero, son of Glaucus, King of Corinth, who with the help of the winged horse Pegasus, slew the monster Chimera.

Bellona   *1909*   The Cruiser of 1909-1921, named after the mythological Roman goddess of fury in war.

Belted Will   *1846*   *L&C1857*   *1872,1887*   1563-1640. Lord William Howard was a border chief, son of the 4th Duke of Norfolk, and Warden of the western marches. He was known as "Belted or Bauld (bold) Will".
The traditional name of early Brampton engines.

Belvidere   *SS1849*   A turret on a house or an elevated summer house from which a good view may be had. Meaning 'Good to see from'. Usually spelt 'Belvedere'.
The town of Belvedere is just along the line from Charlton between Greenwich and Woolwich. Both this engine and *Angerstein* were built by W.J.& J.Garforth & Co., Dukinfield Foundry, near Ashton-under-Lyne, Lancs. and may have been ordered by Mr.John Robinson McClean, lessee of the South Staffordshire Railway. (See *Angerstein*)

Benbow   *1902*   The Battleship of 1885-1909, named after Admiral John Benbow, 1653-1702, who died from wounds after fighting a French squadron for five days off Jamaica.

Berengaria   *1909*   The daughter of the King of Navarre, who became the Queen of King Richard I. Born c.1163, married and crowned 1191, and died post 1230.

Berenice   *1909*   History provides six Berenices to choose from. Perhaps the outstanding one is the wife of Ptolemy III, King of Egypt, 246-221BC. It is also a town in ancient Egypt, and the title of two 17th century Tragedies. It was also the name of the first successful steamship built for the East India Company.

Bescot   *SS1849*   The village in the West Midlands between Birmingham and Wolverhampton, served by the South Staffordshire Railway.

Bessemer	*1879*	Henry. When many names from the Webb Precursors were passed unchanged to Whale's Precursors, *Bessemer* was changed to *Henry Bessemer*.
Bevere	*1870,1890, 1923*	Bevere Manor was the home of Richard Moon (later Sir Richard) in the parish of Claines near Worcester.
Big Ben	*WJ1855*	This was the name of the hour bell of the clock at the Houses of Parliament, Westminster. The date 1855 presents a problem. See Chapter 7.
Billy	*1875*	This narrow gauge locomotive was named after William Rylance, the foreman at Crewe in charge of a group of men assigned by Mr.Webb for special projects. He used to sign drawings and work sheets "Wm. Rylance & Co.". Thus at first glance it might appear that there was a 'works' within the 'Works'. At the time of his death he was still an L&NWR employee.
Bilston	*SS1858*	The Staffordshire village near Wolverhampton served by the South Staffordshire Railway.
Birkenhead	*C&B1845, BL&CJ1849, B1853*	The town on the west bank of the River Mersey, Cheshire.
Birmingham	*SS1849*	The city mostly in Warwickshire served by the South Staffordshire Railway.
Bittern	*L&M1843, 1853*	A wading bird, allied to the heron.
Black Diamond	*1899*	A euphemism for coal. A very old locomotive name, first used in 1826 on No.3 of the Stockton and Darlington Railway. The choice of this name at the time of Queen Victoria's Diamond Jubilee might suggest there was a connection between this name and *Jubilee*, coming as close as it did to its nameplate incorporating the two *red* diamonds.
Black Prince	*1897*	The Iron Frigate of 1861-1903, named after Edward, Prince of Wales, the eldest son of King Edward III, so nicknamed because of his martial deeds.
Black Watch	*1899*	Raised in 1730 for the protection of Edinburgh, and known as the 43rd. or Highland Regiment in 1739, a title changed to "42nd Regiment " in 1749 and again in 1759 to the "42nd or Highland Regiment". The full title from 1881 was "The Black Watch (Royal Highland Regiment. 42nd and 73rd Foot.)". Alleged to be Queen Victoria's favourite. The title is derived from the fact that all bright colours had been removed from their tartan, and because the Regiment was employed to "watch" the Highlands. "Watches" were first formed to prevent cattle-lifting.
Blackpool	*1915*	A seaside resort in Lancashire served by the Company.
Blazer	*BL&CJ1857*	A name which, when taken in the context of trail-blazer, is akin to 'precedent'; it may also be evocative, as in 'Fire Queen'. One of the meanings of the word to be found in OED is 'Comet'.
Blenheim	*1849, 1860, 1864, 1900*	A village in Bavaria, where Marlborough defeated the French and Bavarians in battle on 13th August 1704. The Cruiser of 1900-1907.
Blenkinsop	*1873 1888*	James Blenkinsop was the Company Solicitor from October 1861, when the company decided to have their own in-house Solicitor. The engine was named as a memorial to him during the year following his death.
Bloodhound	*1911*	A dog, remarkable for the acuteness of its power of scent.
Bloxwich	*SS1858*	The town in Staffordshire, near Walsall.
Boadicea	*1878 1903*	The British Queen, of the Iceni, who died AD62. The Corvette of 1875-1905.
Boarhound	*1911*	A large hound used for hunting wild boar.
Bonaventure	*1911*	The Cruiser of 1892-1920. There was a 'bonaventure mizen', a small mast at the very stern of a ship, from which the cruiser may have derived her name. It was also a type of boat or ship which had gone out of use by 1614.
Boniface	*1909*	A term for a sleek, good tempered and jolly landlord. The name of the abbot in Sir Walter Scott's novel 'The Monastery', and also the name of nine Popes, the Saint of Devon, 680-754, and of the 47th Archbishop of Canterbury, 1245-1273.

Booth	*1853,1857* *1870,1890*	1788-1869. Henry, Secretary, Treasurer and then General Manager of the Liverpool & Manchester Railway, Secretary of the Grand Junction Railway and then Joint Secretary (Northern) of the L&NWR from 1846-1859. A Director of the Company from October 1848 until May 1859 . It was he who suggested to Robert Stephenson the use of a water-tube boiler, which was largely responsible for the success of the *Rocket*. He was also the inventor of the screw coupling.
Breadalbane	*1880* *1894,1923*	John Campbell, the Most Honourable the 2nd Marquis of Breadalbane, KG was Lord Chamberlain 1848-1852 and 1853-1858, and a Director of the Company until his death in 1862, when the marquessate became extinct, but was later revived.
Bret Harte	*1914*	1836-1902. Poet. Francis Bret Harte, American.
Briareus	*GJ1841,1851,1872*	A giant with fifty heads and one hundred hands, the offspring of Heaven and Earth.
Brindley	*1866, 1873,1905*	1716-1772. James, the great canal builder.
Britain	*St.Helens ?date*	The country.
Britannia	*1869* *1889*	The ancient name for Roman Britain. The fact that this was one of three, the others being *Hibernia* and *Scotia*, makes it most unlikely that the name referred to the first Cunard liner, which had made her maiden voyage from Liverpool on 4th July 1840.
Britannic	*1884* *1905*	The White Star liner of 1874. Iron, single screw 5,000 gross tons. She held the Blue Riband jointly with her sister ship the Germanic 1876-1879, became a troopship to South Africa c.1900, and was broken up in 1903. The Battleship of 1904 - 9th November 1918. Sunk off Cape Trafalgar by U-50.
British Empire	*1911*	Named to commemorate the Coronation of King George V on 22nd June 1911.
Britomart	*1909*	A female knight in Spenser's 'Faerie Queene', personifying chastity. The name means 'Sweet Maiden'.
Brook	*H&M1847*	Named "In honour of Joseph Brook Esq. of Greenhead, Huddersfield, Director and Deputy Chairman of the Huddersfield & Manchester Railway and afterwards of the L&NWR". (Wool merchant William Leigh Brook, of the same family, cotton spinner, was a member of the provisional committee set up to launch the Huddersfield & Manchester Canal Company c.1844).
Brougham	*L&C1857* *1870,1893,1907*	1778-1868. Henry Peter, created Baron Brougham in 1866, was a prominent Regency and Victorian lawyer and politician. He gave his name to a carriage, as did Stanhope and Phaeton. Brougham Hall, Westmorland (near Penrith) is to this day the family residence.
Bucephalus	*1849* *1850,1872,1906*	The favourite charger of Alexander the Great.
Buckingham	*1870* *1890,1922*	1823-1889. When Richard Grenville was Chairman of the Company from 1853-1861 he was the Marquis of Buckingham. He resigned on succeeding his father, to become the 3rd Duke of Buckingham and Chandos.
Buckland	*1882* *1896,1909*	1784-1856. William, geologist, in 1840 discovered with Jean Agassiz evidence of glacial action in Scotland. He was installed Dean of Westminster 27th November 1846.
Buffalo	*L&M1839* *1860,1861, 1875, 1909*	The name given to a number of animals of great strength. One is the domestic ox of India, another is found wild in all parts of Africa, and both these are a different species from the American bison.
Bulldog	*1853,1872,1921*	The English dog of remarkable courage, formerly used for bull baiting.
Bull Dog	*1915*	The division of the name into two words is certainly unusual. It is found in a 1908 tool catalogue as the "Bull Dog Wire Grip", the more you pull the tighter it grips. (O.E.D.)The nameplate was, significantly, fixed **above** the defaced *Dachshund*.
Bullfinch *L&M1845,1855,1857*		The bird.

Bulwer Lytton	1913	1803-1873. Novelist and dramatist. Edward George Bulwer-Lytton, 1st Baron.
Bunsen	1868 1888,1922	1811-1899. Robert Wilhelm von Bunsen was the great experimental chemist and pioneer of chemical spectroscopy. He invented the Bunsen Burner, which used coal gas for heating.
Burmah	1872	The country. A Burmese delegation visited Britain in 1872.
Burton	SS1849	The Staffordshire town on the River Trent served by the South Staffordshire Railway.
Bury	B&L1832	1794-1858. Edward, the locomotive pioneer was Locomotive Superintendent of the London & Birmingham Railway, was elected a Fellow of the Royal Society in 1844 because of his contributions to locomotive design and his successful management of the L&B Locomotive Department, but in the early days of the L&NWR resigned from his position at Wolverton on health grounds in 1847.
Byron	1866,1891	1788-1824. George Gordon, Lord Byron, the poet.
Byzantium	1909	The Greek city, founded 657BC, renamed Constantinople AD330, and now known as Istanbul.
Cadmus	1850,1872	The son of Agenor, King of Phoenicia. He was sent in search of his sister, Europa and was helped by five warriors spawned when he killed a dragon and sowed its teeth. He eventually married Hermione, daughter of Venus. He is said to have introduced the Greek alphabet.
Cæsar	1903	The Battleship of 1896-1921, named after the cognomen of Gaius Julius, Roman dictator and general who was assassinated on the Ides of March 44BC, at the age of about 56.
Caithness	1872	1821-1881. James Sinclair, 14th Earl of Caithness, F.R.S. was inventor of the steam carriage for use on macadam roads, a Director of the Highland Railway, and of the L&NWR in 1865. The engine was built at Wolverton in 1861, and was named by Webb in honour of the Earl, recently appointed a Director.
Caledonian	L&M1832 to GJ Contractors	The second locomotive built by Messrs. Galloway, Bowman and Glasgow at their Caledonian Foundry, Great Bridgewater Street, Manchester.
Caliban	GJ1837 1854,1872,1884,1893,1915	Prospero's slave in Shakespeare's "The Tempest"; a rude misshapen fellow, son of Sycorax.
Cambrian	1849	Welsh. Cambria is the mediaeval Latin for Wales.
Camilla	GJ1838 1846,1872	In Roman legend the queen of the Volsci who led her people into battle against Aeneas, but was killed. According to Virgil's "Aeneid" she was exceedingly swift over land or water.
Camperdown	1901	The Battleship of 1885-1908, named after the naval battle on 11th October 1797 when Admiral Duncan fought the Dutch off the coast of north Holland, in which heavy casualties were sustained on both sides. The British, however, captured eleven ships, but lost none.
Canada	1911	A self-governing British Dominion in North America. The locomotive was named to celebrate coronation year, 1911.
Candidate	1847,1874,1905	One who seeks office.
Canning	1847, 1857 1922	1770-1827. George, Statesman, Foreign Secretary, was Prime Minister of Great Britain and Ireland during 1827. 1812-1862. Charles John Canning (1st Earl) was the third son of George Canning, Postmaster-General 1852-55, and Governor-General of India in 1856.
Cannock	SS1858	The town in Staffordshire, eight miles from Walsall, served by the South Staffordshire Railway.
Canopus	1899	The Battleship of 1897-1920, named after the brightest star in the constellation Carina, and the ancient Egyptian port fifteen miles east of Alexandria.
Captain Fryatt	1917	In Memory of Charles Algernon Fryatt, Captain of the Great Eastern Railway Company's Steamship T.S.S.'Brussels' captured by the Germans on Thursday 22nd June 1916. The vessel had earlier distinguished

herself by attempting to ram the German submarine which attacked her. He was executed in Brugge (Bruges) on 27th July. His body was exhumed after the war, given a State Funeral at St.Paul's Cathedral, and conveyed thence by special train to be interred in Dovercourt Cemetery.

Caractacus	*1880* *1896*	Leader of the Britons against the Romans in the 1st century AD. He impressed Claudius so greatly by his bearing in captivity in Rome that he was freed. An alternative name for Caractacus is Caradoc.
Caradoc	*1849* *1875,1894*	Probably named after one of the four naval Holyhead packets built in 1847, later to achieve distinction as the floating headquarters of Lord Raglan during the Crimean War. A possible alternative might be Sir John Caradoc, 1799-1873, 2nd Baron Howden, British Minister to Brazil, 1847-1850. It was through his efforts that the British blockade of Buenos Aires was lifted in 1847.
Carlisle	*W&FJ1847* *1872*	The city on the English - Scottish border, and the location of the L&NWR Permanent Way Department. The Lord Carlisle of "Lord Carlisle's Railways" (RCTS Publication) was George Howard, 6th Earl, who died in 1848. The connection he had with the W&FJ is not known. The name chosen by Mr.S.B.Worthington of the L&NWR Engineering Department for the engine he purchased from the Manchester Sheffield and Lincolnshire Railway in 1863. The engine had been named *Watkin* after Mr.(later Sir) Edward Watkin of that Company and had been used as an inspection engine coupled to a small saloon.
Carnarvon	*1915*	The county-town of Carnarvonshire, North Wales, served by the Company.
Carnarvonshire	*1910*	A county of North Wales served by the Company.
Castor	*1848,1857* *1860,1866,1894* *1916*	A son of Zeus and Leda, twin brother of Pollux, both of whom sailed with Jason on the Argo. The Light Cruiser of 1915, which took a leading role in the battle of Jutland, and received several hits. Sold 1936.
Cato	*1855*	He was a Liverpool shipbuilder, J.Cato, after whom a Paddle Steamer had been named in 1849, and which ultimately belonged to the London Tilbury & Southend Railway Company. An unlikely alternative is Marcus Porcius Cato, Roman soldier and statesman 234-149BC.
Cavalier	*1899*	A horseman; a knight or gentleman soldier, in particular a supporter of King Charles I.
Cedric	*WJ1864, 1878* *1905*	Cedric the Saxon was a principal character in Sir Walter Scott's 'Ivanhoe'. (See *Gurth*) The White Star liner of 1903 of 21,000 gross tons, which lasted until 1931.
Celtic	*1890* *1907*	The White Star liner of 1872-1893 of 3,850 gross tons. The White Star liner of 1901-1928 of 21,000 gross tons. Celtic is the word applied to the peoples and language of the Irish, Manx, Welsh, ancient Cornish, Breton and Scottish Gaels.
Centaur	*GJ1837* *GJ1842,1853,1879.1895*	The beast of mythology, half horse and half man.
Centipede	*1855*	A many-legged arthropod.
Centurion	*1899*	The Battleship of 1892-1910, named after the rank of a Roman officer in charge of a "Century", or eighty men.
Cerberus	*GJ1837* *1844,1857,1857,1878,1905*	The three headed dog, guardian of the entrance to the infernal regions.
Chaffinch	*L&M1845,1853*	The bird.
Challenger	*1911*	HMS Challenger, built 1858, was used as a 'Survey Ship' between 1872 and 1888, for oceanography, under the command of Captain Sir George Nares. 'The Challenger Expedition' took place between December 1872 and May 1876 for experiments in deep sea soundings. This is another of the 'Ships of Discovery' series.
Champion	*1848* *1874,1904*	One who comes forward to defend a cause; the first in its class. Literally it means 'one who holds the field'. French Le champ.
Chandos	*1854*	1823-1889. Richard Grenville, Marquis of Chandos was elected Chairman of the Company in October

	1860,1862	1853, an office which he resigned in 1861. He was MP for Buckinghamshire from 1846 to 1857, and became *1864,1878,1896* 3rd Duke of Buckingham on the death of his father in 1861. He resigned his directorship in 1880. Another instance of two engines being named after the same person, the other one 'Buckingham'. (Vide *The Auditor*)
Charles Dickens	*1882,1913*	1812-1870 Charles John Huffam Dickens, author.
Charles H.Dent	*1916*	He was General Manager of the Great Northern Railway, a son of Admiral C.B.C.Dent, sometime the Company's Marine Superintendent. (See *Sir Francis Dent*)
Charles H.Mason	*1903*	Charles Henry Mason made his first official appearance as lieutenant to the Company Solicitor, Mr.R.F.Roberts, in 1874 at the public enquiry at Wigan into the accident the previous February near Euxton Junction. He succeeded Mr.Roberts as Company Solicitor. He died on 29th December 1902.
Charles James Lever	*1914*	1806-1872 The Irish novelist.
Charles J. Cropper	*1914*	Charles James Cropper of Ellergreen, Burneside, Kendal was Chairman of James Cropper & Co. Ltd. paper mills of Burneside, and in 1900 was the nominee of the L&NWR to the Board of Directors of the Cockermouth, Keswick & Penrith Railway, and was appointed a Director of the L&NWR in 1907. In 1876 he had married a daughter of the 1st Viscount Knutsford and was thus related to the Holland (later Holland- Hibbert) family. He died in 1924.
Charles Kingsley	*1913*	1819-1875 The poet and novelist.
Charles Lamb	*1914*	1775-1834 The essayist and critic.
Charles N. Lawrence	*1914*	1855-1927 The Honourable Charles Napier Lawrence, created Baron Kingsgate in 1923 was a Director of the Company Lawrence *1913* 1884-1922, Deputy-Chairman in 1904, and Chairman in 1921 following the resignation of Sir Gilbert Claughton. He became the first Chairman of the LMS (1923-4). He was the third son of John Laird Mair Lawrence (1811-1879), first Lord Lawrence of the Punjab.
Charles Wolfe	*1913*	1791-1823 The Irish poet.
Charon	*GJ1840* *1852,1861,1892*	The son of Erebus. The ferryman of the river Styx which flowed nine times round the Infernal Regions.
Cheshire	*1909*	The English County served by the Company.
Chester	*BL&CJ1849*	The city and county-town of Cheshire.
Chillington	*1849* *1850,1875* *1895,1909*	Chillington Hall near Wolverhampton was the seat of the Giffard family, which has a long and notable history. According to D.H.Stuart it was the residence of a Director. On the available evidence it seems improbable that Henri V. Giffard was a member of this family, and if so, not a close one. (See *Giffard*)
Chimera	*ExNU* *1848,1860,1863, 1890*	A monster having a lion's head, a goat's body and the tail of a dragon, and which vomited flames.
City of Carlisle	*1886,1906*	The Iredale liner, sailing from Liverpool.
City of Chester	*1886,1906*	The Inman liner of 1873 of 4,600 gross tons, sailing from Liverpool. She was transferred to the American Line in 1893 and renamed "Chester".
City of Chicago	*1884*	The Inman liner of 1883, lost in fog off the Old Head of Kinsale on 5th July 1893.
City of Dublin	*1888,1906*	The Inman liner of 1864, sailing from Liverpool. Sold 1873.
City of Edinburgh	*1886* *1906*	The Inman liner, sailing from Liverpool.
City of Glasgow	*1886,1906*	The Inman liner of 1850, sailing from Liverpool. Sold 1854.

City of Lichfield	1888 1906	The City, in Staffordshire on the Trent Valley line.
City of Liverpool	1886 1906	Named after the City at the time of the Exhibition there in 1886 at which the engine was exhibited.
City of London	1888, 1906	The Inman liner, sailing from Liverpool 1863-1879.
City of Manchester	1886 1906	The Inman liner, sailing from Liverpool 1851-1871.
City of New York	1888	The Inman liner of 1888-1923, of 10,500 gross tons, transferred to the American line in 1893 and renamed 'New York'.
City of Paris	1888 1906	The Liverpool, New York & Philadelphia Steamship Company's liner of 1865-1884 of 2,651 gross tons which had contended with the Cunarder 'Russia' for the Blue Riband in 1867. It was the first British liner to be steered from the bridge. By 1888 her successor in name was being constructed, of 10,650 gross tons, and she held the Blue Riband in 1889 and 1892, but was transferred to the American Line in 1893 and renamed 'Paris'.
C.J.Bowen Cooke	1920	1859-1920. Charles John Bowen Cooke began his career with the Company in 1875, was Chief Mechanical Engineer from 1909-1920, and died on 18th October 1920.
Clanricarde	1849 1906	1802-1874. Ulick John de Burgh, 1st Marquis of Clanricarde was the only son of the 13th Earl of Clanricarde and was Postmaster-General from 1846-1852.
Clarence	B&L1832	The name of Edward Bury's Foundry, Liverpool in 1832 (King William IV had been the Duke of Clarence).
Clarendon	1849 1851, 1873, 1893	1800-1870. George William Frederick Villiers, 4th Earl was British Foreign Secretary under four Prime Ministers, and known as "The Great Lord Clarendon".
Clio	GJ1838, 1848, 1922	The muse of history and epic poetry.
Clive	1863, 1907	1725-1774. Robert, Lord Clive was the British soldier and administrator, and founder of the British Empire in India. He was known as 'Clive of India'.
Clwyd	VofC1858	The river and valley in Flintshire and Denbighshire, which runs through the Vale of Clwyd and enters the sea west of Rhyl.
Clyde	St.Helens, 1850 1863 1907	The River. By this time the name would have referred to Lord Clyde (1793-1863), formerly Sir Colin Campbell, who finally achieved the relief of Lucknow in 1857. He was created Baron Clyde in 1858, and became a Field Marshal in 1862.
Cocker	C&W1847	The river in West Cumberland which flows fifteen miles north-west through Buttermere, Crummock Water and the Lorton Valley to the Derwent at Cockermouth.
Collingwood	1900	The Battleship of 1882-1907, named after Admiral Cuthbert Collingwood (1750-1810), Nelson's second in command at Trafalgar.
Colonel	1847	An army officer holding the highest regimental rank.
Colonel Lockwood	1914	Colonel the Right Honourable Amelius Richard Mark Lockwood, CVO, was born in 1847, served with the Coldsteam Guards 1866-1883. and became a Director of the Company in 1898. He was MP for West Essex 1892-1917, and was created Baron Lambourne in 1917. He died in 1928.
Colossus	GJ1841 1851, 1874 1899	The Colossus of Rhodes was a great statue of the sun god Helios, some 120ft high and listed as one of the seven wonders of the ancient world. It was destroyed by an earthquake in 224BC. The Battleship of 1882-1908.
Columbine	GJ1838 1845, 1872, 1875	The sweetheart of Harlequin. A character from mediaeval Italian comedy.
Columbus	1866, 1888	1451-1506. Christopher, the navigator who discovered America in 1492.

Colwyn Bay	*1915*	The coastal resort in Denbighshire, North Wales, served by the Company.
Combermere	*1863* *1907*	1773-1865. Sir Stapleton Cotton, 1st Viscount Combermere. was commander of Wellington's cavalry in the Peninsular War, and promoted Field Marshal 1855. The Title is derived from Combermere, Cheshire and his statue stands outside the castle gates at Chester.
Comet	*L&M1830/37* *1847*	A nebulous body revolving round the sun in an eccentric orbit.
Commodore	*C&B1840* *1847,1880,1896*	A naval officer below rear-admiral, and above captain.
Commonwealth	*1903*	The Commonwealth of Australia which had been formed in 1901. The Battleship of 1903-1921. She was a sister ship of the Dominion, the Hindostan and the Hibernia (q.v.)
Compound	*1883*	Literally 'Composed of two or more ingredients', and in this instance of locomotive cylinders of differing steam pressure. This was the name given to the 1883 Experiment Compound.
Condor	*L&M1846* *1853,1877,1896,1916*	The large vulture of the Andes.
Conqueror	*1911*	The Battleship of 1911-1922.
Constance	*1866* *1893*	Lady Constance Villiers, daughter of the 4th Earl of Clarendon, married in 1864 the 16th Earl of Derby, of Knowsley Hall. The Earl had no issue, and so in 1893 her husband succeeded and Constance became Countess of Derby. Two other ladies names were used at the same time, namely Adelaide and Henrietta, and it is not known who they were.
Conway	*1848* *1872,1915*	The town in Carnarvonshire, North Wales served by the Chester & Holyhead Railway, opened in 1848; the river there has the same name.
Cook	*1866,1889*	1728-1779. Captain James Cook, English explorer.
Coptic	*1890* *1906*	The White Star liner 1882-1906 of 4,350 gross tons and a sister ship to the Arabic. Coptic is the language of the Copts, the early native Christians of Egypt and their successors, and used when referring to all things appertaining to them.
Coquette	*1911*	The Destroyer of 1897, sunk by a mine off the East Coast on 7th March 1916. A coquette was a minx or female flirt.
Cornwall	*1847* *1905,reinstated 1911*	The County in which Richard Trevithick was born.
Coronation	*1911*	To honour the coronation of King George V on 22nd June 1911.
Corunna	*1868* *1893*	To commemorate the victory gained by Sir John Moore on 16th January 1809 during the Peninsular War. He lost his life in achieving it. Corunna lies in north-west Spain.
Cossack	*9.1854*	The warlike race noted for their skilled horsemanship. The screw corvette seized in 1854 while under construction for the Russian Navy, which saw active service during the Crimean War.
Councillor	*1847,1872*	A member of a council.
Countess	*1866,1891*	The wife or widow of an earl or count.
Courier	*1847* *1854,1877,1896*	A messenger sent with all speed to deliver letters or dispatches. Originally a 'running' messenger.
Crane	*L&M1842,1852*	The migratory wading bird with long legs, neck and bill.
Cressy	*1903*	The Cruiser of 1899, which was torpedoed on 29th August 1914, and was named in honour of the battle, in

which King Edward III defeated the French Army on 26th August 1346. Crecy, as it is spelt nowadays, lies in Northern France about fifteen kilometres north of Abbeville.

Crewe	*1853*	The Cheshire town in which the L&NWR locomotive works was situated, and the Headquarters of the Northern Division.
Cricket	*BL&CJ1856*	A straight-winged insect.
Cromwell	*1866* *1890*	1599-1658. Oliver, Statesman and Politician, Lord Protector of the Commonwealth of England, Ireland and Scotland defeated the forces of King Charles I at Marston Moor and Naseby, and promoted the King's execution.
Cross Fell	*L&C1859*	The highest mountain of the Pennine Range, East Cumberland. Altitude 2,930 ft.
Crow	*L&M1844,1853*	The bird.
Croxteth	*1852* *1860,1864,1889,1923*	Croxteth Hall, West Kirby, Liverpool was the residence of the Earl of Sefton. (See *Sefton*)
Crusader	*1899*	One engaged in a crusade or military expedition, originally a member of a campaign of Christians against Mohameddans.
Cuckoo	*L&M1846* *1856,1872,1879,1894*	A bird, noted for depositing its eggs in other birds' nests
Cumberland	*1903*	The 'Monmouth' class Cruiser 1902-1921. This was one of a class of ten cruisers, all named after Counties.
Cyclops	*L&M1836* *1851,1873,1884,1905*	One of a group of one-eyed giants dwelling in Sicily.
Cygnet	*L&M1842* *1852,1861*	The young swan.
Cyprus	*1911*	A Crown Colony in the eastern Mediterranean Sea, a name given to commemorate the year of King George V's Coronation.
Czar	*3.1854*	The title of the Emperor of Russia. This is a surprising choice of name, for this was the very month that Britain declared war on Russia (27th) after several months of mounting anti-Russian feeling.
Czar of Russia	*1915*	Emperor Nicholas II, a first cousin of King George V, born in 1868, fought with us in a common cause, assumed supreme command of Russian armies in 1915, and was executed in 1918.
Dachshund	*1911*	A short-legged German hound formerly used for badger hunting. The name was struck out in 1915 by a single red line, and a plate worded 'Bull Dog' fixed above it. It remained thus until 1921. The name 'Dachshund' was not used again.
Daedalus	*1847* *1872*	The highly inventive Greek who formed the Cretan labyrinth. He made himself wings and flew from Crete across the archipelago.
Dagmar	*1868,1891*	1847-1928. She was the second daughter of King Christian IX of Denmark, who married Prince Alexander of Russia on 9th November 1866. On his accession to the throne as Tsar Alexander III of all the Russias in 1881, she took the title Tsarina Marca. Her elder sister, Alexandra, married Albert Edward, Prince of Wales in 1863 and became Queen Alexandra in 1900.
Dalemain	*GJ1846* *L&C1857,1872*	The residence of Colonel Edward W.Hasell (1796-1872), Chairman of the Lancaster & Carlisle Railway at its opening in 1846.
Dalton	*1866,1890* *1922*	1766-1844. John, English chemist and natural philosopher, whose most important investigations concerned the Atomic Theory. He was colour-blind, and was also famed for his work on the condition, known as Daltonism. (See *Doctor Dalton*).
Danby Lodge	*1903*	The residence of Sir John ('Navvy') Scott, at Darlington.
Daphne	*1865*	The daughter of the river god Peneus, who was loved by Apollo and was turned at her own request into a bay tree

	1907	to evade him.
Dart	*L&M1830/36*	A pointed missile designed to be thrown or blown as a weapon.
Dee	*BL&CJ1849/56* *1851,St.Helens 1860*	The river flowing through Denbighshire, Flintshire and Cheshire to the Irish Sea.
Deerhound	*1911*	A large rough-coated dog, once used for deer hunting.
Defiance	*1911*	The Torpedo Training School at Devonport 1884-1931.
Delamere	*1848* *1872,1907*	A royal hunting forest in Norman times in Cheshire. A favourite resort of kings and noblemen in earlier days, and in the 17th Century a Barony (later Lordship) held by the Booth family. Thomas Cholmondeley was created 1st Baron Delamere in 1821. Lord Delamere paid a fee of £15 in 1846 to Trevithick for a 'premium' for an apprentice at Crewe.
Delhi	*1868,1890*	The Indian town, re-captured on 20th September 1857 during the Indian Mutiny.
Denbighshire	*1910*	A Welsh County served by the Company.
Derby	*1852* *1872,1880* *SS1858*	1799-1869. Lord Edward Stanley was born at Knowsley Park, and became the 14th Earl of Derby on the death of his father in June 1851. (See *Stanley*) The county town of Derbyshire served by the South Staffordshire Railway.
Derbyshire	*1909*	An English County served by the Company.
Derwent	*W&FI1846* *C&W1854*	The river which flows for 33 miles to Derwent Water, thence to Bassenthwaite Lake and on to the Solway Firth at Workington.
Deva	*GJ1845*	The Roman name for Chester.
Diadem	*1901*	The Cruiser of 1896-1921. A diadem is a crown worn as a symbol of sovereignty, or a badge of loyalty.
Diamond	*1848*	The hardest and most valuable of all the precious stones.
Dickie	*1875*	The son of the Crewe Works foreman William Rylance. (See *Billy*)
Diomed	*GJ1838* *1849,1860,1863,1892*	Hero of the siege of Troy, second in bravery only to Achilles.
Director	*1852,1873,1888*	One appointed to direct the affairs of a company.
Disraeli	*1877* *1894,1922*	1804-1881. Benjamin, man of letters and politician was Prime Minister of Great Britain and Ireland 1868, 1874-1880. He was created Earl of Beaconsfield in 1876.
Doctor Dalton	*GJ1837*	Almost certainly the same person as 'Dalton' (q.v.) who was a scientist associated with Manchester and its University. John Dalton was born near Cockermouth and lived at Kendal for several years before moving to Manchester in 1793. He was a keen mountaineer/fellwalker and ascended Helvellyn between thirty and forty times. In Steel's Guide to the L&C Railway (1846) a Doctor Dalton is quoted as an authority (along with a couple of others) on the heights of the Lake District Mountains, which he calculated by barometrical variations, with remarkable accuracy.
Dominion	*1903*	The Battleship of 1903-1921. Both locomotive and ship were specifically named to honour the Dominion of Canada.
Don	*1852*	The river which flows for 70 miles from near the Cheshire border through Sheffield, Rotherham and Doncaster to the Ouse at Goole.
Doric	*1890,1907*	The White Star liner of 1883-1911 of 4,700 gross tons. Doric is the oldest of the Grecian orders of architecture.
Dot	*1887*	An apt name for a small locomotive, which worked for a while on the Crewe Works narrow gauge system, before moving to Horwich.

Dovedale	1915	The valley of the River Dove, which forms the boundary between Staffordshire and Derbyshire, near the L&NWR branch line from Buxton to Ashbourne. 'The valley of the black or dark river'.
Dragon	GJ1837 1845,1855,1874,1904	A fiery mouthed creature. Also a snake or lizard with wings.
Drake	1866 1890 1910	1540-1596. Admiral Sir Francis circumnavigated the globe and was prominent in the defeat of the Spanish Armada. 1577-1580. He died of a fever and was buried at sea off Porto Bello on 28th January 1596. The Cruiser, built 1902 and sunk on 3rd October 1917 by U-79 in Rathlin Sound.
Dreadnought	BL&CJ1856,1884 1904	Probably just a bold-sounding name for an impressive new class of locomotive. The 1884 name is followed by *Titan* and *Thunderer*, all three being new names to the L&NWR. Other companies had used the name, e.g. Edward Bury's first engine built in 1830, a Bristol & Gloucester one in 1844, and the GWR in 1846 amidst a series which shows clearly that it was not a warship. There was, however, the Battleship of 1875-1908.
Dromedary	1847	A camel with one hump, bred and used for riding.
Druid	C&B1845 1851,1874,1904	A priest of a religious system in ancient Celtic Britain and Gaul. The Cruiser, built 1902 and sunk on 3rd October 1917 by U79 in Rathlin Sound.
Duchess	L&PJ1840 1866,1891	The wife or widow of a Duke.
Duchess of Lancaster	L&C1859,1880,1897	It is believed that Queen Victoria sometimes travelled incognito under this title. She was herself the Duke, and in Lancashire the Royal toast is 'The Queen, Duke of Lancaster'.
Dudley	SS1849	The Worcestershire town eight miles north-west of Birmingham, served by the South Staffordshire Railway.
Duke	1847,1872	The highest hereditary title in the peerage.
Duke of Albany	1882	1853-1884. Prince Leopold was the fourth and youngest son of Queen Victoria.
Duke of Connaught	1882 1896,1922	1850-1943. Prince Arthur was the third son of Queen Victoria who was created Duke in 1874.
Duke of Sutherland	1913	Cromartie Sutherland-Leveson-Gower KG, the 4th Duke, was born in 1851, and died in 1913, having been a Director of the Company for many years. He was at one time MP for Sutherland. His grandfather the 2nd Duke had been a Director of the Liverpool & Manchester Railway, and his father, the Marquis of Stafford who became the 3rd Duke in 1861 had joined the Company Board in 1854, and died in 1893, having served on the Board for thirty-eight years. The 5th Duke, 1888-1963, is not recorded as having succeeded his father as a Director.
Dunrobin	1869 1870,1885,1905	Dunrobin Castle, which lies between Golspie and Brora on the east coast of Sutherland, was the residence of the Duke of Sutherland.
Dwarf	1853	Any person or thing which is much below the ordinary size of its species.
Eagle	GJ1837 1844,1854,1857	Any diurnal bird of prey of the genus *Aquila*, most being of large size, with great strength, powers of flight and keenness of vision.
Eamont	L&C1857 1870,1893	The river which issues from Ullswater and flows nine miles north-east to the Eden four and a half miles east of Penrith.
Earl	1847,1872	A nobleman, third in rank, next below marquis.
Earlestown	1859 1881	A town to the west of Newton-le-Willows, where the Company's Wagon Works were situated. The town was named after Mr. (Later Sir) Hardman Earle (q.v.).
Eclipse	L&M1835 1848,1873,1893	Possibly named after that most famous racehorse. 1764-1770 'It will be Eclipse first, the rest nowhere' was the comment made by Dennis O'Reilly at Epsom on 3rd May 1769 before it ran its first race. Whether the L&M Directors had the racehorse in mind is impossible to say, but the three locomotives delivered from Tayleurs at the time were "Rapid", "Speedwell" and "Eclipse", so speed was in their minds. An eclipse is an interception of light in the sky, as for example that of the sun falling upon the moon by the earth causing the moon to be in shadow.
	1913	The Second Class Cruiser of 1894-1921.

E.C.Trench	*1916*	1869-1960. Ernest Frederic Crosbie Trench, CBE was Chief Engineer of the Company from 1909-1922, and of the LMS in 1923. In publications relating to the L&NWR he is usually referred to as E.F.C.Trench: it is strange that the engine name omitted the 'F'.
Economist	*1883*	One skilled in economics.
Eden *1846, St.Helens1849* *L&C1857, 1859, 1864, 1893*		The river, 65 miles long, which rises in Westmorland, and flows for most of its length through Cumberland to Carlisle and the Solway.
Edith	*1865, 1907*	Edith was the name of Sir Richard Moon's daughter who was born in 1851 and died in Bath in 1947, at a wonderful old age. The Iron Paddle Steamer 'Edith', of 758 gross tons, owned by the Company was built in 1870 by R.Stephenson & Co. and she and her sister ships 'Eleanor' and 'Isabella' were undoubtedly also named after Sir Richard's relations. (See *Eleanor* and *Isabella*)
Edith Cavell	*1915*	Edith Louise Cavell was the British nurse and heroine, born on 4th December 1865 and executed by the Germans on 12th October 1915 for assisting Allied soldiers to escape from German occupied Belgium. Her body lies buried beside Norwich Cathedral.
Edward Gibbon	*1914*	1737-1794. Historian. The author of 'Decline and Fall of the Roman Empire'.
Edward Tootal	*1875* *1895, 1913*	He was a Manchester cotton goods manufacturer who was appointed a Company Director on 21st February 1851. He was still an active Director twenty years later, and died in the autumn of 1874.
Egeria	*1865, 1905*	The nymph who instructed and advised Numa. She was changed into a fountain by the goddess Diana.
Eglinton	*1852* *1872, 1879, 1905*	1812-1861. Archibald William Montgomerie was 13th Earl of Eglinton, whose name became widely known in connection with the famous tournament held at Eglinton Castle near Ardrossan, Ayrshire in 1839, in which Prince Louis Napoleon (Napoleon III) took part, and which is described in Disraeli's *Endymion*. He was appointed Lord Lieutenant of Ireland by the Earl of Derby in 1852 and 1858-1859.
Eleanor	*1865* *1907*	The name of Sir Richard Moon's wife, born on 5th February 1820, and also of his daughter. His wife's maiden name was Brocklebank and she was half sister to Ralph Brocklebank (q.v.). Her death on 31st January 1891 caused Sir Richard great grief. The Company's Iron Paddle Steamer of 917 gross tons built in 1872 by R.Stephenson & Co. was named after one or the other or both of these ladies. She was lost in January 1881 by stranding on Leestone Point, County Down and replaced by the P.S. Eleanor II, a similar vessel, later that year. (See *Edith* and *Isabella*)
Elector	*1848*	One who elects.
Elephant	*L&M1839, 1847*	The largest of existing land mammals, having thick skin, a long flexible trunk, and a pair of tusks.
Elgin	*2.1863*	1811-1863. James Bruce was 8th Earl of Elgin and 12th Earl of Kincardine, Governor-General of Canada 1846-1855, Postmaster-General 1859-1860 and then Viceroy and Governor-General of India from 1862. He died in office on 20th November 1863.
Elk	*1852*	The largest of the deer family.
Elkhound	*1911*	A large and powerful Scandinavian dog originally used to hunt elk.
Eller	*C&W1864*	There is a hamlet of this name south-east of Brougham and also of a stream which joins the River Derwent west of Cockermouth.
Ellesmere	*1849* *1859, 1863, 1893*	1800-1857. Francis Egerton was 1st Earl of Ellesmere, of Worsley Hall, Manchester, and of Shropshire. He was the second son of the 2nd Marquis of Stafford, 1st Duke of Sutherland. The Earldom was created in 1846. This is also the name of a Shropshire town. and of a sheet of water in the 'Shropshire Lakes District'.
Elwy	*VofC1858*	The river which rises near Gwyther, Denbighshire and flows twenty miles north-east to the Clwyd near St.Asaph. 'Strong flow river'.
Emerald	*1848, 1879, 1905*	The precious stone, a form of beryl, of green colour.
Emperor	*1848* *1857, 1884, 1905*	The sovereign or supreme monarch of an empire.

| Empress | *1884,1905* | The consort of an emperor; a woman who governs an empire. |

| Enchantress | *1911* | The Admiralty Yacht of 1903-1935. The name means a woman who charms, or a sorceress or dealer in enchantments. |

| E.Nettlefold | *1911* | Edward D.Nettlefold of Harborne Hall, Birmingham became a Director of the Company in 1901 and retired in 1909, shortly before his death. He was also a Director of Guest Keen and Nettlefold, and was associated with Joseph Chamberlain in business and politics. |

| Engineer | *1897,1923* | The Permanent Way Department's locomotive, for the use of the Chief Engineer. |

Engineer. Bangor
Engineer Birmingham
Engineer-Crewe
Engineer Lancaster
Engineer Liverpool   For the details and dates when
Engineer Manchester   locomotives received Engineer
Engineer Northampton   names, please refer to Table 12.
Engineer Stafford
Engineer South Wales
Engineer Swansea
Engineer Walsall
Engineer Watford
Engineer Wolverton

| Envoy | *1848,1857 1877,1894* | A diplomatic agent, next in rank below an ambassador. One sent on a mission of any sort. |

| Erebus | *GJ1838 1846 1860 1907* | The son of Chaos and the brother of Night. A place of darkness at the entrance to Hades. By this time the name might be associated with the screw Discovery Ship which had sailed under Sir John Franklin in search of the North West Passage in 1845. The search was abandoned in 1848, and the ship struck off in 1854, although the fate of the expedition was not resolved until 1859. So she may have been in the public mind at that time. Another possibility is that the 1907 name refers to the ship 'Invincible' built in 1864 and renamed 'Erebus' c.1905. See description for 'Invincible'. |

| Esk | *SS1853* | A river in Cumberland. The origin of this name is obscure. Both this locomotive and *Justin* were built at the same time by E.B.Wilson & Co., and their names may have a common, or linked source. See *Justin*. This name has sometimes appeared as 'Eske', but this is believed to have come about through a misreading of a clerk's handwriting in the Crewe document - Trevithick's list of 13th March 1855 - where the 'k' has a curlicue, as also have 'Cossack' and 'Turk'. |

| Ethelred | *1862 1909* | The King of the West Saxons from 866-871. The King of the English from 968-1016, whose nickname was 'Ethelred the Unready'. |

| Etna | *L&M1831/37 1854,1860,1862,1879,1905* | The volcano in Sicily. |

| E.Tootal Broadhurst | *1914* | Sir Edward Tootal Broadhurst, Bart. became a Director of the Company in 1906. He was a prominent Manchester businessman, and nephew of Edward Tootal (q.v.). He died aged 63 on 2nd February 1922. |

| Eunomia | *1865 1909* | The daughter of the goddess Themis, who was regarded as the symbol of orderliness. In Greek 'Eu' + 'Nomos' means 'Good' + 'Law'. |

| Euphrates | *1885,1904* | The Troop Ship of 1866-1895, named after the largest river in western Asia. |

| Euryalus | *1903* | The Armoured Cruiser of 1901-1920, named after the friend of Nisus who was slain by Volscens when he rushed to avenge Nisus' death. |

| Euston | *1854* | The Earl of Euston is the subsidiary title of the Duke of Grafton, used as a courtesy title by his son. He owned the site upon which the London terminus of the L&NWR was built, the first of the London main line termini to be opened. The site was named Euston Square after his home village of Euston which lies to the north of Bury |

St.Edmunds in Suffolk.
Old English: EFES-TUN, 'Riverbank-homestead'

| | 1895 | The name was applied at the time of the opening of the Waterloo tunnel route to Riverside Station Liverpool. A newspaper report states that on 13th June 1895 "The train was drawn by the *Euston*, a special engine constructed for tunnel work." (See *Liverpool*) |

Euxine — 1854, 1874, 1893
The P&O liner of 1847-1869 of 1,150 gross tons, an iron paddle steamer, which trooped to the Black Sea in 1854 during the Crimean War.
The Greek name for the Black Sea. 'Hospitable'

Excelsior — W&FJ1856
Henry Longfellow's poem of this title was published in 1841, and has been popular and well known ever since.

Experiment — L&M1833, 1882, 1905
A test or trial of a method or equipment before general adoption for use.
The first locomotive to carry this name was built by Robert Stephenson in 1827. It was also the name of the first locomotive produced by Thomas Sharp and Richard Roberts in February 1833. The name was revived by Mr. Webb for the first of his three cylinder compound locomotives in 1882, and revived again by Mr. Whale for his first 4-6-0 in 1905.

Express — 1883, 1905
A special messenger or conveyance.

Faerie Queene — 1862, 1906
The allegorical romance of chivalry, by Edmund Spenser. 1590.

Fairbairn — 1854, 1877, 1898
1789-1874. Sir William was a Scottish born engineer who established an engineering business in Manchester in 1817 at which many locomotives were built. From 1835 until 1849 he owned a shipyard in Millwall, after which he turned to bridge building, and with Robert Stephenson constructed the tubular bridge over the Menai Straits. He was elected a Fellow of the Royal Society in 1850, and created a Baronet in 1869.

Falaba — 1916
To commemorate the loss of the Elder Dempster liner of 4,086 gross tons, formerly owned by the Cie Belge Maritime du Congo, which left Liverpool on 27th March 1915 and was torpedoed and sunk the following day after five minutes warning by U-28, 38 miles west of Smalls lighthouse. 104 lives were lost. The liner was named after the populous town in north Sierra Leone about 190 miles north-east of Freetown.

Falcon — GJ1837, 1844, 1855
The diurnal bird of prey. The hawk trained for falconry.

Falstaff — 1855, 1858, 1864, 1893, 1915
Sir John, a fat sensual and boastful knight, full of wit; the boon companion of Henry Prince of Wales in Shakespeare's plays.
One of a small number of Shakespearean names, suggesting a short-lived plan to have such a series.

Fame — 1848, 1874, 1905
High reputation, renown.
There was a 3rd Rate warship of this name. 1841-1850.
Possibly the anglicised version of 'Fama', the powerful goddess usually depicted blowing a trumpet.

Faraday — 1866, 1887, 1909
1791-1867. Michael was the great English physicist and chemist, at one time assistant to Sir Humphrey Davy. In 1850 he researched into atmospheric magnetism, and invented the dynamo.

Felicia Hemans — 1914
1793-1835. The poet, Felicia Dorothea Hemans.

Fire Queen — 1911
The name first appeared on a Padarn Railway 0-4-0 in 1848, and later on an iron steamship of 1879 plying between Liverpool and Glasgow, sold to Turkey in 1907.
This name occurs among the series of George the Fifth class locomotives named after vessels of exploration, and may therefore refer to an iron paddle steamer of 1847-1863, or a yacht purchased by the Royal Navy and used between 1882-1920, possibly for survey or exploration. It must be noted, however, that both ships were named 'Firequeen', a single word.
Whatever the source, this was an attractive name for a locomotive, or a ship.

Firefly — L&M1833, 1848, 1860, 1865, 1890
A small nocturnal luminous winged beetle.

Flamingo — L&M1846, 1853
A genus of birds with very long neck and legs, rosy-red in colour when in full plumage.

Flintshire — 1910
A County in North Wales served by the Company.

Florence	*1872* *1891*	Lady Florence Sutherland-Leveson-Gower was the eldest daughter of the 3rd Duke of Sutherland, a Company Director at the time.
Fly	*1853*	An insect. This was also the name of one of the first class carriages on the Liverpool & Manchester Railway.
Flying Fox	*1899*	The racehorse which won the Derby, the 2000 guineas and the St.Leger in 1899, owned by the Duke of Westminster, a Director of the Company at the time.
Forerunner	*BL&CJ1857,* *1861*	A messenger sent ahead. Whether the 1861 locomotive carried the name or not remains in doubt.
Formidable	*1902*	The Battleship of 1898, which was torpedoed in 1st January 1915 by U-24 off Portland Bill.
Forth	*St.Helens,1852*	The river which runs through Perthshire and Stirlingshire and is 116 miles long to the mouth of the estuary.
Fortuna	*1865,1909*	The blind goddess of good luck. ('Fortes fortuna adjuvat' - 'Fortune favours the brave'.)
Foxhound	*1911*	A hound for hunting foxes.
Francis Bacon	*1914*	This name was only borne while the engine was in Crewe works nearing completion. It was renamed *G.P.Neele* before going into service. Francis Bacon 1561-1626 was statesman, essayist and philosopher.
Francis Stevenson	*1902*	He was the Chief Engineer of the Company from 1879 to his death on 1st February 1902.
Franklin	*1866* *1891*	1706-1790. Benjamin Franklin was the American author, inventor, scientist and diplomat. He took part in the drafting of the United States Constitution. A second remote possibility is that the engine might have been named after Sir John Franklin, the explorer, who disappeared while seeking the North West Passage in 1847.
Frederick Baynes	*1914*	He was a member of the Lancashire cotton trade, who became a Director of the Company in 1903. He was born in 1848, and died on 12th November 1917.
Friar	*ExNU* *1849,1857,1884,1906*	A member of a mendicant religious brotherhood. A name paired with *Nun* (but not with *Monk*).
Frobisher	*1866* *1888,1922*	c.1535-1594. Admiral Sir Martin was the English navigator and explorer, who fought with distinction against the Spanish Armada.
F.S.P. Wolferstan	*1910*	Francis Stafford Pipe Wolferstan became a Director of the Company in 1879, and died in 1900.
Fury	*L&M1831,1853*	One of the Erinyes, the goddesses and avengers of iniquity.
F.W.Webb	*1910*	1836-1906. Francis William Webb was articled to Trevithick as a pupil at Crewe on 6th August 1851 at the age of fifteen, and received the appointment of Locomotive Superintendent of the Company on 1st October 1871, a post which was redesignated Chief Mechanical Engineer (in the 1880s?). He remained in office until August 1903, when he retired and went to live in Bournemouth where he died almost three years later. The name was chosen in 1910 by Bowen Cooke to mark appreciation of his predecessor but one. He was truly 'the giant of Crewe'.
Fylde	*L&C1857*	The low, level region of Lancashire between the estuaries of the Wyre and the Ribble.
Gaelic	*1890,1907*	The White Star liner of 1885-1904 of 4,200 gross tons. One branch of the Celtic languages. Scots Gaelic is still spoken in the Highlands of Scotland and the Western Isles.
Galatea	*1902*	The Armoured Cruiser. 1857-1905, named after the sea-nymph who was loved by Acis whom Polyphemus killed. She changed the dead Acis into a fountain.
Gallipoli	*1916*	A peninsula at the north-west end of the Dardanelles. The Gallipoli Campaign lasted from April 1915 to January 1916. The locomotive was named to commemorate the many who lost their lives, and the successful evacuation without loss of life on 15th and 16th December 1915.

Galtfaenan	VofC1859	The residence in Denbigh of Mr. Townshend Mainwaring, MP, the first Chairman of the Vale of Clwyd Railway.
Ganymede	1868	The beautiful youth who was cupbearer to Zeus.
	1887, 1905	Also the largest moon of the planet Jupiter.
Gardner	P&L1856	Probably a worthy person associated with the Preston & Longridge Railway, identity not as yet discovered.
Gazelle	1855	One of the genus of small swift antelopes.
General	1847, 1872, 1878	The commander of an army.
General Joffre	1915	1852-1931. Joseph-Jacques-Cesaire Joffre was Commander in Chief of the French Armies, 1914-1916.
George Findlay	1894, 1909	Sir George Findlay was born on 18th May 1829, appointed Goods Manager in 1864, Chief Traffic Manager of the Company in 1874, and General Manager in 1880. The Ribbon of the Legion of Honour in France and a knighthood at home in 1892 were the special rewards of his valuable life. He died in office on 26th March 1893.
George Macpherson	1916	He was a businessman with interests in the Midlands and Durham, who was Chairman of the Birmingham Canal Navigations which was leased to the L&NWR, of which he became a Director in 1909. He died in 1924.
George the Fifth	1910	King of Great Britain and Ireland and Emperor of India, from 1910-1936.
George Whale	1910	He was born on 7th December 1842 and became the Company's Chief Mechanical Engineer 1903-1909 in succession to Francis Webb. He died at Hove 7th March 1910, aged 67.
Germanic	1884, 1905	The White Star liner of 1875, Iron, single screw, of 5,000 gross tons.
Gheber	BL&CJ1857	A Guebre. A fire-worshipper. A Parsee. A Zoroastrian.
Giant	1853	A mythological being of superhuman size and strength.
Gibraltar	1911	The Crown Possession consisting of a rocky promontory near the southern extremity of Spain. The locomotive was named to celebrate coronation year 1911.
Giffard	1879	1825-1882. Henri V. Giffard was a Frenchman who in 1858 invented the injector. The Giffard injectors were first used at Crewe on the Problem class and consisted of bulky equipment carried on the sides of the firebox. Alternatively, the Giffard family of Chillington Hall in Staffordshire had a long and notable history, living close by the L&NWR main line. (See *Chillington*)
Giraffe	1849	A very long necked ruminant African ungulate.
	1850, 1875, 1895	
Gladiator	1868, 1888	A professional fighter with sword or other weapon against man or beast in the Roman amphitheatre.
Gladstone	1866	1809-1898. William Ewart was Prime Minister of Great Britain 1868-1874, 1880-1885, February to August
	1889	1886 and 1892-1894.
Glatton	1900	The Turret Ship of 1871-1903 named after the village in Huntingdonshire where a Mr. Wells, builder of the first ship of that name (a 4th Rate of 1795) owned an estate.
Glendower	1852	c1354-1416. Owen was the Welsh leader known as Prince of Wales who led a struggle for independence against
	1860, 1861, 1906	King Henry IV. He is also a character in Shakespeare's 'Henry the Fourth (Part 1)'.
Glowworm	1855	An insect; a beetle which has the power under her full control of emitting light.
	1858, 1863, 1892, 1914	
Glyn	1851, 1872	1797-1873. George Carr Glyn was a banker, Chairman of the London & Birmingham Railway 1837-1846 and first Chairman of the L&NWR, 1846-1852, sometime MP for Kendal. He was created Baron Wolverton in 1869.
Glynllivon	1867	Glynllifon Park (Recent spelling) lies five miles south of Carnarvon alongside the railway to Afon Wen.
	Carnarvon Railway	In 1860 Glynllivon Castle was the residence of Spencer Bulkeley Wynne, 3rd Lord Newborough, High Sheriff of Anglesea in 1847, and a Deputy-Lieutenant for Carnarvon.

Gnome	*BL&CJ1857*	A misshapen elemental spirit dwelling in the bowels of the earth; guardian of mines and quarries.
Goldfinch	*L&M1845, 1853, 1857*	The song-bird, so named from the colour of its wings.
Goldsmith	*1869*	The name was very short-lived, and may have referred to Oliver Goldsmith (q.v.).
Goliah	*L&M1831/39 1847*	An early-Victorian alternative spelling of Goliath.
Goliath	*St.Helens 1854*	Of Gath, the Philistine giant who was slain by David.
	1900	A Battleship, built in 1898 and sunk by Turkish torpedoes on 13th May 1915.

Good Hope *1903* The Armoured Cruiser, built in 1899 and lost in action at Coronel on 1st November 1914, named after the cape at the south-west corner of Africa, near Cape Town.

Gorgon *GJ1838, 1847* Anything unusually hideous. One of the three monsters, which had snakes on its head instead of hair.

G.P.Neele *1914* George Potter Neele began his railway career in 1847 with the South Staffordshire Railway and joined the L&NWR in 1861. He became Superintendent of the Line, retired in 1895, and died aged 95 in 1920.

Grasmere *K&W1851, 1862* A village in Westmorland, well known for its lake.

Grasshopper *L&CJ1857* A straight-winged jumping insect of the locust family.

Greater Britain *1891, 1908* A phrase which was used to mean "The whole British Empire".
The name accurately reflects the spirit of the end of the 19th century, when many believed that human society was steadily advancing from good to better. It was a 'land of hope and glory'.

Greenbank
Brockley Lane Branch 1894 "Greenbank Sidings" was the alternative name for the Brockley Lane Branch.

Greyhound *1853* A hound of great swiftness and keenness of sight used for hunting and racing.
1885, 1905 This was also the name of one of the first class carriages on the Liverpool & Manchester Railway.

Greystock *1865* The name of the Samson class engine is sometimes recorded as being spelt 'Greystocke' but Scott gives it as 'Greystock' until 4th December 1891, when the spelling was altered to 'Greystoke'.

Greystoke *GJ1846 L&C1857 1891* A village in Cumbria west of Penrith. Greystoke Castle was the residence of Henry Howard, the Deputy Chairman of the Lancaster & Carlisle Railway. The name Greystoke is spoken locally with the emphasis on the first syllable, and thus the change of name in 1891 barely affected its pronunciation. Henry Howard (1850-1914) inherited the Greystoke estates, and was a Director of the Cockermouth, Keswick and Penrith Railway from 1876 and Chairman from 1910.

G.R.Jebb *1917* George Jebb was for many years in charge of the engineering side of the Birmingham Canal Navigations, and Engineer of the Shropshire Union Railways & Canal Company, and in that capacity had a seat on the L&NWR Board. As a 'life-long friend of Francis Webb' he was a mourner at his funeral in Bournemouth. He is described in a press report on Sir Richard Moon's funeral as representing the Birmingham Canal Company.

Grouse *1911* A species of game-bird.

Gurth *WJ1863* The swineherd of Cedric the Saxon in Sir Walter Scott's Ivanhoe. (See *Cedric*)

Guy Calthrop
1916 until March 1919 See *Sir Guy Calthrop*.

Hampden *1866 1892, 1922* 1594-1643. John, English parliamentary leader opposed to King Charles I (concerning 'Ship Money'). He was Oliver Cromwell's first cousin.

Hannibal *1902* The Battleship of 1896-1920, named after the famous Carthaginian general of the Second Punic War.

Harbinger *1852, 1874, 1904* A forerunner. One who goes ahead.

Hardinge *1854* 1785-1856. Field Marshal Sir Henry, soldier and statesman, was Governor General of India 1844-1848, and

| | *1858* | became the 1st Viscount Hardinge of Lahore in 1846. |

Hardman   *1855*
1858,1863,1890

1814-1874. Frederick was a novelist and journalist and a frequent contributor to Blackwood's Magazine. He was born in Manchester.

Hardwicke   *1852*
1873,1892

1799-1873. Charles Philip Yorke, 4th Earl of Hardwicke, the admiral and politician became Postmaster-General in 1852.

Harlequin   *GJ1838*
1846,1860,1907

One who dances through the world; only visible to Columbine.
A conventional clown in the improvised Italian comedy.
This was also the name of one of the first class carriages on the Liverpool & Manchester Railway.

Harpy   *GJ1837*
1846,1872,1885,1905

A fierce, filthy monster in mythology, half woman, half bird, and the minister of divine vengeance.

Harrier   *1911*

A hound for hunting hares; a cross country runner; a species of falcon.
The name comes in the midst of the series of George the Fifth class 'Vessels of Discovery', but no trace has so far been found of any such vessel.

Harrowby   *1853*
1878,1905

1762-1847. Dudley Ryder, 1st Earl of Harrowby, was Foreign Secretary in 1809 under his intimate friend William Pitt. Lord President of the Council 1812-1827. The title is derived from Harrowby Hall, near Grantham. He lived at Sandon, near Stafford.
The 2nd Earl, also Dudley Ryder, was MP for Liverpool 1832-1847, Deputy Lieutenant for Staffordshire in 1853, President of the British Association 1854, Chancellor of the Duchy of Lancaster 1854-1855 and Lord Privy Seal 1855-1857.

Harvey Combe *L&B1835*

1784-1853. He was master of the Old Berkeley Hunt, whose territory was disturbed by the building of the London & Birmingham Railway in Hertfordshire. The name was used for a contractors locomotive in 1835, which was later owned by the L&B 1837-1843.

Haulier   *1893*

One who, or that which hauls. The locomotive delivered to the L&NWR in November 1895 with this name was later renamed *Platelayer*.

Havelock   *1863*
1905

1795-1857. General Sir Henry Havelock, KCB died as a result of defending Lucknow during the Indian Mutiny.

Hawk *GJ1838,1847,1859*

One of the many species of birds of prey.

Hawkstone   *1849*
1860,1861

An estate in Shropshire.
The residence of the 2nd Viscount Hill (Rowland Hill), who was born in 1800, succeeded to the title in 1842, and died in 1875. An ancestor, Sir Rowland Hill, was Lord Mayor of London in 1555, and according to N.Pevsner in his "Houses in Shropshire" there is no known connection with Sir Rowland of the Penny Post fame.

Hecate   *GJ1837*
1846,1872,1884,1905

The threefold goddess, the daughter of Perses and Asteria, known in the heavens as Luna, on earth as Diana and in the infernal regions as Hecate or Persephone or Proserpine. She presided over witchcraft.

Hecla   *GJ1837*
W&FJ1856
1860,1864,1895

A volcano in Iceland.
A name carried by several warships; It was also the name of the ship in which William Edward Parry sailed on the expedition to the North Pole and got to within 8 degrees of it in 1819/1820.

Hector   *1853,1857*
1870,1892

The eldest son of Priam, the bravest of warriors and leader of the Trojan forces. He was killed by Achilles.

Helvellyn   *1846*
1872,1878,1904

A peak in the Lake District on the borders of Cumberland and Westmorland. The two counties were combined as Cumbria in 1974.

Henrietta   *1866*
1890

Henrietta, Constance and Adelaide were all 'new' names given to Samsons in January 1866. It has not proved possible to discover who she was. (See *Adelaide* and *Constance*) It is improbable that the locomotive was named after the daughter of King Henry IV of France, or of King Charles I.

Henry Bessemer	*1894,1907*	1813-1898. Sir Henry Bessemer was the inventor of the 'Bessemer process' of steel manufacture involving the decarbonisation of cast iron by forcing a blast of air through a mass of metal when in the molten state. One of his plants was installed at Crewe Works in 1864-1865, the first "blow" of steel taking place on 22nd September 1864. (See *Bessemer*)
Henry Cort	*1879 1898,1909*	1740-1800. He was born at Lancaster, and devised the reverberatory puddling process for converting pig iron into wrought iron.
Henry Crosfield	*1871 1890,1913*	In 1850 he was appointed a member of the shareholders' committee formed to give an opinion on the future management of the Company. From 1864 he became Company Auditor, Liverpool and gave the Company more than 30 years of distinguished service. He achieved the distinction of having two locomotives named after him at the same time, the other being *The Auditor*. He died on 18th February 1882, highly esteemed by all his fellow members on the Board.
Henry Maudslay	*1898,1911*	1771-1831. He was an engineer who worked with Richard Roberts and Thomas Telford and did more than any other man to develop the engineer's self-acting lathe in regard to its essential mechanism.
Henry Pease	*1882,1894*	1807-1881. He was the son of Edward Pease who had been closely connected with the construction of the Stockton & Darlington Railway, and was MP for South Durham 1857-1865. He was a most prominent railway person, being a Director of the Cockermouth Keswick & Penrith Railway as nominee of the Stockton & Darlington Railway, and of the North Eastern Railway until his death, Chairman of the former and a Director of the latter, and Director of the Tees Valley Railway, the Eden Valley Railway and the South Durham & Lancashire Union Railway. He was an ardent worker for peace.
Henry Ward	*1910*	He was a Staffordshire ironmaster of Penkridge, who died there aged 76 in 1904 having been a Director of the Company for thirty years.
Henry W. Longfellow	*1913*	1807-1882. Henry Wadsworth , American poet, who wrote "Excelsior" and "Luck of Edenhall".
Herald	*1851,1872 1885,1905*	Originally an officer of state having the duty of making royal or state proclamations. An officer of the College of Arms and also of the Court of Lord Lyon.
Hercules	*L&M1835 1850,1856,1859,1863,1877,1897*	The Greek hero of superhuman strength and vigour.
Herefordshire	*1909*	An English County served by the Company.
Hermione	*1911*	The Cruiser, 1893-1921, named after the daughter of Menelaus and Helen, who married Orestes after helping him to murder her husband Pyrrhus.
Hero	*1848 St.Helens 1853,1860,1864,1890*	The priestess of Aphrodite, who was in love with Leander.
Herod	*GJ1840,1855*	The reason for this choice is unclear, but may refer to the Kings of the Jews of that name.
Heron	*L&M1841, 1852,1861*	A wading bird with long neck and legs.
Herschel	*1866 1890,1909*	1792-1871. Sir John Frederick William, Baronet, astronomer, mathematician and chemist, was involved in photography from its earliest days. He lies buried in Westminster Abbey.
Hertfordshire	*1909*	An English County served by the Company.
Hibernia	*1869 1888 1915*	Vernon & Co built a ship named Hibernia for the Chester & Holyhead Railway in 1847-8. This Hibernia was the turbine steamer of 1,594 gross tons of the Company's North Wales service to Ireland of the 1913-1914 fleet, which was herself named after an earlier vessel of the Chester and Holyhead Railway's 1849 fleet purchased by the L&NWR in 1859. She was renamed Tara when used for naval service during the Great War. (See *Tara*) The first locomotive to carry this name was designed by Richard Roberts in 1834 for service on the Dublin & Kingstown Railway. Hibernia is the Roman name for Ireland.

Himalaya	*1885* *1905*	The mountain range in North India. In 1885. The name is paired with Niagara, and both probably refer to geographical wonders.
Hindostan	*1903*	Named after the Battleship of 1903-1923. A Persian word, being the name given to the land of the Hindus in the central plain of India, spelt thus at the time the locomotive was named, but now more commonly spelt Hindustan to produce as accurately as possible the pronunciation in the original tongue.
Hirondelle	*C&B1840*	The French name for swallow.
Holland Hibbert	*1913*	The Honourable Arthur Henry Holland-Hibbert of Munden, near Watford was appointed a Director of the Company in 1880, and succeeded as the 3rd Viscount Knutsford in 1931. He died on 16th January 1935. Note that the locomotive nameplate did not include a hyphen.
Holyhead	*1915*	The port in Anglesey serving Ireland.
Hood	*1903*	The Battleship of 1891, which was sunk as a blockship at Portland in 1914. Admiral Samuel, Viscount Hood, 1724-1816, was the most distinguished of several Admirals of this name.
Hope	*1851*	The final entity in Pandora's box. A stagecoach name.
Hornet	*GJ1838,1848*	A large wasp.
Hotspur	*1851* *1874,1896,1915*	1364-1403. Henry (or Harry) Percy was son of the 1st Earl of Northumberland, who predeceased his father. The term 'Hotspur' is derived from his character, for he was 'a fiery person with scant control over his temper'. Another Shakespearean character, from "Henry IV, Part 1."
Howe	*1903*	The Battleship of 1885-1910, which was named after the Admiral, Richard Lord Howe of 1726-1799, who in 1794 was victor over the French on 'The Glorious First of June'.
Huddersfield	*H&M1847*	The town in the West Riding of Yorkshire. The engine was ceremonially named by Joseph Brook, Deputy Chairman of the Huddersfield & Manchester Railway & Canal Company at Heaton Lodge on 2nd August 1847.
Hugh Myddleton	*1898,1909*	1560-1631. Sir Hugh was the Promoter of the New River Scheme for supplying water to London, and built the canal from Ware to Islington. His name was sometimes spelt Myddelton.
Huish	*1853,1857*	Captain Mark Huish was General Manager of the L&NWR from its inception in July 1846. He resigned in November 1858.
Humphrey Davy	*1880,1895*	1778-1829. Sir Humphry was the chemist, and inventor in 1816 of a safety lamp for mines. Note that the locomotive's name was not spelt the way he used himself.
Hurricane	*1854* *1906*	Shakespeare uses the word 'hurricanoes' in King Lear Act 3, Scene 2, as a description of a storm. In the 18th century it was a term for a riot, so called because of the hustle and noise that took place. In more recent times it means a violent storm, the strongest force on the Beaufort scale.
Huskisson	*1847* *1857,1885,1904*	1770-1830. The Right Honourable William, MP for Liverpool and President of the Board of Trade was fatally injured at the opening of the Liverpool & Manchester Railway on the 15th September 1830.
Hydra	*1846,1872* *1883,1905*	The poisonous many-headed snake living in the Lernean marshes near Argos, destroyed by Hercules as one of his twelve labours.
Hyperion	*GJ1840* *1850,1906*	One of the Titans, the son of Uranus and Gaea. Also the title of a poem by Keats.
Ida	*1853,1858*	There are several Mount Idas in Asia Minor and Greece with various myths attached; the mount near Troy was the site of the Judgement of Paris. According to one myth, Ida was a nymph of Crete who went into Phrygia where she gave her name to a mountain in that country. It would appear doubtful that this is the name of a close relative of anyone with connections with the Company, for it predates by thirteen years any other such names.

Ilion	*1868,1888,1906*	A Greek town in the vicinity of Troy.

Ilion *1868,1888,1906* A Greek town in the vicinity of Troy.

Illustrious *1902,1923* The Battleship of 1896-1920.

Implacable *1899* The Battleship of 1899-1921.

India *1911* The country of southern Asia, consisting of the present day India, Pakistan and Bangladesh. The locomotive was named to celebrate the coronation of King George V as Emperor of India in 1911.

Inflexible *1899* The Battleship of 1876-1903.

Ingestre *1846,1872,1923* Ingestre Hall was the seat of the Chetwynd family, Earls Talbot, near Stafford.

Ingleboro *L&C1857,1859* The mountain 2373 ft. with the distinctive flat top visible from the Lancaster & Carlisle Railway.

Inglewood *L&C1857,1872* The forest which originally covered most of the area between Penrith and Carlisle.

Intrepid *1900* The Cruiser of 1891-1918, sunk as a blockship at Zeebrugge on 23rd April 1918.

Invincible *1899* The Ironclad of 1864, which was renamed Erebus in 1904 for use as a Training Ship.

Ionic *1890,1906* The White Star liner of 1883, 4,750 gross tons which was used as a troopship in the Boer War and sold to the Aberdeen line in 1900.
One of the three orders of Grecian architecture.

Iron Duke *1897 1899* The Battleship of 1870-1906, named after The Duke of Wellington (1769-1852), so called because of his iron will.

Irresistible *1899* The Battleship of 1898, which was sunk by a torpedo fired from the shore, Dardanelles, on 18th March 1915.

Irwell *1852 St.Helens 1856* The river which rises on the east Lancashire border and flows 30 miles, through Manchester and into the Mersey at Irlam.

Isabella *1873 1892* This was the name of one of Sir Richard Moon's many sisters.
It was also the name of the Company's Iron Paddle Steamer of 831 gross tons built by Laird Bros. of Birkenhead in 1877, and as in the case of 'Edith' and of 'Eleanor' the locomotives and the vessels were named after the same ladies. (See *Edith* and *Eleanor*)

Isis *1853, 1874,1893* The principal goddess of ancient Egypt, and goddess of the moon. She was the daughter of Keb and Nut (Earth and Sky) and sister and wife of Osiris.
There was also a 4th Rate naval vessel of 1819-1867.
Possibly the River, tributary of the Thames, but seen in context with the other names of 1853, unlikely.

I.T.Williams *1917 until Dec, 1919* See *Sir Thomas Williams*.

Ivanhoe *1863 1906* The title of one of Sir Walter Scott's novels, and another name for Ivinghoe, a village in Buckinghamshire near Tring, Hertfordshire.

Ixion *1848,1873,1893* King of the Lapithae, who was bound to a revolving wheel of fire as a punishment for his boastfulness.

J.A.Bright *1914* John Albert Bright, 1848-1924, was a Director of the Company at the time of his election as MP for Birmingham on 15th April 1889, and was son of the celebrated John Bright. (q.v.).

J.A.F.Aspinall *1916* Sir John Audley Frederick Aspinall received his early training at Crewe, becoming Chief Mechanical Engineer, then General Manager of the L&YR. He died aged 85 on 19th January 1937.

James Bishop *1916* He was the Company Secretary from April 1904 to 31st December 1921.

Japan *1872* The Country. A Japanese Delegation visited Britain in that year.

Jason *GJ1838, 1847,1857,1879,1905* The hero of the Greek legend, leader of the sailors in the Argo on the expedition into the Black Sea to capture the fleece of the golden ram.

J.Bruce Ismay	*1914*	1862-1937. Joseph Bruce Ismay, shipowner and son of T.H.Ismay was appointed a Director of the Company in 1901, and later became a Director of the LMS.
Jeanie Deans	*1890,1907*	The heroine of Sir Walter Scott's novel 'The Heart of Midlothian'.
Jim Crow	*1894*	The name of a musical routine entitled "Jump Jim Crow", first performed by its author Thomas Dartmouth Rice in 1828. In those days it was a pseudonym for a renegade or turncoat. The word 'Crow' in this context has no connection with 'Crowbar'. Nevertheless a 'Jim Crow' was a term used by railwaymen to refer to a platelayer's tool for bending rails. If one can use such a tool to bend a rail, why not also use one to bend a live language?
John Bateson	*1910*	Of Wavertree, Liverpool became a Director of the Company in 1877, and died aged 85 on 7th February 1901.
John Bright	*1869* *1892*	1811-1889. He was the statesman, and partner in "Cobden and Bright", founders of the Anti-Corn Law League in 1833, and were largely responsible for the Reform Bill of 1867.
John Hick	*1894* *1913*	He was a Civil Engineer, MP for Bolton 1868-1880 and a Director of the Company from 1871 until his death aged 78 in February 1894.
John Keats	*1913*	1795-1821. The poet.
John Mayall	*1885* *1891,1913*	1803-1876. He was a cotton spinner, born at Lydgate near Ashton under Lyne, who entered the cotton spinning business in about 1824 and set up at Mossley in 1828. By the 1870s the largest specialised cotton spinner in the world (but no weaving). He was largely responsible for the growth of the Pennine town of Mossley, and lived and died there.
John O'Gaunt *L&PJ1840,1849,L&C1859,1874,1895*		1340-1399. Duke of Lancaster, the fourth son of King Edward III.
John o Gaunt	*1913*	The locomotive so named in February 1913. It was a new plate, not provided with an apostrophe, nor with the customary full stop, and the 'o' was somewhat less than full size.
John O'Groat	*1849,1874* *1895,1922*	Jan Groot was a Dutchman who bought land on the north-eastern tip of Scotland in the reign of King James IV, and settled there.
John Penn	*1898* *1909*	He was a Director of the Great Eastern Railway Company, MP for Lewisham, the son of John Penn FRS, formerly head of John Penn & Sons, Marine Engineers, Greenwich and Deptford.
John Ramsbottom	*1872,1888*	He was born on 11th September 1814 at Todmorden, Yorkshire and died at Alderley Edge, Cheshire on 20th May 1897. He was Locomotive Superintendent of the Manchester & Birmingham Railway, taking charge of Longsight Works, from 23rd May 1842 until July 1846. He became District Superintendent of the L&NWR M&B Division (renamed the North Eastern Division in 1849) from then until August 1857, and of the Northern Division from then until March 1862, when he succeeded Trevithick as L&NWR Locomotive Superintendent, in the post from which he retired on grounds of failing health on 30th September 1871. The name was chosen by Mr.Webb when he succeeded him in that office. Mr.Ramsbottom became a Director of the L&Y and of Beyer, Peacock & Co.
John Rennie	*1878,1898,1913*	1761-1821. He was the Civil Engineer in bridge, canal and harbour building, FRS 1798. He built the Waterloo, Southwark and London Bridges over the Thames, and is buried in St.Paul's Cathedral. Another possibility might be Sir John Rennie, 1794-1874, who surveyed the Liverpool & Manchester Railway.
John Ruskin	*1913*	1819-1900. The writer and critic. He was honoured with a locomotive name despite his expressed view that 'An England of railways would see the end of all natural beauty.'.
John Smith *St.Helens1855*		A railway contractor who lived in the St.Helens area, who became a Director of the St.Helens Railway and was probably for a time chairman of its locomotive committee.
Joshua Radcliffe *1878,1896*		He was Deputy Chairman of the Lancashire & Yorkshire Railway. He retired from that post in March 1883.
J.P.Bickersteth	*1910*	John Pares Bickersteth became a Director of the Company in 1868, was Chairman of the Locomotive and Engineering Committee, and became Deputy Chairman of the Company Board in 1873. He died in 1909

having been a Director for forty one years.

Jubilee	*1897*	The Diamond Jubilee of Queen Victoria's accession to the Throne, 20th June 1897. The nameplates included a red diamond at each end of the lettering, with the result that the name has appeared from time to time in print as "Diamond Jubilee".

Jupiter   *L&M1831*   The supreme deity in Roman mythology, the giver of victory and justice.
The largest of the planets.
1903   The Battleship of 1895-1920.

Justin   *SS1853*   The origin of this name is obscure. Both this locomotive and *Esk* were built at the same time by E.B.Wilson & Co., and their names may have a common, or linked source. (See *Esk*)

Kelpie   *WJ1855*   In Scottish fairy-lore a spirit of the waters in the form of a horse. Every lake had its Water-Horse.

Kendal   *L&C1859*   The largest town in Westmorland. Derived from its old name Kirkbie Kendal, 'Kirkbie in Kent-dale' or 'Church-town in (River) Kent Valley'.

Kestrel   *1854*   The small falcon. The commonest bird of prey in the British Isles.
1879,1895,1915

King Arthur   *1901*   The British Chieftain of the 6th Century. Possibly a legendary figure. This is another of the Jubilee class locomotives named after "historical" folk popularly known for the legends that have been built around them.

King Edward VII   *1901*   King, Emperor, from 1901-1910.

King Lear   *WJ1861*   The title of one of William Shakespeare's Plays.

King of Italy   *1915*   1869-1947. Victor Emmanuel III, King 1900-1946 assumed supreme command of the Italian land and naval forces in 1915.

King of Serbia   *1915*   1844-1921. Peter I, of Serbia acceded to the throne in 1903. He was with the Serbian army in 1914 -1915, although by that time he was a septuagenarian.

King of the   *1915*   1875-1934. Albert acceded to the throne in 1909, led the Belgian army in spirited resistance against the German
Belgians   invasion in 1914, and was killed in an accident.

Kingfisher *L&M1841,1851*   The brilliantly plumaged bird.

Kitchener   *1915*   See *Lord Kitchener.*

Knighton   *Knighton 1861*   An Urban District in East Radnor, Wales.

Knowsley   *1846*   Knowsley Hall was the seat of the Earl of Derby.
1872,1883,1905   The village lies to the east of Liverpool.

La France   *1900*   So named for the Paris Universal Exposition of 1900.

Lady Beatrice   *1875*   1857-1944. She was fifth daughter and youngest child of Queen Victoria, who married in 1885 Prince Henry of Battenburg. (See *Beatrice* and *Princess Beatrice*)

Lady Godiva   *1903,1923*   This is another of the Jubilee class locomotives named after real people who have become well known because of a legend associated with them. Lady Godiva was the wife of Leofric, Earl of Mercia. To prevent him imposing exactions on his tenants in 1040, she rode naked on horseback through the streets of Coventry. Through the course of time the legend has been somewhat embellished.

Lady of the Lake   It seems probable that when the name first appeared the Directors of the Kendal & Windermere Railway might
K&W1850   have had Lake Windermere in mind. The pioneer vessel on the Lake, built in 1845 had been given that name, and in many instances we find a close affinity between the names of ships and locomotives sharing the same part of the country.
1860,1862,1906   The name's appearance in later years is more likely to have associations either with Vivienne, the mistress of

Merlin in the Arthurian legends, or Ellen Douglas in Sir Walter Scott's poem "The Lady of the Lake" of 1809/1810, when the lake would be Loch Katrine.

Lancashire	*1909*	An English County served by the Company.
Lancashire Witch	*B&L1828*	The locomotive was described at its naming ceremony as 'beautiful', and the witch as 'universally attractive'; to quote S.P.B.Mais, "An orbed maiden with white fire laden".
Lancaster	*L&PJ1840*	The "Roman fort on the River Lune", the ancient county town of Lancashire.
L/Corpl.J.A.Christie V.C.	*1922*	John Alexander Christie 1/4th (County of London) Battalion The London Regiment (Finsbury Rifles) was awarded the Victoria Cross for most conspicuous gallantry on Bald Hill, Fija, near Jerusalem, on 21st and 22nd December 1917. Before the war he served as a Parcels Clerk with the L&NWR at Euston. He did not return to railway employment, and died at Stockport on 10th September 1967, aged 72. He was popularly known as 'Jock'.
Landrail	*1911*	The corncrake; a bird which is a summer visitor.
Lang Meg	*L&C1859* *1875,1906*	The present day 'Long Meg', in Cumbria. It is a large stone in a bronze age circle at Hunsonby, north-east of Penrith. The other stones are her daughters.
Langdale	*K&W1850* *1865,1872*	The Langdales of the Kendal & Windermere Railway would be the two valleys of Great and Little Langdale west of Ambleside.
Lapwing	*L&M1843* *St.Helens 1853,1878.1906*	The peewit, a bird of the plover family.
Latona	*1855,1860,1864*	The mother of 'The Latonian Twins' Apollo and Diana.
Lawrence	*1880* *1895*	1811-1879. John Laird Mair Lawrence was Governor of the Punjab at the time of the Mutiny, and was created 1st Baron Lawrence of the Punjab in 1869. He was Governor General of India, and lies buried in Westminster Abbey. By this time Charles N.Lawrence, one of Baron Lawrence's sons had been a Director of the Company for seven years, and some, especially railwaymen, could have associated this name with him, even though the general public might not. By 1913, when the name was removed to avoid confusion with the new Claughton 'Charles N.Lawrence' it is evident the name was associated with Charles, by then Deputy-Chairman of the Board.
Lazonby	*L&C1857* *1880*	A village north-east of Penrith. Lazonby Hall was the residence of Lt.Col.Maclean, a Director of the Lancaster & Carlisle Railway.
Leamington	*1915*	The Warwickshire resort served by the company.
Leamington Spa	*1915*	The omission of 'Spa' was swiftly rectified.
Leander	*1848* *1860,1906*	The person who swam the Hellespont nightly to visit his beloved Hero, and who unfortunately was drowned in doing so.
Leeds	*L&M1833*	The city in Yorkshire where the locomotive was built by Fenton, Murray & Jackson.
Leicestershire	*1909*	An English County served by the Company.
Leopard	*L&M1838*	A large and ferocious carnivore of the cat group, known by its spots, which it may not change.
Levens	*L&C1857* *1879,1906*	The village near Kendal, and a Hall, near the Lancaster & Carlisle Railway. The Howards of Levens Hall were distantly related to the Howards of Greystoke, but they do not seem to have had a Director of the railway amongst them. They may however have owned land near Burton and Holme which was sold to the railway.
Leviathan	*1849,1872,1885* *1904*	A dragon or sea monster of great size and strength. The Cruiser of 1901-1920.
Lewis Carroll	*1914*	1832-1898. The Reverend Charles Lutwidge Dodgson, author and mathematician.

Lichfield	*SS1849*	The city in Staffordshire served by the South Staffordshire Railway.
Lightning	*L&M1836,1849* *1872,1888,1909*	A flash of light due to a discharge of atmospheric electricity.
Lily	*1848,1860*	The flower. (See *Rose* and *Violet*)
Linnet	*L&M1845,* *1853,1857*	The small song-bird of the Finch family.
Lion	*L&M1838,1857*	The carnivore remarkable for its strength and roar.
Little England *Sandy & Potton, 1863*		Built in 1848, bought second hand from George England & Co. and undoubtedly named after him or his firm. There were several locomotives with this name and it is difficult to know which is which. It is likely that the one that was shown by England at the 1851 Exhibition carried nameplates, and may have gone to the Sandy & Potton Railway, but there remains an element of uncertainty whether this was an appropriate nickname or the actual nameplate.
Liver	*L&M1833* *1850,1874,1895*	A mythical bird invented by 17th Century antiquarians to account for the name of the City of Liverpool. It appears on the City Coat of Arms as a heraldic cormorant.
Liverpool	*?B&L1830*	1770-1828. Robert Banks Jenkinson, the 2nd Earl of Liverpool was Prime Minister of Great Britain and Ireland from 1812-1827.
	1848	The Headquarters of the L&NWR in the north and formerly of the Grand Junction Railway. This name is paired with the Southern Division's *London* (q.v.).
	1895	The 1895 name was applied in time for the opening of Riverside Station in June of that year, and refers to the city, the ocean-going terminal. (See *Euston*)
Livingstone	*1868* *1891,1915*	1813-1873. David, the Scottish missionary and explorer who crossed Africa in 1853.
Llandrindod	*1915*	The spa town (Llandrindod Wells) in Radnorshire Central Wales, served by the Company.
Llandudno	*1915*	The North Wales coastal resort in Carnarvonshire served by the Company.
Llewellyn	*1848*	Probably named after one of the four naval Holyhead packets built in 1847. (See *Banshee* and *Caradoc*)
	1877,1897,1923	1173-1240. The Prince of Wales, Llewellyn Ab Iowerth was in 1201 the greatest prince in Wales and supported the English barons against King John. Or: c1225-1282. The grandson of the above, Llewellyn ap Gruffydd, Prince of Wales, who supported the English barons under Simon de Montfort against King Henry III. He became King of Wales in 1246. The name is usually spelt 'Llewelyn'.
Loadstone	*1852,* *1874,1894,1915*	Magnetic oxide of iron, used as a magnet compass, or 'stone that guides'. The word may also be spelt Lodestone.
Locke	*1852* *Ex B'head1860* *1861,1862,1907*	1805-1860. Joseph Locke was Engineer-in-Chief of the Grand Junction Railway, and the Lancaster & Carlisle Railway. He was a civil and mechanical engineer. He was born at Attercliffe, just outside Sheffield on 9th August 1805, and died on 18th September 1860. The Times obituary notice classed him with Stephenson and Brunel as 'one of the great triumvirate of the engineering world', and he has a memorial window in Westminster Abbey.
Locomotion	*1871*	The act or motion of moving from place to place. This must be reckoned the ideal name for a locomotive.
London	*1847*	The capital of England and seat of government of the United Kingdom. The engine was named thus because London was the Headquarters of the L&NWR, and formerly of the L&B. (See *Liverpool*)
Lonsdale	*GJ1846,WJ1847* *W&FJ1847* *W&FJ1864* *L&C1857,1872*	It is uncertain after whom or what these two early locomotives were named; possibly the district. The Earl of Lonsdale lived at Lowther Castle, was Chairman of the Whitehaven & Furness Junction Railway, and Postmaster General 1841-1846. (See *Lowther*) 'The valley of the Lune', through which the Lancaster & Carlisle Railway passed in the Lowgill to Tebay section.

Lord Byron	*1913*	1788-1824. George Gordon Byron, the poet. 6th Baron Byron 1798.
Lord Faber	*1914*	1847-1920, The Right Honourable Lord Edward Beckett Faber was a banker who became a Leeds Director of the Company in 1895. He was sometime MP for Andover. Created Baron 1905.
Lord Kenyon	*1916*	Lloyd Tyrell-Kenyon, Colonel the Right Honourable Lord Kenyon, was a landowner in North Wales and ADC to King George V, who became a Director of the Company in 1907 and who died aged 63 in 1927.
Lord Kitchener	*1914*	1850-1916. Horatio Herbert, Field Marshal Earl Kitchener of Khartoum and Broome, was Secretary of State for War in 1914, and famous for the poster, depicting his face and the words 'Your Country Needs You!', and was drowned on 5th June 1916 in the sinking of HMS Hampshire off Orkney.
Lord Loch	*1910*	Henry Brougham Loch PC GCB GCMG DCL had a most distinguished career in the Royal Navy and the Army, and was elected to the L&NWR Board of Directors in 1882. He relinquished his seat on the Board in 1884 when he was appointed Governor of Victoria (Australia), a post he held until 1889 when he became Governor of Cape Colony until 1894. He was re-elected to the Board in 1894. He was created Baron Loch in 1895, and died in 1900 aged 73.
Lord of the Isles	*1863* *1909*	Lord Ronald, the Lord of the Isles in Sir Walter Scott's poem of that title published in 1815.
Lord Rathmore	*1913*	1838-1919. The Hon. David Robert Plunket was a Barrister and KC. One time MP for Dublin University and Solicitor General (Ireland) he was created Baron Rathmore 1895. He became a Director of the Company in 1897, and died on 22nd August 1919 aged 80.
Lord Stalbridge	*1913*	1837-1912. As Lord Richard de Aquila Grosvenor he was appointed a Director of the Company in 1870, and was Chairman from 1891 until 1911. He was Liberal MP for Flintshire from 1861 for twenty five years, Vice-Chamberlain Royal Household 1872-1874, and was created Baron Stalbridge in 1886. He was the younger son of the 2nd Marquis of Westminster, the 1st Duke of Westminster. (See *Lupus*)
Lowther	*1846* *Whitehaven* *Junction 1846* *L&C1857* *1875,1896*	The river which flows for seventeen miles from Hawes Water past Bampton, Lowther Castle and Clifton to the Eamont at Brougham Castle. 1787-1872. Lord William Lowther (2nd Earl of Lonsdale) pulled down Lowther Hall in 1808 and built Lowther Castle. He was one of the original Directors of the Lancaster & Carlisle Railway. He was Postmaster-General 1841-1846. (See *Lonsdale*)
Loyalty	*1913*	A name given in honour of the visit of King George V and Queen Mary to Crewe Locomotive Works on 21st April 1913, the day when Robert Turnbull and Frank Ree were knighted.
Lucifer	*GJ1839* *1848,1872*	The name of the archangel who fell from heaven and became the Devil, or Satan. Venus, the Morning Star.
Luck of Edenhall	*L&C1857* *1874,1894*	The name is derived from a legend connected with the crystal drinking glass of Eden Hall, the family seat of the Musgraves near Penrith. In Henry Longfellow's poem inspired by and translated from one by Uhland based on the legend are two lines which read:- "Should the goblet break or fall, Farewell the Luck of Edenhall."
Lucknow	*1868,1891,1922*	The town in India which was relieved on 17th November 1857 during the Indian Mutiny.
Lune	*1846,L&C1857* *S.Helens ?date 1872*	The river which rises in Westmorland and flows for 45 miles past Tebay, Kirkby Lonsdale and Lancaster to the Irish Sea.
Lupus	*C&B1840*	Latin for 'Wolf', This was the nickname of the 1st Earl of Chester from the 1070s, who died in 1101. The 1st Duke of Westminster, elevated from a Marquisate in 1874 was Hugh Lupus Grosvenor (1825-1899), so the name has an oblique reference to two later Directors, Lord Stalbridge and the Duke of Westminster.
Lusitania	*1916*	In memory of the loss of the Cunard liner of 32,000 gross tons built in 1907 and holder in July that year of the Blue Riband, which was torpedoed and sunk by enemy action on 7th May 1915 off the Old Head of Kinsale while returning from New York to Liverpool. 1,198 lives were lost, of whom 128 were United States citizens. Lusitania was the Roman Province roughly corresponding to Portugal.

Lynx	*GJ1837,1846*	A creature of mythology, half dog and half panther.
	1871,1894	A species of the cat family having tufted ears and a short tail.
Mabel	*1880,1896*	The mother of George Stephenson and grandmother of Robert, whose maiden name was Carr. The locomotive of this name took part in the Stephenson Centenary celebrations at Newcastle in 1881.
Maberley	*1854*	1798-1885 William Leader Maberly, was MP for several constituencies 1819-1834, then Secretary to the General
	1872	Post-Office. He vigorously opposed the introduction of the Penny Post, delayed improvement of any kind in the postal services, and spoke of Rowland Hill as "that man from Birmingham". By all accounts he spelt his name "Maberly".
Madge	*1871,1891*	The tombstone of the wife of John Ramsbottom gives her name as Mary Ann but J.N.Maskelyne refers to her as Madge. It is quite possible that she was called 'Madge' by her family and close friends.
Magdala	*1869,1892*	A fortified city in Abyssinia, ruthlessly ruled by King Theodore who imprisoned the British Consul and others, and which was captured by an army commanded by General Robert Napier on 13th April 1868. He was elevated to the peerage as Baron Napier of Magdala on 17th July 1868.
Magistrate	*1847*	A public civil officer, invested with a certain judicial authority.
Magnet	*1852*	The loadstone; a piece of magnetised iron or steel.
		A stagecoach name.
Magnificent	*1901*	The Battleship of 1894-1918.
Maintenance	*1890*	The act of maintaining. A suitable name for a Permanent Way Department locomotive.
Majestic	*L&M1830/36,*	'Having majesty or dignity of person or experience'.
1855,Ex B'head 1860,1862,1863		
		The name of 1855 was one of three given that year to commemorate the Crimean War, the other two being *Nightingale* and *Banshee*. HMS Majestic was a large warship carrying twelve 8in. guns and sixty eight 32 pounders, and served in the Baltic in 1854-5.
	1909	The White Star liner of 1890-1914 of 9,950 gross tons and sister ship of the Teutonic.
		A Battleship built in 1895, and sunk in 1915 off Cape Helles.
Malta	*1911*	A Crown Colony in the central Mediterranean Sea. The locomotive was named to celebrate coronation year 1911.
Mammoth	*L&M1839*	An extinct species of elephant of the Pleistocene age, some of which were of immense size.
1849,1872,1885,1905		
Marathon	*L&M1838*	The place of battle on the north-east coast of Attica between the Persians and the Athenians in 490BC after
	1862,1878	which the news of victory was borne to Athens by a swift runner named Pheidippides. When the Olympic
	1896,1922	Games was revived in 1896 at Athens the distance was reckoned to be 26 miles and 385 yards, and the race was called "The Marathon".
Marchioness of Stafford	*1885*	Millicent was the eldest daughter of the 4th Earl of Rosslyn, who in 1884 married the Marquis, son of the 3rd Duke of Sutherland and a Director of the Company. She later became Duchess of Sutherland.
Mark Twain	*1914*	1835-1910. The pen name of Samuel Langhorne Clemens, the American author.
Marlborough	*1866,1893,*	1650-1722. John Churchill, 1st Duke of Marlborough is one of England's greatest generals, victor at Blenheim,
	1909	Ramillies, Malplaquet and Oudenarde.
Marmion	*1863,1907*	Lord Marmion was the hero of the Sir Walter Scott's romantic poem.
Marquis	*1847*	A title in the peerage below Duke and above Earl.
1850,1873,1874,1904		
Marquis Douro		This was one of the titles of the Duke of Wellington, used as a courtesy title by his eldest son. The River Douro
	B&L1838,1850	was crossed by Wellington's troops on 12th May 1809, and Oporto was liberated on the same day. Wellington

Ex B'head 1860 *1865,1893*		was known to the Portugese soldiers as Douro and was thus happy to have the same name bestowed on his eldest son. This name has sometimes been recorded as *Marquis of Douro*.

Marron   *C&W1849*   The river which rises on Blake Fell and flows nine miles north to the Derwent near Workington.

Mars   *L&M1831*
       W&FJ1857
       1903
The sun's planet next farthest out from the earth, named after the god of war in Roman mythology, father of Romulus and Remus.
The Battleship of 1896-1921.

Martin   *L&M1842*
1850,1860,1864,1894
The bird, a member of the swallow family.

Maryport   *WJ1847*   The coastal town in Cumberland on the Solway Firth.

Mastodon   *L&M1839*
1849,1872,1879,1892
An extinct species of elephant.

Mayor   *1847*   The chief of a municipal corporation.

Mazeppa   *1849*
       1861,1906
1644-1709. Ivan Stepanovitch Mazeppa-Kalodinsky, a Cossack military commander, the hero of Lord Byron's poem. There was a London stage performance of "Mazeppa" in 1844.

McConnell   *SS1858*   James Edward McConnell was born in Fermoy, County Cork on 1st January 1815 and was appointed Locomotive Superintendent of the Birmingham & Gloucester Railway from July 1841 until February 1847 when he succeeded Edward Bury at Wolverton. He resigned in February 1862, and died on 11th June 1883 aged 68.

Medea   *GJ1836*
1848,1872,1879,1895
The daughter of the King of Colchis, who married Jason and helped him to obtain the Golden Fleece.

Medusa   *GJ1838*
1846,1872,1885,1905
The chief of the Gorgons, a beautiful maiden transformed by Athena into a monster so hideous that all who looked on her were turned to stone. She was therefore beheaded by Perseus.

Megatherion   *1848*   There is no such word in the O.E.D. A megatherium, however is an extinct gigantic toothless animal of the Pleistocene Age. Some sources give the name *Megatherium*, but S.S.Scott in his manuscript emphasised the '**ion**' by bold script underlined. Livesey and Baxter have followed suit.

Memnon   *BL&CJ1854*
1855.1861,1864, 1892
The oriental prince who in the Trojan War went to the assistance of Priam and was slain by Achilles.

Menai   *1848,1860,1864*   The straits between North Wales and Anglesey.

Mercury   *L&M1831*
1855,1878,1895
The planet nearest to the sun, named after Jupiter's messenger with winged hat and sandals; the god of eloquence.

Merlin   *GJ1838*
       1854
       1903
King Arthur's bard, and a wizard of Arthurian legend; a blend of fact and fiction.
The Bird, one of the smaller hawks, and one of several such names given to locomotives in that year.
The Sloop of 1901-1923 and a Survey Vessel in 1906.

Merrie Carlisle
    L&C1859,1877,1895
The City of Carlisle.

Mersey   *GJ1849*
       BL&CJ 1849/52
St.Helens ?date,1860,1907
The river formed by the rivers Goyt and Tame at Stockport, which flows into Liverpool Bay. Its length is 70 miles including the estuary.

Messenger   *1853*
       1884,1905
One who conveys a message; a forerunner.
'Queen's (or King's) Messenger' was a title given to one responsible for the conveyance of "Diplomatic Bags" for the Foreign and Commonwealth Office, and it was the duty of the railways to give speedy passage to such a person.

Meteor   *L&M1830/7*
1849,1877,1913
A rock from outer space rendered luminous by friction with the earth's atmosphere. A shooting star - a small meteorite.

Middlesex	*1909*	An English County served by the Company.
Midge	*1870*	Any minute fly or gnat.
Miles MacInnes	*1910*	He was the eldest son of General John MacInnes, banker and MP(Lib) for Hexham 1885-1892/3-5. He moved to Rickerby House, Carlisle in 1876 and joined the L&NWR Board of Directors in November that year as a nominee of the Cockermouth Keswick & Penrith Railway Board, and continued as a Director of both Boards for the next thirty years until his death aged 79 in 1909. The Secretary of the L&NWR Temperance Union in Carlisle wrote "We have lost our very best friend, on whom railwaymen of the LNWR line have looked for help when in trouble and also in our Christian and temperance work.". He was also Vice President of the Church Missionary Society.
Milo	*L&M1832/6*	The celebrated Greek athlete in his youth capable of prodigious feats of strength.
Milton	*1866,1890,1916*	1608-1674. John, the poet, blind from the age of 44, for the last 22 years of his life.
Minerva	*1868,1888*	One of the three chief divinities of Roman mythology. The goddess of wisdom.
	1915	The 2nd Class Cruiser of 1895-1920 which served in the Dardanelles.
Minotaur	*1851*	A monster with a bull's head and a man's body, kept in the labyrinth in Crete.
	1857,1870,1887	
Miranda	*7.1854*	The Corvette built in 1851 which served with distinction in the Russian War. She was presumably named after
	1878,1897	the daughter of Prospero, in Shakespeare's "The Tempest".
Monarch	*1848,1860,1907*	The supreme ruler of a state, usually hereditary.
Monk	*ExNU1846,1856*	A member of a religious order for men.
	BL&CJ1849?	The BL&CJR locomotive probably recalls the members of the Benedictine Priory, who had owned the ferry rights which the railway was seeking to revive.
Monmouthshire	*1909*	An English County at the time served by the Company. (Since 1974 part of Wales, known as Gwent.)
Moonstone	*1915*	A felspar exhibiting moonlike light reflections. A name first used a month or so after *Loadstone* was reintroduced, and thus probably not associated with Wilkie Collins' Novel of that name.
Moor Hen	*1911*	The name plate was inscribed with two separate words. The small coot-like bird. According to the Oxford English Dictionary the word is always hyphenated 'and never found as a single word'; but the scientific word now accepted as correct and used by The Wildfowl & Wetlands Trust and other agencies is 'Moorhen'.
Morecambe	*L&C1859*	The Lancashire town on the west coast. There is a Morecambe Lodge three miles north of Carnforth.
Murdock	*1866*	1754-1839. William Murdoch was employed in 1777 with Boulton & Watt at Soho, after which he was sent to
	1888	Cornwall by James Watt to look after pumping engines. He made the first self -propelled vehicle in Britain, the little 3-wheeler of 1784 now in the Birmingham Museum, and may thus be considered the ancestor of all cars and locomotives. He was also a pioneer in the gas industry, and is buried in Handsworth Parish Church. He changed his surname to Murdock to try to overcome the English inability to pronouce the Scottish "ch" to his liking.
Napier	*1851*	1782-1853. Lieut.General Sir Charles James Napier had a distinguished career in India, was a pall-bearer at the Duke of Wellington's funeral, and has a statue in St.Paul's Cathedral.
	1872	1810-1890. General Robert Cornelis Napier had a most distinguished career in India and elsewhere, and his exploits at Magdala (q.v.) indicate but a fraction of his greatness. He was made Fellow of the Royal Society in 1869.
Napoleon	*1863*	1808-1873. Emperor Napoleon III of France, the nephew of Napoleon Bonaparte, was President of the Second
	1905	Republic from 1850 until 1852, and Emperor from then until 1871. He concluded an alliance with Great Britain prior to the Crimean War. He died at Chislehurst.
Narcissus	*1847,1873,1890*	The youth who fell in love with his reflection in the water of a fountain and was changed into a flower.
Nasmyth	*1854*	1808-1890. James was the inventor of the steam hammer and founder of the Bridgewater Foundry at Patricroft,

	1878,1893	Locomotive Manufacturers.

Nasr Ed Din   *1873*   A name in Persian script, carried temporarily by Problem class No 806 in June 1873 to honour the visit of the Shah of Persia to Crewe Works. It is understood that the nameplate reads from right to left the words 'Nasr Ed Din Shah'. His dates were 1845-1896.

Navvie   *St.Helens*   Originally a labourer employed for cutting canals for navigation. Nowadays usually spelt 'Navvy'.
(or Navvy)   *?date*

Nelson   *B&L1833*   1758-1805. Admiral Horatio, 1st Viscount Nelson. A successful commander in naval battles, culminating at the
    1848   battle of Trafalgar, during which he was mortally wounded.
    1903   The iron armoured frigate of 7,473 tons built by Elder in 1876, which became a training ship in 1902, was sold in 1910 and broken up in Holland.

Neptune   *1903*   The Battleship of 1878-1903, named after the Roman god of the sea, and one of the planets discovered in 1846 as a result of predictions by John Couch Adams, a Cambridge mathematician and U.J.J.Verrier, a Frenchman.

Nestor   *1855*   The King of Pylos, the oldest and most experienced of the chieftains who took part in the siege of Troy.

Newby   *L&C1857*   Newby Grange, Crosby, Carlisle was the residence of William Nicholson Hodgson, Director of the Lancaster & Carlisle Railway and from 1860 of the L&NWR. He was also a Director of the Cockermouth Kendal and Penrith Railway as a nominee of the L&NWR from 1863, and died in 1876.

Newcomen *1866,1890,1910*   1663-1729. Thomas, the inventor of the first practical steam engine.

Newton   *W&N1831*   Newton-le-Willows, a general railway exchange point at the time.
    1866,1888   1642-1727. Sir Isaac, natural philosopher and mathematician was President of the Royal Society in 1703 and lies buried in Westminster Abbey. This was the first of a series of names of famous people.

New Zealand   *1911*   Named after the self-governing British Dominion to celebrate coronation year 1911.

Niagara   *1885*   The river, 31 miles long, between Lake Erie and Lake Ontario on the Canadian - United States border famous for
    1905   the Falls 160ft high situated half way along it. (See *Himalaya*)

Nightingale   *1855*   1820-1910. Florence, the English nurse and founder of trained nursing as a profession for women who was in charge of the hospital at Scutari during the Crimean War, and earned the byname 'Lady of the Lamp' from making her rounds at night. This was one of three names given that year to commemorate the Crimean War. (See *Banshee* and *Majestic*)

Nipper.   *1867*   A slang term for a little boy, and also a good choice of name for a hand tool well used in and around Crewe Works.

North Star   *L&M1830*   Polaris, the pole star and the final one in the tail of the Little Bear.
    L&PJ1840,1847,1892

North Western   *1847,1873*   The abbreviated version of the full title "London & North Western", which had been formed in 1846. The name
    1887,1906   had no hyphen. It is interesting to note that the words are hyphenated in the company seal, in the Rule Book, by G.P.Neele in his "Railway Reminiscences", and in books by George Findlay, C.J.Bowen Cooke, and in C.Williams' locomotive registers.

Northumberland   *1909*   The most northerly English County. A curious choice since it was not served by the Company.

Northumbrian   *L&M1830*   The locomotive built by Robert Stephenson & Co. at Newcastle-upon-Tyne in Northumberland, and which led the procession of trains at the opening of the Liverpool & Manchester Railway in 1830. The name was at first intended to be 'Northumberland' but was changed to honour the Northumbrian George Stephenson.

Novelty   *1868*   The first locomotive of this name, which took part in the Rainhill trials, is believed to have been named after a
    1892   theatre. It was designed by John Braithwaite and John Ericsson and built in London. Subsequent uses of the name relate to this pioneer locomotive.

Nubian   *1911*   The Destroyer of 1909-1916, which was badly damaged by a torpedo on 27th October 1916, and was joined to HMS Zulu also damaged, to become HMS Zubian.

Nun	*ExNU1841*	A woman devoted to the religious life in a convent.
	1849,1857	A name paired with *Friar*.
Oberon	*GJ1838*	The King of the Fairies, the husband of Titania. Folk-lore.
	1848,W&FJ1851,	Also a character in Shakespeare's 'A Midsummer Night's Dream'.
	1874,1904	
Oceanic	*1889*	The White Star liner of 1871-1895 of 3,708 gross tons.
	1907	The White Star liner of 1899-1913 of 17,250 gross tons.
		The name means 'Of or pertaining to the ocean'.
Odin	*GJ1840,1851*	The Scandinavian god of wisdom, poetry, war and agriculture, who in Norse mythology was the father of the
	1872,1879	gods and protector of warriors and sailors. One might have expected such a versatile god to have found his name
	1895	on a mixed-traffic locomotive.
	1916	There was a sloop of this name which served in the Mesopotamian Campaign in 1915.
Oliver Goldsmith	*1913*	1728-1774. The poet, author and playwright. (See *Goldsmith*)
Onyx	*1848,1860*	A variety of agate lined with streaks of dark and white chalcedony.
	1864,1893,1916	
Oregon	*1884,1905*	The Guion liner of 1883, Iron, single screw of 7,400 gross tons, named after the north-western Pacific American
		State, bought by the Cunard Line in 1884, and holder of the Blue Riband 1884-1885. She sank on 14th March
		1886 in the approaches to New York following a collision.
Orion	*L&M1834*	One of the chief constellations, mentioned by Homer, Amos and Job.
		A giant and a hunter, noted for his beauty who was killed by an arrow shot by Artemis.
	1902	The Armoured Corvette of 1879-1909, when she was renamed 'Orontes' for use as a depot ship at Malta. Sold
		1913.
Osprey	*L&M1846,*	The fish-hawk. A large sea-bird preying on fish.
	1856,1872	
Ostrich	*L&M1842*	A flightless bird of southern and eastern Africa.
1854,1860,1865,1890,1913		
Otterhound	*1911*	A hound used for hunting the otter.
Ousel	*1854*	The ancient name for the blackbird.
Outram	*1863*	1803-1863. Sir James, who helped Havelock to defeat the Shah of Persia at Herat in 1856 and again with
		Havelock reinforced the garrison at Lucknow in 1857 before it was finally relieved by Sir Colin Campbell.
Owl *L&M1842,1853,1860*		A nocturnal bird of prey.
Owzell	*L&M1845*	See 'Ousel'.
Oxfordshire	*1909*	An English County served by the Company.
Pacific	*1889*	The White Star liner of 1851 named after the Pacific Ocean, so called by Magellan in October/November 1520
	1907	when he first sighted it and found the sea so calm. She held the Blue Riband at one time.
Palmerston	*1863*	1784-1865. Henry John Temple, 3rd Viscount from 1802 was Prime Minister of Great Britain and Ireland
		1855-1858 and 1859-1865.
Pandora	*B&L1838*	The first woman, made by Vulcan, whose box contained every imaginable evil and, last of all, Hope.
	1865,1905	
Panopea	*1865,1905*	A sea nymph, one of the Nereids.

Panther	*L&M1839*	The leopard; applied also to the puma and the jaguar.
Partridge *L&M1843,1854,1872,1911*		A game bird.
Patentee	*L&M1834*	One who has obtained a patent, or that which has been patented. The locomotive was the first six wheeled engine to be built, for the Liverpool & Manchester Railway in 1834. It later became a generic term for the earliest batch of such engines, "The Patentees", notorious for the weakness of their crank axles.
Pathfinder	*1911*	A Scout Cruiser formerly the Fastnet (renamed 1903), which was torpedoed on 5th September 1914 by U-21 in the North Sea.
Patience	*1875* *1897,1922*	The quality of calmness and composure, and the second in the trio of engines named after the virtues 'Pluck, Patience and Perseverance'.
Patriot	*1920*	"In memory of the fallen L & N W R employees 1914-1919".
Patterdale	*L&C1857* *1869,1893*	The village at the south end of Ullswater. Patterdale Hall was the residence of William Marshall MP, a Director of the Lancaster & Carlisle Railway.
Peacock	*1853*	The game-bird, allied to the stork.
Peak	*C&HP1883*	The district crossed by the Cromford and High Peak Railway on the way to its northern terminus at Whaley Bridge on the Peak Forest Canal.
Pearl	*1848,1857,* *1879,1906*	A concretion of mother of pearl around some foreign body within the shell of various bivalve molluscs.
Peel	*B&L1840* *1850* *1862,1905*	1788-1850. Sir Robert was Prime Minister of Great Britain and Ireland from 1834-1835 and from 1841-1846. He was responsible for the repeal of the Corn Laws in 1846. The engine was named shortly before his death on 2nd July. He was a personal friend of Edward Tootal, and had opened the L&NWR Trent Valley line in 1847.
Peerless	*1848*	Matchless, having no equal.
Pegasus	*GJ1838/42* *1854,1880,1894,1915*	A winged horse ridden by Bellerophon when he slew the monster Chimera.
Pelican	*L&M1841,1852*	A fish-eating bird.
Pelsall	*SS1851*	A village in Staffordshire served by the South Staffordshire Railway.
Penguin	*L&M1844* *1853,1884,1905*	The flightless sea-bird, found wild only in the southern hemisphere.
Penmaenmawr *1852* *1857,1870,1893,1913*		The Carnarvonshire town on the North coast of Wales.
Penrith Beacon *L&C1859,1875,1897*		A beacon hill on the north-eastern outskirts of Penrith.
Percy Bysshe Shelley	*1914*	1792-1822. The poet.
Perseus	*1911*	The son of Zeus, Andromeda's lover who saved her from a sea-monster and beheaded Medusa.
Perseverance	*1875,1897*	Persistence in anything undertaken. The third in the trio of virtues, following 'Pluck' and 'Patience'.
Persia	*1916*	In memory of the Peninsular and Oriental liner of 7,974 gross tons built in 1900 and torpedoed without warning by U-38 in the eastern Mediterranean on 30th December 1915 with heavy loss of life, 334 persons in all.

Pet	1865	A popular member of Crewe Locomotive Works.
Petrel	L&M1844	A family numbering several species, of long-winged dark-plumaged sea-birds.
	WJJ1852, 1856,1872,1879,1895,1916	
Petteril	L&C1857	The river which rises near Penruddock and flows 21 miles north-east and then north-west to the Eden at Carlisle.
Phaeton	1847	The son of Phoebus the sun-god, who undertook to drive his father's chariot and upset it over Athens.
	1872,1890,1913	
Phalaris	GJ1837	The Sicilian tyrant c.570BC notorious for his cruelty, not least for heating prisoners in a bronze bull named after him.
	1844,1854,1873,1893,1907	
Phantom	GJ1839	A spirit or apparition.
	1848,1877,1894	
P.H.Chambres	1911	He was a member of a prominent landowning family of Trefnant, Denbighshire. Philip Henry Chambres was elected a Director of the Company from 1885-1907. He died in 1909.
Pheasant	L&M1842	A game-bird.
	1851,1860,1872,1879,1895,1909	
Phlegethon	GJ1841,1853	A river of liquid fire in Hades.
Phoebus	GJ1838	An epithet of Apollo, god of the sun.
	GJ1841,1850,1860,1862	
Phoenix	L&M1830/6	A fabulous Arabian bird which immolated itself on a fire after a five hundred year life span, and then rose with
	WJ1852	new life from the ashes.
Phosphorus	GJ1840	The morning star, Lucifer; the planet Venus at dawn.
	1850,1860,1907	A non-metallic element undergoing slow combustion in air at ordinary temperatures and appearing luminous in the dark.
Pilot	1847,1877,1896	A director of one's course, one qualified to steer a vessel in harbour approaches, etc.
Pioneer	1872,1888	One who goes ahead to prepare the way; An explorer.
Pitt	1866,1888	1759-1806. William, the younger was Prime Minister of Great Britain from 1783-1801 and of Great Britain and Ireland 1804-1806.
Planet	L&M1830	A celestial body, revolving in an orbit around the sun.
	1866,1893,1913	
Platelayer	1914	A railway workman employed to lay and repair the rails, these originally having been termed 'plates'.
Pluck	1875,1894	Courage, heart, spirit. The first of the trio of engines named after the virtues, 'Pluck, Patience and Perseverance'.
Pluto	L&M1832	In mythology the ruler of the infernal regions, the son of Saturn and brother of Jupiter and Neptune.
	1851,1857,1870,1888,1916	
Plynlimmon	1878	A mountain in the Cambrian range, near Aberystwyth.
	1896,1915	
Pollux	1848,1857	The twin brother of Castor.
Polyphemus	1846,1872	The son of Poseidon, the largest and fiercest of the Cyclops, who was blinded by Odysseus in Sicily.
	1900	The Torpedo Ram of 1881-1903.
Powerful	1900	The Cruiser of 1895 until November 1919 when she was renamed 'Impregnable' for use as a Training Ship. Sold 1929.

Powis	*1849,1850*	1785-1848. Edward Herbert, 2nd Earl of Powis was MP for Ludlow from 1806 until his succession to the peerage in 1839. He achieved popularity with the clergy and the universities, and in 1847 opposed Prince Albert as candidate for the Chancellorship of Cambridge University, losing by only a slender majority. He died accidentally and tragically in January 1848.
Precedent	*1875,1895,1915*	An example to follow. Mr. Webb gave this name to the prototype of his largest wheeled (6ft.6in.) 2-4-0s.
Precursor	*1850*	A forerunner; one who precedes,
	1874	The name was revived in April 1874 by Mr. Webb as appropriate for the first of his smallest (5ft.6in.) 2-4-0s.
	1904	The name was revived once again by Mr. Whale in March 1904 for the first of his 4-4-0s.
Premier	*1846*	That which is 'First' or 'Principal'. The Prime Minister of Great Britain and Ireland, and of certain British
	1872,1888,1923	Dominions, and some other states. The L&NWR was widely known as 'The Premier Line'.
President	*1849*	The chief of a republic: One who presides.
	1850,1872,1906	
President Garfield	*1882,1895*	1831-1881. James Garfield was President of the United States of America in 1881, and was assassinated.
President Lincoln	*1882*	1809-1865. Abraham Lincoln was President of the United States of America from 1861 until his assassination on
	1895,1909	15th April 1865.
President Washington	*1882,1894*	1732-1799. George Washington was the first President of the United States of America from 1789-1797. In 1881 the Duke of Sutherland and a party of L&NWR Directors visited the USA and were received by President Garfield at the White House. To commemorate this visit three 'Jumbos' were named as shown above.
Preston	*L&C1859*	The Lancashire town.
Priam	*SS1855*	King of Troy, slain in old age at the siege by Pyrrhus the son of Achilles.
Prince	*GJ1845*	A sovereign, a ruler, especially of a principality.
Prince Albert	*1847,1872,1890*	1819-1861. Francis Charles Augustus Albert Emanuel was the Prince Consort, from 1840 the dearly loved husband of Queen Victoria.
	1922	1895-1952. Albert Frederick Arthur George was the second son of King George V and later became King George VI.
Prince Alfred	*1863*	1844-1900. He was the second son of Queen Victoria, who succeeded his paternal uncle Duke Ernst II as Duke of Saxe-Coburg and Gotha. He later became Duke of Edinburgh.
Prince Arthur	*1853*	1850-1942. He was the third son of Queen Victoria, who later became Duke of Connaught.
Prince Ernest	*1853,1857*	1845-1923. Prince Ernest Augustus, son of King George V of Hanover, and Duke of Cumberland was Crown Prince in 1851, succeeded as Duke in 1878, but was deprived of the title in 1917. He visited London in 1853 with his parents.
Prince Eugene	*1853*	Duke of Savoy, the Emperor Leopold I's great general in the War of the Spanish Succession and fought beside
	Ex B'head 1860,1872	Marlborough in the battles of Blenheim, Oudenarde and Malplaquet.
Prince George	*1894*	1865-1936. He was the second son of the Prince of Wales and Princess Alexandra, who later became King George V.
	1907	1902-1942. He was the fourth son of the Prince and Princess of Wales, who later became Duke of Kent.
Prince Leopold	*1877,1897*	1853-1884. He was the fourth son of Queen Victoria, later to become Duke of Albany.
Prince of Wales	*1852,1862*	He was the eldest son of Queen Victoria, who became King Edward VII.
	1906	He was the second and only surviving son of King Edward VII, later to become King George V.
	1911	1894-1972. Edward Albert Christian George Andrew Patrick David was the eldest son of King George V, later to become King Edward VIII and after his abdication, Duke of Windsor.
	1924	The same person as above, but the engine was so named because he was President of the British Empire Exhibition at which the locomotive was exhibited.

Prince Oscar   *1862*   He was a Prince of Sweden, who visited Crewe Works in May 1862.

Princess   *GJ1845*   *1871*   The daughter of a sovereign; the consort of a prince.

Princess Alexandra   *1863*   1844-1925. She was a Princess of Denmark, who married the Prince of Wales in 1863 and later became Queen Alexandra. A name possibly given as a wedding welcome into the Royal Family.

              1909   1891-1959. Alexandra Victoria was the elder daughter of Princess Louise (1867-1931). She was declared a Princess on 9th November 1905, her grandfather King Edward VII's birthday, and married Prince Arthur of Connaught in 1913.

Princess Alice   *1863*   1843-1878. She was the third child of Queen Victoria. She married in July 1862, and the name might have been a belated wedding gift.

              1907   1883-1981. She was the daughter of Prince Leopold and Princess Helena, who married the Earl of Athlone in 1904, and lived to the very great age of ninety-seven, thus becoming the last surviving grand-daughter of Queen Victoria.

Princess Beatrice   *1877*   1857-1944. She was the fifth daughter and youngest child of Queen Victoria, who in 1885 married Prince Henry of Battenburg. (See *Beatrice* and *Lady Beatrice*)

Princess Helena   *1866*   1846-1923. The third daughter of Queen Victoria, who in 1866 married Prince Christian of Schleswig-Holstein.
              1888   Maybe it was a wedding commemoration.

Princess Louise   1848-1939. She was the fourth daughter of Queen Victoria, who in 1871 married the Marquess of Lorne, heir to
1877,1896,1922   the 8th Duke of Argyll.
       1867-1931, She was the eldest daughter of King Edward VII, whose elder daughter was Princess Alexandra, 1891-1959 (q.v.).

Princess May   *1894,1906*   1867-1953. She was the daughter of the Duke of Teck and great grand-daughter of King George III, who married the Duke of York in 1893, and when he ascended the throne in 1910 became Queen Mary.

Princess Royal   *1862*   A title given in 1841 to Princess Victoria, the first child of Queen Victoria, born 21st November 1840.

Private E. Sykes V.C.   Ernest Sykes. 27th (S) Battalion Northumberland Fusiliers, was awarded the Victoria Cross (London Gazette 8th
    1922,1926   June 1917) for most conspicuous bravery and devotion to duty while in France. Prior to the war he was a platelayer at Micklehurst, and afterwards returned to L&NWR employment. At the time the engine was named he was employed as a ticket-collector at Stalybridge. He ultimately became a guard, and served in the Home Guard in the Second World War. He died on 3rd August 1949 aged 64, and is buried at Woodfield cemetery.

Private W. Wood V.C. *1922*   Wilfred Wood. 10th (Service) Battalion Northumberland Fusiliers was awarded the Victoria Cross for most
              1926   conspicuous bravery and initiative on 28th October 1918 near Casa Van, Italy. He joined the L&NWR in 1916 as a cleaner in the locomotive department. After the war he was promoted to fireman, and driver, and retired from British Railways on 27th August 1960 as Supervisor at Longsight Motive Power Depot. He died on 3rd January 1982, aged 84, and was cremated at Stockport.

Problem   *1848,1859,1905*   A question proposed for solution, as for example a prototype locomotive's development might raise.

Prometheus   *GL1838/41*   One of the Titans, the bestower of fire, which he had stolen from heaven and celebrated in mythology as a
     1849,1861   benefactor of mankind.
              1906   The Third Class Cruiser of 1898 until May 1914, when it was sold despite the fear of war.

Proserpine   *1856*   The wife of Pluto, Queen of the Shades, and in Greek known as Persephone.
   1872,1877,1894

Prospero   *GJ1837*   The rightful Duke of Milan in Shakespeare's "The Tempest".
  1854,1873,1896,1907

Psyche   *1865,1905*   A beautiful maiden beloved by Cupid. The personified and deified soul or spirit.

Ptarmigan   *1854,1911*   A bird of the grouse family.

Puck	*1866* *1893,1913*	A mischievous sprite of popular folklore. One of this name appears in Shakespeare's "Midsummer Night's Dream".
Python	*GJ1841* *1853,1874,1905*	The serpent slain by Apollo. A non-venomus snake of the boa constrictor family.
Quail	*1854,1911*	Britain's smallest game-bird. A summer visitor.
Queen Alexandra	*1901*	1844-1925. She was the wife of King Edward VII.
Queen Empress	*1893,1906*	The two titles of Queen Victoria, the former by The Act of Settlement 1701, and the latter by proclamation at a Durbar held at Delhi on 1st January 1877. The choice of name was most appropriate, for the locomotive was a British exhibit at the Chicago Exposition World's Fair in 1893, and received the highest award.
Queen Mab	*WJ1861*	The female elf, employed as a midwife to deliver men's brains of dreams. Not to be confused with Titania, the Queen of King Oberon, for the word 'queen' as applied to Mab does not imply sovereignty, but simply 'female'. Folk-lore, and see Shakespeare's 'Romeo and Juliet 1, 4.'.
Queen Mary	*1910*	1867-1953. She was the wife of King George V.
Queen of the Belgians	*1915*	1876-1965. Elizabeth was the wife of King Albert I, and a Princess of Bavaria.
Quernmore	*L&C1857* *1870,1891*	A village two miles east of Lancaster close to the Lancaster & Carlisle Railway. Quernmore Park was the residence of William Garnett, a Director of that Company.
Quicksilver	*1852* *1860,1864*	The metallic element Mercury. A stage-coach name.
Racehorse	*1911*	Another of the small number of names of vessels of exploration and discovery. There was a ketch of this name, which had previously been a French privateer named *Marquis de Vandruell* captured in 1757; it was later fitted for use in Arctic exploration, and in 1773/6 attempted to find (along with HMS 'Carcass') the North-East passage into the Pacific. Captured December 1776 by the American *Andrea Dorea* and destroyed on 15th November 1777 by the Royal Navy in Delaware Bay. There was also a Destroyer of 1902-1920 with this name.
Raglan	*10.1854* *1872*	1788-1855. Lord Fitzroy Somerset, younger son of 5th Duke of Beaufort was created Baron Raglan 1852, promoted Field Marshal November 1854, and commanded the British Forces in Crimea. He died there on 28th June 1855 following the failure of the assault upon Sebastopol. He was a most brave and loyal man who had lost an arm at the battle of Waterloo.
Raleigh	*1866* *1888*	1552-1618. Sir Walter is generally regarded as being an admiral, by virtue of having been given the title of "Vice Admiral of Devon and Cornwall" in 1585, but this was purely a legal and administrative post, and he is mentioned in the Encylopaedia Britannica only as an explorer.
Ralph Brocklebank	*1913*	He was a shipping magnate who lived at Houghton Hall and a Liverpool Director of the Company from 1882-1895.
Ramillies	*1900*	The Battleship of 1892-1913, named after the victory in battle over the French on 23rd May 1706 at a village of that name south-east of Brussels.
Rapid	*L&M1835*	An appropriate choice of name for a locomotive, and paired with that of its successor 'Speedwell', and one which had appeared in earlier times on the London - Nottingham stagecoach.
Raven	*L&M1843* *1853,1888* *St.Helens 1863*	The largest bird of the crow family. "Raven" is a word closely associated with St.Helens. "The Raven" is an inn sited in Raven Street across the road from the Station, where it is said the Directors sometimes assembled. The British Cast Glass Plate Company, dating from 1786 was at Ravenshead, St.Helens and is now a part of Pilkington.
Raymond Poincaré	*1915*	1860-1934. He was the French Prime Minister in 1912 and President of the 3rd Republic 1913-1920, who largely determined the policy that led to France's involvement in the Great War.

Fig. 82   Sir Richard Moon. Company Chairman 1861-1891

L&NWR Society Photograph Collection A66.

R.B.Sheridan	*1914*	1751-1816. Richard Brinsley Butler Sheridan, the author.
Red Gauntlet	*1863,1909*	The title of one of Sir Walter Scott's novels was 'Redgauntlet', a single word. Other railway companies used the single word, and it is not known why the L&NWR used two.
Redbreast	*L&M1845,1851*	The robin, so named because of the colour of its breast.
Redstart	*L&M1845 1856,1857*	The migratory bird, allied to the redbreast, both being members of the Thrush family.
Redwing	*L&M1844,1854*	The thrush, having a red patch under its wings.
Renown	*1899*	The Battleship of 1895-1914.
Resolution	*1899*	The Battleship of 1892-1914.
Revenge	*1902*	The Battleship of 1892-1915, when she was renamed 'Redoubtable' and classed as a 'Bombarding Ship'. Sold 1919.
Reynard	*1853,1875,1897*	The fox. The reason for this choice of name is obscure. An HMS Reynard was lost in the China Seas in 1851, but this would seem an unlikely source.

Rhinoceros	*1847*	A large pachydermatous ungulate with either one or two horns on the nose.
Ribble	*P&W1847* *St.Helens 1856* *L&C1857,1872*	The river which rises at Ribblehead in the former West Riding of Yorkshire and flows past Settle, Clitheroe and Preston to the Irish Sea.
Richard Arkwright	*1898* *1913*	1732-1792. He was the inventor who solved the problem of mechanical spinning, and was knighted in 1786.
Richard Cobden	*1873,1890,1922*	1804-1865. He was the politician noted for being instrumental in the repeal of the Corn Laws in 1846.
Richd Francis Roberts	*1884*	He was the L&NWR Company Solicitor, 1874, who had died suddenly on 27th October 1883, and one held in high affection throughout the Company. He was buried at Bridport.
Richard Moon	*1894,1906*	1814-1899. He was a member, with Henry Crosfield, of the shareholders' committee appointed in 1850 to give an opinion on the future management of the L&NWR, and who was made a Director of the Company on 21st February 1851. He was Chairman from 1861 until 1891 and was created a baronet in 1887. He died on 17th November 1899, aged 85.
Richard Trevithick	*1894,1906*	1771-1833. He was the pioneer of steam traction, at Pen-y-darran and father of Francis who was 'Foreman of Locomotives' at Crewe from 1843 until his retirement on 9th May 1857.
Rickerby	*L&C1857*	Rickerby House, Carlisle, was the residence in 1846 of George Head, banker, one of the original Directors of the Lancaster & Carlisle Railway, who left it in his Will in 1876 to Miles MacInnes. The house was retained by the MacInnes family until 1914.
Robert Benson	*1875,1896*	He was a Director of the Company from 1844 until his death early in 1875, having previously been a Director of the London & Birmingham Railway. He became Deputy Chairman in 1853, retiring from office in 1858.
Robert Burns	*1913*	1759-1796. The Scottish poet.
Robert L. Stevenson	*1913*	1850-1894. Robert Louis (baptised Lewis) Balfour Stevenson, the author.
Robert Southey	*1913*	1774-1843. The Poet Laureate from 1813.
Roberts	*1859* *1864* *1894*	Richard was the inventor in 1825 of the self-acting mule in cotton-spinning machinery, and partner in the firm Sharp, Roberts & Co. which branched into locomotive building beginning with the 'Experiment' of 1833, which he designed. He later worked with Thomas Telford and Henry Maudslay. For most people by this time the name would signify Earl Roberts of Kandahar (1832-1914) who was Field Marshal and Commander-in-Chief South Africa during the Boer War.
Robin Hood	*1899*	The 1320 Pipe Roll for Yorkshire lists a 'Robertus Hood fugitivus' from which might come the traditional outlaw and hero of English ballads, but there are several other possibilities as to who he actually was. He figures as Locksley in Sir Walter Scott's 'Ivanhoe', and a host of legendary tales have been woven around him. This is one more of the Jubilee class locomotives named after such folk.
Rob Roy	*1899*	A Waverley novel by Sir Walter Scott of 1818. The nickname of the noted Scots outlaw 'Robert the Red' who lived from 1671 to 1754. He is the Scots equivalent of Robin Hood, and is yet another of the Jubilee class series named after such people.
Rocket	*L&M1829* *1852,1878,1897*	Robert Stephenson & Co.'s locomotive, winner of the Rainhill trials, for which it had been built. He chose the name himself, an imaginative one for a locomotive, in that a rocket is a projectile propelled by the regulated expansion of a gas, and developed latterly by Sir William Congreave for use in the Napoleonic War. (As opposed to Arrow or Dart which are projected by an instantaneous applied force). An article in the March 1825 'Quarterly Review' on the subject of Railways gave him the idea for this name.
Roderic (or Roderick)	*L&M1838* *1847*	The chief character in Sir Walter Scott's poem "The Vision of Don Roderick", published in 1811. Don Roderick was traditionally the last Gothic King of Spain. The name sometimes appears as "Roderick", as for example in Samuel Scott's list of the L&M locomotive stock in 1840, but even he is inconsistent about the 'k'.
Roebuck	*1847*	The male of the roe, a small species of deer.

	1911	This is another of the locomotives named after vessels of exploration or discovery. The 'Roebuck' was William Dampier's ship on his exploration of New Holland (Australia) in 1699. She foundered off Ascension Island in February 1701, and the wreck and her bronze ship's bell were discovered in February 2001, almost 300 years later to the day. There was also a Destroyer of 1901-1919 with this name.
Rokeby	*L&M1838*	Sir Walter Scott's poem "Rokeby" appeared in 1813. It is dedicated to John B.S.Morritt Esq., and the scene is laid in his demesne at Rokeby, a village in the North Riding, fourteen miles west of Darlington.
Rose	*1848,1857*	The flower. (See *Lily* and *Violet*)
Rowland Hill	*1854,1872* *1886,1905*	1795-1879. He was first an educationalist reckoned to be on a par with Arnold of Rugby. As an administrative reformer he was the originator of the penny post and of adhesive postage stamps, Secretary to the Postmaster-General 1846, Secretary to the Post Office 1854-1864, FRS 1857 and received a knighthood in 1860.
Royal George	*1899*	Her Majesty's Yacht. Built 1817, Harbour Service 1843, and broken up in 1905. The name dates back to 1714 when it was carried by a warship in honour of King George I, and successive warships of the same name honoured the next three of the 'Four Georges'.
Royal Oak	*1902*	The Battleship of 1892-1914, named after the tree near Boscobel north-west of Wolverhampton in which King Charles II hid after his escape from the field of battle at Worcester in 1651.
Royal Sovereign	*1900*	The Battleship of 1891-1913. This name had appeared on successive warships since 1509, and the vessel of 1637-1696 had formerly been the celebrated 'Sovereign of the Seas'.
Ruby	*1848*	The precious stone.
Rupert Guinness	*1914*	The Hon.Rupert Edward Guinness CMG was a Director of the Company in 1904.
Russell	*1847* *1860*	1792-1878. John, 1st.Earl 1861 was Prime Minister of the United Kingdom of Great Britain and Ireland 1846-1852 and 1865-1866.
St.Arnaud	*12.1854* *1858*	1798-1854. Marechal Arnaud Jacques Le Roy de Sainte-Arnaud organised the Coup d'Etat in December 1851 which made Napoleon Emperor, was appointed Minister for War by Napoleon III on 11th March 1854, and was Commander-in-Chief of the French Forces in the Crimea. He resigned on 26th September and died on board a ship crossing the Black Sea. He was buried at Les Invalides on 16th October 1854.
St.David	*B&L1841* *1848,1872*	The Patron Saint of Wales.
St.George	*1848* *1874,1893* *1913*	The Patron Saint of England. The Cruiser of 1892-1920. HMS St.George is listed as "A Discovery Ship", of 1701-1716, and may possibly be another of the George the Fifth class series commemorating such vessels. What discoveries she may have made have not come to light.
St.Germans	*1854*	1798-1877. Lord Edward Granville Eliot, 3rd Earl of St.Germans was Chief Secretary of State for Ireland in 1841 and was appointed Postmaster-General by Peel in 1846. Another example of the Company's fondness for PMG names. The name has at times appeared in print erroneously as "St.Germain".
St.Patrick	*1848,1874,1893*	The Patron Saint of Ireland.
Saddleback	*1846* *L&C1857,1879.1893.1913*	A mountain in the Lake District, north-east of Keswick.
Saddleworth	*H&M1847*	The town in the West Riding of Yorkshire twelve miles south-west of Huddersfield.
Safety	*SS1858*	Freedom from danger, hurt, injury or loss. It was also the London to Cambridge stagecoach.
Salamander	*B&L1831*	A tailed amphibian, fabled at one time to be able to live in fire.
Salopian	*1849,1875,1896*	A man of Shropshire, and also the name of the London to Shrewsbury stagecoach.

Samson	L&M1831/9	The son of Manoah of the tribe of Dan, an Israelite Judge, a man of great strength.
1848,1859,1863,1892,1916		

Sandon   1846,1872   The village about five miles north of Stafford in which lay the home of Viscount Sandon, the 1st Earl of Harrowby.

Sankey   *St.Helens ?date*   The Sankey Brook, whose valley is crossed by the celebrated viaduct on the Liverpool & Manchester Railway. Many of the Company's engines were named after rivers, so why not commemorate the local stream. It is also the name of the canal which extends from St.Helens to Warrington and Widnes.

Sanspareil   *B&L1829*   'Sans Pareil' is French for 'Without Equal'.
1866,1893,1907   The name chosen by Timothy Hackworth for the locomotive he built and sent to compete in the Rainhill Trials. Hackworth's choice was not original, for the Sans Pareil was also a warship, a 3rd Rate prize taken on the Glorious First of June 1794, and not broken up until 1842; it was also a stagecoach name.

Saracen   *GJ1837*   A nomadic Arab; later, a Moslem opponent of the Crusaders.
GJ1842,1852   In Arthurian legend, the term was used for any unbaptised person of whatever race.
St.Helens 1858,1861,1909

Sarmatian   1884   The Allan Line ship of 3,611 gross tons, built in Greenock in 1871 for the Liverpool - Montreal trade.
1905   Pertaining to Sarmatia, an ancient territory extending from the Vistula to the Volga. The Sarmatians were Iranian nomads, military horsemen, especially active between 179BC and AD200.

Saturn   *L&M1831*   One of the planets, named after the mythological Roman deity who devoured all his children except Jupiter.
1852,1861,1905

Scorpion   *GJ1837*   An arachnid with lobster-like claws and a six-jointed tail ending with a sting
1852 St.Helens 1852,1861,1905

Scotia   1869,1870   The Cunard Liner RMS Scotia of 1861 of 3,871 gross tons was described as 'the finest and last of the ocean going
1892,1922   paddle steamers'. Scotia is the sixth century name for that part of western Scotland south of Fort William.

Scott   1866,1890,1916   1771-1832. Sir Walter, author and poet, who was created baronet in 1820.

Scottish Chief   1894,1906   The Head of a clan, or 'Chieftain'.

Sedbergh   *L&C1859*   The railway line from Lowgill to Ingleton was under construction when this engine was named. At this time the town was in the West Riding of Yorkshire. 'Flat topped hill'.

Sedgwick   *L&C1857*   A village between Carnforth and Kendal adjacent to the Lancaster & Carlisle Railway. Sedgwick House was the
1870,1888   residence of John Wakefield, one of the original Directors of that Railway.

Sefton   1852   The Earldom was created in 1791 when Baron Croxteth became the 1st Earl, and by 1852 the 3rd Earl of Sefton
1857,1860,1873   was resident at the family seat at Croxteth Hall. He was succeeded by his son William Philip Molyneux who became the 4th Earl in 1855.
The locomotives of 1852 and 1857 presumably relate to the 3rd and 4th Earls respectively.

Senator   1847,1874,1904   A member of a Senate; a counsellor.

Serpent   1855,1874   A reptile with an elongated scaly body, which moves by means of its ribs and scales.

Servia   1884,1905   The Cunard liner of 1881-1901 of 7,392 gross tons, built by J.and G.Thomson.

Severn   *St.Helens 1859*   The river, 180 miles long which rises near Llanidloes, flows east to Shrewsbury, and then south through Worcester to the Severn Estuary.

Shah of Persia   1873,1893   The Shah, an Oriental potentate, visited Crewe Works on 28th June 1873. (See *Nasr Ed Din*)

Shakespeare   1866   1564-1616. William, poet and dramatist.
1890,1911

Shamrock	*1868,1891,1907*	The plant, the lesser trefoil; The emblem of Ireland.

Shannon
Sandy & Potton 1857   The locomotive was named on 17th June 1857 after HMS Shannon, an iron steam frigate of 1855-1871, then under the command of Captain William Peel VC, Royal Navy, the owner of the Sandy & Potton Railway. Captain Peel had won the Victoria Cross on 25th October 1854 with the Guards, defending Balaklava against the Russian attempt to capture it. He was related to Sir Robert Peel, the politician.

St.Helens1859   The River in Ireland.

Shap   *ExL&C1846*   The village south of Penrith, near the summit of the line between Carnforth and Carlisle.
L&C1857,1859,1864,1893

Shark   *GJ1837*   A voracious salt-water fish.
1845,1854,1874,1894

1916   The Destroyer of 1912 - 31.5.1916, lost at Jutland after heroic action.

Shooting Star   *1883,1905*   A picturesque name for a meteor.

Shropshire   *1909*   An English County served by the Company.

Simoom   *1854*   HMS Simoom, the Frigate of 1849-1887 used as a troopship on active service in the Baltic in 1854 during the Crimean War, and named after the hot dry wind which blows at intervals across Asiatic and African deserts during spring and summer.
1904

Simoon   *1874*   An alternative spelling of 'Simoom', (O.E.D.).

Sir Alexander Cockburn   Sir Alexander James Edmund Cockburn, 10th Baronet was Lord Chief Justice of England from 1874-1880.
1880,1896

Sir Arthur Lawley   *1916*   The Hon. Sir Arthur C.Lawley, GCSI, GCIE, KCMG, Governor of Western Australia 1901-1902, Lieutenant Governor of the Transvaal 1902-1906, Governor of Madras from 1905- 1911and appointed a Director of the Company in 1912. In 1931 he became the 6th Baron Wenlock, and died aged 72 the following year.

Sir Charles   *L&CH1863*   Sir Charles Henry Rouse-Boughton, the 11th baronet, was Chairman of the Trustees of the Ludlow & Clee Hill Railway. He was also Chairman of the Shrewsbury and Hereford and Central Wales Railways until their amalgamation with the London & North Western and Great Western Railways. He died aged 81 in 1906.

Sir Charles Cust   *1921*   1860-1932. Equerry to the Duke of York, later King George V from 1892, the 3rd Baronet, who frequently liaised with the Company's officers concerning the working of Royal Trains. Experience indicated that it might be helpful to have a locomotive named after him, and he is said to have been delighted.

Sir Francis Dent   *1916*   He joined the L&NWR in 1884 at the age of eighteen, and became District Traffic Manager in 1901, London & District Goods Traffic Manager from 1902-1907, when he moved to the South Eastern & Chatham Railway to be their General Manager from 1911-1920. He was a son of Admiral C.B.C.Dent, sometime Marine Superintendent of the L&NWR. He died in 1955.

Sir Frank Ree   *1913*   L&NWR Goods Manager in 1893 and was General Manager of the Company from 1909, until his death in 1914. He received a knighthood on 21st April 1913 at Crewe on the occasion of the Royal Visit to the Works.

Sir Frederick Harrison *1913*   He entered L&NWR employment in 1864 at the age of twenty, was trained by Mr.George Findlay, and joined Mr.G.P.Neele in 1875 as Assistant Superintendent of the Line. He next became Chief Goods Manager in 1885, General Manager 1893-1908, and a Director of the Company in 1909. He was also Deputy Chairman of the South Eastern & Chatham Railway. He died in 1914.

Sir Gilbert Claughton *1913*   Gilbert Henry Claughton was born in 1856, was apprenticed with Beyer Peacock, then became Chief Mineral Agent for his uncle the Earl of Dudley. He joined the L&NWR Directors in 1905, became a Deputy-Chairman in 1910 and was elected Chairman in 1911 and held that office until shortly before his death on 27th June 1921. He was created 1st Baronet in June 1912.

Sir Guy Calthrop
March 1919   Calthrop Guy Spencer Calthrop, born 1870, was the General Manager of the Company from October 1914 until the time of his death in 1919. From 1917 he was also Controller of Coal Mines, and in 1919 received a baronetcy.

Sir Hardman Earle   *1877*   1792-1877. Although at first a strong opponent of railways, he became a Director of the Grand Junction Railway

	1895	and a member of the L&NWR Amalgamated Board of 1845, a Director of the Company, Chairman of the Locomotive Committee in Liverpool, created 1st.Baronet in 1869 and was still an active member of the Board right up to the time of his death. At which time he was the oldest railway director in the country.
Sir Herbert Walker	*1916*	Herbert Ashcombe Walker was born in 1868 and had spent the early part of his career from 1885-1912 with the L&NWR, becoming Assistant to the General Manager in 1911. He became General Manager of the London & South Western Railway Company in 1912, Chairman of the wartime Railway Executive Committee, then Chairman of the Southern Railway until 1937. He died in 1949.
Sir Herbert Walker K.C.B. *April 1917*		The nameplate was altered when he became a Knight Commander of the British Empire.
Sir John French	*1915*	1852-1925. Field Marshal, 1st Earl of Ypres and Commander of the British Army on the Western Front in the Great War until December 1915, when he was replaced by Haig.
Sir Robert Turnbull	*1913*	He entered L&NWR service in 1868 at the age of sixteen. In 1875 he joined Mr.G.P.Neele's staff, succeeding him as Superintendent of the Line from 1895-1914, and General Manager from February to October 1914, when he retired, becoming a Company Director from 1915-1922. He received a knighthood on 21st April 1913 at Crewe, on the occasion of the Royal visit to the Works. He was also Director of the London Brighton & South Coast Railway from 1915-1922, and of the Southern Railway until his death in 1925.
Sir Salar Jung	*1877* *1897*	Nawab Sir Salar Jung was Chief Minister of Hyderabad, and had supported the British side during the Indian Mutiny, and been made GCSI in 1870. He visited Crewe Works in 1876 as the guest of the Duke of Sutherland, and again two years later. He died in 1883.
Sir Thomas Brooke	*1910*	He was a Yorkshire Director of the Company, who took his seat on the Board in February 1882, was chairman of several committees and a member of the Joint Committee of the L&NWR/L&Y Joint lines. He was made Baronet in 1899, and died aged 78 in 1908.
Sir Thomas Williams *December 1919*		Thomas Williams was Acting General Manager of the Company from 1917-1919, and General Manager from 1919-1920. He became a Director of the LMS until 1939, and died aged 88 in 1941. (See *I.T.Williams*)
Sir W.S.Gilbert	*1914*	1836-1911. William Schwenck Gilbert, the playwright, and librettist.
Siren	*1848,1873,1893*	A mythical monster, half woman and half bird, the sweetness of whose singing enticed sailors to their doom.
Sirius	*GJ1838* *1855, WJ1857* *1873,1895*	The Dog Star, the brightest in the sky. The 'Sirius' was a small Irish coastal steamer of 703 tons built in 1837 and chartered by Junicus Smith to compete with Brunel's 'Great Western'. She set out from Cork on 5th April 1838 for New York and arrived first, by four hours.
Sirocco *GJ1842,1854,1874,1904*	*GJ1837*	The hot south wind from the Sahara. The Italian name for Simoom.
Sister Dora	*1894*	Miss Dorothy Wyndlow Pattison was a nurse whose personality and career were outstanding. She was put in charge of a new hospital built in Walsall in 1868, and in 1875 single -handedly and with great heroism ran an Epidemic hospital there during a smallpox epidemic. She died of cancer at the age of 46 on Christmas Eve 1878, and her obituary in the *Daily Telegraph* said: "What Florence Nightingale did for Military hospitals, Dorothy Pattison accomplished in civil duty." Her statue was set up in the middle of Walsall.
Sisyphus	*1868,1891,1909*	The King of Corinth who was condemned for ever to the unending rolling of a stone to a hill-top.
Skiddaw *L&C1857 ,1874,1893*	*ExGJ1850*	A mountain in Cumberland, altitude 3,053 ft. north of Keswick in the Lake District.
Smeaton	*1866,1888,1916*	1724-1792. John, the engineer and instrument maker.
Snake *1855,1858,1884,1905*		A long reptile without developed limbs.
Snipe	*1854,1911*	A bird having a long straight bill and by repute the fastest flying game bird.

Snowdon	*1848, 1875*	The highest mountain in Wales, in Carnarvonshire, altitude 3560ft. south of Llanberis.
Soho	*B&L1834*	The Bolton & Leigh engine was built by Benjamin Hick and Son at their Soho Ironworks, Bolton.
	1861	A district near Smethwick where the foundry of Boulton & Watt was situated.
Solway	*1855*	The Firth. 'Ford of the pole (firth)'.
Soult	*1862*	1769-1851. Nicholas-Jean de Dieu, Duc de Dalmatie, the French military leader who opposed Wellington.
South Africa	*1911*	One of the self-governing Dominions, a name which celebrated coronation year 1911.
Speedwell	*L&M1835*	An apt choice of name, following that of its immediate predecessor *Rapid*. Rail travel must truly have seemed very speedy and successful.
Speke	*1868, 1891*	1827-1864. John Hanning Speke, the British explorer and the first European to reach and name Lake Victoria on 30th July 1858.
		A District of Liverpool. There is a Speke Hall, also Speke Junction.
Sphinx	*GJ1841*	An ancient monster, in Greek mythology having the head of a woman, the body of a lion, and wings, and in
	1851, 1874, 1893, 1916	Egyptian, a lion with the head and breast of a man and wingless.
Spitfire	*ExL&C1846*	An irascible person, whose angry words are like fire spat from the mouth of a fire-eater.
	1857, 1860, 1864, 1893	
S.R.Graves	*1873*	Samuel Robert Graves was a Liverpool shipowner, Mayor of Liverpool in 1860, who became a Director of the Company in 1864, and was MP for Liverpool 1865 until his death which took place suddenly at the Euston Hotel in January 1873, aged 54.
Stafford	*SS1849*	The County town of Staffordshire. See also *Marchioness of Stafford*.
Staffordshire	*1888, 1913*	An English County served by the Company.
	1909	
Stag	*SS1853*	The male red deer.
		It was also the name of the Shrewsbury stagecoach.
Staghound	*1911*	A large and powerful dog formerly kept for stag hunting. It is an alternative name for a deerhound.
Standedge	*H&M1847*	The location of the canal and rail tunnels through the Pennines on the Huddersfield & Manchester Railway & Canal.
Stanley	*1850*	1789-1869. Edward George Geoffrey Smith Stanley, the son of the 13th Earl of Derby who used the courtesy title Lord Stanley until his father's death in June 1851. Prime Minister of Great Britain and Ireland February to December 1852, February 1858 to June 1859 and July 1866 until February 1868. (See *Derby*)
Star	*L&M1836*	A celestial body, especially self-luminous and apparently fixed in space.
	St.Helens 1852, 1847, 1860	
Starling	*L&M1845*	A passerine bird.
	1854, 1857	
Stentor	*GJ1837, 1854, 1922*	The Greek 'herald' in the Trojan war who had a voice as loud as fifty men.
Stephenson	*1851*	i) 1781-1848. George, engineer and pioneer of steam traction. He died on 12th August 1848. and lies buried at Holy Trinity Church, Chesterfield.
	1862, 1906	ii) 1803-1859. Robert, the son of George, mechanical and civil engineer. FRS 1849. He was Chief Engineer of the London & Birmingham Railway.
Stewart	*L&C1859*	Charles Edward. Joint Secretary (London) of the Company from 1847-1859 and Company Secretary from then
	1861, 1877, 1897	until his resignation in 1866.
Stork	*L&M1842*	The large wading bird.
	1852, 1872, 1886, 1905	

Fig. 83 George Stephenson.

L&NWR Postcard Set 1. (Fred Gray Collection).

Sultan	*GJ1839,1848,1872*	A Mohameddan sovereign.
	1900	The Battleship of 1870, purchased in 1878, in 1906 transferred to Harbour Service, and not broken up until 1946.
Sun	*L&M1831/7*	The heavenly body at the heart of the solar system around which the planets revolve in elliptic orbits.
	St.Helens c1859	
Sunbeam	*GJ1838*	A ray of sunlight.
	1857,1884,1905	
Superb	*1900*	The Battleship purchased in 1878 and in service until 1906. An earlier ship had been in Nelson's fleet, and is celebrated in Newbolt's poem. "The old Superb was barnacled, and green as grass below".
Sutherland	*1851,1859*	The 2nd Duke of Sutherland was a Director of the Liverpool & Manchester Railway. He died in 1861.
	1864	The 3rd Duke of Sutherland, 1828-1892, was a Director of the L&NWR 1852-1892, and the promoter of many railways in the Scottish Highlands. He served a full apprenticeship under McConnell at Wolverton.
	1893	The 4th Duke of Sutherland. The name was removed in 1913 when the Claughton class locomotive was named *Duke of Sutherland*.
Suvla Bay	*1916*	A bay of the Gallipoli Peninsula at which one of the surprise attacks was effected during the ill-fated attempt in the Great War to occupy the Dardanelles. The name was given to commemorate the evacuation carried out without serious loss in December 1915.
Swallow	*L&M1841,1849*	Any of the numerous species of passerine migratory birds except the Martin.
Swan	*L&M1842*	A large long necked aquatic bird.
St.Helens1848/9,1853,St.Helens 1856?,1872		
Swift	*1851,1872*	John Swift, of the firm of Carter, Swift & Wagstaffe, solicitors to the L&NWR, from L&M days until October 1861, when he was succeeded by James Blenkinsop. In the summer of 1840 he arranged the purchase of the land on which Crewe Works was built. The name of the firm of solicitors acting for the Liverpool & Manchester Railway after December 1831 was "Clay and Swift".

Swiftsure	*L&M1834* *1888*	An Elizabethan compound name said to signify 'Swift pursuer', one frequently applied to ships of the Royal Navy, the first in 1621. The name was surely chosen to advertise the ability of the engine to haul its load swiftly and safely to its destination. Subsequent names in the Liverpool & Manchester list are the Tayleur pair of 1835, *Rapid* and *Speedwell*.
	1905	A Battleship of 1904-1920 which saw service in the Dardanelles in 1915.
Sybil	*GJ1838* *1849,1860 ,1874,1894*	A woman endowed with the ability to foretell the future. A Roman Prophetess.
Sydney Smith	*1913*	1771-1845. The writer and divine.
Sylph	*SS1863*	An elemental spirit of air, so named in the Middle Ages.
Syren	*GJ1839*	One of the mythical monsters half woman and half bird said by the Greek poets to entice seamen to their death. The replacement locomotive of June 1848 was named *Siren*. See above.
Talavera	*1868* *1890*	In commemoration of the battle fought during the Peninsular War on 27th July 1809 at a village south-west of Madrid, which despite heavy losses was deemed to be a victory.
Talbot	*1848*	1777-1849. Sir Charles Chetwynd Talbot, the 2nd Earl Talbot, was Lord Lieutenant of Staffordshire from 1812 until the time of his death at Ingestre Hall.
Talisman	*GJ1838/41,1849* *Ex B'head 1860* *1865,1890,1923*	A charm, or magical figure or form of words; from the Greek 'Telisma' meaning 'Mystery'. Sir Walter Scott's novel "The Talisman" was published in 1825.
Tamerlane	*GJ1838,1843* *1854,1872* *1886,1904*	1336-1405. The Tartar conqueror, immortalised in Elizabethan drama. This was also the name of the first locomotive to be completed at Crewe Works, on 20th October 1843. A verse composed in 1887 by David Atkinson, a fitter in the wheel shop at Crewe runs:- "And on the twentieth day October 'forty three TAMERLANE cleared the way First of three thousand."
Tantalus	*GJ1840* *1850,1860,1905*	The son of Zeus and Pluto who was condemned to be tantalised for ever for having revealed the secrets of the gods.
Tara	*1916*	To commemorate the loss on 5th November 1915 of H.M.S.Tara, formerly the Company's T.S.S.Hibernia, of 1,594 gross tons, built in 1900, taken over by the Admiralty in 1914 and which as an armed boarding ship was torpedoed and sunk by U-35 while making for Sollum. The ninety five survivors became Turkish prisoners of war. Tara was the Seat of the Irish Kings from ancient times, in County Meath.
Tartarus	*GJ1838* *1859,1864,1893*	The mythical deep and sunless abyss, the infernal regions, placed according to Homer far below Hades.
Tebay	*L&C1859*	A village in Westmorland, important as the depot for the Shap banking engines.
Telford	*1866,1890,1922*	1757-1834. Thomas Telford was a notable civil engineer and builder of roads, canals and bridges.
Temeraire	*1900*	The Ironclad 1878-1904 when she was renamed 'Indus II' for use as a Training Ship. The French for 'Daring'. An earlier ship of this name was the subject of a poem by Newbolt and a painting by Turner, "The Fighting Temeraire".
Tennyson	*1869* *1885,1891,1922*	1809-1892. Alfred, Lord Tennyson, Poet Laureate in 1850, and created Baron in 1884.
Terrier	*1855* *1858,1863,1890,1909*	A group of several breeds of dog, e.g."Yorkshire" "Airedale". A register in which lands of private persons or corporations are described.
Teutonic	*1889* *1905*	The White Star liner 1889-1914 of 9,950 gross tons, designed for rapid conversion to cruiser in an emergency, and converted in 1914. Bought by the Royal Navy in August 1915. She became a Troopship in 1919 and was broken up in 1922. Teutonic means 'Of the Germans.' The engine was renamed 'The Tsar' in November 1914.

Thalaba	*GJ1838, GJ1841, 1850, 1860, 1865, 1890, 1923*	The hero in Robert Southey's poem 'Thalaba the Destroyer'.
The Auditor	*1878, 1894*	Henry Crosfield, the Company Auditor.
The Duke of Edinburgh	*1866, 1888*	Prince Alfred, 1844-1900. The second son of Queen Victoria, who visited Crewe Works in the summer of 1866.
The Earl of Chester	*1866 1893*	A title of the Prince of Wales.
The Nile	*1868, 1891, 1916*	To commemorate the battle which took place in Aboukir Bay off Egypt on 1st August 1798.
Theodore	*1855*	There are plenty of possible choices. The most probable is Theodore of Magdala, who had at the time the engine was named enjoyed friendly relations with Great Britain, and had been in power as Emperor of Ethiopia since that year. (See *Magdala*)
Theorem	*1847 1860, 1864, 1893*	A proposition to be proved by a chain of reasoning.
The Queen	*1847 1872, 1892*	Her Majesty Queen Victoria.
Theseus	*1849, 1872*	The chief hero of Attica in Greek legend, one of whose mighty deeds was to have slain the Minotaur.
The Tsar *or*	*1914*	A name removed when the Prince of Wales class locomotive was named *Czar of Russia* in 1915.
The Tzar	*1914*	There has been debate over whether the name was "Tsar", or "Tzar", but no photograph has come to light to determine the issue. The name was only carried for just over a year.
T.H.Ismay	*1900*	1837-23.11.1899. Thomas Henry Ismay was the founder, with others, of the famous White Star Line. He is described by G.P.Neele as being "one of our own Board of Directors" on the occasion of the trial trip of the "Teutonic" in July 1889. The engine was named in his memory
Thomas B. Macaulay	*1913*	1800-1859. Thomas Babington Macaulay, historian and poet, who was created a Baron in 1857.
Thomas Campbell	*1913*	1777-1844. The poet.
Thomas Carlyle	*1882, 1894*	1795-1881. The essayist.
Thomas Gray	*1914*	1716-1771. The poet.
Thomas Houghton	*1910*	He began his career as a junior clerk with the Manchester & Birmingham Railway, and came to Euston on its absorption with the L&NWR, rising to become the L&NWR Assistant Goods Manager in 1874, and Company Secretary from 1890 to 1902.
Thomas Moore	*1913*	1779-1852. The poet.
Thomas Savery	*1898, 1909*	c.1650-1715. The English engineer and inventor, who built the first steam engine, and later joined Thomas Newcomen in his work.
Thunderbolt	*1848 1874, 1904*	From Jupiter's armoury. According to the myth he held a sceptre in his left hand and thunderbolts in his right. A supposed dart, formerly believed to be the destructive force of a lightning-flash on striking any object.
Thunderer	*L&M1836 1885, 1905*	One who, or that which thunders. A suitable name for a steam locomotive. Possibly named after the Turret Ship of 1872-1909, or maybe as an allusion to "The Times" newspaper.
Tiger	*L&M1838 1850, 1860, 1905*	The large Asiatic feline carnivore.
Tiny	*1862*	Small in size and scale.
Tipton	*SS1858*	A village in Staffordshire served by the South Staffordshire Railway.

Name	Reference	Description

Titan *L&M1834,1884,1904* One of the twelve primordial beings of enormous strength and size, of which six were male and six female.

Titania *W&FJ1851* The wife of Oberon, Queen of the Fairies. Folk-lore.

T.J.Hare *1910* Theodore Julius Hare was born in 1839, appointed a Director of the Company in 1885, and was Chairman of the Railway Clearing House for a few weeks until his sudden death in 1907.

Tomlinson *B.L.Sidings1884* Sir William E.H.Tomlinson was the owner of the Brockley Lane Sidings, Preston.

Topsy *1867* The name of the small black character in 'Uncle Tom's Cabin'. (1852 - the best selling book of the 19th Century) A term of affection, and highly suitable for a small black Works locomotive.

Torch *GJ1838,1849,1872* A light carried in the hand.

Tornado *1862,1906* A violent storm with constantly changing wind direction.

Touchstone *C&B1840* A black flinty slate used by means of a touch-needle to ascertain the purity of gold or silver. Hence meaning any test or criterion. It is possible this name refers to the clown in Shakespeare's "As You Like It".

Trafalgar *1848 1860,1864 1900* To commemorate the defeat of the French Navy by the Fleet under the command of Admiral Nelson on 21st October 1805 off Cape Trafalgar in Spain, west of Gibraltar.
The Battleship of 1887-1911.

Traveller *1911* One who travels.
There is a possibility that this is another of the George the Fifth class named after vessels of discovery. There was a wooden screw gunboat of 1856, sold in 1864. Her early sale may suggest there was an interested buyer. The absence of the name of the buyer could indicate further use, since shipbreakers are usually recorded, with the date on which the ship was broken up.
It was also the name of one of the first class carriages on the Liverpool & Manchester Railway.

Trent *St.Helens 1860* The second longest river completely in England, about 170 miles long. This engine went from the Manchester & Birmingham Railway in April 1860, to become St.Helens No 2, and was named *Trent* in keeping with their custom of using the names of rivers. It came to the L&NWR on 1st July 1864 as their No 1364, and was sold almost at once, leaving the name available for re-use, but, as it transpired, with a new origin.
August 1864 1890,1916 The "Trent Incident" began during the American Civil War, when on November 8th 1861 two Confederate Commissioners were seized by the U.S.Navy from the neutral British ship 'Trent' on the high seas. Popular opinion demanded that war be declared, but the British Government demanded an apology, which was made by the U.S.Secretary of State on December 26th, and the two Commissioners were released shortly afterwards.
The L&NWR played a significant part in relation to this incident, being responsible for conveying dispatches from the British Ambassador in Washington between Holyhead and Euston on January 9th 1862 in five hours at the highest possible speed.

Trentham *1846 1872,1883,1905* Trentham Hall near Stoke-on-Trent was one of the seats of the Leveson-Gower family. George Granville Sutherland Leveson-Gower became 2nd Duke of Sutherland in 1833, and the title taken by his son was Marquess of Stafford.

Trevithick *1859 1864* This name refers to Francis Trevithick who was born on 12th June 1812 and died on 27th October 1877 at Penzance, having retired from being 'Foreman of Locomotives' at Crewe twenty years previously. His father was already remembered by *Cornwall*. (See *Richard Trevithick*).

Triplex *1895* The name given by Webb to the 2-2-2 simple No.54 *Medusa*, which had been converted to an experimental two cylinder Compound in 1878, and again rebuilt as a Triple-expansion Compound in August of that year.

Tubal *1853 1860,1864,1890,1906* The first Engineer. The grandson of Noah and son of Zillah, who 'made tools out of bronze and iron'. Genesis chapter 4, verse 22.

Tubal Cain *WJ1854* The same person as Tubal.

Turk *9.1854 1860,1864,1892* The Turks were allies of the United Kingdom and France in the Crimean War.

Twin Sisters	B&L?1828	So named because the 1828 Bolton & Leigh locomotive had two boilers. (Note that S.S.Scott's typescript has *Twin Brothers* in error.)
Tyne	St.Helens	The river in Northumberland.
Typhon	GJ1841 1853,1873,1890,1913	The son of Tartarus and father of Cerberus, the hundred-headed and flame-breathing monster and the father of all winds.
Ulleswater	L&C1857/9	Ullswater Lake forms part of the Cumberland-Westmorland boundary. The name is found spelt 'Ulleswater' in various documents in the 19th Century.
Umpire	1855,1872	One to whom sole decisions on questions or controversies are entrusted. The name of the London - Liverpool stagecoach.
Una	1852,1872	The personification of Truth in Spenser's "Faerie Queene".
Underley	L&C1859	Underley Grange lies on the east bank of the River Lune. Underley Hall lies on the west bank of the River Lune north of Kirby Lonsdale. The Hall was the residence from 1840 of William Thompson, Lord Mayor of London 1828/29 and MP for Westmorland, a former Penydarren ironmaster.
Unicorn	1849 1860,1874,1896	The mythological beast having one horn. The British and North America Royal Mail Steam Packet Company's vessel of 700 tons hired by Cunard to make the first mail run from Liverpool to the United States in May 1840.
Union	B&L1836	The Bolton & Leigh engine was the first built by Rothwell, Hick & Rothwell at their Union Foundry, Bolton, established about 1801 and so possibly indirectly named after the union with Ireland. Alternatively it might have been named to celebrate a junction, and if so, probably the Leigh and Kenyon Junction.
Utilis	B&L1832	The Latin for 'Useful'.
Vampire	GJ1838 1848,1874,1896	A fabulous being, usually in the form of a bloodsucking bat.
Vandal	GJ1839 1848,1872,1885,1904	A member of a Teutonic race from the Baltic who despoiled Rome and ravaged Gaul in the 5th Century. Hence a wilful ignorant destroyer of anything worthy of preservation.
Vanguard	1911	The Battleship built in 1909 and sunk by explosion in Scapa Flow on 9th July 1917.
Varna	9.1854	A port on the Black Sea. In the Crimean War this was Marshal St.Arnaud's Headquarters and the advance base for the attack on Sebastopol. The British contingent finally left Varna on 7th September despite no decision having yet been taken about where the expedition was to land!
Vauxhall	SS1858	A suburb in the north-east of Birmingham served by the South Staffordshire Railway.
Velocipede	1847,1883,1906	An early form of bicycle without pedals; A dandy horse.
Venus	L&M1831	The second planet from the sun, named after the goddess of sexual love and beauty.
Vernon	1850	Vernon was a prominent Liverpool surname, and a street name. Thomas Vernon & Co. was a firm of shipbuilders and locomotive manufacturers active in Liverpool at this time. They also supplied the boilers for the two new engines working the rope haulage system at Edge Hill in 1834, and were the builders of *Prince George* which ran trials over the L&M in the summer of 1838. The firm also built the ship Hibernia for the Chester & Holyhead Railway in 1847-8. A John Vernon was a partner in the firm of Bury, Curtis & Kennedy.
Vesta	L&M1831/37,1855	The virgin goddess of the hearth.
Vesuvius	L&M1836 1888,1905	The volcano in Italy near Naples.
Veteran	B&L1831	One who has grown old in any service or art.

Viceroy	*1853*	The governor of a kingdom or country ruling as his sovereign's representative.
Victor	*1883,1905*	One who conquers, or wins a contest.
Victor Hugo	*1913*	1802-1885. Victor Marie Hugo, the French poet, dramatist and novelist.
Victoria	*B&L1837*	Her Majesty Queen Victoria, born on 24th May 1819, who acceded to the Throne on 20th June 1837.
	L&M1839	Only Whishaw lists an L&M locomotive of this name, and his entry must be regarded with caution.
L&PJ1840,C&B1845,1862,1907		
Victoria and Albert	*1901*	The Royal Yacht of 1897-1954, named after the Queen and her late Consort.
Victorious	*1901*	The Battleship of 1895-1916.
Victory	*L&M1831*	Nelson's Flagship. The name was first used on the Liverpool & Manchester Railway's No.22, then on the Bolton
	B&L1842	& Leigh engine of 1842, and later on an L&NWR 'DX' in 1860.
	1860	It was also the name of one of the first class carriages on the Liverpool & Manchester Railway.
Vimiera	*1868,1891*	To commemorate the battle in which the English defeated the French in Portugal on 21st August 1808.
Vindictive	*1923*	The Cruiser built in 1897, which took part in the attack on Zeebrugge on 23rd April 1918, sunk as a blockship at Ostend on 9th/10th May, raised in August 1920, and broken up.
Violet	*1848*	The flower. The short firebox locomotive of 1848 was one of three named *Lily, Rose* and *Violet*.
Ex B'head 1860,1861,1863		There was a ship of this name in the Dublin Steam Packet Line, serving Holyhead from 1836-1852.
	1893	There was a L&NWR vessel of this name 1880-1902.
Viper	*SS1852*	A venonous snake.
Virago	*1855*	Literally a man-like woman. A term used to describe a scolding shrew.
Viscount	*1847,1874,1905*	A title next in rank above a baron and below an earl.
Vizier	*GJ1837/42*	The chief minister or councillor of state in a Moslem community.
1854,1874,1905		
Volante	*BL&CJ1856*	Lord Clement's racehorse, winner of The Oaks in 1792. 'Volant' means 'Flying, passing through the air'.
Voltigeur	*BL&CJ1856*	Lord Zetland's racehorse, winner of the St.Leger in 1850. A former French light infantryman, or sharpshooter.
Vulcan	*L&M1831*	The son of Jupiter and Juno, god of fire and worker of metals. The patron of all craftsmen.
	1851,1857	This was also the name of the locomotive building factory at Newton-le-Willows, north of Warrington.
WJ 1860,1870,1888,1915		
Vulture	*GJ1838*	A carrion-eating bird of prey, with great powers of flight.
1847,1872,1878,1905		
Walsall	*SS1849*	A town in Staffordshire eight miles north-west of Birmingham served by the South Staffordshire Railway.
Warrington	*W&N1831*	A town in Lancashire (now in Cheshire), midway between Liverpool and Manchester.
Warrior	*9.1854*	A fighting or military man, especially when veteran or distinguished.
	1874,1900	The Iron Armoured Ship (Ironclad) of 1860-1904, when she was renamed 'Vernon II', for use as a Training Ship.
Warwickshire	*1909*	An English County served by the Company.
Wasp	*1849,1850,1872*	The insect.
Waterloo	*1848*	To commemorate Wellington's victory in battle over Napoleon Bonaparte on 18th June 1815 at a village of this
	1860,1864,1889	name south of Brussels.

Watt	1848 1859,1906	1736-1819. James, the great British engineer and inventor of the steam engine improved by the use of condensers.
Waverley	1863 1905	The title of Sir Walter Scott's first novel, a name derived from Waverley Abbey, near Farnham, Surrey.
W.C.Brocklehurst	1910	1818-1900. William Coare Brocklehurst of Butley Hall, Prestbury, was a Director of the Company from 1876-1895. He was head of a silk manufacturing firm, and MP for Macclesfield, 1868-1880.
W.E.Dorrington	1914	William Edward Dorrington became a Director of the Company in 1894.
Weaver	BL&CJ1853	The river which rises near the Shropshire border and flows through Cheshire to the Mersey near Runcorn. It is 45 miles long. Liverpool trains leave the West Coast Main Line at Weaver Junction.
Wednesbury	SS1849	The Staffordshire town near Wolverhampton served by the South Staffordshire Railway.
Wellington	B&L1836 1848,1862,1909	1769-1852. Arthur Wellesley, 1st Duke, from 1814, was the British Army Commander at the battle of Waterloo, and Prime Minister of Great Britain and Ireland 1828-1830. This was also the name of one of the first class carriages on the Liverpool & Manchester Railway.
Wennington	L&C1859	A village eleven miles north-east of Lancaster, with a station on the "Little" North Western Railway. It later became the junction for the Midland Railway to Lancaster Green Ayre and the Furness & Midland Joint Railway to Carnforth, giving connection with the Furness Railway. The L&NWR had running powers between Carnforth and Wennington, but they were not used. 'Wennington' means 'The farm on the dark river'.
Westminster	1910	1825-1899. Hugh Lupus Grosvenor, son of the 2nd Marquess of Westminster, succeeded as the 3rd Marquess in 1869, and was created Duke of Westminster in 1874. He was a Company Director, and his was the last of the 1910 series of names of deceased Directors.
Westmorland	1909	An English County served by the Company.
Wheatstone	1882 1897	1802-1875. Sir Charles, physicist and scientist, FRS 1836, who invented the electric telegraph, which could be said to have made safety on railways more possible. He was knighted in 1861.
(White Raven)		There was no engine of this name. (See *Raven*)
Whitehaven	WFJc1846	The 'harbour by the white headland', in Cumberland.
Whitworth	1859 1865,1889	1803-1887. Sir Joseph, pioneer in precision toolmaking and engineering, instigator of a uniform system of screw threads, and President of the Institution of Mechanical Engineers in 1856. He was closely associated with the Company and endowed the Crewe "Whitworth Scholarships'.
Widgeon	1911	A duck, migratory and a winter visitor.
Wild Duck	1911	The Mallard. Britain's most common and best known duck.
Wildfire	L&M1830 GJ1837,1844 1855,1874,1890	This was the name chosen by Robert Stephenson for the locomotive he delivered to the Liverpool & Manchester Railway on 18th January 1830, It was renamed *Meteor* about a fortnight later at the beginning of February, when the L&M Directors decided from then on to choose the names for their locomotives. Another name for lightning, and for 'Will-o'-the Wisp' .
William Baker	1879	The first Chief Engineer of the L&NWR, who held office from 1858 until his death on 20th December 1878 at the early age of 62. Among his most noted works were the viaduct at Stockport, the bridge over the Mersey at Runcorn, and that of the West London Extension Railway over the Thames at Battersea.
William Cawkwell	1894,1906	Goods Manager of the Lancashire & Yorkshire Railway Company, who became L&NWR General Manager 1858-1874, was elected a Director in 1873 and became Deputy Chairman in 1884.
William Cowper	1914	1731-1800. The poet.

William Froude	*1898,1913*	1810-1879. The English engineer and naval architect. FRS 1870.
William Siemens	*1898, 1913*	1823-1883. Sir Charles William, engineer. He was the pioneer of the 'Open hearth' furnace and of the regenerative principles for the conservation of energy. A "Siemens - Marten" gas-fired furnace was built at Crewe in 1865. He was knighted in 1883.
Windermere *GJ1846 P&W1846/7 K&W1850,1855,1857,1915*		A lake in Westmorland and Lancashire, the largest in England. The town near the lake, and the terminus of the branch line from Oxenholme.
Wirral	*C&B1840*	The low-lying peninsula between the Mersey and the Dee. 'Wirral' means 'The river meadows where the bog myrtle grows'.
Witch	*GJ1837 1846,1871,1891,1916*	A female wizard. A woman supposed to have dealings with the devil.
Wizard	*GJ1837 1856,1877,1895*	One skilled in magic.
W.M.Thackeray	*1914*	1811-1863. William Makepeace Thackeray, the author.
Wolfe	*1866,1890*	1726-1759. James, General, who died as Commander of the British Army at the capture of Quebec.
Wolfhound	*1911*	A dog used for wolf hunting.
Wolverhampton	*SS1849*	The Staffordshire town, served by the South Staffordshire Railway; 'The high farm of Wufrun'.
Wolverine	*1911*	The Destroyer of 1910, lost in a collision in 1917.
Woodcock	*1854,1911*	A bird allied to the snipe but with shorter and stronger legs.
Woodlark	*L&M1845 1851,1862,1864,1895*	A species of the lark, which perches on trees.
Worcestershire	*1910*	An English County served by the Company.
Wordsworth *GJ1846,1873,1891,1909*		1770-1850. William Wordsworth, the Poet Laureate from 1843.
Wyre	*1851 1872,1879,1896*	The river 26 miles long which flows past Garstang and Poulton-le-Fylde to the Irish Sea at Fleetwood. In April 1850 five Preston & Wyre Railway locomotives were handed over to the L&NWR of which one was probably named *Wyre*, and withdrawn at once. If this is so, the name dates from the 1840s.
York	*L&M1836*	The city, and county town of Yorkshire.
Yorkshire	*1910*	An English County served by the Company.
Zamiel	*GJ1837 1845,1856,1873 1890,1915*	The forest Demon-huntsman who supplied Caspar with seven unerring magic bullets, cast in diabolical circumstances. (Weber's Opera "Der Freischutz" 1821) Another name for 'Samiel' or 'Simoom'. The hot dry wind sometimes coming from North Africa.
Zeno	*BL&CJ1857 1865,1894*	The Greek philosopher, founder of the Stoics, born in Cyprus but who became famous in Athens.
Zillah	*C&B1840 BL&CJ1857 1865,1890,1911*	The mother of Tubal (Tubal Cain), and thus "the mother of all engineers". Genesis chapter 4, verse 19. Zillah is the Hebrew word for 'Shade'.
Zopyrus	*BL&CJ1857 1865,1894*	The follower of Darius who was largely responsible for his success in capturing Babylon.
Zygia	*BL&CJ1857 1865,1893*	The 'surname' of the goddess Hera, presiding over marriage. The verb in appropriately derived from the verb 'To yoke'.

CHAPTER EIGHT
NAMES REQUIRING AMPLIFICATION OR SPECIAL MENTION

AIREY
Newton class 2-4-0 No 1678 *Airey*, built in April 1868.

An alternative source might possibly be George Bidden Airy (1801-1892), who became Astronomer Royal in 1835 and was also a member of the Gauge Commission which came down in favour of the 4ft 8 1/2in standard for our mainland railways. He was incidentally responsible for the adoption of Greenwich Mean Time in 1880.

If this explanation is correct it would incur another instance of a misspelt name, as in the cases of *Maberley* and *Humphrey Davy*.

ALDAM
Huddersfield & Manchester 2-2-2 No 1 *Aldam*

The engine already bore its name on Saturday 24th July 1847. A contemporary account says 'At nine o'clock in the morning the first engine and tender named 'The Aldam' steamed into the town (Huddersfield). It was named after the chairman of the company and described as being very hansome and powerful'. - Stanley Chadwick 'Railway Wonder' Pt.1. 1974. A naming ceremony took place on 2nd August at Heaton Lodge, performed by Joseph Brook, the Deputy Chairman of the Company.

ANGERSTEIN
South Staffordshire Railway 0-4-2 No 11 *Angerstein* built by W.J.& J.Garforth & Co. DukinfieldFoundry, near Ashton-under-Lyne, Lancs. in 1850

The origin of the name is uncertain.

It might relate to a Mr.John *Angerstein* who had a wharf on the Thames and who, two years after the locomotive was named, built a branch line from his wharf to the South Eastern Railway from Charlton between Greenwich and Woolwich. Just along the line is *Belvedere*. John Robinson McClean, lessee of the South Staffs Railway, who probably ordered these engines lived in Kent and died at Stonehouse, presumably the small place just north of Strood.

Alternatively it might refer to the well known John Julius *Angerstein*, 1735-1823. A Russian born merchant, philanthropist, and amateur in fine art, whose art collection formed the nucleus of the National Gallery in 1824. He was introduced to Lloyds in its 'coffee house' days, and became an underwriter; instrumental in establishing Lloyds as the major institution we know today. A friend of Sir Thomas Lawrence.

There is an Angerstein Lane in Blackheath/Greenwich.

ARAB
LFB Goods DA No 346 *Arab*, built in September 1854, at the height of the Crimean War.

This might be a name associated with the Battle of the Danube during the Russian War. The "Arab Tabia" was a newly constructed earthwork about 150 yards long. The Russians could not storm the Abd-ul-Mejid, the key to Silistra, until the Arab Tabia was taken. Two English Officers were in command of a detachment of well-disciplined Egyptians, armed with the French Miniè (rifle), and by Albanians armed with matchlocks. From 28th April 1854 for week after week the Russians bombarded and assaulted it, and "all Europe hung on the fate of the fortress, while with painful slowness the allied armies crept to the aid of the Turks." Silistra was never taken, and the allies won the Battle of the Danube.

Alternatively the name had been given to a Brig-sloop built in 1847, and before that to three successive warships captured from the French in 1795, 1797 and 1798 and also to another Brig-sloop built in 1812 and wrecked in 1823.

The GWR had an *Arab* in 1841, paired with a *Mazeppa* a stagecoach name, and a London & South Western Railway "Hercules" class received the name *Arab* in April 1853, which obviously was not related to the "Arab Tabia", so the possibility remains that the source of the name is in fact the breed of horse.

ARGUS
Dreadnought class 2-(2-2)-0 No 2056 *Argus*.

Argus was the nom de plume of Mr William H.Moss who had written lengthy articles in "The Engineer" between September 1885 and the following January severely critical of the efficiency of Mr.Webb's three cylinder compounds. This three cylinder compound locomotive, completed at Crewe in December 1885 and bearing his adversary's pseudonym was his only, and friendly reply. For many years Argus' identity remained a secret. But he continued to make his feelings on locomotive policy known to the L&NWR authorities and one of his letters written in February 1914 addressed to Sir Gilbert Claughton was received by Mr.James Bishop the Company Secretary and passed on to him. Sir Gilbert's reply was terse, "The writer has been known to us for many years." The letter was signed by "Wm.H.Moss". The secret was out. Who would have imagined that such a monster lurked behind a front door of a house in Sheridan Street, Manor Park?

BAYING
Newton class 2-4-0 No 1746 *Baying* built in November 1869.

The name was carried for just about two months until January 1870, when the name was changed to *Bevere*.

No person's name or place or house in Great Britain has come to light. Could it be the present Beijing (Peking) of China? The name of Beijing has changed many times over during the past 140 years. And why it was changed so rapidly to *Bevere* will possibly never be known. Might this have been the time when Richard Moon moved into the great house there?

BELVIDERE
South Staffordshire Railway 0-4-2 No 10 *Belvidere*,built by W.J.& J.Garforth & Co. in 1850.

It is curious to find *Belvidere* spelt with an 'i', but this might have been a misspelling on the part of Trevithick's clerk at Crewe when compiling the L&NWR list. It is spelt in this way in all old references to this engine. Belvedere is six miles distant from Angerstein's Wharf of the Thames. See the reference to *Angerstein* above.

BIG BEN
Whitehaven & Furness Junction Railway 0-6-0No 11 *Big Ben* of August 1855.

The date presents a problem. The bell was cast by Warners of Cripplegate (London) at Stockton-on-Tess in 1856, cracked in 1857, recast by George Mears, Whitechapel (London) in 1858, and delivered to site in May that year. But the decision to name the bell "Big Ben" may have been announced as early as 1855.

Sir Benjamin Hall, MP for Marylebone and of Welsh extraction whose nickname was "Big Ben" had connections with the bell etc. as "Commissioner of Woods and Forests" (precursor of "Minister of Works"), but there is no firm evidence that the bell recalls him.

There was a London boxer of this time, but this seems an unlikely solution.

The connection with the W.& F.J.is unknown.

COSSACK
LFB Goods DA No 347 *Cossack*, built in September 1854,at the height of the Crimean War.

As in the case of Arab there is more than one possible source.

The first, suggested by the fact that the name was a direct successor to *Arab*, is one of the warlike race inhabiting the south-eastern steppes of Russia, noted for their military service and skilled horsemanship.

The second is that on the outbreak of the Crimean War, the Russian warship "Witjas", a screw corvette, was being built at Northfleet and was seized on 8th April 1854, completed, and renamed HMS *Cossack*. By September 1854 it is likely that the warship was uppermost in the public consciousness for the name appears among other warships then on active service in the Baltic and Black Seas.

There have been several locomotives of this name. The first use of it appears to be on London & South Western Railway No 6 of July 1839. It would seem likely that their "Sussex" class engine was named in September 1852 after the racehorse which won the Derby in 1847, making it a popular one at the time. The Great Western waited until November 1862 before introducing the name on a member of their "Caliph" class.

ESK and JUSTIN
South Staffordshire Railway 2-4-0 Nos 18 *Esk* and 19 *Justin* built by E.B.Wilson & Co. in May 1853.

Attempts have been made to solve the sources of *Esk* and *Justin* by finding some link between the two names. For example, there was a Justinhaugh Station on the Caledonian Railway on the Forfar - Brechin line with the River South Esk right beside it. There is also a well known old pub 58 miles distant called the Justinlees Inn in Eskbank, with the Rivers North and South Esk close by. (This last river is not the same as the one mentioned above.) Yet another trail leads to Ireland, for County Cork is the homeland of the Justins, and John Robinson McClean, lessee of the South Staffs Railway, who probably ordered these engines, may have been born in Belfast, where there are two loughs and a river called Eske. So maybe Trevithick's clerk's curlicue was an 'e' after all. The source or sources of these two names have yet to be discovered.

FORERUNNER
DX 0-6-0 No 442 *Forerunner*.

Doubts have been expressed as to whether this locomotive carried this name. Scott in his manuscript has "?Forerunner", Livesey is doubtful, Stuart is quite definite and says "Nameplate never fitted", and Nock in 'The Premier Line' writes "This name was intended, but the engine No.442 never actually carried the name." On the other hand both Harris and Baxter include the name without comment. The BL&CJ 0-6-0 from which the name and number came was sold in March 1861, the same month in which the DX was completed and this of course made it an obvious choice. On balance it would appear that the name *Forerunner* was intended, but never used.

GERMANIC
Experiment Compound 333 *Germanic* built in February 1884.

The liner had a long and chequered career, holding the Blue Riband with her sister ship the Britannic 1876-1879. She heeled over and sank in a New York blizzard in 1899, was raised and served as a troopship to South Africa during the Boer War, sold to Turkey in 1910, torpedoed in the sea of Marmara by a British submarine in 1915, raised a second time to sail between Istanbul and New York in 1920-1921, and was not broken up until 1950. The adventures of the nameplates were no less chequered, the letters 'Germanic' being

partially obliterated on Whale Experiment 372 in 1914 after the outbreak of war, and a plate worded 'Belgic' fixed above. Both plates were removed in 1921 and replaced by a standard style 'Belgic'.

GOLIAH / GOLIATH
The name of the Biblical strong man is spelled GOLIATH in the Version of Scripture authorised by King James, and is in current use today.

However the spelling GOLIAH appears in some early locomotive stock lists, such as the L&MR stock list of December 1842, and by Trevithick in his letter of July 1847 and in his list of March 1855, and again when the name was removed from the SFB Goods engine on 9th August 1875. (See Appendix 2).

Ahrons in "The British Steam Railway Locomotive 1825-1925 includes the "T" when referring to the L&M engine of 1831. Samuel Scott's "The List of Locomotives up to 1840 inclusive" has GOLIATH for No 15, and both he and Livesey give the same for the 1847 engine. thus using the spelling of their day. It would appear most likely that all three were mistaken.

It is most likely that the St.Helens No 25 built in 1854 was named GOLIATH, and beyond question so was the Jubilee No 1927 of 1900.

IDA
LFB Goods DA No 311 *Ida* built in May 1853.

Everard Beauchamp writes "I recently came across a massive historical novel entitled 'Ida - the mystery of the nun's grave at Vale Royal Abbey' by John Henry Cooke (Published 1912). Vale Royal Abbey is alongside the L&NWR between Winsford and Hartford just north of Crewe. There is also a Monks Well on the map. Might there be a connection with the 1853 engine name?"

JEANIE DEANS
No 1304 *Jeanie Deans*

A name which appeared in March 1890 on the fourth of the Teutonic class in the midst of a series of White Star Liners. How this came about is recorded in 'The Locomotive' of 15th March 1939. Her name was suggested to Mr.Webb by Mr.Alfred Rosling Bennett (1850-1928), the Chairman of the Engineering Section of the Edinburgh Exhibition of 1890, and he responded at once with a gesture that was regarded as a great compliment to that City and to the memory of (Sir Walter Scott) the author of "The Heart of Midlothian". Many of Scott's characters were real people whose identity was masked by fictitious names. In this case it was a certain Helen Walker who walked from Edinburgh to London to plead with Queen Anne for mercy for her sister Effie, condemned to death for the murder of her illegitimate child. The Heart of Midlothian was the old Tolbooth Gaol in Edinburgh, demolished in 1817.

Mr.Bennett was the author of "The Chronicles of Boulton's Siding", "Historic Locomotives" etc..

JOHN MAYALL
Newton class 2-4-0 No 1747 *Tennyson* was renamed *John Mayall* in December 1885.

The source given in "LMS Locomotive Names" was that the locomotive was named after the pioneer in the Daguerreotype process, who became a celebrated portrait photographer, and not least to the Royal Household. His studio in London at the time the locomotive was named was equipped with the most powerful electric lighting of its time.

General opinion, however, prefers John Mayall the cotton spinner as a much more likely source of this name.

LA FRANCE

Jubilee 1926 *La France* was not in fact the 4,000th locomotive to have been built at Crewe, but somewhere near it. Crewe numbers *3784* and *3785* were never used, and "Precedent" class 861 *Amazon* for whom Crewe number *3783* had been allocated, was not "Renewed" until September 1901.

MERRIE CARLISLE
Lancaster & Carlisle 2-2-2 No 72 *Merrie Carlisle*, built in 1859 by W.D.Fairbairn & Sons.

The old ballad 'The Marriage of Sir Gawaine' begins "King Arthur lives in mery Carlisle and seemly is to see..." In the Arthurian Legends, 'The Healing of Sir Urre', Book XIX, v.,10-14, we read that the healing took place in 'Carlshylle' on the Anglo Scottish borders at Pentecoste when the Round Table was assembled there; it was a cause of much thanksgiving and merriment, a high feste, and jousting won by the restored Sir Urre, after which followed the wedding of his sister to Sir Gawaine.

MIRANDA
LFB Pass (Raven class) No 341 *Miranda*, built in July 1854

There was a partial blockade of the White Sea in July 1854 by a small squadron of three British ships - *Eurydice, Brisk,* and *Miranda.* In June the squadron bombarded Kola in northern Lapland and entered the White Sea. An attack was made on Solovetski Island in the Gulf of Onega. where the squadron boarded and examined over 300 merchant vessels, capturing any that could be fairly claimed as prizes. The news must have reached Crewe very swiftly.

MONK
The Chester & Birkenhead Railway 2-2-2 No 8 *Birkenhead* built about April 1845 by Jones & Potts, and renamed *Monk*, following the amalgamation with the Birkenhead, Lancashire & Cheshire Junction Railway in 1847.

The Benedictine Prior of Birkenhead was granted the ferry rights in 1330. These passed into lay ownership c1540, and devolved to the Woodside Ferry. A rival crossing claiming to be the true ancient ferry was started by the Monks Ferry Co in 1835. This was challenged in court, who ruled in favour of the Woodside crossing. Monks Ferry ceased, and the assets were purchased by the Chester & Birkenhead Railway c 1840, together with their ferryboats, named Monk, Abbey and Dolphin. They already owned shares in the Woodside Ferry. The Chester & Birkenhead Railway amalgamated with the Birkenhead Lancashire & Cheshire Junction Railway on 22 July 1847, and restarted the Monks Ferry. The former possessed a locomotive delivered in 1845, No 8 named *Birkenhead*. When the combined Company in March 1849 purchased a No 11, and gave it the name *Birkenhead*, their No 8 was renamed *Monk*. By this time they had restarted Monks Ferry in conjunction with an extension of the line to the riverside, and it must be assumed it was renamed either after the Benedictine Prior of 1330, or after their ferryboat "Monk", itself presumably, indirectly named after him.

In 1859 the companies which had amalgamated in 1847 were now called The Birkenhead Railway, so when their No 8 *Monk* came into the LNWR Northern Division in November 1860, to avoid duplication with No 180 *Monk* which had come to the L&NWR in 1847 from the North Union, it was renamed *Violet*, and given the associated number 224.

MORECAMBE
Lancaster & Carlisle 2-4-0 Goods No 82 *Morecambe*, built in 1859 by Robert Stephenson & Co.

The name appeared some two years before the Lancaster & Carlisle

Railway reached the town when Morecambe was little more than a village. Until 1889 it was officially named Poulton-le-Sands, but the name had been current in railway circles long before that. So was this a Director's residence? There is a Morecambe Lodge three miles north of Carnforth. G.P.Neele writes "From Hest Bank a short line, opened in September 1864, ran to Morecambe, into the terminus of the Midland Railway there; Morecambe was the only seaside town in the North in the possession of that Company, and they dealt with it in the most liberal manner in all their Excursion announcements from Yorkshire towns. So little interest did the North-Western Company then take in the place that, although the branch from Hest Bank was originally a double line, it was arranged to take up one set of rails and work it as a single line."

Recent research shows that the line was authorised by the Lancaster and Carlisle Railway Act 1859, the year the locomotive ws delivered, and was opened in 1861, so that its naming might have taken place in anticipation of its opening.

PRINCE EUGENE
LFB Pass (Prince Ernest class) No 316 *Prince Eugene*, built in August 1853.

The name presents some difficulty. It appears immediately after *Prince Ernest* and *Prince Arthur*, which would suggest a reference to a third living member of some royal family, but Prince Ernest was an only son, and it has not proved possible to discover any European Prince of this name at the time.

QUEEN EMPRESS
Greater Britain class 2-(2-2)-2 No 2054 *Queen Empress*, built May 1893.

An alternative rendering is "Queen-Empress", repeatedly used by Charles Rous-Marten and by a contributor who gave himself the title "Brunel Redivivus" in articles in The Railway Magazine in 1901 and 1902. On the Teutonic class engine of 1893, the words "Queen" and "Empress" were on separate plates on the two splashers over the driving wheels, and so obviously there was no hyphen; neither was there one on the single straight plates on the Experiment class engine of 1906. Nevertheless Her Majesty's Titles when referred to together quite properly invoke the hyphen.

SISTER DORA

Samson class 2158 *Serpent* was withdrawn in August 1894, for rebuilding to become a member of the Waterloo class. Samuel Scott's manuscript records that the name was changed to *Sister Dora* on 17th November 1894. This is an instance of a person who had attained a degree of popularity sufficient to displace an existing name. This devoted nurse had in fact achieved distinction by her devotion to her patients in Walsall as far back as 1878, but the fact was that No 2158 was shedded at Burton on Trent and ran regularly through Walsall on the Derby - Birmingham trains makes it reasonable to suppose that the idea of giving a local engine her name came by popular request from the community at Walsall, who were understandably grateful to her and very proud of her. Small wonder that her name should still appear on diesel locomotives in the 1990s to keep her memory alive and as an incentive to our late 20th and early 21st century railway enthusiasts to find out who she was.

SOHO
The Bolton & Leigh 0-4-2 of 1838, and the SFB Pass SF No 125 so named during the half year ending May 1850.

The name 'Soho' originated in the pleasure gardens of London, and was chosen by Boulton and Watt to be the name of the manufactory they established in 1765 near to Soho Park in Birmingham. Soho

Foundry was opened in 1796 by Boulton & Watt a mile or so away in Smethwick and Soho was used to describe the surrounding district. The name was copied by others including B.Hick & Son for their factory in Bolton.

SOULT
Problem class 2-2-2 No 804 *Soult,* built in November 1862.

Marshal Soult was recalled from exile as a royalist supporter of King Louis- Philippe, and in July 1838 while he was the French Ambassador to Great Britain he travelled at the Duke of Wellington's suggestion on the London & Birmingham Railway from Euston to Denbigh Hall, and from Rugby to Birmingham, continuing on the Grand Junction Railway to Liverpool.

SWIFT
SFB Goods DA No 274 *Swift,* built in November 1851.

It seems unlikely that the locomotive was named after a bird, not being one the 'Bird' class built between 1841 and 1845.

In support of the solicitor as the preferred choice, the surname Swift appears in Thomas' "The Liverpool and Manchester Railway" in which on page 225 it states "George Pritt, the Company's Law Clerk, died in December 1831, The firm's partner William Clay succeeded him, and the firm became Clay and **Swift**." From which it may be deduced that from very early times, a solicitor of the name Swift is likely to have had dealings with both the L&M and the L&NWR.

THE TSAR
Precursor class 4-4-0 No 2583 *Teutonic* was renamed *Tsar* in November 1914.

There has been debate over whether the name was "Tsar", or "Tzar", and no photograph has come to light to determine the issue. The name was only carried until December 1915 when the name was changed again to *Moonstone*.

UNICORN
SFB Pass SF No 233 *Unicorn* built in March 1849.

A possible but unlikely alternative source might be HMS Unicorn, the oldest Royal Navy ship in service in 1849, and still afloat at the present time. This 5th Rate is a wooden frigate launched on 30th March 1824, which became a Powder Hulk in 1860, was the RNR Depot at Dundee from 1873 and is now preserved there.

INDEX OF NAMES, TABLES AND NUMBERS

Numbers in italics are Crewe, or Motion Numbers
Those in ordinary type are the Running \numbers

Booth	*241 308 1309 3071*
Breadalbane	*2401 3508 5559*
Bret Harte	*5189*
Briareus	GJ67 *188 995*
Brindley	*929 3343 4512*
Britain	St.H17
Britannia	*1284 3056*
Britannic	*2737 4507*
British Empire	*5001*
Britomart	*4848*
Brook	H&M46
Brougham	L&C17 *1300 3346 4678*
Bucephalus	(253) *253 780 4545*
Buckingham	*1289 3070 5390*
Buckland	*2507 3657 4784*
Buffalo	L&M67 *364 452 1908 4789*
Bull Dog	*4990*
Bulldog	*238 627 4990*
Bullfinch	L&M94 *341 371*
Bulwer Lytton	*5179*
Bunsen	*1173 3026 5507*
Burmah	993
Burton	SS5
Byron	*983 3248*
Byzantium	*4841*
Cadmus	256 789
Cæsar	*4288*
Caithness	1199
Caledonian	L&M28
Caliban	GJ17 *310 602 1697 3376 5266*
Cambrian	249 *1921 3684*
Camilla	GJ38 *38 889*
Camperdown	*4132*
Canada	*5003*
Candidate	170 *1806 4511*
Canning	110 *378 5453*
Cannock	SS24
Canopus	*3938*
Captain Fryatt	*5368*
Caractacus	*2402 3613*
Caradoc	246 *1919 3494*
Carlisle	PW Dept
Carnarvon	*5239*
Carnarvonshire	*4867*
Castor	199 *375* 199 *882 3450 5307*
Cato	*330*
Cavalier	*3935*
Cedric	W&FJ18 *2238 4466*
Celtic	*3110 4671*
Centaur	GJ12i GJ12ii *283 2279 3463*
Centipede	*343*
Centurion	*3936*
Cerberus	GJ18 *310 365 2236 4467*
	384
Chaffinch	L&M95 *267 342*
Challenger	*5011*
Champion	226 *1804 4457*
Chandos	*284 325 547 2228 3659*
Charles Dickens	*2510 5118*
Charles H.Dent	*5345*
Charles H.Mason	*4289*

Charles J.Cropper	*5235*
Charles James Lever	*5195*
Charles Kingsley	*5176*
Charles Lamb	*5192*
Charles N.Lawrence	*5146*
Charles Wolfe	*5168*
Charon	GJ65 *221 513 627 3133*
Cheshire	*4851*
Chester	BL&CJ12
Chillington	(243) *243 1915 3557 4785*
Chimera	Ex-NU177 *455 626 3116*
City of Carlisle	*2897 4550*
City of Chester	*2898 4551*
City of Chicago	*2742*
City of Dublin	*3015 4552*
City of Edinburgh	*2900 4553*
City of Glasgow	*2901 4554*
City of Lichfield	*3016 4555*
City of Liverpool	*2899 4556*
City of London	*3014 4557*
City of Manchester	*2896 4558*
City of New York	*3012*
City of Paris	*3013 4559*
C.J.Bowen Cooke	*5532*
Clanricarde	235 *4620*
Clarendon	(264) *264 1687 3351*
Clio	GJ53 *53 5376*
Clive	*601 4660*
Clwyd	VofC1
Clyde	St.H26 *602 4667*
Cocker	C&W2
Collingwood	*4049*
Colonel	188
Colonel Lockwood	*5230*
Colossus	GJ66 *193 1812 3937*
Columbine	GJ49 *49 850*
Columbus	*997 3055 5377*
Colwyn Bay	*5243*
Combermere	*491 4682*
Comet	L&M5 L&M55 166
Commodore	175 *529* 2403 3683*
Commonwealth	*4290*
Compound	*2625*
Condor	L&M100 *242 2049 3685 5271*
Conqueror	*5036*
Constance	*884 3367*
Conway	207 1183 *5244*
Cook	*996 3060*
Coptic	*3108 4530*
Coquette	*5033*
Cornwall	173 *4512*
Coronation	*5000*
Corunna	*1161 3347*
Cossack	*302 1809 4447*
Councillor	112 981
Countess	*985 3200*
Courier	176 *313 2044 3598*
Crane	L&M78 *253*
Cressy	*4291*
Crewe	*252*
Cricket	BL&CJ39
Cromwell	*998 3148*

222

Cross Fell	L&C80
Crow	L&M87 *266*
Croxteth	*206 436 730 3114 5510*
Crusader	*3934*
Cuckoo	L&M103 *360* 1185 *2283 3449*
Cumberland	*4292*
Cyclops	L&M46 *184 1697 2744 4477*
Cygnet	L&M80 *219 528*
Cyprus	*5009*
Czar	*273*
Czar of Russia	*5298*
Dachshund	*4990*
Dædalus	98 896
Dagmar	*1162 3196*
Dalemain	GJ80 L&C22 854
Dalton	*926 3066 5501*
Danby Lodge	PW Dept.
Daphne	*836 4661*
Dart	L&M4 L&M48
Dee	*186* BL&CJ14 BL&CJ38 St.H27
Deerhound	*4996*
Defiance	*5037*
Delamere	228 1198 *4679*
Delhi	*1168 3146*
Denbighshire	*4868*
Derby	*213* SS23 1187 *2406*
Derbyshire	*4852*
Derwent	C&W1
Deva	GJ74
Diadem	*4130*
Diamond	191
Dickie	Crewe NG
Diomed	GJ52 52 *449 633 3136*
Director	*218 1686 3054*
Disraeli	*2048 3510 5483*
Doctor Dalton	GJ19
Dominion	*4293*
Don	*230*
Doric	*3106 4670*
Dovedale	*5246*
Dragon	GJ10 *350 1813 4448*
Drake	*993 3059 4985*
Dreadnought	BL&CJ40 *2795 4444*
Dromedary	168
Druid	*191* C&B7 *1808 4449*
Duchess	L&PJ *986 3251*
Duchess of Lancaster	L&C71 *2404 3730*
Dudley	SS1
Duke	99 891
Duke of Albany	*2504*
Duke of Connaught	*2505 3597 5383*
Duke of Sutherland	*5142*
Dunrobin	*1287 1303 2886 4478*
Dwarf	PW Dept
Eagle	GJ20 *313 385*
Eamont	L&C18 *1301 3344*
Earl	100 626
Earlestown	Wagon Wks
Eclipse	L&M40 202 *1696 3370 5133*
Economist	*2626*

E.C.Trench	*5342*
Eden	87 L&C7 St.H7 *404 683 3356*
Edith	*830 4668*
Edith Cavell	*5304*
Edward Gibbon	*5194*
Edward Tootal	*1904 3575 5126*
Egeria	*839 4468*
Eglinton	*216* 1182 *2253 4479*
Eleanor	*831 4669*
Elector	189
Elephant	L&M65 113
Elgin	*603*
Elk	*231*
Elkhound	*4997*
Eller	C&W5
Ellesmere	245 *423 625 3354*
Elwy	VofC2
Emerald	195 *388 2255 4486*
Emperor	217 *389 2753 4495*
Empress	*331 2752 4496*
Enchantress	*5034*
E.Nettlefold	*4978*
Envoy	209 *374 2043 3509*
Erebus	GJ33i GJ33ii *426 4663*
Esk	SS18
Ethelred	*587 4780*
Etna	L&M20 L&M51 *289 343 550 2254*
	4521
E.Tootal Broadhurst	*5234*
Eunomia	*837 4781*
Euphrates	*2888 4458*
Euryalus	*4335*
Euston	*286 1960*
Euxine	*320 1845 3355*
Experiment	L&M32 *2500 4505*
Express	*2672 4497*
Faerie Queene	*588 4547*
Fairbairn	*297 2051 3782*
Falaba	*5322*
Falcon	GJ5 *349*
Falstaff	*326 401 689 3381 5264*
Fame	197 *1821 4522*
Faraday	*927 2999 4776*
Felicia Hemans	*5186*
Fire Queen	*5012*
Firefly	L&M31 231 231 *789 3123*
Flamingo	L&M102 *250*
Flintshire	*4869*
Florence	*1485 3245*
Fly	*234*
Flying Fox	*3945*
Forerunner	BC&LJ13 *479*
Formidable	*4197*
Forth	St.H13
Fortuna	*838 4772*
Foxhound	*4995*
Francis Stevenson	*4204*
Franklin	987 *3201*
Frederick Baynes	*5231*
Friar	Ex NU178 *381* 178 *2750 4531*
Frobisher	*995 3029 5520*

F.S.P.Wolferston	*4972*
Fury	L&M21 *240*
F.W.Webb	*4981*
Fylde	L&C16
Gaelic	*3111 4672*
Galatea	*4198*
Gallipoli	*5317*
Galtfaenan	VofC3
Ganymede	*1164 3001 4523*
Gardner (Gardiner)	P&L
Gazelle	*340*
General	174 1184 *2224*
General Joffre	*5297*
George Findlay	*3472 4830*
George Macpherson	*5337*
George the Fifth	*4970*
George Whale	*4982*
Germanic	*2738 4508*
Gheber	BL&CJ14
Giant	*233*
Gibraltar	*5007*
Giffard	*2252*
Giraffe	(242) 243 *1909 3560*
Gladiator	*1179 3048*
Gladstone	*988 3061*
Glatton	*4002*
Glendower	*202* 280 ex-C&B 7 *470 4621*
Glowworm	*327 403 629 3140 3283*
Glyn	*183 768*
Glynllivon	Carnarvonshire
Gnome	BL&CJ12
Goldfinch	L&M93 *265 387*
Goldsmith	*1288*
Goliah	L&M15
	L&M68
Goliath	122 St.H25 *4001*
Good Hope	*4294*
Gorgon	GJ41 41
G.R.Jebb	*5367*
G.P.Neele	*5196*
Grasmere	K&W/L&C69 *553*
Grasshopper	BL&CJ6
Greater Britain	*3292 4771*
Greenbank	BS2586
Greyhound	*269 2890 4487*
Greystock	*780*
Greystoke	GJ81 L&C23 *780 3137 4779*
Grouse	*5027*
Gurth	W&FJ17
Guy Calthrop	*5340*
Hampden	*999 3284 5454*
Hannibal	*4199*
Harbinger	*207 1803 4416*
Hardinge	*278 396*
Hardman	*323 399 631 3121*
Hardwicke	*224 1688 3286*
Harlequin	GJ44i GJ44ii *427 4680*
Harpy	GJ25i GJ25ii *893 2892 4513*
Harrier	*5013*
Harrowby	*263 2237 4488*

Harvey Combe	L&B
Havelock	*599 4480*
Hawk	GJ37 37 37
Hawkstone	236 236 *483*
Hecate	GJ4i GJ4ii 848 *2747 4489*
Hecla	GJ2 W&FJ2 *450 731 3454*
Hector	*237* 304 *1308 3285*
Helvellyn	94 890 *2231 4418*
Henrietta	*883 3117*
Henry Bessemer	*3476 4685*
Henry Cort	*2250 3859 4831*
Henry Crosfield	*1380 3147 5127*
Henry Maudslay	*3861 4980*
Henry Pease	*2509 3531*
Henry W.Longfellow	*5177*
Henry Ward	*4976*
Herald	263 765 *2893 4498*
Hercules	L&M39 261 St.H4 *420 2047 3781*
Herefordshire	*4853*
Hermione	*5039*
Hero	192 St.H23 *444 680 3126*
Herod	GJ63 *348*
Heron	L&M72 *211 523*
Herschel	*922 3057 4777*
Hertfordshire	*4854*
Hibernia	*1285 3023 5262*
Himalaya	*2804 4460*
Hindostan	*4336*
Holland Hibbert	*5143*
Holyhead	*5245*
Hood	*4337*
Hope	*192*
Hornet	GJ50 50
Hotspur	*196 1848 3470 5265*
Howe	*4338*
Huddersfield	H&M45
Hugh Myddleton	*3862 4832*
Huish	243 309
Humphrey Davy	*2409 3573*
Hurricane	*275 4622*
Huskisson	380 169 *2894 4459*
Hydra	95 888 *2628 4491*
Hyperion	GJ62 62 *4549*
Ida	247 *394*
Ilion	*1163 3031 4537*
Illustrious	*4200 5553*
Implacable	*3940*
India	*5002*
Inflexible	*3942*
Ingestre	GJ85 856 *5382*
Ingleboro	L&C14 400
Inglewood	L&C13 607
Intrepid	*3996*
Invincible	*3939*
Ionic	*3107 4532*
Iron Duke	*3856 3928*
Irresistible	*3941*
Irwell	*204* St.H3
Isabella	*1691 3288*
Isis	*244 1855 3380*
I.T.Williams	*5369*

Name	References
Ivanhoe	*596 4631*
Ixion	232 *1699 3366*
J.A.Bright	*5227*
J.A.F.Aspinall	*5346*
James Bishop	*5341*
Japan	991
Jason	GJ40 40 *386 2256 4469*
J.Bruce Ismay	*5232*
Jeanie Deans	*3105 4689*
Jim Crow	NG
John Bateson	*4973*
John Bright	*1281 3283*
John Hick	*3505 5119*
John Keats	*5169*
John Mayall	*1283 3193 5124*
John o'Gaunt	250 L&C74 *1849 3458*
John o Gaunt	*3995*
John o'Groat	252 *1847 3462 5511*
John Penn	*3863 4834*
John Ramsbottom	*1479 3050*
John Rennie	*2229 3864 5120*
John Ruskin	*5174*
John Smith	St.H6
Joshua Radcliffe	*2220 3682*
J.P.Bickersteth	*4987*
Jubilee	*3856*
Jupiter	L&M14 *4339*
Justin	SS19
Kelpie	W&FJ11
Kendal	L&C77
Kestrel	*290 2284 3457 5267*
King Arthur	*4133*
King Edward VII	*4126*
King of Italy	*5301*
King of Serbia	*5300*
King of the Belgians	*5299*
Kingfisher	L&M71 *189*
King Lear	W&FJ9
Kitchener	NG
Knighton	Knighton
Knowsley	91 887 *2670 4499*
La France	*4000*
Lady Beatrice	*1917*
Lady Godiva	*4340 5550*
Lady of the Lake	K&W/L&C68 *433 531 4623*
Lancashire	*4855*
Lancaster	L&PJ
Landrail	*5021*
Lang Meg	L&C73 *2232 4533*
Langdale	529* K&W/L&C66 603
Lapwing	L&M 85/St.H18 *264 2233 4534*
Latona	332 364 Ex-BL&CJ15
Lawrence	*2408 3596*
Lazonby	L&C25 *2407*
L/Corpl.J.A.Christie V.C.	*5513*
Leamington	*5242*
Leamington Spa	*5242*
Leander	196 *467 4632*
Leeds	L&M30
Leicestershire	*4856*
Leopard	L&M62
Levens	L&C15 *2257 4535*
Leviathan	244 1001 *2800 4450*
Lewis Carroll	*5188*
Lichfield	SS4
Lightning	L&M45 114 *1487 3027 4838*
Lily	222 466
Linnet	L&M92 *257 379*
Lion	L&M57 *370*
Little England	S&P
Liver	L&M26 262 *1857 3455*
Liverpool	245 *1961*
Livingstone	*1174 3244 5258*
Llandrindod	*5240*
Llandudno	*5237*
Llewellyn	225 *2050 3726 5561*
Loadstone	*217 1856 3443 5263*
Locke	*200* 278 Ex-BL&CJ20 *471 584 4666*
Locomotion	*220*
London	200
Lonsdale	GJ78 L&C11 840 W&FJ19
Lord Byron	*5180*
Lord Faber	*5229*
Lord Kenyon	*5339*
Lord Kitchener	*5236*
Lord Loch	*4975*
Lord of the Isles	*594 4782*
Lord Rathmore	*5144*
Lord Stalbridge	*5137*
Lowther	90 L&C21 *1913 3599*
Loyalty	*5131*
Lucifer	GJ55 55 1004
Luck of Edenhall	L&C8 *1850 3447*
Lucknow	*1167 3194 5475*
Lune	88 L&C6 St.H28 615
Lusitania	*5321*
Lynx	GJ16i GJ16ii *1384 3353*
Mabel	*2400 3614*
Maberley	*272* 1200
Madge	*1381 3247*
Magdala	*1280 3282*
Magistrate	107
Magnet	*226*
Magnificent	*4129*
Majestic	L&M10 368 ex-BL&CJ24
	L&M50 *337 551 492 4773*
Malta	*5008*
Mammoth	L&M61 247 978 *2802 4461*
Marathon	*282 2223 3611 5497*
Marchioness of Stafford	*2798*
Mark Twain	*5187*
Marlborough	*990 3349 4839*
Marmion	*595 4665*
Marquis	102 102 *1691 1807 4442*
Marquis Douro	B&L14 124 124 ex-BL&CJ41 *788 3363*
Marron	C&W3
Mars	L&M12 *4341*
Martin	L&M70 129 *510 687 3445*
Maryport	WJ4
Mastodon	L&M63 119 625 *2287 3141*

Mayor	108
Mazeppa	234 *524 4633*
McConnell	SS26
Medea	GJ46 46 623 *2286 3460*
Medusa	GJ54i GJ54ii 999 *2889 4481*
Megatherion	212
Memnon	*324* 356 Ex-BL&CJ27 *485 732 3132*
Menai	206 500 *432*
Mercury	L&M11 *339 2222 3571*
Merlin	GJ27 *309 4342*
Merrie Carlisle	L&C72 *2038 3535*
Mersey	GJ77 BL&CJ13 BL&CJ23 St.H16i St.H16ii *440 4664*
Messenger	*270 2748 4482*
Meteor	L&M3 L&M54 115 *2041 5136*
Middlesex	*4857*
Midge	Crewe NG
Miles MacInnes	*4988*
Milo	L&M25 L&M47
Milton	*982 3069 5275*
Minerva	*1175 3028 5257*
Minotaur	*190* 271 *1304 2996*
Miranda	*287 2221 3728*
Monarch	230 468 *4662*
Monk	NU19 *361* C&B8 BL&CJ11
Monmouthshire	*4858*
Moonstone	*4527*
Moor Hen	*5022*
Morcambe	L&C82
Murdock	*928 3052*
Napier	265 917
Napoleon	*493 4538*
Narcissus	186 *1694 3131*
Nasmyth	*298 2225 3490*
Nasr Ed Din	*598*
Navvie	St.H1
Nelson	219 *4343*
Neptune	*4344*
Nestor	*335*
New Zealand	*5005*
Newby	L&C2
Newcomen	*923 3068 4986*
Newton	*920 3047*
Niagara	*2803 4470*
Nightingale	*336*
Nipper	Crewe NG
North Star	L&M8 *888 3139*
North Western	171 *1689 2997 4624*
Northumberland	*4859*
Northumbrian	L&M7
Novelty	*1176 3291*
Nubian	*5015*
Nun	Ex-NU179 179 *383*
Oberon	GJ48 48 *1819 4419*
Oceanic	*3103 4673*
Odin	GJ64 *198* 847 *2281 3459 5316*
Oliver Goldsmith	*5172*
Onyx	211 *445 681 3372 5312*
Oregon	*2739 4514*
Orion	L&M35 *4201*

Osprey	L&M106 *362* 703
Ostrich	L&M74 *280* 133 *881 3122 3369*
Otterhound	*4993*
Ousel	*316*
Outram	*600*
Owl	L&M75 *282* 443
Owzell	L&M97
Oxfordshire	*4860*
Pacific	*3104 4674*
Palmerston	*490 4625*
Pandora	*833 4500*
Panopea	*835 4471*
Panther	L&M64
Partridge	L&M83 *300* 617 *5025*
Patentee	L&M33
Pathfinder	*5035*
Patience	*1906 3746 5509*
Patriot	*5375 5502*
Patterdale	L&C5 *1288 3350*
Peacock	*236*
Pearl	193 *382 2258 4536*
Peel	B&L 127 *533 4525*
Peerless	190
Pegasus	GJ31i GJ31ii *285 2405 3493 5260*
Pelican	L&M73 *214*
Pelsall	SS12
Penguin	L&M90 *268 2751 4515*
Penmaenmawr	*227* 295 *1307 3348 5130*
Penrith Beacon	L&C75 *1914 3727*
Percy Bysshe Shelley	*5193*
Perseus	*5014*
Perseverance	*1907 3742*
Persia	*5324*
Pet	Crewe NG
Petrel	L&M91 *358* 838 *2285 3461 5274*
Petteril	L&C12
P.H.Chambres	*4979*
Phaeton	104 *1486 3145 5132*
Phalaris	GJ15 *317 1701 3361 4675*
Phantom	GJ56 56 *2046 3532*
Pheasant	L&M82 141 141 666 *2288 3451 4778*
Phlegethon	GJ72 *245*
Phoebus	GJ34 34 34 ex-BL&CJ34 *552*
Phœnix	L&M6 L&M49 W&FJ6
Phosphorus	GJ1 61 *429 4681*
Pilot	181 *2042 3658*
Pioneer	*1480 3049*
Pitt	*989 3025*
Planet	L&M9 *889 3371 5135*
Platelayer	NG
Pluck	*1905 3491*
Pluto	L&M27 *197 276 1306 3053 5308*
Plynlimmon	*2227 3681 5259*
Pollux	200 *376*
Polyphemus	96 892 *4003*
Powerful	*3998*
Powis	(239) 239
Precedent	*1902 3534 5261*
Precursor	255 *1802 4415*
Premier	93 *1484 3046 5500*
President	(238) 238 *1007 4626*

President Garfield	2501 3556			
President Lincoln	2502 3558 4786			
President Washington	2503 3533			
Preston	L&C76			
Priam	SS20			
Prince	GJ73			
Prince Albert	GJ73 1482 3144 5489			
Prince Alfred	593			
Prince Arthur	255			
Prince Ernest	254 392			
Prince Eugene	256 316 ex-BL&CJ21			
Prince George	3473 4686			
Prince Leopold	2036 3780			
Prince of Wales	222 532 4635 5030 5752			
Prince Oscar	489			
Princess	GJ19 1385 3142			
Princess Alexandra	592 4835			
Princess Alice	591 4683			
Princess Beatrice	1917			
Princess Helena	984 3045			
Princess Louise	2035 3656 5546			
Princess May	3474 4636			
Princess Royal	590			
Private E.Sykes V.C.	5517 5557			
Private W.Wood V.C.	5530 5560			
Problem	424 4524			
Prometheus	GJ28i GJ28ii 28 525 4634			
Proserpine	356 1006 2052 3506			
Prospero	GJ13 311 1692 3468 4687			
Psyche	834 4501			
Ptarmigan	293 5024			
Puck	885 3359 3596			
Python	GJ69 249 1818 4502			
Quail	294 5020			
Queen Alexandra	4127			
Queen Empress	3435 4637			
Queen Mab	W&FJ10			
Queen Mary	4971			
Queen of the Belgians	5305			
Quernmore	L&C4 1287 3242			
Quicksilver	225 496 438			
Racehorse	5016			
Raglan	306 996			
Raleigh	994 3030			
Ralph Brocklebank	5145			
Ramillies	4004			
Rapid	L&M37			
Raven	L&M86 281 St.H21 3017			
Raymond Poincaré	5302			
R.B.Sheridan	5183			
Red Gauntlet	597 4774			
Redbreast	L&M99 187			
Redstart	L&M98 357 373			
Redwing	L&M88 291			
Renown	3943			
Resolution	3944			
Revenge	4203			
Reynard	260 1911 3744			
Rhinocerus	167			
Ribble	363 P&WHDR/St.H10 L&C19 630			

Richard Arkwright	3858 5123
Richard Cobden	1685 3062 5444
Richard Moon	3477 4627
Richard Trevithick	3479 4548
Richd Francis Rober	2734
Rickerby	L&C1
Rob Roy	3929
Robert Benson	1903 3615
Robert Burns	5173
Robert L.Stevenson	5182
Robert Southey	5167
Roberts	407 733 3441
Robin Hood	3931
Rocket	L&M1 223 2226 3743
Roderic	L&M60 118
Roebuck	182 5017
Rokeby	L&M59
Rose	223 390
Rowland Hill	271 1008 2905 4526
Royal George	3933
Royal Oak	4202
Royal Sovereign	4050
Ruby	194
Rupert Guinness	5233
Russell	111 442
St.Arnaud	318 397
St.David	205 740
St.Germans	276
St.George	203 1844 3382 5128
St.Patrick	208 1842 3375
Saddleback	GJ84 L&C10 2280 3378 5129
Saddleworth	H&M/S Div4
Safety	SS15
Salopian	248 1920 3600
Samson	L&M13 L&M66 120 419 624 3135 5276
Sandon	GJ 86 855
Sankey	St.H8
Sanspareil	887 3373 4688
Saracen	GJ 1i GJ1ii/St.H12 208 526 4783
Sarmatian	2743 4509
Saturn	L&M16
Scorpion	GJ 7/St.H15 209 527 4492
Scotia	1286 1302 3290 5451
Scott	981 3143 5272
Scottish Chief	3475 4628
Sedbergh	L&C78
Sedgwick	L&C3 1286 3044
Sefton	210 391 285 ex-BL&CJ22
Senator	106 1815 4451
Serpent	344 1860
Servia	2736 4516
Severn	St.H19
Shah of Persia	1684 3345
Shakespeare	980 3064 4635
Shamrock	1165 3250 4676
Shannon	St.H22 S&P
Shap	214 ex-L&C1
	L&C20 214 685 3358
Shark	GJ3 319 1861 3444 5313
Shooting Star	2673 4503

Shropshire	*4861*
Simoom	*274 4440*
Simoon	*1816*
Sir Alexander Cockburn	*2406 3660*
Sir Arthur Lawley	*5338*
Sir Charles	L&CH
Sir Charles Cust	*5565*
Sir Francis Dent	*5344*
Sir Frank Ree	*5139*
Sir Frederick Harrison	*5140*
Sir Gilbert Claughton	*5117*
Sir Guy Calthrop	*5340*
Sir Hardman Earle	*2034 3559*
Sir Herbert Walker	*5343*
Sir Herbert Walker K.C.B.	*5343*
Sir John French	*5303*
Sir Robert Turnbull	*5138*
Sir Salar Jung	*2037 3745*
Sir Thomas Brooke	*4977*
Sir Thomas Williams	*5369*
Sir W.S.Gilbert	*5190*
Siren	58 *1700 3374*
Sirius	GJ30 *321* W&FJ13 *1693 3464*
Sirocco	GJ 24i GJ24ii *279 1811 4452*
Sister Dora	*3453*
Sisyphus	*1177 3150 4836*
Skiddaw	83 L&C9 *1846 3383*
Smeaton	*925 3022 5311*
Snake	*342 398 2749 4517*
Snipe	*296 5026*
Snowdon	227 *1918*
Soho	B&L16 125 *522*
Solway	C&W4
Soult	*586*
South Africa	*5006*
Speedwell	L&M38
Speke	*1178 3249*
Sphinx	GJ70 *70 1858 3456 5273*
Spitfire	215 *366 435 735 3360*
S.R.Graves	*1690 3051 5125*
Stafford	SS6
Staffordshire	*4862*
Stag	SS17
Staghound	*4998*
Standedge	H&M/S Div 246
Stanley	257
Star	L&M41 65 St.H14 *464*
Starling	L&M96 *315 372*
Stentor	GJ6 *314 5470*
Stephenson	*201 530 4638*
Stewart	398 498 *2045 3777*
Stork	L&M77 *215 992 2903 4518*
Sultan	GJ57 *57 977 4052*
Sun	L&M17 L&M53 164 St.H20
Sunbeam	GJ42 *377 2746 4493*
Superb	*4051*
Sutherland	266 *422 734 3369*
Suvla Bay	*5319*
Swallow	L&M69/St.H9 128
Swan	L&M79/St.H5 *251* 629
Swift	*194* 717
Swiftsure	L&M 36 *3021 4462*

Sybil	GJ45 45 45 *1854 3446*
Sydney Smith	*5170*
Sylph	SS14
Syren	GJ58
Talavera	*1166 3065*
Talbot	213
Talisman	GJ35 35 35 ex-BL&CJ 35 *786 3127 5521*
Tamerlane	GJ2 *292* 1003 *2904 4417*
Tantalus	GJ60 60 *428 4472*
Tara	*5326*
Tartarus	GJ39 *405 682 3365*
Tebay	L&C79
Telford	*924 3149 5447*
Temeraire	*4053*
Tennyson	*1283 1303 3151 5380*
Terrier	*325 400 628 3118 4788*
Teutonic	*3102 4527*
T.H.Ismay	*3995*
Thalaba	GJ36 36 36 ex-BL&CJ 36 *787 3128 5544*
The Auditor	*2219 3492*
The Duke of Edinburgh	*921 3043*
The Earl of Chester	*880 3368*
The Nile	*1170 3197 5309*
The Queen	109 *1481 3287*
The Tsar	*4527*
Theodore	*328*
Theorem	183 *454 686 3384*
Theseus	254 1002
Thomas B.Macaulay	*5178*
Thomas Campbell	*5181*
Thomas Carlyle	*2508 3507*
Thomas Gray	*5184*
Thomas Houghton	*4989*
Thomas Moore	*5175*
Thomas Savery	*3865 4833*
Thunderbolt	204 *1817 4453*
Thunderer	L&M44 BL&CJ37 *2797 4463*
Tiger	L&M58 117 *465 4519*
Tiny	Crewe NG
Tipton	SS29
Titan	L&M34 *2796 4441*
T.J.Hare	*4983*
Tomlinson	BS2587
Topsy	Crewe NG
Torch	GJ51 51 895
Tornado	*585 4629*
Touchstone	C&B3
Trafalgar	221 495 *448 4054*
Traveller	*5018*
Trent	St.H2 *738 3115 5314*
Trentham	92 894 *2669 4483*
Trevithick	*257 406*
Triplex	54
Tubal	*248 439 736 3124 4539*
Tubal Cain	W&FJ8
Turk	*301 434 737 3138*
Tyne	St.H11
Typhon	GJ71 *246 1698 3129 5134*

Ulleswater	L&C81 397
Umpire	*329* 1000
Una	*229* 998
Underley	L&C83
Unicorn	233 233 *1859 3469*
Vampire	GJ43 43 *1851 3466*
Vandal	GJ59 59 980 *2891 4454*
Vanguard	*5019*
Varna	*304*
Vauxhall	SS27
Velocipede	187 *2627 4528*
Venus	L&M18
Vernon	251
Vesta	L&M24
	L&M56 *334*
Vesuvius	L&M43 *3018 4464*
Viceroy	*261*
Victor	*2671 4484*
Victor Hugo	*5171*
Victoria	(L&M69,1) L&PJ *589 4684*
Victoria and Albert	*4128*
Victorious	*4134*
Victory	B&L11
	L&M22 *453*
Vimiera	*1169 3192*
Vindictive	*5541*
Violet	224 224 ex-C&B8 *469 632 3357*
Viper	SS 16
Virago	*346*
Viscount	105 *1814 4473*
Vizier	GJ23i GJ23ii *299 1805 4504*
Volante	BL&CJ32
Voltigeur	BL&CJ33
Vulcan	L&M19 *195* W&FJ14 275 *1305 3024*
	5269
Vulture	GJ47 47 853 *2234 4494*
Walsall	SS2
Warrior	*305 1820 3999*
Warwickshire	*4863*
Wasp	(*241*) 241 979
Waterloo	220 *446 684 3112*
Watt	229 *425 4529*
Waverley	*598 4474*
W.C.Brocklehurst	*4974*
W.E.Dorrington	*5228*
Weaver	BL&CJ26
Wednesbury	SS3
Wellington	218 *529 4775*
Wennington	L&C70
Westminster	*4984*
Westmorland	*4864*
Wheatstone	*2506 3729*
(White Raven)	St.H21
Whitworth	*408 781 3113*
Widgeon	*5028*
Wild Duck	*5023*
Wildfire	GJ8 *322 1843 3130*
William Baker	*2251*
William Cawkwell	*3478 4639*
William Cowper	*5191*

William Froude	*3860 5121*
William Siemens	*3866 5122*
Windermere	GJ83 *333 393* P&WHDR K&W
	259/L&C67 *5228*
Wirral	C&B1
Witch	GJ14i GJ14ii *1383 3198 5310*
Wizard	GJ21 *354 2053 3574*
W.M.Thackeray	*5185*
Wolfe	*991 3067*
Wolfhound	*4991*
Wolverhampton	SS9
Wolverine	*5038*
Woodcock	295 *5029*
Woodlark	L&M89 *199 548 688 3452*
Worcestershire	*4865*
Wordsworth	GJ82 *1682 3199 4837*
Wyre	*185 614 2282 3467*
York	L&M42
Yorkshire	*4866*
Zamiel	GJ11 *359 1695 3120 4866 5268*
Zeno	BL&CJ1 *782 3448*
Zillah	BL&CJ5 *785 3119 4131*
Zopyrus	BL&CJ2 *783 3442*
Zygia	BL&CJ4 *784 3362*

ACKNOWLEDGMENTS

The publication of LMS LOCOMOTIVE NAMES in 1994 resulted in quite a considerable correspondence, all of a helpful and friendly nature, and much of it relating to the names of London & North Western Locomotives which came into London Midland and Scottish stock in 1923. Apart from those who have died, I have lost none of the friends I mentioned in that book, and have gained many new ones who have contributed out of the store of their own knowledge of the subject. Their work has not been in vain: I have sifted through the letters and information I have received, and have included everything in the way of additions and corrections that I considered ought to be included in this L&NWR LOCOMOTIVE NAMES book.

I wish to record my gratitude for the help and guidance so many have given me, and particularly to Messrs Hugh Ballantyne, Roger Bell, Michael Bentley, Everard Beauchamp, Reg Bond, the late Harold Bowtell, Mike Burnett, David Camis, Greg Child, Brian Cooke, John Edgington, Bernard Harding, Clive Holden, Harry Jack, the late Professor Mike Page, Alan Pearsall, E.V.Richards, J.W.P.Rowledge, Edward Talbot, Richard Taylor, John True, David Walker, John Ward and the late Willie Yeadon, together with all those others who have helped, namely the members of the Crimean War Research Association, of Greenwich Public Library, St.Helens Town Hall and Local History Archives Library, Huddersfield Public Library, The Jockey Club, Shropshire County Council and of the Wildfowl & Wetlands Trust.

Everard Beauchamp, Reg Bond, Bernard Harding, Clive Holden, Harry Jack, Peter Rowledge, Ted Talbot, Dick Taylor, David Walker and others have proved themselves indefatiguable proof readers, and have spent countless hours and burned much tobacco (well, some of them) at their task, and deserve special mention. Between them they have given me advice and corrected errors of every kind. I owe them a huge debt of gratitude.

July 2002 John Goodman

BIBLIOGRAPHY

E.L.Ahrons	The British Steam Railway Locomotive 1825-1925.
Christopher Awdry	Encyclopaedia of British Railway Companies. Patrick Stephens Ltd. 1990.
Peter E.Baughan	A Regional History of the Railways of Great Britain Volume 11 North and Mid Wales. David & Charles 1980.
D.Baxter (Ed).	British Locomotive Catalogue Vols 2A/2B/3A/3B, Moorland 1978/1979/1982/1982.
R.Bell & E.Talbot.	The Locomotive Nameplates of the London & North Western Railway Premier Portfolio 3, London & North Western Railway Society 1984.
R.L.V.ffrench Blake.	Extracts from "The Crimean War".
Bonner Smith & Dewar	"Russian War, 1854".
Board of Trade	Reports 11.1841 (Bradshaw).
Harold D.Bowtell	Rails through Lakeland. Silver Link Publishing Ltd. 1988.
D.L.Bradley	A Locomotive History of Railways on The Isle of Wight RCTS 1982.
J.J.Colledge	Ships of the Royal Navy.
Brian Cooke	The Grand Crimean Central Railway.
C.P.Davis.	The Webb 'Experiment' Compounds. Premier Portfolio 4, London & North Western Society 1985.
P.C.Dewhurst	"The Locomotive" March 1955. Commentary on "Railway Locomotives down to the end of 1831".
Dictionary of National Biography.	Oxford University Press 1917 (1959-1960 Reprint).
Duckworth & Langmuir	"Railway and other Steamers".
David Eggenberger	"A Dictionary of Battles" 1967.
Stephen P.Goodall	The Vale of Clwyd Railway. 1982.
M.D.Greville	Chronology of the Railways of Lancashire and Cheshire. Journal of the Railway & Canal Historical Society 1981.
Clive Hardy	E.E.Wilson & Co. Locomotive Works list. Thomas Aleksandr 1981.
Hargreaves	Locomotive list of 21st November 1845 (LNW Archives, Kew).
Harry Jack.	The L.N.W.R.Bloomers Wolverton's 7ft Singles. Premier Portfolio 6, London & North Western Society 1987. Locomotives of the LNWR Southern Division R.C.T.S. 2001.
James	A Chronology of the Construction of Britain's Railways 1776-1855. Ian Allen 1983.
Gwyn Briwnant Jones & Denis Dunstone	The Origins of the LMS in South Wales. Gomer Press 1998.
H.F.F.Livesey.	The Locomotives of the L.N.W.R., The Railway Publishing Co. 1948.
James W.Lowe	British Steam Locomotive Builders. Goose & Son 1975.
E.T.MacDermot	History of the Great Western Railway, Volume 1 Great Western Railway Company 1927.
Capt.T.D.Manning and Cmdr.C.E.	Walker British Warship Names 1969.

J.Marshall	A Biographical Dictionary of Railway Engineers, David & Charles 1978.
Navy Record Society	The Russian War, Official Correspondence 1943.
G.P.Neele.	Railway Reminiscences 1889.
O.S.Nock	Premier Line, The story of London & North Western Locomotives Ian Allen 1952.
O.S.Nock.	The LNWR Precursor Family, David & Charles 1966.
O.S.Nock.	North Western Ian Allen 1968.
Colin Reed	Premier Portfolio 10, London & North Western Society 1992 "Gateway to the West".
RCTS	The Locomotives of the Great Western Railway Part 3. 1956.
M.C.Reed	The London & North Western Railway. Atlantic Transport Publishers 1996.
E.E.Robinson Jnr.	The L.& N.W.R. 4-cylinder 4-4-0 Compound Passenger Engines & the 4-cylinder "Renown" Class Simples 1932, and the Corrigenda subsequently published.
E.E.Robinson Jnr.	The Claughton and Baby Scot classes 1934, and the Supplement published later containing Addenda and Corrigenda.
J.W.P.Rowledge	Locomotives Illustrated No 121 L&NWR 2-4-0s and 3 cyl Compounds.
S.S.Scott	Locomotives of the LNWR (Part 3) Typescript.
Ray Shill	"Some Notes on John Hargreaves Junior and His Locomotives" Journal of the Railway & Canal Historical Society No 146 November 1990.
D.H.Stuart & Brian Read	Loco Profile No 15 "The Crewe Types" Profile Publications 1971.
Edward Talbot	An Illustrated History of LNWR Engines. Oxford Publishing Co. 1985. 'Argus' Revealed. British Railway Journal No.17. 1987.
J.M.Tolson	The St.Helens Railway. Oakwood Press 1982.
R.H.G.Thomas.	"The Liverpool and Manchester Railway". Batsford 1980.
C.H.A.Townley, C.A.Appleton, F.D.Smith, J.A.Peden.	"The Industrial Railways of Bolton, Bury and the Manchester Coalfield Part1. Bolton and Bury." Runpast Publishing 1994
Russell Wear	The Locomotive Builders of Kilmarnock. Industrial Railway Record No.69. 1977.
C.Williams.	A Register of all the Locomotives now in use 1912.
C.Williams	A Register of all the Locomotives now in use on the London & North-Western Railway, Author 1922.
C.Williams	Supplement to the Register (1922 Edition) of London & North-Western Locomotives, Author 1924.
Willie B.Yeadon.	A Compendium of LNWR Locomotives 1912-1949 Part One Passenger Tender Engines, Challenger Publications 1995.
F.Whishaw	The Railways of Great Britain and Ireland (List of locomotives) London 1841.

Magazines, Periodicals:
 Railnews.
 Steam Days.
 Steam World.
 The Railway Magazine.
 The Railway Observer.
 The Journal of the Stephenson Locomotive Society.
 The LNWR Society Premier News and the Society Journal.

A SEQUEL TO

LMS LOCOMOTIVE NAMES

THE NAMED LOCOMOTIVES OF THE
LONDON, MIDLAND AND SCOTTISH RAILWAY
AND ITS CONSTITUENT COMPANIES

JOHN GOODMAN

THE RAILWAY CORRESPONDENCE AND TRAVEL SOCIETY

2002

Fowler 2-6-4T 2313 *The Prince.* Note the date of the Prince of Wales visit to Derby visible under the "E" of Prince, 24.4.28

(John Ward Collection)

CONTENTS

LMS SEQUEL

PREFACE

My interest in railways and in locomotives especially began at an early age and one of my most cherished possessions was a copy of "Great Western Railway Engines Names, Numbers, Types and Classes". Each summer holiday the family exchanged houses, my grandparents coming to look after our home in Birmingham, while we all went to theirs in Paignton, where the house was in sight of the railway. Some of the family preferred to spend the day on the beach, but this member of it was usually to be found on a seat in Victoria Park near the level crossing, waiting for the bell to ring and the level crossing gates to open for the next train. The journeys there and back via Bristol Temple Meads were of course memorable. I carefully underlined the named engines that came my way, and kept a notebook containing the numbers of those which were unnamed.

From home I preferred to go into the City by train rather than by bus, and for 2d return made my way to New Street Station and back; but to my regret I knew of no LMS equivalent of the GWR books, and began to compile my own lists of their named engines - thus making the occasional mistake - for instance noting down what I believed to be "Edith Flavell", setting out from Crewe on an Up Express. After all, we had a boy of that surname in my form at school!

Then one day I found at the bookstall on New Street Station "Locomotives of the LMS Past & Present" by The Locomotive Publishing Co. Ltd, and was delighted to find on page 44 onwards a "List of Named Engines". I have it to this day. It included the information that 6161 was named *The King's Own* and so it must have been published late in 1930. Just what I wanted! Or was it? For the book informed me that 5014 was named *Murdoch*, whereas I had written it down as I stood by it at Rugby before travelling behind it to Lubenham, and felt sure I had spelled it correctly as *Murdock*. Then I noticed that both 5311 and 5317 were named *Express*, which was unbelievable, and as I discovered later the lists contain more than a dozen errors.

To add to the confusion, the Railway Magazine later published a list of LMS engine names faithfully copying every error in that book. How many errors, once having appeared in print have been copied again and again. Many of the errors in my book, which I have corrected here have in fact been "source errors".

It was comforting to realise that I wasn't the only list-maker to make mistakes.

To cut a long story short, I have made many many errors since then, but so to a greater or lesser degree have the compilers and publishers of the many lists I have since studied.

So, shortly after "LMS LOCOMOTIVE NAMES" appeared in 1994, several readers wrote pointing out errors in it, of which there are an embarrassingly large number; but they also provided a mass of additional information. To my wholehearted appreciation the entire work has been scrutinised as if under a microscope, and I owe it to many readers that this Sequel has been made possible, and in particular I want to pay tribute to Reg Bond, Bernard Harding, Clive Holden, Ron Simpson, Ray Townsin and John True who must have spent countless hours proof-reading, checking and doing research on every detail of the book, and without whom this new work could never have been attempted or published.

The question "Who was responble for choosing engine names?" crops up from time to time. I addressed the subject briefly in my Preface to "LMS Locomotive Names" by writing "Who chose them?". One answer has recently emerged in a letter from W.A.Stanier to T.F.Coleman, the Chief Draughtsman at Derby, dated 20th April 1936 in connection with the naming of the Stanier Class 5 4-6-0 Locomotives, and signed by him.

An extract reads:- "With reference to your letter of the 17th instant, notification was received from the Vice-President in February last that it had been decided to name Engines Nos. 5157 and 5158 "Glasgow Highlander" and "Glasgow Yeomanry" respectively".

All I hope is that this "SEQUEL" to "LMS Locomotive Names" will, together with its predecessor, provide us with a reasonably comprehensive and accurate version of the fine collection of names that appeared on LMS locomotives.

And I was at least correct about that name *Murdock*!

JOHN GOODMAN
May 2001

Fig. 84   Renewed Precedent 1488 *Murdock,* at Carlisle.

Locomotive & General Railway Photographs 22686. (Everard Beauchamp Collection).

Chapter 1

INTRODUCTION

The correct title of what was given as "The Amalgamation Act 1921" was "The Railways Act 1921".

At the time of the formation of the LMS on 1st January 1923 there were eight hundred and eleven named locomotives, as follows:-

Caledonian Railway	1
Cleator & Workington Junction Railway	6
Glasgow & South Western Railway	1
Leek & Manifold Valley Light Railway	2
Knott End Railway	4
Highland Railway	84
London & North Western Railway	667
North Staffordshire Railway	3
Departmental Stock Standard Gauge	12
At Crewe Works (Narrow gauge)	7
At Horwich Works (Narrow gauge)	8
Permanent Way Department (Narrow gauge)	3
Belfast & Northern Counties Railway	5
Ballycastle Railway (Narrow gauge)	2
Dundalk Newry & Greenore Railway	6
	Total 811

The named locomtives, by classes, at the birth of British Railways were:-

L&NWR Survivors	5
Departmental Stock	4
Class 5	4
Patriot	37
Jubilee	191
Royal Scot	71
Princess Royal	12
Princess Coronation	37
Highland Railway Survivors	14
Northern Counties Committee	31
Dundalk Newry & Greenore Railway	5
	Total 411

To sum up, the LMS began life in 1923 with eight hundred and eleven named locomotives, and ended up in December 1947 with four hundred and eleven.

Chapter 2

LONDON & NORTH WESTERN RAILWAY

Additional information Details:-

Renewed Precedent L&NWR 2190 (LMS 5000)was named *Beatrice* from 4.1875 until sometime later that same year, and then *Lady Beatrice* until 13th March 1877, when it was renamed *Princess Beatrice*.

Renown class LMS No (5134) was named *John O Gaunt* and photographs have established that the plates included neither the apostrophe nor a full stop. The plates were new and were not those carried on the L&NWR Waterloo class 2-4-0 No 1163.

Alfred the Great class 1961 LMS 5140 carried the name *Albermarle* for a few months until the spelling was corrected.

George the Fifth class LMS 25348 *Coronation*. Despite the claim on the nameplate, it wasn't in fact the 5,000th engine built at Crewe Works, but was assigned the 5,000th Crewe motion number.

George the Fifth class 5409 *Dovedale* was renumbered 25409 at Rugby Works.

Experiment class 5492 *Sanspareil* retained its name until withdrawal in December 1928.

Prince of Wales class. Precise dates for the earliest withdrawals of the class have come to light. The first to go was 5632 *Bret Harte* on September 5th 1933, followed by 5688/52/22/06 later that month,

Fig. 85   Renown 1921 *John O Gaunt*

Photograph by G.J.Alcock (Everard Beauchamp Collection).

Fig. 86   Waterloo 1163 *John O Gaunt*

L&GRP No. 15120 (Everard Beauchamp Collection).

and 5600/9/10/39/49 in October.

Claughton class. 5946 *Duke of Connaught.*, 5953 *Buckingham.*, 5966 *Bunsen.* and 6004 *Princess Louise*, all had the fullstop at the end of the name.

The nameplates of *L/CORPL J.A.CHRISTIE V.C.* have in the abbreviated `Corporal' two dots under a raised smaller capital `L'

6023 *Sir Charles Cust* was permanently named in 12.1921. The nameplate dates from 10.1921, used temporarily on other locomotives of the class for Royal train working.

The nameplates of *C.J.Bowen Cooke* show no sign of any alteration of the building date; The accounts of a plate dated May 1920 having been brazed over are a myth. Even though the locomotive had an official building date of May 1920 it was not completed until October. The number 2059 was not available until after the withdrawal of the "Bill Bailey" that September.

The L&NWR intrusion into LMS times had a singular effect upon some of the 1923 nameplates. It has been established that the January pair, *Talisman* and *Ingestre* had the letters "L & N W R Co." on their plates, and that those named from then on had instead the letters

"LMS". Each plate also contained the building date of the locomotive concerned.

Amendments:-
Precursor class 4-4-0

Date of Naming	LMS Number	Date of Naming	LMS Number
9.1905	5213	3.1904	5285
7.1905	5214	4.1905	5287
10.1905	5225	11.1904	5289
7.1905	5274	2.1905	5299

Published lists of these dates vary slightly, and this occurs particularly when the date comes at the end of one month and the start of the next; the dates listed above tally with the table published in W.Yeadon's "Compendium of LNWR Locomotives 1912-1949 Part One" (April 1995).

Corrections:-

Details:-

The nameplates of *Cornwall* are 3in deep, with letters of 2 1/2in.
  George the Fifth class. The standard nameplate length was 4ft 9in.
  Claughton class. The name was removed from 6004 *Princess Louise*. in December 1936.
  During 1922 a start was made towards naming the whole class. Three received the names of L&NWR employees who had won the Victoria Cross during the War, one after the warship *Vindictive*. Thus on 1st January 1923, fifty named Claughtons came into LMS Stock. During 1923, ten others were given some of the old familiar L&NWR names, bringing the final named total to sixty.

There were sundry other errors in this chapter which may be summarised best in the following table, but for a full record please refer to "L&NWR Locomotive Names".

The corrections are:-

Locomotive of class	L&NWR Number	LMS Number	Name	Date withdrawal
Renewed		(5004)	*Minotaur*	12.1927
Precedent		5013	*Pioneer*	1.1928
		5023	*Dagmar*	2.1932
		(5028)	*Ariadne*	9.1925
	2192	(5043)	*Caradoc*	
		5075	*Balmoral*	8.1931
Waterloo		5084	*Bee*	1.1932
(or Whitworth)		(5089)	*North Star*	
		5104	*Woodlark*	9.1931
Precursor		5199	*Cedric*	12.1933
		5221	*Vizier*	12.1930
		5222	*Alaska*	9.1933
		5312	*Velocipede*	12.1935
			(The name was removed in July 1933)	
George the Fifth	25324		*John Bateson*	11.1938
	2512	5338	*Thomas Houghton*	
Experiment		5461	*City of London (25461)*	
		5475	*Ivanhoe*	6.1935
		5476	*Leander*	8.1931
		5479	*Shakespeare*	1.12.1934
			(Cut up 17.10.1935)	
		5524	*Babylon*	1.1932
		5529	*Berenice*	12.1933
	25532		*Britomart*	9.1934
Prince of Wales	25642		*King of the Belgians*	3.1936
	25643		*King of Serbia*	11.1934
	1352	5653		
	1379	5654		
	1484	5655		
	1084	5656		
	1346	5657		
	2417	5658	*Atlas*	
	2442	5659		
Claughton		5921	*Sir Arthur Lawley*	1.12.1934
		(5976)		
		(5988)		
		6008	*Lady Godiva*	6.2.1933
		5999	*Vinductor* name removed 9.1936	

Additional information:-

The LMS Re-numbering Scheme of February 1934
The scheme was evolved to reduce to a minimum the amount of renumbering which had to be undertaken in order to bring all standard engines into numbers below 10,000.

Stage A IMMEDIATE RE-NUMBERING

Increase by 20,000
2-4-0   5001
4-6-0   Experiments between 5500 and 5552 inclusive
        5502/4/6/8/9/11/4/23/5/6/8/31/2/9/48/51/2 (5506wdn)

4-6-0   Prince of Wales 5600 - 5664 inclusive
        5601-5/7/8/11-21/3-31/3-8/40-8/50/1/3-64

5500-10 (5971/02/59/85/7/49/74/36, 6010/05/12)

5511-9   (5942/66/58/83/92/82/52, 6006/8)
5520-2   (5954/33/73)
5523-9   (6026, 5907/16/63/44/96/26)
5530-5   (6022/27/11, 5905/35/97)
5536-41   (6018/15/00. 5925/01/03)

Stage B ENGINES TO BE RE-NUMBERED AS THEY PASS THROUGH SHOPS

Increase by 20,000

0-6-0ST   7334

Experiment and Prince of Wales classes between 5450 and 5845 inclusive

      5456/7/60-2/6/73/5/9/87/8/91/7

and   5665-87/9-5845

    (25672 - Crewe 3.4.1934 and 25694 - Crewe 3.4.1934
already dealt with)

Stage C OTHER NON-STANDARD ENGINES,

having numbers below 10,000 will only be re-numbered as and when existing numbers are encroached upon by standard engines. The non-standard engines will then have 20,000 added to their existing numbers

Note: The above lists are an extract taken from the full documents to contain only those engines which carried names.

Later research on the progress of this scheme has resulted in:-

Precursor class

    5231/9/41/3/4/6/8/50/70/4/6/8/80/1/3/5/89/90/5/6,
    5301/3/5/6/8/9/12-8

were withdrawn before the 20,000 prefix was announced.

5284 was renumbered 25284   This one should have been renumbered under Stage C "when their numbers were required for new construction", but it was done on 11.8.1936 at Rugby Works shortly before, it is assumed, some major fault was found.   The locomotive was towed to Crewe, and was withdrawn eleven days later on 22.8.1936.

George the Fifth class

5344 was withdrawn without being renumbered.

5409 was renumbered on 4.6.1937; Class 5 No 5409 was built in
    mid September 1937.

Experiment class

5457/60-2/6/75/9/87/8/91/7, 5506/23/6/39/48/51
were withdrawn without being renumbered.

Fig. 87   5600 *Prince of Wales,* one of the first of the class to be withdrawn, on 21st November 1933.

Photograph by C.J.Alcock (Everard Beauchamp Collection).

Fig. 88   The nameplate of Claughton *Lady Godiva*. Note the letters "LMS" at the left end of the plate.

(J.Mander Collection).

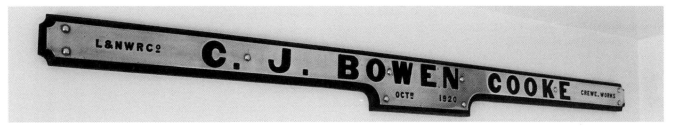

Fig. 89   The nameplate *C.J.Bowen Cooke.*

(Michael Bentley).

Glossary
Additional information and corrections of fact:-

The vast majority of new information and corrected entries will be found in the glossaries in L&NWR Locomotive Names. Included here are those of particular interest and importance.

Albion	1915	The engine of 1915 was named after the Battleship of 1901-1919, which served in the Dardanelles 1915.
Castor	1916	The Light Cruiser of 1915, which took a leading role in the battle of Jutland, and received several hits. Sold 1936.
Colossus	1899	The Battleship of 1882-1908.
Condor	1916	This was also the name of C.J.Bowen Cooke's yacht.
Delhi	1868 1890	The Indian town, re-captured in September during the Indian Mutiny. Delhi did not become the Capital of India until 1912.
Edith Cavell	1915	She was executed on 12th October 1915, and is buried beside Norwich Cathedral.
John Mayall	1885 1913	It is far more likely that the engine was named after the specialised cotton spinner, of Mossley. 1803-1876.
Leamington		Renamed `Leamington Spa` later in 1915.
Minerva	1915	The 2nd Class Cruiser of 1895-1920 which served in the Dardanelles.
Novelty	1829 1892 1928 1936	There appear to be several ways of spelling "Ericson". One old print which appears in The Railway Magazine Volume 67 page 181 refers to him as "Erricsson of London", where the double `s` is written in continental fashion, but the most usual form is "Ericsson".
President	1850 1906	No British Railway had a President until Sir Josiah Stamp in LMS days.
St.George		By 1913 she had been converted into a Destroyer Depot Ship, and as such might not have warranted a name. This was however also the name of another "Discovery ship", of 1701-1716.
Shark	1916	The Destroyer of 1912 - 31.5.1916, lost at Jutland.
Wyre	1851 1896	The historical details given were not quite correct. The Preston & Wyre Railway, Harbour & Dock Co was leased to the Manchester & Leeds Railway in 1847, with the latter changing its name later that year to the Lancashire & Yorkshire Railway. In 1849 the Preston & Wyre lines were vested jointly in the LYR and L&NWR and it remained a joint line until the LYR and L&NWR amalgamated on 1 January 1922, just prior to the Grouping.

Glossary   The names proposed but never applied.

Additional information and corrections of fact:-

Duke of Edinburgh	This appears to have been just the revival of a former name, for there does not seem to have been a Duke of Edinburgh in 1923.				
Florence	The proposed re-use of this name in 1923 might possibly have been to honour the wife of Mr.H.P.M.Beames, Chief Mechanical Engineer of the L&NWR 1921.				
Marchioness of Stafford	In 1924 her name was Dorothy Hilda, who had married Francis Edward Fitzherbert-Stafford, 12th Baron Stafford in 1903.				
Outram	The engine was not named after Benjamin, the Canal engineer, but after Sir James Outram, who helped Havelock reinforce the garrison at Lucknow before it was finally relieved by Sir Colin Campbell.				
William Baker	Some sources give Robert Stephenson the title "Chief Engineer", 1846-1858, but he acted in his capacity as a consultant; William Baker was on the L&NWR staff, and was thus from 1858-1878 the company's first Chief				

Chapter 3

OTHER ENGLISH CONSTITUENTS

The Knott End Railway

Incorporated in 1864 as The Garstang and Knot End Railway, it opened in 1870 from Garstang to Pilling only. The company was in receivership between 1874 and 1897. It was purchased by a separate Knott End Railway Company in 1908, who completed the line between Pilling and Knott End. Passenger service was withdrawn on 31st March 1930, but it remained open in parts for goods and coal traffic until the final section to Garstang Town closed in August 1965.

LMS Number	Name	Type	Date and builder		Withdrawn
11300	*Jubilee Queen*	0-6-0ST	1897	Hudswell, Clarke No 484	11.3.1926
(11301)	*New Century*	0-6-0ST	1900	Hudswell, Clarke No 559	22.10.1925
(11302)	*Knott End*	0-6-0T	1908	Manning, Wardle & Co. No 1732	6.1924
11680	*Blackpool*	2-6-0T	1909	Manning, Wardle & Co. No 1747	10.1927

Jubilee Queen and *Blackpool* were overhauled and painted at Crewe in 1924.

Cleator & Workington Junction Railway

Promoted by firms connected with the local iron industry in objection to the high tariffs of existing railways, the line opened in 1879 from Cleator Moor to Workington, in 1882 from Distington to Rowrah, and in 1887 from Workington to Linefoot.

LMS Number	C&WJR Number	Name	Type	Builder/Number/Date		Withdrawn
	5	*Moresby Hall*	0-6-0ST	R.Stephenson & Co.	2692/1892	
11564	6	*Brigham Hill*	0-6-0ST	R.Stephenson & Co.	2813/1894	11.12.1926
11565	7	*Ponsonby Hall*	0-6-0ST	R.Stephenson & Co.	2846/1896	10.12.1927
11566	8	*Hutton Hall*	0-6-0ST	Peckett	1134/1907	3.12.1927
11567	9	*Millgrove*	0-6-0ST	Peckett	1340/1917	12.5.1928
11568	10	*Skiddaw Lodge*	0-6-0ST	Hudswell, Clarke & Co.	1400/1920	22.6.1932

Moresby Hall was withdrawn before the LMS numbering scheme was drawn up, and was seen in a scrapyard at Barrow in May 1924. 11564-7 were cut up soon after withdrawal, and 11568 was sold to R.Fraser & Sons, Hebburn-on-Tyne w/e 26.6.1932, rebuilt by Ridley, Shaw of Middlesbrough 1949, later to Hartley Main Colliery, N.C.B. No 21, and scrapped at Seaton Dalaval, 21.8.1956.

Moresby Hall A Director's Residence, Moresby lies about two miles NNE of Whitehaven.

North Staffordshire Railway

THE LEEK & MANIFOLD VALLEY LIGHT RAILWAY

1. *E.R.Calthrop*   2. *J.B.Earle*

Both locomotives were 2-6-4T and were built by Messrs Kitson & Co. in 1904. No 2 was Works No 4257, and No 1 4258.

There were no fullstops after the numerals on the plates.

The line closed in March 1934. No 1 was withdrawn in December 1936, and bought by Geo. Cohen, Sons & Co. Ltd., contractors of Stanningley near Bradford, Yorks, but was used on dismantling of the railway, and scrapped at Waterhouses October 1937. No 2 had gone to Crewe Works by October 1934, and was stored until sold to Geo. Cohen, Sons & Co. Ltd. in May 1937, moved to their yard at Stanningley and scrapped.

E.R.Calthrop Everard Richard Calthrop (1857-1927) was the eldest brother of Sir Guy Calthrop.

CALDON LOW QUARRY

This narrow gauge railway ran from Caldon Quarry to Froghall Wharf on Caldon Canal. The area around Froghall is noted for its profusion of frogs. (and presumably toads!).

There were three locomotives:

Frog and *Toad* were both built in 1877 by Henry Hughes & Company, of Loughborough. There is no date on *Toad*'s builder's plate, and it is known that the firm went out of business c.1878. The engines were acquired by the North Staffordshire Railway in May 1887.

Bobs was built in August 1901 by Messrs W.G.Bagnall Ltd, of Stafford (Works No 1634).

Bobs This was the nickname of Field Marshal Earl Roberts of Kandahar, C-in-C during the South African War.

Chapter 4

DEPARTMENTAL LOCOMOTIVES
The Engineers

Several more precise dates concerning the Engineers have come to light:-

Engineer	Class	No.	Name	Dates
Engineer	Samson	885	*Vampire*	5.1897 - 5.1923
	Waterloo	792	*Theorem* (5099)	5.1923 - 6.1932
Engineer.Bangor	Samson	1166	*Wyre*	1.1902 - 14.12.1925
Engineer-Crewe	Waterloo	209	*Petrel*	7.1914 - 5.1932
Engineer Lancaster	Samson	414	*Prospero*	4.1903 - 2.1924
	Waterloo	737	*Roberts* (5100)	2.1924 - 7.1935
Engineer Liverpool	Waterloo	742	*Spitfire*	7.1921 - 3.10.1932
Engineer Manchester	Waterloo	2156	*Sphinx*	6.1914 - 9.1927
Engineer Northampton	Samson	209	*Petrel*	1.1902 - 5.1923
	Waterloo	468	*Wildfire* (5086)	5.1923 - 12.1927
Engineer South Wales	Waterloo	485	*Euxine*	2.1921 - 12.1931
	Waterloo		*Engineer-Crewe*	5.1932 - 8.1933

(Replaced by M.R. 155, later 20155. The nameplates had been removed at least by February 1937. Withdrawn 28.10.1950)

Engineer Walsall	Samson	2151	*Baltic*	c1904 - 6.1923
	Waterloo	609	*The Earl of Chester* (5094)	6.1923 - 2.1928
Engineer Watford	Samson	773	*Centaur*	7.1895 - 5.1923
	Waterloo	793	*Martin* (5101)	5.1923 - 13.12.1935

(Withdrawn from service as Engineer Watford on 13.12.1935, and replaced by M.R.20008 on that date, but not withdrawn until April 1936)

"Spare Engine"	Samson	2157	*Unicorn*	11.1901 - 5.1923
(unnamed)	Samson		*Engineer*	5.1923 - 3.1925

The photograph on page 46 of "LMS Locomotive Names" of *Engineer-Crewe* is "Waterloo class 209 *Petrel*", and not as indicated in the caption.

L&NWR "Special Tank" 0-6-0T No 8 *Earlestown*. The number 2359 was removed in May 1881. It was cut up at Crewe in November 1957.

Fig. 90   A contrast in nameplate sizes and styles. *Topsy* and *Earlestown*.

(Roger Bell).

Permanent Way Department.   2ft 6in gauge

Jim Crow   0-4-2ST Built by Hudswell, Clarke of Leeds, Works No 340, 3.1894 and still in existence in 1939.

Platelayer 0-4-0ST Built by W.G.Bagnall of Stafford, No 1410 of 1893, and delivered in November 1895 to Crewe with the name *Haulier*. Sold by LMS probably in 1941 to T.W.Ward Ltd., Templeborough, and although not recorded in their books, probably cut up. Date of change of name not known, but likely to have taken place early in its career. A photograph dated 27th March 1938 shows a nameplate possibly painted on a plate which was riveted or bolted to the cabside.

Kitchener 0-4-0ST Built by W.G.Bagnall of Stafford No 1999 of 1915. Its withdrawal date is not known, but it was still in existence in 1939.

Glossary

Haulier 1893 One who hauls.

Jim Crow   A platelayer's tool for bending rails. Not in O.E.D., so possibly railwaymen's slang.

L&NWR 0-4-0T. Crewe Works   18in gauge.

Name	Type	Built	Withdrawn
Tiny	0-4-0T	5.1862	25.3.1928, and cut up 2.5.1928
Pet	0-4-0T	6.1865	4.1929 Preserved
Nipper.	0-4-0T	1.1867	P10.1929 and not cut up until 12.2.1931
Topsy.	0-4-0T	1.1867	P10.1929 ditto
Midge	0-4-0T	11.1870	P10.1929 ditto
Billy.	0-4-0T	7.1875	P1.1931 Sold to J.Cashmore, Scrap Merchants, Great Bridge, near Dudley.
Dickie	0-4-0T	5.1876	P10.1929 and not cut up until 12.2.1931

Period 10 1929 was the four weeks ending 5.10.1929.

L&Y 0-4-0ST, with tender. Horwich Works 18in gauge.

Dot   Built 1887 (BP 2817/87) Worked initially in Beyer, Peacock's Works at Gorton Foundry, Manchester, then inside Crewe Works, and finally at Horwich. Withdrawn 1930 and now preserved at The Narrow Gauge Railway Museum, Towyn.

Robin Built 1887 Withdrawn between 1.3.1936 and 21.2.1937.

Wren Built 1887 Withdrawn 1961, and displayed on a plinth in Horwich Works Erecting Shop in July 1961 and now at the

Period 1 1931 was the four weeks ending 24.1.1931
There is evidence that *Tiny*, the first to be built, in 1862, was known as "The dwarf loco." until a name was chosen for it. All were built in the L&NWR works at Crewe, but were not allotted Crewe (Motion) numbers. *Billy* and *Dickie* were constructed by a team of men who worked for Mr.Webb on special projects under the foremanship of Mr.William Rylance, who signed himself as `Wm. Rylance & Co.`.

5519 *Crewe* A diesel locomotive. (Hudswell Clarke & Co. D563 of 12.1930) became ZM9 at Horwich where the nameplate was removed shortly after its arrival there in June 1935. It was replaced by another diesel locomotive ZM32 in October 1957.

Glossary

Topsy   Perhaps this was a reference to the character in "Uncle Tom's Cabin" who just 'grow'd'.

National Railway Museum, York. Prior to withdrawal it appeared in British Railways livery.

Wasp Built 1891 Horwich Withdrawn between 1.3.1936 and 4.1937.

Fly   Built 1891 Withdrawn 1930.

Mouse Built 1899 Withdrawn between 1.3.1936 and 4.1937.

Midget Built 1899 Withdrawn 1933.

Bee   Built 1901 Withdrawn 1930.

Miscellaneious Vehicles

Danby Lodge Standard gauge.

An 0-6-0ST built in March 1903 by Manning, Wardle No 1595 for John Scott (later Sir John) for the Grassholme Reservoir construction. It was bought in 1919 by the L&NWR from the Ministry of Munitions, Chilwell, and was used in widening the Standedge Tunnel, then in 1928-9 on work at Rolleston west curve, Notts. and in 1930-2 on widening at Mirfield, Yorks. It ended its days at Beeston in 1948. It had typical Manning, Wardle nameplates, cast, with raised lettering which were fixed to the locomotive's saddle tanks.

It was not included in the departmental stock, but was listed, together with other engines, (e.g. *Kitchener* and *Platelayer* of the P.W.Dept. and the narrow gauge Horwich Works engines) under "Miscellaneous Vehicles".

No 10 *Batley* 3ft gauge 0-4-0ST, built July 1924 (Bagnall 2233) and bought 1945 for use at the Beeston creosote works. Withdrawn w/e 22.10.1955.

Glossary

Batley 1945   The town in West Yorkshire, where the locomotive worked between 1926 and 1928, when owned by Lehane, Mackenzie & Shand for working on reservoir construction at Brownhill for Batley Corporation.

Chapter 5
LMS BUILT LOCOMOTIVES
Fowler 2-6-4T class 4P

2313 *The Prince*   The Prince of Wales visited Derby on 21st February, and painted under the "E" of "Prince", in small lettering was the date 21.2.28.

Class 5. 2 cyl. 4-6-0

According to a letter from Mr.W.A.Stanier to Mr.T.F.Coleman at Derby dated 20th April, the decision to name engines of this class can be traced back to February 1936. It refers to Engine No 5157 to be "Glasgow Highlander" and 5158 "Glasgow Yeomanry", and mentions that the ceremony in connection with 5157 had already taken place. Dates of naming were:-

5154	*Lanarkshire Yeomanry*	8.4.1937	
		5156	*Ayrshire Yeomanry*
			Earl of Carrick's Own
5157	*The Glasgow Highlander*	6.3.1936	
		5158	*Glasgow Yeomanry*
			Field Brigade R.A.T.A.

19.6.1936	
22.5.1936	

Some St.Rollox drawings have survived showing proposed designs for the Class 5 nameplates. One dated 24.2.36 depicts *The Glasgow Highlander* in a straight line, and another (undated) shows *The Ayrshire Yeoman* in the curved style finally adopted (with the words *The Ayrshire Yeomanry*) but with the *Earl of Carricks Own* in a straight line, and without an apostrophe. Several attempts were made before the design for *Glasgow Yeomanry* was finally approved; the first plan dated 5.4.36 shows a large radius curved two line plate worded "Queen's Own Royal" (top line) and "Glasgow Yeomanry" (lower line), with the plaque above; the second shows a stepped plate with the three words in the top line smaller, and the third a standard one line plate "Glasgow Yeomanry" but this time with the plaque below, and the fourth shows a design similar to the previous one but with the shorter radius which was finally adopted.

What is evident is that a great deal of thought and discussion was centred on the design of these plates.

A note in the Railway Magazine 1937 Volume 80 page 307 from Mr.D.S.Barrie reads:- "Class 5 5154 is to be renamed *Lanarkshire Yeomanry*", which suggests that for a short while it might have been named "The Lanarkshire Yeomanry".

5155 *Queen's Edinburgh.*

Two Memos from Mr.Stanier, one to Mr.H.G.Ivatt at St.Rollox, and one to Mr.J.Ballantyne at Glasgow, dated 19th February 1937 say that the name "Queen's Edinburgh" had been allocated to Engine No.5155, and that Engine No.5154 or Engine No.5159 be chosen to bear the name "Lanarkshire Yeomanry".

In 1937 Mr.D.S.M.Barrie includes 5155 *Queen's Edinburgh* in his "Modern Locomotives of the LMS", a book issued with the authority of the LMS.

The evidence continues with an official Memo dated 3rd March 1938 from the Chief Mechanical & Electrical Engineer's Department at Derby headed 'NAMING OF 4-6-0 2-CYLINDER MIXED TRAFFIC ENGINES' containing a list which includes "5155 *Queen's,Edinburgh* With plaque" and in which the typewritten apostrophe has been crossed out in ink, and an ink comma inserted in the space between the 's' and the 'E' close to the 's'.

This is followed by an official reply from Derby to an enquiry made on 28th July 1939 by a member of the public, a Mr.Seddon, in which he had asked about the names of specific engines. It includes:- "Engine No.5155 is not named" and is dated 3rd August 1939.

The next known official record is a Memo, also from Derby, dated 28th July 1944 and headed NAMING OF LOCOMOTIVES which states "Where it has not been possible to obtain the information from photographs, the engines given below have been specially examined in order to ascertain the correct names:-", and included in a list of fourteen, five by photographs, and the rest by examination, we find "5155 *Queens, Edinburgh*" (by examination). Apart from 6161 whose name was erroneously checked against a photograph 14 years out of date, all the names are correct to the last detail, but the placing of a comma in the case of 5155 causes one to raise an eyebrow. The fact that 6125 and 6137 are listed "with crest", indicates that 5155 did not have one, despite the Memo of 3rd March 1938.

There is strong evidence therefore that 5155 received its name sometime during the War, which, according to Peter Rowledge in "Engines of the LMS" was in 1942.

Finally in a "List of engines bearing names, correct at 30 Sept.1945" headed C.M.& E.E. Department, London Road Offices, Derby, 5154-5158 are listed, and beside the entry for 5155 *Queens, Edinburgh* is found, in pencil "? Name removed". When and by whom these words were added is, of course, unknown. Maybe he had read page 355 of the Nov/Dec.1944 issue of the Railway Magazine where we find "LMSR 4-6-0s No.5155 "The Queen's Edinburgh" (and 5514, 5518 and 6144) have had their names removed", and believed this to be correct.

On the other hand, no photograph of 5155 with a name has come to light, and according to the late Mr.A.G.Dunbar, who worked for many years in St.Rollox Works and later in St.Rollox shed, and was undoubtedly a reliable authority on the subject, "Class 5 5155 never received a name". Mr.Barrie, too, in 1982 wrote that there were "only four named Class 5MT locomotives".

It seems to me on balance that there was a 5155 *Queen's Edinburgh*, (with the apostrophe, as written by Mr.Stanier) and that up to the present day it remains impossible to be precise about the dates of application and removal of the nameplates.

Patriot Class 4-6-0

Naming date	Name removed	Number		Name
24.11.1933		5971	(5500)	*Croxteth*
25.2.1937			5500	*Patriot In Memory of the Fallen L.&.N.W.R. Employees 1914-1919*
13.11.1930	10.3.1937	5902	(5501)	*Sir Frank Ree*
17.4.1937			5501	*St Dunstan's*
5.6.1937		(5959)	5502	*Royal Naval Division*
8.7.1938		(5985)	5503	*The Leicestershire Regiment*
3.11.1948			(45503	*The Royal Leicestershire Regiment)*
10.4.1937		(5987)	5504	*Royal Signals*
8.1947		(5949)	5505	*The Royal Army Ordnance Corps*
15.9.1948		(5974)	(45506	*The Royal Pioneer Corps)*
20.11.1937		(5936)	5507	*Royal Tank Corps*
10.11.1951		(6005)	(45509	*The Derbyshire Yeomanry)*
12.1.1938		(5942)	5511	*Isle of Man*
Late 1933		5966	5512	*Bunsen*
9.7.1938 to 1941 and from 26.3.1947		(5983)	5514	*Holyhead*
15.1.1939		(5992)	5515	*Caernarvon*
31.7.1938		(5982)	5516	*The Bedfordshire and Hertfordshire Regiment*
9.6.1939 to mid 1942 and from 26.3.1947		(6006)	5518	*Bradshaw*
25.2.1933		6008	(5519)	*Lady Godiva*
28.3.1938		(5954)	5520	*Llandudno*
14.1.1938		(5933)	5521	*Rhyl*
22.3.1939		(5973)	5522	*Prestatyn*
20.6.1938		(6026)	5523	*Bangor*
14.3.1933	9.3.1937	5907	(5524)	*Sir Frederick Harrison*
23.3.1937			5524	*Blackpool*
22.3.1933	23.8.1937	5916	5525	*E.Tootal Broadhurst*
14.1.1938			5525	*Colwyn Bay*
6.10.1937		(5963)	5526	*Morecambe and Heysham*
15.9.1937		(5944)	5527	*Southport*
2.10.1959		(5996)	(45528	*R.E.M.E.)*
6.4.1933	7.9.1937	5926	5529	*Sir Herbert Walker K.C.B.*
w/e 24.7.1948			(45529	*Stephenson)*
10.3.1937		(6022)	5530	*Sir Frank Ree*
14.1.1938		(6027)	5531	*Sir Frederick Harrison*
10.4.1933		6011	(5532)	*Illustrious*
11.4.1933		5905	(5533)	*Lord Rathmore*
27.8.1937		(5935)	5534	*E.Tootal Broadhurst*
19.4.1938		(5997)	5535	*Sir Herbert Walker K.C.B.*
4.5.1933		6018	(5536)	*Private W.Wood, V.C.*
19.7.1933		6015	(5537)	*Private E.Sykes V.C.*
4.11.1938		(6000)	5538	*Giggleswick*
22.7.1933		5925	(5539)	*E.C.Trench*
7.8.1933		5901	(5540)	*Sir Robert Turnbull*
15.8.1933		5903	(5541)	*Duke of Sutherland*
30.7.1940			5543	*Home Guard*
3.11.1948			(45545	*Planet)*
18.7.1938			5546	*Fleetwood*
18.12.1937			5548	*Lytham St.Annes*

Numbers in brackets in column 4 are those which the locomotive, already named, was given as a result of the 1934 Renumbering Scheme.

5971 was seen carrying blank nameplate fixtures as early as 1.7.1931. According to one observer, 5514 *Holyhead* was still named in January 1939 being seen both then, and during the summer of 1940 with nameplates covered, presumably pending a naming ceremony. Another source however quotes a possible date for the removal of the name *Holyhead* from 5514 as 15.1.1939.

The nameplates of 5514 had been removed by the end of 1941 and those of 5518 by the middle of 1942.

5503/5/16, and in British Railways time 45506/9 had two line plates.

5501 *St Dunstan's* had a badge format plate.

The 'OF' in the plates *Isle of Man* and *Duke of Sutherland* appear in full size letters, as also the 'ST' in *Lytham St.Annes*.

In order to fit the nineteen letters into a single line plate, the 'AND' in *Morecambe and Heysham* was in smaller letters set on the base line.

The Coat of Arms above the nameplate of 5511 *Isle of Man* included the motto "*QUOCUNQUE JECERIS STABIT*" or "Wherever you throw it, it will stand."

The second plate of 45503 when revised to incorporate the Royal prefix was stepped, making it off-standard for a two row plate.

The plates of 45545 *Planet* were new, and not those formerly carried on Royal Scot 6131.

There were two styles of mounting the nameplate above the splasher.

The first had the nameplate almost flush with the top of the splasher, whilst the second had the nameplate raised about 2 1/2 inches above it. In the case of 5511 *Isle of Man*, the plates was raised to start with, and flush when the coat of arms were added.

5902 *Sir Frank Ree* was photographed in works grey with a longer than usual nameplate and with the words spaced further apart. A photograph of the engine in service shows it with a shorter nameplate similar in style to other members of the class.

Names selected in 1942, but never used:-

5505 Wemyss Bay	5529 Air Training Corps	5549 R.A.M.C.
5509 Commando	5542 Dunoon	5550 Sir Henry Fowler
5513 Sir W.A.Stanier	5545 The Royal Marine	5551 Rothesay

Names selected in 1948, but never used:-

Vulcan	Velocipede	Dragon
Goliath	Champion	
Courier	Harlequin	

Disposal of plates.

One of the nameplates from 45536 was presented in 1976 to Mr.Wilfred Wood, V.C., and he in turn presented it to his old school, Norbury Church of England Primary School.

Glossary

R.A.M.C.   The Royal Army Medical Corps began during the Crimean War as "The Medical Staff Corps", a very short-lived title, as it became the "Army Hospital Corps" in 1857.

Sir Henry Fowler was CME MR 1909-1922, and CME LMS 1925-1930.

Sir William Stanier was appointed CME LMS in 1932.

Jubilee class 4-6-0

Naming dates:-

A handwritten list of naming dates probably attributable to C.Williams has come to light which provides for the first time in print, the dates "With nameplates off works". It appears to have been compiled during February 1937, since it includes the naming of 5555 *Quebec* on 8th February 1937, and none after that. A few of these dates agree with those printed in "LMS Locomotive Names" and many are close to within a day or two. For simplicity of presentation the list is reproduced here:-

"With nameplates off Works"

5552	29.4.1935	5592	22.1.1936	5625	10.11.1936
5554	11.3.1936	5593	27.5.1936	5627	17.4.1936
5555	8.2.1937	5594	20.3.1936	5628	11.3.1936
5557	31.10.1936	5595	15.2.1936	5629	2.2.1937
5558	27.10.1936	5596	8.6.1936	5630	1.4.1936
5559	13.1.1937	5597	26.3.1936	5631	29.1.1936
5560	2.9.1936	5598	20.4.1936	5632	17.2.1936
5561	4.6.1936	5599	21.7.1936	5633	23.3.1936
5562	21.2.1936	5600	22.6.1936	5636	22.4.1936
5563	24.1.1936	5601	20.7.1936	5637	27.3.1936
5564	27.1.1936	5602	7.5.1936	5638	14.4.1936
5565	24.2.1936	5603	24.2.1936	5640	16.3.1936
5566	23.4.1936	5604	11.5.1936	5642	3.4.1936*
5567	16.3.1936	5605	28.7.1936	5647	27.4.1936
5568	21.9.1936	5606	21.9.1936	5648	29.6.1936
5569	10.2.1936	5607	20.7.1936	5651	29.1.1936
5570	16.1.1936	5608	13.3.1936	5653	16.4.1936

5571	4.5.1936	5609	22.9.1936	5654	29.5.1936
5572	24.3.1936	5610	24.2.1936	5656	4.3.1936
5573	10.2.1936	5611	24.12.1936	5657	3.2.1936
5574	26.5.1936	5613	16.3.1936	5658	23.1.1936
5579	2.10.1936	5614	11.1.1937	5659	2.3.1936
5582	13.10.1936	5616	6.8.1936	5661	4.2.1936
5585	30.6.1936	5618	27.3.1936	5662	11.3.1936
5586	2.4.1936	5619	8.4.1936	5664	7.4.1936
5587	11.5.1936	5621	30.7.1936	5665	26.11.1935*
5588	8.10.1936	5622	10.3.1936	5668	4.2.1937
5589	21.2.1936	5623	23.12.1936	5669	26.1.1937
5591	21.4.1936	5624	23.1.1936		

* 5642 "Booked off new 24.4.1935 Tender 4559"
* 5665 "Without nameplate, Off Works 18.11.1935, New"

5612	Fitted at Derby Plates sent	29.6.1936
5615		15.6.1936
5634		15.5.1936
5635		11.6.1936
5639		11.6.1936
5649		27.5.1936
5660		19.6.1936
5663		29.4.1936

"Named as built"

5680	31.12.1935	5701	24.4.1936	5722	24.8.1936
5681	31.12.1935	5702	5.5.1936	5723	26.8.1936
5682	6.1.1936	5703	6.5.1936	5724	2.9.1936
5683	16.1.1936	5704	11.5.1936	5725	25.9.1936
5684	6.2.1936	5705	21.5.1936	5726	9.10.1936
5685	31.1.1936	5706	26.5.1936	5727	12.10.1936
5686	5.2.1936	5707	27.5.1936	5728	7.10.1936
5687	10.2.1936	5708	1.6.1936	5729	13.10.1936
5688	24.2.1936	5709	3.6.1936	5730	16.10.1936
5689	28.2.1936*	5710	8.6.1936	5731	21.10.1936
5690	9.3.1936	5711	19.6.1936	5732	29.10.1936
5691	11.3.1936	5712	24.6.1936	5733	2.11.1936
5692	19.3.1936	5713	29.6.1936	5734	11.11.1936
5693	19.3.1936	5714	1.7.1936	5735	16.11.1936
5694	25.3.1936	5715	3.7.1936	5736	25.11.1936
5695	26.3.1936	5716	3.7.1936	5737	23.11.1936
5696	2.4.1936	5717	21.7.1936	5738	30.11.1936
5697	7.4.1936	5718	27.7.1936	5739	9.12.1936
5698	8.4.1936	5719	3.8.1936	5740	19.12.1936
5699	15.4.1936	5720	17.8.1936	5741	29.12.1936
5700	20.4.1936	5721	26.8.1936	5742	31.12.1936

* 5689 "*Ajax* Fitted at Crewe North Shed 13.3.1936"

This concludes the lists, and not included in them, because they had yet to be named are:-

5553	24.3.1937	5617	7.9.1937	5667	25.2.1937
5556	8.3.1937	5620	19.3.1937	5670	1.3.1937
5575	13.11.1937	5626	9.4.1937	5671	22.3.1937
5576	9.12.1937	5643	30.10.1937	5672	4.3.1937
5577	30.9.1937	5644	6.11.1937	5673	8.3.1937
5578	3.3.1938	5645	3.9.1937	5674	1.4.1937
5580	18.2.1938	5646	11.9.1937	5675	18.3.1937
5581	30.3.1938	5650	15.2.1937	5676	14.5.1937
5583	29.1.1938	5652	3.6.1937	5677	22.3.1937
5584	12.2.1938	5655	11.6.1937	5678	16.3.1937
5590	11.6.37	5666	See Note 4 below	5679	29.6.1937

Fig. 91   5706 *Express* before receiving the badge.

(Ray Townsin Collection).

Fig. 92   Close-up of *Express* nameplate and badge.

(Ray Townsin Collection).

On the evidence of the internal correspondence there is no doubt that in the lists there appear a few omissions and errors:-

1. The exchange of identities between 5552 and 5642 needs to be made clear. Old 5552 was built 10.5.1934, and entered traffic with Tender 4559, and entered traffic as 5642 on 29.4.1935 nameless. 5552 (formerly 5642) entered traffic on 24.4.1935, having been named a week earlier on 17.4.1935 and not as would appear from the list above on 29.4.1935.

2. The list of those "Fitted at Derby".
5641 is known to have been fitted at Derby and should be added to the list. 5663 should be deleted, since the correspondence gives the date of naming as 5.4.1937, the date of its return to traffic from Crewe after a Heavy General Overhaul. It may be however that the plates were sent to Derby 29.4.1936, in which case the entry is correct but misleading, and that their fitting to the engine was overlooked at the time. The plates for 5617 were also sent to Derby, but were overlooked, and were sent on to Patricroft Shed and fitted there.

3. The list of those "Named as built".
Engine History Cards give:-

| 5703 | 5.5.1936 | 5716 | 4.7.1936 | 5718 | 30.7.1936 |

4. 5666 Cornwallis. As indicated above the date of naming is uncertain. It is not included in the handwritten list, and it may be presumed that the writer had no information that it had been named prior to 8th February 1937. There is a letter from CME Crewe to Euston dated 1.3.1937 in which this date has been crossed out and 1.1.1937 substituted. 5666 was 'in shops' from 13.2.1937 until 1.3.1937. On balance therefore it would seem that 1.3.1937 would be the correct date.

5. To ensure that the naming date of every member of the class is included in this analysis, an additional list is set out here:-

Fitted at Derby	Plates sent	Naming date
5612	29.6.1936	23.4.1937
5615	15.6.1936	12.5.1936
5634	15.5.1936	16.5.1936
5635	11.6.1936	12.6.1936
5639	11.6.1936	12.6.1936
5649	27.5.1936	29.5.1936
5660	19.6.1936	9.7.1936
5641	Not listed	5.5.1936
(5663	29.4.1936	5.4.1937)

5612 came into shops from 8.2.1937 until 23.4.1937.
The relative dates for the most part make good sense, and that 5615 was said to have been named before the plates were sent is probably a simple clerical error. It looks for all the world as if 5663 was listed by mistake for 5641.

Details:-

5603 *Solomon Islands* A study of the list of the names selected shows that the names of members of the British Empire were chosen in alphabetical order. This name stands out as an exception, and it is

reasonable to assume that the intention in the first instance was to have the name *British Solomon Islands*, as found at that time on the protectorate's flag.

5616 was renamed *Malta G.C.* ex works 19.10.1943, and the new nameplates were officially unveiled at Euston on 4.11.1943.

5633 *Trans-Jordan*. named 23.3.1936, lost its name in June 1946, and was renamed *Aden* 22.8.1946 in preparation for the ceremony on 4.9.1946.

5648 was named *Wemyss* (Spelling error in "LMS Locomotive Names")

5665 The nameplate *Lord Rutherford of Nelson* had smaller lettering on the second line of the plate.

5678 was named *De Robeck* (Spelling error in "LMS Locomotive Names")

45700 *Britannia*'s name was removed 10.5.1951, and the new plates *Amethyst* were fitted 21.9.1951 for an official photograph.

5706 *Express*, when new, had the nameplates in the normal position, almost flush above the splasher, but when the plaque was fitted on it, the nameplate had to be raised higher than normal.

5731 *Perseverance* The nameplates were new, since those originally intended for use on the Royal Scot class engine had by then been scrapped.

5736 There was no diphthong in *Phoenix*.

5739 *Ulster* In the photograph taken on the 16th November 1936 with the group of four fitters, three of whom are seen holding the plates of 5740-2, the backplate for a plaque on 5739 is clearly visible. This makes it appear possible the engine was fitted with plaques for an official photograph, and that they were removed prior to entering traffic.

45739 *Ulster* Photographic evidence indicates that the plaques had been removed (but not the backplate) by 23rd February 1952, possibly at the time of an intermediate repair on 24th December 1951. The backplates presumably were taken off during a heavy repair in the summer of 1953.

5596 *Bahamas* was provided after restoration with a plaque above the nameplate.

The plates

A material difference between the Patriot and Jubilee classes was that the introduction of the taper boiler meant that the whole of the centre splasher was now available for positioning a nameplate. Several versions of the official Engine Diagram show the nameplate above the centre splasher, but no engine ever appeared in this (typically Great Western) guise, and the nameplates were fitted above the splasher over the leading coupled wheels.

The plates were cast in brass, curved, with raised lettering. The vast majority were made at Crewe and had letters 2 7/8in high. Those provided for 5576-8/80/1/3/4 were made at St.Rollox, and were readily distinguishable, having letters 3in high, somewhat thinner, and more closely spaced.

The following table has been compiled from internal correspondence:-

		Named	Cast at		Fitted		
5575	*Madras*	13.11.1937	Crewe		St.Rollox		
5576	*Bombay*	9.12.1937	St.Rollox		" "		
5577	*Bengal*	30. 9.1937	" "	"	" "	"	"
5578	*United Provinces*	3. 3.1938	" "	"	" "	"	"
5579	*Punjab*	2.10.1936	Crewe		Crewe		
5580	*Burma*	18. 2.1938	St.Rollox		Aberdeen?		
5581	*Bihar and Orissa*	30. 3.1938	" "		St.Rollox		
5582	*Central Provinces*	13.10.1936	Crewe		Crewe		
5583	*Assam*	29. 1.1938	St.Rollox		St.Rollox		
5584	*North West Frontier*	12. 2.1938	St.Rollox		Perth?		
5643	*Rodney*	30.10.1937	Crewe		St.Rollox		
5644	*Howe*	6.11.1937	St.Rollox		" "		
5645	*Collingwood*	3. 9.1937	" "	"	" "	"	"
5646	*Napier*	11. 9.1937	Crewe		" "		

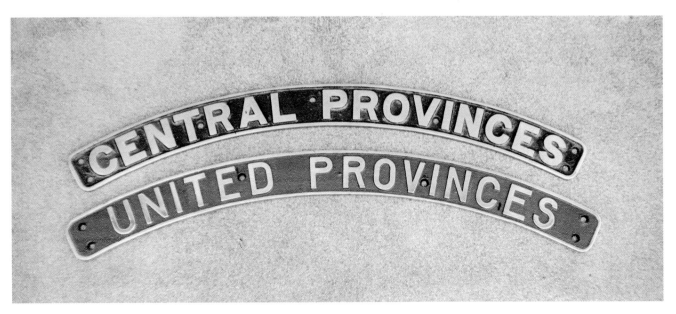

Fig. 93 The nameplates of 5582 *Central Provinces*, (Crewe) and 5578 *United Provinces*, (St. Rollox), showing the difference in the style of lettering.

(Ray Townsin Collection).

Additional information and corrections to the Glossary in LMS Locomotive Names:-

Glossary

Agamemnon	The Battleship of 1907-1926, which saw service in the Dardanelles in 1915.
Ajax	The Cruiser of 1934-1949, which came into prominence in the sinking of the Admiral Graf Spee in 1939, as did also HMS Achilles.
Anson	1697-1762 Admiral George, Lord Anson circumnavigated the globe 1740-1744.
Barfleur	The Naval Battle off Cherbourg in May 1692.
Beatty	1871-1936. He commanded the Battle-cruiser squadron at Jutland, and succeeded Jellicoe as C-in-C the Grand Fleet from November 1916 until the end of the war.
Camperdown	The Naval Battle against the Dutch off the coast of North Holland on 11th October 1797.
Cochrane	1758-1832. Admiral Sir Alexander Forrester Inglis Cochrane. 1775-1860. Admiral Thomas Cochrane, Earl of Dundonald. 1789-1872. Admiral Sir Thomas John Cochrane.
Collingwood	1750-1810. Admiral Cuthbert, Lord Collingwood was second in command to Nelson at Trafalgar.
Colossus	The Battleship of 1911-1928, which took part in the Battle of Jutland.
Defence	The Cruiser of 1907 which was lost at Jutland 31.5.1916.
Dreadnought	The Battleship of 1906-1921, the first of the big gun turbine driven battleships.
Hood	The most distinguished admiral was Samuel (not Horace) Hood.
Howe	1726-1799. Admiral Richard, Earl Howe.
Inflexible	The Battle Cruiser of 1907-1921, which saw action at the Falklands in 1914, the Dardanelles in 1915, and Jutland 1916.
Invincible	The Battle Cruiser of 1907 - 31.5.1916, which took part in the Falklands victory as Sturdee's flagship, but was lost at Jutland.
Kempenfelt	1718-1782. Admiral Richard.
Malta G.C.	The George Cross was awarded `For Gallantry` on 15th April 1942, at the height of the Luftwaffe offensive, and presented on 13th September that year.
Minotaur	The Armoured Cruiser of 1906-1920, which saw service at Jutland.
Neptune	The Cruiser of 1933, which was mined in 1941. Since many Jubilees were named after warships which had seen service at Jutland, this might also have been named after the Battleship of 1911-1921.
Polyphemus	This is an exception, in that it seems to be the only Jubilee ship's name which did not refer to one which had served in the fleet during the reign of King George V.
Renown	HMS Renown fulfilled the role of Royal Yacht for several cruises in the inter-war years.
Revenge	The Battleship of 1915-1948.
Shovell	1650-1797. Admiral Sir Cloudsley. The spelling Cloudsley is given elsewhere as Clowdisley (DNB) and Cloudesley (Thorne). The DNB states that Clowdisley is a common surname in Norfolk, where Shovell was baptised.
Swiftsure	The Battleship of 1904-1920, which saw service in the Dardanelles in 1915.

Valiant	The Battleship of 1914-1948, which was in action at Jutland, and at Matapan in 1941.
Warspite	The Battleship of 1915-1947, which had a most distinguished career, from Jutland in 1916 to Matapan in 1941, and right through the Second World War.
Wemyss	1864-1933. Admiral Rosslyn Erskine Wester, lst Baron Wemyss.

Royal Scot class 4-6-0

Additional information, and corrections to "LMS Locomotive Names"

Date of Naming	Number	Name	Date of Naming	Number	Name
25.7.1927	6100	Royal Scot	By 4.1928	6114	Coldstream Guardsman
By 4.1928	6101	Royal Scots Grey	"	6115	Scots Guardsman
3.1928	6102	Black Watch	"	6116	Irish Guardsman
By 4.1928	6103	Royal Scots Fusilier	"	6117	Welsh Guardsman
"	6104	Scottish Borderer	"	6118	Royal Welch Fusilier
"	6105	Cameron Highlander	"	6119	Lancashire Fusilier
"	6106	Gordon Highlander	"	6120	Royal Inniskilling Fusilier
"	6107	Argyll and Sutherland Highlander	"	6121	H.L.I.
"	6108	Seaforth Highlander	22.1.1949	(46121	Highland Light Infantry The City of Glasgow Regiment)
"	6109	Royal Engineer			
3.1928	6110	Grenadier Guardsman	By 4.1928	6122	Royal Ulster Rifleman
By 4.1928	6111	Royal Fusilier	"	6123	Royal Irish Fusilier
"	6112	Sherwood Forester	"	6124	London Scottish
3.1928	6113	Cameronian			

Date of Naming	Number	First Name	Date of Renaming	Second Name
3.1928	6125	Lancashire Witch	19.9.1935	3rd Carabinier
By 4.1928	6126	Sanspareil	16.8.1935	Royal Army Service Corps
"	6127	Novelty	10.12.1935	briefly The Old Contemptible
			28.11.1936	Old Contemptibles 1914 Aug.5 to Nov.22
"	6128	Meteor	22.9.1936	The Lovat Scouts
"	6129	Comet	3.12.1935	The Scottish Horse
"	6130	Liverpool	3.1935	The West Yorkshire Regiment
"	6131	Planet	26.3.1936	The Royal Warwickshire Regiment
"	6132	Phoenix	27.4.1936	The King's Regiment Liverpool
"	6133	Vulcan	3.9.1936	The Green Howards
3.1928	6134	Atlas	25.8.1936	The Cheshire Regiment
By 4.1928	6135	Samson	12.5.1936	The East Lancashire Regiment
"	6136	Goliath	28.4.1936	The Border Regiment
"	6137	Vesta	21.9.1936	The Prince of Wales's Volunteers South Lancashire
"	6138	Fury	23.10.1929	The London Irish Rifleman
3.1928	6139	Ajax	20.3.1936	The Welch Regiment
By 4.1928	6140	Hector	27.5.1936	The King's Royal Rifle Corps
"	6141	Caledonian	12.5.1936	The North Staffordshire Regiment
"	6142	Lion	14.10.1936	The York & Lancaster Regiment
"	6143	Mail	24.7.1934	The South Staffordshire Regiment
"	6144	Ostrich	1.1935	Honourable Artillery Company
3.1928	6145	Condor	12.1935	The Duke of Wellington's Regt. (West Riding)
By 4.1928	6146	Jenny Lind	5.5.1936	The Rifle Brigade
"	6147	Courier	25.7.1935	The Northamptonshire Regiment
"	6148	Velocipede	24.5.1935	The Manchester Regiment
"	6149	Lady of the Lake	10.6.1936	The Middlesex Regiment

10.1930	6150	*The Life Guardsman*		
"	6151	*The Royal Horse Guardsman*		
"	6152	*The King's Dragoon Guardsman*		
"	6153	*The Royal Dragoon*		
"	6154	*The Hussar*		
By 6.8.1930	6155	*The Lancer*		
By 8.8.1930	6156	*The South Wales Borderer*		
10.1938	6157	*The Royal Artilleryman*		
7.7.1931	6158	*The Loyal Regiment*		
10.1931	6159	*The Royal Air Force*		
Late 1932	6160	*Queen Victoria's Rifleman*		
9.1930	6161	*The King's Own*	7.1.1931	*King's Own*
Late 1932	6162	*Queen's Westminster Rifleman*		
"	6163	*Civil Service Rifleman*		
"	6164	*The Artists' Rifleman*		
"	6165	*The Ranger 12th London Regt.*		
"	6166	*London Rifle Brigade*		
"	6167	*The Hertfordshire Regiment*		
12.1930	6168	*The Girl Guide*		
27.10.1930	6169	*The Boy Scout*		
12.1929	6399	*Fury*	11.1935 6170	*British Legion*

Sundry Details:-

6100 *Royal Scot* was officially taken into stock 28.7.1927.

6112 *Sherwood Forester* carried a plate fitted on the splasher under the nameplate giving a record of its workings for the regiment. One of the plates is on public display in Derby Museum & Art Gallery. It measures 10in horizontally by 8in vertically with corners of 1in radius, and the lettering is engraved with black filling. It reads:-

HAULED SPECIAL TRAIN

1ST.BATTALION.	WILLESDEN TO LICHFIELD.	15-11-32.
5TH.BATTALION.	CREWE TO HOLYHEAD.	30-7-33.
2ND.BATTALION.	LIVERPOOL TO DERBY.	8-11-47.
5TH.BATTALION.	ROTHERHAM TO DERBY.	18-6-60.
8TH.BATTALION.	NOTTINGHAM TO LONDON.	30-7-60.
5TH /8TH.BATTALION.	NOTTINGHAM TO LONDON.	24-6-61.
5TH./8TH.BATTALION.	LONDON TO DERBY.	8-7-61.

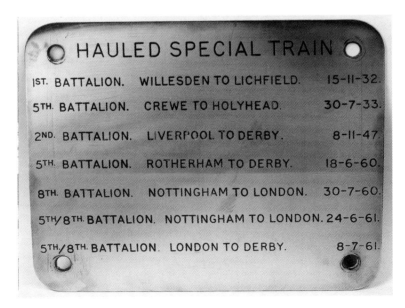

Fig. 94 The plate fixed to the splasher of Royal Scot class 6112 *Sherwood Forester.*

Copyright (Derby Museums and Art Gallery).

6127 *Old Contemptibles* The plates depicted their badge, and were cast in bronze.

6144 *Honourable Artillery Company* came into Crewe on 18th March 1938 for plaques of the regimental crest to be fitted.

6159 was photographed at Derby on 13th August 1940, newly built and incorrectly named *The Life Guardsman.*

6167 was temporarily named *The London Irish Rifleman* to haul the regiment from London to Heysham, 6138 being under repair at the time. The date was sometime around the end of July 1931.

6169 had been named *The Boy Scout,* but without the badge, by 27.10.1930; Ceremony, with badge, 9.12.1930.

6170 *British Legion* was named on 2.11.1935. White metal was used to match the Legion's badge.

46121 *Highland Light Infantry The City of Glasgow Regiment*'s nameplates were fixed at Crewe 5.1.1949, but the locomotive was noted running nameless on 13.1.1949. The nameplates were stepped.

History of the Naming of the Class

6100-49 were built under Derby Order 6829 of February 1927, and the nameplates of 6100 were cast at Derby and charged to this Order Number.

Additional information comes from a letter from Mr.E.A.Langridge in the Journal of the Stephenson Locomotive Society in 1967 page 120:-

"The loco. came down to Derby without nameplates. The write-up and pictures first handed out to the press has no name plate or brackets. After a few days....it was put on the L.M.S. "make a break" turn - 10.47 Derby to St.Pancras, via Nottingham, 40 min. turn round time at St.Pancras, back with 2.25 to Derby (arr 4.55 p.m.). Under great secrecy the name plates *Royal Scot* were cast and put on the splashers and the loco. sent to Euston for an unveiling ceremony on the new train."

The nameplates of *Royal Scot* were made at Derby under Order 6829 (February 1927).

The height of the single line plate was 4 1/2in, and that of the double line plates varied slightly, between 8 1/16in and 8 1/8in.

There appears to have been considerable confusion about what should be the name of the second of the class. The first mention appears in "The Locomotive" of August 15, 1927 and says "The second engine of the class No 6101 is to bear the name "Highland Chieftain". On the other hand Minute 1714 of the Board dated 27th October 1927 gave approval that it should be "Highland Chief", whereas the LMS Magazine of October 1927 on page 343 states "The second engine (of the class) No.6126, which is illustrated above, is to bear the name *Highland Chieftain.*" This illustration is of 6126, unnamed, and with the number painted on the tender. A Note on page 182 in the June 1928 of the same Magazine refers to this statement and goes on to say "It was originally intended that No 6126 should bear the name "Highland Chieftain". To add to the confusion, in the Railway Magazine for October 1927 page 334 four observers wrote to report "No.6101 is named "Highland Chieftain.", which would lead readers to suppose they had actually set eyes on it! Whatever be the rights and wrongs of all these statements, No.6101 was carrying the name *Royal Scots Grey* by April 1928 and a photograph attributed to The Scotsman

appeared in the LMS Magazine for December 1929 page 412 of the engine drawing the first trainload of Royal Scots Greys troops leaving Edinburgh for Tidworth on Wednesday 6th November. The appropriateness of locomotives having regimental names and the extent to which the Armed Forces used the railways in the course of their movements can be seen by the mention that in this instance the main body of the regiment left Edinburgh in four detachments consisting in all of 10 officers, 343 N.C.O.s and men, 43 wives, 47 children, 302 horses and about 53 tons of baggage.

Fig. 95 The nameplate and right-facing plaque of *Hector.*
Real Photographs Ltd (Ray Townsin Collection).

The addition of plaques to the nameplates

1) Pioneer Locomotives.

It has been observed that, whereas the official drawings from which the illustrations in "LMS Locomotive Names" were made, all depict the locomotive facing left, many other photographs (including those of 6137/8/40/2/5) show them facing right. It seems certain that every pair of plaques were made with one of each. It is significant that none of the locomotive drawings of the plaques contain any lettering or numerals, making them reversible.

Fig.64 in "LMS Locomotive Names" shows the engine on the plaque facing left, and is presumably on the left hand splasher. The ancient engine and its modern counterpart always went in the same direction!

All these plaques were fitted on the splasher below the nameplate.

Their dimensions were approximately 10 1/2in by 6in.

It needs to be pointed out that the facsimile details of the historic locomotives are not always precisely correct.

For example:-

PERSEVERANCE was built privately for the Rainhill trials of 1829, and was not purchased by the Liverpool & Manchester Railway.

SANSPAREIL was built privately for the Rainhill trials and only afterwards purchased by the L&M.

NOVELTY was built privately for the Rainhill trials, after which a request by the L&M to purchase it was refused by the owner.

LIVERPOOL was initially used on ballasting work during the final stages of the building of the L&M, but was not purchased by them.

MAIL There was no such engine named MAIL, and the name refers to a class of engines and the fact that they hauled the mail trains. Furthermore they worked on the North Midland Railway, and not the Midland Counties.

CONDOR was built in March 1846, and not in 1845.

2) Regimental.

These plaques, or crests, were paid for and provided by the regiments concerned and remained their property, thus satisfying English law which makes it illegal to bear arms to which one is not entitled. Hence at the ceremonies at which they were unveiled, an L.M.S. representative received them as a gift on behalf of the Company.

These plaques were fitted either on the splasher below the nameplate, or on a backplate above it.

Those fixed below were on 6102/16/8/20/2/3/38/58/61/8/9.
Those fixed above were on 6103/7/9/12/3/24/6/8-37/9/41/4-9/66, and in post LMS days 46121.

6139 and 6140 were provided with a backplate above the name, but for some unknown reason no plaque was ever affixed.

Fig. 96   From a photograph of 46140, showing clearly the backplate upon which no plaque was ever fixed. Taken at Holbeck 17th June 1961.

Photograph A.G.Ellis (John Ward Collection).

The Final Years

Many plates were sold properly to collectors, and a few were presented by British Railways to appropriate people and organisations. One of the first to go in this way was a plate from 46131 which went in 1963 to the Royal Warwickshire Regiment, and which, after being kept for a while at Budbrooke Barracks was moved to Warwick Castle for display there. A plate from 46148 was presented ceremonially to the Manchester Regiment at Ashton-under-Lyne on 1st June 1965, a plate and a plaque from 46157 to 252 Regiment R.A. where they were installed in the regiment's armoury at Stockport, and those of 46121 to the Royal Highland Fusiliers for display in their regimental museum. A nameplate and the fleur-de-lys badge of *The Boy Scout* were presented in 1965 to the Boy Scouts Association together with a framed photograph of the engine, for display in Baden-Powell House, London; and those of *The Girl Guide* to the Girl Guide Association on 9th November 1966 just under thirty-six years after their unveiling at Euston by Lady Baden-Powell.

These, together with many others are examples of such presentations,

and serve to underline the goodwill of British Railways at the time of the ending of steam traction.

Princess Royal class 4-6-2

6200 was photographed before going into service in works grey with the nameplate "*Princess Royal*", but this style was never used.

Glossary (Addition and correction)

6206 *Princess Marie Louise* was the younger sister of Princess Helena Victoria.

6211 *Queen Maud* 1869-1938   She was the third daughter of King Edward VII.

Princess Coronation class 4-6-2

6230 *Duchess of Buccleuch* (Spelling correction).

6244 *King George VI* was named on 5.6.1941.

6248 *City of Leeds* was named on 2.12.1943.

6252 *City of Leicester* was named on 8.10.1944

6253 *City of St Albans* was named on 17.8.1946.

6256 *Sir William A.Stanier, F.R.S.* is the correct style of the nameplate. There is a square headed comma after the word "*Stanier*", and the full stops in "*F.R.S.*" are similarly square headed.

Details:-

6249 *City of Sheffield* The stainless steel plates were made following a suggestion made at the time of the naming ceremony, jointly by Firth-Vickers Stainless Steel Limited and the Lord Mayor. The company volunteered to make and present the nameplates, and the LMS accepted the offer as a symbol of the close ties between the railway and the industry of Sheffield. These plates were fitted at Crewe in 1945.

46257 *City of Salford* was built in February 1948. An official photograph dated 26th February 1948 shows this locomotive in works grey numbered 6257M and named, but it did not enter service at that time due to problems with the cast steel rear truck, which was replaced by a fabricated one. It was released to traffic in May 1948, basically in the LMS 1946 livery but with the number 46257 and with BRITISH RAILWAYS in full on the tender, and it was in this condition at the time of the naming ceremony in June.

There is a conflict of evidence as to whether plaques of the Coat of Arms of Salford were ever fitted. The Railway Observer states "Plaques of the Arms of Salford have been affixed" but an examination of photographs of 46257 shows that they were not carried.

Disposal of plates

46243 *City of Lancaster* One plate was presented on 26th June 1965 to Lancaster City Council and is on display in Lancaster City Museum.

Duchess of Atholl   She was Katharine Marjory, fourth daughter of Sir James Henry Ramsey, 10th Bart. of Banff.

Duchess of Buccleuch   She was Vreda Esther Mary, the daughter of Major W.F.Lascelles.

Duchess of Gloucester   She was the third daughter of the 7th Duke of Buccleuch.

Duchess of Montrose   She was the wife of the 6th Duke of Montrose.

Duchess of Norfolk   She was the widow of Henry Fitzalan Howard, her name was Gwendolen, and she was in her own right Baroness Herries.

Duchess of Rutland   She is stated to be the daughter of Francis John Tennant of Innes, Morayshire. (Burke's p.2330)

Duchess of Sutherland   She was Mistress of the Robes to Queen Mary 1916-1921.

Lady Patricia   She was H.R.H.Lady Patricia Ramsay. (Spelling)

Princess Alexandra   The locomotive was named in 1937 after the   daughter of the Duke and Duchess of Kent, Alexandra Helen Elizabeth Olga Christabel, born on 25th December 1936.

Chapter 6
The Regimental Names

As forecast in the Prelude to Chapter 10 of "LMS Locomotive Names" at the foot of page 125, extra suggestions relating to the Glossary have come to hand. and many of the sources have subsequently been improved, corrected and altered.

It seemed best to group together here the regimental additions and corrections for the benefit of those who might be particularly interested in Royal Scot and other regimentally named engines. It must be stressed that the names listed below are not the complete list of the LMS regimental names.

Regimental history is a specialised enterprise, and though there is very much agreement, not every authority on the subject gives precisely the same information. These notes are based on Crystal, Griffen, Hallows, Henderson, Encyclopaedia Britannica, and Everyman's Encyclopaedia.

Black Watch
The "42nd Foot", raised in 1730 for the protection of Edinburgh, and known as the "43rd or Highland Regiment" in 1739, a title changed to "42nd Regiment" in 1751, and again in 1758 to the "42nd or Royal Highland Regiment". The full title from 1881 was "The Black Watch (Royal Highlanders)", and from 1920 "The Black Watch (Royal Highland Regiment)".

Cameronian
Formed in 1688 after the martyrdom of Richard Cameron, and placed 26th in line in 1751, linked in 1881 with the "90th", which had been raised as "The Perthshire Volunteers" in 1794. The full regimental title was "The Cameronians (The Scottish Rifles)".

Civil Service Rifleman
The 15th Battalion of the London Regiment, merged with the Queen's Westminster Rifles in 1922. (q.v.)

Glasgow Yeomanry
First raised in 1797 in the Glasgow area, and re-raised subsequently. Converted in 1920 to form an Artillery Brigade.

Grenadier Guardsman
Raised in 1656 by Lord Wentworth for the service of King Charles II in France. Known as the "1st Foot Guards" until 1815, when at Waterloo they defeated grenadiers of Napoleon's Imperial Guard, after which the Prince Regent conferred upon them their present title.

H.L.I.
The initials of "The Highland Light Infantry".

Highland Light Infantry
The City of Glasgow Regiment
An amalgamation in 1881 of 1) The "73rd (Highland) Regiment" of 1777, which successively became the "71st (Highland) Regiment" in 1786, the "71st (Highland) Regiment" in 1808, and a year later the "71st (Highland) Light Infantry", and 2) The "74th (Highland) Regiment" of 1787. In 1923 it is recorded that the regiment's full title was "Highland Light Infantry (City of Glasgow Regiment)", but note that the nameplate did not include the brackets.

Honourable Artillery Company
The oldest unit in the British Army, formed in 1537, when granted a charter of incorporation by King Henry VIII. A London Territorial Army unit, proposed as the 26th Battalion of the London Regiment, but declined and remained unnumbered.

King's Own
Formed as the "Tangier Regiment" in 1680, it became successively "The Queen Consort's Regiment" in 1684, "The Queen's Marines" in 1702, "The King's Own Regiment" in 1715, the "4th, or King's Own Regiment" in 1751, "The 4th (The King's Own Royal) Regiment" in 1867, and in 1881 the full title was "King's Own (Royal Lancaster Regiment)". In 1920 the title was changed to "The King's Own Royal Regiment (Lancaster)".

London Rifle Brigade
The 5th Battalion of the London Regiment.

Old Contemptibles
"This was the taunt hurled by the Kaiser at the British Expeditionary Force, who were in action a week later at Mons, and in October at Ypres." - The Times 18th August 1994.

Queen Victoria's Rifleman
The 9th Battalion of the London Regiment.

Queen's Edinburgh	The 4th/5th Battalion (Queen's Edinburgh), The Royal Scots, a formation which traced its descent from the 1st Edinburgh (City) Rifle Volunteer Corps, formed in 1859 by the merger of several rifle corps already existing within the city.
Queen's Westminster Rifleman	The 16th Battalion of the London Regiment.
Royal Army Service Corps	The Corps was founded in 1889 as the "Army Service Corps" from a multitude of smaller formations, the earliest being the "Corps of Royal Waggoners" in 1794. The 'Royal' prefix was granted in recognition of the Corps' achievements in the Great War.
Royal Fusilier	Formed in 1665 as the "Royall Regiment of Fusileers", known from 1751 as the "7th or Royal Fuziliers", and since 1881 under their full title "Royal Fusiliers (City of London Regiment)".
Royal Inniskilling Fusilier	Raised by King William III either in 1689 or 1690 and called "Tiffen's Regiment", or as sometimes found "Tiffin's Regiment". In 1751 a complete change of name found them "The 27th or The Inniskilling Regiment". The "27th" and the "108th" were merged in 1881 to become "The Royal Inniskilling Fusiliers".
Royal Irish Fusilier	Formed by an amalgamation in 1881 of 1) The "87th (Prince of Wales's Own Irish) Regiment" of 1793 which in 1811 became the "87th (Prince of Wales's Own Irish)" and in 1827 "87th (Royal Irish Fusiliers)", and 2) The "89th (Princess Victoria's)" of 1865.
Royal Naval Division	Fought with distinction in World War I. (Not WWII) The Division was raised from Royal Navy reservists and, although still officially sailors, they fought as soldiers in Gallipoli and France.
Royal Scot	"The 1st Foot" was formed in 1625, and is thus a highly suitable name for the first of the class. The title "1st Foot" signified that it was the senior regiment of the Infantry of the Line. The Regiment was known in 1633 as "Sir John Hepburn's Regiment", and in 1684 "The Royal Regiment of Foote". In 1751, it became "The 1st or Royal Scots Regiment", and by 1881 "The Lothian Regiment (Royal Scots)", and in 1882 "The Royal Scots (Lothian Regiment)". In 1920 the full title was "The Royal Scots (The Royal Regiment)".
Royal Scots Fusilier	"The Earl of Mar's Regiment" was formed in 1678, became "The Scotch Fuzileers" in 1685, "The North British Fuzileers" in 1707, with Royal prefix granted in 1712, and were placed "21st Foot" in 1751. Its present title dates from 1881.
Royal Tank Corps	Formed as the "Heavy Branch of the Machine Gun Corps" in 1916, becoming "The Tank Corps" in 1917, and receiving the Royal prefix in 1923. Note that in 1939 it was renamed "Royal Tank Regiment" on the formation of the "Royal Armoured Corps".
Royal Ulster Rifleman	They belonged to the "86th" and "83rd Foot". The former were raised in Ireland in 1793, known as the "83rd (County of Dublin) Regiment" from 1859. The latter, also in 1793, were known as the "86th or Leinster Regiment" in 1809, and the "86th (Royal County Down)" in 1812. They were combined in 1881 as "The Royal Irish Rifles", and renamed "The Royal Ulster Rifles" in 1920. Rowland Hill served as an officer in the "86th"
Scottish Borderer	Formed in 1689 as "The Earl of Leven's Regiment", or the "Edinburgh Regiment", which in 1751 became the "25th or Edinburgh Regiment". In 1782 the title was the "25th (Sussex) Regiment", and in 1805 the "25th" or "King's Own Borderers". In 1887 its full title became "The King's Own Scottish Borderers".
Sherwood Forester	The "Sherwood Foresters (Derbyshire) Regiment" was a combination in 1881 of "Houghton's" of 1741 later the "45th (1st Nottinghamshire Regiment)" and the "95th (Derbyshire) Regiment" of 1823. The 1st Battalion fought at Talavera. In 1902 the regiment was retitled "The Sherwood Foresters (Nottinghamshire and Derbyshire Regiment)", and their full title at the time the engine was named was "Sherwood Foresters (Derbyshire Regiment)".

The Artists' Rifleman	The 28th Battalion of the London Regiment, raised in 1859.
The Bedfordshire and Hertfordshire Regiment	The "16th Regiment" of 1809 became the "Bedfordshire Regiment" in 1881, and so many Hertfordshire men had served in the Bedfordshire Regiment in the Great War that in 1919 the regiment was renamed in their recognition.
The Border Regiment	Formed in 1881 as an amalgamation of 1) "Lord Lucas's Regiment" of 1702, the "34th Regiment" of 1751, the "34th (Cumberland) Regiment" of 1782, and 2) the "55th Regiment" of 1755, which became the "55th (Westmoreland) Regiment" in 1782. Since then the title has been simply "The Border Regiment".
The Cheshire Regiment	Formed in 1689 as "The Duke of Norfolk's Regiment", it became the "22nd Regiment of Foot" in 1751, the "22nd (Cheshire) Regiment" in 1782, and "The Cheshire Regiment (22nd Foot)" in 1881.
The Duke of Wellington's Regt. (West Riding)	The regimental title did not abbreviate the word "Regiment", as did the locomotive name. It was formed in 1881 from 1) "33rd Earl of Huntingdon's Regiment" of 1702, the "33rd Regiment" of 1751, the "33rd (1st Yorkshire, West Riding) Regiment" of 1782, the "33rd (Duke of Wellington's Regiment)" in 1853, and 2) The "76th 'Hindoostan' Regiment" of 1787, known as the "76th Regiment" of 1812.
The East Lancashire Regiment	Formed in 1881 from a merger of 1) "Sanderson's Marines" of 1702, which became the "30th Regiment" in 1751, and the "30th (Cambridgeshire) Regiment" in 1782, and 2) "The 59th Regiment" of 1753, which became "The 59th (2nd Nottinghamshire) Regiment" of 1782.
The King's Dragoon Guardsman	First formed in 1685 as "Queen's Regiment of Horse", it became "The King's Horse" in 1714, and has been known by the full title of "1st or King's Dragoon Guards" since 1746.
The King's Regiment Liverpool	First known in 1685 as "Princess Anne of Denmark's Regiment", it became "The King's Regiment" in 1714, the "8th or King's Regiment" in 1751, and "The King's Liverpool Regiment" in 1881. In 1920 the title "The King's Regiment (Liverpool)" was adopted.
The Lancer	A lancer is a cavalry soldier armed with a lance. In 1930 there were four regiments of Lancers, 1) "9th (Queen's Royal Lancers)" of 1830, 2) "12th (Prince of Wales's Royal Lancers)" of 1816, 3) "17th Lancers (Duke of Cambridge's Own)" and "21st (The Empress of India's)" who were combined in 1922 to form the "17th/21st Lancers" and 4) "16th (The Queen's) Lancers" of 1816 and "5th (Royal Irish) Lancers" of 1858 who combined in 1922 to form the "16th/5th The Queen's Royal Lancers".
The Life Guardsman	The senior regiment of the British Army, which stemmed from the "Horse Guards" of 1660 who escorted King Charles II to London from exile in Belgium, and which since 1788 had consisted of the 1st and 2nd Life Guards. These two troops merged in 1922 to become simply "The Life Guards".
The London Irish Rifleman	In 1929 this was the 18th Battalion of the London Regiment, which in 1937 became part of the Royal Ulster Rifles.
The Loyal Regiment	Formed in 1881 as "Loyal North Lancashire Regiment" from 1) "Mordaunt's" of 1741 who were later known as the "47th (Lancashire) Regiment", and 2) the "81st (Loyal Lincoln Volunteers)" of 1793. The 1881 amalgamation was of the "47th" and the "81st". The title was changed in 1920 from "The Loyal North Lancashire Regiment" to "The Loyal Regiment (North Lancashire)".
The Manchester Regiment	Formed in 1881 from the "63rd West Suffolk Regiment" of 1782 and the "96th Regiment" of 1824. The "63rd" with "King's" had begun in 1685 as "Princess Anne of Denmark's Regiment" and were one regiment until the 2nd Battalion was designated the "63rd Regiment of Foot" in 1758.

The Northamptonshire Regiment

Formed as the "48th Regiment" in 1751 ("Cholmondeley's" of 1740), the "48th (Northamptonshire)" of 1782, together with the "58th (Rutlandshire)", also of 1782. These two merged in 1881 to form the present regiment. The 2nd Battalion which later became "The Rutlandshire" had been formed in 1755.

The North Staffordshire Regiment

Formed in 1881 from the "64th (2nd) Staffordshire Regiment" of 1758 and the "98th" in 1824, which acquired the title "98th (The Prince of Wales's) Regiment" in 1876.

The Rifle Brigade

Known as "The Rifle Corps" in 1800, the "95th (Rifle) Regiment" in 1802, "The Rifle Brigade" in 1816, "The Prince Consort's Own Rifle Brigade" in 1862, and "The Rifle Brigade (Prince Consort's Own)" in 1920.

The Royal Army Ordnance Corps

The Corps traces its descent from the early 15th Century, In 1895 the "Military Stores Department" became the "Army Ordnance Department" (Officers), and "Army Ordnance Corps" (Other Ranks). These two were amalgamated in 1919 and granted the Royal prefix, to become "The Royal Army Ordnance Corps".

The Royal Artilleryman

Two permanent Companies were formed in 1716 and were joined in 1722 by the Gibraltar and Minorca Companies to form the "Royal Regiment of Artillery", and in 1882 were joined by the Corps of Artillery Drivers. In 1899 it was separated into "The Royal Garrison Artillery" and "The Royal Field Artillery", then reunified in 1924 to become once more "The Royal Regiment of Artillery".

The Royal Horse Guardsman

Formed in 1660 as "The Royal Regiment of Horse", quickly to become in January 1661 "The Earl of Oxford's Regiment", and by 1684 "Royal Regiment of Horse Guards". In 1746 it became "Royal Horse Guards Blue", and finally in 1821 "Royal Horse Guards (The Blues)", forming from then on part of the Household Cavalry.

The Royal Pioneer Corps

This was a successor to the Labour Corps of the Great War, the "Auxiliary Military Pioneer Corps" formed soon after the outbreak of the Second World War in 1939. That title was short-lived, lasting only until renamed "The Pioneer Corps" in July 1940. It was granted the Royal prefix in November 1946.

The South Staffordshire Regiment

Formed in 1881 from the "38th Foot" raised in 1705, which became the "38th (1st Stafforshire) Regiment" of 1792, and the "80th Staffordshire Volunteers" of 1793.

The South Wales Borderer

First known in 1689 as "Dering's Regiment", then as the "24th Regiment" in 1751, the "24th (2nd Warwickshire) Regiment" in 1782, and as "The South Wales Borderers" since 1881.

The Welch Regiment

An amalgamation in 1881 of 1) "Fielding's Invalids" of 1719, known as the "41st or Invalids Regiment" in 1751, the "41st" in 1787 and the "41st (Welch)" in 1831, together with 2) "The 69th Regiment" of 1756, in 1782 known as the "69th South Lincolnshire Regiment".

Note that 'Welsh' was changed to 'Welch' in 1920, or 1922. Authorities differ on the year in question.

The West Yorkshire Regiment

Started as "Hales's Regiment" in 1685, the "14th Regiment" in 1751, "The 14th (Bedfordshire Regiment)" in 1782, the "14th (Buckinghamshire Regiment)" in 1809, the "Prince of Wales's Own" in 1876, "The Prince of Wales's Own (West Yorkshire) Regiment" in 1881, and finally in 1920 "The West Yorkshire Regiment (The Prince of Wales's Own)".

The York & Lancaster Regiment

Dating from 1881, when the "69th Foot" of 1758, and the "84th" of 1793 which became the "York & Lancaster Regiment" in 1800 (or 1808) were combined.

3rd Carabinier

A merger in 1922 between 1) "Earl of Plymouth's Horse" of 1685, which became the "3rd Dragoon Guards" in 1747, and the "3rd or Prince of Wales's Dragoon Guards" in 1765, and 2) "Lumley's Horse" of 1685, which successively became the "King's Carabiniers" in 1691, the "3rd Irish Horse: The Carabiniers" in 1747, and the "6th Dragoon Guards (The Carabiniers)" in 1788, later the "3rd/6th Dragoon Guards", which became "3rd Carabiniers (Prince of Wales's Dragoon Guards)" in 1928.

Chapter 7
SCOTTISH CONSTITUENTS
The Caledonian Railway

CR No 779 LMS No 14335 *Breadalbane*. The name was removed in January 1925.

The Company rarely provided names for its locomotives. No 124, a Drummond 4-4-0, built in 1886 by Dubs & Co. for the International Exhibition at Edinburgh, and purchased afterwards by the Company, later received the name *Eglinton*, most probably after it was transferred to Ardrossan in 1890 to work the Arran Express boat train, in honour of the Earl of Eglinton on whose estate the town of Ardrossan was built; the name was removed prior to the 1914-18 war. It was allotted the number 14296, but was withdrawn in 1925 without carrying it.

No 79 *Carbrook* was built in 1889 by the Company, and named in 1895, but also lost it before the Great War. It survived until 1928, long enough to have been repainted LMS red with the number 14297.

The first of the 4-4-0s built in 1896 was No 721, and received the name *Dunalastair*, the name by which the series of classes, the "Dunalastair II, III and IV"s became known as improvements and developments were made. The name was removed when the locomotive was under repair at St.Rollox late in 1918.

Two of the class, Nos 723 *Victoria* and 724 *Jubilee* were named in 1897, but lost their names after 1900 following Her Majesty's death, and certainly by 1901 and 1903 respectively.

No 766 *Dunalastair 2nd* was the prototype of its class, variously referred to in literature as "the second class of Dunalastairs", or "Dunalastair 2nds", but more generally (even if incorrectly) as the "Dunalastair II" class. The engine was originally named *Dunalastair 2nd* in May-June 1898, and remained thus for about a year. There is photographic evidence in 1910 that, like No 721, its name was simply *Dunalastair* and during the intervening years it may never have been painted with the Roman "II". Whichever be the case, the name was removed before the War.

The '49' class 4-6-0, No 50 *Sir James Thompson* was built in 1903, followed in 1906 by '903' class 4-6-0 No 903 *Cardean*, by '908' class No 909 *Sir James King* and No 911 *Barochan*. The names were removed from *Sir James King* and *Barochan* during the war years; *Cardean* came into works early in 1920 and *Sir James Thompson* at about the same time, and lost theirs then.

For interest the details are set out below:-

CR No	LMS No	Name	Class	Withdrawn
124	(14296)	*(Eglinton)*	-	28.8.1925
79	14297	*(Carbrook)*	`Carbrook`	30.11.1928
721	14311	*(Dunalastair)*	`Dunalastair I`	14.10.1931
723	14313	*(Victoria)*	`Dunalastair I`	4.7.1933
724	14314	*(Jubilee)*	`Dunalastair I`	27 or 31.12.1930
766	14430	*(Dunalastair 2nd)*	`Dunalastair II` (superheated)	w/e 25.1.1936
779	14335	*Breadalbane*	`Dunalastair II`	14.10.1939
50	14751	*(Sir James Thompson)*	`49`	18.3.1933
903	14752	*(Cardean)*	`903`	12.12.1930
909	14610	*(Sir James King)*	`908`	4.7.1933
911	14612	*(Barochan)*	`908`	4.11.1931

Caption Fig 80 in LMS Locomotive Names should read "CR 4-6-0 911 *Barochan* on a Gourock train in Glasgow Central on 1st August 1911".

Glossary

Carbrook   The estate near Stirling of J.C.Bolton, Chairman of the Caledonian Railway, 1880-1897.

Dunalastair   The home near Kinloch Rannoch of J.C.Bunten, Chairman of the Caledonian Railway, 1897-1901.

The 'River' class 4-6-0

Additional information:-

The name *River Tummel* is given in Hawthorn Leslie`s order book as *River Beauly*

Glasgow & South Western Railway 4-4-0

G&SWR Number	LMS Number	Name	Date of Withdrawal
394	14509	*Lord Glenarthur*	16.11.1934

This was the only named engine belonging to the Company at the time, and the first to be named since a 2-4-0 *Galloway* in 1858.

The Highland Railway

Eighty-four named Highland Railway engines came into LMS stock, and were allocated LMS numbers. The LMS numbers were applied swiftly in 1923.

Strath class 4-4-0

HR Number	Builder		Date	Name	LMS Number	Withdrawn
89	Neilson	(4428)	1892	*SIR GEORGE*	14271	13.9.1930
92A	"	(4431)	1892	*STRATHDEARN*	14272	1.3.1930
94	"	(4433)	1892	*STRATHTAY*	(14273)	21.3.1925
95	"	(4434)	1892	*STRATHCARRON*	14274	27.12.1930*
98	"	(4437)	1892	*GLENTRUIM*	14275	15.11.1930
100	"	(4439)	1892	*GLENBRUAR*	14276	1.3.1930

* Variously given as 30.12.1930

According to the list of names originally intended, No 94 was to have been *Strathglass*, No 97 *Glenbruar* and No 100 *Glenmore*. Before completion however instructions were given for No 94 to be *Strathtay* and for Nos 97 and 100 to exchange names.

Additional information. It will be convenient to list here:-

Named locomotives which survived into LMS times
It was decided in August 1923 that these should be withdrawn, and shortly afterwards they were sold or scrapped. They are listed below roughly in order of their building date.

Glenbarry class 2-2-2 later 2-4-0
Built by Neilson & Co. 11.1863

35A (*ISLA BANK*)		(Seen at work on a permanent way train in December 1923)

Duke class 4-4-0
Built at Lochgorm 1884-1888

67 } (*CROMARTIE*)	renumbered 2.1923
70A}	and withdrawn 8.1923 (See note below)
72A (*GRANGE*)	Sold 3.12.23?
73A (*ROSEHAUGH*)	
75A (*BREADALBANE*)	Broken up at Kilmarnock 1925
84A (*DOCHFOUR*)	Broken up at Kilmarnock 1925

Clyde Bogie class 4-4-0
Built by Clyde Locomotive Co. 1886

76A (*BRUCE*)	Withdrawn 1924 Broken up at Lochgorm Works 1925
77A (*LOVAT*)	Broken up at Kilmarnock 1925
78A (*LOCHALSH*)	Sold 6.11.1923 to Arrol Jackson
79A (*ATHOLL*)	Broken up at Kilmarnock 1924/5
80A (*STAFFORD*)	Sold 1.11.1923 to Arrol Jackson
81A (*COLVILLE*)	Broken up at Lochgorm Works 1925
83A (*MONKLAND*)	Sold 3.1.1924 to Arrol Jackson

Strath class 4-4-0
Built by Neilson & Co. Ltd. 1892

90A (*GRANDTULLY*)	Sold 13.12.1923 to Arrol Jackson
91A (*STRATHSPEY*)	Broken up at Kilmarnock 1924/5
93A (*STRATHNAIRN*)	Sold 14.12.1923 to Arrol Jackson
96A (*GLENTILT*)	Sold 5.12.1923 to Arrol Jackson
97A (*GLENMORE*)	Sold 8.11.1923 to Arrol Jackson
99A (*GLENTROMIE*)	Sold 15.12.1923 to Arrol Jackson

In addition, listed below are:-
Previously named locomotives which came into LMS stock

Erstwhile name		Name removed	LMS Number	

Clyde Bogie class 4-4-0
Built by Clyde Locomotive Co. 9.1886

82A	(*FIFE*)	1900		
renamed	(*DURN*)	1916	14278	Withdrawn 4.1930

Jones Tank class 2-4-0T (later 4-4-0T)
Built at Lochgorm 1878-9

58	(*BURGHEAD*)	1900	15011	Withdrawn 2.1928
59	(*HIGHLANDER*)	1900	15010	Withdrawn 11.1932
50 ex 17	(*ABERFELDY*)	1906	15012	Withdrawn 11.1929

Passenger Tank class (Drummond) 0-4-4T
Built at Lochgorm 9.1905

40	(*GORDON LENNOX*)c	1920	15052	Withdrawn 12.1930

And a further three, withdrawn in 1923, which did not come into LMS stock:-

Special Tank class 2-4-0T
Built by Kitson of Leeds 8.1870
Rebuilt and named 1896

118A	(*GORDON CASTLE*)	1900		Withdrawn 8.1923

Small Goods 2-4-0
Built by Sharp, Stewart & Co. 11.1863

27A	(*CONON*)			Withdrawn 8.1923

Medium Goods 2-4-0
.Built by Sharp, Stewart & Co. 5.1864

37A e 42	(*LENTRAN*)			Withdrawn 8.1923

It is useful to mention here the history of LMS 14277, because this is a locomotive which has caused considerable puzzlement and diversity of opinions among historians, causing many different interpretations to appear in print. The first point in the context of this work is to make clear is that it was not named at the time of the amalgamation of the railways, but the fact that it has frequently been associated with the name *Cromartie* merits this mention.

Which engine went into LMS stock and became 14277? Here is the answer.

HR No 67 was one of the Duke class, built in August 1874 named *The Duke*, and renamed *Cromartie* in January 1877. Upon the amalgamation in 1923, it was decided that this No 67, despite the fact that it had been extensively overhauled in 1921, should be withdrawn and not go into LMS stock.

Instead it was decided that HR No 70 of the Skye Bogie class, built at Lochgorm Works in May 1882, and unnamed, although it had been on the duplicate list as No 70A since 1915, was fit for traffic and should go into LMS stock. So in February 1923, No 70A, which had never been named was renumbered 67, because the number 70 had by then gone to *Loch Ashie*. A few months later it became LMS 14277; and No 67 was renumbered 70A, retaining its name *Cromartie*. The `new` 70A was soon withdrawn, went into storage in sidings at Culloden Moor, and was ultimately scrapped.

Loch class 4-4-0
Withdrawal dates:-

14379	13.3.1948	14385	6.4.1950	14391	18.7.1941
14380	22.11.1941	14386	5.8.1938	14392	19.4.1947
14381	9.3.1940	14387	31.12.1930	14393	23.11.1934
14382	31.12.1940	14388	31.12.1930	14394	19.9.1936
14383	10.9.1934	14389	25.2.1931	14395	20.11.1935
14384	27.8.1938	14390	30.1.1937	14396	10.9.1934

The location of the Lochs appears in Cormack and Stevenson`s "Highland Railway Locomotives" Book 1.

'Small Ben' class 4-4-0

British Railways renumbering, and amended withdrawal dates:-

14397	5.2.1949	(54397)		14407	24.3.1931		
14398	12.2.1953	54398	10.1950	14408	21.6.1947		
14399	22.4.1952	54399	1.1951	14409	28.3.1950	(54409)	
14400	21.9.1946			14410	10.12.1949	(54410)	
14401	16.10.1948	(54401)		14411	26.9.1936*		
14402	9.12.1939**			14412	19.4.1947		
14403	12.2.1949	(54403)		14413	30.12.1933		
14404	16.10.1950	54404	10.1948	14414	30.12.1933		
14405	9.9.1944			14415	8.5.1948	(54415)	
14406	2.8.1947			14416	21.8.1948	(54416)	

The correct spelling of 14407 is **BEN MACDHUI**.

There is a builder's photograph of H.R. No 1 with the name *Ben Nevis* (Later to be LMS No 14397 *BEN-Y-GLOE*).

14379 lost its name during the war, but this was later restored. The locomotive was noted at Aviemore on 15.3.1945, once more named *Loch Insh*, and in very fine condition externally.

Withdrawal was not always final:-

* An unusual visitor to Ardrossan late in 1936 was the former HR 14411 *Ben Loyal*, which had come down to Kilmarnock to be scrapped, but was put into further use from Hurlford.

** For some two years after withdrawal, 14402 *BEN ARMIN*, still "fairly complete though dirty and decrepit", functioned as a stationary boiler on carriage warming duties at Ayr.

'Large Ben' class 4-4-0

Withdrawal dates:-

14417	23.5.1936	14419	3.10.1935	14421	24.10.1932
14418	26.12.1932	14420	27.3.1934	14422	4.3.1937***

*** 14422 *BEN A'CHAORUINN*, the last of its class to be withdrawn, somewhat ingloriously finished its career by supplying steam to Inverness Station Laundry while the laundry boiler was in course of replacement, before being dispatched to Kilmarnock for scrapping.

Snaigow and Durn 4-4-0

HR Number	LMS Number	Name	Date of Withdrawal
73	14522	*SNAIGOW*	9.4.1936
74	14523	*DURN*	11.4.1935

Castle class 4-6-0

Withdrawal dates:-

14675	4.8.1939	14682	5.11.1943	14689	26.8.1944
14676	21.9.1937	14683	17.4.1937	14690	19.4.1947
14677	25.2.1939	14684	13.1.1940	14691	9.9.1938
14678	9.2.1946	14685	20.1.1945	14692	23.3.1946
14679	22.2.1936	14686	13.7.1946	14693	11.4.1935
14680	14.5.1930	14687	7.5.1935		
14681	21.9.1946	14688	2.2.1935		

14678 was withdrawn w/e 1.7.1939, and reinstated w/e 14.9.1940
14689　　　　　　　w/e 29.4.1939,　　　　　w/e 10.5.1941

HR Livery. As with all ex-Highland Railway classes in LMS days, the name appeared first in serif style, and from the late 1930s onwards in plain block lettering.

Clan class 4-6-0

Withdrawal dates:-

14762	7.6.1947	14765	20.1.1945	14768	10.3.1945
14763	5.8.1944	14766	18.3.1944	14769	8.10.1943
14764	14.2.1948	54767	30.1.1950		

Strathpeffer Tank class 0-4-4T

Withdrawal date:-

15050   21.12.1929

Passenger Tank class (Drummond) 0-4-4T

Withdrawal date:-

15051   (55051 5.1949)   22.6.1956

Lochgorm Tank class (Stroudley) 0-6-0T

Withdrawal dates:-

16118	12.1927	16119	26.12.1932	16383	10.1.1927

Name Styles
The height of the lettering in LMS days was 4in. at least up to 1928.

14397 was withdrawn in February 1949 as *BEN-Y-GLOE*.
14416 *BEN A`BHUIRD* appeared as *BEN-A-BHUIRD* sometime between June 1943 and August 1945. (Photographic evidence)

Glossary

Glasgow & South Western Railway:-
Lord Glenarthur was a Director of the Company, and Chairman 1920-1922.

Highland Railway Names (Additional):-

(ABERFELDY)	The branch where HR 50 (ex 17) worked for a while. A town in Perthshire, the name of which came from the Gaelic for the name of a follower of St.Ninian. *
(ATHOLL)	The Duke of Atholl, a Director.
(BRUCE)	The Hon.Thomas Charles Bruce, Deputy Chairman 1865, and Chairman 1885-1891.
(BURGHEAD)	The branch where HR 58 worked for a time. From the Norse "a ford or shelter." a fishing village in Morayshire.*
(COLVILLE)	Lord Colville of Culross.
(CONON)	Geographical.
(DOCHFOUR)	The residence at the north-east end of Loch Ness of James R.Baillie. a Director. OR "James E.Bailey Esq.," The name is derived from the old Flemish meaning "Pasture land".
(FIFE)	The Earl of Fife, a Director.
(HIGHLANDER)	A general name of no specific significance.
(ISLA BANK)	The residence at Keith of George Kynoch, a Director. The name sometimes appears spelt ISLABANK, and as the residence of James W.Kynoch, Esq. Director. The name is derived from the River Isla.*
(LENTRAM)	Geographical.
(LOVAT) (ROSEHAUGH)	Lord Lovat, head of the Fraser Clan, a Director, and large shareholder. The residence near Avoch, Ross-shire of James D.Fletcher, a Director. OR. The estate in Ross-shire owned by Douglas Fletcher Esq., Director. The name is derived from the Gaelic meaning a "promontary".*

* Information derived from Alan G.Dunbar, SLS Journal 1958 page 182ff.

Additional information and corrections of fact:-

BEN MHEADHOIN	The name has sometimes appeared in print as Mheadoin and Mheadhouin, but photographic evidence (See Cormack and Stevenson's Highland Railway Locomotives Book 2, Figure 69 on page 80) shows the name in March 1924 to be Ben Mheadhoin.
BEN MACDHUI	Macdhui. (Spelling corrections)
BEN NA CAILLICH	In Druid lore Beira held sway from the Feast of Samhuinn (modern Hallowe'en) to the Beltane festival in late spring.
(GRANDTULLY)	The residence of W.Steuart Fotheringham Esq.

Chapter 8
NORTHERN IRELAND
Northern Counties Committee
(formerly the Belfast & Northern Counties Railway)

Additional information and corrections:-

33 *Galgorm Castle* was built at Belfast in 1890. In November 1926 it was renewed as a 4-4-0 "U1", renumbered 3, and retained its name *Galgorm Castle*.

It carried the name *Galgorm Castle* from 1926 until 12.1932 when it was renamed *Glanaan*.

"Mountain" class 4-4-0 "A1"

67 *Slieveanorra* Delete all reference. The name was allotted, but the locomotive was withdrawn without receiving its name.
69 *Slieve Bane* The B&NCR Number was 9.
Several references exist which give this name as a single word *Slievebane*, but there is photographic evidence that two separate words is correct.

"County" class 4-4-0 "B3"

60 *County Donegal* was named 6.1932

Light Compound 2-4-0 "C1"

57 *Galgorm Castle* The B&NCR Number was 57.

Heavy Compound 4-4-0 "D"

55 *Parkmount* was withdrawn in 1940, reinstated in 1942 and finally withdrawn in 1944.

Superheated Simple 4-4-0 "D1"

50 *Jubilee* Its former class was 4-4-0 "D".

Class "A"

58 *Lurigethan* Delete all reference. The name was allotted but never applied.

"Glen" class 4-4-0 "U1"

3 *Glenaan* The naming date was 12.1932.
4 *Glenariff* The naming date was 1.1931.

"Castle" class 4-4-0 "U2"

71 *Glenarm Castle* The B&NCR Number was 69.
Two Castle class names have at times appeared in error in print as *Cara Castle* and *Lisanoure Castle*

"Mogul" class 2-6-0 "W"

The naming date for 97 *Earl of Ulster* was 5.7.1935.
Names were considered in the first instance for Moguls 90-3:-

90 *Earl of Ulster*	92 *Richard de Burgh*
91 *Sorley Bay*	93 *John de Courcy*

Years of withdrawal:-

1949 4A (formerly 4), 33	1960 76, 78
1950 34, 65,	1961 80, 84, 96
1954 62, 64, 66, 69	1963 74 to Belfast Transport Museum
1956 75, 79, 82, 83, 90, (101)	1964 95, 98
1957 81, 87. 92,	1965 91, 93, 94, 97, 99
1959 100, 103	

The table published in the Railway Magazine for June 1931 gives details of the NCC stock of that time. It includes a list of the engines already named, and indicates the intention of giving names to all the Mountain and Castle class engines. For some reason three Mountains and four Counties never received them.

The ornate style of the characteristic is NCC numberplate made the "7" somewhat reminiscent of an invertd "2"; the numerals in fact were not reversible.

They would have been:-

58 *Lurigethan*	Class "A1"		70 *Portmuck Castle*	Class "U2"
59 *Craiggore*	(Formerly Class "A")		72 *Shane's Castle*	(Formerly class "U")
63 *Ben Bradagh*	ditto		73 *Carn Castle*	ditto
			77 *Ballygalley Castle*	ditto

Dundalk, Newry & Greenore Railway

The Crewe numbers of Nos.1-6, were *1509-11/1962/3* and *3877*.

5 *Carlingford* was withdrawn 10.1928, and cut up 11.1928.

All five 0-6-0STs were withdrawn in 1951, and the line closed on 31.12.1951.

The date of Adam Macrory's significant role in the formation of the Dundalk & Greenore Railway was in 1863 (not 1873 as stated)

The County Donegal Railways Joint Committee 3ft 0in gauge

This table is reset, following subsequent information:-

			Builder and date	Withdrawn	Scrapped
2-4-0T Class 1			Sharp, Stewart & Co. 1881		
	1	*Alice*		1926	
	(2	*Blanche* and 3 *Lydia*		1912)	
4-6-0T Class 2			Neilson, Reid & Co. 1893		
	4	*Meenglas*		1935	
	5	*Drumboe*		1931	
	6	*Inver*		1931	
	7	*Finn*		1931	
	8	*Foyle*		1935	8.1937
	9	*Columbkille*		1935	After 8.1937
4-4-4T Class 3			Neilson, Reid & Co. 1902		
	10	*Sir James*		1933	
	11	*Hercules*		1933	

				Renumbered in 1937	Withdrawn
4-6-4T Class 4			Nasmyth, Wilson & Co. 1904		
	12	*Eske*		9	1954
	13	*Owenea*		10	Early 1953
	14	*Erne*		11	1959
	15	*Mourne*		(12)	Early 1953

				Renumbered and renamed before 12.1936	Withdrawn
2-6-4T Class 5			Nasmyth, Wilson & Co. 1907		
	16	*Donegal*		4 *Meenglas*	1959
	17	*Glenties*		5 *Drumboe*	1969
	18	*Killybegs*		6 *Columbkille*	1959
	19	*Letterkenny*		(7 *Finn*)	1940
	20	*Raphoe*		8 *Foyle*	1954
2-6-4T Class 5A			Nasmyth, Wilson & Co. 1907		
	21	*Bellyshannon*	Renumbered 1 in 1917 and renamed *Alice* in 1928		1959
	2A	*Strabane*	Renumbered and renamed 2 *Blanche* in 1928		1959
	3A	*Stranorlar*	Renumbered and renamed 3 *Lydia* in 1928		1959

Details:-

Class 4 No 12 *Mourne* was officially renumbered 15 but the number was never changed on the engine.

Class 5 No 8 received the nameplates from the old Class 2 of that number, as also most probably did Nos 4, 5 and 6.

No 19 *Letterkenny* was withdrawn without being renumbered or renamed, and the frames, cab, and side tanks were to be seen at Stranloar in 1950, with numberplates "19" and nameplates *Letterkenny* still in place.

No 18 *Killybegs* was officially supposed to be re-named *Glencolumbkille*, and is listed as such in the Railway Observer Supplement of March 1937, and in the RCTS Stock Book of 1939. The Stock Book of 1946 lists it as *Columbkille*.
Class 5A locomotives received the original nameplates of the first Number 1 - 3.

Gardner 74 HP Diesel 11 *Phoenix* was built in 1928 as a vertical boiler steam tractor by Atkinson Walker of Wigan at Atkinson`s Frenchwood works in Preston, similar in principle to the "Sentinel" locomotives. It ran successfully and unnamed on the Clogher Valley Railway in 1929, and was converted to a diesel locomotive at Dundalk works in 1932, and named during 1937. It was withdrawn in 1961.

Glossary

Additional information:-

Columbkille	The home village of Sir James Musgrave (q.v.).
Drumboe	The residence in County Donegal of Sir Samuel Hercules Hayes, Bart.
Hercules	Named after Sir Samuel Hercules Hayes, Bart. Chairman of the Fenn Valley Railway, 1887-1892, and Director of the Donegal Valley Railway from 1892. He was the son-in-law of the 4th Viscount Lifford.
Phoenix	So named because the locomotive had been converted from steam to diesel, and so had 'risen from the ashes'.
Raphoe	The 'Blue Guide' refers to Raphoe as a village.
Sir James	Sir James Musgrave 1826-1904 (Bart.1897) Partner in Musgrave Bros., Belfast Ironfounders. Chairman Belfast Harbour Board. Deputy Chairman WDR from 1873; Chairman Donegal Railway 1896-1904.

Class 2 Nos 4 - 9 were said to have been named after the towns or villages of the residences of Company Directors.

Chapter 9
THE DUPLICATION OF NAMES

Name	First engine Number	Second engine Number	Period of Overlap		
Achilles	5290	5697	7.4.1936	to	10.10.1936
Ajax	5190	6139	3.1928	to	9.9.1928
Arethusa	5671	5696	2.4.1936	to	9.1936
Atlas	5658	6134	3.1928	to	7.1933
Bee	Horwich Works	5084	1.1.1923	to	1930
Blackpool	11680	5407	1.1.1923	to	10.1927
Breadalbane	CR779/14335	6017	3.1923	to	1.1925
Condor	5672	6145	3.1928	to	7.1933
Coronation	5348	6220	15.5.1937	to	22.6.1940
Courier	5057	6147	4.1928	to	12.1928
Cyprus	5359	5605	28.7.1936	to	9.1936
Express	5311	5706	26.5.1936	to	9.1936
Gibraltar	5356	5608	13.3.1936	to	9.1936
Goliath	5116	6136	4.1928	to	10.12.1931
Hector	5035	6140	4.1928	to	7.1928
Holyhead	DN&GR(I)6	5408	1.1923	to	24.4.1937
		5514	9.7.1938	briefly and from	26.3.1947
India	5350	5574	26.5.1936	to by	10.11.1936
Jubilee	NCC(I)50	5156	1.1923	to	12.1931
King Edward VII	5185	NCC(I)3	1.1923	to	18.2.1930
King George VI	NCC(I)99	6244	6.1941	to	31.12.1947
Lady of the Lake	5468	6149	4.1928	to	31.12.1928
Liverpool	7334/27334	6130	4.1928	to	3.1935
Malta	5358	5616	6.8.1936	to	9.1936
Meteor	5398	6128	4.1928	to	7.1933
Novelty	5036	6127	4.1928	to	1.7.1928
Planet	5397	6131	4.1928	to	7.1933
Queen Alexandra	5145	NCC(I)34	1.1923	to	11.1928
Queen Elizabeth	NCC(I)100	6221	1938	to	31.12.1947
Samson	5682	6135	4.1928	to	7.1933
Sanspareil	5492	6126	4.1928	to	12.1928
Silver Jubilee	5552	NCC(I)96	18.5.1935	to	31.12.1947
South Africa	5355	5571	4.5.1936	to	4.7.1936
Thunderer	5310	5703	5.5.1936	to	9.1936
Velocipede	5312	6148	4.1928	to	7.1933
Vulcan	5669	6133	4.1928	to	17.4.1937

Chapter 10
CEREMONIES (NAMES AND PLAQUES)

It appears probable that until 1975 the LMS locomotive naming ceremony files were kept at Derby London Midland Region CM&EE headquarters, but were then thrown out and destroyed. The undergoing entries have been assembled from cuttings in the railway press and in newspapers.

6122 Royal Ulster Rifleman
There is believed to have been a naming ceremony, sometime possibly before 1929, but the date has not been discovered.

1929
24th October 6138 *The London Irish Rifleman*
At Euston by Lt.Col.Pilkington, in the presence of Sir Josiah Stamp, Mr.J.H.Follows, Sir Henry Fowler, Mr.C.Byrom and other officers of the LMS. The engine was working a troop train taking the Royal Ulster Rifles from Euston to Ireland. In attendance were Pipers and a Guard of Honour.

1930
Saturday 21st June 6123 *Royal Irish Fusilier*
At Euston. Lt.General Sir Thomas E.Scott, KCB, CIE, DSO presented plaques bearing the crest of the regiment, and in doing so said that the railway company had paid them a great compliment in giving their name to the engine which conveyed members of the regiment to their homes when they came back on leave from foreign service. The plaques bear the words "*Faugh-a-Ballagh*", Gaelic for "Clear the Way", the motto of the regiment. They were received on behalf of the LMS by Mr.John Quirey, Vice-President of the Company. Driver W.Bull and Fireman J.Kilmore (both of Crewe) were on the footplate.

Wednesday 15th October 6102 *Black Watch*
At Glasgow Central when the plaques bearing the regimental crest, the gift of the Black Watch Association, were unveiled. Major George D.Pullar, OBE, TD unveiled them, and Mr.Robert Killin, CBE, General Superintendent of the Northern Division of the LMS accepted their custody. It was noted that Sir Robert Munro, the first colonel of the regiment, appointed in 1736 was an ancestor of Sir Robert Munro, one of the present Scottish Directors of the LMSR. This was the first Scottish Regiment to make such a presentation.

9th December 6168 *The Girl Guide* and 6169 *The Boy Scout*
At Euston by Lady and Lord Baden-Powell respectively.

1931
7th January 6161 *King's Own*
Formerly named *The King's Own*, the locomotive was renamed at Euston by Brig.Gen.F.B.Matthews CB,DSO, the 2nd Battalion having disembarked at Southampton the same day after overseas service and travelled to London for the ceremony. 6161 then conveyed them to Lichfield.

1933
16th June 6112 *Sherwood Forester*
At Derby in the C.M.E. Department of the Works, by Major R.L.Sherbrooke, commanding officer of the Depot, Normanton Barracks, who was invited by Captain H.P.M.Beames, deputy C.M.E. Derby, to unveil the nameplate and regimental plaque. The ceremony was attended by the civic authorities, regimental officers, a representative from the regiment, and the band of the 1st Battalion Sherwood Foresters.

17th June 6109 *Royal Engineer*
Naming ceremony at Derby.

22nd July 6167 *The Hertfordshire Regiment*
At Watford Station. Brigadier General the Viscount Hampden KCB, CMG, Colonel of the Regiment and Lord Lieutenant of Hertfordshire unveiled the plates. The Mayor of Watford was present, and the LMS was represented by Viscount Knutsford JP, DL.

1935
24th June 6130 *The West Yorkshire Regiment*
At Wellington Station, Leeds. Plaques were added by the Colonel of the Regiment, General Sir C.J.Deverell, KCB.

2nd August 6103 *Royal Scots Fusilier*
At Ayr Station. Presentation of plaques by Lord Trenchard, Colonel of the Regiment. The plaques were received by Mr. Charles Kerr, Chairman of the LMS Scottish Local Committee.

17th October 6147 *The Northamptonshire Regiment*
At Northampton (Castle) Station. Plaques were unveiled by Lady Knox, wife of Sir Harry Knox, KCB, DSO, Colonel in Chief of the Regiment and were accepted on behalf of the LMS by Mr.E.J.H.Lemon, Vice-President. Detachments of the regiment from Aldershot, Peterborough and Huntingdon travelled to be present at the occasion, and the Mayor and a distinguished company were there. (An instance of excellent coverage.)

12th November 6170 *British Legion*
At Euston by Earl Jellicoe. He was not well at the time, but insisted on fulfilling his obligations at this and various other Remembrance ceremonies. The strain was too much for him and he died a week later.

7th December 6129 *The Scottish Horse*
At Perth General Station His Grace the Duke of Atholl unveiled a plaque bearing the crest of the Regiment. The gift was acknowledged on behalf of the Company by Mr.Charles Kerr, chairman of the Scottish Local Committee. The engine driver, Mr.John Sprunt, was a former sergeant who had fought with the regiment in the Boer War under the Duke of Atholl himself.

10th December 5665 *Lord Rutherford of Nelson*
At St. Pancras station by Master Pat Fowler, grandson of Lord Rutherford prior to the departure of the special train to Derby on the occasion of the opening of the LMS Research Centre.

1936
14th January 6126 *Royal Army Service Corps*
At Euston by Major-General W.K.Tarver CB, CMG, Colonel-Commandant, RASC in the presence of Mr.E.B.Fielden, Deputy Chairman of the Company. The Corps presented a replica of their crest, which had been fixed above the nameplate.

6th March 5157 *The Glasgow Highlander*
At Glasgow Central Station by Mrs.A.H.Menzies, wife of the Honorary Colonel of the Battalion. Sir Robert Bruce, one of the Scottish directors, accepted the plaques on behalf of the Company. It was appropriate that the ceremony took place on the platform from which the regiment had set out to France in 1914.

16th March 6113 *Cameronian*
At Glasgow Central Station, when plaques were added.

22nd May 5158 *Glasgow Yeomanry*
At Glasgow Central Station.

Saturday 6th June 6136 *The Border Regiment*
At the Citadel station, Carlisle. There was a guard of honour of twenty men from the Castle, which was inspected by the Mayor at the start of the proceedings. Major W.F.H.Chambers, MC performed the ceremony of unveiling the plaque, the gift of the Regiment. Sir Robert Creig MC, LlD, DSc. represented the LMS Company, and the engine was in charge of Driver John A.Forster and Fireman James Bradley, MM, both of whom had served in the Regiment during the Great War. The ceremony ended with the Band of the 4th Battalion playing "John Peel", The Border Regiment marching tune.
The plates had been fitted at St.Rollox on 28th April.

13th June 6141 *The North Staffordshire Regiment*
At Stoke-on-Trent by Sir Francis Joseph, a Director of the LMS.

19th June 5156 *Ayrshire Yeomanry*

30th June 6125 *3rd Carabinier*
At Euston by Sir Josiah Stamp.

Sunday 4th October 6145 *The Duke of Wellington's Regt. (West Riding)* at Halifax.
The naming ceremony was performed by Brig.Gen.P.A.Turner, Colonel of the Duke of Wellington's Regiment. Among the civic guests were the Mayors and Mayoresses of Halifax and Brighouse, and the Mayor of Huddersfield. Driver G.S.Seed and Fireman A.Marsh both of Low Moor were old members of the Regiment. The Regiment provided the plaque to affix to the name plate.

27th November 6127 *Old Contemptibles*
At Euston by General Sir Felix Ready,President the O.C. Association. The LMS was represented by Mr.W.V.Wood, a Vice-President of the Company.

1937

23rd March 5524 *Blackpool*
At Blackpool Central by the Mayor of Blackpool, Alderman W.S.Ashton, on the occasion of a visit by Sir Josiah Stamp who, later in the day was presented with the Freedom of the Borough.

8th April 5154 *Lanarkshire Yeomanry*
Named by the Colonel of the Regiment, Sir John Usher.

10th April 5504 *Royal Signals*
At Euston (Platform 1) by Brigadier H.Clementi Smith, Colonel Commandant of the Royal Corps of Signals. Mr.W.A.Stanier, Chief Mechanical Engineer of the LMS welcomed the Corps on behalf of the Company.

17th April 5501 *St Dunstan's*
At Euston (Platform 1) by Sir Ian Fraser, CBE, MP.

27th May 5595 *Southern Rhodesia*
At Euston by their Prime Minister Dr.Huggins.

5th June 5502 *Royal Naval Division*
At Euston by Mr.Winston Churchill.

11th July 6124 *London Scottish*
At Euston by Colonel L.D.Henderson, MC, TD, Commanding Officer of the London Scottish (14th London Regiment).

Note: 5518 *Bradshaw* was seen running with names covered on 15th July 1937, and so presumably a naming ceremony was intended.

6th October 5526 *Morecambe and Heysham*
At Morecambe Promenade Station by the Mayor, Mr.Michael Benson. (Plaques were fitted later, in December)

14th October 6137 *The Prince of Wales's Volunteers South Lancashire*
At Warrington Bank Quay Station.

18th December 5548 *Lytham St.Annes* At St.Annes-on-the Sea by The Mayor of Lytham St.Annes in the presence of Mr.Ashton Davies.

20th November 5507 *Royal Tank Corps*
At Euston, on the twentieth anniversary of the battle of Cambrai. The ceremony was performed by Major-General Sir Ernest Swinton, KBE, CB, DSO, the representative Colonel Commandant of the Royal Tank Corps. The Company was represented by Mr.W.A.Stanier. The engine was in the charge of Driver H.R.Prince who had served with the Corps and was mentioned three times in despatches, and Fireman G.H.Sorrell who had served with the Corps from 1918 to 1920. After the ceremony they were each presented with an inscribed silver tankard.

1938

26th January 5560 *Prince Edward Island*
At Euston.

26th January 5564 *New South Wales*
At Euston by Mr.A.E.Heath CMG, Agent General of New South Wales. A detachment and band of the Royal Navy took part in the ceremony in recognition of the fact that Captain Arthur Phillips, RN was in command of the Brig "Supply", which had landed sailors 150 years before.

Note: 5520 *Llandudno* and 6144 *Honourable Artillery Company* were observed on 8th May 1938 with nameplates covered, presumably in preparation for naming ceremonies.

14th May 5511 *Isle of Man*
The Coat of Arms were added to the nameplates at this time. (No mention of place of ceremony.)

16th June 5525 *Colwyn Bay*
At Platform 1 of Colwyn Bay Station by the Mayor, Alderman Robert Howard. Mr Ashton Davies OBE, Chief Commercial Manager of the LMS presided, and with him was Lord Colwyn, a Director. The platform was described as "A Blaze of Colour". The ceremony was not without incident. The Mayor had two tries at smashing the bottle of champagne. The first time the hammer dropped from his hand onto the permanent way; another was produced, and at the second attempt he succeeded. (North Wales

Pioneer 23rd June)

20th June 6131 *The Royal Warwickshire Regiment*
At New St. Station, Birmingham by Brigadier C.T.Tomes, DSO, Colonel of the Regiment in the presence of Mr.W.A.Stanier, CME, and Brigadier General Sir Walter Ludlow and the Lord Mayor of Birmingham. The plaques were presented by Lt.Col.P.M.Brooke-Hitching.

Wednesday 6th July 5523 *Bangor*
At Bangor by the Mayor, Councillor W.Owen, by breaking a bottle of champagne over the nameplate, and emphasising the first syllable of the name "Bangor". The arrangements were made by Mr.L.C.Brittlebank, District Goods and Passenger Manager, Chester. The engine was manned by Driver E.Williams and Fireman O.Edwards. Notable among the guests was Dr.Green, Archbishop of Wales.

8th July 5503 *The Leicestershire Regiment*
At Leicester, London Road by Brigadier General B.C.Dent.

Sunday 31st July 5516 *The Bedfordshire and Hertfordshire Regiment*
As part of the celebrations of the 250th anniversary of the County Regiment, the engine was named at Midland Road Station, Bedford by the Colonel of the Regiment, Lieut. General Sir Henry Jackson, in the presence of Lord Luke (Lord Lieutenant of Bedfordshire), the Mayor of Bedford (Ald.W.E.Sowter MBE), the High Sheriff of Bedfordshire (Mr.J.H.Staddon), the Bishop of St. Albans, and Mr.D.S.Inman (District Goods and Passenger Manager). A Guard of Honour consisted of men of the 2nd and 5th Battalions. Both Driver P.W.Pegg and Fireman A.Fitzgerald had served in the Regiment. The Bishop offered a prayer, and it is understood that a brass plate inside the engine's cab recorded its dedication.

4th November 5538 *Giggleswick*
At Settle by Mr E.H.Partridge, Head Master of Giggleswick School. Mr.H.A.Hooks presided and pupils of the school were present.

During February 5515 *Caernarvon*
'Quietly' in the presence of the town's civic dignitaries.

Note: 5518 *Bradshaw* was noted on 15th July 1939 running with names covered, from which it was presumed that a naming ceremony was pending. Whether or not one ever took place is not known.

1940

30th July 5543 *Home Guard*
At Euston by Lt.Gen. Sir Henry Pownall, KBE,CB, MC, Inspector General of the Home Guard. (This was the first ceremony since the outbreak of war.)

1943

20th July 6245 *City of London*
At Euston by the Lord Mayor, Sir Samuel G.Joseph, in the presence of Sir Thomas Royden, Chairman of the LMS. Driver Freestone, who had been awarded the BEM for services during air raids and Fireman D.H.Saville were in charge at the ceremony.

3rd September 6246 *City of Manchester*
At Manchester Victoria by the Lord Mayor of Manchester, Alderman J.S.Hill. This was the first recorded visit of the class to Manchester (Victoria). At the ceremony Driver W.Wood, VC, of Newton Heath was in charge of the locomotive.

21st September 6247 *City of Liverpool*
At Liverpool Lime Street by the Lord Mayor.

4th November 5616 *Malta G.C.*
At Euston. Renamed by Lt.Gen.Sir William Dobbie, former GOC Malta.

2nd December 6248 *City of Leeds*
At Leeds City Station by the Lord Mayor, Alderman Albert Hayes, JP.

1944

20th June 6250 *City of Lichfield*
At Lichfield Trent Valley Station by the Mayor, Miss Agnes M.Thompson, in the presence of Lord Royden, Chairman of the LMS.

9th October 6252 *City of Leicester*
At Leicester by the Lord Mayor, in the presence of the Lady Mayoress and many prominent persons of the City. The LMS was represented by Mr.G.L.Darbyshire, Vice-President, and Mr.H.Tandy. the Leicester Goods and Passenger Manager. The locomotive was on display the following day at Campbell Street sidings.

1st November 6249 *City of Sheffield*
At Sheffield by the Lord Mayor, Councillor S.H.Marshall, in the presence of Sir Harold Hartley, Vice-President of the LMS accompanied by officials of Samuel Fox & Sons whose firm made the replacement stainless steel nameplates fitted at Crewe in 1945.

1945

20th March 6235 *City of Birmingham*
At Birmingham New Street Station by the Lord Mayor.

4th October 6251 *City of Nottingham*
At Nottingham. It marked the occasion inauspiciously by getting derailed at the south end of the station.

6th November 6240 *City of Coventry*
At Coventry Eaton Road Station by the Mayor, who also presented plaques of the City Coat of Arms, in the presence of Sir Harold Hartley, Vice-President of the L.M.S. Two railwaymen with distinguished records were in charge of the locomotive, Driver C.M.Brett MM, who had served in both World Wars and Fireman Jonathan Birch who had come through the evacuation at Dunkirk. According to the Coventry Evening Telegraph the locomotive mileage at the time was 395,565.

1946

4th September 5633 *Aden*
At Euston. Renamed by Lt.Col.Sir Bernard Reilly KCMG,CIE,OBE who was the first Governor when it became a colony in 1937. Sir Robert Burrows, Chairman of the LMS was present.

20th September 6254 *City of Stoke-on-Trent*
At Stoke-on-Trent by the Lord Mayor, Councillor Percy Williams JP in the presence of Sir Francis Joseph, Director LMS. This was the first occasion of a 4-6-2 visiting the city. It worked to Stoke via orton Bridge and Stone. The City Coat of Arms were not applied until 1947. They were the gift of the Corporation and after being affixed were inspected by the Lord Mayor and Lady Mayoress, Alderman and Mrs.H.Leason, the Town Clerk, and Sir Francis Joseph, Director LMS.

13th December 6133 *The Green Howards*
At Leeds City Station. General Sir Harold E.Franklyn, Colonel of the Regiment unveiled the regimental crests. These were the gift of Sir Robert Ropner whose son-in-law Lt.Col.C.M.Hull MC was second in command of the 6th Battalion. Mr.R.A.Riddles, a Vice-

President of the LMS presided. Driver Wallace was on the footplate, and had served in the regiment in the First World War; he was accompanied by his son Fireman Charlie Wallace, who had earlier been a driver in the Royal Engineers in France during the Second World War.

1947

Friday 31st January 5739 *Ulster*
At Euston. The plaques of the Coat of Arms of Ulster, mounted above the nameplates of the engine, were presented by Lady Brooke, wife of Capt.The Rt.Hon.Sir Basil Brooke, Bart, CBE MC DL MP, Prime Minister of Northern Ireland. The ceremony was attended by many distinguished guests and was presided over by Sir Robert Burrows, Chairman of the LMS.

15th April 6134 *The Cheshire Regiment*
At Chester (General) Station. Brigadier G.P.Harding unveiled the nameplate and plaque, in the presence of Field Marshal Montgomery and Sir Robert Burrows, Chairman of the LMS. The Field Marshall drove the locomotive through the station after the ceremony.

28th June 6135 *The East Lancashire Regiment*
At Preston. Plaques of the crest were unveiled by Brigadier J.W.Pendlebury, DSO, MC, in the presence of Sir Robert Burrows, Chairman of the LMS.

During August 5505 *The Royal Army Ordnance Corps*
The locomotive was named without any special ceremony because of the austere conditions prevailing at the time. The plaques were the gift of the Corps, made during 1947.

17th December 6256 *Sir William A.Stanier, F.R.S.*
At Euston. Sir Robert Burrows, Chairman of the LMS, presided at the ceremony.

British Railways

1948

3rd June 46257 *City of Salford*
At Manchester Exchange by the Mayor of Salford, Alderman J.Brentnall.

12th August 45529 *Stephenson*
At Chesterfield (Market Place) Station. Renamed for George Stephenson's centenary celebrations.

15th September 45506 *The Royal Pioneer Corps*
At Euston by Field Marshal Viscount Montgomery. The plaques were presented by the R.P.C. Association.

18th September 46112 *Sherwood Forester*
At Nottingham. New plaques presented by Brigadier P.N.White, Colonel of the Regiment. Driver Croll and Fireman Follon, both ex-Foresters, were on the footplate, wearing their medals.

1949

22nd January 46121 *Highland Light Infantry The City of Glasgow Regiment*
At Glasgow Central Station, when plaques were presented by the Lord Provost of Glasgow. A Guard of Honour was provided by the Regiment.

8th September NCC101 *Lord Massereene*
At York Road Station, Belfast, by Lord Massereene in a brief ceremony prior to the departure of the Londonderry train.

1951

10th November 45509 *The Derbyshire Yeomanry*
At Derby Midland Station. Officially named by Colonel Sir Ian Walker, Colonel of the Regiment, and the regimental crests were presented by Lt.Col.J.Crompton-Inglefield.

1958

12th December 45610 *Ghana*
At Euston. Renamed by His Excellency Mr.E.O.Asafu-Adjaye, High Commissioner of Ghana. Mr.David Blee, General Manager of the London Midland Region of British Railways presided.

1969

October 6115 *Scots Guardsman*
At Dinting, Glossop by Lt.J.A.Napier.
(After the locomotive's restoration for preservation.)

Chapter 11
THE APPENDIX
London Tilbury & Southend Railway

Details of Locomotive classes, Builders and Makers numbers:-

(1)	**The "No 1" class 4-4-2T**	**Nos 1-36**		
	1-12 Sharp, Stewart & Co	1880		2880-2891
	13-8 ditto	1881		2969-71/3018-20
	19-30 ditto	1884		3217-28
	31-6 Nasmyth, Wilson & Co.	1892		425-30
(2)	**Originally the "No 37" class 4-4-2T**	**Nos 37-48**		
	37-42 Sharp, Stewart & Co.	1897		4245-50
	43-8 Dubs & Co.	1898		3666-71
(4)	**The "No 51" class 4-4-2T**	**Nos 51-68**		
	51-62 Sharp, Stewart & Co.	1900		4653-64
	63-8 The North British Locomotive Co.Ltd.	1903		15744-9
(5)	**The "No 69" class 0-6-2T**	**Nos 69-78/83-6**		
	69-74 North British Loco.Co.Ltd.	1903		15750-5
	75-8 ditto	1908		18504-7
	83-6 Beyer, Peacock & Co.	1912		5604-7
(6)	**The "No 79" class 4-4-2T**	**Nos 79-82**		
	R.Stephenson & Co.	1909		3366-9
(7)	**The "No 87" class 4-6-4T**	**Nos 87-94**		
	Beyer, Peacock & Co.	1912		5608-15

Additional Information:

6 *Upton Park* and 17 *Thames Haven*
    There is photographic evidence that at some time both names had a hyphen separating the two words, (*Upton-Park* and *Thames-Haven*).

80 *Thundersley* Immediately below the name is a replica of the gold medal awarded at the Imperial International Exhibition held at Shepherd's
    Bush in 1909.

Names proposed but never applied, for the twelve engines that were delivered from Beyer, Peacock in 1912 after the MR takeover:-

For the 0-6-2T "69" class.

83 *Ealing*	Western terminus of Ealing to Southend through service
84 *Vange*	A small village near Pitsea
85 *Hammersmith*	One of the District Railway's main stations in west London and served by the Ealing to Southend through service
86 *Richmond*	Served by the District Railway, but no through service to Southend

For the 4-6-4T "87" class.

87 *Henry Doughty Browne*	Chairman LTS 1883-1906
88 *James Rolls Hoare*	Deputy Chairman in 1912
89 *Cecil Brown*	Director in 1912
90 *Francis Claughton Mathews*	Director in 1912
91 *Herbert Morton Jessel*	Director in 1912
92 *James Round*	Director in 1912
93 *Frederick Whiney*	Director in 1912

94 *Arthur Lewis Stride*   Chairman from 1906 and Managing Director in 1912

Concerning the names for the "Baltic" Tanks the only thing that is certain is the Mr.Robert Harben Whitelegg intended that they should be named after past and present Directors of the Company. There exist two hypothetical lists, both alleged to have been suggested by Mr.R.A.C.Nunn, one being as listed above, the other containing the same names, but starting with "Arthur Lewis Stride", and giving expanded names for Nos 91 and 92 as "Capt.(later Col.Sir) Herbert Morton Jessel" and "The Rt. Hon. James Round" respectively.

A scale model of No 94 is painted in the green livery of the Railway, and is named *Arthur Lewis Stride*, who was Chairman of theLTSR at the time of the amalgamation with the Midland.

Corrections:

31 *St Pancras*   Delete the full stop in "St.".
The lettering was in capitals, with the T half size in the upper half of the lettering space and underlined.
40 For *Blackhorse Road* read *Black Horse Road*.
59 *Holloway* Delete *Road* (renamed *Holloway* in 1911).
62 *Camden Town*   For *Town* read *Road*.
78 *Dagenham Docks* For *Docks* read *Dock*.

Sources differ in respect of the renamings of these engines, but Kenneth Leech is undoubtedly a most reliable historian, and the following list has been derived from his articles in the Stephenson Locomotive Society Journal in 1940:-

9	*Purfleet - Black Horse Road*	1911/2	45	*Burdett Road - Shoeburyness*	1911
13	*Benfleet - Commercial Road*	1911/2	55	*Wellington Road - Bow Road*	1903
18	*Shoeburyness - Burdett Road*	1911/2	58	*Hornsey Road - Hornsey*	1911
22	*East Horndon - Tilbury Docks*	1911/2	60	*Highgate Road - Highgate*	1911
40	*Black Horse Road - Benfleet*	1911	62	*Camden Road - Camden*	1911
42	*Commercial Road - East Horndon*	1911			

Very recent study of the LT&SR/MR Register at the Public Record Office, Kew shows that the renamings of LT&SR Nos 9/13/32 and 51 are correctly recorded on pages 201-203 of LMS Locomotive Names, and were not as listed above by Kenneth Leech.

Glossary

Kenneth Leech, writing in the Stephenson Locomotive Society Journal in 1940, says "All the tank engines had names, starting off with the names of stations on the line, and (when the supply of these ran dry) continuing with the names of stations to which the Tilbury Company had running powers; finally the names of parishes in Essex served by the railway were pressed into service, and even so the very last engine named, No 82 *Crowstone*, was named after a rock in the Thames estuary, near Southend."

Crowstone The obelisk dates from 1837 and replaced one of 1755. Until 31st March 1909, the year of building and naming of the locomotive, it was visited by the Lord Mayor, Sheriffs etc. of London, after which shipping up-stream lay with the Port of London Authority.

Midland Railway

Midland Railway 377 was 'renewed' in 1923 as a Class 483 and not withdrawn until 1955 - but of the original *Beatrice* there was probably little or nothing left, even before 1923.

The Severn and Wye and Severn Bridge Railway

The line was vested jointly in the Midland Railway and the Great Western Railway in 1894.
Three 0-6-0Ts built by Vulcan Founrdy came to the MR when the locomotive stock was divided between the MR and the GWR in October 1895, of which two survived the Amalgamation in 1923.

Name	MR Number	MR 1907 Number	Built	Withdrawn
(Sharpness)	1124A	1606	3.1880	1.1924
(Forester)	1124A	1608	6.1886	12.1924

ACKNOWLEDGMENTS

The publication of LMS LOCOMOTIVE NAMES in 1994 resulted in quite a considerable correspondence, all of a helpful and friendly nature, and much of it relating to the names of London & North Western Locomotives which came into London Midland and Scottish stock in 1923. Apart from those who have died, I have lost none of the friends I mentioned in that book, and have gained many new ones who have contributed out of the store of their own knowledge of the subject. Their work has not been in vain: I have sifted through the letters and information I have received, and have included everything in the way of additions and corrections that I considered ought to be included in this L&NWR LOCOMOTIVE NAMES book.

I wish to record my gratitude for the help and guidance so many have given me, and particularly to Messrs Hugh Ballantyne, Roger Bell, Michael Bentley, Everard Beauchamp, Reg Bond, the late Harold Bowtell, Mike Burnett, David Camis, Greg Child, Brian Cooke, John Edgington, Bernard Harding, Clive Holden, Harry Jack, the late Professor Mike Page, Alan Pearsall, E.V.Richards, J.W.P.Rowledge, Edward Talbot, Richard Taylor, John True, David Walker, John Ward and the late Willie Yeadon, together with all those others who have helped, namely the members of the Crimean War Research Association, of Greenwich Public Library, St.Helens Town Hall and Local History Archives Library, Huddersfield Public Library, The Jockey Club, Shropshire County Council and of the Wildfowl & Wetlands Trust.

Everard Beauchamp, Reg Bond, Bernard Harding, Clive Holden, Harry Jack, Peter Rowledge, Ted Talbot, Dick Taylor, David Walker and others have proved themselves indefatiguable proof readers, and have spent countless hours and burned much tobacco (well, some of them) at their task, and deserve special mention. Between them they have given me advice and corrected errors of every kind. I owe them a huge debt of gratitude.

July 2002 John Goodman

BIBLIOGRAPHY

E.L.Ahrons	The British Steam Railway Locomotive 1825-1925.
Christopher Awdry	Encyclopaedia of British Railway Companies. Patrick Stephens Ltd. 1990.
Peter E.Baughan	A Regional History of the Railways of Great Britain Volume 11 North and Mid Wales. David & Charles 1980.
D.Baxter (Ed).	British Locomotive Catalogue Vols 2A/2B/3A/3B, Moorland 1978/1979/1982/1982.
R.Bell & E.Talbot.	The Locomotive Nameplates of the London & North Western Railway Premier Portfolio 3, London & North Western Railway Society 1984.
R.L.V.ffrench Blake.	Extracts from "The Crimean War".
Bonner Smith & Dewar	"Russian War, 1854".
Board of Trade	Reports 11.1841 (Bradshaw).
Harold D.Bowtell	Rails through Lakeland. Silver Link Publishing Ltd. 1988.
D.L.Bradley	A Locomotive History of Railways on The Isle of Wight RCTS 1982.
J.J.Colledge	Ships of the Royal Navy.
Brian Cooke	The Grand Crimean Central Railway.
C.P.Davis.	The Webb 'Experiment' Compounds. Premier Portfolio 4, London & North Western Society 1985.
P.C.Dewhurst	"The Locomotive" March 1955. Commentary on "Railway Locomotives down to the end of 1831".
Dictionary of National Biography.	Oxford University Press 1917 (1959-1960 Reprint).
Duckworth & Langmuir	"Railway and other Steamers".
David Eggenberger	"A Dictionary of Battles" 1967.
Stephen P.Goodall	The Vale of Clwyd Railway. 1982.
M.D.Greville	Chronology of the Railways of Lancashire and Cheshire. Journal of the Railway & Canal Historical Society 1981.
Clive Hardy	E.E.Wilson & Co. Locomotive Works list. Thomas Aleksandr 1981.
Hargreaves	Locomotive list of 21st November 1845 (LNW Archives, Kew).
Harry Jack.	The L.N.W.R.Bloomers Wolverton's 7ft Singles. Premier Portfolio 6, London & North Western Society 1987. Locomotives of the LNWR Southern Division R.C.T.S. 2001.
James	A Chronology of the Construction of Britain's Railways 1776-1855. Ian Allen 1983.
Gwyn Briwnant Jones & Denis Dunstone	The Origins of the LMS in South Wales. Gomer Press 1998.
H.F.F.Livesey.	The Locomotives of the L.N.W.R., The Railway Publishing Co. 1948.
James W.Lowe	British Steam Locomotive Builders. Goose & Son 1975.
E.T.MacDermot	History of the Great Western Railway, Volume 1 Great Western Railway Company 1927.
Capt.T.D.Manning and Cmdr.C.E.	Walker British Warship Names 1969.

| J.Marshall | A Biographical Dictionary of Railway Engineers, David & Charles 1978. |

Navy Record Society — The Russian War, Official Correspondence 1943.

G.P.Neele. — Railway Reminiscences 1889.

O.S.Nock — Premier Line, The story of London & North Western Locomotives Ian Allen 1952.

O.S.Nock. — The LNWR Precursor Family, David & Charles 1966.

O.S.Nock. — North Western Ian Allen 1968.

Colin Reed — Premier Portfolio 10, London & North Western Society 1992 "Gateway to the West".

RCTS — The Locomotives of the Great Western Railway Part 3. 1956.

M.C.Reed — The London & North Western Railway. Atlantic Transport Publishers 1996.

E.E.Robinson Jnr. — The L.& N.W.R. 4-cylinder 4-4-0 Compound Passenger Engines & the 4-cylinder "Renown" Class Simples 1932, and the Corrigenda subsequently published.

E.E.Robinson Jnr. — The Claughton and Baby Scot classes 1934, and the Supplement published later containing Addenda and Corrigenda.

J.W.P.Rowledge — Locomotives Illustrated No 121 L&NWR 2-4-0s and 3 cyl Compounds.

S.S.Scott — Locomotives of the LNWR (Part 3) Typescript.

Ray Shill — "Some Notes on John Hargreaves Junior and His Locomotives" Journal of the Railway & Canal Historical Society No 146 November 1990.

D.H.Stuart & Brian Read — Loco Profile No 15 "The Crewe Types" Profile Publications 1971.

Edward Talbot — An Illustrated History of LNWR Engines. Oxford Publishing Co. 1985.
'Argus' Revealed. British Railway Journal No.17. 1987.

J.M.Tolson — The St.Helens Railway. Oakwood Press 1982.

R.H.G.Thomas. — "The Liverpool and Manchester Railway". Batsford 1980.

C.H.A.Townley, C.A.Appleton, F.D.Smith, J.A.Peden. — "The Industrial Railways of Bolton, Bury and the Manchester Coalfield Part1. Bolton and Bury." Runpast Publishing 1994

Russell Wear — The Locomotive Builders of Kilmarnock. Industrial Railway Record No.69. 1977.

C.Williams. — A Register of all the Locomotives now in use 1912.

C.Williams — A Register of all the Locomotives now in use on the London & North-Western Railway, Author 1922.

C.Williams — Supplement to the Register (1922 Edition) of London & North-Western Locomotives, Author 1924.

Willie B.Yeadon. — A Compendium of LNWR Locomotives 1912-1949 Part One Passenger Tender Engines, Challenger Publications 1995.

F.Whishaw — The Railways of Great Britain and Ireland (List of locomotives) London 1841.

Magazines, Periodicals:
 Railnews.
 Steam Days.
 Steam World.
 The Railway Magazine.
 The Railway Observer.
 The Journal of the Stephenson Locomotive Society.
 The LNWR Society Premier News and the Society Journal.

RAISING STEAM ON THE LMS
The Evolution of LMS Locomotive Boilers

This absorbing read opens at Grouping with an LMS Locomotive fleet of poor steaming designs unsuited to the heavy and growing traffic levels. The Board's historic decision to hire Stanier from the rival Great Western and his revolutionary work to equip the LMS with a more suitable fleet revolved around more effective raising and use of steam. The complete story is presented here, from early LMS practice based on pre-Grouping designs, through Stanier's importation of GWR practices, early results and comprehensive details of his design improvements culminating in the largest British pacifics, the Coronation class. The neccessary technical content is presented by author Arthur Cook concisely in useful tables and an Appendix, allowing the text to be presented in an infectious, readable style. Readers can almost imagine themselves in the mutual improvement classes at the running shed!

Casebound, page size 180 x 235mm, 233 pages, 138 photographs and drawings, including one in colour.

LMS DIESELS
Locomotives and Railcars

Today's British motive power fleet ia a tribute to the pioneering work of the LMS. C1 56, 58, 60 and HST power cars use AC generators based on the 10800 *Hawk* development and C1 77 electrics used LMS designed bogies. C1 40, 50 and DP2 used LMS designed engines and Peak C1 44-46 used cab design from the famous 10000 and 10001. Our first generation dmmus owe much to the 1938 80000-2 LMS railcars. And, of course, our C1 08 and 11 bear testimony to the quality of their LMS design 60 years ago. Author Edgar Richards takes readers through the fascinating history of LMS diesel development. From the first steam converion in 1932 to the rugged 0-6-0 shunters built in large numbers for war service at home and abroad, the revolutionary main line 10000, 10100 and 10800, and the Michelin, Coventry and LMS railcars, in total 208 locomotives, 15 railcars and 5 trolleys were operated by the LMS. Full details of their design, construction, modification, liveries, allocation and use are included. The book includes much new material and is highly recommended.

Casebound, 219 pages, 125 illustrations.

GREAT NORTHERN LOCOMOTIVE HISTORY

This major four volume work covers the complete story of the Great Northern Railway, Doncaster Works and its locomotives, from earliest days to The Grouping. Each class is covered from all six designers - Cubitt, Bury, Sturrock, Stirling, Ivatt and Gresley. 1,553 Doncaster built engines are covered, plus those bought in. Their robust design was demonstrated by almost half of the GN stock passed to the LNER at Grouping surviving into British Railway ownership 25 years later.

The set totals 804 pages with 738 illustrations. Buy the complete set or individual volumes.

BRITISH RAILWAYS STANDARD STEAM LOCOMOTIVES
Volume 1 Background to Standarisation and the Pacific Classes
Volume 3 The Tank Engine Classes

Immediately British Railway was formed in January 1948, Robert Riddles was instructed to design a series of standard locomotives to modernise secondary route power. Railway enthusiasts from Penzance to Wick became familiar with their high running plates. The Society presents for the first time the complete story of British locomotives standardisation from the days of the Robinson ROD 2-8-0s to the twelve BR Standard designs totalling 999 locomotives. Paul Chancellor and Peter Gilbert present the Standards design history and for each of the 66 locomotives in the popular Britannia, Duke and Clan classes (Vol 1) and the 230 engines of the three tank classes (Vol 3) its complete construction, modification, diagram, allocation and use. With their construction at all six main workshops, local livery variations and national use, there is something for everyone to savour in these books.

Casebound, page size 212 x 272mm, Vol 1 184 pages, 151 illustrations including 17 in colour,
Vol 3 168 pages, 189 photographs including 16 colour

RCTS Publications List

*UK Post Free
Overseas add 40%

Title of Book	ISBN No	*Price
Locomotives of the LMS		
Locomotives of the LNWR Southern Division		
L & BR, LNWR and Wolverton Loco Works	0901115894	£27.95
Raising Steam on the LMS	0901115851	£24.95
LMS Diesels	0901115762	£19.95
LMS Locomotive Names	0901115797	£18.95
Highland Railway Locomotives 1855-1895	0901115649	£12.95
Highland Railway Locomotives 1895-1923	090111572X	£16.95

SPECIAL OFFER set of Highland Railway Locomotives		£23.50

Title of Book	ISBN No	*Price
The Birkenhead Railway	0901115878	£14.95
BR Standard Steam Locomotives:		
Vol 1 Background and the Pacifics	0901115819	£19.95
Vol 3 The Tank Engine Classes	0901115770	£19.95

SPECIAL OFFER BUY THIS BOOK WITH ANOTHER FOR JUST £5.00		
Western Change-Summer Saturdays in the West	0901115789	£15.95

Title of Book	ISBN No	*Price
The Railways of Keynsham	0901115827	£9.95
The Great Northern Railway in the East Midlands		
The Erewash Valley lines, Pinxton Branch,		
Awsworth-Ilkeston, Heanor & Stanton Branches	0901115886	£15.95
Nottingham Vic, GC, Leen Valley Network	090111586X	£14.95
Colwick Yards, London Rd-Gedling-Basford	0901115843	£13,95
The High Level Bridge and Newcastle Central Station	1873513283	£9.95
Gt. Northern Locomotive History		
1: 1847 - 1866	0901115614	£12.95
2: 1867 - 1895	0901115746	£19.95
3A: 1896 - 1911	090111569X	£19.95
3B: 1911 - 1923	0901115703	£16.95

SPECIAL OFFER set of Gt Northern Loco History		£40.95

Title of Book	ISBN No	*Price
A Travellers Guide to Robin Hood line	0901115835	£2.95
Locomotives of the LNER:		
Part 1 Preliminary Survey	0901115118	£12.95
Part 2A Tender Engines A1-A10	0901115258	£14.95
Part 2B Tender Engines Classes B1-B19	0901115738	£13.95
Part 9A Tank Engine Classes L1-L19	0901115401	£10.95
Part 9B Tank Engines Q1-25	090111541X	£10.95
Part 10A Department Stock, Engine Sheds,		
Boiler and Tendering Number	0901115657	£10.95

Available from:-

Hon Assitant Publications Officer, Hazelhurst, Tiverton Road, Bampton, Devon, EX16 9LJ.

When ordering please quote reference LNWN1